HOLT McDOUGAL

Virginia

UNITED STATES HISTORY

CIVIL WAR TO PRESENT

correlated to the

Virginia Curriculum Framework

for United States History: 1865 to the Present

CONTENTS

LESSONS WITH EMBEDDED VIRGINIA CONTENT EXPECTATIONS

Look for the Virginia symbol throughout this book. It highlights targeted content expectations to help you master the state standards.

Virginia Reviewers

Curtis Ashley
Matoaca Middle School
Matoaca, VA

Howard Goldberg
Seneca Ridge Middle School
Sterling, VA

Michelle J. Gotico
Poe Middle School
Annandale, VA

James Brian Mason
Lake Braddock Secondary School
Burke, VA

Will McClain
Short Pump Middle School
Glen Allen, VA

Erik Sassak
Farmwell Station Middle School
Ashburn, VA

ISBN-13: 978-0-55-403344-0
ISBN-10: 0-55-403344-5
2 3 4 5 6 7 8 9 0868 12 11 10
4500245646

United States History: 1865 to the Present

As you read the following pages and work through the Virginia Curriculum Framework, you will discover the big ideas and key concepts that your teacher expects you to learn and understand.

You will see four things:

1 **>)**
what the framework and standards actually say

2 **Essential Understandings**
an explanation to help you understand the big ideas within the standard

3 **Essential Questions**
the questions you will be able to answer when you have mastered the standard

4 **Essential Skills**
the social studies skills you will develop as you learn the standard

Virginia
Old Dominion State

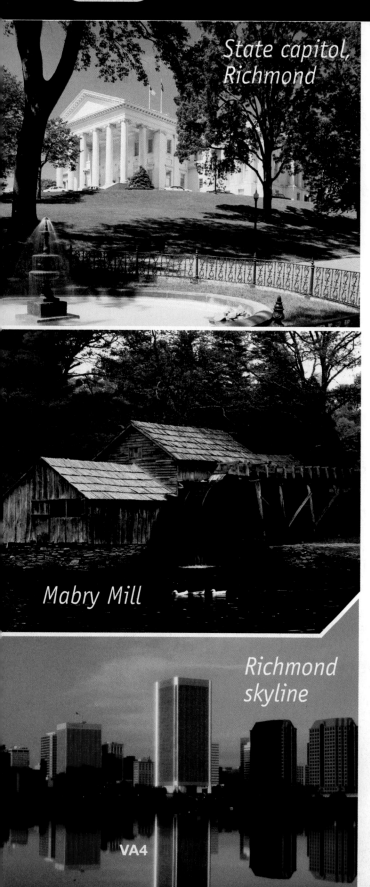

State capitol, Richmond

Mabry Mill

Richmond skyline

VA4

Virginia Curriculum Framework : United States History: 1865 to the Present

>Standard USII.1

The student will demonstrate skills for historical and geographical analysis, and responsible citizenship, including the ability to

1a) analyze and interpret primary and secondary source documents to increase understanding of events and life in United States history from 1865 to the present

1b) make connections between past and present;

1c) sequence events in United States history from 1865 to the present;

1d) interpret ideas and events from different historical perspectives;

1e) evaluate and debate issues orally and in writing;

1f) analyze and interpret maps that include major physical features;

1g) use parallels of latitude and meridians of longitude to describe hemispheric location;

1h) interpret patriotic slogans and excerpts from notable speeches and documents.

1i) identify the costs and benefits of specific choices made including the consequences, both intended and unintended, of the decision and how people and nations responded to positive and negative incentives.

The skills identified in standard USII.1a-i are cited under the "Essential Skills" heading of each standard for *United States History: 1865 to the Present* with the exception of "e" (evaluate and debate issues orally and in writing). Students should have opportunities to practice speaking and writing. Teachers should incorporate these skills into instruction throughout the year.

Flowering Dogwood, state flower

Cardinal, state bird

>Standard USII.2

The student will use maps, globes, photographs, pictures, or tables for

2a) **explaining how physical features and climate influenced the movement of people westward**

Essential Understandings

During the nineteenth century, people's perceptions and use of the Great Plains changed.

Technological advances allowed people to live in more challenging environments.

Essential Questions

How did people's perceptions and use of the Great Plains change after the Civil War?

How did people adapt to life in challenging environments?

Essential Skills

Analyze and interpret primary and secondary source documents to increase understanding of events and life in United States history. (USII.1a)

Analyze and interpret maps that include major physical features. (USII.1f)

2b) **explaining relationships among natural resources, transportation, and industrial development after 1865;**

Essential Understandings

Advances in transportation linked resources, products, and markets.

Monticello

Manufacturing areas were clustered near centers of population.

Essential Questions

How did advances in transportation link resources, products, and markets?

What are some examples of manufacturing areas that were located near centers of population?

Essential Skills

Make connections between past and present. (USII.1b)

Sequence events in United States history. (USII.1c)

Analyze and interpret maps that include major physical features. (USII.1f)

2c) locating the 50 states and the cities most significant to the historical development of the United States.

Essential Understandings

A state is an example of a political region. States may be grouped as part of different regions, depending upon the criteria used.

Cities serve as centers of trade and have political, economic, and cultural significance.

Essential Questions

What is one way of grouping the 50 states?

What are some examples of cities that historically have had political, economic, and/or cultural significance to the development of the United States?

Essential Skills

Make connections between past and present. (USII.1b)

Analyze and interpret maps that include major physical features. (USII.1f)

Use parallels of latitude and meridians of longitude to describe hemispheric location. (USII.1g)

Smith Mountain Lake

>Standard USII.3

The student will demonstrate knowledge of the effects of Reconstruction on American life by

3a) analyzing the impact of the 13th, 14th, and 15th Amendments to the Constitution of the United States of America;

Essential Understandings

The 13th, 14th, and 15th Amendments to the Constitution of the United States of America address the issues of slavery and guarantee equal protection under the law for all citizens.

Essential Questions

What are the basic provisions of the 13th, 14th, and 15th Amendments?

Essential Skills

Analyze and interpret primary and secondary source documents to increase understanding of events and life in United States history. (USII.1a)

Make connections between the past and the present. (USII.1b)

Sequence events in United States history. (USII.1c)

Interpret ideas and events from different historical perspectives. (USII.1d)

3b) describing the impact of Reconstruction policies on the South and North;

Essential Understandings

The Reconstruction policies were harsh and created problems in the South.

Rosslyn

Reconstruction attempted to give meaning to the freedom that the former enslaved African Americans had achieved.

Essential Questions
What were the Reconstruction policies for the South?

Essential Skills
Analyze and interpret primary and secondary source documents to increase understanding of events and life in United States history. (USII.1a)

Sequence events in United States history. (USII.1c)

Interpret ideas and events from different historical perspectives. (USII.1d)

3c) describing the legacy of Abraham Lincoln, Robert E. Lee, and Frederick Douglass.

Essential Understandings
The actions of Abraham Lincoln, Robert E. Lee, and Frederick Douglass created lasting impacts.

Essential Questions
What were the lasting impacts of Abraham Lincoln, Robert E. Lee, and Frederick Douglass?

>Standard USII.4

The student will demonstrate knowledge of how life changed after the Civil War by

4a) identifying the reasons for westward expansion, including its impact on American Indians;

Essential Understandings
New opportunities and technological advances led to westward migration following the Civil War.

Essential Questions
Why did westward expansion occur?

How did the lives of American Indians change with western expansion?

Shenandoah National Park

Essential Skills

Analyze and interpret primary and secondary source documents to increase understanding of events and life in United States history. (USII.1a)

Interpret ideas and events from different historical perspectives. (USII.1d)

4b) **explaining the reasons for the increase in immigration, growth of cities, new inventions, and challenges arising from this expansion;**

Essential Understandings

Population changes, growth of cities, and new inventions produced interaction and often conflict between different cultural groups.

Population changes, growth of cities, and new inventions produced problems in urban areas.

Inventions had both positive and negative effects on society.

Essential Questions

Why did immigration increase?

Why did cities develop?

What inventions created great change and industrial growth in the United States?

What challenges faced Americans as a result of those social and technological changes?

Essential Skills

Make connections between past and present. (USII.1b)

Sequence events in United States history. (USII.1c)

Interpret ideas and events from different historical perspectives. (USII.1d)

Analyze and interpret maps that include major physical features. (USII.1f)

Blue Ridge Mountains

4c) describing racial segregation, the rise of "Jim Crow," and other constraints faced by African Americans and other groups in the post-Reconstruction South;

Essential Understandings

Discrimination against African Americans continued after Reconstruction.

"Jim Crow" laws institutionalized a system of legal segregation.

African Americans differed in their responses to discrimination and "Jim Crow."

Essential Questions

What is racial segregation?

How were African Americans discriminated against?

How did African Americans respond to discrimination and "Jim Crow"?

Essential Skills

Analyze and interpret primary and secondary source documents to increase understanding of events and life in United States history. (USII.1a)

Make connections between past and present. (USII.1b)

Sequence events in United States history. (USII.1c)

Interpret ideas and events from different historical perspectives. (USII.1d)

4d) explaining the impact of new inventions, the rise of big business, the growth of industry, and life on American farms;

Essential Understandings

Between the Civil War and World War I, the United States was transformed from an agricultural to an industrial nation.

Essential Questions

What created the rise in big business?

What factors caused the growth of industry?

How did industrialization and the rise in big business influence life on American farms?

Essential Skills

Make connections between past and present. (USII.1b)

Sequence events in United States history. (USII.1c)

Richmond

Analyze and interpret maps that include major physical features. (USII.1f)

4e) describing the impact of the Progressive Movement on child labor, working conditions, the rise of organized labor, women's suffrage, and the temperance movement.

Essential Understandings

The effects of industrialization led to the rise of organized labor and important workplace reforms.

Essential Questions

How did the reforms of the Progressive Movement change the United States?

How did workers respond to the negative effects of industrialization?

Essential Skills

Analyze and interpret primary and secondary source documents to increase understanding of events and life in United States history. (USII.1a)

Make connections between past and present. (USII.1b)

Sequence events in United States history. (USII.1c)

Interpret ideas and events from different historical perspectives. (USII.1d)

>Standard USII.5

The student will demonstrate knowledge of the changing role of the United States from the late nineteenth century through World War I by

5a) explaining the reasons for and results of the Spanish American War;

Essential Understandings

The United States emerged as a world power as a result of victory over Spain in the Spanish American War.

Economic interests and public opinion often influence U.S. involvement in international affairs.

Essential Questions

What were the reasons for the Spanish American War?

What were the results of the Spanish American War?

Little River

Essential Skills

Analyze and interpret primary and secondary source documents to increase understanding of events and life in United States history. (USII.1a)

Sequence events in United States history. (USII.1c)

5b) describing Theodore Roosevelt's impact on the foreign policy of the United States;

Essential Understandings

Roosevelt expanded the Monroe Doctrine as a way to prevent European involvement in the affairs of Caribbean and South American countries.

Essential Questions

What were Theodore Roosevelt's foreign polices, and what were their impacts on the United States?

Essential Skills

Analyze and interpret primary and secondary source documents to increase understanding of events and life in United States; (USII.1a)

Make connections between past and present; (USII.1b)

5c) explaining the reasons for the United States' involvement in World War I and its international leadership role at the conclusion of the war.

Essential Understandings

The United States involvement in World War I ended a long tradition of avoiding involvement in European conflicts and set the stage for the United States to emerge as a global superpower later in the 20th century.

There were disagreements about the extent to which the United States should participate in world affairs.

Essential Questions

What were the reasons for the United States becoming involved in World War I?

Who were the Allies?

Who were the Central Powers?

In what ways did the United States provide leadership at the conclusion of the war?

Essential Skills

Analyze and interpret primary and secondary source documents to increase understanding of events and life in United States history. (USII.1a)

Sequence events in United States history. (USII.1c)

Interpret ideas and events from different historical perspectives. (USII.1d)

>Standard USII.6

The student will demonstrate knowledge of the social, economic, and technological changes of the early twentieth century by

6a) explaining how developments in factory and labor productivity and transportation (including the use of the automobile), communication, and rural electrification changed American life;

Essential Understandings

Technology extended progress into all areas of American life, including neglected rural areas.

Essential Questions

How was social and economic life in the early twentieth century different from that of the late nineteenth century?

What factors increased factory and labor productivity?

Norfolk

Essential Skills

Make connections between past and present. (USII.1b)

Interpret ideas and events. (USII.1d)

6b) describing the social and economic changes that took place, including prohibition, and the Great Migration north and west;

Essential Understandings

Reforms in the early twentieth century could not legislate how people behaved.

Economic conditions and violence led to the migration of people.

Essential Questions

What was Prohibition, and how effective was it?

Why did African Americans migrate to northern cities?

What were the economic changes Prohibition was imposed by a constitutional amendment that made it illegal to manufacture, transport, and sell alcoholic beverages?

Essential Skills

Interpret ideas and events from different historical perspectives. (USII.1d)

Analyze and interpret maps that include major physical features. (USII.1f)

6c) examining art, literature, and music from the 1920s and 1930s, emphasizing Langston Hughes, Duke Ellington, Georgia O'Keeffe, and the Harlem Renaissance;

Essential Understandings

The 1920s and 1930s were important decades for American art, literature, and music.

Shenandoah Valley

The leaders of the Harlem Renaissance drew upon the heritage of black culture to establish themselves as powerful forces for cultural change.

Essential Questions

Who were the leaders in art, literature, and music?

What were their contributions?

How did the Harlem Renaissance influence American life?

Essential Skills

Analyze and interpret primary and secondary source documents to increase understanding of events and life in United States history. (USII.1a)

Sequence events in United States history. (USII.1c)

Interpret ideas and events from different historical perspectives. (USII.1d)

6d) identifying the causes of the Great Depression, its impact on Americans, and the major features of Franklin D. Roosevelt's New Deal.

Essential Understandings

The optimism of the 1920s concealed problems in the American economic system and attitudes about the role of government in controlling the economy.

The Great Depression had a widespread and severe impact on American life.

Franklin Roosevelt's New Deal used government programs to help the nation recover from the Depression.

Essential Questions

What were the causes of the Great Depression?

How were the lives of Americans affected by the Great Depression?

What were the major features of the New Deal?

Mount Vernon

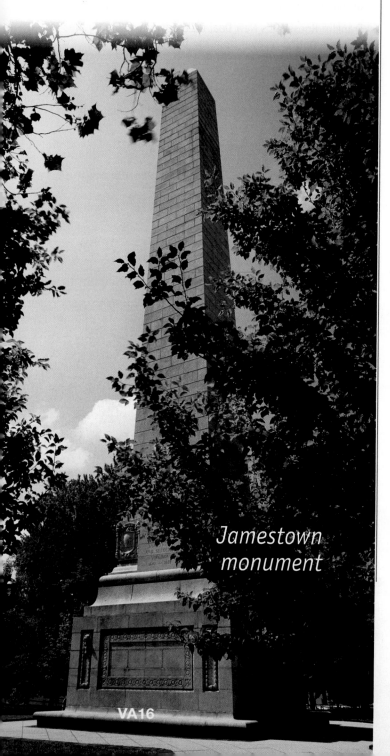

Jamestown monument

Essential Skills

Make connections between past and present. (USII.1b)

Sequence events in United States history. (USII.1c)

Interpret ideas and events from different historical perspectives. (USII.1d)

>Standard USII.7

The student will demonstrate knowledge of the major causes and effects of American involvement in World War II by

7a) identifying the causes and events that led to American involvement in the war, including the attack on Pearl Harbor;

Essential Understandings

Political and economic conditions in Europe following World War I led to the rise of fascism and to World War II.

The rise of fascism threatened peace in Europe and Asia.

As conflict grew in Europe and Asia, American foreign policy evolved from neutrality to direct involvement.

Essential Questions

How did post-World War I Europe set the stage for World War II?

How did the rise of fascism affect world events following World War I?

How did American policy toward events in Europe and Asia change over time?

Essential Skills

Make connections between past and present. (USII.1b)

Sequence events in United States history. (USII.1c)

Interpret ideas and events from different historical perspectives. (USII.1d)

Analyze and interpret maps that include major physical features. (USII.1f)

7b) locating and describing the major events and turning points of the war in Europe and the Pacific;

Essential Understandings

Despite initial Axis success in both Europe and the Pacific, the Allies persevered and ultimately defeated Germany and Japan.

The Holocaust is an example of prejudice and discrimination taken to the extreme.

Essential Questions
What were the major events and turning points of World War II?

What was the Holocaust?

Essential Skills
Sequence events in United States history. (USII.1c)

Interpret events from different historical perspectives. (USII.1d)

Analyze and interpret maps that include major physical features. (USII.1f)

7c) describing the impact of World War II on the home front.

Essential Understandings
World War II affected every aspect of American life.

Americans were asked to make sacrifices in support of the war effort and the ideas for which we fought.

Essential Questions
How did Americans at home support the war effort?

What effect did the war have on race relations in America?

Essential Skills
Make connections between past and present. (USII.1b)

Sequence events in United States history. (USII.1c)

Interpret ideas and events from different historical perspectives. (USII.1d)

State capitol

>Standard USII.8

The student will demonstrate knowledge of the economic, social, and political transformation of the United States and the world between the end of World War II and the present by

8a) describing the rebuilding of Europe and Japan after World War II, the emergence of the United States as a superpower, and the establishment of the United Nations;

Essential Understandings

Learning from the mistakes of the past, the United States accepted its role as a world superpower, helping to rebuild Europe and Japan and taking the leading role in establishing the United Nations.

Essential Questions

How did the United States help rebuild postwar Europe and Japan?

Essential Skills

Analyze and interpret primary and secondary source documents to increase understanding of events and life in United States history. (USII.1a)

Make connections between past and present. (USII.1b)

Sequence events in United States history. (USII.1c)

Interpret ideas and events from different historical perspectives. (USII.1d)

Shenandoah National Park

8b) describing the conversion from a wartime to a peacetime economy;

Essential Understandings

Following World War II, Americans prospered due to an expanding economy stimulated by America's involvement in the war.

Essential Questions

What contributed to the prosperity of Americans following World War II?

Essential Skills

Make connections between past and present. (USII.1b)

8c) identifying the role of America's military and veterans in defending freedom during the Cold War, including the wars in Korea and Vietnam, the Cuban missile crisis, the collapse of communism in Europe, and the rise of new challenges;

Essential Understandings

The United States and the Soviet Union emerged from World War II as world powers, triggering a rivalry over ideology and national security.

Since World War II, the United States has been directly involved in various conflicts that reflected the divisions created by Cold War tensions and hostilities.

The tension between the free world and the communist world caused divisiveness at home and abroad.

The Cold War was the central organizing principle in foreign affairs for 40 years.

Shenandoah National Park

VA19

Essential Questions

How and why did the Cold War begin?

What have been the major conflicts and confrontations involving America in the post-World War II era?

How did Cold War tensions cause divisiveness at home?

How did communism collapse in Europe?

How were the challenges after the Cold War different from earlier challenges?

Essential Skills

Analyze and interpret primary and secondary source documents to increase understanding of events and life in United States history. (USII.1a)

Make connections between past and present. (USII.1b)

Sequence events in United States history. (USII.1c)

Interpret ideas and events from different historical perspectives. (USII.1d)

Analyze and interpret maps that include major physical features. (USII.1f)

8d) **describing the changing patterns of society, including expanded educational and economic opportunities for military veterans, women, and minorities;**

Essential Understandings

Changing patterns in American society at the end of World War II changed the way most Americans lived and worked.

Essential Questions

What factors led to changing patterns of society in the post-World War II era?

What policies and programs expanded educational and employment opportunities for the military, women, and minorities?

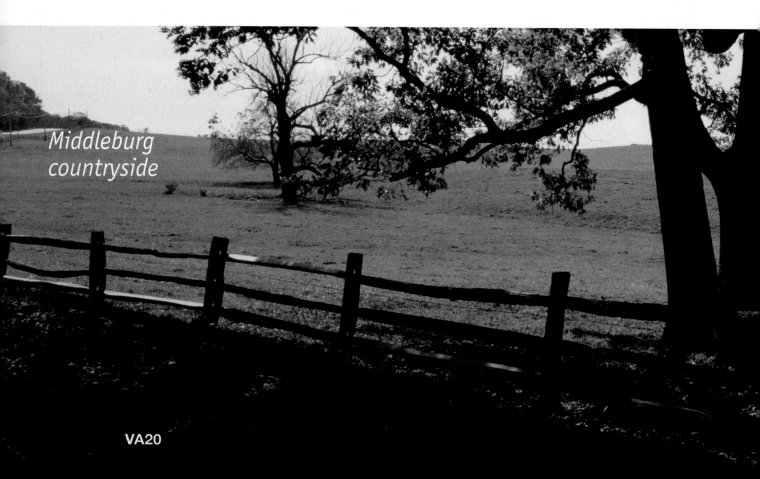

Middleburg countryside

Essential Skills

Make connections between past and present. (USII.1b)

Sequence events in United States history. (USII.1c)

Interpret ideas and events from different historical perspectives. (USII.1d)

Interpret slogans and documents. (USII.1h)

8e) **describing how international trade and globalization have impacted American life.**

Essential Understandings

Between the end of World War II and the present, the world has been marked by an increase in globalization and interdependence.

Essential Questions

How has globalization impacted American life?

Essential Skills

Identify the costs and benefits of specific choices made including the consequences, both intended and unintended, of the decision and how people and nations responded to positive and negative incentives. (USII.1f)

>Standard USII.9

The student will demonstrate knowledge of the key domestic and international issues during the second half of the twentieth century by

9a) **examining the Civil Rights Movement and the changing role of women;**

Virginia
Old Dominion State

Blue Ridge Mountains

Essential Understandings

The Civil Rights Movement resulted in legislation that ensured constitutional rights to all citizens regardless of race.

Women activists were inspired by the achievements of the Civil Rights Movement and took action to gain equality for themselves, particularly in the workplace.

Essential Questions

What were some effects of segregation on American society?

How did the African American struggle for equality become a mass movement?

How did the law support the struggle for equality for African Americans?

How were women disadvantaged in the workplace?

What actions were taken to improve conditions for women?

9b) **describing the development of new technologies in communication, entertainment, and business and their impact on American life;**

Essential Understandings

After the war, Americans turned their energies to the development of peacetime technologies.

Essential Questions

New technologies in communication, entertainment, and business have dramatically affected American life?

Which industries benefited the most from the new technologies?

What impact did the new technologies have on American life?

How have new technologies in communication, entertainment, and business affected American life?

Essential Skills

Make connections between past and present. (USII.1b)

Sequence events in United States history. (USII.1c)

Identify the costs and benefits of specific choices made including the consequences, both intended and unintended, of the decision and how people and nations responded to positive and negative incentives. (USII.1f)

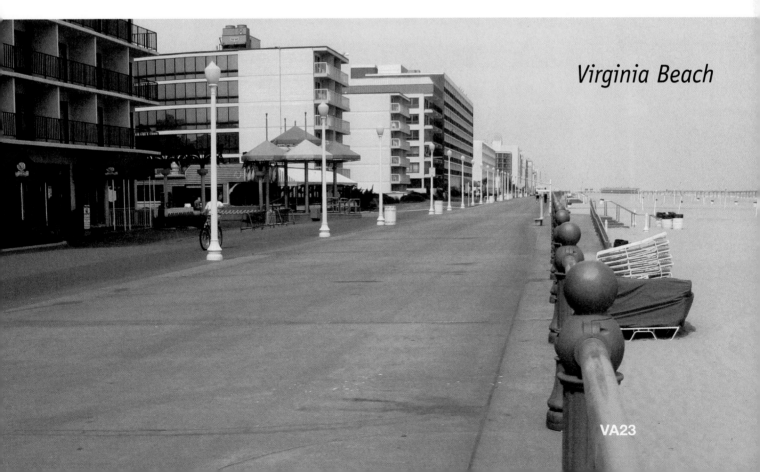

Virginia Beach

9c) **identifying how individual citizens from the time period influenced America scientifically, culturally, academically, and economically;**

Essential Understandings

Individual citizens have influenced America scientifically, culturally, academically, and economically.

Essential Questions

How have individual citizens influenced America scientifically, culturally, academically, and economically?

9d) **examining American foreign policy, immigration, the global environment, and other emerging issues.**

Essential Understandings

American foreign policy, immigration policies, energy policies, environmental policies affect both people in the United States and in other countries.

Essential Questions

How have American foreign policy, immigration policies, energy policies, environmental policies affected both people in the United States and in other countries?

Essential Skills

Identify the costs and benefits of specific choices made including the consequences, both intended and unintended, of the decision and how people and nations responded to positive and negative incentives. (USII.1f)

Alexandria

Virginia Standards Practice

How does *United States History: Civil War to the Present*, help me practice the Virginia Curriculum Framework?

United States History: Civil War to the Present provides complete coverage of the Virginia Standards of Learning. To help you use your textbook to learn and practice the standards, use the standards practice questions.

> This box indicates the curriculum framework that you will be practicing. It includes the framework itself as well as an explanation of what the framework means to you.

How can I use the Virginia Standards Practice?

▶ Each framework has practice questions. You will see that each question focuses on a particular standard of learning.

▶ As you study the book with your class, ask yourself the questions found here.

▶ There are multiple questions for each standard. Each of these questions addresses one of the standards of learning.

▶ If you have trouble answering the question, refer to your textbook to find the answer.

Virginia Standards Practice

VA USII.1

The student will demonstrate skills for historical and geographical analysis, and responsible citizenship.

What it means to you:
You will learn the skills necessary to succeed as a student of United States history.

Below are questions to help you practice standard USII.1.

1

> "The face of war is the face of death . . . The decision to use the atomic bomb was a decision that brought death to over a hundred thousand Japanese. No explanation can change that fact and I do not wish to gloss it over. But this deliberate, premeditated destruction was our least abhorrent choice."
> —Secretary of War Henry Stimson on the bombing of Hiroshima and Nagasaki

According to the quote, what did President Harry Truman's Secretary of War believe about the costs and benefits of dropping the atomic bomb?

A Dropping the bomb was the worst decision the United States could have made.

B The choice to drop the bomb was not thoroughly considered.

C No one cared about the cost of lives as long as the bombing ended the war.

D Although the decision was costly, it was the best option available.

2 A research paper on the causes of World War I is an example of a —

F manuscript

G primary source

H secondary source

J historical document

3 Why were the reform movements of the late nineteenth century and the early twentieth century important?

A Many of the reforms are still in force today.

B They prevented the rise of large corporations.

C Most of the reforms have since been overturned.

D The reform movements had no significant impact.

4 Meridians are used to pinpoint locations in terms of —

F north and south

G elevation

H east and west

J mileage

5 Which of the following events would fit on a time line that showed events between the end of World War II and the beginning of the Vietnam War?

A the bombing of Hiroshima

B the My Lai Massacre

C the Battle of Belleau Wood

D the Korean War

6

> William McKinley assassinated
> stock market crash
> Spanish-American War
> Alaska purchased from Russia

Which of the following reflects the correct chronological order of the above events?

F Spanish-American War, William McKinley assassinated, stock market crash, Alaska purchased from Russia

G William McKinley assassinated, stock market crash, Alaska purchased from Russia, Spanish-American War

H Alaska purchased from Russia, Spanish-American War, William McKinley assassinated, stock market crash

J stock market Crash, Alaska purchased from Russia, Spanish-American War, William McKinley assassinated

7

According to the map, where were the cattle being driven?

A to market cities on rail lines

B to capitals of midwestern states

C to rivers to water the cattle

D to major meat packing centers

8 Meridians are used to pinpoint locations in terms of —

F North and South

G Elevation

H East and West

J Mileage

9 What concern was President Franklin D. Roosevelt speaking about when he said the famous lines, "The only thing we have to fear is fear itself"?

A fears of foreign invasion

B concerns about the Depression

C misgivings over his policies

D anxieties about the afterlife

10 Which of the following slogans was used during the period of Reconstruction following the Civil War?

F "Forty acres and a mule"

G "Give me Liberty, or give me Death"

H "We shall overcome"

J "Ask not what your country can do for you"

Virginia Standards Practice

USII.2

| The student will use maps, globes, photographs, pictures, or tables. | **What it means to you:** You will learn to gather geographic information from maps, globes, photographs, pictures, and tables. |

Below are questions to help you practice standard USII.2.

1 How did the public's perception of the Great Plains change after the Civil War?

- **A** Most people wanted the Great Plains to be used for American Indian reservations.
- **B** Because of technology, the region was seen as a place worth settling.
- **C** The Great Plains were perceived as nothing more than a barren wasteland.
- **D** Settlers saw the Great Plains as an obstacle to moving to the West Coast.

2 All of the following are key physical feature of the Great Plains EXCEPT —

- **F** rising flatlands
- **G** heavy erosion
- **H** abundant rain
- **J** dust storms

3 The invention of barbed wire resulted in —

- **A** the end of the open range
- **B** a boom in the steel industry
- **C** decreased ranching competition
- **D** the rise of the cattle kingdom

4 Which of the following states is a part of the non-contiguous United States?

- **F** Maine
- **G** Alaska
- **H** Virginia
- **J** Florida

5 The windmill made it easier for western farmers to acquire —

- **A** flour
- **B** energy
- **C** heat
- **D** water

6 Manufacturing centers developed around what areas?

- **F** population centers
- **G** rural communities
- **H** the western plains
- **J** major waterways

7 What city became the center of American steel production?

- **A** Detroit
- **B** Washington, D.C.
- **C** Pittsburgh
- **D** Kansas City

8 Advancements in transportation affected American industry by —

- **F** moving settlers out west with greater ease and speed
- **G** moving the army to areas of conflict with Native Americans
- **H** moving cattle to major meatpacking cities
- **J** moving natural resources to factories in the East

9 Which of the following cities most likely had a large textile industry in the late 1800s?
A San Francisco
B Chicago
C Boston
D San Antonio

10

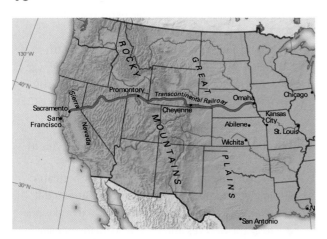

How did the geographic features of the American West affect the building of the Transcontinental Railroad?
F The flatness of the Great Plains made the work easy.
G Competition was high to build more tracks at a quicker pace.
H Food and supplies were hard to come by on the Great Plains.
J Railroad companies relied on immigrants for labor.

11 Ohio, Indiana, and Illinois are located in what region?
A Pacific
B Northeast
C Rocky Mountains
D Midwest

12 Which cities on the east and west coasts served as important gateways for immigrants coming to the United States?
F Boston and Los Angeles
G Charleston and Portland
H Jacksonville and Seattle
J New York and San Francisco

13 In which territory, now a state, did the Central Pacific and Union Pacific railroads meet?
A Utah
B Colorado
C Wyoming
D Oregon

14 The Wright brothers took the first motorized airplane flight in what state?
F Georgia
G South Carolina
H North Carolina
J Virginia

Virginia Standards Practice

USII.3

The student will demonstrate knowledge of the effects of Reconstruction on America.

What it means to you:
You will learn about the outcomes of the Reconstruction after the Civil War.

Below are questions to help you practice standard USII.3.

1 The Thirteenth Amendment —
  A established the Freedmen's Bureau
  B abolished slavery in the United States
  C gave African Americans the right to vote
  D granted citizenship to African Americans

2 All of the following were provisions of the Fourteenth Amendment EXCEPT —
  F a definition of citizens
  G equal protection for all citizen**s**
  H citizenship for Native Americans
  J federal court review of state laws

3 Which of the following was used to deny African Americans their rights under the Fifteenth Amendment?
  A poll taxes
  B segregation
  C sharecropping
  D Jim Crow laws

4 Under President Andrew Johnson's plan, what did southern states have to ratify to rejoin the Union?
  F Emancipation Proclamation
  G Thirteenth Amendment
  H Reconstruction Acts
  J Fifteenth Amendment

5 The Freedmen's Bureau was established to —
  A keep carpetbaggers out of the South
  B aid enslaved persons traveling to the North
  C help black and white southerners after the war
  D oppose Confederate forces still fighting in the South

6 What was the purpose of the Civil Rights Act of 1866?
  F to provide equal rights for African Americans
  G to give support to the Freedmen's Bureau Bill
  H to enable poor whites in the South to find work
  J to grant 40 acres and a mule to all former slaves

7 A carpetbagger was —
  A the same thing as a scalawag, or a "greedy rascal"
  B a northern Republican who moved to the South after the war
  C a nickname for southern Democrats who opposed the Reconstruction
  D a formerly enslaved person who traveled west on the railways

8

> "The future condition of the conquered power depends on the will of the conqueror. They must come in as new states or remain as conquered provinces. Congress . . . is the only power that can act in the matter."
> —Thaddeus Stevens

How did Congressman Thaddeus Stevens view the South?
  F as a sore loser
  G as a misguided friend
  H as a conquered territory
  J as an unsettled province

9

HOPES RAISED AND DENIED

Slavery	Freedom	Rights Denied
• No rights	• Slavery banned	• Sharecropping system created cycle of debt
• Forced labor	• Free to work for wages	
• No freedom of movement without permission	• Could move and live anywhere	• Ability to vote and hold office restricted
• Family members sold away from one another	• Many families reunited	• White leadership regained control of southern state governments
• No representation in government	• Could serve in political office	

What right did African Americans gain during Reconstruction that was later restricted?

A the right to work for wages

B the right to reunite with family

C the right to be freed from slavery

D the right to hold political office

10 **What brought Reconstruction to an end?**

F the New South

G the Ku Klux Klan

H the Enforcement Acts

J the Compromise of 1877

11 **General Robert E. Lee went on to become the president of what institution?**

A Washington University

B College of William and Mary

C University of Virginia

D James Madison University.

12 **What did Abraham Lincoln's Ten Percent Plan offer to southern states after the Civil War?**

F punishment

G occupation

H amnesty

J money

13 **Frederick Douglass believed that the work of the abolitionists was not over until African Americans received the right to —**

A work

B vote

C pray

D travel

USII.4

The student will demonstrate knowledge of how life changed after the Civil War.	**What it means to you:** You will learn how life in the United States changed after the Civil War.

Below are questions to help you practice standard USII.4.

1 The Indian Wars that were fought from the 1870s through the 1890s resulted in which of the following?

A Native Americans were moved onto reservations.

B Native Americans were given rights to their lands.

C Native Americans were relocated to the West Coast.

D Native American leaders agreed to share their lands.

2 Which group that settled in the West during the 1870s became known as Exodusters?

F Chinese immigrants

G German immigrants

H white Americans from the East

J African Americans from the South

3 Which of the following was NOT one of the reasons for westward expansion?

A new opportunities for land ownership

B increase in available transportation

C fair treatment for immigrants

D hope to strike it rich in mining

4 Chief Joseph led the Nez Percé on a 1,400-mile trek to —

F Texas

G Canada

H Mexico

J California

5 Thomas Edison's greatest innovations involved —

A airplanes

B electricity

C the telegraph

D the telephone

6

What does this map illustrate about the new immigrants coming to the United States in the late 1800s?

F They were mainly settled in rural areas.

G They were mainly Protestant Christians.

H They came from southern and eastern Europe.

J They came from northern and western Europe.

7 Political machines often gained power by —
A changing the gold standard
B promising to reduce immigration
C organizing reformers to reduce corruption
D helping and reaching out to immigrants

8 What was the effect of the Jim Crow laws?
F They separated whites and African Americans.
G They moved Native Americans to reservations.
H They created the system of sharecropping.
J They improved race relations in the South.

9 What African American leader helped to found the National Association for the Advancement of Colored People (NAACP)?
A Ida B. Wells
B W. E. B. Du Bois
C Elizabeth Cady Stanton
D George Edmund Haynes

10 Booker T. Washington believed that the best way for African Americans to achieve equality was to —
F fight to overturn Jim Crow legislation
G improve educational and economic opportunities
H migrate to urban communities in the north
J elect African Americans to government offices

11 Which business tycoon built a fortune on shipping and railroads?
A Andrew Carnegie
B J. P. Morgan
C Cornelius Vanderbilt
D John D. Rockefeller

12 All of the following were factors that resulted in a growth in American industry EXCEPT —
F an abundance of new inventions
G a growing immigrant workforce
H the organization of labor unions
J access to raw materials and energy

13

U.S. OIL PRODUCTION, 1880–1910

Source: *Historical Statistics of the United States*

Based on the graph, during which period did U.S. oil production skyrocket?
A 1880–1890
B 1880–1900
C 1890–1900
D 1900–1910

14 The Homestead strike involved protesting workers from what industry?
F steel
G oil
H railroad
J mining

15 Women gained the right to vote with the passage of what amendment to the Constitution?
A Eighteenth Amendment
B Nineteenth Amendment
C Twentieth Amendment
D Twenty First Amendment

16 The movement to prohibit the manufacture, sale, and transportation of alcohol was known as the —
F labor movement
G suffrage movement
H progressive movement
J temperance movement

Virginia Standards Practice

VA USII.5

The student will demonstrate knowledge of the changing role of the United States from the late nineteenth century through World War I.

What it means to you:
You will learn how the part the United States played in world affairs changed during the beginning of the twentieth century.

Below are questions to help you practice standard USII.5.

1 Sensationalist news reporting during the late 1800s became known as —
- A imperial journalism
- B "big stick" journalism
- C yellow journalism
- D propaganda journalism

2 Which of the following events helped to start the Spanish-American War?
- F the Boxer Rebellion
- G the sinking of the USS *Maine*
- H the formation of the Anti-Imperialist League
- J the adoption of the Platt Amendment

3 As a result of the Spanish-American War, the United States gained control of —
- A California and Texas
- B Cuba, Mexico, and Texas
- C Cuba, the Panama Canal, and the Philippines
- D Cuba, Guam, Puerto Rico, and the Philippines

4 What document allowed the United States to interfere in Cuban affairs?
- F Platt Amendment
- G Teller Amendment
- H Open Door Policy
- J Cuba Agreement

5

How many locks did ships have to travel through from Balboa to Colón?
- A two
- B three
- C four
- D five

6 The Roosevelt Corollary was meant to —
- F help Cuba remain independent
- G establish permanent military bases worldwide
- H protect U.S. economic interests in Latin America
- J increase European colonization in Latin America

7 What was an outcome of President Theodore Roosevelt's "Big Stick" policy?

A strained relations with Europe

B U.S. economic downturns

C Latin American revolutions

D American influence abroad

8 All of the following were reasons the United States entered World War I EXCEPT —

F economic ties to Germany

G inability to stay neutral

H the Zimmermann telegraph

J German submarine warfare

9 Americans who supported isolationism during World War I wanted —

A the United States to remain neutral

B the United States to help the Allied forces

C the United States to try to establish a peace

D the United States to defeat the Central Powers

10 What was the name of the British passenger liner carrying 128 Americans that was sunk by a German submarine?

F U-boat

G *Sussex*

H *Lusitania*

J *Marne*

11 What type of warfare kept World War I at a stalemate for the first few years of fighting?

A submarine warfare

B trench warfare

C hand-to-hand combat

D cannon warfare

12 All of the following were Central Powers EXCEPT —

F Germany

G Austria-Hungary

H Bulgaria

J Russia

13 President Woodrow Wilson's plan for peace after World War I was —

A the Treaty of Versailles

B the League of Nations

C the Fourteen Points

D self-determination

Virginia Standards Practice

 USII.6

The student will demonstrate knowledge of the social, economic, and technological changes of the early twentieth century.

What it means to you:
You will learn how life changed in the United States during the first half of the twentieth century.

Below are questions to help you practice standard USII.6.

1 How did the growth of the automobile industry affect the U.S. economy during the 1920s?
  A It led to the expansion of welfare.
  B It led to a decrease in the use of credit.
  C It led to the growth of related industries.
  D It led to a population decrease in urban areas.

2 All of the following are examples of Henry Ford's innovative business practices EXCEPT —
  F the moving assembly line
  G outsourced manufacturing
  H higher wages for employees
  J installment plans for buyers

3 The radio and movies led to the —
  A development of a national culture
  B decline of interest in reading
  C fear of communist infiltration
  D invention of jazz music

4 Which of the following is a result of prohibition?
  F Alcohol was completely removed from the United States.
  G Social gatherings took place only in the home.
  H Bootlegging led to a rise in organized crime.
  J Americans moved overseas to be able to drink.

5 Prohibition was the result of which amendment?
  A Twelfth Amendment
  B Fourteenth Amendment
  C Sixteenth Amendment
  D Eighteenth Amendment

6 During the Great Migration, African Americans moved —
  F north and west
  G south and west
  H north and east
  J south and east

7 Which of the following is a reason for the Great Migration?
  A There were areas of the country where discrimination did not exist.
  B African Americans wanted to find jobs with higher wages.
  C More jobs were available in rural areas of the country.
  D African Americans received lands taken from Native Americans.

8 Who was the American composer famous for incorporating the sounds of jazz music in his compositions?
  F Louis Armstrong
  G George Gershwin
  H Jelly Roll Morton
  J Aaron Copeland

9 The Harlem Renaissance was the revival of African American —
  A history
  B religion
  C education
  D culture

10

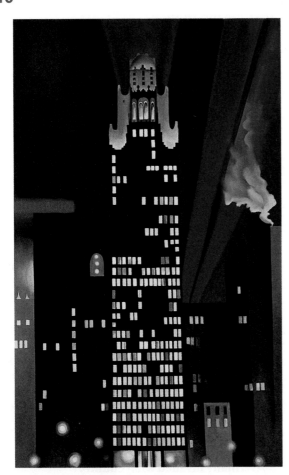

This painting of an urban landscape is most likely the work of —
F   Georgia O'Keeffe
G   John Steinbeck
H   Jacob Lawrence
J   Bessie Smith

11 All of the following were leaders in the Harlem Renaissance EXCEPT —
A   Langston Hughes
B   Duke Ellington
C   John Steinbeck
D   Jacob Lawrence

12 What period was the focus of the writings of F. Scott Fitzgerald?
F   World War I
G   the Great Depression
H   the Jazz Age
J   the Harlem Renaissance

13

Based on the chart, what was a major financial cause of the 1929 stock market crash?
A   severe labor shortages
B   unrealistic rises in stock prices
C   skyrocketing profits in farming
D   large increases in consumer spending

14 All of the following were New Deal programs EXCEPT —
F   the Federal Reserve System
G   the Rural Electrification Administration
H   the Tennessee Valley Authority
J   the Works Progress Administration

15 At the height of the Great Depression, how many workers were without jobs?
A   one-tenth
B   one-fifth
C   one-fourth
D   one-half

Virginia Standards Practice

USII.7

The student will demonstrate knowledge of the major causes and effects of American involvement in World War II.

What it means to you:
You will learn about what caused World War II and the impact it had on the United States.

Below are questions to help you practice standard USII.7.

1 What is the name for the political philosophy in which total power is given to a dictator and individual freedoms are denied?

A communism

B fascism

C monarchy

D socialism

2 In the aftermath of World War I, Germany was angry about being forced to —

F join the League of Nations

G make reparation payments

H give up lands it had invaded

J hold democratic elections

3 All of the following nations were Axis Powers EXCEPT —

A Germany

B Italy

C Soviet Union

D Japan

4 Who was the prime minister of Great Britain during World War II?

F Franklin D. Roosevelt

G Harry Truman

H Neville Chamberlain

J Winston Churchill

5

> Battle of Britain
> Munich Conference
> Japan's invasion of China
> invasion of the Rhineland

Which of the following places these events in the correct chronological order?

A Japan's invasion of China, invasion of the Rhineland, Munich Conference, Battle of Britain

B Munich Conference, Battle of Britain, invasion of the Rhineland, Japan's invasion of China

C Battle of Britain, Munich Conference, Japan's invasion of China, invasion of the Rhineland

D invasion of the Rhineland, Japan's invasion of China, Battle of Britain, Munich Conference

6 World War II officially began when Nazi Germany invaded what country?

F France

G Belgium

H Poland

J Austria

7 The Lend-Lease Act enabled the United States to —

A lend money to nations fighting the Axis Powers

B send troops to fight with Britain and France

C remain neutral until the bombing of Pearl Harbor

D send aid to anyone vital to U.S. defense

8

This map depicts what important battle?
F   Battle of Pearl Harbor
G   D-Day
H   Battle of Stalingrad
J   Battle of the Bulge

9 **The turning point in the war in the Pacific was —**
A   the Battle of Leyte Gulf
B   the Bataan Death March
C   the Battle of Midway
D   the Battle of the Coral Sea

10 **The Nazi slaughter of Jews during World War II stemmed from prejudice known as what?**
F   Nazism
G   fascism
H   communism
J   anti-Semitism

11 **Adolf Hitler's "final solution" employed the use of —**
A   concentration camps
B   deportation
C   military occupation
D   re-education

12 **U.S. involvement in World War II finally brought an end to what?**
F   the League of Nations
G   tensions over communism
H   the Great Depression
J   international conflicts

13 **Rosie the Riveter became a war-time symbol for —**
A   the war front at home
B   American isolationism
C   conservation efforts
D   female empowerment

14 **What group was the target of fear in the United States and was subsequently relocated to internment camps during the war?**
F   African Americans
G   Japanese Americans
H   German Americans
J   Communist Americans

USII.8

The student will demonstrate knowledge of the economic, social, and political transformation of the United States and the world between the end of World War II and the present.

What it means to you:
You will learn how American society, politics, and economics has changed from World War II to now.

Below are questions to help you practice standard USII.8.

1

The Iron Curtain was a division between —
A East Germany and West Germany
B the winners and losers of World War II
C Europe and Asia
D the communist east and democratic west

2 The Marshall Plan was used to help Europe's economy recover after the war in hopes of —
F rebuilding ties with the Soviet Union
G undoing the effects of the Great Depression
H preventing the spread of communism
J establishing the United States as a world super power

3 Which of the following nations helped to establish the United Nations?
A China
B Germany
C France
D Japan

4 How did the United States' relationship with Japan change after the war?
F Japan became a territory governed by the United States.
G Japan became a strong ally of the United States.
H Japan sought to undermine the United Nations.
J Japan became a strong ally of the Soviet Union.

5 All of the following are changes that occurred to the post war U.S. economy EXCEPT —
A a boom in the production of consumer goods
B a rise in the size and power of labor unions
C an increase in the number of female workers
D an expansion of the use of credit for purchases

6 Why was the conflict between the United States and the Soviet Union referred to as the Cold War?
F It was fought in the northern regions of the Soviet Union.
G It occurred during the winter after World War II.
H *Cold* was a slang term referring to the Soviet Union.
J It was characterized by tensions but no actual fighting.

7 What was the name of the philosophy that said the United States should go to the verge of war to oppose communism?

A détente

B brinkmanship

C dollar diplomacy

D containment

8 Why did the United States enter the Korean War?

F North Korea requested U.S. aid.

G U.S. leaders wanted to colonize Korea.

H U.S. leaders feared North Korea might attack.

J U.S. leaders wanted to contain communism's spread.

9 The theory that communism would spread if the United States did not intervene in South Vietnam was known as the —

A Vietnam theory

B Cold War theory

C domino theory

D collapse theory

10 What instigated the Cuban missile crisis?

F the completion of the Berlin Wall

G the United States blockade around Cuba

H the Bay of Pigs invasion of Cuba

J the conclusion of the Korean War

11 What was the nickname for the legislation that provided veterans with money for school and loans for houses, farms, and businesses?

A the G.I. Bill

B the Cold War Bill

C the Baby Boom Bill

D the Beatnik Bill

12

> *"There was always the assumption, even when I was getting my graduate degree in education, that any work I did was temporary, something to do until I assumed my principal role in life which was to be the perfect wife and mother, supported by my husband."*
> —Sally Ann Carter, quoted in *The Fifties: A Women's Oral History*, by Brett Harvey

This quote illustrates the traditional expectation that women would —

F contribute to the "Baby Boom"

G get a college education

H work in the home as a mother

J marry a man returning from the war

13 Eleanor Roosevelt, wife of President Franklin D. Roosevelt, worked to advance civil rights in what role?

A U.S. senator

B UN delegate

C U.S. ambassador

D First Lady

14 What term describes the increasing economic integration of the world's nations following World War II?

F globalization

G communication

H internationalism

J diplomacy

15 One effect of the increased connections between the United States and the rest of the world is —

A an increase in global conflicts

B a surge in emigration

C the outsourcing of jobs

D the rising cost of trade

Virginia Standards Practice

 USII.9

The student will demonstrate knowledge of the key domestic and international issues during the second half of the twentieth and early twenty-first centuries.

What it means to you:
You will learn about the important issues for the United States and the world in the late twentieth and early twenty-first centuries.

Below are questions to help you practice standard USII.9.

1 Rosa Parks's arrest in 1955 led to integrated —
   A city buses
   B public schools
   C universities
   D restaurants

2 Which landmark Supreme Court case led to the integration of public schools in the United States?
   F *Reynolds* v. *Sims*
   G *Miranda* v. *Arizona*
   H Gideon v. *Wainwright*
   J *Brown* v. *Board of Education of Topeka, Kansas*

3

This photograph is an example of what form of protest?
   A freedom riding
   B petitioning
   C sit–ins
   D boycotting

4 What strategy did Martin Luther King Jr. and several other civil rights leaders employ?
   F forced repatriation
   G non violent resistance
   H white accommodation
   J group armed resistance

5 What was the purpose of the failed Equal Rights Amendment?
   A to end to the practice of racial segregation
   B to promote democracy in communist countries
   C to provide cheap low-income housing
   D to outlaw discrimination based on sex

6 Who was the author of *The Feminine Mystique?*
   F Shirley Chisholm
   G Betty Friedan
   H Judy Heumann
   J Phyllis Schlafly

7 How has nationwide access to information and entertainment changed American culture?
   A It has increased regional variation.
   B It has reduced interest in the arts.
   C It has decreased regional variation.
   D It has reduced racial differences.

8 **What is one way that new technology might affect where people choose to live?**

F Technology makes it cheaper to travel around the world for vacation.

G People move less often because it is easier to communicate across large distances.

H Technology improves the quality of life in areas once considered less habitable.

J Technology has had no effect on where people choose to live.

9 **The American scientist Charles Drew is known for his work with —**

A the atomic bomb

B computer chips

C the polio vaccine

D plasma and blood

10 **Who was the American dancer and choreographer who was known for her pioneering work in modern dance?**

F Martha Graham

G Audrey Hepburn

H Sylvia Plath

J Ella Fitzgerald

11

"We are watching something historic happening, and it will affect the world . . . the same way the scientific method, the invention of printing, and the arrival of the Industrial Age did."
        —Bill Gates, quoted in *Newsweek*

Bill Gates is describing what has come to be known as —

A the Industrial Revolution

B the Globalization Revolution

C the Information Revolution

D the Computer Revolution

12 **What group currently constitutes the largest minority group in the United States?**

F African Americans

G Hispanic Americans

H Asian Americans

J Arab Americans

13 **Those who worry about global warming are concerned about the rising amount of what in Earth's atmosphere?**

A carbon dioxide

B ozone particles

C fossil fuels

D solar rays

14 **The air offensive against Iraq after it invaded neighboring Kuwait, was known as —**

F the Persian Gulf Conflict

G the Iraq War

H the War on Terror

J Operation Desert Storm

15 **Which of the following is NOT one of the diseases that are threatening the developing world?**

A malaria

B influenza

C AIDS

D tuberculosis

Virginia: Physical

NJ

DE

MARYLAND

PENNSYLVANIA

OHIO

WEST VIRGINIA

KENTUCKY

TENNESSEE

NORTH CAROLINA

Eastern Shore

ATLANTIC OCEAN

Chesapeake Bay

Coastal Plain

Piedmont Plateau

York River

Rappahannock River

Pamunkey River

James River

Nottoway River

Roanoke River

Potomac River

South Fork Shenandoah River

Lake Gaston

John H. Kerr Res.

Leesville Lake

Philpott Res.

Smith Mt. Lake

Claytor Lake

Stony Man Mtn. 4,011 ft (1,223 m)

Hawksbill Mtn. 4,051 ft (1,236 m)

Shenandoah Valley

Shenandoah Mountain

Allegheny Mountains

Blue Ridge Mountains

Great Valley

Bald Knob 4,229 ft (1,289 m)

APPALACHIAN MOUNTAINS

Highest Point: Mount Rogers 5,729 ft (1,746 m)

Whitetop Mtn. 5,520 ft (1,682 m)

Black Mtn. 4,145 ft (1,263 m)

ELEVATION

Feet		Meters
3,000		900
1,500		450
600		180
300		90
(Sea level) 0		0 (Sea level)
Below sea level		Below sea level

0   25   50 Miles

0   25   50 Kilometers

Projection: Albers Equal Area

N E S W

Virginia Maps and Facts

Virginia: Political

NJ

DE

MARYLAND

PENNSYLVANIA

OHIO

WEST VIRGINIA

KENTUCKY

TENNESSEE

NORTH CAROLINA

ATLANTIC OCEAN

Chesapeake Bay

CHINCOTEAGUE N.W.R.
Chincoteague

Potomac River

Shenandoah River
South Fork Shenandoah River

Rappahannock River

Pamunkey River

York River

James River

Nottoway River

Roanoke River

Washington, D.C.
Arlington
Falls Church
Alexandria
Leesburg
Herndon
Vienna
Fairfax
Manassas
Warrenton
Front Royal
SHENANDOAH NATIONAL PARK
Culpeper
Fredericksburg
Winchester
Charlottesville
Harrisonburg
Staunton
Waynesboro
Lexington
Buena Vista
Covington
Salem
Roanoke
Bedford
Lynchburg
Farmville
Richmond
Chester
Colonial Heights
Petersburg
Hopewell
Williamsburg
Gloucester
Newport News
Hampton
Norfolk
Virginia Beach
Chesapeake
Portsmouth
Suffolk
Franklin
GREAT DISMAL SWAMP N.W.R.
Emporia
South Hill
Lake Gaston
John H. Kerr Res.
South Boston
Danville
Martinsville
Rocky Mount
Philpot Res.
Smith Mt. Lake
Leesville Lake
Blacksburg
Christiansburg
Radford
Claytor Lake
Pulaski
Galax
Wytheville
MT. ROGERS N.R.A.
Marion
Bluefield
Norton
Abingdon
Bristol

Legend

★ State capital
• Other cities

0   25   50 Miles
0   25   50 Kilometers

Projection: Albers Equal Area

N E S W

Governors of the State of Virginia

Commonwealth Governors

Patrick Henry (1776–1779)

Thomas Jefferson (1779–1781)

William Fleming (June 4, 1781–June 12, 1781)

Thomas Nelson, Jr.
(June 12, 1781–November, 1781)

David Jameson (November 22-30, 1781)

Benjamin Harrison (1781–1784)

Patrick Henry (1784–1786)

Edmund Randolph (1786–1788)

State Governors

Beverley Randolph (1788–1791)

Henry Lee (1791–1794)

Robert Brooke (1794–1796)

James Wood (1796–1799)

Hardin Burnley (December 7-11, 1799)

John Pendleton (December 11–19, 1799)

James Monroe (1799–1802)

John Page (1802–1805)

William H. Cabell (1805–1808)

John Tyler, Sr. (1808–1811)

George William Smith (January 15–19, 1811)

James Monroe (January 19-April 3, 1811)

George William Smith (April 3–Dec. 6, 1811)

George William Smith (December 6–26, 1811)

Peyton Randolph
(December 27, 1811–January 2, 1812)

James Barbour (1812–1814)

Wilson Cary Nicholas (1814–1816)

James P. Preston (1816–1819)

Thomas Mann Randolph (1819–1822)

James Pleasants, Jr. (1822–1825)

John Tyler, Jr. (1825–1827)

William B. Giles (1827–1830)

John Floyd (1830–1834)

Littleton Waller Tazewell (1834–1836)

Wyndham Robertson (1836–1837)

David Campbell (1837–1840)

Thomas Walker Gilmer (1840–1841)

John Mercer Patton (March 20-31, 1841)

John Rutherford (1841–1842)

John M. Gregory (1842–1843)

James McDowell (1843–1846)

William Smith (1846–1849)

John Buchanan Floyd (1849–1852)

Joseph Johnson (1852–1856)

Henry Alexander Wise (1856–1860)

John Letcher (1860–1864)

William Smith (1864–1865)

Francis Harrison Pierpont (1865–1868)

Henry H. Wells (1868–1869)

Gilbert C. Walker (1869–1874)

James Lawson Kemper (1874–1878)

Frederick W. M. Holliday (1878–1882)

William E. Cameron (1882–1886)

Fitzhugh Lee (1886–1890)

Philip W. McKinney (1890–1894)

Charles T. O'Ferrall (1894–1898)

James Hoge Tyler (1898–1902)

Andrew Jackson Montague (1902–1906)

Claude A. Swanson (1906–1910)

William Hodges Mann (1910–1914)

Henry Carter Stuart (1914–1918)

Westmoreland Davis (1918–1922)

E. Lee Trinkle (1922–1926)

Harry Flood Byrd, Sr. (1926–1930)

John Garland Pollard (1930–1934)

George C. Peery (1934–1938)

James H. Price (1938–1942)

Colgate W. Darden, Jr. (1942–1946)

William M. Tuck (1946–1950)

John S. Battle (1950–1954)

Thomas B. Stanley (1954–1958)

J. Lindsay Almond, Jr. (1958–1962)

Albertis S. Harrison, Jr. (1962–1966)

Mills E. Godwin, Jr. (1966–1970)

A. Linwood Holton, Jr. (1970–1974)

Mills E. Godwin, Jr. (1974–1978)

John Dalton (1978–1982)

Charles S. Robb (1982–1986)

Gerald L. Baliles (1986–1990)

L. Douglas Wilder (1990–1994)

George F. Allen (1994–1998)

James (Jim) Gilmore III (1998–2002)

Mark Warner (2002–2006)

Tim Kaine (2006–   )

Virginia Government

Executive Branch

Carries out the laws and policies of state government

Governor
- Elected by voters to a four-year term
- Cannot serve consecutive terms
- Appoints officials and some judges for temporary succession in the event of a vacancy
- Signs bills into law but can also veto bills

Lieutenant Governor
- Elected by voters to a four-year term
- Holds various responsibilities including replacing the governor should he or she leave office

Attorney General
- Serves as the state's chief legal advisor
- Issues advisory opinions and defends the state in legal matters

Legislative Branch

Makes state laws

Bicameral System
- The General Assembly has two houses–Senate and House of Delegates
- Both houses take part in drafting and passing laws
- General Assembly can override the governor's veto with a two-thirds vote in each house

State Senate
- 40 members
- Elected to four-year terms
- No term limits

State House of Delegates
- 100 members
- Elected to two-year terms
- No term limits

Judicial Branch

Decides conflicts and questions about the law

Circuit Courts
- Hear civil and criminal cases
- Consists of 131 judges
- Judges elected by General Assembly to eight-year terms

Court of Appeals
- Hears appeals from the lower courts
- Consists of eleven judges
- Elected by the General Assembly to eight-year terms

Supreme Court of Virginia
- Highest appellate court in the state
- Consists of eleven justices
- Justices elected by the General Assembly to twelve-year terms

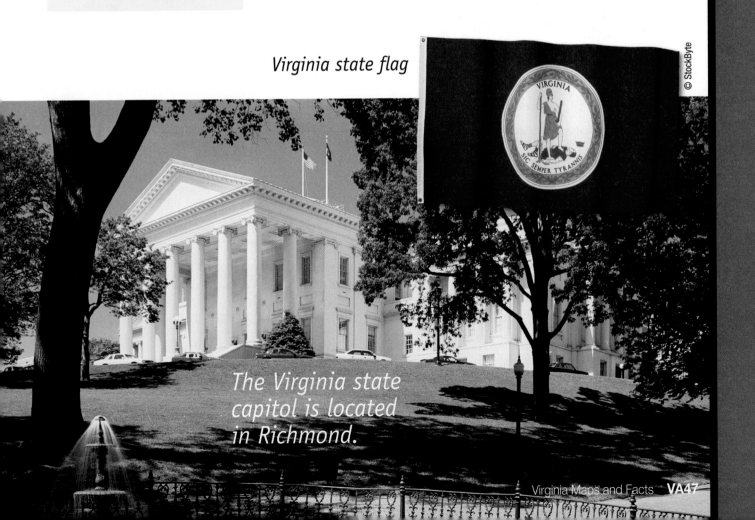

Virginia state flag

The Virginia state capitol is located in Richmond.

© StockByte

Virginia Facts

State tree	Dogwood
State bird	Cardinal
State fish	Brook Trout
State dog	American Foxhound
State insect	Tiger Swallowtail Butterfly
State shell	oyster shell
State flower	Dogwood
State boat	Chesapeake Bay deadrise
State dance	square dance
State beverage	milk
State fossil	Chesapecten jeffersonius
State bat	Virginia big-eared bat
Capital	Richmond
Year of Statehood	June 25, 1788
Nickname	The Old Dominion state
Motto	Sic Semper Tyrannis (Thus Always to Tyrants)
Song	"Carry Me Back to Old Virginia"
Highest Elevation	Mt. Rogers, 5,729 feet above sea level
Lowest Elevation	Atlantic Ocean, sea level
Total area	about 42,770 square miles
National rank in total area	35
Total Coastline	112 miles
Largest city (population)	Virginia Beach
Largest natural freshwater lake	Lake Drummond
Number of counties	95
Population (2006)	7,642,884
National rank in population	12
Length (North to South)	about 440 miles
Width (East to West)	about 200 miles

The Cardinal is the Virginia state bird.

The Dogwood is the Virginia state flower.

HOLT McDOUGAL

Virginia

United States History
Civil War to the Present

William Deverell
Deborah Gray White

HOLT McDOUGAL
a division of Houghton Mifflin Harcourt

Authors

William Deverell

William Deverell is Professor of History at the University of Southern California. He is the author of *Railroad Crossing: Californians and the Railroad, 1850-1910* and *Whitewashed Adobe: The Rise of Los Angeles and the Remaking of the Mexican Past*. He is the editor of the *Blackwell Companion to the American West*. With Greg Hise, he co-authored *Eden by Design: The 1930 Olmsted-Bartholomew Plan for the Los Angeles Region* and co-edited *Land of Sunshine: The Environmental History of Metropolitan Los Angeles*. He is the former chairman of the California Council for the Humanities.

Deborah Gray White

Deborah Gray White, a former New York City school teacher, is Distinguished Professor of History at Rutgers University in New Brunswick, New Jersey. A specialist in American history and the history of African Americans, she is the author of several books, including: *Ar'n't I A Woman? Female Slaves in the Plantation South; Too Heavy a Load: Black Women in Defense of Themselves, 1894-1994*; and *Let My People Go, African Americans 1804-1860*, Volume 4 in the *Young Oxford History of African Americans*.

ISBN-13 978-0-03-099550-7

ISBN-10 0-03-099550-7

3 4 5 6 7 8 9 0868 12 11 10 09
4500245646

Program Consultants

Contributing Author

Kylene Beers, Ed.D.

Senior Reading Advisor to
Secondary Schools
Teachers College Reading and
Writing Project
Columbia University
New York City, New York

A former middle school
teacher, Dr. Beers has turned her
commitment to helping struggling readers into the major focus
of her research, writing, speaking,
and teaching. She is the former
editor of the National Council
of Teachers of English (NCTE)
literacy journal *Voices from the
Middle*. Currently serving NCTE
as vice president, she will assume
the presidency in 2008. Her published works include *When Kids
Can't Read: What Teachers Can Do*
(Heinemann, 2002).

General Editor

Frances Marie Gipson

Secondary Literacy
Los Angeles Unified School
District
Los Angeles, California

In her current position, Frances
Gipson guides reform work for
secondary instruction and supports its implementation. She
has designed curriculum at the
district, state, and national levels.
Her leadership of a coaching col-
laborative with Subject
Matter Projects of the University of California at Los Angeles
evolved from her commitment to
rigorous instruction and to meeting the needs of diverse learners.

Senior Literature and Writing Specialist

Carol Jago

English Department Chairperson
Santa Monica High School
Santa Monica, California

An English teacher at the middle
and high school levels for 26
years, Carol Jago also directs the
reading and literature project at
UCLA and writes a weekly education column for the Los Angeles
Times. She has been published in
numerous professional journals
and has authored several books,
including *Cohesive Writing: Why
Concept is Not Enough* (Boynton/
Cook, 2002).

Consultants

Martha H. Ball, M.A.

Religion Consultant
Utah 3Rs Project Director
Utah State Office of Education
Salt Lake City, Utah

John Ferguson, M.T.S., J.D.

Senior Religion Consultant
Assistant Professor
Political Science/Criminal Justice
Howard Payne University
Brownwood, Texas

J. Frank Malaret

Senior Consultant
Dean, Downtown and West
Sacramento Outreach Centers
Sacramento City College
Sacramento, California

Kimberly A. Plummer, M.A.

Senior Consultant
History-Social Science Educator/
Advisor
Holt, Rinehart & Winston

Galit Reichlin

Associate Director
Middle Eastern Affairs and
International Analysis
Anti-Defamation League
(Reviewed Chapter 30 for
Middle East content)

Andrés Reséndez, Ph.D.

Senior Consultant,
Assistant Professor
Department of History
University of California at Davis
Davis, California

Academic Reviewers

Anne C. Bailey, Ph.D.
Spelman College
Atlanta, Georgia

Albert Camarillo, Ph.D.
Department of History
Stanford University

Larry Conyers, Ph.D.
Department of Anthropology
University of Denver

Willard Gatewood, Ph.D.
Emeritus Alumni Distinguished
    Professor, Department of
    History
University of Arkansas

Christopher Hendricks, Ph.D.
Department of History
Armstrong Atlantic State
    University
Savannah, Georgia

Skip Hyser, Ph.D.
Department of History
James Madison University
Harrisonburg, Virginia

Yasuhide Kawashima
Department of History
University of Texas at El Paso

Brenda E. Stevenson, Ph.D.
Department of History
UCLA
Los Angeles, California

David Switzer, Ph.D.
Department of Social Studies
Plymouth State University
Plymouth, New Hampshire

Jessica Wang, Ph.D.
Department of History
UCLA
Los Angeles, California

Nan Woodruff, Ph.D
Department of History
Pennsylvania State University

Craig Yirush, Ph.D.
Department of History
UCLA
Los Angeles, California

Educational Reviewers

Nelson Acevedo
New York City Alternative
    Schools and Programs
New York, New York

Henry Assetto
Twin Valley High School
Elverson, Pennsylvania

John Bilsky
Linton Middle School
Penn Hills, Pennsylvania

Julie Chan, Ed.D.
Director, Literacy Instruction
Newport-Mesa Unified School
    District
Costa Mesa, California

Kermit Cummings
Cockeysville Middle School
Baltimore County Public Schools
Baltimore, Maryland

Katherine A. DeForge
Social Studies Chair
Marcellus Central School
Marcellus, New York

Sandra Eades
Ridgely Middle School
Lutherville, Maryland

Ed Felten
Coopersville Public School
    District
Coopersville, Michigan

Tim Gearhart
Daniel Lewis Middle School
Paso Robles, California

Stacy Goldman
Lincoln Middle School
Berwyn, Illinois

Joseph P. Macary
Supervisor of Social Studies
Waterbury Public Schools
Waterbury, Connecticut

Carol Eiler Moore
Dundalk Middle School
Dundalk, Maryland

Tina Nelson
Baltimore County Public School
    District
Baltimore, Maryland

Ann-Jean Paci
Sheepshead Bay High School
Brooklyn, New York

Anthony Powell
Edmund W. Miles Middle School
Amityville, New York

Linda Prior
Floyd T. Binns Middle School
Culpeper County, Virginia

Wendy Schanberger
Hereford Middle School
Monkton, Maryland

Sue A. Shinn
Culpeper Middle School
Culpeper, Virginia

Kathleen Torquata
Lincoln Middle School
Berwyn, Illinois

Contents

UNIT 5 The Nation Breaks Apart (1861–1877)

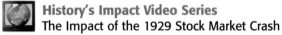
From the Collections of Henry Ford Museum and Greenfield Village

Features

Charts, Graphs, and Tables

Analyze information presented visually to learn more about history.

CHARTS

INFOGRAPHICS

Analyze and interpret information from graphics.

TIME LINES

See how key events are related in time.

Points of View

See how different people have interpreted historical issues in different ways.

Historic Documents

Examine key documents that have shaped U.S. history.

Social Studies Skills

Learn, practice, and apply the skills you need to study and analyze history.

Reading Social Studies

Learn and practice skills that will help you read your social studies lesson.

FOCUS ON WRITING AND SPEAKING

Use writing and speaking to study and reflect on the events and people who made history.

Interdisciplinary Connections

Learn history through connections to other disciplines.

Writing Workshop

Learn to write about history.

Political Cartoons

Interpret political cartoons to learn about U.S. history.

Supreme Court Decisions

Study the impact of Supreme Court decisions on U.S. history.

Literature in History

Learn about the beliefs and experiences of people who lived in other times and places through literature pieces.

Primary Sources

Read and analyze the exact words of important people and documents as related to the study of U.S. history.

Maps

Interpret maps to see where important events happened and analyze how geography has influenced history.

Reading like a Historian

Historians use paintings along with many other tools to help understand the past. The famous painting on the next page, *Washington Crossing the Delaware*, captures the determination of Patriot leaders and soldiers to endure brutal conditions in the hope of winning their struggle for liberty. As you study United States history, you too will learn how to use different historical sources to **Read like a Historian.**

To find out more about reading like a historian and the historical sources that follow, visit

go.hrw.com
More Online
KEYWORD: HISTORIAN

By Frances Marie Gipson
Secondary Literacy Coordinator
Los Angeles Unified School District, Los Angeles, California

What Does It Mean to Read like a Historian?

In your history class you will be doing a lot of reading, thinking, and problem-solving. Much of your reading and thinking will center on different types of texts or materials. Since you are in a history class reading all sorts of things, a question to consider is, "What does it mean to think, read, and solve problems like a historian?"

Historians work with different types of sources to understand and learn from history. Two categories of sources are **primary** and **secondary** sources.

Primary Sources are historical documents, written accounts by a firsthand witness, or objects that have survived from the past. A study of primary sources might include letters, government documents, diaries, photographs, art objects, stamps, coins, and even clothing.

Secondary Sources are accounts of past events created by people some time after the events happened. This textbook and other books written about historical events are examples of secondary sources.

As you learn more about your work as a historian, you will begin to ask questions and analyze historical materials. You will be working as a detective, digging into history to create a richer understanding of the mysteries of the past.

How to Analyze
Written Sources

> ### "Spain's Victory of Peace"
>
> To five hundred thousand Cubans starved or otherwise murdered have been added an American battleship and three hundred American sailors lost as the direct result of the dilatory [delaying] policy of our government toward Spain. If we had stopped the war in Cuba when duty and policy alike urged us to do the *Maine* would have been afloat today, and three hundred homes, now desolate, would have been unscathed [safe from harm].
>
> — *New York Journal*, February 17, 1898

Asking questions can help you determine the relevance and importance of written primary sources, such as this newspaper editorial about the sinking of an American warship. As you analyze the primary source above and the primary and secondary sources included in this textbook, ask yourself questions like the ones below.

- **Who created the source and why?**

- **Did the writer have firsthand knowledge of the event, or does he report what others saw or heard?**

- **Was the writer a neutral party, or did the author have opinions or interests that might have influenced what was recorded?**

- **Did the writer wish to inform or persuade others?**

- **Was the information recorded during the event, immediately after the event, or after some lapse of time?**

The Attack on Lawrence, Kansas

"Sheriff Jones, again at the head of an army of Missourians, marched into Lawrence. In broad daylight, they threw the printing presses of two newspapers into a river. They burned down the Free State Hotel and other buildings. Antislavery Kansans seethed with rage. Here is how one eyewitness described the attack: *Sheriff Jones, after looking at the flames rising from the hotel and saying that it was 'the happiest day of his life,' dismissed the troops and they began their lawless destruction.*"

–John A. Garraty, from *The Story of America*, 1994

When reading secondary sources, such as the description of the attack on Lawrence, Kansas, historians ask additional questions to seek understanding. They try to source the text, build evidence, and interpret the message that is being conveyed. For historians, reading is a quest to find evidence to answer or challenge a historical problem. As you study secondary sources, ask questions like the ones below.

- Who is the author? What do I know about this author?

- Did the author have firsthand information? What is the author's relationship to the event?

- What might be the author's motivation in writing this piece?

- What type of evidence did the author look at?

- Are any assumptions or biases present?

- How does this document fit into the larger context of the events I am studying?

- What kind of source is it?

- Is the source an original?

- Is the content probable or reasonable?

- What does the date tell me about the event?

- What do I already know about this topic that will help me understand more of what I am reading?

How to Analyze an Artifact

Artifacts, such as this phonograph invented by Thomas Edison, take many forms. They might be coins, stone tools, pieces of clothing, or even items found in your backpack. As you study artifacts in this textbook, ask yourself questions like the ones below.

- Why was this object created?

- When and where would it have been used?

- What does the artifact tell me about the technology available at the time it was created?

- What can it tell me about the life and times of the people who used it?

- How does the artifact help to make sense of the time period?

How to Analyze a Historical Map

Maps, such as this one from 1719 of New France, are symbolic representations of places shown in relation to one another. All maps necessarily include some details and leave out others. As you study maps in this textbook, ask questions like the ones below.

- When and where was the map produced?

- What details has the mapmaker chosen to include (or exclude) on this map?

- Why was the map drawn?

- How can I determine if the map is accurate?

- How are maps used to analyze the past, present, and future?

How to Analyze a Photograph

Photographs, like the one above of African American soldiers during the Civil War, are another important source for historians. One way to study a photograph is to write down everything you think is important about it. Then divide the image into four sections and describe the important elements from each section. As you study photographs in this textbook, ask questions like the ones below.

- What is the subject of the photograph?
- What does the image reveal about its subject?
- What is the setting for the photograph?
- What other details can I observe?
- When and where in the past was the photograph created?
- How can I describe the photographer's point of view?

How to Analyze a Political Cartoon

In 1871 Thomas Nast published this cartoon—"Who Stole the People's Money?"—poking fun at corruption in politics. As you study political cartoons in this textbook, use the following helpful tips and questions.

- List the parts of the political cartoon and the importance of each part.

- Describe the focus or significance of the political cartoon.

- Do the captions and call-out boxes clarify the political cartoon's purpose?

- Does the cartoon help me understand the information that I am studying in my textbook better?

Become an Active Reader

by Dr. Kylene Beers

Did you ever think you would begin reading your social studies book by reading about reading? Actually, it makes better sense than you might think. You would probably make sure you learned some soccer skills and strategies before playing in a game. Similarly, you need to learn some reading skills and strategies before reading your social studies book. In other words, you need to make sure you know whatever you need to know in order to read this book successfully.

Tip #1
Use the Reading Social Studies Pages

Take advantage of the two pages on reading at the beginning of every chapter. Those pages introduce the chapter themes; explain a reading skill or strategy; and identify key terms, people, and academic vocabulary.

Themes

Why are themes important? They help our minds organize facts and information. For example, when we talk about baseball, we may talk about types of pitches. When we talk about movies, we may discuss animation.

Historians are no different. When they discuss history or social studies, they tend to think about some common themes: Economics, Geography, Religion, Politics, Society and Culture, and Science and Technology.

Reading Skill or Strategy

Good readers use a number of skills and strategies to make sure they understand what they are reading. These lessons will give you the tools you need to read and understand social studies.

Key Terms, People, and Academic Vocabulary

Before you read the chapter, review these words and think about them. Have you heard the word before? What do you already know about the people? Then watch for these words and their meanings as you read the chapter.

Gives you practice in the reading skill or strategy

Tells which theme or themes are important in the chapter

Explains a skill or strategy good readers use

Identifies the important words in the chapter

Tip #2
Read like a Skilled Reader

You will never get better at reading your social studies book—or any book for that matter—unless you spend some time thinking about how to be a better reader.

Skilled readers do the following:

- They preview what they are supposed to read before they actually begin reading. They look for vocabulary words, titles of sections, information in the margin, or maps or charts they should study.

- They divide their notebook paper into two columns. They title one column "Notes from the Chapter" and the other column "Questions or Comments I Have."

- They take notes in both columns as they read.

- They read like **active readers**. The Active Reading list below shows you what that means.

- They use clues in the text to help them figure out where the text is going. The best clues are called signal words.

  Chronological Order Signal Words:
  first, second, third, before, after, later, next, following that, earlier, finally

  Cause and Effect Signal Words:
  because of, due to, as a result of, the reason for, therefore, consequently

  Comparison/Contrast Signal Words:
  likewise, also, as well as, similarly, on the other hand

Active Reading

Successful readers are **active readers**. These readers know that it is up to them to figure out what the text means. Here are some steps you can take to become an active, and successful, reader.

Predict what will happen next based on what has already happened. When your predictions don't match what happens in the text, reread the confusing parts.

Question what is happening as you read. Constantly ask yourself why things have happened, what things mean, and what caused certain events.

Summarize what you are reading frequently. Do not try to summarize the entire chapter! Read a bit and then summarize it. Then read on.

Connect what is happening in the part you're reading to what you have already read.

Clarify your understanding. Stop occasionally to ask yourself whether you are confused by anything. You may need to reread to clarify, or you may need to read further and collect more information before you can understand.

Visualize what is happening in the text. Try to see the events or places in your mind by drawing maps, making charts, or jotting down notes about what you are reading.

Tip #3
Pay Attention to Vocabulary

It is no fun to read something when you don't know what the words mean, but you can't learn new words if you only use or read the words you already know. In this book, we know we have probably used some words you don't know. But, we have followed a pattern as we have used more difficult words.

Key Terms and People

At the beginning of each section you will find a list of key terms or people that you will need to know. Be on the lookout for those words as you read through the section.

...men's Bureau

In 1865 Congress established the **Freedmen's Bureau**, an agency providing relief for freed-people and certain poor people in the South.

Freedmen's Bureau

In 1865 Congress established the **Freedmen's Bureau**, an agency providing relief for freed-people and certain poor people in the South. The Bureau had a difficult job. At its high point, about 900 agents served the entire South. Bureau commissioner Oliver O. Howard eventually decided to use the Bureau's limited budget to distribute food to the poor and to provide education and legal help for freed-people. The Bureau also helped African American war veterans.

The Freedmen's Bureau played an important role in establishing more schools in the South. Laws against educating slaves meant that most freedpeople had never learned to read or write. Before the war ended, however, northern groups, such as the American Missionary Association, began providing books and teachers to African Americans. The teachers were mostly women who were committed to helping freedpeople. One teacher said of her students, "I never before saw children so eager to learn . . . It is wonderful how [they] . . . can have so great a desire for

knowledge, and such a capacity for attaining [reaching] it."

After the war, some freedpeople organized their own education efforts. For example, Freedmen's Bureau agents found that some African Americans had opened schools in abandoned buildings. Many white southerners continued to believe that African Americans should not be educated. Despite opposition, by 1869 more than 150,000 African American students were attending more than 3,000 schools. The Freedmen's Bureau also helped establish a number of universities for African Americans, including Howard and Fisk universities.

Students quickly filled the new classrooms. Working adults attended classes in the evening. African Americans hoped that education would help them to understand and protect their rights and to enable them to find better jobs. Both black and white southerners benefited from the effort to provide greater access to education in the South.

READING CHECK Analyzing How did the Freedmen's Bureau help reform education in the South?

Helping the Freedpeople

Congress created the Freedmen's Bureau to help freedpeople and poor southerners recover from the Civil War. The Bureau assisted people by:
- providing supplies and medical services
- establishing schools
- supervising contracts between freedpeople and employers
- taking care of lands abandoned or captured during the war

What role did the Freedmen's Bureau play during Reconstruction?

556

Damaged South

Tired southern soldiers returned home to find that the world they had known before the war was gone. Cities, towns, and farms had been ruined. Because of high food prices and widespread crop failures, many southerners faced starvation. The Confederate money held by most southerners was now worthless. Banks failed, and merchants had gone bankrupt because people could not pay their debts.

Former Confederate general Braxton Bragg was one of many southerners who faced economic hardship. He found that *"all, all* was lost, except my debts." In South Carolina, Mary Boykin Chesnut wrote in her diary about the isolation she experienced after the war. "We are shut in here . . . All RR's [railroads] destroyed—bridges gone. We are cut off from the world."

Lincoln's Plan

President Abraham Lincoln wanted to reunite the nation as quickly and painlessly as possible. He had proposed a plan for readmitting the southern states even before the war ended. Called the **Ten Percent Plan**, it offered southerners amnesty, or official pardon, for all illegal acts supporting the rebellion. To receive amnesty, southerners had to do two things. They had to swear an oath of loyalty to the United States. They also had to agree that slavery was illegal. Once 10 percent of voters in

a state made these pledges, they could form a new government. The state then could be readmitted to the Union.

Louisiana quickly elected a new state legislature under the Ten Percent Plan. Other southern states that had been occupied by Union troops soon followed Louisiana back into the United States.

Wade-Davis Bill

Some politicians argued that Congress, not the president, should control the southern states' return to the Union. They believed that Congress had the power to admit new states. Also, many Republican members of Congress thought the Ten Percent Plan did not go far enough. A senator from Michigan expressed their views.

"The people of the North are not such fools as to . . . turn around and say to the traitors, 'all you have to do [to return] is . . . take an oath that henceforth you will be true to the Government.'"
–Senator Jacob Howard, quoted in *Reconstruction: America's Unfinished Revolution, 1863–1877*, by Eric Foner

Two Republicans—Senator Benjamin Wade and Representative Henry Davis—had an alternative to Lincoln's plan. Following **procedures** of the Wade-Davis bill, a state had to meet two conditions before it could rejoin the Union. First, it had to ban slavery. Second, a majority of adult males in the state had to take the loyalty oath.

ACADEMIC VOCABULARY
procedure
a series of steps taken to accomplish a task

War destroyed Richmond, Virginia, once the capital of the Confederacy.

553

ACADEMIC VOCABULARY
procedure
a series of steps taken to accomplish a task

Academic Vocabulary

When we use a word that is important in all classes, not just social studies, we define it in the margin under the heading *Academic Vocabulary*. You will run into these academic words in other textbooks, so you should learn what they mean while reading this book.

Words to Know

As you read this social studies textbook, you will be more successful if you know or learn the meanings of the words on this page. There are two types of words listed here. The first list contains academic words, the words we discussed at the bottom of the previous page. These words are important in all classes, not just social studies. The second list contains words that are special to this particular topic of social studies, U.S. history.

Academic Words

acquire	to get
advocate	to plead in favor of
aspects	parts
authority	power, right to rule
concrete	specific, real
consequences	the effects of a particular event or events
establish	to set up or create
execute	to perform, carry out
facilitate	to bring about
factor	cause
ideal	ideas or goals that people try to live up to
implement	to put in place
implications	effects of a decision
incentive	something that leads people to follow a certain course of action
innovation	a new idea or way of doing something
motive	a reason for doing something
neutral	unbiased, not favoring either side in a conflict
principle	basic belief, rule, or law
procedure	a series of steps taken to accomplish a task
process	a series of steps by which a task is accomplished
role	1. a part or function 2. assigned behavior
strategy	a plan for fighting a battle or war
traditional	customary, time-honored
values	ideas that people hold dear and try to live by
vary/various	1. to be different 2. of many types

Social Studies Words

AD	refers to dates after Jesus's birth
BC	refers to dates before Jesus's birth
BCE	refers to "Before Common Era," dates before the birth of Jesus
CE	refers to "Common Era," dates after Jesus's birth
century	a period of 100 years
civilization	the culture of a particular time or place
climate	the weather conditions in a certain area over a long period of time
culture	the knowledge, beliefs, customs, and values of a group of people
custom	a repeated practice; tradition
democracy	governmental rule by the people, usually on a majority rule principle
economy	the system in which people make and exchange goods and services
geography	the study of the earth's physical and cultural features
independence	freedom from forceful rule
monarchy	governmental rule by one person, a king or queen
North	the region of the United States sometimes defined by the states that did not secede from the Union during the Civil War
rebellion	an organized resistance to the established government
society	a group of people who share common traditions
South	the region of the United States sometimes defined by the states that seceded from the Union to form the Confederate States of America

Mapping the Earth

A **globe** is a scale model of the earth. It is useful for showing the entire earth or studying large areas of the earth's surface.

A pattern of lines circles the globe in east-west and north-south directions. It is called a **grid**. The intersection of these imaginary lines helps us find places on the earth.

The east-west lines in the grid are lines of **latitude**. Lines of latitude are called **parallels** because they are always parallel to each other. These imaginary lines measure distance north and south of the **equator**. The equator is an imaginary line that circles the globe halfway between the North and South Poles. Parallels measure distance from the equator in **degrees**. The symbol for degrees is °. Degrees are further divided into **minutes**. The symbol for minutes is ´. There are 60 minutes in a degree. Parallels north of the equator are labeled with an N. Those south of the equator are labeled with an S.

The north-south lines are lines of **longitude**. Lines of longitude are called **meridians**. These imaginary lines pass through the Poles. They measure distance east and west of the **prime meridian**. The prime meridian is an imaginary line that runs through Greenwich, England. It represents 0° longitude.

Lines of latitude range from 0°, for locations on the equator, to 90°N or 90°S, for locations at the Poles. Lines of longitude range from 0° on the prime meridian to 180° on a meridian in the mid-Pacific Ocean. Meridians west of the prime meridian to 180° are labeled with a W. Those east of the prime meridian to 180° are labeled with an E.

Lines of Latitude

Lines of Longitude

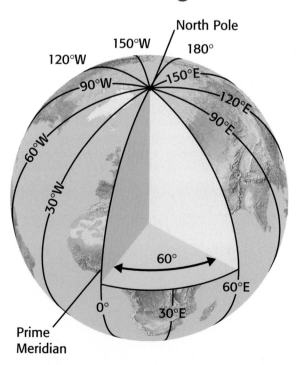

The equator divides the globe into two halves, called **hemispheres**. The half north of the equator is the Northern Hemisphere. The southern half is the Southern Hemisphere. The prime meridian and the 180° meridian divide the world into the Eastern Hemisphere and the Western Hemisphere. However, the prime meridian runs right through Europe and Africa. To avoid dividing these continents between two hemispheres, some mapmakers divide the Eastern and Western hemispheres at 20°W. This places all of Europe and Africa in the Eastern Hemisphere.

Our planet's land surface is divided into seven large landmasses, called **continents**. They are identified in the maps on this page. Landmasses smaller than continents and completely surrounded by water are called **islands**.

Geographers also organize Earth's water surface into parts. The largest is the world ocean. Geographers divide the world ocean into the Pacific Ocean, the Atlantic Ocean, the Indian Ocean, and the Arctic Ocean. Lakes and seas are smaller bodies of water.

Northern Hemisphere

Southern Hemisphere

Western Hemisphere

Eastern Hemisphere

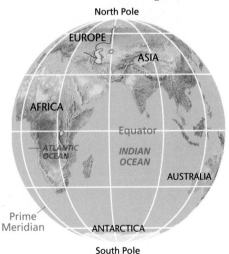

Mapmaking

A **map** is a flat diagram of all or part of the earth's surface. Mapmakers have created different ways of showing our round planet on flat maps. These different ways are called **map projections**. Because the earth is round, there is no way to show it accurately in a flat map. All flat maps are distorted in some way. Mapmakers must choose the type of map projection that is best for their purposes. Many map projections are one of three kinds: cylindrical, conic, or flat-plane.

Paper cylinder

Mercator projection

Cylindrical Projections

Cylindrical projections are based on a cylinder wrapped around the globe. The cylinder touches the globe only at the equator. The meridians are pulled apart and are parallel to each other instead of meeting at the Poles. This causes landmasses near the Poles to appear larger than they really are. The map below is a Mercator projection, one type of cylindrical projection. The Mercator projection is useful for navigators because it shows true direction and shape. However, it distorts the size of land areas near the Poles.

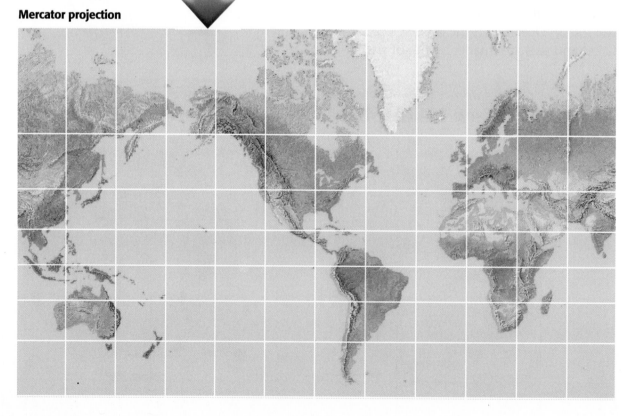

Conic Projections

Conic projections are based on a cone placed over the globe. A conic projection is most accurate along the lines of latitude where it touches the globe. It retains almost true shape and size. Conic projections are most useful for showing areas that have long east-west dimensions, such as the United States.

Paper cone

Conic projection

Flat-Plane Projections

Flat-plane projections are based on a plane touching the globe at one point, such as at the North Pole or South Pole. A flat-plane projection is useful for showing true direction for airplane pilots and ship navigators. It also shows true area. However, it distorts the true shapes of land masses.

Flat plane

Flat-plane projection

Map Essentials

Maps are like messages sent out in code. Mapmakers provide certain elements that help us translate these codes. These elements help us understand the message they are presenting about a particular part of the world. Of these elements, almost all maps have titles, directional indicators, scales, and legends. The map below has all four of these elements, plus a fifth—a locator map.

❶ Title

A map's **title** shows what the subject of the map is. The map title is usually the first thing you should look at when studying a map, because it tells you what the map is trying to show.

Battles in the East

PENNSYLVANIA

| | Union state |
| West Virginia (Separated from Virginia in 1861 and joined the Union in 1863) |
| Confederate state |
| Union forces |
| Union victory |
| Confederate forces |
| Confederate victory |

0   15   30 Miles
0   15   30 Kilometers

WEST VIRGINIA

Potomac

Shenandoah Valley

LEE

McCLELLAN

MARYLAND

River

POPE

Washington

Manassas Junction

Bull Run
July 1861 &
Aug. 1862

LEE

Chesapeake Bay

Fair Oaks
May–June
1862

LEE

Richmond

James River

York R.

McCLELLAN

Seven Days
June 1862

Yorktown

N
W   E
S

VIRGINIA

ATLANTIC OCEAN

❷ Compass Rose

A directional indicator shows which way north, south, east, and west lie on the map. Some mapmakers use a "north arrow," which points toward the North Pole. Remember, "north" is not always at the top of a map. The way a map is drawn and the location of directions on that map depend on the perspective of the mapmaker. Most maps in this textbook indicate direction by using a compass rose. A **compass rose** has arrows that point to all four principal directions, as shown.

❸ Scale

Mapmakers use scales to show the distances between points on a map. Scales may appear on maps in several different forms. The maps in this textbook provide a bar **scale**. Scales give distances in miles and kilometers.

To find the distance between two points on the map, place a piece of paper so that the edge connects the two points. Mark the location of each point on the paper with a line or dot. Then, compare the distance between the two dots with the map's bar scale. The number on the top of the scale gives the distance in miles. The number on the bottom gives the distance in kilometers. Because the distances are given in large intervals, you may have to approximate the actual distance on the scale.

❹ Legend

The **legend**, or key, explains what the symbols on the map represent. Point symbols are used to specify the location of things, such as cities, that do not take up much space on the map. Some legends, such as the one shown here, show colors that represent certain elevations. Other maps might have legends with symbols or colors that represent things such as roads. Legends can also show economic resources, land use, population density, and climate.

❺ Locator Map

A locator map shows where in the world the area on the map is located. The area shown on the main map is shown in red on the locator map. The locator map also shows surrounding areas so the map reader can see how the information on the map relates to neighboring lands.

Working with Maps

The Atlas at the back of this textbook includes both physical and political maps. Physical maps, like the one you just saw and the one below, show the major physical features in a region. These features include things like mountain ranges, rivers, islands, and plains. Political maps show the major political features of a region, such as countries and their borders, capitals, and other important cities.

Topographic Maps

Some maps are topographic maps. A topographic map, like this one, shows the shape of the earth's surface using contour lines. Contour lines are imaginary lines connecting points of the same elevation above sea level. The distance between the lines represents the distance between points on the earth's surface. If the lines are close together, the feature is more steep than if the lines are far apart. Symbols on topographic maps represent natural and manmade features such as rivers, mountains, roads, and even buildings. Name five symbols you see on this topographic map.

Dale, Indiana

Lake/pond, perennial
Elevation contour
Highway, primary
Highway, dual
Railroad, single track
Road, light-duty, paved
Road, minor
Stream, perennial

0   0.5   1 Mile
0   0.5   1 Kilometer

The Louisiana Purchase

Legend:
- U.S. states and territories in 1804
- Louisiana Purchase
- Disputed by United States and Britain
- Lewis and Clark's Expedition, 1804–1806
- Pike's Expedition, 1806–1807

Historical Map

In this textbook, most of the maps you will study are historical maps. Historical maps, such as this one, are maps that show information about the past. This information might be which lands an empire controlled or where a certain group of people lived. Often colors are used to indicate the different things on the map. What does this map show?

Route Map

One special type of historical map is called a route map. A route map, like the one above, shows the route, or path, that someone or something followed. Route maps can show things like trade routes, invasion routes, or the journeys and travels of people. If more than one route is shown, several arrows of different colors may be used. What does this route map show?

The maps in this textbook will help you study and understand history. By working with these maps, you will see where important events happened, where people moved, and how the United States grew and changed. In studying these maps, you will learn how geography has influenced history.

Geographic Dictionary

OCEAN
a large body of water

CORAL REEF
an ocean ridge made up of skeletal remains of tiny sea animals

GULF
a large part of the ocean that extends into land

PENINSULA
an area of land that sticks out into a lake or ocean

BAY
part of a large body of water that is smaller than a gulf

ISLAND
an area of land surrounded entirely by water

ISTHMUS
a narrow piece of land connecting two larger land areas

DELTA
an area where a river deposits soil into the ocean

STRAIT
a narrow body of water connecting two larger bodies of water

SINKHOLE
a circular depression formed when the roof of a cave collapses

WETLAND
an area of land covered by shallow water

RIVER
a natural flow of water that runs through the land

LAKE
an inland body of water

FOREST
an area of densely wooded land

COAST
an area of land
near the ocean

MOUNTAIN
an area of rugged
land that generally
rises higher than
2,000 feet

VALLEY
an area of low
land between
hills or mountains

GLACIER
a large area of
slow-moving ice

VOLCANO
an opening in Earth's crust
where lava, ash, and gases erupt

CANYON
a deep, narrow valley
with steep walls

HILL
a rounded, elevated
area of land smaller
than a mountain

PLAIN
a nearly
flat area

DUNE
a hill of sand
shaped by wind

OASIS
an area in the
desert with a
water source

DESERT
an extremely dry area with
little water and few plants

PLATEAU
a large, flat,
elevated
area of land

The Five Themes of Geography

Geography is the study of the world's people and places. As you can imagine, studying the entire world is a big job. To make the job easier, geographers have created the Five Themes of Geography. They are: **Location, Place, Human-Environment Interaction, Movement,** and **Region**. You can think of the Five Themes as five windows you can look through to study a place. If you looked at the same place through five different windows, you would have five different perspectives, or viewpoints, of the place. Using the Five Themes in this way will help you better understand the world's people and places.

1 Location The first thing to study about a place is its location. Where is it? Every place has an absolute location—its exact location on Earth. A place also has a relative location—its location in relation to other places. Use the theme of location to ask questions like, "Where is this place located, and how has its location affected it?"

2 Place Every place in the world is unique and has its own personality and character. Some things that can make a place unique include its weather, plants and animals, history, and the people that live there. Use the theme of place to ask questions like, "What are the unique features of this place, and how are they important?"

3 Human-Environment Interaction People interact with their environment in many ways. They use land to grow food and local materials to build houses. At the same time, a place's environment influences how people live. For example, if the weather is cold, people wear warm clothes. Use the theme of human-environment interaction to ask questions like, "What is this place's environment like, and how does it affect the people who live there?"

4 Movement The world is constantly changing, and places are affected by the movement of people, goods, ideas, and physical forces. For example, people come and go, new businesses begin, and rivers change their course. Use the theme of movement to ask questions like, "How is this place changing, and why?"

5 Region A region is an area that has one or more features that make it different from surrounding areas. A desert, a country, and a coastal area are all regions. Geographers use regions to break the world into smaller pieces that are easier to study. Use the theme of region to ask questions like "What common features does this area share, and how is it different from other areas?"

1

LOCATION
The United States is located in the Western Hemisphere. Forty-eight of the states are located between Mexico and Canada. This location has good farmland, many resources, and many different natural environments.

Canada

4

5

United States

1

3

Mexico

2

PLACE
New York City is one of the most powerful cities in the world. The people of New York also make the city one of the most ethnically diverse places in the world.

3

HUMAN-ENVIRONMENT INTERACTION
People near Las Vegas, Nevada, transform the desert landscape by building new neighborhoods. Americans modify their environment in many other ways—by controlling rivers, building roads, and creating farmland.

5

REGION
The United States is a political region with one government. At the same time, smaller regions can be found inside the country, such as the Badlands in South Dakota.

4

MOVEMENT
People, goods, and ideas are constantly moving to and from places such as Seattle, Washington. As some places grow, others get smaller, but every place is always changing.

How to Make This Book Work for You

Studying U.S. history will be easy for you using this textbook. Take a few minutes to become familiar with the easy-to-use structure and special features of this history book. See how this U.S. history textbook will make history come alive for you!

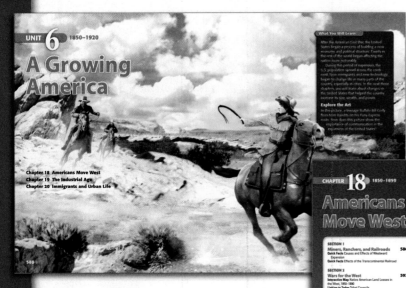

Unit

Each chapter of this textbook is part of a unit of study focusing on a particular time period. Each unit opener provides an illustration, painting, or photograph that gives you an overview of the exciting topics that you will study in the unit.

Chapter

Each chapter begins with a chapter-opener introduction where the sections of the chapter are listed out, and ends with Chapter Review pages and a Standardized Test Practice page.

Reading Social Studies These chapter-level reading lessons teach you skills and provide opportunities for practice to help you read the textbook more successfully. Within each chapter there is a point-of-reference *Focus on Reading* note in the margin to demonstrate the reading skill for the chapter. There are also questions in the Chapter Review activity to make sure that you understand the reading skill.

Social Studies Skills The Social Studies Skills lessons, which appear at the end of each chapter, give you an opportunity to learn and use a skill that you will most likely use again while in school. You will also be given a chance to make sure that you understand each skill by answering related questions in the Chapter Review activity.

Section

The Section opener pages include: Main Idea statements, an overarching Big Idea statement, and Key Terms and People. In addition, each section includes the following special features.

If You Were There . . . introductions begin each section with a situation for you to respond to, placing you in the time period and in a situation related to the content that you will be studying in the section.

Building Background sections connect what will be covered in this section with what you studied in the previous section.

Short sections of content organize the information in each section into small chunks of text that you should not find too overwhelming.

The Taking Notes feature allows you to write down the most important information from the section in a usable format.

Miners, Ranchers, and Railroads

What You Will Learn...

Main Ideas
1. A mining boom brought growth to the West.
2. The demand for cattle created a short-lived Cattle Kingdom on the Great Plains.
3. East and West were connected by the transcontinental railroad.

The Big Idea
As more settlers moved West, mining, ranching, and railroads soon transformed the western landscape.

Key Terms
frontier, *p. 586*
Comstock Lode, *p. 587*
boomtowns, *p. 588*
Cattle Kingdom, *p. 589*
cattle drive, *p. 589*
Chisholm Trail, *p. 589*
Pony Express, *p. 590*
transcontinental railroad, *p. 590*

TAKING NOTES As you read the following section, take notes on the kinds of economic opportunities that people found in the West. Organize your notes in a table like the one below.

Opportunities in the West

586 CHAPTER 18

If YOU were there...

You are a cowboy in Texas in 1875. You love life on the open range, the quiet nights, and the freedom. You even like the hard work of the long cattle drives to Kansas. But you know that times are changing. Homesteaders are moving in and fencing off their lands. Some of the older cowboys say it's time to settle down and buy a small ranch. You hope that they're not right.

What would make you give up a cowboy's life?

BUILDING BACKGROUND In the years following the Civil War, the U.S. population grew rapidly. Settlements in the West increased. More discoveries of gold and silver attracted adventurers, while the open range drew others. Thousands of former Civil War soldiers also joined the move West.

Mining Boom Brings Growth

During the years surrounding the War, most Americans had thought of the Great Plains and other western lands as the Great American Desert. In the years following the Civil War, Americans witnessed the rapid growth of the U.S. population and the spread of settlements throughout the West. With the admission of the state of California to the Union in 1850, the western boundary of the American **frontier**—an undeveloped area—had reached the Pacific Ocean.

The frontier changed dramatically as more and more people moved westward. Settlers built homes, fenced off land, and laid out ranches and farms. Miners, ranchers, and farmers remade the landscape of the West as they adapted to their new surroundings. The geography of the West was further changed by the development and expansion of a large and successful railroad industry that moved the West's natural resources to eastern markets. Gold and silver were the most valuable natural resources, and mining companies used the growing railroad network to bring these precious metals to the East.

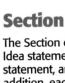

Effects of the Transcontinental Railroad
- Increased settlement of the West
- Increased business activity and East-West trade
- Helped make the railroad industry one of the most powerful in the country

Results of the Railroad

The transcontinental railroad increased both economic growth and the population in the West. Railroad companies provided better transportation for people and goods. They also sold land to settlers, which encouraged people to move West.

New railroads helped businesses. Western timber companies, miners, ranchers, and farmers shipped wood, metals, meat, and grain east by railroad. In exchange, eastern businesses shipped manufactured goods to the West. As trade between regions increased, the idea that the U.S. economy was inter-

THE IMPACT TODAY
Today's businesses ship goods across the country using railroads, the interstate highway system, and airplanes.

dependent became [...] perceptions of [...] railroad schedules began to unite areas that had before existed under different times. Four continental time zones were established in 1883.

Railroad companies encouraged people to put their money into the railroad business, which they did—sometimes unwisely. Railroad speculation and the collapse of railroad owner Jay Cooke's banking firm helped start the Panic of 1873. By the 1880s, many small western railroads were deeply in debt. Despite such setbacks, Americans remained interested in railroad investments. By 1890 there were about 164,000 more miles of track in operation than in 1865. Railroads had become one of the biggest industries in the United States.

READING CHECK Finding Main Ideas How did the railroad affect the development of the West?

SUMMARY AND PREVIEW In this section you learned about the increased settlement of the West. In the next section you will learn about conflicts with Native Americans.

Reading Check questions end each section of content so that you can test whether or not you understand what you have just studied.

Summary and Preview statements connect what you have just studied in the section to what you will study in the next section.

Section Assessment boxes provide an opportunity for you to make sure that you understand the main ideas of the section. We also provide assessment practice online!

Section 1 Assessment

Reviewing Ideas, Terms, and People
1. **a. Recall** Why did Americans move West in the years following the Civil War?
   b. Draw Conclusions What effect did the discovery of the **Comstock Lode** have on the West?
   c. Evaluate Do you think women were important to the success of mining towns? Why or why not?
2. **a. Recall** What led to the cattle boom in the West?
   b. Analyze Why was there competition between ranchers and farmers to settle in the Great Plains?
   c. Evaluate What played the biggest role in ending the **Cattle Kingdom**? Why?
3. **a. Recall** When and where did the Union Pacific and Central Pacific lines meet?
   b. Make Generalizations How do you think the **transcontinental railroad** improved people's lives?

Critical Thinking
4. **Comparing** Review your notes about opportunities in the West. Then use a graphic organizer like the one below to list the effects of these opportunities.

Opportunity	Effect

FOCUS ON WRITING
5. **Taking Notes on Mining, Ranching, and the Railroads** As you read this section, take notes on how mining, ranching, and railroads changed the West. How might a railroad worker feel about these changes?

go.hrw.com
Online Quiz
KEYWORD: SC7 HP18

592 CHAPTER 18

Beginnings of a Nation:

A Review of United States History to 1860

BUILDING BACKGROUND The first settlers in the Americas came in small groups from Asia over the course of thousands of years. Much later, European colonists arrived. Europeans combined their traditions with the opportunities and environment of the Americas to create brand-new societies and, eventually, new nations.

Our Colonial Heritage

Reading Focus *As you read, think about the kinds of people who arrived in the Americas to make a new home.* Most historians agree that the first people came to North America from Asia by crossing the Bering Land Bridge between 38,000 and 10,000 B.C. As they spread through the Americas, these early Native Americans created many societies—groups that share a set of common values and traditions.

Land and climate had a dramatic impact on these early societies. Some places were good for farming or had a rich supply of wild animals and plants. In these areas large groups of people lived in villages. This was true in the Pacific Coast and parts of the East and Southwest. Other parts of North America had less game and were too dry and cold for farming. In these regions Native Americans lived in smaller groups and had to move often to find food. Farther south, in modern-day Mexico and Peru, Native Americans called the Aztec and the Inca each built powerful empires.

Contact and Colonies

The Atlantic and Pacific Oceans kept the Americas isolated from the rest of the world for many years. By the A.D. 1400s, however, Europeans were exploring the seas. They wanted to find overseas routes to the valuable Asian silk and spice trade. Portuguese sailors traveled east around the southern tip of Africa to reach Asia. Christopher Columbus convinced the king and queen of Spain to support his search for a western sea route. In 1492 Columbus's small fleet crossed the Atlantic Ocean. The ships landed not in Asia, as Columbus believed, but on an island in the Bahamas.

Ships such as these were used by European explorers.

Early Beginnings, 38,000 B.C.–1492

c. 38,000 to 10,000 B.C.
The first humans settle in North America.

1492 Christopher Columbus sails across the Atlantic Ocean and reaches the Americas.

38,000 BC

1492

C. A.D. 1200 The Aztec occupy central Mexico.

- **1620** The Pilgrims sign the Mayflower Compact, one of the first attempts at self-government in the colonies.

Other Europeans soon came to the Americas. Spanish soldiers called conquistadores conquered the Aztec and Inca and claimed their lands, encouraging Spain to carve out an empire in the Americas. Spain's success led countries such as France, the Netherlands, Sweden, and England to form their own colonies in North America.

The English Colonies

England founded thirteen colonies in North America, in three general regions, each with its own unique characteristics. The first permanent English settlement in North America was Jamestown, in what is now Virginia. Jamestown colonists came seeking wealth. Other colonists, such as the Pilgrims and the English Catholics who founded Maryland, came seeking religious freedom. All found many challenges and opportunities awaiting them in a new land.

The Southern Colonies

Virginia, Maryland, Georgia, and North and South Carolina made up the southern colonies. Like later colonists in New England, the early Virginia settlers relied on the aid of local Native Americans to survive the harsh conditions they faced. The southern economy depended upon growing cash crops such as tobacco and rice. The biggest farms were called plantations. At first indentured servants did much of the work on these plantations. By the 1700s, however, enslaved Africans had replaced indentured servants as the main source of labor. The southern colonies used harsh laws called slave codes to control and punish slaves.

The New England Colonies

New England consisted of Massachusetts, Connecticut, New Hampshire, and Rhode Island. Pilgrims and Puritans seeking religious freedom founded New England. They built a diverse economy based on shipping, fishing, farming, and manufacturing. Puritan families valued education

The Colonies, 1607–1765

April 6, 1607
English settlers found Jamestown, the first permanent English settlement in North America.

1607

Reconstruction of the Jamestown colony

1620 The Pilgrims arrive in New England to found the Plymouth Colony.

1630 Puritan colonists arrive in New England and found the Massachusetts Bay Colony.

Anne Hutchinson

and built schools for their children. Politics and religion were closely connected, with only church members allowed to vote or hold office. The center of politics was the town meeting, where people met to discuss local issues. Conflict over religious beliefs led Puritan leaders to banish people like Anne Hutchinson and Roger Williams from Massachusetts.

The Middle Colonies

The middle colonies included New York, New Jersey, Pennsylvania, and Delaware. They combined qualities of the New England and southern colonies. Like New England, they had many towns and were centers of trade with Britain and the West Indies. Like the southern colonies, the middle colonies grew large amounts of crops, mainly wheat, barley, and oats. Indentured servants and, to a lesser degree, slaves did much of the labor.

Creating a Nation

Two shared events helped unite colonists living in very different areas. In the 1730s and 1740s, a Christian religious movement called the Great Awakening swept the colonies. It drew people from all walks of life to hear sermons about spiritual equality and social issues. In 1754 the French and Indian War began, pitting the British colonists against French colonists and their Indian allies. The British won the war in 1763. This victory encouraged colonists to settle farther west.

The Thirteen Colonies

Thirteen Colonies

NEW FRANCE

MAINE (PART OF MASS. COLONY)

NEW HAMPSHIRE

MASSACHUSETTS

NEW YORK

RHODE ISLAND

Land claimed by New York and New Hampshire

CONNECTICUT

PENNSYLVANIA

NEW JERSEY

MARYLAND

DELAWARE

ATLANTIC OCEAN

VIRGINIA

APPALACHIAN MOUNTAINS

NORTH CAROLINA

ATLANTIC OCEAN

SOUTH CAROLINA

GEORGIA

New England colonies
Middle colonies
Southern colonies

0   100   200 Miles
0   100   200 Kilometers

SPANISH FLORIDA

1647 The General Court of Massachusetts orders the creation of public schools.

1765

1664 The English capture the Dutch colony of New Amsterdam, renaming it New York.

1690s The Salem witch trials take place in Massachusetts.

Peter Stuyvesant was forced to surrender New Amsterdam to the English in 1664.

- **1775** The "shot heard 'round the world" begins the Revolutionary War at the Battle of Concord.
- **1776** The Declaration of Independence is approved by Congress on July 4.

Road to War

To pay for the war, Parliament passed new taxes on colonial goods such as sugar, paper products, and tea. Many colonists saw this as "taxation without representation," because they had no officials representing them in Parliament. They responded by boycotting, or refusing to buy, British goods. Tensions rose. When British troops fired on a Boston mob in 1770, colonists were outraged. When colonists dumped British tea into the Boston Harbor in 1773, Parliament was furious. Soon British troops occupied Boston and closed its harbor.

The American Revolution

Colonial delegates met at the First Continental Congress and decided to prepare for war. When British troops tried to destroy a supply of weapons at Lexington and Concord, Massachusetts, colonial minutemen fought back, beginning the Revolutionary War. At the Second Continental Congress, delegates put George Washington in charge of the Continental Army.

A widely read pamphlet by Thomas Paine called *Common Sense* argued that the colonies should declare independence, and that the people, not kings, should make the laws. On July 4, 1776, the United States of America was born when the Continental Congress approved the Declaration of Independence.

The Patriots, or supporters of independence, lacked a well-trained army, but they knew the land on which they fought. They had few victories until defeating the British in the Battle of Saratoga. This win convinced France and Spain to become their allies. After a brutal winter at Valley Forge and a shift to fighting in the South, the Patriots finally won the decisive victory at Yorktown in 1781. Great Britain recognized U.S. independence in the Treaty of Paris of 1783.

A New Nation, 1765–1787

1776 George Washington and his troops crossed the partially frozen Delaware River on the night of December 25, 1776. This daring act led to a key Patriot victory at the Battle of Trenton.

1765

1765 The Stamp Act taxes newspapers, licenses, and other colonial paper products.

Tax stamp

1770 The Boston Massacre occurs when British soldiers fire on a crowd of colonists, killing five men.

1773 The Boston Tea Party takes place when colonists protest the Tea Act by dumping British tea into Boston Harbor.

Boston Massacre

A New Nation

Reading Focus *As you read, identify the problems of the young nation and the steps taken to strengthen it.* The new United States needed a government to lead it. American political ideas were shaped by European and colonial models. English examples included Magna Carta and the English Bill of Rights. Magna Carta had made the king subject to law, while the Bill of Rights gave Parliament greater power. Enlightenment philosophers also influenced American political ideas. John Locke claimed that rulers and their people were bound by a social contract. Baron de Montesquieu called for the separation of government powers. Americans also had their own models of self-government, such as town meetings, the Mayflower Compact, and the principles set forth in the Declaration of Independence.

KEY FACTS

- **1639** The people of Connecticut create the first written constitution in the English colonies.
- **1689** The English Bill of Rights is created.

Forming a Government

The Second Continental Congress drafted the Articles of Confederation, the first national constitution. The Articles created a Congress with limited powers. There was no executive branch or judicial system. To organize western settlement, Congress passed the Northwest Ordinance of 1787, creating the Northwest Territory. The law allowed new territories to join the Union as equal states.

National Challenges

The weakness of the new Congress caused many problems, especially with the economy. Great Britain and Spain cut American merchants off from trade and made them pay high taxes on imports and exports. Trade laws also varied from state to state, hurting businesses. In an effort to pay high war debts, some states printed too much paper money. This money soon became worthless, causing inflation. When poor farmers in Massachusetts faced high taxes, they joined Shays's Rebellion against the state courts. Although the rebellion failed, to many people it was a sign that a change in the government was needed.

Daniel Shays, at the top of the steps, blocks the courthouse in Massachusetts. By shutting down the courts, farmers hoped to stop the government from selling their land.

1781 The Articles of Confederation are ratified, establishing the first national government of the United States.

1783 The Treaty of Paris of 1783 ends the Revolutionary War and recognizes the independence of the United States.

1787 Shays's Rebellion ends in Massachusetts.

1781 Washington defeats Cornwallis at the Battle of Yorktown.

Battle of Yorktown

1787

The British scuttled, or purposely sank, dozens of their ships. This formed a barrier that kept the French ships from coming too close.

N W E S

French Navy

Choissey

Tarleton

Scuttled British Ships

York River

French Navy

Yorktown
Cornwallis

Rochambeau

Field of British Surrender

- **May 1787** The Constitutional Convention begins in Philadelphia.

The Constitutional Convention

The states held a Constitutional Convention in 1787 to improve the Articles of Confederation. Insteasd of rewriting the Articles, however, the convention drafted a new document. Delegates included Benjamin Franklin, Alexander Hamilton, James Madison, and George Washington. The delegates debated many issues. The Great Compromise created a two-house Congress where each state has an equal voice in the Senate and larger states have more representation in the House of Representatives. The Three-Fifths Compromise counted three-fifths of the slave population when determining representation. These compromises settled disputes between large and small states and northern and southern states. Opponents of the new Constitution, called Antifederalists, objected to the plan for a stronger central government. Supporters of the Constitution, called Federalists, won the public debate by convincing people that the new government would not only provide security but also protect their rights.

Strengths of the Constitution
most power held by national government
three branches of government
executive branch led by president
legislative branch has many powers
firm system of checks and balances

The Constitution

The system of government established by the Constitution is called federalism. Under federalism powers are divided between the states and the federal, or national, government. States keep control over many issues, such as local government and local laws. The power of the federal government is divided among three branches. The legislative branch, or Congress, passes laws. The executive branch, made up of the president and many departments, makes sure the laws are carried out. The judicial branch, consisting of the national courts, interprets laws and punishes criminals. A system of checks and balances keeps any one branch from becoming too

Weaknesses of the Articles of Confederation
• most power held by states
• one branch of government
• legislative branch has few powers
• no executive branch
• no judicial system
• no system of checks and balances

Creating the Constitution, 1787–1800

1787 Delaware becomes the first state to ratify the Constitution.

1788 The *Federalist Papers* supporting the Constitution are collected and published.

Alexander Hamilton, John Jay, and James Madison authored the *Federalist Papers*.

1787

1789 Congress passes the Judiciary Act of 1789, setting up the federal court system.

1791 Officials choose the site of the nation's future capital, which becomes Washington, D.C.

1791 The first 10 amendments to the Constitution, known as the Bill of Rights, are ratified.

This painting shows the signing of the Constitution on September 17, 1787.

powerful. For example, the president can veto a law passed by Congress. The Constitution also allows the people to ratify amendments that change the document to adjust to changing times. Citizens have not only rights but also responsibilities under federalism. Fulfilling these duties helps the system work fairly and effectively for all Americans.

Washington's Presidency

General George Washington was elected as the first U.S. president. Congress created executive departments to help the president run the country, and Washington set up a cabinet to help advise him. Secretary of State Thomas Jefferson and Secretary of the Treasury Alexander Hamilton disagreed on many important issues, including the size and purpose of government, financing the government, and interpreting the Constitution. Their disagreements helped shape the young nation.

Foreign and domestic conflicts disrupted the peace during Washington's administration. The United States tried to remain neutral in European conflicts, but the U.S. Army did go to war with Native American forces in the Northwest Territory. The government faced angry farmers when Congress passed a tax on American whiskey. Washington led an army to end the so-called Whiskey Rebellion.

Washington decided not to run for reelection in 1796 after two terms in office. In his farewell address, Washington advised future leaders to maintain U.S. neutrality in foreign affairs and to avoid the dangers of political parties. Political divisions between followers of Jefferson and Hamilton contributed to the growth of political parties, however.

- **1788** The Constitution goes into effect after New Hampshire becomes the ninth state to ratify it.
- **1789** George Washington is elected as the first president of the United States.
- **1791** Congress establishes the first Bank of the United States.

George Washington

1794 Angry farmers begin the Whiskey Rebellion against the federal government.

1796 George Washington gives his Farewell Address to the country after two terms in office.

1800

A tax collector is tarred and feathered during the Whiskey Rebellion.

- **1803** The United States purchases Louisiana from France.
- **1804** The Lewis and Clark expedition sets out to explore the Louisiana Purchase.
- **1812** The U.S. Congress declares war on Great Britain.

The New Republic

Reading Focus *As you read, notice how the young republic was different from the nation you live in today.* Federalist John Adams defeated Democratic-Republican Thomas Jefferson in the 1796 presidential election. During Adams's term, the United States nearly went to war with France. When Democratic-Republicans who supported France criticized the Federalists for their actions toward France, Congress passed the Alien and Sedition Acts. These laws limited freedom of speech and the press. Jefferson and others called these acts unconstitutional.

The American Republic

The election of 1800 pitted Adams and Jefferson against each other again. Jefferson won the election after a bitter campaign. This victory marked the first peaceful change of power from one political party to another in U.S. history.

Jefferson's Era

During Jefferson's presidency the Supreme Court increased its power with the case *Marbury* v. *Madison*. Chief Justice John Marshall's ruling established the power of judicial review, which allows the Court to declare an act of Congress unconstitutional. One of Jefferson's biggest achievements as president was agreeing to the Louisiana Purchase, which nearly doubled the size of the United States. He then sent the Lewis and Clark expedition to explore this vast new territory.

War and Peace

Jefferson tried unsuccessfully to protect American neutrality with France and Great Britain. Both countries captured U.S. ships trading with the enemy. Efforts to ban trade with these countries only hurt Americans. The British also supported Native Americans who opposed American settlement in the West. As a result, President James Madison called for war against Britain. During the War of 1812, neither side gained any territory.

The New Republic, 1800–1840

1801 Thomas Jefferson is elected president of the United States.

1803 Chief Justice John Marshall establishes the principle of judicial review in the case *Marbury* v. *Madison*.

1814 Great Britain and the United States sign the Treaty of Ghent, ending the War of 1812.

1800

1806 Lewis and Clark return home after reaching the Pacific Ocean.

Thomas Jefferson

Meriwether Lewis and William Clark

Growing Nationalism

A positive outcome of the war was that it boosted American patriotism and confidence. President James Monroe issued the Monroe Doctrine, warning Europeans not to interfere in the Western Hemisphere. Political conflict declined from 1815 to 1825, called the Era of Good Feelings. States built new roads and canals—like the Erie Canal—to link regions together. Writers such as Washington Irving and painters like the members of the Hudson River school created new American styles of art. Yet one threat to unity remained. Northern and southern states disagreed about whether to let slavery expand westward. The Missouri Compromise of 1820 tried to keep the balance between the number of slave and free states. It was only a temporary solution, however.

The Age of Jackson

By 1828 many states had passed laws increasing suffrage for white men. This led to an era of a rise in popular politics, which became known as Jacksonian Democracy, after politician Andrew Jackson. Jackson's defeat in 1824 led his supporters to create the Democratic Party. Many saw his victory in the 1828 presidential election as a win for the common people.

Jackson faced a major crisis when South Carolina threatened to leave the Union if Congress did not lower taxes on imports. Jackson opposed the view that states could reject, or nullify, laws of Congress and the crisis ended. Jackson did not always support federal authority, however. He opposed the Second Bank of the United States because he felt it favored the rich. The Supreme Court had declared the Bank to be constitutional in *McCulloch* v. *Maryland*. Still, Jackson was able to kill public support for the Bank. After he left office, the loss of the Bank helped cause the economic depression called the Panic of 1837. This crisis hurt the Democratic Party and helped the Whig Party win the presidential election of 1840.

1832 South Carolina starts the Nullification Crisis by declaring federal tariffs null and void.

c. 1824 Supporters of Andrew Jackson found the Democratic Party.

1834 The Whig Party is formed to oppose Jackson.

1840

1819 The Supreme Court rules in *McCulloch* v. *Maryland* that the Bank of the United States is constitutional.

Jackson is shown fighting a monster representing the national bank in this cartoon.

Andrew Jackson

The Nation Expands

Reading Focus *As you read, identify differences between the North and the South.* As America's population grew, settlers looked for more territory. In 1830 Congress passed the Indian Removal Act with the support of President Jackson. This law allowed the removal of Native Americans living east of the Mississippi to western land known as Indian Territory. Groups such as the Cherokee protested the law. Not even a Supreme Court ruling in their favor could save them, however. In 1838 several thousand Cherokee died on the march west known as the Trail of Tears.

Manifest Destiny

Indian removal did not stop more Americans from pushing even farther westward. Fur trappers were some of the first Americans to reach the Rockies. Later, thousands of pioneers followed the 2,000-mile-long Oregon Trail to the Pacific Northwest. Thousands more settled in the Mexican province of Texas. The Mexican government grew worried that these Americans were disobeying Mexican laws. When Mexico banned further American settlement, tempers flared. In 1836 Texas rebelled against Mexico and won its independence.

Many Americans began to believe that America had a manifest destiny, or obvious fate, to settle all the way to the Pacific Ocean. Soon there were calls to annex Texas and Oregon. President James K. Polk gained Oregon peacefully by treaty with Great Britain. But the conflict over Texas led to the Mexican-American War. The overwhelming U.S. victory in that war led Mexico to grant huge pieces of land to the United States. This so-called Mexican Cession included California and most of the present-day American Southwest.

The Nation Expands, 1830–1850

1830

1836 Texas wins independence from Mexico.

1830 American Peter Cooper builds the locomotive called *Tom Thumb.*

1938 During the Trail of Tears, thousands of Cherokee died from disease, starvation, and harsh weather. They were forced to walk hundreds of miles to their new land in the West. Other Native Americans were also moved, with similar results.

The discovery of gold in California brought a rush of miners from all over the world. These included some of the first Chinese immigrants to America. California's population and economy boomed as a result of this Gold Rush. By 1850 California had become the 31st state.

The Industrial North

As pioneers headed West, new industries grew in the Northeast. The first American factories used water-powered machines to make cloth. Inventor Eli Whitney later came up with the idea of interchangeable parts, which helped make mass production and less expensive goods possible. Factories employed men, women, and children to run the machinery. Workers toiled long hours in difficult conditions, often for little pay. Labor reform efforts had little success. Some workers formed unions and used strikes to demand better treatment.

The Transportation Revolution

Steamboats and steam-powered trains made transportation faster and cheaper than ever before. By 1860 the United States had nearly 30,000 miles of railroads and hundreds of steamboats. Communication also improved with the invention of the telegraph, which carried messages across wires. These changes helped fuel economic growth.

Immigration and City Life

Steam power also allowed factories to move from the countryside to the cities. City populations boomed, thanks to new jobs and the arrival of several million immigrants. Most of these people came from Ireland and Germany, fleeing famine or political troubles. Many immigrants faced prejudice from other Americans. Industry and city growth helped create a new middle class of managers and skilled workers. The downsides of city growth were overcrowding, crime, disease, and the threat of fires.

KEY FACTS

- **1793** The first U.S. textile mill opens in Pawtucket, Rhode Island.
- **1798** Eli Whitney proposes to mass produce muskets using interchangeable parts.
- **1807** Robert Fulton successfully sails the first full-sized steamboat, the *Clermont*.
- **1814** Francis Lowell opens his first mill in Waltham, Massachusetts.

1846 The United States declares war on Mexico.

1849 Thousands of "forty-niners" come to California in search of gold.

1848 The United States and Mexico sign the Treaty of Guadalupe Hidalgo, ending the Mexican-American War.

1850

The Cherokee during the Trail of Tears

KEY FACTS

- **1793** Eli Whitney patents the cotton gin.
- **1790s to early 1800s** The Second Great Awakening sweeps the nation.
- **1848** The first public meeting on women's rights in the United States is held in Seneca Falls, New York.

The Agricultural South

Compared to the North, the South had less industry and fewer big cities. As a result, fewer immigrants settled in the region. Instead, the South remained rural and agricultural, relying on cash crops for its wealth.

The Cotton Boom

The first southern cash crops were tobacco, rice, and indigo. Eli Whitney's invention of the cotton gin in 1793 made cotton the South's biggest crop. The gin quickly removed seeds from cotton fibers. The demand for cotton boomed as textile mills in the American North and in Great Britain grew. The South became a major player in world trade and was sometimes called the Cotton Kingdom.

The Slave System

Cotton brought wealth but also increased the demand for slave labor to grow and process the crop. Only about one-third of white southerners had slaves. Yeomen farmers and poor whites owned few or no slaves, but most defended the slave system. Many slaves lived on the small number of large plantations owned by wealthy planters. On big plantations most slaves worked in the fields, while some had specific skilled jobs like carpentry. Slaves' living conditions were poor and the punishments they faced harsh. Slave codes limited slaves' right to travel and banned them from schools. Still, enslaved people kept alive African customs and expressed themselves through folktales and spirituals. Some slaves even led rebellions, though these were rare and severely punished.

American Society, 1830–1855

1830

1831 Nat Turner leads an unsuccessful slave rebellion in Virginia.

An illustration of Nat Turner's rebellion

1833 William Lloyd Garrison helps found the American Anti-Slavery Society.

1840 The United States produces more than half of the world's cotton.

U.S. Cotton Production, 1800–1860

Cotton (in 100,000 bales)

24
20
16
12
8
4
0

1800   1820   1840   1860

Year

New Movements in Society

Some Americans formed the abolitionist movement to oppose slavery. Former slaves Frederick Douglass and Sojourner Truth were two leading abolitionists. Abolitionists used speeches and newspapers to spread their antislavery messages. They based many speeches and articles on the ideas of equality found in the Declaration of Independence. Abolitionists fought against laws that protected slavery, including laws that made it illegal to help runaway slaves.

Abolition was just one of the many reform movements that arose in the United States. The religious revival called the Second Great Awakening triggered a wave of reform efforts. Some people supported the temperance movement, which tried to stop alcohol abuse. They blamed alcohol for problems of society such as crime and poverty. Others called for prison and education reform, such as better treatment for prisoners and more public schools for children. Reformers helped spread education to African Americans and women by opening schools that would accept them.

Women who took part in the abolition movement, like Elizabeth Cady Stanton, began to demand more rights for women as well. Stanton and other reformers called for women's suffrage, or the right to vote. Some claimed that women did not have an obligation to follow the laws of a nation that did not let them vote. These were just the first steps toward gaining equal rights for many Americans.

1849 Harriet Tubman escapes slavery and soon begins leading fugitive slaves to freedom through the Underground Railroad.

Harriet Tubman

1855

1855 The photograph above of the 1855 class at Oberlin College shows the slow integration of African Americans into previously white colleges.

- **1852** Harriet Beecher Stowe publishes *Uncle Tom's Cabin*.
- **1854** Congress passes the Kansas-Nebraska Act.
- **1857** The Supreme Court issues the *Dred Scott* decision.
- **1861** Seven southern states leave the Union and form the Confederacy.

The Nation Breaks Apart

Reading Focus *As you read, list the sequence of events leading to the Civil War.* By 1850 the North and South had grown apart in many ways. The regions had different economies, different societies, and different goals. People in one region knew fairly little about their fellow citizens in another part of the country. As both regions pushed westward, their differences led to conflict.

Deepening Divisions

Many northerners did not want slavery to spread to the West. Some opposed it for moral reasons, while others felt it would take jobs from white workers. After the Mexican-American War, Representative David Wilmot said that slavery should be banned in the new lands gained by the United States. Southerners strongly opposed this idea. In the North, the Free-Soil Party arose to oppose the spread of slavery.

Failed Compromises

The addition of California as a state threatened to upset the political balance between slave and free states in the Union. An unequal balance would affect the political make up of the Senate. The North already had an edge in the House of Representatives. Henry Clay offered the Compromise of 1850 to keep the peace. California joined the Union as a free state, but other territories in the Southwest would be allowed to choose whether to allow slavery. The Kansas-Nebraska Act later applied the same approach by allowing new territories in the Midwest to support or oppose slavery. Neither of these compromises kept the peace for long.

Bleeding Kansas

The Compromise of 1850 introduced a law called the Fugitive Slave Act. This made it easier to capture runaway slaves hiding in the North. The law angered many northerners. Those opposed to slavery were equally upset

The Nation Breaks Apart, 1850–1860

1850 California enters the Union as a free state.

1854 The Republican Party is formed to oppose the spread of slavery.

1850

1854 The Kansas-Nebraska Act is passed, organizing the territories of Kansas and Nebraska.

California +2 senators

Northern free states 30 senators

Southern slave states 30 senators

when the Kansas-Nebraska Act opened the door to the spread of slavery in the Midwest. The Missouri Compromise had once banned slavery in that region. Harriet Beecher Stowe's popular antislavery novel *Uncle Tom's Cabin* fanned these flames by upsetting many southerners. So when the Kansas Territory was opened, pro- and antislavery settlers rushed in. Each side was determined to control the territory. The result was a series of attacks and killings by both groups that shocked the nation.

Prelude to War

Northerners received another shock with the Supreme Court's ruling in the *Dred Scott* case. The Court ruled that African Americans could not be U.S. citizens and that Congress could not ban slavery in any of the territories. This decision boosted support for the new Republican Party, which opposed the spread of slavery to the West.

Abolitionist John Brown stunned the South when he attacked Harper's Ferry, Virginia, trying to start a slave rebellion. Many northerners called Brown a hero. The election of 1860 took place in this bitter atmosphere. Republican Abraham Lincoln won the election without winning a single electoral vote from the South, upsetting southern leaders. They feared that Lincoln would ban slavery. Such a move would destroy the South's economy and change its society. South Carolina, Mississippi, Florida, Alabama, Georgia, Louisiana, and Texas responded to Lincoln's win by withdrawing from the Union. They formed the Confederate States of America, or the Confederacy. Lincoln insisted that the Confederate states could not simply leave the Union or keep the federal property within their borders. The stage was set for a terrible conflict pitting North against South.

SUMMARY AND PREVIEW America had moved from a collection of loose-knit colonies to an independent, united country, to a nation divided over issues such as slavery. Now the nation faced the terrible prospect of a civil war that would threaten its very existence.

Abraham Lincoln

Stephen Douglas

1858 Republican Abraham Lincoln and Democrat Stephen Douglas hold the Lincoln–Douglas debates in Illinois over the issue of slavery.

1860

1859 Abolitionist John Brown leads a raid on Harper's Ferry.

1860 Abraham Lincoln wins the U.S. presidential election.

Lincoln ran for U.S. Senate in Illinois against Douglas in 1858. The two men debated seven times at various locations around the state. Lincoln lost the election but gained national recognition.

The Nation Breaks Apart

Chapter 16 The Civil War
Chapter 17 Reconstruction

When compromise after compromise failed, the United States was divided by war. The American Civil War tested the strength of the bond between the states. During the Civil War, Americans fought each other on battlefields and in government. Ideas about slavery and sovereignty led many soldiers to fight. Eventually the nation was reunited, but deep scars remained. In the next two chapters, you will learn about the war and the period after when rebuilding the South became a priority.

Explore the Art

This painting is titled *Fight for the Colors*. It shows Union and Confederate troops at the Battle of Gettysburg, which began in Pennsylvania on July 1, 1863. This 3-day battle was the largest and bloodiest in the Civil War.

What aspects of the Civil War does this picture show?

The Civil War

Virginia Standards of Learning

USII.1 The student will demonstrate skills for historical and geographical analysis, and responsible citizenship, including the ability to

a) analyze and interpret primary and secondary source documents to increase understanding of events and life in United States history from 1865 to the present; **b)** make connections between past and present; **c)** sequence events in United States history from 1865 to the present; **d)** interpret ideas and events from different historical perspectives; **e)** evaluate and debate issues orally and in writing; **f)** analyze and interpret maps that include major physical features

USII.2 The student will use maps, globes, photographs, pictures, or tables for

c) locating the 50 states and the cities most significant to the historical development of the United States

USII.3 The student will demonstrate knowledge of the effects of Reconstruction on American life by

c) describing the legacy of Abraham Lincoln, Robert E. Lee, and Frederick Douglass

FOCUS ON WRITING

Writing a Newspaper Article For most of this nation's history, newspapers have been an important way for citizens to learn about what is happening in the United States. In this chapter you will read about the main events of the Civil War. Then you will choose one of these events and write a newspaper article about it.

UNITED STATES

1861 Confederate guns open fire on Fort Sumter on April 12. Confederates win the first battle of the Civil War on July 21 at Bull Run in Virginia.

1861

WORLD

1861 Great Britain and France decide to buy cotton from Egypt instead of from the Confederacy.

HOLT

History's Impact
▶ **video series**
Watch the video to understand the impact of the Civil War.

What You Will Learn...

In this chapter you will learn how the resources of the North enabled it to defeat the South in the Civil War. Among those who marched off to war were these drummer boys of the Union army.

1862 The *Monitor* fights the *Virginia* on March 9.

1863 The Emancipation Proclamation is issued on January 1.

1865 General Robert E. Lee surrenders to General Ulysses S. Grant on April 9.

1862 | **1863** | **1864** | **1865**

1862 An imperial decree expels foreigners from Japan.

1864 With the support of French troops, Archduke Maximilian of Austria becomes emperor of Mexico.

1864 The Taiping Rebellion in China ends after the capture of Nanjing in July.

Reading Social Studies

by Kylene Beers

Focus on Themes As you read this chapter about the Civil War, you will see that this was a time in our history dominated by two major concerns: **politics** and **society and culture**. You will not only read about the political decisions made during this war, but also you will see how the war affected all of American society. You will read about the causes and the key events during the war and the many consequences of this war. This chapter tells of one of the most important events in our history.

Supporting Facts and Details

Focus on Reading Main ideas and big ideas are just that, ideas. How do we know what those ideas really mean?

Understanding Ideas and Their Support A main idea or big idea may be a kind of summary statement, or it may be a statement of the author's opinion. Either way, a good reader looks to see what support—facts and various kinds of details—the writer provides. If the writer doesn't provide good support, the ideas may not be trustworthy.

Notice how the passage below uses facts and details to support the main idea.

Civil War armies fought in the ancient battlefield formation that produced massive casualties. Endless rows of troops fired directly at one another, with cannonballs landing amid them. When the order was given, soldiers would attach bayonets to their guns and rush toward their enemy. Men died to gain every inch of ground. . .

Despite the huge battlefield losses, the biggest killer in the Civil War was not the fighting. It was diseases such as typhoid, pneumonia, and tuberculosis. Nearly twice as many soldiers died of illnesses as died in combat.

From Chapter 16, p. 533

> The main idea is stated first.

> These sentences provide details about the challenges soldiers faced.

> The writer concludes with some facts as support.

Writers support propositions with . . .

1. **Facts and statistics**—statements that can be proved; facts in number form
2. **Examples**—specific instances that illustrate the facts
3. **Anecdotes**—brief stories that help explain the facts
4. **Definitions**—explanation of unusual terms or words
5. **Comments from the experts or eyewitnesses**—statements from reliable sources

Virginia Standards of Learning

Reading 6.5e Organize the main idea and details to form a summary.

You Try It!

The following passage is from the chapter you are about to read. As you read it, look for the writer's main idea and support.

> In February 1862, Grant led an assault force into Tennessee. With help from navy gunboats, Grant's Army of the Tennessee took two outposts on key rivers in the west. On February 6, he captured Fort Henry on the Tennessee River. Several days later he took Fort Donelson on the Cumberland River.
>
> Fort Donelson's commander asked for the terms of surrender. Grant replied, "No terms except an unconditional and immediate surrender can be accepted." The fort surrendered. The North gave a new name to Grant's initials: "Unconditional Surrender" Grant.

From Chapter 16, pp. 522–523

After you read the passage, answer the following questions.

1. Which sentence best states the writer's main idea?
   a. The fort surrendered.
   b. In February 1862, Grant led an assault force into Tennessee.
   c. Fort Donelson's commander asked for the terms of surrender.

2. Which method of support is not used to support the main idea?
   a. facts
   b. comments from experts or eyewitnesses
   c. anecdotes

3. Which sentence in this passage provides a comment from an expert or eyewitness?

> **As you read Chapter 16,** pay attention to the details that the writers have chosen to support their main ideas.

Key Terms and People

Chapter 16

Section 1
Abraham Lincoln *(p. 510)*
Fort Sumter *(p. 511)*
border states *(p. 512)*
Winfield Scott *(p. 513)*
cotton diplomacy *(p. 513)*

Section 2
Thomas "Stonewall" Jackson *(p. 517)*
First Battle of Bull Run *(p. 517)*
George B. McClellan *(p. 517)*
Robert E. Lee *(p. 518)*
Seven Days' Battles *(p. 518)*
Second Battle of Bull Run *(p. 518)*
Battle of Antietam *(p. 519)*
ironclads *(p. 520)*

Section 3
Ulysses S. Grant *(p. 522)*
Battle of Shiloh *(p. 523)*
David Farragut *(p. 524)*
Siege of Vicksburg *(p. 524)*

Section 4
abolitionists *(p. 529)*
emancipation *(p. 529)*
Emancipation Proclamation *(p. 529)*
Frederick Douglass *(p. 530)*
William Lloyd Garrison *(p. 530)*
contrabands *(p. 531)*
54th Massachusetts Infantry *(p. 531)*
Copperheads *(p. 532)*
habeas corpus *(p. 532)*
Clara Barton *(p. 534)*

Section 5
Battle of Gettysburg *(p. 537)*
George Pickett *(p. 539)*
Pickett's Charge *(p. 539)*
Gettysburg Address *(p. 540)*
Wilderness Campaign *(p. 540)*
William Tecumseh Sherman *(p. 541)*
total war *(p. 542)*
Appomattox Courthouse *(p. 542)*

Academic Vocabulary

In this chapter, you will learn the following academic words:

innovation *(p. 520)*
execute *(p. 540)*

The War Begins

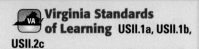 **Virginia Standards of Learning** USII.1a, USII.1b, USII.2c

What You Will Learn...

Main Ideas

1. Following the outbreak of war at Fort Sumter, Americans chose sides.
2. The Union and the Confederacy prepared for war.

The Big Idea

Civil war broke out between the North and the South in 1861.

Key Terms and People

Abraham Lincoln, *p. 510*
Fort Sumter, *p. 511*
border states, *p. 512*
Winfield Scott, *p. 513*
cotton diplomacy, *p. 513*

TAKING NOTES As you read, take notes on the Civil War and how Americans chose sides and how each side prepared for the war.

	Choosing Sides	Preparing for War
North		
South		

If **YOU** were there...

You are a college student in Charleston in early 1861. Seven southern states have left the Union and formed their own government. All-out war seems unavoidable. Your friends have begun to volunteer for either the Union or the Confederate forces. You are torn between loyalty to your home state and to the United States.

Would you join the Union or the Confederate army?

BUILDING BACKGROUND The divisions within the United States reached a breaking point with the election of Abraham Lincoln in 1860. Several southern states angrily left the Union to form a new confederation. In border states such as Virginia and Kentucky, people were divided. The question now was whether the United States could survive as a disunified country.

Americans Choose Sides

Furious at the election of Republican **Abraham Lincoln** and fearing a federal invasion, seven southern states had seceded. The new commander in chief tried desperately to save the Union.

In his inaugural address, Lincoln promised not to end slavery where it existed. The federal government "will not assail [attack] you. You can have no conflict without being yourselves the aggressors," he said, trying to calm southerners' fears. However, Lincoln also stated his intention to preserve the Union. He believed that saving the Union would help to save democracy. If the Union and its government failed, then monarchs could say that people were unable to rule themselves. As a result, Lincoln refused to recognize secession, declaring the Union to be "unbroken."

In fact, after decades of painful compromises, the Union was badly broken. From the lower South, a battle cry was arising, born out of fear, rage—and excitement. Confederate officials began seizing branches of the federal mint, arsenals, and military outposts. In a last ditch effort to avoid war between the states, Secretary of State Seward suggested a united effort of threatening war against Spain and France for interfering in Mexico and the Caribbean. In the highly charged atmosphere, it would take only a spark to unleash the heat of war.

Fort Sumter

Charleston

In Charleston, all activity came to a complete stop. Citizens crowded rooftops to watch the battle.

Castle Pinckney

Charleston Harbor

Charleston
ATLANTIC OCEAN

Shots fired at the ironclad battery did little damage.

The first shot fired on Fort Sumter was fired from Fort Johnson.

Fort Johnson

Fort Sumter

Fort Moultrie

Fort Sumter was strategically placed to control Charleston Harbor.

Cummings Point

Atlantic Ocean

The first shots of the Civil War were fired at Fort Sumter, South Carolina. Although no one was killed there, the bloodiest war in the country's history had begun.

GEOGRAPHY SKILLS | **INTERPRETING MAPS**

1. **Human-Environment Interaction** Why would the Union Army need to resupply Fort Sumter?
2. **Place** What advantages would a floating battery have?

In 1861, that spark occurred at **Fort Sumter**, a federal outpost in Charleston, South Carolina, that was attacked by Confederate troops, beginning the Civil War. Determined to seize the fortress—which controlled the entrance to Charleston harbor—the Confederates ringed the harbor with heavy guns. Instead of surrendering the fort, Lincoln decided to send in ships to provide badly needed supplies to defend the fort. Confederate officials demanded that the federal troops evacuate. The fort's commander, Major Robert Anderson, refused.

Before sunrise on April 12, 1861, Confederate guns opened fire on Fort Sumter. A witness wrote that the first shots brought "every soldier in the harbor to his feet, and every man, woman, and child in the city of Charleston from their beds." The Civil War had begun.

The fort, although massive, stood little chance. Its heavy guns faced the Atlantic Ocean, not the shore. After 34 hours of cannon blasts, Fort Sumter surrendered. "The last ray of hope for preserving the Union has expired at the assault upon Fort Sumter . . ." Lincoln wrote.

Reaction to Lincoln's Call

The fall of Fort Sumter stunned the North. Lincoln declared the South to be in a state of rebellion and asked state governors for 75,000 militiamen to put down the rebellion. States now had to choose: Would they secede, or would they stay in the Union? Democratic Senator Stephen Douglas, speaking in support of Lincoln's call for troops, declared, "There can be no neutrals in this war, *only patriots*—or *traitors*."

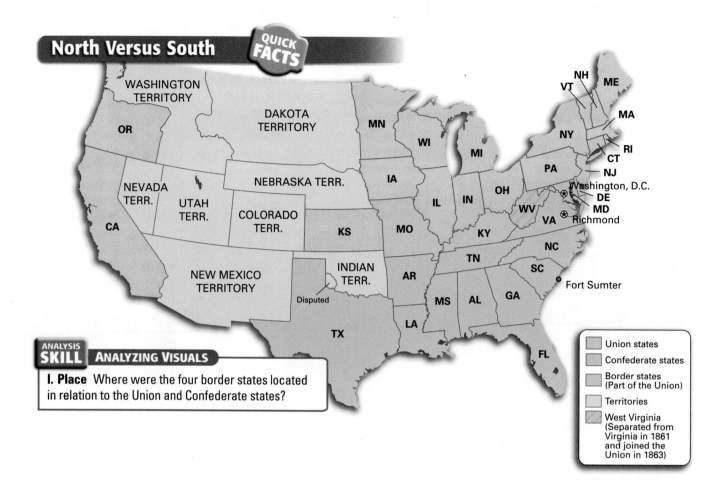

North Versus South — QUICK FACTS

WASHINGTON TERRITORY
DAKOTA TERRITORY
OR
MN
WI
MI
NH
VT
ME
MA
NY
PA
RI
CT
NJ
NEVADA TERR.
UTAH TERR.
NEBRASKA TERR.
IA
IL
IN
OH
Washington, D.C.
DE
MD
CA
COLORADO TERR.
KS
MO
WV
VA
Richmond
KY
NC
NEW MEXICO TERRITORY
INDIAN TERR.
Disputed
AR
TN
SC
Fort Sumter
MS
AL
GA
TX
LA
FL

Legend:
- Union states
- Confederate states
- Border states (Part of the Union)
- Territories
- West Virginia (Separated from Virginia in 1861 and joined the Union in 1863)

ANALYSIS SKILL — ANALYZING VISUALS

1. Place Where were the four border states located in relation to the Union and Confederate states?

Pennsylvania, New Jersey, and the states north of them rallied to the president's call. The crucial slave states of the Upper South—North Carolina, Tennessee, Virginia, and Arkansas—seceded. They provided soldiers and supplies to the South. Mary Boykin Chesnut, whose husband became a Confederate congressman, wrote in her diary:

"I did not know that one could live in such days of excitement…Everybody tells you half of something, and then rushes off…to hear the last news."
—Mary Boykin Chesnut, quoted in *Mary Chesnut's Civil War*, edited by C. Vann Woodward

Wedged between the North and the South were the key **border states** of Delaware, Kentucky, Maryland, and Missouri—slave states that did not join the Confederacy. Kentucky and Missouri controlled parts of important rivers. Maryland separated the Union capital, Washington, D.C., from the North.

People in the border states were deeply divided on the war. The president's own wife, Mary Todd Lincoln, had four brothers from Kentucky who fought for the Confederacy. Lincoln sent federal troops into the border states to help keep them in the Union. He also sent soldiers into western Virginia, where Union loyalties were strong. West Virginia set up its own state government in 1863.

Northern Resources

Numbers tell an important story about the Civil War. Consider the North's advantages. It could draw soldiers and workers from a population of 22 million. The South had only 5.5 million people to draw from. One of the greatest advantages in the North was the region's network of roads, canals, and railroads. Some 22,000 miles of railroad track could move soldiers and supplies throughout the North. The South had only about 9,000 miles of track.

In the North, the Civil War stimulated economic growth. To supply the military, the production of coal, iron, wheat, and wool increased. Also, the export of corn, wheat, beef, and pork to Europe doubled. In the South, the export of resources decreased because of the Union blockade.

Finally, the Union had money. It had a more developed economy, banking system, and a currency called greenbacks. The South had to start printing its own Confederate dollars. Some states printed their own money, too. This led to financial chaos.

Taking advantage of the Union's strengths, General **Winfield Scott** developed a two-part strategy: (1) destroy the South's economy with a naval blockade of southern ports; (2) gain control of the Mississippi River to divide the South. Other leaders urged an attack on Richmond, Virginia, the Confederate capital.

Southern Resources

The Confederacy had advantages as well. With its strong military tradition, the South put many brilliant officers into battle. Southern farms provided food for its armies. The South's best advantage, however, was strategic. It needed only to defend itself until the North grew tired of fighting.

The North had to invade and control the South. To accomplish this, the Union army had to travel huge distances. For example, the distance from northern Virginia to central Georgia is about the length of Scotland and England combined. Because of distances such as this, the North had to maintain long supply lines.

In addition, wilderness covered much of the South. Armies found this land difficult to cross. Also, in Virginia, many of the rivers ran from east to west. Because of this, they formed a natural defense against an army that attacked from the north to the south. As a result, Northern generals were often forced to attack Confederate troops from the side rather than from the front. Furthermore, because southerners fought mostly on their home soil, they were often familiar with the area.

The South hoped to wear down the North and to capture Washington, D.C. Confederate president Jefferson Davis also tried to win foreign allies through **cotton diplomacy**. This was the idea that Great Britain would support the Confederacy because it needed the South's raw cotton to supply its booming textile industry. Cotton diplomacy did not work as the South had hoped. Britain had large supplies of cotton, and it got more from India and Egypt.

READING CHECK **Comparing** What advantages did the North and South have leading up to the war?

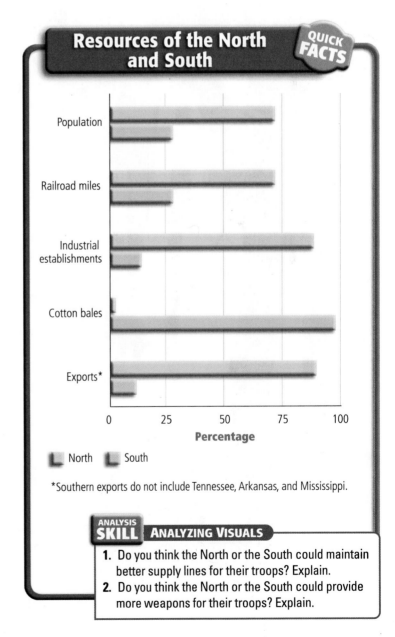

Resources of the North and South

QUICK FACTS

*Southern exports do not include Tennessee, Arkansas, and Mississippi.

ANALYSIS SKILL **ANALYZING VISUALS**

1. Do you think the North or the South could maintain better supply lines for their troops? Explain.
2. Do you think the North or the South could provide more weapons for their troops? Explain.

Union and Confederate Soldiers

Early in the war, uniforms differed greatly, especially in the Confederate army. Uniforms became simpler and more standard as the war dragged on.

The soldiers carried food, extra ammunition, and other items in their haversacks.

Each soldier was armed with a bayonet, a knife that can be attached to the barrel of a rifle. The bayonets were stored in scabbards on their belts.

Both soldiers were also armed with single-shot, muzzle-loading rifles.

Confederate Soldier

Union Soldier

ANALYSIS SKILL **ANALYZING VISUALS**

How are the Union and Confederate uniforms and equipment similar and different?

Preparing for War

The North and the South now rushed to war. Neither side was prepared for the tragedy to come.

Volunteer Armies

Volunteer militias had sparked the revolution that created the United States. Now they would battle for its future. At the start of the war, the Union army had only 16,000 soldiers. Within months that number had swelled to a half million. Southern men rose up to defend their land and their ways of life. Virginian Thomas Webber came to fight "against the invading foe [enemy] who now pollute the sacred soil of my beloved native state." When Union soldiers asked one captured rebel why he was fighting, he replied, "I'm fighting because you're down here."

Helping the Troops

Civilians on both sides helped those in uniform. They raised money, provided aid for soldiers and their families, and ran emergency hospitals. Dr. Elizabeth Blackwell, the first woman to receive a license to practice medicine, organized a group that pressured President Lincoln to form the U.S. Sanitary Commission in June 1861. The Sanitary, as it was called, was run by clergyman Henry Bellows. Tens of thousands of volunteers worked with the U.S. Sanitary Commission to send bandages, medicines, and food to Union army camps and hospitals. Some 3,000 women served as nurses in the Union army.

Training the Soldiers

Both the Union and Confederate armies faced shortages of clothing, food, and even rifles. Most troops lacked standard uniforms and simply wore their own clothes. Eventually, each side chose a color for their uniforms. The Union chose blue. The Confederates wore gray.

The problem with volunteers was that many of them had no idea how to fight. Schoolteachers, farmers, and laborers all had to learn the combat basics of marching, shooting, and using bayonets.

In a letter to a friend, a Union soldier described life in the training camp.

"We have been wading through mud knee deep all winter … For the last two weeks we have been drilled almost to death. Squad drill from 6 to 7 A.M. Company drill from 9 to 11 A.M. Batallion Drill from 2 to 4 1/2 P.M. Dress Parade from 5 to 5 1/2 P.M. and non-commissioned officers' school from 7 to 8 in the evening. If we don't soon become a well drilled Regiment, we ought to."

—David R. P. Shoemaker, 1862

With visions of glory and action, many young soldiers were eager to fight. They would not have to wait long.

Discipline and drill were used to turn raw volunteers into an efficient fighting machine. During a battle, the success or failure of a regiment often depended on its discipline—how well it responded to orders.

Volunteers also learned how to use rifles. Eventually, soldiers were expected to be able to load, aim, and fire their rifles three times in one minute. The quality of the weapons provided varied greatly. Most soldiers favored the Springfield and Enfield rifles for their accuracy. On the other hand, soldiers often complained about their Austrian and Belgian rifles. A soldier remarked, "I don't believe one could hit the broadside of a barn with them."

The Union army provided the infantry with two-person tents. However, soldiers often discarded these tents in favor of more portable ones. The Confederate army did not usually issue tents. Instead, Confederates often used tents that were captured from the Union army.

READING CHECK **Summarizing** How did soldiers and civilians prepare for war?

SUMMARY AND PREVIEW As citizens chose sides in the Civil War, civilians and soldiers alike became involved in the war effort. In the next section you will learn about some early battles in the war, both on land and at sea.

Section 1 Assessment

go.hrw.com
Online Quiz
KEYWORD: SB7 HP16

Reviewing Ideas, Terms, and People

1. **a. Identify** What event triggered the war between the Union and the Confederacy?
   b. Contrast How did the Union's strategy differ from that of the Confederacy?
   c. Evaluate Which side do you believe was best prepared for war? Explain your answer.
2. **a. Describe** How did women take part in the war?
   b. Summarize In what ways were the armies of the North and South unprepared for war?
   c. Elaborate Why did men volunteer to fight in the war?

Critical Thinking

3. **Comparing and Contrasting** Review your notes on the preparations for war by the North and the South.

Then copy the graphic organizer shown below and use it to show the strengths and weaknesses of each side in the war.

	Union	Confederacy
Strengths		
Weaknesses		

FOCUS ON WRITING

4. **Taking Notes on the War's Beginning** As you read this section, take notes on the crisis at Fort Sumter and on the recruiting and training of the armies. Be sure to answer the following questions: Who? Where? When? Why? and How?

The War in the East

Virginia Standards of Learning USII.1a, USII.1b, USII.1d, USII.2c, USII.3c

What You Will Learn...

Main Ideas

1. Union and Confederate forces fought for control of the war in Virginia.
2. The Battle of Antietam gave the North a slight advantage.
3. The Confederacy attempted to break the Union naval blockade.

The Big Idea

Confederate and Union forces faced off in Virginia and at sea.

Key Terms and People

Thomas "Stonewall" Jackson, *p. 517*
First Battle of Bull Run, *p. 517*
George B. McClellan, *p. 517*
Robert E. Lee, *p. 518*
Seven Days' Battles, *p. 518*
Second Battle of Bull Run, *p. 518*
Battle of Antietam, *p. 519*
ironclads, *p. 520*

TAKING NOTES As you read, take notes on the battles in the east and at sea and the winners of each. Write your notes in a chart like the one below.

Battle	Winner

If YOU were there...

You live in Washington, D.C., in July 1861. You and your friends are on your way to Manassas, near Washington, to watch the battle there. Everyone expects a quick Union victory. Your wagon is loaded with food for a picnic, and people are in a holiday mood. You see some members of Congress riding toward Manassas, too. Maybe this battle will end the war!

Why would you want to watch this battle?

BUILDING BACKGROUND The shots fired at Fort Sumter made the war a reality. Neither the North nor the South was really prepared. Each side had some advantages—more industry and railroads in the North, a military tradition in the South. The war in the East centered in the region around the two capitals: Washington, D.C., and Richmond, Virginia.

War in Virginia

The troops that met in the first major battle of the Civil War found that it was no picnic. In July 1861, Lincoln ordered General Irvin McDowell to lead his 35,000-man army from the Union capital, Washington, to the Confederate capital, Richmond. The soldiers were barely trained. McDowell complained that they "stopped every moment to pick blackberries or get water; they would not keep in the ranks." The first day's march covered only five miles.

Bull Run/Manassas

McDowell's army was headed to Manassas, Virginia, an important railroad junction. If McDowell could seize Manassas, he would control the best route to the Confederate capital. Some 22,000 Confederate troops under the command of General Pierre G. T. Beauregard were waiting for McDowell and his troops along a creek called Bull Run. For two days, Union troops tried to find a way around the Confederates. During that time, Beauregard requested assistance, and

General Joseph E. Johnston headed toward Manassas with another 10,000 Confederate troops. By July 21, 1861, they had all arrived.

That morning, Union troops managed to cross the creek and drive back the left side of the Confederate line. Yet one unit held firmly in place.

"There is Jackson standing like a stone wall!" cried one southern officer. "Rally behind the Virginians!" At that moment, General **Thomas "Stonewall" Jackson** earned his famous nickname.

A steady stream of Virginia volunteers arrived to counter the attack. The Confederates surged forward, letting out their terrifying "rebel yell." One eyewitness described the awful scene.

"There is smoke, dust, wild talking, shouting; hissings, howlings, explosions. It is a new, strange, unanticipated experience to the soldiers of both armies, far different from what they thought it would be."

—Charles Coffin,
quoted in *Voices of the Civil War* by Richard Wheeler

The battle raged through the day, with rebel soldiers still arriving. Finally, the weary Union troops gave out. They tried to make an orderly retreat back across the creek, but the roads were clogged with the fancy carriages of panicked spectators. The Union army scattered in the chaos.

The Confederates lacked the strength to push north and capture Washington, D.C. But clearly, the rebels had won the day. The **First Battle of Bull Run** was the first major battle of the Civil War, and the Confederates' victory. The battle is also known as the First Battle of Manassas. It shattered the North's hopes of winning the war quickly.

More Battles in Virginia

The shock at Bull Run persuaded Lincoln of the need for a better trained army. He put his hopes in General **George B. McClellan**. The general assembled a highly disciplined force of 100,000 soldiers called the Army of the Potomac. The careful McClellan spent months training. However, because

Battles in the East

Union state

West Virginia (Separated from Virginia in 1861 and joined the Union in 1863)

Confederate state

→ Union forces

✴ Union victory

→ Confederate forces

✴ Confederate victory

0 15 30 Miles
0 15 30 Kilometers

go.hrw.com
Interactive Map
KEYWORD: SB7 CH16

GEOGRAPHY SKILLS **INTERPRETING MAPS**

1. **Location** Which battle was fought in Maryland?
2. **Human-Environment Interaction** How did geography influence the movement of forces?

he overestimated the size of the Confederate army, McClellan hesitated to attack. Lincoln grew impatient. Finally, in the spring of 1862, McClellan launched an effort to capture Richmond called the "Peninsular Campaign." Instead of marching south for a direct assault, McClellan slowly brought his force through the peninsula between the James and York rivers. More time slipped away.

The South feared that McClellan would receive reinforcements from Washington. To prevent this, Stonewall Jackson launched an attack toward Washington. Although the attack was pushed back, it prevented the Union from sending reinforcements to McClellan.

THE IMPACT TODAY

Many Americans continue to be fascinated by the Civil War. Some history buffs regularly stage re-enactments of famous battles, complete with uniforms, guns, and bayonets.

In June 1862, with McClellan's force poised outside Richmond, the Confederate army in Virginia came under the command of General **Robert E. Lee**. A graduate of the U.S. Military Academy at West Point, Lee had served in the Mexican War and had led federal troops at Harpers Ferry. Lee was willing to take risks and make unpredictable moves to throw Union forces off balance.

During the summer of 1862, Lee strengthened his positions. On June 26, he attacked, launching a series of clashes known as the **Seven Days' Battles** that forced the Union army to retreat from near Richmond. Confederate General D. H. Hill described one failed attack. "It was not war—it was murder," he said. Lee saved Richmond and forced McClellan to retreat.

A frustrated Lincoln ordered General John Pope to march directly on Richmond from Washington. Pope told his soldiers, "Let us look before us and not behind. Success and glory are in the advance."

Jackson wanted to defeat Pope's army before it could join up with McClellan's larger Army of the Potomac. Jackson's troops met Pope's Union forces on the battlefield in August in 1862. The three-day battle became known as the **Second Battle of Bull Run**, or the Second Battle of Manassas.

The first day's fighting was savage. Captain George Fairfield of the 7th Wisconsin regiment later recalled, "What a slaughter! No one appeared to know the object of the fight, and there we stood for one hour, the men falling all around." The fighting ended in a stalemate.

On the second day, Pope found Jackson's troops along an unfinished railroad grade. Pope hurled his men against the Confederates. But the attacks were pushed back with heavy casualties on both sides.

On the third day, the Confederates crushed the Union army's assault and forced it to retreat in defeat. The Confederates had won a major victory, and General Robert E. Lee decided it was time to take the war to the North.

READING CHECK **Sequencing** List in order the events that forced Union troops out of Virginia.

Eyewitness at Antietam

Battle of Antietam

Confederate leaders hoped to follow up Lee's successes in Virginia with a major victory on northern soil. On September 4, 1862, some 40,000 Confederate soldiers began crossing into Maryland. General Robert E. Lee decided to divide his army. He sent about half of his troops, under the command of Stonewall Jackson, to Harpers Ferry. There they defeated a Union force and captured the town. Meanwhile, Lee arrived in the town of Frederick and issued a Proclamation to the People of Maryland, urging them to join the Confederates. However, his words would not be enough to convince Marylanders to abandon the Union. Union soldiers, however, found a copy of Lee's battle plan, which had been left at an abandoned Confederate camp. General McClellan learned that Lee had divided his army in order to attack Harpers Ferry. However, McClellan hesitated to attack. As a result, the Confederates had time to reunite.

The two armies met along Antietam Creek in Maryland on September 17, 1862. The battle lasted for hours. By the end of the day, the Union had suffered more than 12,000 casualties. The Confederates endured more than 13,000 casualties. Union officer A. H. Nickerson later recalled, "It seemed that everybody near me was killed." The **Battle of Antietam,** also known as the Battle of Sharpsburg, was the bloodiest single-day battle of the Civil War—and of U.S. history. More soldiers were killed and wounded at the Battle of Antietam than the deaths of all Americans in the American Revolution, War of 1812, and Mexican-American War combined.

During the battle, McClellan kept four divisions of soldiers in reserve and refused to use them to attack Lee's devastated army. McClellan was convinced that Lee was massing reserves for a counterattack. Those reserves did not exist. Despite this blunder, Antietam was an important victory. Lee's northward advance had been stopped.

James Hope was a professional artist who joined the Union army. Too sick to fight at Antietam, Hope was reassigned to work as a scout and a mapmaker. He sketched scenes from the battle as it happened and later used his sketches to make paintings like this one. This scene is of early morning on the battlefield. This painting doesn't represent a particular moment, but is meant to show a series of events.

ANALYSIS SKILL **ANALYZING VISUALS**

How is this painting different from modern war reporting?

READING CHECK **Analyzing** Why was the Battle of Antietam significant?

POLITICAL CARTOON
Anaconda Plan

This cartoon shows visually the North's plan to cut off supplies to the South through naval blockades, a strategy called the Anaconda Plan.

Why is the snake's head red, white, and blue?

How does the cartoonist show what the snake represents?

ANALYSIS SKILL | **ANALYZING PRIMARY SOURCES**

Why do you think the plan was called the Anaconda Plan?

Breaking the Union's Blockade

While the two armies fought for control of the land, the Union navy controlled the sea. The North had most of the U.S. Navy's small fleet, and many experienced naval officers had remained loyal to the Union. The North also had enough industry to build more ships. The Confederacy turned to British companies for new ships.

The Union's Naval Strategy

ACADEMIC VOCABULARY

innovation a new idea or way of doing something

The Union navy quickly mobilized to set up a blockade of southern ports. The blockade largely prevented the South from selling or receiving goods, and it seriously damaged the southern economy.

The blockade was hard to maintain because the Union navy had to patrol thousands of miles of coastline from Virginia to Texas. The South used small, fast ships to outrun the larger Union warships. Most of these blockade runners traveled to the Bahamas or Nassau to buy supplies for the Confederacy. These ships, however, could not make up for the South's loss of trade. The Union blockade reduced the number of ships entering southern ports from 6,000 to 800 per year.

Clash of the Ironclads

Hoping to take away the Union's advantage at sea, the Confederacy turned to a new type of warship—**ironclads**, or ships heavily armored with iron. The British government neglected to stop these ships from being delivered, in violation of its pledge of neutrality. The Confederates had captured a Union steamship, the *Merrimack*, and turned it into an ironclad, renamed the *Virginia*. One Union sailor described the **innovation** as "a huge half-submerged crocodile." In early March 1862, the ironclad sailed into Hampton Roads, Virginia, an important waterway guarded by Union ships. Before nightfall, the *Virginia* easily sank two of the Union's wooden warships, while it received minor damage.

Union Blockade

Union states
Confederate states
Union blockade

0   100   200 Miles
0   100   200 Kilometers

Washington, D.C.
Hampton Roads
Richmond

Monitor battles *Virginia* at Hampton Roads.

Charleston

80°W
30°N

ATLANTIC OCEAN

New Orleans

Gulf of Mexico

90°W
Tropic of Cancer

GEOGRAPHY SKILLS **INTERPRETING MAPS**

Location What major port cities in the South were affected by the blockade?

The Union navy had already built its own ironclad, the *Monitor*, designed by Swedish-born engineer John Ericsson. Ericsson's ship had unusual new features, such as a revolving gun tower. One Confederate soldier called the *Monitor* "a tin can on a shingle!" Although small, the *Monitor* carried powerful guns and had thick plating.

When the *Virginia* returned to Hampton Roads later that month, the *Monitor* was waiting. After several hours of fighting, neither ship was seriously damaged, but the *Monitor* forced the *Virginia* to withdraw. This success saved the Union fleet and continued the blockade. The clash of the ironclads also signaled a revolution in naval warfare. The days of wooden warships powered by wind and sails were drawing to a close.

READING CHECK **Evaluating** How effective was the Union blockade?

SUMMARY AND PREVIEW The early battles of the Civil War were centered in the East. In the next section you will read about battles in the West.

THE IMPACT TODAY

The *Monitor* sank in North Carolina in the winter of 1862. The shipwreck was located by scientists in 1973, and remains of the ship are part of the exhibit at the USS *Monitor* Center, which opened in 2007.

Section 2 Assessment

go.hrw.com
Online Quiz
KEYWORD: SB7 HP16

Reviewing Ideas, Terms, and People

1. **a. Identify** List the early battles in the East and the outcome of each battle.
   b. Elaborate Why do you think the Union lost the **First Battle of Bull Run**?
2. **a. Describe** What costly mistake did the Confederacy make before the **Battle of Antietam**?
   b. Analyze What was the outcome of the Battle of Antietam, and what effect did it have on both the North and the South?
   c. Elaborate Why do you think General **George B. McClellan** did not finish off General **Robert E. Lee**'s troops when he had the chance?
3. **a. Describe** What was the Union's strategy in the war at sea?
   b. Draw Conclusions Why were **ironclads** more successful than older, wooden ships?

Critical Thinking

4. **Supporting a Point of View** Review your notes on the battles in the east and at sea. Then copy the graphic organizer below and use it to show which three conflicts you think were the most significant and why.

Most Significant	Why

FOCUS ON WRITING

5. **Taking Notes on the War in the East** As you read this section, take notes on the First Battle of Bull Run, the Seven Days' Battles, the Second Battle of Bull Run, and the Battle of Antietam. Be sure to answer the following questions: Who? Where? When? Why? and How?

The War in the West

Virginia Standards of Learning USII.1b, USII.1f, USII.2c

What You Will Learn...

Main Ideas

1. Union strategy in the West centered on control of the Mississippi River.
2. Confederate and Union troops struggled for dominance in the Far West.

The Big Idea

Fighting in the Civil War spread to the western United States.

Key Terms and People

Ulysses S. Grant, *p. 522*
Battle of Shiloh, *p. 523*
David Farragut, *p. 524*
Siege of Vicksburg, *p. 524*

TAKING NOTES As you read, take notes on Civil War battles in the West. Write your notes in a graphic organizer like the one below.

Battles in the West
1.
2.
3.
4.
5.
6.

If YOU were there...

You live in the city of Vicksburg, set on high bluffs above the Mississippi River. Vicksburg is vital to the control of the river, and Confederate defenses are strong. But the Union general is determined to take the town. For weeks, you have been surrounded and besieged. Cannon shells burst overhead, day and night. Some have fallen on nearby homes. Supplies of food are running low.

How would you survive this siege?

BUILDING BACKGROUND The Civil War was fought on many fronts, all across the continent and even at sea. In the East, fighting was at first concentrated in Virginia. In the West, cities and forts along the Mississippi River were the main target of Union forces. Northern control of the river would cut off the western states of the Confederacy.

Union Strategy in the West

While Lincoln fumed over the cautious, hesitant General McClellan, he had no such problems with **Ulysses S. Grant**. Bold and restless, Grant grew impatient when he was asked to lead defensive maneuvers. He wanted to be on the attack. As a commander of forces in the Union's western campaign, he would get his wish.

The western campaign focused on taking control of the Mississippi River. This strategy would cut off the eastern part of the Confederacy from sources of food production in Arkansas, Louisiana, and Texas. From bases on the Mississippi, the Union army could attack southern communication and transportation networks.

In February 1862, Grant led an assault force into Tennessee. With help from navy gunboats, Grant's Army of the Tennessee took two outposts on key rivers in the west. On February 6, he captured Fort Henry on the Tennessee River. Several days later he took Fort Donelson on the Cumberland River.

Fort Donelson's commander asked for the terms of surrender. Grant replied, "No terms except an unconditional and immediate

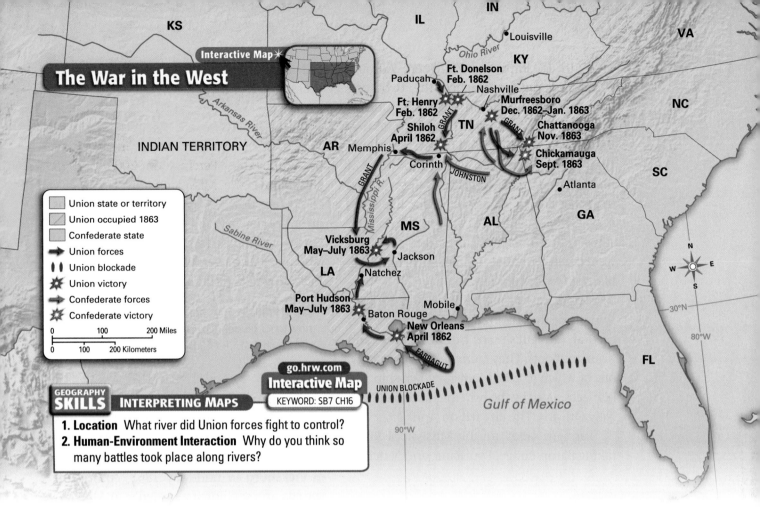

The War in the West

Interactive Map

Legend:
- Union state or territory
- Union occupied 1863
- Confederate state
- → Union forces
- ‖ Union blockade
- ✷ Union victory
- → Confederate forces
- ✷ Confederate victory

0   100   200 Miles
0 100 200 Kilometers

go.hrw.com
Interactive Map
KEYWORD: SB7 CH16

GEOGRAPHY SKILLS INTERPRETING MAPS

1. **Location** What river did Union forces fight to control?
2. **Human-Environment Interaction** Why do you think so many battles took place along rivers?

Map labels: KS, IL, IN, VA, KY, Louisville, Ohio River, Paducah, Ft. Donelson Feb. 1862, Nashville, Murfreesboro Dec. 1862–Jan. 1863, NC, Ft. Henry Feb. 1862, Shiloh April 1862, TN, Chattanooga Nov. 1863, Chickamauga Sept. 1863, SC, Arkansas River, INDIAN TERRITORY, AR, Memphis, Corinth, JOHNSTON, Atlanta, GA, MS, AL, Sabine River, Mississippi R., Vicksburg May–July 1863, Jackson, LA, Natchez, Port Hudson May–July 1863, Baton Rouge, New Orleans April 1862, Mobile, FARRAGUT, UNION BLOCKADE, Gulf of Mexico, FL, 30°N, 80°W, 90°W

---

surrender can be accepted." The fort surrendered. The North gave a new name to Grant's initials: "Unconditional Surrender" Grant.

Advancing south in Tennessee, General Grant paused near Shiloh Church to await the arrival of the Army of the Ohio. Grant knew that the large rebel army of General A. S. Johnston was nearby in Corinth, Mississippi, but he did not expect an attack. Instead of setting up defenses, he worked on drilling his new recruits.

In the early morning of April 6, 1862, the rebels sprang on Grant's sleepy camp. This began the **Battle of Shiloh**, in which the Union army gained greater control of the Mississippi River valley.

During the bloody two-day battle, each side gained and lost ground. Johnston was killed on the first day. The arrival of the Ohio force helped Grant regain territory and push the enemy back into Mississippi. The armies finally gave out, each with about 10,000 casualties. Both sides claimed victory, but, in fact, the victor was Grant.

The Fall of New Orleans

As Grant battled his way down the Mississippi, the Union navy prepared to blast its way upriver to meet him. The first obstacle was the port of New Orleans, the largest city in the Confederacy and the gateway to the Mississippi River.

BIOGRAPHY

David Farragut
(1801–1870)

David Farragut was born in Tennessee to a Spanish father and an American mother. At age seven Farragut was adopted by a family friend who agreed to train the young boy for the navy. Farragut received his first navy position—midshipman at large—at age nine and commanded his first vessel at 12. He spent the rest of his life in the U.S. Navy. Farragut led key attacks on the southern ports of Vicksburg and New Orleans.

Drawing Inferences How did Farragut help the war effort of the North?

With 18 ships and 700 men, Admiral **David Farragut** approached the two forts that guarded the entrance to New Orleans from the Gulf of Mexico. Unable to destroy the forts, Farragut decided to race past them.

The risky operation would take place at night. Farragut had his wooden ships wrapped in heavy chains to protect them like ironclads. Sailors slapped Mississippi mud on the ships' hulls to make them hard to see. Trees were tied to the masts to make the ships look like the forested shore.

Before dawn on April 24, 1862, the warships made their daring dash. The Confederates fired at Farragut's ships from the shore and from gunboats. They launched burning rafts, one of which scorched Farragut's own ship. But his fleet slipped by the twin forts and made it to New Orleans. The city fell on April 29.

Farragut sailed up the Mississippi River, taking Baton Rouge, Louisiana, and Natchez, Mississippi. He then approached the city of Vicksburg, Mississippi.

The Siege of Vicksburg

Vicksburg's geography made invasion all but impossible. Perched on 200-foot-high cliffs above the Mississippi River, the city could rain down firepower on enemy ships or on soldiers trying to scale the cliffs. Deep gorges surrounded the city, turning back land assaults. Nevertheless, Farragut ordered Vicksburg to surrender.

"Mississippians don't know, and refuse to learn, how to surrender … If Commodore Farragut … can teach them, let [him] come and try."

—Colonel James L. Autry, military commander of Vicksburg

Farragut's guns had trouble reaching the city above. It was up to General Grant. His solution was to starve the city into surrender.

General Grant's troops began the **Siege of Vicksburg** in mid-May 1863, cutting off the city and shelling it repeatedly. As food ran out, residents and soldiers survived by eating horses, dogs, and rats. "We are utterly cut off from the world, surrounded by a circle of fire," wrote one woman. "People do nothing

Primary Source

SPEECH
Response to Farragut

The mayor of New Orleans considered the surrender of the city to the Union navy:

"We yield to physical force alone and maintain allegiance to the Confederate States; beyond this, a due respect for our dignity, our rights and the flag of our country does not, I think, permit us to go."

–Mayor John T. Monroe,
quoted in *Confederate Military History, Vol. 10*

ANALYSIS SKILL **ANALYZING PRIMARY SOURCES**

How does Monroe's statement reveal his attitude about surrender?

but eat what they can get, sleep when they can, and dodge the shells."

The Confederate soldiers were also sick and hungry. In late June a group of soldiers sent their commander a warning.

"The army is now ripe for mutiny [rebellion], unless it can be fed. If you can't feed us, you'd better surrender us, horrible as the idea is."

—Confederate soldiers at Vicksburg to General John C. Pemberton, 1863

On July 4, Pemberton surrendered. Grant immediately sent food to the soldiers and civilians. He later claimed that "the fate of the Confederacy was sealed when Vicksburg fell."

READING CHECK Summarizing How did the Union gain control of the Mississippi River?

Struggle for the Far West

Early on in the war, the Union halted several attempts by Confederate armies to control lands west of the Mississippi. In August 1861, a Union detachment from Colorado turned back a Confederate force at Glorieta Pass. Union volunteers also defeated rebel forces at Arizona's Pichaco Pass.

Confederate attempts to take the border state of Missouri also collapsed. Failing to seize the federal arsenal at St. Louis in mid-1861, the rebels fell back to Pea Ridge in northwest Arkansas. There, in March 1862, they attacked again, aided by some 800 Cherokee. The Indians hoped the Confederates would give them greater freedom. In addition, slavery was legal in Indian Territory, and some Native Americans who were slaveholders supported the Confederacy. Despite being outnumbered, Union forces won the Battle of Pea Ridge. The Union defense of Missouri held.

Pro-Confederate forces remained active in the region throughout the war. They attacked Union forts and raided towns in Missouri and Kansas, forcing Union commanders to keep valuable troops stationed in the area.

READING CHECK Analyzing What was the importance of the fighting in the Far West?

SUMMARY AND PREVIEW The North and the South continued their struggle with battles in the West. A number of key battles took place in the Western theater, and several important Union leaders emerged from these battles. One, Ulysses S. Grant, would soon become even more important to the Union army. In the next section you will learn about the lives of civilians, enslaved Africans, and soldiers during the war.

go.hrw.com
Online Quiz
KEYWORD: SB7 HP16

Section 3 Assessment

Reviewing Ideas, Terms, and People

1. a. **Identify** What role did **Ulysses S. Grant** play in the war in the West?
   b. **Explain** Why was the **Battle of Shiloh** important?
   c. **Elaborate** Do you think President Lincoln would have approved of Grant's actions in the West? Why or why not?

2. a. **Describe** How did the Union take New Orleans, and why was it an important victory?
   b. **Draw Conclusions** How were civilians affected by the **Siege of Vicksburg**?
   c. **Predict** What might be some possible results of the Union victory at Vicksburg?

Critical Thinking

3. **Identifying Cause and Effect** Review your notes on Union strategy in the West. Then copy this graphic organizer and use it to show the causes and effects of each battle.

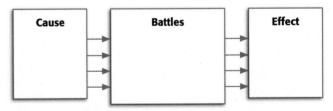

Cause	Battles	Effect

FOCUS ON WRITING

4. **Taking Notes on the War in the West** As you read this section, take notes on the fight for the Mississippi River and the Siege of Vicksburg. Be sure to answer the following questions: Who? Where? When? Why? and How?

The Vicksburg Strategy

"Vicksburg is the key!" President Abraham Lincoln declared. "The war can never be brought to a close until that key is in our pocket." Vicksburg was so important because of its location on the Mississippi River, a vital trade route and supply line. Union ships couldn't get past the Confederate guns mounted on the high bluffs of Vicksburg. Capturing Vicksburg would give the Union control of the Mississippi, stealing a vital supply line and splitting the Confederacy in two. The task fell to General Ulysses S. Grant.

5 **The Siege of Vicksburg** Grant now had 30,000 Confederate troops trapped in Vicksburg. After two assaults on the city failed, Grant was forced to lay siege. After six weeks of bombardment, the Confederates surrendered on July 4, 1863. Grant's bold campaign had given the Union control of the Mississippi River.

Vicksburg

1 **Grant Crosses into Louisiana** General Grant planned to attack Vicksburg from the North, but the swampy land made attack from that direction difficult. So, Grant crossed the Mississippi River into Louisiana and marched south.

Port Gibson

2 **Grant Moves East** Grant's troops met up with their supply boats here and crossed back into Mississippi. In a daring gamble, Grant decided to move without a supply line, allowing his army to move quickly.

3 **Port Gibson** A skirmish at Port Gibson proved that the Confederates could not defend the Mississippi line.

UNION
CONTROL

CONFEDERATE
CONTROL

Ironclads

Union ironclads were vital to the Vicksburg campaign. These gunboats protected Grant's troops when they crossed the Mississippi. Later, they bombarded Vicksburg during the siege of the city.

4

The Battle of Jackson Grant defeated a Confederate army at Jackson and then moved on to Vicksburg. This prevented Confederate forces from reinforcing Vicksburg.

BIOGRAPHY

Ulysses S. Grant
(1822–1885)

Ulysses S. Grant was born in April 1822 in New York. Grant attended West Point and fought in the Mexican-American War. He resigned in 1854 and worked at various jobs in farming, real estate, and retail. When the Civil War started, he joined the Union army and was quickly promoted to general. After the Civil War, Grant rode a wave of popularity to become president of the United States.

GEOGRAPHY
SKILLS INTERPRETING MAPS

1. Location Why was Vicksburg's location so important?

2. Place What natural features made Vicksburg difficult to attack?

Daily Life during the War

🔷 Virginia Standards of Learning USII.1b, USII.2c, USII.3c

What You Will Learn...

Main Ideas

1. The Emancipation Proclamation freed slaves in Confederate states.
2. African Americans participated in the war in a variety of ways.
3. President Lincoln faced opposition to the war.
4. Life was difficult for soldiers and civilians alike.

The Big Idea

The lives of many Americans were affected by the Civil War.

Key Terms and People

abolitionists, *p. 529*
emancipation, *p. 529*
Emancipation Proclamation, *p. 529*
Frederick Douglass, *p. 530*
William Lloyd Garrison, *p. 530*
contrabands, *p. 531*
54th Massachusetts Infantry, *p. 531*
Copperheads, *p. 532*
habeas corpus, *p. 532*
Clara Barton, *p. 534*

TAKING NOTES As you read, take notes on the effects of the Civil War on the lives of African Americans, soldiers, and women and children. Write your notes in a graphic organizer like the one below.

How the Civil War affected	
African Americans	
Soldiers	
Women and children	

If YOU were there...

You live in Maryland in 1864. Your father and brothers are in the Union army, and you want to do your part in the war. You hear that a woman in Washington, D.C., is supplying medicines and caring for wounded soldiers on the battlefield. She is looking for volunteers. You know the work will be dangerous, for you'll be in the line of fire. You might be shot or even killed.

Would you join the nurses on the battlefield?

BUILDING BACKGROUND The Civil War touched almost all Americans. Some 3 million men fought in the two armies. Thousands of other men and women worked behind the lines, providing food, supplies, medical care, and other necessary services. Civilians could not escape the effects of war, as the fighting destroyed farms, homes, and cities.

Emancipation Proclamation

Emancipation Proclamation

At the heart of the nation's bloody struggle were millions of enslaved African Americans. **Abolitionists**, or people who worked to end slavery, urged President Lincoln to free them.

In an 1858 speech, Lincoln declared, "There is no reason in the world why the negro is not entitled to all the natural rights numerated in the Declaration of Independence—the right to life, liberty, and the pursuit of happiness." Yet as president, Lincoln found **emancipation**, or the freeing of slaves, to be a difficult issue. He did not believe he had the constitutional power. He also worried about the effects of emancipation.

Lincoln Issues the Proclamation

Northerners had a range of opinions about abolishing slavery.

- The Democratic Party, which included many laborers, opposed emancipation. Laborers feared that freed slaves would come north and take their jobs at lower wages.
- Abolitionists argued that the war was pointless if it did not win freedom for African Americans. They warned that the Union would remain divided until the problem was resolved.

The painting at left shows Lincoln and his cabinet after the signing of the Emancipation Proclamation. Above is a photo of former slaves who were freed by the proclamation.

How do you think the Emancipation Proclamation would affect the Civil War?

Emancipation Proclamation

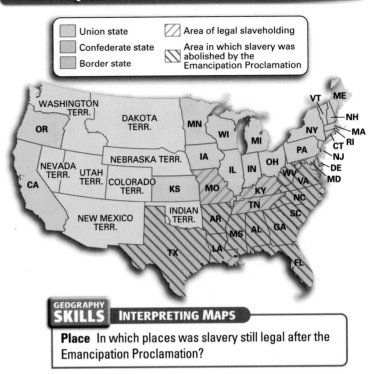

Legend:
- Union state
- Confederate state
- Border state
- Area of legal slaveholding
- Area in which slavery was abolished by the Emancipation Proclamation

GEOGRAPHY SKILLS — INTERPRETING MAPS

Place In which places was slavery still legal after the Emancipation Proclamation?

- Lincoln worried about losing support for the war. Previous wartime Confiscation Acts that had attempted to free the slaves had been unpopular in the border states.
- Others, including Secretary of War Edwin Stanton, agreed with Lincoln that the use of slave labor was helping the Confederacy make war. Therefore, as commander in chief, the president could free the slaves in all rebellious states. Freed African Americans could then be recruited into the Union army.

For several weeks in 1862, Lincoln worked intensely, thinking, writing, and rewriting. He finally wrote the **Emancipation Proclamation**, the order to free the Confederate slaves. The proclamation declared that:

" ...all persons held as slaves within any State or designated part of a State the people whereof shall then be in rebellion against the United States shall be then, thenceforward, and forever free. "
—Emancipation Proclamation, 1862

The Emancipation Proclamation was a military order that freed slaves only in areas

New Soldiers

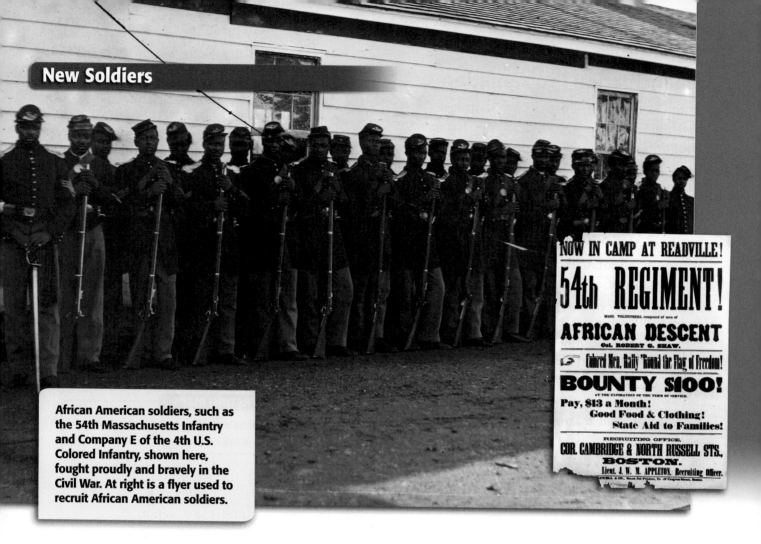

African American soldiers, such as the 54th Massachusetts Infantry and Company E of the 4th U.S. Colored Infantry, shown here, fought proudly and bravely in the Civil War. At right is a flyer used to recruit African American soldiers.

NOW IN CAMP AT READVILLE!
54th REGIMENT!
MASS. VOLUNTEERS, composed of men of
AFRICAN DESCENT
Col. ROBERT G. SHAW.
Colored Men, Rally 'Round the Flag of Freedom!
BOUNTY $100!
AT THE EXPIRATION OF THE TERM OF SERVICE.
Pay, $13 a Month!
Good Food & Clothing!
State Aid to Families!
RECRUITING OFFICE.
COR. CAMBRIDGE & NORTH RUSSELL STS.,
BOSTON.
Lieut. J. W. M. APPLETON, Recruiting Officer.

controlled by the Confederacy. In fact, the proclamation had little immediate effect. It was impossible for the federal government to enforce the proclamation in the areas where it actually applied—the states in rebellion that were not under federal control. The proclamation did not stop slavery in the border states, where the federal government would have had the power to enforce it. The words written in the Emancipation Proclamation were powerful, but the impact of the document was more symbolic than real. It defined what the Union was fighting against, and discouraged Britain from aiding the Confederacy.

Lincoln wanted to be in a strong position in the war before announcing his plan. The Battle of Antietam gave him the victory he needed. He issued the Emancipation Proclamation on September 22, 1862. The proclamation went into effect on January 1, 1863.

Reaction to the Proclamation

On New Year's Eve, 1862 worshippers at many African American churches prayed, sang, and gave thanks. When the clocks struck midnight, millions were free. Abolitionists rejoiced. African-American abolitionist **Frederick Douglass** called January 1, 1863, "the great day which is to determine the destiny not only of the American Republic, but that of the American Continent."

Abolitionist **William Lloyd Garrison** was quick to note, however, that "slavery, as a system" continued to exist in the loyal slave states. Yet, the proclamation encouraged many enslaved Africans to escape when the Union troops came near. They flocked to the Union camps and followed them for protection. The loss of slaves crippled the South's ability to wage war.

READING CHECK Finding Main Ideas How did northerners view the Emancipation Proclamation?

LETTER
June 23, 1863

Joseph E. Williams, an African American soldier and recruiter from Pennsylvania, wrote this letter describing why African Americans fought for the Union.

"We are now determined to hold every step which has been offered to us as citizens of the United States for our elevation [benefit], which represent justice, the purity, the truth, and aspiration [hope] of heaven. We must learn deeply to realize the duty, the moral and political necessity for the benefit of our race...Every consideration of honor, of interest, and of duty to God and man, requires that we should be true to our trust."

—quoted in *A Grand Army of Black Men*, edited by Edwin S. Redkey

ANALYSIS SKILL ANALYZING PRIMARY SOURCES

Why did Williams think being soldiers was so important for African Americans?

African Americans Participate in the War

As the war casualties climbed, the Union needed even more troops. African Americans were ready to volunteer. Not all white northerners were ready to accept them, but eventually they had to. Frederick Douglass believed that military service would help African Americans gain rights.

"Once let the black man get upon his person the brass letters, U.S.; ... and a musket on his shoulder and bullets in his pocket, and there is no power on earth which can deny that he has earned the right to citizenship."

—Frederick Douglass, quoted in *The Life and Writings of Frederick Douglass, Vol. 3*

Congress began allowing the army to sign up African American volunteers as laborers in July 1862. The War Department also gave **contrabands**, or escaped slaves, the right to join the Union army in South Carolina. Free African Americans in Louisiana and Kansas also formed their own units in the Union army. By the spring of 1863, African American army units were proving themselves in combat. They took part in a Union attack on Port Hudson, Louisiana, in May.

One unit stood out above the others. The **54th Massachusetts Infantry** consisted mostly of free African Americans. In July 1863 this regiment led a heroic charge on South Carolina's Fort Wagner. The 54th took heavy fire and suffered huge casualties in the failed operation. About half the regiment was killed, wounded, or captured. Edward L. Pierce, a correspondent for the *New York Tribune*, wrote, "The Fifty-fourth did well and nobly...They moved up as gallantly as any troops could, and with their enthusiasm they deserved a better fate." The bravery of the 54th regiment made it the most celebrated African American unit of the war.

About 180,000 African Americans served with the Union army. They received $10 a month, while white soldiers got $13. They were usually led by white officers, some from abolitionist families.

African Americans faced special horrors on the battlefield. Confederates often killed their black captives or sold them into slavery. In the 1864 election, Lincoln suggested rewarding African American soldiers by giving them the right to vote.

READING CHECK Analyzing Information
How did African Americans support the Union?

Growing Opposition

The deepening shadows in Lincoln's face reflected the huge responsibilities he carried. Besides running the war, he had to deal with growing tensions in the North.

Copperheads

As the months rolled on and the number of dead continued to increase, a group of northern Democrats began speaking out against the war. Led by U.S. Representative Clement L. Vallandigham of Ohio, they called themselves Peace Democrats. Their enemies called them Copperheads, comparing them to a poisonous snake. The name stuck.

Many **Copperheads** were midwesterners that sympathized with the South and opposed abolition. They believed the war was not necessary and called for its end. Vallandigham asked what the war had gained, and then said, "Let the dead at Fredericksburg and Vicksburg answer."

Lincoln saw the Copperheads as a threat to support of the war effort. To silence them, he suspended the right of habeas corpus.

Habeas corpus is a constitutional protection against unlawful imprisonment. Ignoring this protection, Union officials jailed their enemies, including some Copperheads, without evidence or trial. Lincoln's action greatly angered Democrats and some Republicans.

Northern Draft

In March 1863, war critics erupted again when Congress approved a draft, or forced military service. For $300, men were allowed to buy their way out of military service. For an unskilled laborer, however, that was nearly a year's wages. Critics of the draft called the Civil War a "rich man's war and a poor man's fight."

In July 1863, riots broke out when African Americans were brought into New York City to replace striking Irish dock workers. The city happened to be holding a war draft at the same time. The two events enraged rioters, who attacked African Americans and draft offices. More than 100 people died.

In this tense situation, the northern Democrats nominated former General George McClellan for president in 1864. They called

Infantry Family

While wealthy civilians could avoid military service, poorer men were drafted to serve in the Union army. This member of the 31st Pennsylvania Infantry brought his family along with him. His wife probably helped the soldier with many daily chores such as cooking and laundry.

Why would soldiers bring their families to live with them in camp?

for an immediate end to the war. Lincoln defeated McClellan in the popular vote, winning by about 400,000 votes out of 4 million cast. The electoral vote was not even close. Lincoln won 212 to 21.

READING CHECK Identifying Cause and Effect Who opposed the war, and how did Lincoln respond to the conflict?

Life for Soldiers and Civilians

Young, fresh recruits in both armies were generally eager to fight. Experienced troops, however, knew better.

On the Battlefield

Civil War armies fought in the ancient battlefield formation that produced massive casualties. Endless rows of troops fired directly at one another, with cannonballs landing amid them. When the order was given, soldiers would attach bayonets to their guns and rush toward their enemy. Men died to gain every inch of ground.

Doctors and nurses in the field saved many lives. Yet they had no medicines to stop infections that developed after soldiers were wounded. Many soldiers endured the horror of having infected legs and arms amputated without painkillers. Infections from minor injuries caused many deaths.

Despite the huge battlefield losses, the biggest killer in the Civil War was not the fighting. It was diseases such as typhoid, pneumonia, and tuberculosis. Nearly twice as many soldiers died of illnesses as died in combat.

Prisoners of War

Military prisoners on both sides lived in unimaginable misery. In prison camps, such as Andersonville, Georgia, and Elmira, New York, soldiers were packed into camps designed to hold only a fraction of their number. Soldiers had little shelter, food, or clothing. Starvation and disease killed thousands of prisoners.

LINKING TO TODAY

Battlefield Communications

The drummer was an essential member of every Civil War unit. Drummers served army commanders by drumming specific beats that directed troop movements during battle. Different beats were used to order troops to prepare to attack, to fire, to cease fire, and to signal a truce. Drummers had to stay near their commanders to hear orders. This meant that the drummers—some as young as nine years old—often saw deadly combat conditions.

The Civil War gave birth to the Signal Corps, the army unit devoted to communications. Today battlefield communications are primarily electronic. Radio, e-mail, facsimile, and telephone messages, often relayed by satellites, enable orders and other information to be transmitted nearly instantaneously all over the globe.

Union Signal Corps

Modern battlefield communications

ANALYSIS SKILL **ANALYZING INFORMATION**

Why is communication so important on the battlefield?

Life as a Civilian

The war effort involved all levels of society. Women as well as people too young or too old for military service worked in factories and on farms. Economy in the North boomed as production and prices soared. The lack of workers caused wages to rise by 43 percent between 1860 and 1865.

THE IMPACT TODAY

The American Red Cross today supplies victims of natural disasters with relief aid.

Women were the backbone of civilian life. On the farms, women and children performed the daily chores usually done by men. One visitor to Iowa in 1862 reported that he "met more women . . . at work in the fields than men." Southern women also managed farms and plantations.

One woman brought strength and comfort to countless wounded Union soldiers. Volunteer **Clara Barton** organized the collection of medicine and supplies for delivery to the battlefield. At the field hospitals,

Clara Barton founded the American Red Cross.

the "angel of the battlefield" soothed the wounded and dying and assisted doctors as bullets flew around her. Barton's work formed the basis for the future American Red Cross.

In the South, Sally Louisa Tompkins established a small hospital in Richmond, Virginia. By the end of the war, it had grown into a major army hospital. Jefferson Davis recognized her value to the war effort by making her a captain in the Confederate army.

READING CHECK **Analyzing** How did women help the war effort on both sides?

SUMMARY AND PREVIEW Many lives were changed by the war. In the next section you will learn about the end of the war.

Section 4 Assessment

go.hrw.com
Online Quiz
KEYWORD: SB7 HP16

Reviewing Ideas, Terms, and People

1. **a. Recall** Why did some Americans want to end slavery?
   b. Contrast How did reactions to the **Emancipation Proclamation** differ?
   c. Elaborate Do you think that the **emancipation** of slaves should have extended to the border states? Explain your answer.
2. **a. Recall** Why did some northerners want to recruit African Americans into the Union army?
   b. Contrast In what ways did African American soldiers face more difficulties than white soldiers did?
3. **a. Identify** Who were **Copperheads**, and why did they oppose the war?
   b. Evaluate Should President Lincoln have suspended the right to **habeas corpus**? Why?
4. **a. Describe** What were conditions like in military camps?
   b. Draw Conclusions How did the war change life on the home front?

Critical Thinking

5. **Identifying Effects** Review your notes. Then copy the graphic organizer below. Use it to summarize the reasons for the Emancipation Proclamation, its main points, and its effects on different people.

> Reasons for the Emancipation Proclamation
>
> ↓
>
> Main points of the Proclamation
>
> ↓
>
> Effect on People's Lives

FOCUS ON WRITING

6. **Taking Notes on Life During the War** As you read this section, take notes on the emancipation of the slaves, African American soldiers, and women who provided medical care for soldiers. Answer the following questions: Who? Where? When? Why? and How?

Abraham Lincoln

What would you do to save the struggling Union?

When did he live? 1809–1865

Where did he live? Abraham Lincoln was born in a log cabin to a poor family in Kentucky. Growing up in Kentucky and Illinois, Lincoln went to school for less than a year. He taught himself law and settled in Springfield, where he practiced law and politics. As president he lived in Washington, D.C. There, at age 56, his life was cut short by an assassin, John Wilkes Booth.

What did he do? The issue of slavery defined Lincoln's political career. He was not an abolitionist, but he strongly opposed extending slavery into the territories. In a series of famous debates against Senator Stephen Douglas of Illinois, Lincoln championed his views on slavery and made a brilliant defense of democracy and the Union. As president, Lincoln led the nation through the Civil War.

Why is he important? Lincoln is one of the great symbols of American democracy. "A house divided against itself cannot stand," he declared in a debate with Douglas. In 1863 Lincoln issued the Emancipation Proclamation. His address to commemorate the bloody battlefield at Gettysburg is widely considered to be one of the best political speeches in American history.

Summarizing Why is Lincoln such an important figure in American history?

Lincoln's address at the dedication of the Gettysburg National Cemetery.

KEY EVENTS

- **1834** Elected to the Illinois legislature
- **1842** Marries Mary Todd
- **1858** Holds series of famous debates with U.S. Senator Stephen Douglas
- **1860** Elected president on November 6
- **1863** Issues the Emancipation Proclamation on January 1
- **1863** Gives the Gettysburg Address on November 19
- **1865** Gives second inaugural address on March 4
- **1865** Shot on April 14; dies the next day

The Tide of War Turns

Virginia Standards of Learning USII.1a, USII.1c, USII.1d, USII.2c, USII.3c

What You Will Learn...

Main Ideas

1. The Union tried to divide the Confederate Army at Fredericksburg, but the attempt failed.
2. The Battle of Gettysburg in 1863 was a major turning point in the war.
3. During 1864, Union campaigns in the East and South dealt crippling blows to the Confederacy.
4. Union troops forced the South to surrender in 1865, ending the Civil War.

The Big Idea

Union victories in 1863, 1864, and 1865 ended the Civil War.

Key Terms and People

Battle of Gettysburg, *p. 537*
George Pickett, *p. 539*
Pickett's Charge, *p. 539*
Gettysburg Address, *p. 540*
Wilderness Campaign, *p. 540*
William Tecumseh Sherman, *p. 541*
total war, *p. 542*
Appomattox Courthouse, *p. 542*

TAKING NOTES Copy the graphic organizer. Use it to recall the events that led to the end of the Civil War.

| July 1–3, 1863 |
| September 2, 1864 |
| May–June, 1864 |
| December 10, 1864 |
| April 2, 1865 |
| April 9, 1865 |

If YOU were there...

You live in southern Pennsylvania in 1863, near a battlefield where thousands died. Now people have come from miles around to dedicate a cemetery here. You are near the front of the crowd. The first speaker impresses everyone with two hours of dramatic words and gestures. Then President Lincoln speaks—just a few minutes of simple words. Many people are disappointed.

Why do you think the president's speech was so short?

BUILDING BACKGROUND Many people, especially in the North, had expected a quick victory, but the war dragged on for years. The balance of victories seemed to seesaw between North and South, and both sides suffered terrible casualties. The last Confederate push into the North ended at Gettysburg in one of the bloodiest battles of the war.

Fredericksburg and Chancellorsville

Frustrated by McClellan's lack of aggression, Lincoln replaced him with General Ambrose E. Burnside as leader of the Army of the Potomac. Burnside favored a swift, decisive attack on Richmond by way of Fredericksburg. In November 1862, he set out with 120,000 troops.

Burnside's tactics surprised General Lee. The Confederate commander had divided his force of 78,000 men. Neither section of the Confederate army was in a good position to defend Fredericksburg. However, Burnside's army experienced delays in crossing the Rappahannock River. These delays allowed Lee's army to reunite and entrench themselves around Fredericksburg. Finally, the Union army crossed the Rappahannock and launched a series of charges. These attacks had heavy casualties and failed to break the Confederate line. Eventually, after suffering about 12,600 casualties, Burnside ordered a retreat. The Confederates had about 5,300 casualties.

Soon Burnside stepped down from his position. Lincoln made General Joseph Hooker the commander of the Army of the Potomac. At the end of April 1863, Hooker and his army of about 138,000 men launched a frontal attack on Fredericksburg. Then Hooker ordered about 115,000 of his troops to split off and approach the Confederate's flank, or side. Hooker's strategy seemed about to work. But for some reason he hesitated and had his flanking troops take a defensive position at Chancellorsville. This town was located a few miles west of Fredericksburg.

The following day, Lee used most of his army (about 60,000 men) to attack Hooker's troops at Chancellorsville. Stonewall Jackson led an attack on Hooker's flank while Lee commanded an assault on the Union front. The Union army was almost cut in two. They managed to form a defensive line, which they held for three days. Then Hooker ordered a retreat.

Lee's army won a major victory. But this victory had severe casualties. During the battle, Lee's trusted general, Stonewall Jackson, was accidentally shot by his own troops. He died a few days later.

READING CHECK **Comparing** What did generals McClellan, Burnside, and Hooker have in common?

Battle of Gettysburg

General Lee launched more attacks within Union territory. As before, his goal was to break the North's will to fight. He also hoped that a victory would convince other nations to recognize the Confederacy.

First Day

In early June 1863, Lee cut across northern Maryland into southern Pennsylvania. His forces gathered west of a small town called Gettysburg. Lee was unaware that Union soldiers were encamped closer to town. He had been suffering from lack of enemy information for three days because his cavalry chief "Jeb" Stuart was not performing his duties. Stuart and his cavalry had gone off on their own raiding party, disobeying Lee's orders.

Another Confederate raiding party went to Gettysburg for boots and other supplies. There, Lee's troops ran right into Union general George G. Meade's cavalry, triggering the **Battle of Gettysburg**, a key battle that finally turned the tide against the Confederates. The battle began on July 1, 1863, when the

Three Days at Gettysburg

Gettysburg was the largest and bloodiest battle of the Civil War. In three days, more than 51,000 soldiers were killed, wounded, captured, or went missing. It was an important victory for the Union, and it stopped Lee's plan of invading the North.

Artillery played a key role in the Battle of Gettysburg on July 1, 1863.

Day One: July 1, 1863

Confederate raiding party and the Union forces began exchanging fire. The larger Confederate forces began to push the Union troops back through Gettysburg.

The Union soldiers regrouped along the high ground of Cemetery Ridge and Culp's Hill. General Lee wanted to prevent the Union forces from entrenching themselves. He therefore ordered General Ewell to attack immediately. However, Ewell hesitated and thereby gave the Federals time to establish an excellent defensive position.

In fact, Confederate General James Longstreet thought that the Union position was almost impossible to overrun. Instead of attacking, he felt that the Confederate army should move east, take a strong defensive position themselves, and wait for the Union forces to attack them. However, General Lee was not convinced. He believed that his troops were invincible.

The Confederates camped at Seminary Ridge, which ran parallel to the Union forces. Both camps called for their main forces to reinforce them and prepare for combat the next day.

Second Day

On July 2, Lee ordered an attack on the left side of the Union line. Lee knew that he could win the battle if his troops captured Little Round Top from the Union forces. From this hill, Lee's troops could easily fire down on the line of Union forces. Union forces and Confederate troops fought viciously for control of Little Round Top. The fighting was particularly fierce on the south side of the hill. There the 20th Maine led by Colonel Joshua Chamberlain battled the 15th Alabama led by Colonel William Oates. Later, when describing the conflict, Oates said, "The blood stood in puddles in some places in the rocks." Eventually, the Union forced the Confederates to pull back from Little Round Top.

Then the Confederates attacked Cemetery Hill and Culp's Hill. The fighting lasted until nightfall. The assault on Cemetery Hill was unsuccessful. The Confederates did manage to take a few trenches on Culp's Hill. Even so, the Union forces still held a strong defensive position by the day's end.

Three Days at Gettysburg (continued)

Day Two: July 2, 1863, 10 a.m.

Union soldiers desperately defended Little Round Top from a fierce Confederate charge.

Pickett's Charge

On the third day of battle, Longstreet again tried to convince Lee not to attack. But Lee thought that the Union forces were severely battered and ready to break. Because of this, he planned to attack the center of the Union line on Cemetery Ridge. Such a tactic, he felt, would not be expected. Indeed, General Meade left only about 5,750 troops to defend the center.

For over an hour, the Confederates shelled Cemetery Ridge with cannon fire. For a while, the Union cannons fired back. Then they slacked off. The Confederates assumed that they had seriously damaged the Union artillery. In reality, the Confederate barrage did little damage.

The task of charging the Union center fell to three divisions of Confederate soldiers. General **George Pickett** commanded the largest unit. In late afternoon, nearly 15,000 men took part in **Pickett's Charge**. For one mile, the Confederates marched slowly up toward Cemetery Ridge. Showered with cannon and rifle fire, they suffered severe losses. But eventually, some of them almost reached their destination. Then Union reinforcements added to the barrage on the rebels. Soon the

Pickett's Charge, July 3, 1863

General George Pickett led his troops across Emmitsburg Road to attack the Union position. He lost more than half of his men in the 50-minute battle.

Interactive Map

PENNSYLVANIA
Gettysburg
Washington, D.C.

Legend:
- Union positions
- Confederate troop movements
- Confederate positions
- Roads

0   0.5   1 Mile
0   0.5   1 Kilometer

go.hrw.com
Interactive Map
KEYWORD: SB7 CH16

GEOGRAPHY **SKILLS** **INTERPRETING MAPS**

1. **Human-Environment Interaction** How do you think geography affected Pickett's Charge?
2. **Movement** In which direction did Pickett's soldiers charge?

Pickett's Charge

Pickett's Charge proved a disaster for the Confederate attackers. Fewer than half of them survived.

Day Three: July 3, 1863, 3 p.m.

Confederates retreated, leaving about 7,500 casualties on the field of battle. Distressed by this defeat, General Lee rode among the survivors and told them, "It is all my fault."

On the fourth day, Lee began to retreat to Virginia. In all, nearly 75,000 Confederate soldiers and 90,000 Union troops had fought during the Battle of Gettysburg.

General Meade decided not to follow Lee's army. This decision angered Lincoln. He felt that Meade had missed an opportunity to crush the Confederates and possibly end the war.

Aftermath of Gettysburg

Gettysburg was a turning point in the war. Lee's troops would never again launch an attack in the North. The Union victory at Gettysburg took place on the day before Grant's capture of Vicksburg, Mississippi. These victories made northerners believe that the war could be won.

In addition, the Union win at Gettysburg helped to end the South's search for foreign influence in the war. After Gettysburg, Great Britain and France refused to provide aid to the Confederacy. The South's attempt at cotton diplomacy failed.

The Gettysburg Address

On November 19, 1863, at the dedicating ceremony of the Gettysburg battlefield cemetery, President Lincoln gave a speech called the **Gettysburg Address**, in which he praised the bravery of Union soldiers and renewed his commitment to winning the Civil War. This short but moving speech is one of the most famous in American history. In one of its frequently quoted lines, Lincoln referenced the Declaration of Independence and its ideals of liberty, equality, and democracy. He reminded listeners that the war was being fought for those reasons.

Lincoln rededicated himself to winning the war and preserving the Union. A difficult road still lay ahead.

READING CHECK Analyzing Why was Gettysburg a turning point?

FOCUS ON READING
The first sentence of the paragraph to the right is a main idea. The rest of this paragraph supports the idea.

ACADEMIC VOCABULARY
execute to perform, carry out

Union Campaigns Cripple the Confederacy

Lincoln had been impressed with General Grant's successes in capturing Vicksburg. He transferred Grant to the East and gave him command of the Union army. In early 1864, Grant forced Lee to fight a series of battles in Virginia that stretched Confederate soldiers and supplies to their limits.

Wilderness Campaign in the East

From May through June, the armies fought in northern and central Virginia. Union troops launched the **Wilderness Campaign**—a series of battles designed to capture the Confederate capital at Richmond, Virginia. The first battle took place in early May, in woods about 50 miles outside of Richmond. Grant then ordered General Meade to Spotsylvania, where the fighting raged for five days.

Over the next month, Union soldiers moved the Confederate troops back toward Richmond. However, Grant experienced his worst defeat at the Battle of Cold Harbor in early June, just 10 miles northeast of Richmond. In only a few hours the Union army suffered 7,000 casualties. The battle delayed Grant's plans to take the Confederate capital.

Union forces had suffered twice as many casualties as the Confederates had, yet Grant continued his strategy. He knew he would be getting additional soldiers, and Lee could not. Grant slowly but surely advanced his troops through Virginia. He told another officer, "I propose to fight it out on this line if it takes all summer."

After Cold Harbor, General Grant moved south of Richmond. He had hoped to take control of the key railroad junction at Petersburg, Virginia. Lee's army, however, formed a solid defense, and Grant could not **execute** his attack. Grant was winning the war, but he still had not captured Richmond. Facing re-election, Lincoln was especially discouraged by this failure.

Final Campaigns

Union state
Union occupied, 1865
Confederate state
➤ Union forces
✦ Union victory
➤ Confederate forces
✦ Confederate victory

0   100   200 Miles
0   100   200 Kilometers

IA · IL · IN · OH · PA · NJ · MD · DE · Washington, D.C. · WV · Richmond · VA · KY · Ohio River · MO · KS · OK · AR · TN · Nashville Dec. 15–16, 1864 · HOOD · APPALACHIAN MTS. · Atlanta Sept. 2, 1864 · SC · NC · Raleigh April 13, 1865 · Wilmington Feb. 22, 1865 · SHERMAN · MS · AL · GA · SHERMAN · Savannah Dec. 21, 1864 · LA · Mississippi River · Pensacola · Gulf of Mexico · FL · 30°N · ATLANTIC OCEAN

0   20   40 Miles
0   20   40 Kilometers

PA · Gettysburg, July 1–3, 1863 · MD · GRANT · LEE · WV · The Wilderness, May 5–7, 1864 · Chancellorsville, May 1–5, 1863 · Washington, D.C. · VA · Spotsylvania Courthouse, May 8–19, 1864 · LEE · Richmond · GRANT · Cold Harbor, June 3, 1864 · Appomattox Courthouse, Apr. 9, 1865– Lee surrenders to Grant · Petersburg, June 1864– April 1865 · Chesapeake Bay · 70°W

GEOGRAPHY SKILLS INTERPRETING MAPS

1. **Movement** About how long was Sherman's March to the Sea from Atlanta to Savannah?
2. **Movement** What challenges do you think Sherman faced on his southern attacks?

Sherman Strikes the South

Lincoln needed a victory for the Union army to help him win re-election in 1864. The bold campaign of General **William Tecumseh Sherman** provided this key victory. Sherman carried out the Union plan to destroy southern railroads and industries.

In the spring of 1864, Sherman marched south from Tennessee with 100,000 troops. His goal was to take Atlanta, Georgia, and knock out an important railroad link. From May through August, Sherman's army moved steadily through the Appalachian Mountains toward Atlanta. Several times, Sherman avoided defenses set up by Confederate general Joseph Johnston.

In July, Sherman was within sight of Atlanta. Confederate president Jefferson Davis gave General John Hood command of Confederate forces in the region. Hood repeatedly attacked Sherman in a final attempt to

save Atlanta, but the Union troops proved stronger. The Confederate troops retreated as Sherman held Atlanta under siege.

Atlanta fell to Sherman's troops on September 2, 1864. Much of the city was destroyed by artillery and fire. Sherman ordered the residents who still remained to leave. Responding to his critics, Sherman later wrote, "War is war, and not popularity-seeking." The loss of Atlanta cost the South an important railroad link and its center of industry.

Many people in the North had been upset with the length of the war. However, the capture of Atlanta showed that progress was being made in defeating the South. This success helped to convince Union voters to re-elect Lincoln in a landslide.

Sherman did not wait long to begin his next campaign. His goal was the port city of Savannah, Georgia. In mid-November 1864,

Sherman left Atlanta with a force of about 60,000 men. He said he would "make Georgia howl!"

During his March to the Sea, Sherman practiced **total war**—destroying civilian and economic resources. Sherman believed that total war would ruin the South's economy and its ability to fight. He ordered his troops to destroy railways, bridges, crops, livestock, and other resources. They burned plantations and freed slaves.

Sherman's army reached Savannah on December 10, 1864. They left behind a path of destruction 60 miles wide. Sherman believed that this march would speed the end of the war. He wanted to break the South's will to fight by marching Union troops through the heart of the Confederacy. In the end, Sherman's destruction of the South led to anger and resentment toward the people of the North that would last for generations.

READING CHECK Drawing Conclusions

How did Sherman hope to help the Union with his total-war strategy?

Causes and Effects of the Civil War

QUICK FACTS

Causes
- Disagreement over the institution of slavery
- Economic differences
- Political differences

Effects
- Slavery ends
- 620,000 Americans killed
- Military districts created
- Southern economy in ruins

ANALYSIS SKILL INTERPRETING CHARTS

How important was slavery to the Civil War?

The South Surrenders

In early April, Sherman closed in on the last Confederate defenders in North Carolina. At the same time, Grant finally broke through the Confederate defenses at Petersburg. On April 2, Lee was forced to retreat from Richmond.

Fighting Ends

By the second week of April 1865, Grant had surrounded Lee's army and demanded the soldiers' surrender. Lee hoped to join other Confederates in fighting in North Carolina, but Grant cut off his escape just west of Richmond. Lee tried some last minute attacks but could not break the Union line. Lee's forces were running low on supplies. General James Longstreet told about the condition of Confederate troops. "Many weary soldiers were picked up . . . some with, many without, arms [weapons],—all asking for food."

Trapped by the Union army, Lee recognized that the situation was hopeless. "There is nothing left for me to do but go and see General Grant," Lee said, "and I would rather die a thousand deaths."

On April 9, 1865, the Union and Confederate leaders met at a home in the small town of **Appomattox Courthouse** where Lee surrendered to Grant, thus ending the Civil War.

During the meeting, Grant assured Lee that his troops would be fed and allowed to keep their horses, and they would not be tried for treason. Then Lee signed the surrender documents. The long, bloody war had finally ended. Grant later wrote that he found the scene at Appomattox Courthouse more tragic than joyful.

"I felt . . . sad and depressed at the downfall of a foe [enemy] who had fought so long and valiantly [bravely], and had suffered so much for a cause, though that cause was, I believe, one of the worst for which a people ever fought."

—Ulysses S. Grant, *Battle Cry of Freedom*

Surrender at Appomattox

Union general Grant rose to shake hands with Confederate general Lee after the surrender. Grant allowed Lee to keep his sword and Lee's men to keep their horses.

Was it important for Grant and Lee to shake hands? Why or why not?

As General Lee returned to his troops, General Grant stopped Union forces from cheering their victory. "The war is over," Grant said with relief. "The rebels are our countrymen again."

The Effects of the War

The Civil War had deep and long-lasting effects. Almost 620,000 Americans lost their lives during the four years of fighting.

The defeat of the South ended slavery there. The majority of former slaves, however, had no homes or jobs. The southern economy was in ruins.

A tremendous amount of hostility remained, even after the fighting had ceased. The war was over, but the question remained: How could the United States be united once more?

READING CHECK **Predicting** What problems might the Union face following the Civil War?

SUMMARY AND PREVIEW After four long years of battles, the Civil War ended with General Lee's surrender at Appomattox Courthouse. In the next chapter you will read about the consequences of the war in the South.

Section 5 Assessment

go.hrw.com
Online Quiz
KEYWORD: SB7 HP16

Reviewing Ideas, Terms, and People

1. **a. Identify** What Confederate general died from his wounds at Chancellorsville?
   b. Draw Conclusions Why was the Union army defeated at Chancellorsville?
2. **a. Identify** What was the **Gettysburg Address**?
   b. Analyze Why was geography important to the outcome of the Battle of Gettysburg?
3. **a. Recall** What was the purpose of the **Wilderness Campaign**?
   b. Draw Conclusions In what way was the capture of Atlanta an important victory for President Lincoln?
4. **a. Identify** What events led to Lee's surrender at **Appomattox Courthouse**?
   b. Summarize What problems did the South face at the end of the war?

Critical Thinking

5. **Supporting a Point of View** Review your notes on the end of the Civil War. Then copy the graphic organizer below. Use it to show the three events in this section that you think contributed most to the end of the Civil War and explain why.

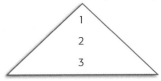

FOCUS ON WRITING

6. **Taking Notes on the End of the War** As you read this section, take notes on the Battle of Gettysburg, the Wilderness Campaign, the fall of Atlanta, and the South's surrender. Be sure to answer the following questions: Who? Where? When? Why? and How?

Social Studies Skills

Interpreting Political Cartoons

Define the Skill

Political cartoons are drawings that express views on important issues. They have been used throughout history to influence public opinion. The ability to interpret political cartoons will help you understand issues and people's attitudes about them.

Learn the Skill

Political cartoons use both words and images to convey their message. They often contain caricatures or symbolism. A caricature is a drawing that exaggerates the features of a person or object. Symbolism is the use of one thing to represent something else. Cartoonists use these techniques to help make their point clear. They also use titles, labels, and captions to get their message across.

Use these steps to interpret political cartoons.

1 Read any title, labels, and caption to identify the cartoon's general topic.

2 Identify the people and objects. Determine if they are exaggerated and, if so, why. Identify any symbols and analyze their meaning.

3 Draw conclusions about the message the cartoonist is trying to convey.

The following cartoon was published in the North in 1863. The cartoonist has used symbols to make his point. Lady Liberty, representing the Union, is being threatened by the Copperheads. The cartoonist has expressed his opinion of these people by drawing them as the poisonous snake for which they were named. This cartoon clearly supports the Union's continuing to fight the war.

Practice the Skill

Apply the guidelines to interpret the cartoon below and answer the questions that follow.

1. What do the tree and the man in it symbolize?

2. What policy or action of President Lincoln is this cartoon supporting?

LINCOLN'S LAST WARNING.
"Now, if you don't come down, I'll cut the Tree from under you."

544   CHAPTER 16

Chapter Review

HOLT

History's Impact
▶ video series
Review the video to answer the closing question:
How do you think the age of a country relates to its citizens' national pride?

Visual Summary

Use the visual summary below to help you review the main ideas of the chapter.

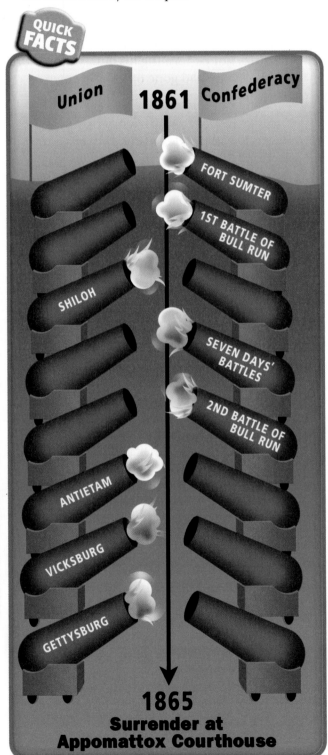

QUICK FACTS

Union — 1861 — Confederacy

FORT SUMTER

1ST BATTLE OF BULL RUN

SHILOH

SEVEN DAYS' BATTLES

2ND BATTLE OF BULL RUN

ANTIETAM

VICKSBURG

GETTYSBURG

1865
Surrender at Appomattox Courthouse

Reviewing Vocabulary, Terms, and People

Match the numbered definitions with the correct terms from the list below.

a. contrabands
b. cotton diplomacy
c. Second Battle of Bull Run
d. Siege of Vicksburg
e. Thomas "Stonewall" Jackson

1. Attack by Union general Ulysses S. Grant that gave the North control of the Mississippi River
2. Confederate general who held off Union attacks and helped the South win the First Battle of Bull Run
3. Important Confederate victory in which General Robert E. Lee defeated Union troops and pushed into Union territory for the first time
4. Southern strategy of using cotton exports to gain Britain's support in the Civil War
5. Term given to escaped slaves from the South

Comprehension and Critical Thinking

SECTION 1 *(Pages 510–515)*

6. a. Identify When and where did fighting in the U.S. Civil War begin?

b. Analyze How did civilians help the war effort in both the North and the South?

c. Elaborate Why do you think the border states chose to remain in the Union despite their support of slavery?

SECTION 2 *(Pages 516–521)*

7. a. Identify What was the first major battle of the war? What was the outcome of the battle?

b. Analyze What was the Union army hoping to accomplish when it marched into Virginia at the start of the war?

c. Evaluate Was the Union's naval blockade of the South successful? Why or why not?

SECTION 3 (Pages 522–525)

8. a. Identify Which side did the Cherokee support in the fighting at Pea Ridge? Why?

b. Draw Conclusions What progress did Union leaders make in the war in the West?

c. Evaluate Which victory in the West was most valuable to the Union? Why?

SECTION 4 (Pages 528–534)

9. a. Describe What responsibilities did women take on during the war?

b. Analyze What opposition to the war did President Lincoln face, and how did he deal with that opposition?

c. Predict What might be some possible problems that the newly freed slaves in the South might face?

SECTION 5 (Pages 536–543)

10. a. Recall When and where did the war finally end?

b. Compare and Contrast How were the efforts of Generals Grant and Sherman at the end of the war similar and different?

c. Elaborate What do you think led to the South's defeat in the Civil War? Explain.

Social Studies Skills

Interpreting Political Cartoons *Use the Social Studies Skills taught in this chapter to answer the question about the political cartoon below.*

11. What do you think the artist is saying about politicians with this cartoon?

Reading Skills

Supporting Facts and Details *Use the Reading Skills taught in this chapter to answer the question about the reading selection below.*

> Lee was unaware that Union soldiers were encamped closer to town. He had been suffering from lack of enemy information for three days because his cavalry chief "Jeb" Stuart was not performing his duties. Stuart and his cavalry had gone off on their own raiding party, disobeying Lee's orders. *(p. 537)*

12. What is the main idea of the above reading selection?

a. "Jeb" Stuart was not performing his duties.

b. Stuart and his cavalry had gone off on their own.

c. Stuart and his cavalry disobeyed Lee's orders.

d. Lee was suffering from a lack of enemy information.

Reviewing Themes

13. Society and Culture What effects did the Civil War have on American society?

14. Politics What political difficulties did the Emancipation Proclamation cause for President Lincoln?

Using the Internet
go.hrw.com KEYWORD: SB7 CH16

15. Activity: Writing a Poem Soldiers in the Civil War came from all walks of life. Despite the hope for glory and adventure, many encountered dangerous and uncomfortable conditions. Enter the activity keyword to learn more about Civil War soldiers. After viewing photographs and reading letters, write a poem describing the life of a soldier. Your poem should reflect on the soldier's emotions and experiences.

FOCUS ON WRITING

16. Write Your Newspaper Article Review your notes. Then choose the subject you think would make the best newspaper article. Write an attention-grabbing headline. Then write your article, giving as many facts as possible.

DIRECTIONS: Read each question and write the letter of the best response.

1 Use the map below to answer the following question.

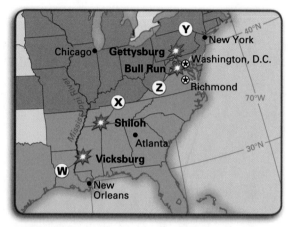

The place where two major battles of the Civil War were fought is indicated on the map by which letter?

A W

B X

C Y

D Z

2 The Battle of Gettysburg was an important battle of the Civil War because

A it was an overwhelming Confederate victory.

B the Union army's advance on the Confederate capital was stopped.

C it ended Lee's hopes of advancing into northern territory.

D it enabled the Union to control the Mississippi River.

3 Overall command of Confederate forces in Virginia during most of the Civil War was held by

A Jefferson Davis.

B William Tecumseh Sherman.

C Thomas "Stonewall" Jackson.

D Robert E. Lee.

4 Which of Lincoln's speeches and writings reflected the statement that "all men are created equal"?

A the Emancipation Proclamation

B the first inaugural address (1861)

C the second inaugural address (1865)

D the Gettysburg Address

5 The tactics that Sherman used against Confederate armies in the South were based on what strategy?

A cutting off troops from their officers

B a naval blockade of southern ports

C destroying the South's resources and economy

D hit-and-run attacks on major southern cities

6 In the War of 1812 the British navy blockaded American seaports in the hope that the U.S. economy would suffer and the United States would surrender. Which Civil War strategy was similar?

A Scott's plan to destroy the southern economy

B Sherman's March to the Sea

C General Ulysses S. Grant's capture of Vicksburg

D Admiral David Farragut's defeat of New Orleans

7 Read the following quote from Grant about Lee's surrender and use it to answer the question below.

> *"*What General Lee's feelings were I do not know. He was a man of much dignity, without expression on his face. It was impossible to say whether he felt inwardly glad that the end had finally come, or felt sad over the result, and was too manly to show it. Whatever his feelings, they were entirely hidden from me.*"*
>
> –Ulysses S. Grant, adapted from *Personal Memoirs of U.S. Grant, Vol. 2*

Document-Based Question What is your opinion about what Lee might have been feeling during his surrender?

Reconstruction

Virginia Standards of Learning

USII.1 The student will demonstrate skills for historical and geographical analysis, and responsible citizenship, including the ability to

a) analyze and interpret primary and secondary source documents to increase understanding of events and life in United States history from 1865 to the present; **b)** make connections between past and present; **c)** sequence events in United States history from 1865 to the present; **d)** interpret ideas and events from different historical perspectives; **e)** evaluate and debate issues orally and in writing; **h)** interpret patriotic slogans and excerpts from notable speeches and documents; **i)** identify the costs and benefits of specific choices made including the consequences, both intended and unintended, of the decision and how people and nations responded to positive and negative incentives

USII.2 The student will use maps, globes, photographs, pictures, or tables for

c) locating the 50 states and the cities most significant to the historical development of the United States

USII.3 The student will demonstrate knowledge of the effects of Reconstruction on American life by

a) analyzing the impact of the 13th, 14th, and 15th Amendments to the Constitution of the United States of America
b) describing the impact of Reconstruction policies on the South and North; **c)** describing the legacy of Abraham Lincoln, Robert E. Lee, and Frederick Douglass

USII.4 The student will demonstrate knowledge of how life changed after the Civil War by

c) describing racial segregation, the rise of "Jim Crow," and other constraints faced by African Americans and other groups in the post-Reconstruction South

FOCUS ON WRITING

Job History When the Civil War ended, it was time to rebuild. People were ready to get back to work. But life had changed for many people and would continue to change. As you read this chapter, think about jobs people may have had during Reconstruction.

UNITED STATES

1865
Abraham Lincoln is assassinated.

1865

WORLD

1865
Black Jamaicans rebel against the wealthy planter class.

What You Will Learn...

The ruins of this Virginia plantation stand as a bleak reminder of the changes brought to the South by the Civil War. In this chapter you will learn about the challenges that faced the nation after the Civil War and attempts to meet those challenges.

1868
President Andrew Johnson is impeached and almost removed from office.

U.S. SENATE
Impeachment of President
ADMIT THE BEARER
MARCH 13, 1868
Geo. T. Brown
Sergeant-at-Arms.
To be taken up at
MAIN ENTRANCE
U.S. SENATE

1870
Hiram Revels becomes the first African American to serve in the U.S. Senate.

1877
The Compromise of 1877 ends Reconstruction.

1870

1875

1880

1868
The Meiji dynasty returns to power in Japan.

1869
The Suez Canal opens, linking the Mediterranean and Red seas.

1871
Otto von Bismarck and Wilhelm I unite Germany.

RECONSTRUCTION **549**

Reading Social Studies

by Kylene Beers

Economics   Geography   Politics   Society and Culture   Science and Technology

Focus on Themes In this chapter you will read about the time immediately after the Civil War. You will see how the government tried to rebuild the South and will learn about how life changed for African Americans after slavery was declared illegal.

You will read about the **political** conflicts that emerged as southern leadership worked to gain control of Reconstruction efforts. Throughout the chapter, you will read how the **culture** of the South changed after the War.

Analyzing Historical Information

Focus on Reading History books are full of information. As you read, you are confronted with names, dates, places, terms, and descriptions on every page. You don't want to have to deal with anything unimportant or untrue.

Identifying Relevant and Essential Information Information in a history book should be relevant to the topic you're studying. It should also be essential

to understanding the topic and be verifiable. Anything else distracts from the material you are studying.

The first passage below includes several pieces of irrelevant and nonessential information. In the second, this information has been removed. Note how much easier the revised passage is to comprehend.

First Passage

President Abraham Lincoln, <u>who was very tall</u>, wanted to reunite the nation as quickly and painlessly as possible. He had proposed a plan for readmitting the southern states even before the war ended, <u>which happened on a Sunday</u>. Called the Ten Percent Plan, it offered southerners amnesty, or official pardon, for all illegal acts supporting the rebellion. <u>Today a group called Amnesty International works to protect the rights of prisoners. Lincoln's plan certainly would have worked if it would have been implemented.</u>

> Lincoln's appearance and the day on which the war ended are not essential facts.

> Amnesty International is not relevant to this topic.

> There is no way to prove the accuracy of the last sentence.

Revised Passage

President Abraham Lincoln wanted to reunite the nation as quickly and painlessly as possible. He had proposed a plan for readmitting the southern states even before the war ended. Called the Ten Percent Plan, it offered southerners amnesty, or official pardon, for all illegal acts supporting the rebellion.

From Chapter 17, p. 553

You Try It!

The following passage is adapted from the chapter you are about to read. As you read, look for irrelevant, nonessential, or unverifiable information.

The Freedmen's Bureau

In 1865 Congress established the Freedmen's Bureau, an agency providing relief for freedpeople and certain poor people in the South. The Bureau had a difficult job. It may have been one of the most difficult jobs ever. At its high point, about 900 agents served the entire South. All 900 people could fit into one hotel ballroom today. Bureau commissioner Oliver O. Howard eventually decided to use the Bureau's limited budget to distribute food to the poor and to provide education and legal help for freedpeople. One common food in the South at that time was salted meat. The Bureau also helped African American war veterans. Today the Department of Veterans' Affairs assists American war veterans.

From Chapter 17, p. 556

After you read the passage, answer the following questions.

1. Which sentence in this passage is unverifiable and should be cut?

2. Find two sentences in this passage that are irrelevant to the discussion of the Freedmen's Bureau. What makes those sentences irrelevant?

3. Look at the last sentence of the passage. Do you think this sentence is essential to the discussion? Why or why not?

As you read Chapter 17, ask yourself what makes the information you are reading essential to a study of Reconstruction.

Key Terms and People

Academic Vocabulary

Success in school is related to knowing academic vocabulary— the words that are frequently used in school assignments and discussions. In this chapter, you will learn the following academic words:

Rebuilding the South

Virginia Standards of Learning USII.3a, USII.3b, USII.3c

What You Will Learn...

Main Ideas

1. President Lincoln and Congress differed in their views as Reconstruction began.
2. The end of the Civil War meant freedom for African Americans in the South.
3. President Johnson's plan began the process of Reconstruction.

The Big Idea

The nation faced many problems in rebuilding the Union.

Key Terms and People

Reconstruction, *p. 552*
Ten Percent Plan, *p. 553*
Thirteenth Amendment, *p. 554*
Freedmen's Bureau, *p. 556*
Andrew Johnson, *p. 557*

TAKING NOTES As you read, take notes on the different ways the U.S. government attempted to reconstruct the south after the Civil War. Write your notes in a graphic organizer like the one below.

Rebuilding and Reconstruction
1.
2.
3.
4.
5.
6.
7.

If YOU were there...

You are a young soldier who has been fighting in the Civil War for many months. Now that the war is over, you are on your way home. During your journey, you pass plantation manor homes, houses, and barns that have been burned down. No one is doing spring planting in the fields. As you near your family's farm, you see that fences and sheds have been destroyed. You wonder what is left of your home and family.

What would you think your future on the farm would be like?

BUILDING BACKGROUND When the Civil War ended, much of the South lay in ruins. Like the young soldier above, many people returned to destroyed homes and farms. Harvests of corn, cotton, rice, and other crops fell far below normal. Many farm animals had been killed or were roaming free. These were some of the challenges in restoring the nation.

Reconstruction Begins

After the Civil War ended in 1865, the U.S. government faced the problem of dealing with the defeated southern states. The challenges of **Reconstruction**, the process of readmitting the former Confederate states to the Union, lasted from 1865 to 1877.

Damaged South

Tired southern soldiers returned home to find that the world they had known before the war was gone. Cities, towns, and farms had been ruined. Because of high food prices and widespread crop failures, many southerners faced starvation. The Confederate money held by most southerners was now worthless. Banks failed, and merchants had gone bankrupt because people could not pay their debts.

Former Confederate general Braxton Bragg was one of many southerners who faced economic hardship. He found that "*all, all* was lost, except my debts." In South Carolina, Mary Boykin Chesnut wrote in her diary about the isolation she experienced after the war. "We are shut in here . . . All RR's [railroads] destroyed—bridges gone. We are cut off from the world."

Lincoln's Plan

President Abraham Lincoln wanted to reunite the nation as quickly and painlessly as possible. He had proposed a plan for readmitting the southern states even before the war ended. Called the **Ten Percent Plan**, it offered southerners amnesty, or official pardon, for all illegal acts supporting the rebellion. To receive amnesty, southerners had to do two things. They had to swear an oath of loyalty to the United States. They also had to agree that slavery was illegal. Once 10 percent of voters in a state made these pledges, they could form a new government. The state then could be readmitted to the Union.

Louisiana quickly elected a new state legislature under the Ten Percent Plan. Other southern states that had been occupied by Union troops soon followed Louisiana back into the United States.

Wade-Davis Bill

Some politicians argued that Congress, not the president, should control the southern states' return to the Union. They believed that Congress had the power to admit new states. Also, many Republican members of Congress thought the Ten Percent Plan did not go far enough. A senator from Michigan expressed their views.

"The people of the North are not such fools as to . . . turn around and say to the traitors, 'all you have to do [to return] is . . . take an oath that henceforth you will be true to the Government.'"

–Senator Jacob Howard, quoted in *Reconstruction: America's Unfinished Revolution, 1863–1877,* by Eric Foner

Two Republicans—Senator Benjamin Wade and Representative Henry Davis—had an alternative to Lincoln's plan. Following **procedures** of the Wade-Davis bill, a state had to meet two conditions before it could rejoin the Union. First, it had to ban slavery. Second, a majority of adult males in the state had to take the loyalty oath.

ACADEMIC VOCABULARY

procedure
a series of steps taken to accomplish a task

War destroyed Richmond, Virginia, once the capital of the Confederacy.

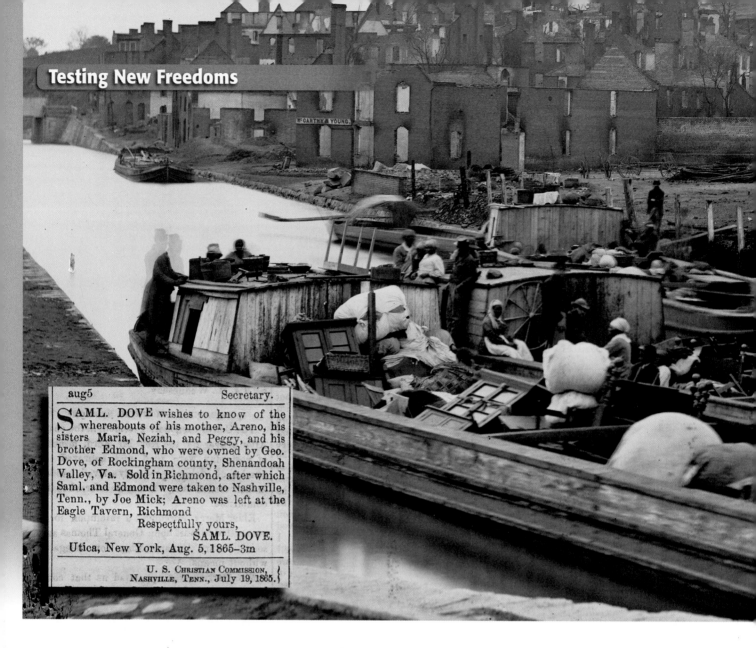

aug5   Secretary.

SAML. DOVE wishes to know of the whereabouts of his mother, Areno, his sisters Maria, Neziah, and Peggy, and his brother Edmond, who were owned by Geo. Dove, of Rockingham county, Shenandoah Valley, Va. Sold in Richmond, after which Saml. and Edmond were taken to Nashville, Tenn., by Joe Mick; Areno was left at the Eagle Tavern, Richmond

Respectfully yours,
SAML. DOVE.

Utica, New York, Aug. 5, 1865–3m

U. S. Christian Commission,
Nashville, Tenn., July 19, 1865.

Under the Wade-Davis bill, only southerners who swore that they had never supported the Confederacy could vote or hold office. In general, the bill was much stricter than the Ten Percent Plan. Its provisions would make it harder for southern states to rejoin the Union quickly.

President Lincoln therefore refused to sign the bill into law. He thought that few southern states would agree to meet its requirements. He believed that his plan would help restore order more quickly.

READING CHECK **Contrasting** How was the Ten Percent Plan different from the Wade-Davis bill?

Freedom for African Americans

One thing Republicans agreed on was abolishing slavery. The Emancipation Proclamation had freed slaves only in areas that had not been occupied by Union forces, not in the border states. Many people feared that the federal courts might someday declare the proclamation unconstitutional.

Slavery Ends

On January 31, 1865, at President Lincoln's urging, Congress proposed the **Thirteenth Amendment**. This amendment made slavery illegal throughout the United States.

The freedpeople at left have packed their household belongings and are leaving Richmond. Many people traveled in search of relatives. Others placed newspaper advertisements looking for long-lost relatives. For other freedpeople, like the couple above, freedom brought the right to marry.

In what ways did former slaves react to freedom?

The amendment was ratified and took effect on December 18, 1865. When abolitionist William Lloyd Garrison heard the news, he declared that his work was now finished. He called for the American Anti-Slavery Society to break up. Not all abolitionists agreed that their work was done, however. Frederick Douglass insisted that "slavery is not abolished until the black man has the ballot [vote]."

Freedom brought important changes to newly freed slaves. Many couples held ceremonies to legalize marriages that had not been recognized under slavery. Many freedpeople searched for relatives who had been sold away from their families years earlier. Others placed newspaper ads seeking information about their children. Many women began to work at home instead of in the fields. Still others adopted children of dead relatives to keep families together. Church members established voluntary associations and mutual-aid societies to help those in need.

Now that they could travel without a pass, many freedpeople moved from mostly white counties to places with more African Americans. Other freedpeople traveled simply to test their new freedom of movement. A South Carolina woman explained this need. "I must go, if I stay here I'll never know I'm free."

For most former slaves, freedom to travel was just the first step on a long road toward equal rights and new ways of life. Adults took new last names and began to insist on being called Mr. or Mrs. as a sign of respect, rather than by their first names or by nicknames. Freedpeople began to demand the same economic and political rights as white citizens. Henry Adams, a former slave, argued that "if I cannot do like a white man I am not free."

Forty Acres to Farm?

Many former slaves wanted their own land to farm. Near the end of the Civil War, Union general William Tecumseh Sherman had issued an order to break up plantations in coastal South Carolina and Georgia. He wanted to divide the land into 40-acre plots and give them to former slaves as compensation for their forced labor before the war.

Many white planters refused to surrender their land. Some freedpeople pointed out that it was only fair that they receive some of this land because their labor had made the plantations prosper. In the end, the U.S. government returned the land to its original owners. At this time, many freedpeople were unsure about where they would live, what kind of work they would do, and what rights they had. Freedoms that were theirs by law were difficult to enforce.

Freedmen's Bureau

In 1865 Congress established the **Freedmen's Bureau**, an agency providing relief for freedpeople and certain poor people in the South. The Bureau had a difficult job. At its high point, about 900 agents served the entire South. Bureau commissioner Oliver O. Howard eventually decided to use the Bureau's limited budget to distribute food to the poor and to provide education and legal help for freedpeople. The Bureau also helped African American war veterans.

The Freedmen's Bureau played an important role in establishing more schools in the South. Laws against educating slaves meant that most freedpeople had never learned to read or write. Before the war ended, however, northern groups, such as the American Missionary Association, began providing books and teachers to African Americans. The teachers were mostly women who were committed to helping freedpeople. One teacher said of her students, "I never before saw children so eager to learn . . . It is wonderful how [they] . . . can have so great a desire for knowledge, and such a capacity for attaining [reaching] it."

After the war, some freedpeople organized their own education efforts. For example, Freedmen's Bureau agents found that some African Americans had opened schools in abandoned buildings. Many white southerners continued to believe that African Americans should not be educated. Despite opposition, by 1869 more than 150,000 African American students were attending more than 3,000 schools. The Freedmen's Bureau also helped establish a number of universities for African Americans, including Howard and Fisk universities.

Students quickly filled the new classrooms. Working adults attended classes in the evening. African Americans hoped that education would help them to understand and protect their rights and to enable them to find better jobs. Both black and white southerners benefited from the effort to provide greater access to education in the South.

READING CHECK **Analyzing** How did the Freedmen's Bureau help reform education in the South?

Helping the Freedpeople

Congress created the Freedmen's Bureau to help freedpeople and poor southerners recover from the Civil War. The Bureau assisted people by:

- providing supplies and medical services
- establishing schools
- supervising contracts between freedpeople and employers
- taking care of lands abandoned or captured during the war

What role did the Freedmen's Bureau play during Reconstruction?

President Johnson's Reconstruction Plan

While the Freedmen's Bureau was helping African Americans, the issue of how the South would politically rejoin the Union remained unresolved. Soon, however, a tragic event ended Lincoln's dream of peacefully reuniting the country.

A New President

On the evening of April 14, 1865, President Lincoln and his wife attended a play at Ford's Theater in Washington, D.C. During the play, John Wilkes Booth, a southerner who opposed Lincoln's policies, sneaked into the president's theater box and shot him. Lincoln was rushed to a boardinghouse across the street, where he died early the next morning. Vice President **Andrew Johnson** was sworn into office quickly. Reconstruction had now become his responsibility. He would have to win the trust of a nation shocked at its leader's death.

Johnson's plan for bringing southern states back into the Union was similar to Lincoln's plan. However, he decided that wealthy southerners and former Confederate officials would need a presidential pardon to receive amnesty. Johnson shocked Radical Republicans by eventually pardoning more than 7,000 people by 1866.

New State Governments

Johnson was a Democrat whom Republicans had put on the ticket in 1864 to appeal to the border states. A former slaveholder, he was a stubborn man who would soon face a hostile Congress.

Johnson offered a mild program for setting up new southern state governments. First, he appointed a temporary governor for each state. Then he required that the states revise their constitutions. Next, voters elected state and federal representatives. The new state government had to declare that secession was illegal. It also had to ratify the Thirteenth Amendment and refuse to pay Confederate debts.

By the end of 1865, all the southern states except Texas had created new governments. Johnson approved them all and declared that the United States was restored. Newly elected representatives came to Washington from each reconstructed southern state. However, Republicans complained that many new representatives had been leaders of the Confederacy. Congress therefore refused to readmit the southern states into the Union. Clearly, the nation was still divided.

READING CHECK **Summarizing** What was President Johnson's plan for Reconstruction?

SUMMARY AND PREVIEW In this section you learned about early plans for Reconstruction. In the next section, you will learn that disagreements about Reconstruction became so serious that the president was almost removed from office.

go.hrw.com
Online Quiz
KEYWORD: SB7 HP17

Section 1 Assessment

Reviewing Ideas, Terms, and People

1. **a. Identify** What does **Reconstruction** mean?
   b. Summarize What was President Lincoln's plan for Reconstruction?
2. **a. Recall** What is the **Thirteenth Amendment**?
   b. Elaborate In your opinion, what was the most important accomplishment of the **Freedmen's Bureau**? Explain.
3. **a. Recall** Why was President Lincoln killed?
   b. Analyze Why did some Americans oppose President Johnson's Reconstruction plan?

Critical Thinking

4. **Summarizing** Review your notes on Reconstruction. Then copy the graphic organizer below and use it to show how African Americans were affected by the end of the war.

African Americans and Reconstruction — Marriages are legalized.

FOCUS ON WRITING

5. **Considering Historical Context** Many people planned to continue doing what they had done before the war. Others planned to start a new life. How do you think events and conditions you just read about might have affected their plans?

The Fight over Reconstruction

Virginia Standards of Learning USII.1a, USII.1d, USII.1h, USII.2c, USII.3a, USII.3b

What You Will Learn...

Main Ideas

1. Black Codes led to opposition to President Johnson's plan for Reconstruction.
2. The Fourteenth Amendment ensured citizenship for African Americans.
3. Radical Republicans in Congress took charge of Reconstruction.
4. The Fifteenth Amendment gave African Americans the right to vote.

The Big Idea

The return to power of the pre-war southern leadership led Republicans in Congress to take control of Reconstruction.

Key Terms and People

Black Codes, *p. 558*
Radical Republicans, *p. 559*
Civil Rights Act of 1866, *p. 560*
Fourteenth Amendment, *p. 561*
Reconstruction Acts, *p. 561*
impeachment, *p. 562*
Fifteenth Amendment, *p. 563*

TAKING NOTES As you read, take notes on how Republicans in Congress took over Reconstruction and how they changed Reconstruction policies. Write your notes in a graphic organizer like the one below.

Issues that Concerned Republicans	Changes by the Republican Congress

If YOU were there...

A member of Congress, you belong to the same political party as the president. But you strongly disagree with his ideas about Reconstruction and civil rights for African Americans. Now some of the president's opponents are trying to remove him from office. You do not think he is a good president. On the other hand, you think removing him would be bad for the unity of the country.

Will you vote to remove the president?

BUILDING BACKGROUND Americans were bitterly divided about what should happen in the South during Reconstruction. They disagreed about ending racial inequality and guaranteeing civil rights for African Americans. These conflicts split political parties. They led to showdowns between Congress and the president. Political fights even threatened the president's job.

Opposition to President Johnson

In 1866 Congress continued to debate the rules for restoring the Union. Meanwhile, new state legislatures approved by President Johnson had already begun passing laws to deny African Americans' civil rights. "This is a white man's government, and intended for white men only," declared Governor Benjamin F. Perry of South Carolina.

Black Codes

Soon, every southern state passed **Black Codes**, or laws that greatly limited the freedom of African Americans. They required African Americans to sign work contracts, creating working conditions similar to those under slavery. In most southern states, any African Americans who could not prove they were employed could be arrested. Their punishment might be one year of work without pay. African Americans were also prevented from owning guns. In addition, they were not allowed to rent property except in cities.

The Black Codes alarmed many Americans. As one Civil War veteran asked, "If you call this freedom, what do you call slavery?"

African Americans organized to oppose the codes. One group sent a petition to officials in South Carolina.

"We simply ask … that the same laws which govern white men shall govern black men … that, in short, we be dealt with as others are—in equity [equality] and justice."

—Petition from an African American convention held in South Carolina, quoted in *There Is a River: The Black Struggle for Freedom in America* by Vincent Harding

Radical Republicans

The Black Codes angered many Republicans. They thought the South was returning to its old ways. Most Republicans were moderates who wanted the South to have loyal state governments. They also believed that African Americans should have rights as citizens. They hoped that the government would not have to force the South to follow federal laws.

Radical Republicans, on the other hand, took a harsher stance. They wanted the federal government to force change in the South. Like the moderates, they thought the Black Codes were cruel and unjust. The Radicals, however, wanted the federal government to be much more involved in Reconstruction. They feared that too many southern leaders remained loyal to the former Confederacy and would not enforce the new laws. Thaddeus Stevens

POLITICAL CARTOON
Supporting Radical Republican Ideas

Republicans were outraged to see former Confederates return to power as leaders of the Democratic Party. This 1868 political cartoon shows former Confederates Raphael Semmes and Nathan Bedford Forrest. Semmes was a Confederate admiral who had captured 62 Union merchant ships during the Civil War. Forrest was a cavalry officer known for brutality who later founded the Ku Klux Klan.

How do the actions of the people in these illustrations support the artist's point of view?

How do events in the background of these illustrations support the artist's point of view?

ANALYSIS SKILL **ANALYZING PRIMARY SOURCES**

Why do you think that the men are shown in their Confederate uniforms?

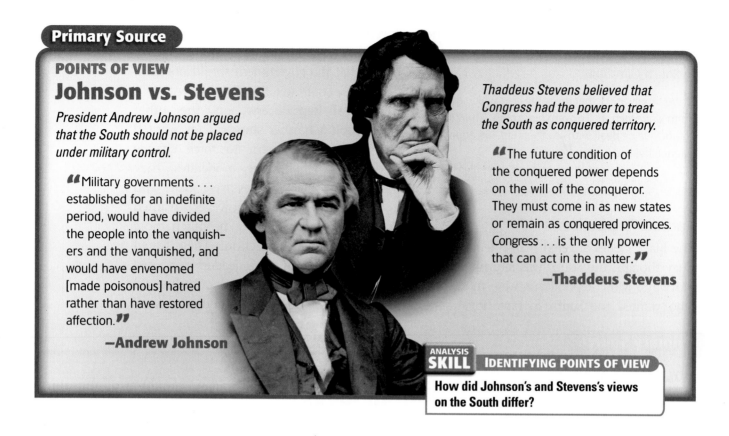

POINTS OF VIEW
Johnson vs. Stevens

President Andrew Johnson argued that the South should not be placed under military control.

"Military governments . . . established for an indefinite period, would have divided the people into the vanquishers and the vanquished, and would have envenomed [made poisonous] hatred rather than have restored affection.**"**

—Andrew Johnson

Thaddeus Stevens believed that Congress had the power to treat the South as conquered territory.

"The future condition of the conquered power depends on the will of the conqueror. They must come in as new states or remain as conquered provinces. Congress . . . is the only power that can act in the matter.**"**

—Thaddeus Stevens

ANALYSIS SKILL | **IDENTIFYING POINTS OF VIEW**

How did Johnson's and Stevens's views on the South differ?

---

of Pennsylvania and Charles Sumner of Massachusetts were the leaders of the Radical Republicans.

A harsh critic of President Johnson, Stevens was known for his honesty and sharp tongue. He wanted economic and political justice for both African Americans and poor white southerners. Sumner had been a strong opponent of slavery before the Civil War. He continued to argue tirelessly for African Americans' civil rights, including the right to vote and the right to fair laws.

Both Stevens and Sumner believed that President Johnson's Reconstruction plan was a failure. Although the Radicals did not control Congress, they began to gain support among moderates when President Johnson ignored criticism of the Black Codes. Stevens believed the federal government could not allow racial inequality to survive.

ACADEMIC VOCABULARY
principle basic belief, rule, or law

READING CHECK Comparing and Contrasting How were Radical Republicans and moderate Republicans similar and different?

Fourteenth Amendment

Urged on by the Radicals in 1866, Congress proposed a new bill. It would give the Freedmen's Bureau more powers. The law would allow the Freedmen's Bureau to use military courts to try people accused of violating African Americans' rights. The bill's supporters hoped that these courts would be fairer than local courts in the South.

Johnson versus Congress

Surprising many members of Congress, Johnson vetoed the Freedmen's Bureau Bill. He insisted that Congress could not pass any new laws until the southern states were represented in Congress. Johnson also argued that the Freedmen's Bureau was unconstitutional.

Republicans responded with the **Civil Rights Act of 1866**. This act provided African Americans with the same legal rights as white Americans. President Johnson once again used his veto power. He argued that the act gave too much power to the federal government. He also rejected the **principle** of equal rights for African Americans. Congress, however, overrode Johnson's veto.

Many Republicans worried about what would happen when the southern states were readmitted. Fearing that the Civil Rights Act might be overturned, the Republicans proposed the **Fourteenth Amendment** in the summer of 1866. The Fourteenth Amendment included the following provisions.

1. It defined all people born or naturalized within the United States, except Native Americans, as citizens.
2. It guaranteed citizens the equal protection of the laws.
3. It said that states could not "deprive any person of life, liberty, or property, without due process of law."
4. It banned many former Confederate officials from holding state or federal offices.
5. It made state laws subject to federal court review.
6. It gave Congress the power to pass any laws needed to enforce it.

1866 Elections

President Johnson and most Democrats opposed the Fourteenth Amendment. As a result, civil rights for African Americans became a key issue in the 1866 congressional elections. To help the Democrats, Johnson traveled around the country defending his Reconstruction plan. Johnson's speaking tour was a disaster. It did little to win votes for the Democratic Party. Johnson even got into arguments with people in the audiences of some of his speaking engagements.

Two major riots in the South also hurt Johnson's campaign. On May 1, 1866, a dispute in Memphis, Tennessee, took place between local police and black Union soldiers. The dispute turned into a three-day wave of violence against African Americans. About three months later, another riot took place during a political demonstration in New Orleans. During that dispute, 34 African Americans and three white Republicans were killed.

READING CHECK **Summarizing** What issue did the Fourteenth Amendment address, and how did it affect the congressional elections of 1866?

Congress Takes Control of Reconstruction

The 1866 elections gave the Republican Party a commanding two-thirds majority in both the House and the Senate. This majority gave the Republicans the power to override any presidential veto. In addition, the Republicans became united as the moderates joined with the Radicals. Together, they called for a new form of Reconstruction.

Reconstruction Acts

In March 1867, Congress passed the first of several **Reconstruction Acts**. These laws divided the South into five districts. A U.S. military commander controlled each district.

Reconstruction Military Districts

■ Military District 1	■ Military District 4	
■ Military District 2	■ Military District 5	
■ Military District 3	**1868** Date former Confederate state was readmitted to Union	

0   150   300 Miles
0 150 300 Kilometers

VA 1870
NC 1868
TN 1866
SC 1868
AR 1868
Disputed
MS 1870
AL 1868
GA 1870
TX 1870
LA 1868
FL 1868
Gulf of Mexico
80°W
30°N
90°W

GEOGRAPHY SKILLS **INTERPRETING MAPS**

1. **Region** Which district consisted of only one state?
2. **Human-Environment Interaction** Do you see any reason why Military District 5 might be more difficult for federal troops to control than the other districts?

The military would remain in control of the South until the southern states rejoined the Union. To be readmitted, a state had to write a new state constitution supporting the Fourteenth Amendment. Finally, the state had to give African American men the right to vote.

Thaddeus Stevens was one of the new Reconstruction Acts' most enthusiastic supporters. He spoke in Congress to defend the acts.

"Have not loyal blacks quite as good a right to choose rulers and make laws as rebel whites? Every man, no matter what his race or color . . .
has an equal right to justice, honesty, and fair play with every other man; and the law should secure him those rights."

–Thaddeus Stevens, quoted in *Sources of the American Republic*, edited by Marvin Meyers et al.

President on Trial

President Johnson strongly disagreed with Stevens. He argued that African Americans did not deserve the same treatment as white people. The Reconstruction Acts, he said, used "powers not granted to the federal government or any one of its branches." Knowing that Johnson did not support its Reconstruction policies, Congress passed a law limiting his power. This law prevented the president from removing cabinet officials without Senate approval. Johnson quickly broke the law by firing Edwin Stanton, the secretary of war.

For the first time in United States history, the House of Representatives responded by voting to impeach the president. **Impeachment** is the process used by a legislative body to bring charges of wrongdoing against a public official. The next step, under Article I of the Constitution, was a trial in the Senate. A two-thirds majority was required to find Johnson guilty and remove him from office.

Although Johnson was unpopular with Republicans, some of them believed he was being judged unfairly. Others did not trust the president pro tempore of the Senate, Benjamin Wade. He would become president if Johnson were removed from office. By a single vote, Senate Republicans failed to convict Johnson. Even so, the trial weakened his power as president.

Election of 1868

Johnson did not run for another term in 1868. The Democrats chose

The Reconstruction Amendments QUICK FACTS

Thirteenth Amendment (1865)
Banned slavery throughout the United States

Fourteenth Amendment (1868)
Overturned the *Dred Scott* case by granting citizenship to all people born in the United States (except for Native Americans)

Fifteenth Amendment (1870)
Gave African American men the right to vote

This Reconstruction-era painting shows African American men voting after passage of the Fifteenth Amendment.

What right did the Fifteenth Amendment protect?

former New York governor Horatio Seymour as their presidential candidate. The Republicans chose Ulysses S. Grant. As a war hero, Grant appealed to many northern voters. He had no political experience but supported the congressional Reconstruction plan. He ran under the slogan "Let Us Have Peace."

Shortly after Grant was nominated, Congress readmitted seven southern states—Alabama, Arkansas, Florida, Georgia, Louisiana, North Carolina, and South Carolina. (Tennessee had already been readmitted in 1866.) Under the terms of readmission, these seven states approved the Fourteenth Amendment. They also agreed to let African American men vote. However, white southerners used violence to try to keep African Americans away from the polls.

Despite such tactics, hundreds of thousands of African Americans voted for Grant and the "party of Lincoln." The *New Orleans Tribune* reported that many former slaves "see clearly enough that the Republican party [is] their political life boat." African American votes helped Grant to win a narrow victory.

READING CHECK Analyzing To what voters did Grant appeal in the presidential election of 1868?

Fifteenth Amendment

After Grant's victory, Congressional Republicans wanted to protect their Reconstruction plan. They worried that the southern states might try to keep black voters from the polls in future elections. Also, some Radical Republicans argued that it was not fair that many northern states still had laws preventing African Americans from voting. After all, every southern state was required to grant suffrage to African American men.

In 1869 Congress proposed the **Fifteenth Amendment**, which gave African American men the right to vote. Abolitionist William Lloyd Garrison praised what he saw as "this wonderful, quiet, sudden transformation of four millions of human beings from . . . the auction block to the ballot-box." The amendment went

into effect in 1870 as one of the last Reconstruction laws passed at the federal level.

The Fifteenth Amendment did not please every reformer, however. Many women were angry because the amendment did not also grant them the right to vote.

READING CHECK Finding Main Ideas How did Radical Republicans take control of Reconstruction?

SUMMARY AND PREVIEW In this section you learned that Congress took control of Reconstruction and took steps to protect the rights of African Americans. In the next section you will learn about increasing opposition to Reconstruction.

---

go.hrw.com
Online Quiz
KEYWORD: SB7 HP17

Section 2 Assessment

Reviewing Ideas, Terms, and People
1. a. **Describe** What were **Black Codes**?
   b. **Make Inferences** Why did Republicans think Johnson's Reconstruction plan was a failure?
2. a. **Recall** What was the **Civil Rights Act of 1866**?
   b. **Summarize** Why was the **Fourteenth Amendment** important?
3. a. **Recall** Why was President Johnson impeached?
   b. **Evaluate** Which element of the **Reconstruction Acts** do you believe was most important? Why?
4. a. **Recall** What does the **Fifteenth Amendment** state?
   b. **Elaborate** Do you think that women should have been included in the Fifteenth Amendment? Explain.

Critical Thinking
5. **Identify** Review your notes on the issues that led Republicans to take over Reconstruction. Then copy the graphic organizer below and use it to identify the main provisions of the Fourteenth Amendment and their effects.

Provisions	Effects

FOCUS ON WRITING

6. **Recognizing Cause-and-Effect Relationships** As you have read in this section, social and political unrest continued long after the war ended. How could this unrest cause people to leave their jobs? What new jobs might they find?

Virginia Standards of Learning USII.1b, USII.1d, USII.1i, USII.2c, USII.3b, USII.4c

What You Will Learn...

Main Ideas

1. Reconstruction governments helped reform the South.
2. The Ku Klux Klan was organized as African Americans moved into positions of power.
3. As Reconstruction ended, the rights of African Americans were restricted.
4. Southern business leaders relied on industry to rebuild the South.

The Big Idea

As Reconstruction ended, African Americans faced new hurdles and the South attempted to rebuild.

Key Terms and People

Hiram Revels, *p. 565*
Ku Klux Klan, *p. 566*
Compromise of 1877, *p. 567*
poll tax, *p. 568*
segregation, *p. 568*
Jim Crow laws, *p. 568*
Plessy v. *Ferguson, p. 569*
sharecropping, *p. 569*

TAKING NOTES As you read, look for information related to the South's efforts to rebuild and the effects on African Americans.

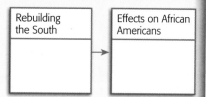

Rebuilding the South	Effects on African Americans

Reconstruction in the South

If YOU were there...

You live on a farm in the South in the 1870s. Times are hard because you do not own your farm. Instead, you and your family work in a landowner's cotton fields. You never seem to earn enough to buy land of your own. Some of your neighbors have decided to give up farming and move to the city. Others are going to work in the textile mills. But you have always been a farmer.

Will you decide to change your way of life?

BUILDING BACKGROUND Reconstruction affected politics and economics in the South. Republican and Democratic politicians fought over policies and programs. New state governments began reforms, but later leaders ended many of them. Some parts of the southern economy improved. However, many farmers, like the family above, went through hard times.

Reconstruction Governments

After Grant became president in 1869, the Republicans seemed stronger than ever. They controlled most southern governments, partly because of the support of African American voters. However, most of the Republican officeholders were unpopular with white southerners.

Carpetbaggers and Scalawags

Some of these office-holders were northern-born Republicans who had moved South after the war. Many white southerners called them carpetbaggers. Supposedly, they had rushed South carrying all their possessions in bags made from carpeting. Many southerners resented these northerners, accusing them—often unfairly—of trying to profit from Reconstruction.

Southern Democrats cared even less for white southern Republicans. They referred to them as scalawags, or greedy rascals. Democrats believed that these southerners had betrayed the South by

African American Representation in the South, 1870

Washington, D.C.

Hiram Revels was the son of former slaves and helped organize African American regiments in the Civil War. Revels was selected to fill the U.S. Senate seat formerly held by Jefferson Davis, president of the Confederacy.

Blanche K. Bruce escaped from slavery and began a school for African Americans before the Civil War. Bruce was the first African American elected to a full six-year term in the U.S. Senate.

● Member of U.S. Congress
○ State legislator

0   150   300 Miles
0   150   300 Kilometers

TN
NC
SC
ATLANTIC OCEAN
30°N
80°W
AL
MS
GA
TX
LA
FL
Gulf of Mexico
95°W   90°W   85°W
25°N

GEOGRAPHY SKILLS | **INTERPRETING MAPS**

1. **Location** Which state had the most African American state legislators?
2. **Region** Which states had the least African American representation?

voting for the Republican Party. Many southern Republicans were small farmers who had supported the Union during the war. Others, like Mississippi governor James Alcorn, were former members of the Whig Party. They preferred to become Republicans rather than join the Democrats.

African American Leaders

African Americans were the largest group of southern Republican voters. During Reconstruction, more than 600 African Americans won election to state legislatures. Some 16 of these politicians were elected to Congress. Other African Americans held local offices in counties throughout the South.

African American politicians came from many backgrounds. **Hiram Revels** was born free in North Carolina and went to college in Illinois. He became a Methodist minister and served as a chaplain in the Union army. In 1870 Revels became the first African American in the U.S. Senate. He took over the seat previously held by Confederate president Jefferson Davis. Unlike Revels, Blanche K. Bruce grew up in slavery in Virginia. Bruce became an important Republican in Mississippi and served one term as a U.S. senator.

State Governments Change Direction

Reconstruction governments provided money for many new programs and organizations in the South. They helped to establish some of the first state-funded public school systems in the South. They also built new hospitals, prisons, and orphanages and passed laws prohibiting discrimination against African Americans.

Southern states under Republican control spent large amounts of money. They aided the construction of railroads, bridges, and public buildings. These improvements were intended to help the southern economy recover from the war. To get the money for these projects, the Reconstruction governments raised taxes and issued bonds.

READING CHECK **Summarizing** What reforms did Reconstruction state governments carry out?

FOCUS ON READING
How does the heading of this section tell you about what you will learn?

Ku Klux Klan

As more African Americans took office, resistance to Reconstruction increased among white southerners. Democrats claimed that the Reconstruction governments were corrupt, illegal, and unjust. They also disliked having federal soldiers stationed in their states. Many white southerners disapproved of African American officeholders. One Democrat noted, "'A white man's government' [is] the most popular rallying cry we have."

In 1866 a group of white southerners in Tennessee created the **Ku Klux Klan**. This secret society opposed civil rights, particularly suffrage, for African Americans. The Klan used violence and terror against African Americans. The group's membership grew rapidly as it spread throughout the South.

Klan members wore robes and disguises to hide their identities. They attacked—and even murdered—African Americans, white Republican voters, and public officials, usually at night.

Local governments did little to stop the violence. Many officials feared the Klan or were sympathetic to its activities. In 1870 and 1871 the federal government took action. Congress passed laws that made it a federal crime to interfere with elections or to deny citizens equal protection under the law.

Within a few years, the Klan was no longer an organized threat. But groups of whites continued to assault African Americans and Republicans throughout the 1870s.

READING CHECK **Drawing Conclusions** Why did southerners join the Ku Klux Klan?

The Ku Klux Klan

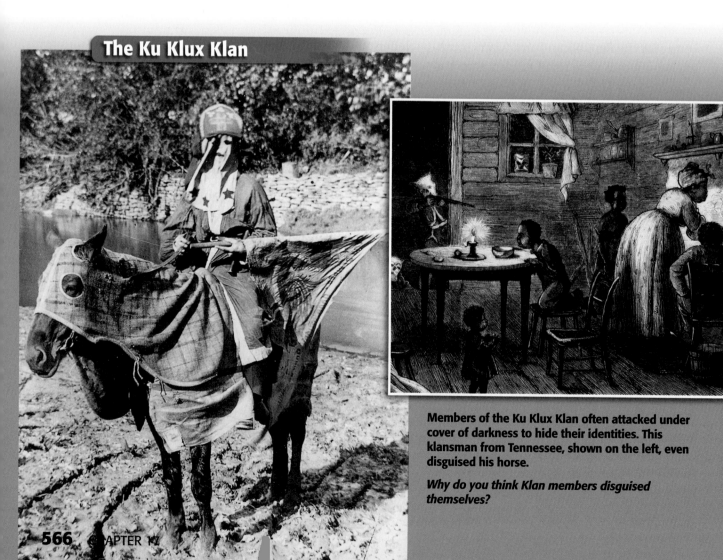

Members of the Ku Klux Klan often attacked under cover of darkness to hide their identities. This klansman from Tennessee, shown on the left, even disguised his horse.

Why do you think Klan members disguised themselves?

Reconstruction Ends

The violence of the Ku Klux Klan was not the only challenge to Reconstruction. Republicans slowly lost control of southern state governments to the Democratic Party. The General Amnesty Act of 1872 allowed former Confederates, except those who had held high ranks, to serve in public office. Many of these former Confederates, most of whom were Democrats, were soon elected to southern governments.

The Republican Party also began losing its power in the North. Although President Grant was re-elected in 1872, financial and political scandals in his administration upset voters. In his first term, a gold-buying scheme in which Grant's cousin took a leading role led to a brief crisis on the stock market called Black Friday. During his second term, his personal secretary was involved in the Whiskey Ring scandal, in which whiskey distillers and public officials worked together to steal liquor taxes from the federal government. Furthermore, people blamed Republican policies for the Panic of 1873.

Panic of 1873

This severe economic downturn began in September 1873 when Jay Cooke and Company, a major investor in railroads and the largest financier of the Union's Civil War effort, declared bankruptcy. The company had lied about the value of land along the side of the Northern Pacific Railroad that it owned and was trying to sell. When the truth leaked out, the company failed.

The failure of such an important business sent panic through the stock market, and investors began selling shares of stock more rapidly than people wanted to buy them. Companies had to buy their shares back from the investors. Soon, 89 of the nation's 364 railroads had failed as well. The failure of almost 18,000 other businesses followed within two years, leaving the nation in an economic crisis. By 1876 unemployment had risen to 14 percent, with an estimated 2 million people out of work. The high unemployment rate set off numerous strikes and protests around the nation, many involving railroad workers. In 1874 the Democrats gained control of the House of Representatives. Northerners were becoming less concerned about southern racism and more concerned about their financial well-being.

Election of 1876

Republicans could tell that northern support for Reconstruction was fading. Voters' attention was shifting to economic problems. In 1874 the Republican Party lost control of the House of Representatives to the Democrats. The Republicans in Congress managed to pass one last civil rights law. The Civil Rights Act of 1875 guaranteed African Americans equal rights in public places, such as theaters and public transportation. But as Americans became increasingly worried about economic problems and government corruption, the Republican Party began to abandon Reconstruction.

Republicans selected Ohio governor Rutherford B. Hayes as their 1876 presidential candidate. He believed in ending federal support of the Reconstruction governments. The Democrats nominated New York governor Samuel J. Tilden. During the election, Democrats in the South again used violence at the polls to keep Republican voters away.

The election between Hayes and Tilden was close. Tilden appeared to have won. Republicans challenged the electoral votes in Oregon and three southern states. A special commission of members of Congress and Supreme Court justices was appointed to settle the issue.

The commission narrowly decided to give all the disputed votes to Hayes. Hayes thus won the presidency by one electoral vote. In the **Compromise of 1877**, the Democrats agreed to accept Hayes's victory. In return, they wanted all remaining federal troops removed from the South. They also asked for funding for internal improvements in the South and

SUPREME COURT DECISIONS

Plessy v. Ferguson (1896)

Background of the Case In 1892, Homer Plessy took a seat in the "whites only" car of a train in Louisiana. He was arrested, put on trial, and convicted of violating Louisiana's segregation law. Plessy argued that the Louisiana law violated the Thirteenth Amendment and denied him the equal protection of the law as guaranteed.

The Court's Ruling

The Court ruled that the Louisiana "separate-but-equal" law was constitutional.

The Court's Reasoning

The Court stated that the Thirteenth and Fourteenth Amendments did not apply. The Court decided that the case had nothing to do with the abolition of slavery mentioned in the Thirteenth Amendment. The justices also ruled that the Fourteenth Amendment was not designed to eliminate social barriers to equality between the races, only political barriers.

Justice John Marshall Harlan disagreed with the Court's ruling. In a dissenting opinion, he wrote that "in respect of civil rights, all citizens are equal before the law."

Why It Matters

Plessy was important because it approved the idea of separate-but-equal facilities for people based on race. The doctrine of separate-but-equal led to segregation in trains, buses, schools, restaurants, and many other social institutions.

The separate-but-equal doctrine led to unequal treatment of minority groups for decades. It was finally struck down by another Supreme Court ruling, *Brown v. Board of Education,* in 1954.

ANALYSIS SKILL **ANALYZING INFORMATION**

1. Why did the Court reject Plessy's arguments?
2. Why was *Plessy* v. *Ferguson* an important Supreme Court case?

---

the appointment of a southern Democrat to the president's cabinet. Shortly after he took office in 1877, President Hayes removed the last of the federal troops from the South.

Redeemers

Gradually, Democrats regained control of state governments in the South. In each state, they moved quickly to get rid of the Reconstruction reforms.

Democrats who brought their party back to power in the South were called Redeemers. They came from a variety of backgrounds. For instance, U.S. senator John T. Morgan of Alabama was a former general in the Confederate army. Newspaper editor Henry Grady of Georgia was interested in promoting southern industry.

Redeemers wanted to reduce the size of state government and limit the rights of African Americans. They lowered state budgets and got rid of a variety of social programs. The Redeemers cut property taxes and cut public funding for schools. They also succeeded in limiting African Americans' civil rights.

African Americans' Rights Restricted

Redeemers set up the poll tax in an effort to deny the vote to African Americans. The **poll tax** was a special tax people had to pay before they could vote.

Some states also targeted African American voters by requiring them to pass a literacy test. A so-called grandfather clause written into law affected men whose fathers or grandfathers could vote before 1867. In those cases, a voter did not have to pay a poll tax or pass a literacy test. As a result, almost every white man could escape the voting restrictions.

Redeemer governments also introduced legal **segregation**, the forced separation of whites and African Americans in public places. **Jim Crow laws**—laws that enforced segregation—became common in southern states in the 1880s.

African Americans challenged Jim Crow laws in court. In 1883, however, the U.S. Supreme Court ruled that the Civil Rights Act of 1875 was unconstitutional. The Court also ruled that the Fourteenth Amendment applied only to the actions of state governments. This ruling allowed private individuals and businesses to practice segregation.

Plessy v. Ferguson

In 1896 the U.S. Supreme Court returned to the issue of segregation. When Homer Plessy, an African American, refused to leave the whites-only Louisiana train car he was riding on, he was arrested and accused of breaking a state law requiring separate cars for blacks and whites. Plessy sued the railroad company and lost. His lawyers argued that the law violated his right to equal treatment under the Fourteenth Amendment. He then appealed to the U.S. Supreme Court. The Supreme Court ruled against Plessy in **Plessy v. Ferguson**. Segregation was allowed, said the Court, if "separate-but-equal" facilities were provided. Among the justices, only John Marshall Harlan disagreed with the Court's decision. He explained his disagreement in a dissenting opinion:

" In the eye of the law, there is in the country no superior, dominant [controlling], ruling class of citizens … Our constitution is color-blind, and neither knows nor tolerates classes among citizens. In respect of civil rights, all citizens are equal before the law. "

—John Marshall Harlan, quoted in *Plessy v. Ferguson: A Brief History with Documents,* edited by Brook Thomas

Despite Harlan's view, segregation became widespread across the country. African Americans were forced to use separate public schools, libraries, and parks. When they existed, these facilities were usually of poorer quality than those created for whites. In practice, these so-called separate-but-equal facilities were separate and unequal.

Farming in the South

Few African Americans in the South could afford to buy or even rent farms. Moving West also was costly. Many African Americans therefore remained on plantations. Others tried to make a living in the cities.

African Americans who stayed on plantations often became part of a system known as **sharecropping**, or sharing the crop. Landowners provided the land, tools, and supplies, and sharecroppers provided the labor. At harvest time, the sharecropper usually had to give most of the crop to the landowner. Whatever remained belonged to the sharecropper. Many sharecroppers hoped to save enough money from selling their share of the crops to one day be able to buy a farm. Unfortunately, only a few ever achieved this dream.

Instead, most sharecroppers lived in a cycle of debt. When they needed food, clothing, or supplies, most families had to buy goods on credit because they had little cash.

Hopes Raised and Denied

Slavery
- No rights
- Forced labor
- No freedom of movement without permission
- Family members sold away from one another
- No representation in government

Freedom
- Slavery banned
- Free to work for wages
- Could move and live anywhere
- Many families reunited
- Could serve in political office

Rights Denied
- Sharecropping system put in place
- Ability to vote and hold office restricted
- White leadership regained control of southern state governments

When sharecroppers sold their crops, they hoped to be able to pay off these debts. However, bad weather, poor harvests, or low crop prices often made this dream impossible.

Sharecroppers usually grew cotton, one of the South's most important cash crops. When too many farmers planted cotton, however, the supply became excessive. As a result, the price per bale of cotton dropped. Many farmers understood the drawbacks of planting cotton. However, farmers felt pressure from banks and others to keep raising cotton. A southern farmer explained why so many sharecroppers depended on cotton:

"Cotton is the thing to get credit on in this country ... You can always sell cotton ... [Y]ou load up your wagon with wheat or corn ...and I doubt some days whether you could sell it."

–Anonymous farmer quoted in *The Promise of the New South*, by Edward L. Ayers

READING CHECK **Finding Main Ideas** How were African Americans' rights restricted?

Rebuilding Southern Industry

The southern economy suffered through cycles of good and bad years as cotton prices went up and down. Some business leaders hoped industry would strengthen the southern economy and create a New South.

Southern Industry

Henry Grady, an Atlanta newspaper editor, was a leader of the New South movement. "The new South presents ... a diversified [varied] industry that meets the complex needs of this complex age," he wrote. Grady and his supporters felt that with its cheap and abundant labor, the South could build factories and provide a workforce for them.

The most successful industrial development in the South involved textile production. Businesspeople built textile mills in many small towns to produce cotton fabric. Many people from rural areas came to work in the mills, but African Americans were not allowed to work in most of them.

"The New South...is stirred with the breath of a new life."

—Henry Grady

Atlanta rebuilt quickly after the war, becoming a leading railroad and industrial center. Newspaper editor Henry Grady gave stirring speeches about the need for industry in the South. He became one of the best-known spokesmen of the "New South."

Why might Grady point to Atlanta as a model for economic change?

Southern Mill Life

Work in the cotton mills appealed to farm families who had trouble making ends meet. As one mill worker explained, "It was a necessity to move and get a job, rather than depend on the farm." Recruiters sent out by the mills promised good wages and steady work.

Entire families often worked in the same cotton mill. Mills employed large numbers of women and children. Many children started working at about the age of 12. Some children started working at an even earlier age. Women did most of the spinning and were valued workers. However, few women had the opportunity to advance within the company.

Many mill workers were proud of the skills they used, but they did not enjoy their work. One unhappy worker described it as "the same thing over and over again . . . The more you do, the more they want done." Workers often labored 12 hours a day, six days a week. Cotton dust and lint filled the air, causing asthma and an illness known as brown-lung disease. Fast-moving machinery caused

injuries and even deaths. Despite the long hours and dangerous working conditions, wages remained low. However, mill work did offer an alternative to farming.

READING CHECK Finding Main Ideas What did southern business leaders hope industry would do?

SUMMARY AND PREVIEW In this section you learned about the end of Reconstruction. In the next chapter you will learn about America's continued westward expansion.

go.hrw.com
Online Quiz
KEYWORD: SB7 HP17

Section 3 Assessment

Reviewing Ideas, Terms, and People

1. a. **Identify** Who were some prominent African American leaders during Reconstruction?
   b. **Evaluate** What do you think was the most important change made by Reconstruction state governments? Explain your answer.
2. a. **Recall** For what reasons did some local governments not stop the **Ku Klux Klan**?
   b. **Draw Conclusions** How did the Ku Klux Klan's use of terror interfere with elections in the South?
3. a. **Recall** How did Reconstruction come to an end?
   b. **Explain** What was the relationship between **Jim Crow laws** and **segregation**?
4. a. **Identify** Who was Henry Grady, and why was he important?
   b. **Predict** What are some possible results of the rise of the "New South"?

Critical Thinking

5. **Identifying Causes and Effects** Review your notes on Reconstruction governments. Then copy the graphic organizer below and use it to show why Reconstruction ended, as well as the results of its end.

| Causes | → | Effect/Cause
End of
Reconstruction | → | Effects |

WRITING JOURNAL

6. **Relating Historical Change to Individual Choice** Despite the difficulties of Reconstruction, the Freedmen's Bureau and plans to bring industry to the "New South" did create new jobs. What might have led people to leave their jobs for new ones?

Social Studies Skills

Chance, Oversight, and Error in History

Understand the Skill

Sometimes, history can seem very routine. One event leads to others which, in turn, lead to still others. You learn to look for cause-and-effect relationships among events. You learn how point of view and bias can influence decisions and actions. These approaches to the study of history imply that the events of the past are orderly and predictable.

In fact, many of the events of the past *are* orderly and predictable! They may seem even more so since they're over and done with, and we know how things turned out. Yet, predictable patterns of behavior *do* exist throughout history. Recognizing them is one of the great values and rewards of studying the past. As the philosopher George Santayana once famously said, "Those who cannot remember the past are condemned to repeat it."

At its most basic level, however, history is people, and people are "human." They make mistakes. Unexpected things happen to them, both good things and bad. This is the unpredictable element of history. The current phrase "stuff happens" is just as true of the past as it is today. Mistakes, oversights, and just plain "dumb luck" have shaped the course of history—and have helped to make the study of it so exciting.

Learn the Skill

California merchant John Sutter decided to build a sawmill along a nearby American river in 1848. He planned to sell the lumber it produced to settlers who were moving into the area. Sutter put James W. Marshall to work building the mill. To install the large water wheel that would power the saw, Marshall first had to deepen the river bed next to the mill. During his digging, he noticed some shiny bits of yellow metal in the water. The result of this accidental find was the California gold rush, which sent thousands of Americans to California, and speeded settlement of the West.

In 1863 the army of Confederate General Robert E. Lee invaded Maryland. The Civil War had been going well for the South. Lee hoped a southern victory on Union soil would convince the British to aid the South in the war. However, a Confederate officer forgot his cigars as his unit left its camp in the Maryland countryside. Wrapped around the cigars was a copy of Lee's battle plans. When a Union soldier came upon the abandoned camp, he spotted the cigars. This chance discovery enabled the Union army to defeat Lee at the Battle of Antietam. The Union victory helped keep the British out of the war. More importantly, it allowed President Lincoln to issue the Emancipation Proclamation and begin the process of ending slavery in the United States.

Practice the Skill

In April 1865 President Lincoln was assassinated while attending the theater in Washington, D.C. Bodyguard John Parker was stationed outside the door of the president's box. However, Parker left his post to find a seat from which he could watch the play. This allowed the killer to enter the box and shoot the unprotected president.

Write an essay about how this chance event altered the course of history. How might Reconstruction, North–South relations, and African Americans' struggle for equality have been different had Lincoln lived?

Chapter Review

HOLT

History's Impact
▶ **video series**
Review the video to answer the closing question:
Name three ways the Thirteenth, Fourteenth, and Fifteenth Amendments are related.

Visual Summary

QUICK FACTS

Use the visual summary below to help you review the main ideas of the chapter.

Reform During Reconstruction, the Freedmen's Bureau opened schools for former slaves and performed other services to help the poorest southerners.

Dispute Differing ideas about how to govern the South led to conflicts between African Americans and white southerners, as well as between Republicans and Democrats.

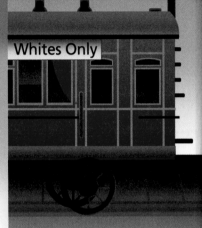

Whites Only

Division After the Compromise of 1877 ended Reconstruction, segregation laws were enacted by southern governments and upheld by the U.S. Supreme Court.

Reviewing Vocabulary, Terms, and People

Complete each sentence by filling in the blank with the correct term or person from the chapter.

1. _____ were laws that allowed racial segregation in public places.

2. The Radical Republicans were led by _____, a member of Congress from Pennsylvania.

3. The period from 1865 to 1877 that focused on reuniting the nation is known as _____.

4. Following the Civil War, many African Americans in the South made a living by participating in the _____ system.

5. After opposing Congress, Andrew Johnson became the first president to face _____ proceedings.

6. The _____ Amendment made slavery in the United States illegal.

7. In 1870 _____ became the first African American to serve in the U.S. Senate.

Comprehension and Critical Thinking

SECTION 1 *(Pages 552–557)*

8. **a. Describe** How did the lives of African Americans change after the Civil War?

 b. Compare and Contrast How was President Johnson's Reconstruction plan similar and different from President Lincoln's Ten Percent Plan?

 c. Evaluate Which of the three Reconstruction plans that were originally proposed do you think would have been the most successful? Why?

SECTION 2 *(Pages 558–563)*

9. **a. Identify** Who were the Radical Republicans, and how did they change Reconstruction?

 b. Analyze How did the debate over the Fourteenth Amendment affect the election of 1866?

 c. Elaborate Do you think Congress was right to impeach President Andrew Johnson? Explain.

SECTION 3 *(Pages 564–571)*

10. **a. Describe** What reforms did Reconstruction governments in the South support?

  b. Draw Conclusions In what ways did southern governments attempt to reverse the accomplishments of Reconstruction?

  c. Evaluate Do you think the South was successful or unsuccessful in its rebuilding efforts? Explain your answer.

Reviewing Themes

11. **Politics** Explain the political struggles that took place during Reconstruction.

12. **Society and Culture** How were the lives of ordinary southerners affected in the years after Reconstruction?

Using the Internet

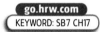
go.hrw.com
KEYWORD: SB7 CH17

13. **Activity: Drawing Conclusions** A challenge for anyone trying to understand Reconstruction is drawing conclusions from primary and secondary sources from the time period. This activity will help you see how complex this can be. Enter the activity keyword, and then rate the credibility of the sources provided. Make sure you explain whether the source is a primary or secondary source, whether or not you think the source is credible, and the reasons for your thoughts.

Reading Skills

Analyzing Historical Information *Use the Reading Skills taught in this chapter to answer the question about the reading selection below.*

Radical Republicans, on the other hand, took a harsher stance. They wanted the Federal government to force change in the South. Like the moderates, they thought the Black Codes were cruel and unjust. *(p. 559)*

14. Which of the following is relevant information for the passage above?

  a. Thaddeus Stevens was a Radical Republican.

  b. Andrew Johnson was a Democrat.

  c. Radical Republicans wanted the federal government to make major changes in the South.

  d. Radical Republicans were eventually removed from power.

Social Studies Skills

Chance, Oversight, and Error in History *Use the Social Studies Skills taught in this chapter to answer the question about the reading selection below.*

Johnson's speaking tour was a disaster. It did little to win votes for the Democratic Party. Johnson even got into arguments with people in the audiences of some of his speaking engagements. *(p. 561)*

15. Which of the following is an example of chance, oversight, or error that affected history?

  a. Johnson got into arguments with audiences.

  b. The tour was a disaster.

  c. The tour did not win votes.

  d. Johnson spoke for the Democratic Party.

FOCUS ON WRITING

16. **Writing a Job History** Review your notes about the changing job scene during Reconstruction. Put yourself in the shoes of a person living then. It could be anyone—a returning soldier, a shopkeeper, a schoolteacher, or a politician. What jobs would that person seek? Why would he or she leave one job for another?

  Write a brief job history for that person during Reconstruction. Include at least four jobs. Make each job description two to four sentences long. End each one with a sentence or two about why the person left that job. Add one sentence explaining why he or she took the next job. Be sure to include specific historical details.

DIRECTIONS: Read each question and write the letter of the best response.

1 Use the map below to answer the following question.

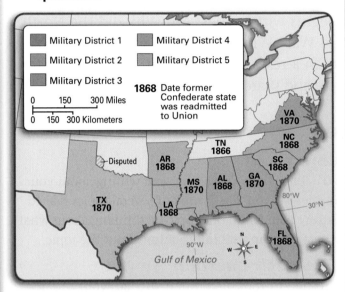

Which military district contained the largest number of states?

A Military District 2

B Military District 3

C Military District 4

D Military District 5

2 What can you infer from the map information?

A South Carolina was difficult to reconstruct.

B The largest number of troops was in Military District 1.

C Military District 5 was the last district to end Reconstruction.

D Tennessee was readmitted to the Union before the other southern states.

3 The quickest approach to reuniting the nation was proposed by the

A Ten Percent Plan.

B Wade-Davis Bill.

C Civil Rights Act of 1866.

D Compromise of 1877.

4 What development convinced Republicans in Congress to take control of Reconstruction from the president?

A President Abraham Lincoln was assassinated by a southern sympathizer.

B President Andrew Johnson vetoed the Wade-Davis bill.

C Southern states began passing Black Codes to restrict African Americans' freedoms.

D White southern women refused to support the Fifteenth Amendment.

5 Which of the following limited opportunities for African Americans in the South after Reconstruction ended?

A Ten Percent plan

B Radical Republicans

C Jim Crow laws

D carpetbaggers

6 Examine the following passage from a northern schoolteacher's letter home and then use it to answer the question.

"Wishing to work where there was the most need—there are so many places where nothing has been done for the freedmen, and where they are sorely persecuted—we came here. A schoolhouse built by the soldiers had just been destroyed by the citizens. The feeling is intensely bitter against anything northern. The affairs of the [Freedmen's] Bureau have been very much mismanaged in Columbus, and our government has been disgraced by the troops who were stationed here."

—Sarah Chase, from *Dear Ones at Home*

Document-Based Question What were some of the problems facing the Freedmen's Bureau in the South?

Assignment

Collect information and write an informative report on a topic related to the Civil War.

TIP **Narrowing the Task** The key to a successful research report is picking a topic that is broad enough that you can find information, but narrow enough that you can cover it in detail. To narrow a subject, focus on one aspect of the larger subject. Then think about whether that one aspect can be broken down into smaller parts. Here's an example of how to narrow a topic:

Too Broad: Civil War Leaders
Less Broad: Civil War Generals
Narrower: Robert E. Lee's Role in the Civil War

A Social Studies Report

All research begins with a question. Why did the North win the Civil War? Why did Abraham Lincoln choose Ulysses S. Grant? In a research report, you find answers to questions like these and share what you learn with your reader.

1. Prewrite

Choosing a Subject

Since you will spend a lot of time researching and writing about your topic, pick one that interests you. First, think of several topics related to the Civil War. Narrow your list to one topic by thinking about what interests you and where you can find information about the topic.

Developing a Research Question

A guiding question related to your topic will help focus your research. For example, here is a research question for the topic "Robert E. Lee's Role in the Civil War": *How did Lee's decision to turn down the leadership of the Union army affect the Civil War?* The answer to this question becomes the thesis, or the big idea of your report.

Finding Historical Information

Use at least three sources of historical information besides your textbook. Good sources include

- books, maps, magazines, newspapers
- television programs, movies, Internet sites, CD-ROMs.

For each source, write down the kinds of information shown below. When taking notes, put a circled number next to each source.

Encyclopedia article
① "Title of Article." Name of Encyclopedia. Edition or year published.
Book
② Author. Title. City of Publication: Publisher, year published.
Magazine or newspaper article
③ Author. "Title of Article." Publication name. Date: page number(s).
Internet site
④ Author (if known). "Document title." Web site. Date of electronic publication. Date information was accessed <url>.

Taking Notes

As you read the source material, take thorough notes on facts, statistics, comparisons, and quotations. Take special care to spell names correctly and to record dates and facts accurately. If you use a direct quotation from a source, copy it word for word and enclose it in quotation marks. Along with each note, include the number of its source and its page number.

Organizing Your Ideas and Information

Informative research reports are usually organized in one of these ways:

- Chronological order (the order in which events occurred)
- Order of importance
- Causes (actions or situations that make something else happen) and effects (what happened as a result of something else).

Use one of these orders to organize your notes in an outline. Here is a partial outline for a paper on Robert E. Lee.

The Thesis/Big Idea: Robert E. Lee's decision to decline the leadership of the Union army had serious consequences for the path of the Civil War.

I. Lee's Military Expertise
   A. Achievements at the U.S. Military Academy
   B. Achievements during the Mexican War
II. Lee's Personality and Character
   A. Intelligence and strength
   B. Honesty and fairness
   C. Daring and courage
III. Lee's Military Victories
   A. Battle of Fredericksburg
   B. Battle of Chancellorsville

TIP **Seeing Different Viewpoints** Consult a variety of sources, including those with different points of view on the topic. Reading sources with different opinions will give you a more complete picture of your subject. For example, reading articles about Robert E. Lee written by a southern writer as well as a northern writer may give you a more balanced view of Lee.

TIP **Recording Others' Ideas** You will be taking three types of notes. **Paraphrases** Restatements of all the ideas in your own words. **Summaries** Brief restatements of only the most important parts. **Direct quotations** The writer's exact words inside quotation marks.

2. Write

You can use this framework to help you write your first draft.

A Writer's Framework

Introduction
- Start with a quote or an interesting historical detail to grab your reader's attention.
- State the main idea of your report.
- Provide any historical background readers need to understand your main idea.

Body
- Present your information under at least three main ideas, using logical order.
- Write at least one paragraph for each of these main ideas.
- Add supporting details, facts, or examples to each paragraph.

Conclusion
- Restate your main idea, using slightly different words.
- Include a general comment about your topic.
- You might comment on how the historical information in your report relates to later historical events.

Studying a Model

Here is a model of a research report. Study it to see how one student developed a paper. The first and the concluding paragraphs are shown in full. The paragraphs in the body of the paper are summarized.

INTRODUCTORY PARAGRAPH

Attention grabber

Statement of thesis

"I cannot raise my hand against my birthplace, my home, my children." With these words, Robert E. Lee changed the course of the Civil War. Abraham Lincoln had turned to Lee as his first choice for commander of the Union army. However, Lee turned Lincoln down, choosing instead to side with his home state of Virginia and take command of the Confederate army. Lee's decision to turn Lincoln down weakened the North and strengthened the Confederates, turning what might have been an easy victory for the North into a long, costly war.

BODY PARAGRAPHS

In the first part of the body, the student points out that Lee graduated from the U.S. Military Academy at West Point, served in the Mexican War, and was a member of the Union army. She goes on to explain that he would have been a strong leader for the North, and his absence made the North weaker.

In the middle of the report, the writer discusses Lee's personality and character. She includes information about the strength of character he showed while in the military academy and while leading the Confederate army. She discusses and gives examples of his intelligence, his daring, his courage, and his honesty.

In the last part of the body of the report, the student provides examples of Lee leading the outnumbered Confederate army to a series of victories. The student provides details of the battles of Fredericksburg and Chancellorsville and explains how a lesser general than Lee may have lost both battles.

CONCLUDING PARAGRAPH

Summary of main points

Restatement of big idea

Lee's brilliant and resourceful leadership bedeviled a series of Union generals. He won battles that most generals would have lost. If Lee had used these skills to lead the larger and more powerful Union army, the Civil War might have ended in months instead of years.

3. Evaluate and Revise

Evaluating and Revising Your Draft

Evaluate your first draft by carefully reading it twice. Ask the questions below to decide which parts of your first draft should be revised.

Evaluation Questions for an Informative Report

- Does the introduction attract the readers' interest and state the big idea/thesis of your report?
- Does the body of your report have at least three paragraphs that develop your big idea? Is the main idea in each paragraph clearly stated?
- Have you included enough information to support each of your main ideas? Are all facts, details, and examples accurate? Are all of them clearly related to the main ideas they support?
- Is the report clearly organized? Does it use chronological order, order of importance, or cause and effect?
- Does the conclusion restate the big idea of your report? Does it end with a general comment about the importance or significance of your topic?
- Have you included at least three sources in your bibliography? Have you included all the sources you used and not any you did not use?

TIP **Organizing Your Time** By creating a schedule and following it, you can avoid that panicky moment when the due date is near and you haven't even started your research. To create your schedule and manage your time, include these six steps.

1 Develop a question and research your topic (10% of your total time).
2 Research and take notes (25%).
3 Write your main idea statement and create an outline (15%).
4 Write a first draft (25%).
5 Evaluate and revise your first draft (15%).
6 Proofread and publish your report (10%).

4. Proofread and Publish

Proofreading

To improve your report before sharing it, check the following:
- The spelling and capitalization of all proper names for people, places, things, and events.
- Punctuation marks around any direct quotation.
- Your list of sources (Works Cited or Bibliography) against a guide to writing research papers. Make sure you follow the examples in the guide when punctuating and capitalizing your source listings.

Publishing

Choose one or more of these ideas to publish your report.
- Share your report with your classmates by turning it into an informative speech.
- Submit your report to an online discussion group that focuses on the Civil War and ask for feedback.
- With your classmates, create a magazine that includes reports on several different topics or post the reports on your school Web site.

5. Practice and Apply

Use the steps and strategies outlined in this workshop to research and write an informative report on the Civil War.

A Growing America

After the American Civil War, the United States began a process of building a new economy and political structure. Events in the rest of the world began affecting the nation more noticeably.

During this period of expansion, the U.S. population spread across the continent. New immigrants and new technology began to change life in many parts of the country, especially in cities. In the next three chapters, you will learn about changes in the United States that helped the country increase its size, wealth, and power.

Explore the Art

In this picture, a teenage Buffalo Bill Cody flees from bandits on his Pony Express route. How does this picture show the importance of communication in the expansion of the United States?

581

Americans Move West

Virginia Standards of Learning

USII.1 The student will demonstrate skills for historical and geographical analysis, and responsible citizenship, including the ability to

a) analyze and interpret primary and secondary source documents to increase understanding of events and life in United States history from 1865 to the present; **b)** make connections between past and present; **c)** sequence events in United States history from 1865 to the present

USII.2 The student will use maps, globes, photographs, pictures, or tables for

a) explaining how physical features and climate influenced the movement of people westward; **b)** explaining relationships among natural resources, transportation, and industrial development after 1865; **c)** locating the 50 states and the cities most significant to the historical development of the United States

USII.4 The student will demonstrate knowledge of how life changed after the Civil War by

a) identifying the reasons for westward expansion, including its impact on American Indians; **d)** explaining the impact of new inventions, the rise of big business, the growth of industry, and life on American farms

FOCUS ON WRITING

Writing a Letter Before telephones and e-mail, one way to communicate with people far away was by letter. In this chapter, you will read about the settlement of the West by European Americans. Suppose you were an Irish immigrant working on a railroad that crossed the Great Plains. What might you have seen or experienced? After you read the chapter, you will write a letter to your sister in Ireland telling her about your experiences.

UNITED STATES

1850

1860 The Pony Express begins delivering mail between East and West.

1860

1855 Paris holds a World's Fair.

WORLD

HOLT

History's Impact

▶ video series

Watch the video to understand the impact of the West on American culture.

What You Will Learn...

In this chapter you will learn about how the great American West changed in the late 1800s. Settlers poured into the region and built mines, ranches, farms, and railroads. In this photo, modern pioneers re-create a wagon journey from the 1800s.

1869 The first transcontinental railroad is completed.

1874 Gold is discovered in the Black Hills of the Dakotas.

1879 Thousands of African Americans migrate from the South to Kansas.

1890 The Massacre at Wounded Knee occurs.

1870

1880

1890

1864 French scientist Louis Pasteur invents the purification process of pasteurization.

1883 The Orient Express railway makes its first run from Paris to Istanbul.

1888 Brazil abolishes slavery.

Reading Social Studies

by Kylene Beers

Economics · Geography · Politics · Society and Culture · Science and Technology

Focus on Themes In this chapter you will follow the development of the United States from the mid-1800s through the 1890s. You will learn that California was admitted to the Union in 1850. You will find out about the struggles that people faced as the movement West continued and people settled the Great Plains. You will learn about the **technological** advancements made during this time as well as the difficult **geographical** obstacles miners and ranchers faced in the West.

Understanding through Questioning

Focus on Reading When newspaper reporters want to get to the heart of a story, they ask certain questions: who, what, when, where, why, and how. When you are reading a history book, you can use the same questions to get to the heart of what happened in the past.

Hypothetical Questions You can also use questions to dig deeper than what is in the text. You can ask hypothetical, or what if, questions. These questions ask what might have happened had events occurred differently. Sometimes asking such questions can help history come alive.

Who? Congress

Where? the West

How? Congress gave land to anyone who agreed to settle on it for five years.

In 1862 Congress passed two important land acts that helped open the West to settlers. The Homestead Act gave government-owned land to small farmers. Any adult who was a U.S. citizen or planned to become one could receive 160 acres of land. In exchange, homesteaders promised to live on the land for five years. The Morrill Act granted more than 17 million acres of federal land to the states. *(p. 600)*

What? encouraged new settlement

When? 1862

Why? Perhaps Congress feared what would happen to western lands if they remained unsettled by U.S. citizens.

What if? If Congress had not passed these laws, U.S. citizens might not have moved West. The United States might not have grown as quickly as it did.

You Try It!

Read the following passage and then answer the questions below.

Building Communities

Women were an important force in the settlement of the frontier. They joined in the hard work of farming and ranching and helped build communities out of the widely spaced farms and small towns. Their role in founding communities facilitated a strong voice in public affairs. Wyoming women, for example, were granted the vote in the new state's constitution, which was approved in 1869. Annie Bidwell, one of the founders of Chico, California, used her influence to support a variety of moral and social causes such as women's suffrage and temperance.

From Chapter 18, p. 602

Answer these questions based on the passage you just read.

1. Who is this passage about?

2. What did they do?

3. When did they do this?

4. How do you think they accomplished it?

5. Why do you think they were able to accomplish so much?

6. How can knowing this information help you understand the past?

7. What if women in the West had been given more rights? Fewer rights? How might the West have been different?

As you read Chapter 18, ask questions like *who, what, when, where, why, how,* and *what if* to help you analyze what you are reading.

Key Terms and People

Chapter 18

Section 1
frontier *(p. 586)*
Comstock Lode *(p. 587)*
boomtowns *(p. 588)*
Cattle Kingdom *(p. 589)*
cattle drive *(p. 589)*
Chisholm Trail *(p. 589)*
Pony Express *(p. 590)*
transcontinental railroad *(p. 590)*

Section 2
Treaty of Fort Laramie *(p. 594)*
reservations *(p. 595)*
Crazy Horse *(p. 595)*
Treaty of Medicine Lodge *(p. 595)*
buffalo soldiers *(p. 596)*
George Armstrong Custer *(p. 596)*
Sitting Bull *(p. 596)*
Battle of the Little Bighorn *(p. 596)*
Massacre at Wounded Knee *(p. 597)*
Long Walk *(p. 597)*
Geronimo *(p. 597)*
Ghost Dance *(p. 598)*
Sarah Winnemucca *(p. 598)*
Dawes General Allotment Act *(p. 598)*

Section 3
Homestead Act *(p. 600)*
Morrill Act *(p. 600)*
Exodusters *(p. 601)*
sodbusters *(p. 601)*
dry farming *(p. 601)*
Annie Bidwell *(p. 602)*
National Grange *(p. 603)*
deflation *(p. 604)*
William Jennings Bryan *(p. 604)*
Populist Party *(p. 604)*

Academic Vocabulary

In this chapter, you will learn the following academic words:

establish *(p. 588)*
facilitate *(p. 602)*

Miners, Ranchers, and Railroads

Virginia Standards of Learning USII.1b, USII.1f, USII.2a, USII.2b, USII.2c, USII.4a, USII.4d

What You Will Learn...

Main Ideas

1. A mining boom brought growth to the West.
2. The demand for cattle created a short-lived Cattle Kingdom on the Great Plains.
3. East and West were connected by the transcontinental railroad.

The Big Idea

As more settlers moved West, mining, ranching, and railroads soon transformed the western landscape.

Key Terms

frontier, *p. 586*
Comstock Lode, *p. 587*
boomtowns, *p. 588*
Cattle Kingdom, *p. 589*
cattle drive, *p. 589*
Chisholm Trail, *p. 589*
Pony Express, *p. 590*
transcontinental railroad, *p. 590*

TAKING NOTES As you read the following section, take notes on the kinds of economic opportunities that people found in the West. Organize your notes in a table like the one below.

Opportunities in the West

If YOU were there...

You are a cowboy in Texas in 1875. You love life on the open range, the quiet nights, and the freedom. You even like the hard work of the long cattle drives to Kansas. But you know that times are changing. Homesteaders are moving in and fencing off their lands. Some of the older cowboys say it's time to settle down and buy a small ranch. You hope that they're not right.

What would make you give up a cowboy's life?

BUILDING BACKGROUND In the years following the Civil War, the U.S. population grew rapidly. Settlements in the West increased. More discoveries of gold and silver attracted adventurers, while the open range drew others. Thousands of former Civil War soldiers also joined the move West.

Mining Boom Brings Growth

During the years surrounding the War, most Americans had thought of the Great Plains and other western lands as the Great American Desert. In the years following the Civil War, Americans witnessed the rapid growth of the U.S. population and the spread of settlements throughout the West. With the admission of the state of California to the Union in 1850, the western boundary of the American **frontier**—an undeveloped area—had reached the Pacific Ocean.

The frontier changed dramatically as more and more people moved westward. Settlers built homes, fenced off land, and laid out ranches and farms. Miners, ranchers, and farmers remade the landscape of the West as they adapted to their new surroundings. The geography of the West was further changed by the development and expansion of a large and successful railroad industry that moved the West's natural resources to eastern markets. Gold and silver were the most valuable natural resources, and mining companies used the growing railroad network to bring these precious metals to the East.

Causes and Effects of Westward Expansion

Causes
- New land for settlers and ranchers
- Mineral resources
- Businesses to support settlers, ranchers, and miners
- Immigration

Effects
- New towns
- Railroads across the continent
- Cattle Kingdom

ANALYSIS SKILL | INTERPRETING CHARTS

What three economic activities attracted people to the West?

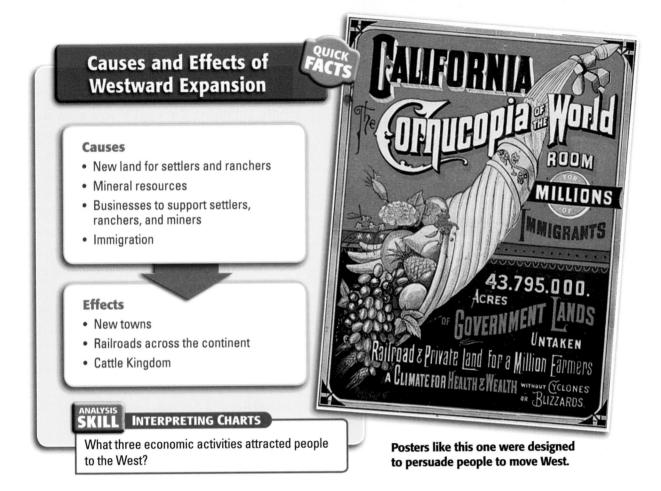

CALIFORNIA The **Cornucopia** OF THE **World**
ROOM FOR MILLIONS OF IMMIGRANTS
43,795,000. ACRES OF GOVERNMENT LANDS UNTAKEN
Railroad & Private Land for a Million Farmers
A CLIMATE FOR HEALTH & WEALTH WITHOUT CYCLONES OR BLIZZARDS.

Posters like this one were designed to persuade people to move West.

Big Business

Most of the precious metals were located in western Nevada. In 1859 miner Henry Comstock discovered a huge deposit of gold and silver in Nevada that became called the **Comstock Lode**. The deposit was incredibly rich and deep. In just the first year after its discovery, the Comstock Lode lured thousands of California miners to Nevada. Over the next 20 years, the Comstock Lode produced more than $500 million worth of gold and silver.

Expensive equipment was needed to remove the silver and gold that were trapped within quartz rock. Larger mining companies bought up land claims from miners who could not afford this machinery. As a result, mining became a big business in the West.

As companies dug bigger and deeper mines, the work became more dangerous. Miners had to use unsafe equipment, such as elevator platforms without protective walls. They worked in dark tunnels and breathed hot, stuffy air. They suffered from lung disease caused by dusty air. Miners often were injured or killed by poorly planned explosions or by cave-ins. Fire was also a great danger. Mining was therefore one of the most dangerous jobs in the country. In the West, worries about safety and pay led miners to form several unions in the 1860s.

Settlers

People from all over the world came to work in the western mines. Some miners came from the eastern United States. Others emigrated from Europe, Central and South America, and Asia. Many Mexican immigrants and Mexican Americans were experienced miners. They were skilled in assaying, or testing, the contents of valuable ore. One newspaper reporter wrote, "Here were congregated the most varied elements of humanity . . . belonging to almost every nationality and every status of life."

New Towns

Mining booms also produced **boomtowns**, communities that grew suddenly when a mine opened. They disappeared just as quickly when the mine closed. Most boomtowns had general stores, saloons, and boardinghouses.

Few women or families lived in boomtowns. "I was never so lonely and homesick in all my life," wrote one young woman. Women washed, cooked, made clothes, and chopped wood. They also raised families, **established** schools, and wrote for newspapers. Their work helped turn some mining camps into successful, permanent towns.

READING CHECK **Summarizing** What risks did miners face?

ACADEMIC VOCABULARY
establish to set up or create

The Cattle Kingdom

The cattle industry was another area of rapid growth. Following the Civil War, a growing economy and population created a greater demand for beef in the East. Cattle worth $3 to $6 each in Texas could be sold for $38 each in Kansas. In New York, they could be sold for $80 each. The most popular breed of cattle was the longhorn. The longhorn spread quickly throughout western Texas. Because these animals needed very little water and could survive harsh weather, they were well-suited to the dry, desert-like environment of western Texas. But how could Texas ranchers move the longhorns to eastern markets?

In 1867 businessman Joseph McCoy discovered a solution. He built pens for cattle in the small town of Abilene, Kansas. The Kansas

Myth and Reality in the Wild West

No episode in American history has given rise to as many myths as the Wild West. Writers of dime novels, popular in the East, helped created the myths in the years after the Civil War. Even today, popular books, television shows, and movies continue to portray the West in ways that are more myth than reality.

Myth: The cowboy was a free-spirited individual.

Reality: Most cowboys were employees. Many joined labor unions and even went on strike.

Myth: Western cowtowns were wild places where cowboys had gunfights, and there was little law and order.

Reality: Most were orderly cities with active law enforcement. Showdowns rarely, if ever, occurred.

Myth: Almost all cowboys were Anglo Americans.

Reality: About 25 percent of cowboys were African Americans, and 12 percent were Hispanic.

Pacific Railroad line went through Abilene. As a result, cattle could be shipped by rail from there. Soon, countless Texas ranchers were making the trip north to Abilene to sell their herds of cattle.

Around the same time, cattle ranching began to expand in the Midwest. The Great Plains from Texas to Canada, where many ranchers raised cattle in the late 1800s, became known as the **Cattle Kingdom**. Ranchers grazed huge herds on public land called the open range. The land had once been occupied by Plains Indians and buffalo herds.

Importance of Cowboys

The workers who took care of the ranchers' cattle were known as cowhands or cowboys. They borrowed many techniques and tools from vaqueros (bah-KER-ohs), Mexican ranch

Marshal Wyatt Earp

Deadwood, South Dakota

hands who cared for cattle and horses. From vaqueros came the western saddle and the lariat—a rope used for lassoing cattle. The cowboys also borrowed the vaqueros' broad felt hat. However, they changed it into the familiar high-peaked cowboy hat.

One of the cowboy's most important and dangerous duties was the **cattle drive**. On these long journeys, cowboys herded cattle to the market or to the northern Plains for grazing. The trips usually lasted several months and covered hundreds of miles. The **Chisholm Trail**, which ran from San Antonio, Texas, to the cattle town of Abilene, Kansas, was one of the earliest and most popular routes for cattle drives. It was blazed, or marked, by Texas cowboy Jesse Chisholm in the late 1860s.

At times, rowdy cowboys made life in cattle towns rough and violent. There were rarely shoot-outs in the street, but there was often disorderly behavior. Law officials such as Wyatt Earp became famous for keeping the peace in cattle towns.

End of the Open Range

As the cattle business boomed, ranchers faced more competition for use of the open range. Farmers began to buy range land on the Great Plains where cattle had once grazed. Small ranchers also began competing with large ranchers for land. Then in 1874, the invention of barbed wire allowed westerners to fence off large amounts of land cheaply. The competition between farmers, large ranchers, and small ranchers increased. This competition led to range wars, or fights for access to land.

Making matters worse, in 1885 and 1886, disaster struck the Cattle Kingdom. The huge cattle herds on the Plains had eaten most of the prairie grass. Unusually severe winters in both years made the ranching situation even worse. Thousands of cattle died, and many ranchers were ruined financially. The Cattle Kingdom had come to an end.

FOCUS ON READING
Ask yourself questions about the information in this paragraph to help you understand the competition between farmers and ranchers.

READING CHECK Drawing Conclusions
Why did the Cattle Kingdom come to an end?

The Transcontinental Railroad

As more Americans began moving West, the need to send goods and information between the East and West increased. Americans searched for ways to improve communication and travel across the country.

In 1860 a system of messengers on horseback called the **Pony Express** began to carry messages west. The messengers carried mail between relay stations on a route about 2,000 miles long. However, telegraph lines, which sent messages faster, quickly put the Pony Express out of business.

Some Americans wanted to build a **transcontinental railroad**—a railroad that would cross the continent and connect the East to the West. The federal government, therefore, passed the Pacific Railway Acts in 1862 and in 1864. These acts gave railroad companies loans and large land grants that could be sold to pay for construction costs. Congress had granted more than 131 million acres of public land to railroad companies. In exchange, the government asked the railroads to carry U.S. mail and troops at a lower cost. Many railroad companies were inspired to begin laying miles of tracks.

Great Race

Two companies, the Central Pacific and the Union Pacific, led the race to complete the transcontinental railroad. In February 1863, the Central Pacific began building east from Sacramento, California. At the end of the year, the Union Pacific started building west from Omaha, Nebraska.

The Union Pacific hired thousands of railroad workers, particularly Irish immigrants. Chinese immigrants made up some 85 percent of the Central Pacific workforce. The railroad's part-owner Leland Stanford praised them, but he paid them less than other laborers. Chinese crews also were given the most dangerous tasks and had to work longer hours than other railroad laborers. They took the job, however, because the $30 a month

Routes West, 1870

When the two lines of the transcontinental railroad met in Promontory, Utah, Leland Stanford drove a celebratory golden spike into the rails.

Railroad
Pony Express
Chisholm Trail
Transcontinental Railroad route

0   200   400 Miles
0   200   400 Kilometers

GEOGRAPHY SKILLS **INTERPRETING MAPS**

Movement According to the map, what was the westernmost city on the transcontinental railroad?

that the Central Pacific paid was as much as 10 times what they could earn in China.

Railroad companies faced many geographic challenges. For example, workers for Central Pacific struggled to cross the Sierra Nevada mountain range in California. Breaking apart its rock formations required setting carefully controlled explosions using large amounts of blasting powder and the explosive nitroglycerin. And in the winter of 1866, snowdrifts more than 60 feet high trapped and killed dozens of workers. Faced with these obstacles, the Central Pacific took four years to lay the first 115 miles of track.

Meanwhile, Union Pacific workers faced harsh weather on the Great Plains. In addition, the company pressured them to work at a rapid pace—at times laying 250 miles of track in six months.

For both railroad companies, providing food and supplies for workers was vital. This job became more difficult in remote areas. The railroad companies consequently often relied on local resources. Professional hunters, such as William "Buffalo Bill" Cody, shot thousands of buffalo to feed Union Pacific workers.

Golden Spike

Congress required the two completed rail lines to connect at Promontory, Utah. On May 10, 1869, a golden spike was used to connect the railroad tie joining the two tracks. Alexander Toponce witnessed the event.

" Governor Stanford, president of the Central Pacific, took the sledge [hammer], and the first time he struck he missed the spike and hit the rail. What a howl went up! Irish, Chinese, Mexicans, and everybody yelled with delight. 'He missed it' . . . Then Stanford tried it again and tapped the spike. "

—Alexander Toponce, quoted in *A Treasury of Railroad Folklore,* edited by B. A. Botkin and Alvin F. Harlo

The railroad companies were not finished, though. Following completion of the transcontinental railroad, companies continued building railroads until the West was crisscrossed with rail lines.

The Central Pacific and Union Pacific connected their tracks at Promontory, Utah, in 1869, completing the transcontinental railroad.

Effects of the Transcontinental Railroad

QUICK FACTS

- Increased settlement of the West
- Increased business activity and East-West trade
- Helped make the railroad industry one of the most powerful in the country

Results of the Railroad

The transcontinental railroad increased both economic growth and the population in the West. Railroad companies provided better transportation for people and goods. They also sold land to settlers, which encouraged people to move West.

New railroads helped businesses. Western timber companies, miners, ranchers, and farmers shipped wood, metals, meat, and grain east by railroad. In exchange, eastern businesses shipped manufactured goods to the West. As trade between regions increased, the idea that the U.S. economy was inter-

THE IMPACT TODAY

Today's businesses ship goods across the country using railroads, the interstate highway system, and airplanes.

dependent became more widespread. Even perceptions of time became more formal as railroad schedules began to unite areas that had before existed under different times. Four continental time zones were established in 1883.

Railroad companies encouraged people to put their money into the railroad business, which they did—sometimes unwisely. Railroad speculation and the collapse of railroad owner Jay Cooke's banking firm helped start the Panic of 1873. By the 1880s, many small western railroads were deeply in debt. Despite such setbacks, Americans remained interested in railroad investments. By 1890 there were about 164,000 more miles of track in operation than in 1865. Railroads had become one of the biggest industries in the United States.

READING CHECK Finding Main Ideas How did the railroad affect the development of the West?

SUMMARY AND PREVIEW In this section you learned about the increased settlement of the West. In the next section you will learn about conflicts with Native Americans.

Section 1 Assessment

go.hrw.com
Online Quiz
KEYWORD: SB7 HP18

Reviewing Ideas, Terms, and People

1. **a. Recall** Why did Americans move West in the years following the Civil War?
   b. Draw Conclusions What effect did the discovery of the **Comstock Lode** have on the West?
   c. Evaluate Do you think women were important to the success of mining towns? Why or why not?
2. **a. Recall** What led to the cattle boom in the West?
   b. Analyze Why was there competition between ranchers and farmers to settle in the Great Plains?
   c. Evaluate What played the biggest role in ending the **Cattle Kingdom**? Why?
3. **a. Recall** When and where did the Union Pacific and Central Pacific lines meet?
   b. Make Generalizations How do you think the **transcontinental railroad** improved people's lives?

Critical Thinking

4. **Comparing** Review your notes about opportunities in the West. Then use a graphic organizer like the one below to list the effects of these opportunities.

Opportunity	Effect

FOCUS ON WRITING

5. **Taking Notes on Mining, Ranching, and the Railroads** As you read this section, take notes on how mining, ranching, and railroads changed the West. How might a railroad worker feel about these changes?

Wars for the West

If YOU were there...

You are a member of the Sioux nation, living in Dakota Territory in 1875. These lands are sacred to your people, and the U.S. government has promised them to you. But now gold has been found here, and the government has ordered you to give up your land. Some Sioux leaders want to fight. Others say that it is of no use, that the soldiers will win.

Would you fight to keep your lands? Why?

BUILDING BACKGROUND Miners, ranchers, and farmers all moved West in the years after the Civil War. The arrival of settlers and the U.S. army to the Great Plains meant the end of the way of life of the Indians who lived there. The coming of the railroad began this destruction, with the killing of thousands of buffalo. Treaties were made but did not protect Indian lands from settlers.

Settlers Encounter the Plains Indians

As miners and settlers began crossing the Great Plains in the mid-1800s, they pressured the federal government for more access to western lands. To protect these travelers, U.S. officials sent agents to negotiate treaties with the Plains Indians.

The Plains Indians lived in the Great Plains, which stretch north into Canada and south into Texas. Indian groups such as the Apache and the Comanche lived in and around Texas and

Virginia Standards of Learning USII.1a, USII.1b, USII.1h, USII.4a

What You Will Learn...

Main Ideas

1. As settlers moved to the Great Plains, they encountered the Plains Indians.
2. The U.S. Army and Native Americans fought in the northern plains, the Southwest, and the Far West.
3. Despite efforts to reform U.S. policy toward Native Americans, conflict continued.

The Big Idea

Native Americans and the U.S. government came into conflict over land in the West.

Key Terms and People

Treaty of Fort Laramie, *p. 594*
reservations, *p. 595*
Crazy Horse, *p. 595*
Treaty of Medicine Lodge, *p. 595*
buffalo soldiers, *p. 596*
George Armstrong Custer, *p. 596*
Sitting Bull, *p. 596*
Battle of the Little Bighorn, *p. 596*
Massacre at Wounded Knee, *p. 597*
Long Walk, *p. 597*
Geronimo, *p. 597*
Ghost Dance, *p. 598*
Sarah Winnemucca, *p. 598*
Dawes General Allotment Act, *p. 598*

TAKING NOTES As you read this section, take notes on the major events in Native Americans' loss of land rights. Organize them in a chart like the one below.

Date	Event

The Plains Indians depended on two animals—the horse and the buffalo.

what is now Oklahoma. The Cheyenne and the Arapaho lived in different regions across the central Plains. The Pawnee lived in parts of Nebraska. To the north were the Sioux. These groups spoke many different languages. However, they used a common sign language to communicate and they shared a similar lifestyle.

Hunting Buffalo

For survival, Plains Indians depended on two animals—the horse and the buffalo. The Spanish brought horses to America in the 1500s. Plains Indians learned to ride horses, and hunters used them to follow buffalo herds year-round. While on horseback, most Plains Indian hunters used a short bow and arrows to shoot buffalo from close range.

Plains Indians used buffalo for food, shelter, clothing, utensils, and tools. Women dried buffalo meat to make jerky. They made tepees and clothing from buffalo hides, and cups and tools from buffalo horns. As one Sioux explained, "When our people killed a buffalo, all of the animal was utilized [used] in some manner; nothing was wasted." The Plains Indians prospered. By 1850, some 75,000 Native Americans lived on the Plains.

Struggle to Keep Land

Miners and settlers were also increasing in numbers—and they wanted Indians' land. The U.S. government tried to avoid disputes by negotiating the **Treaty of Fort Laramie**, the first major treaty between the U.S. government and Plains Indians. Two years later, several southern Plains nations signed a treaty at Fort Atkinson in Nebraska. These treaties recognized Indian claims to most of the Great Plains. They also allowed the United States to build forts and roads and to travel across Indian homelands. The U.S. government promised to pay for any damages to Indian lands.

★ Interactive Map

Native American Land Loss in the West, 1850–1890

Land lost by Native Americans
- 1850–1870
- 1870–1890
- Reservations in 1890
- UTE Native American group

0   200   400 Miles
0   200   400 Kilometers

Battles and Treaties of the Indian Wars

1. Treaties at Fort Laramie, 1851 and 1868
2. Treaty at Fort Atkinson, 1853
3. Sand Creek Massacre, 1864
4. Fetterman Massacre, 1866
5. Treaty of Medicine Lodge, 1867
6. Battle of the Little Bighorn, 1876
7. Battle of the Rosebud, 1876
8. Wounded Knee Massacre, 1890

go.hrw.com
Interactive Map
KEYWORD: SB7 CH18

GEOGRAPHY **SKILLS** INTERPRETING MAPS

Region In what regions did Native Americans lose land in the late 1800s?

Tribal Councils

Native Americans have long held tribal councils to make decisions on behalf of the group. Today this tradition of Native American government continues. There are more than 500 tribal governments in the United States. Tribal governments provide a wide range of services, including law enforcement, health care, and education. Here, a member of the Blackfoot Tribal Council addresses the Montana state legislature.

ANALYSIS SKILL **ANALYZING INFORMATION**

What types of services do tribal governments provide?

The treaties did not keep the peace for long. In 1858 the discovery of gold in what is now Colorado brought thousands of miners to the West. They soon clashed with the Cheyenne and the Arapaho. In 1861 the U.S. government negotiated new treaties with Plains Indians. These treaties created **reservations**, areas of federal land set aside for Native Americans. The government expected Indians to stay on the reservations, which made hunting buffalo almost impossible.

Pioneers and miners continued to cross the Great Plains. Many miners used the Bozeman Trail. To protect them, the U.S. Army built forts along the trail, which ran through favored Sioux hunting grounds. The Sioux responded with war. In late 1866, **Crazy Horse** and a group of Sioux ambushed and killed 81 cavalry troops.

In 1868, under the Second Treaty of Fort Laramie, the government agreed to close the Bozeman Trail, abandon the forts, and provide reservation land to the Sioux.

The U.S. government also negotiated for southern Plains Indians to move off their land. In the 1867 **Treaty of Medicine Lodge**, most southern Plains Indians agreed to live on reservations. However, many Indians did not want to give up their hunting grounds. Fighting soon broke out between the Comanche and Texans. The U.S. Army and the Texas Rangers were unable to defeat the Comanche, so they cut off the Comanche's access to food and water. In 1875 the last of the Comanche war leaders surrendered.

READING CHECK **Summarizing** What was the federal policy toward the Plains Indians in the 1860s and 1870s?

Two Views of a Historic Battle

CONNECT TO THE ARTS

Art historians have identified about 1,000 paintings of the Battle of the Little Bighorn. The painting on this page was painted in 1899. The painting on the next page is one of the many colored-pencil drawings of the battle done by Red Horse, who participated in the fight. He drew them five years after the battle.

How do these paintings show the influences of different cultures?

The Native Americans are shown surrounding a small force of U.S. soldiers.

General Custer is shown standing among his men as he fires.

Fighting on the Plains

In the northern Plains, Southwest, and Far West, Native Americans continued to resist being moved to and confined on reservations. The U.S. government sent troops, including African American cavalry, who the Indians called **buffalo soldiers**, into the area to force the Indians to leave.

Battles on the Northern Plains

As fighting on the southern Plains came to an end, new trouble started in the north. In 1874 Lieutenant Colonel **George Armstrong Custer**'s soldiers discovered gold in the Black Hills of the Dakotas. **Sitting Bull**, a leader of the Lakota Sioux, protested U.S. demands for the land.

"What treaty that the whites have kept has the red man broken? Not one. What treaty that the white man ever made with us have they kept? Not one."
—Sitting Bull, quoted in *Touch the Earth* by T. C. McLuhan

Other Sioux leaders listened to Sitting Bull and refused to give up land. Fighting soon broke out between the army and the Sioux.

On June 25, 1876, Custer's scouts found a Sioux camp along the Little Bighorn River in Montana Territory. Leading 264 of his soldiers, Custer raced ahead without waiting for any supporting forces. In the **Battle of the Little Bighorn**, Sioux forces led by Crazy Horse and Sitting Bull surrounded and defeated Custer and his troops. Newspapers called the battle "Custer's Last Stand" because his entire command was killed. It was the worst defeat the U.S. Army suffered in the West. The Battle of the Little Bighorn was also the Sioux's last major victory.

In 1881 Sitting Bull and a few followers returned from Canada where they had moved. They had run out of food during the hard winter. They joined the Sioux on Standing Rock Reservation in Dakota Territory.

These are wounded men.

The U.S. Army is shown on horseback in this painting.

Almost a decade later, in 1890, while following orders to arrest Sitting Bull, reservation police killed him. Many Sioux left the reservations in protest. Later that year, the U.S. Army shot and killed about 150 Sioux near Wounded Knee Creek in South Dakota. This **Massacre at Wounded Knee** was the last major incident on the Great Plains.

Southwest

The Navajo lived in what became Arizona and New Mexico. In 1863 the Navajo refused to settle on a reservation. In response, U.S. troops made raids on the Navajo's fields, homes, and livestock.

When the Navajo ran out of food and shelter, they started surrendering to the U.S. Army. In 1864 the army led Navajo captives on the **Long Walk**. On this 300-mile march the Navajo were forced to walk across the desert to a reservation in Bosque Redondo, New Mexico. Along the way, countless Navajo died.

Far West

The United States had promised to let the peaceful Nez Percé keep their land in Oregon. Within a few years, however, the government ordered the Nez Percé to a reservation in what is now Idaho. Before leaving, a few angry Nez Percé killed some local settlers and tried to escape to Canada. Near the border, U.S. troops overtook them and sent them to a reservation in what is now Oklahoma.

Final Battles

By the 1880s, most Native Americans had stopped fighting. The Apache of the Southwest, however, continued to battle the U.S. Army. A Chiricahua Apache named **Geronimo** and his band of raiders avoided capture for many years. In September 1886 Geronimo surrendered, ending the Apache armed resistance.

READING CHECK **Contrasting** How did the Apache resistance differ from that of the Navajo?

Conflict Continues

By the 1870s, many Native Americans lived on reservations, where land was usually not useful for farming or buffalo hunting. Many Indians were starving.

A Paiute Indian named Wovoka began a religious movement, the **Ghost Dance**, that predicted the arrival of paradise for Native Americans. In this paradise, the buffalo herds would return and the settlers would disappear.

U.S. officials did not understand the meaning of the Ghost Dance. They feared it would lead to rebellion, so they tried to end the movement, which had spread to other groups, including the Sioux. After the massacre in 1890 at Wounded Knee, the Ghost Dance movement gradually died out.

In the late 1870s, a Paiute Indian named **Sarah Winnemucca** called for reform. She gave lectures on problems of the reservation system. Writer Helen Hunt Jackson published a book that pushed for reform of U.S. Indian policy in 1881.

Sarah Winnemucca spoke out for the fair treatment of her people.

Some reformers believed that Native Americans should adopt the ways of white people. The **Dawes General Allotment Act** of 1887 tried to lessen traditional influences on Indian society by making land ownership private rather than shared. The act also promised—but failed to deliver—U.S. citizenship to Native Americans. After breaking up reservation land, the government sold the acreage remaining. The Act took about two-thirds of Indian land.

READING CHECK **Evaluating** How did reformers try to influence Native Americans' lives?

SUMMARY AND PREVIEW In this section you read about conflict in the settlement of the West. In the next section you will learn more about Great Plains settlers.

---

go.hrw.com
Online Quiz
KEYWORD: SB7 HP18

Section 2 Assessment

Reviewing Ideas, Terms, and People

1. **a. Describe** What animals did Plains Indians depend on, and how did they use those animals?
   b. Analyze How did U.S. policy toward the Plains Indians change in the late 1850s?
   c. Elaborate Would you have agreed to move to a **reservation**? Why or why not?
2. **a. Describe** What events led to the **Battle of the Little Bighorn**?
   b. Elaborate Why do you think most Indian groups eventually stopped resisting the United States?
3. **a. Describe** How did the **Dawes General Allotment Act** affect American Indians?
   b. Predict What effect do you think the **Massacre at Wounded Knee** would have on relations between Plains Indians and the United States?

Critical Thinking

4. **Identifying Cause and Effect** Review your notes about Native American land losses. Organize the events in a time line like the one below.

   1851   1864 1867   1887

FOCUS ON WRITING

5. **Reading about the Wars for the West** As you read this section, take notes on the wars between the U.S. government and the Plains Indians. How might a railroad worker have experienced these conflicts?

Chief Joseph

What would you do to protect your home and your ways of life?

When did he live? 1840–1904

Where did he live? Chief Joseph lived in the Wallowa Valley, the Nez Percé homeland, in present-day Oregon.

What did he do? Chief Joseph led his people in an effort to hold on to the Nez Percé homeland and to avoid war with the United States. For years, Joseph and a band of Nez Percé refused to move as white settlers moved into the valley. Finally, after being threatened with attack, Joseph gave in. An army led by General Oliver Otis Howard eventually chased the Nez Percé across Idaho, Wyoming, and Montana. They were sent to a reservation in what is now Oklahoma, where many died.

Why is he so important? Chief Joseph's surrender speech earned him a place in American history. The band of 700 people, including only 200 warriors, made a courageous three-month, 1,400-mile trek, hoping to cross into Canada for protection. Exhausted, hungry, and freezing, Joseph's people collapsed just short of the Canadian border. In later years, the chief spoke about what had happened.

Cause and Effect What brought suffering to Chief Joseph and his people?

Chief Joseph of the Nez Percé nation tried to protect his people from the advancement of white settlers.

Speech

"I am tired of fighting. Our chiefs are killed … The old men are all dead … It is cold, and we have no blankets. The little children are freezing to death. My people, some of them, have run away to the hills, and have no blankets, no food. No one knows where they are—perhaps freezing to death. I want to have time to look for my children, and see how many of them I can find. Maybe I shall find them among the dead. Hear me, my chiefs! I am tired. My heart is sick and sad. From where the sun now stands I will fight no more forever."

—Chief Joseph of the Nez Percé, surrender speech, October 5, 1877

Farming and Populism

Virginia Standards of Learning USII.1a, USII.1c, USII.2a, USII.2b, USII.2c, USII.4a, USII.4d

What You Will Learn...

Main Ideas

1. Many Americans started new lives on the Great Plains.
2. Economic challenges led to the creation of farmers' political groups.
3. By the 1890s, the western frontier had come to an end.

The Big Idea

Settlers on the Great Plains created new communities and unique political groups.

Key Terms and People

Homestead Act, *p. 600*
Morrill Act, *p. 600*
Exodusters, *p. 601*
sodbusters, *p. 601*
dry farming, *p. 601*
Annie Bidwell, *p. 602*
National Grange, *p. 603*
deflation, *p. 604*
William Jennings Bryan, *p. 604*
Populist Party, *p. 604*

TAKING NOTES As you read this section, take notes on the reasons for the rise of populism. Organize your notes in a graphic organizer like the one below.

Rise of Populism

If YOU were there...

You are a female schoolteacher in Wisconsin in 1880. You live and teach in a small town, but you grew up on a farm and are used to hard work. Now you are thinking about moving West to claim free land from the government. You could teach in a school there, too. You think it would be an exciting adventure, but your family is horrified that a single woman would move West on her own.

Would you decide to become a homesteader?

BUILDING BACKGROUND By the 1870s and 1880s, the Great Plains had been "tamed" and made more welcoming to settlers. The end of the open cattle range was coming, and the Indian wars were nearly over. The government moved to encourage permanent settlements in the West by offering land to homesteaders.

New Lives on the Plains

In 1862 Congress passed two important land grant acts that helped open the West to settlers. The **Homestead Act** gave government-owned land to small farmers. Any adult who was a U.S. citizen or planned to become one could receive 160 acres of land. In exchange, homesteaders promised to live on the land for five years. The **Morrill Act** granted more than 17 million acres of federal land to the states. The act required each state to sell this land and to use the money to build colleges to teach agriculture and engineering.

Settling the Plains

People from all over the country moved West. Many farming families moved from areas where farmland was becoming scarce or expensive, such as New England. Many single women moved West. The Homestead Act granted land to unmarried women, which was unusual for the time.

The promise of land and a life free of discrimination also drew a large group of African Americans West. In 1879 some

20,000 to 40,000 southern African Americans moved to Kansas. Known as **Exodusters**, these southerners made a mass exodus, or departure, from the South. A number of black communities soon developed.

Western homesteads also were attractive to immigrants. Norwegian, Swedish, Danish, German, and Czech immigrants formed many small communities on the Great Plains.

Farming the Plains

Plains farmers had many unique challenges. The seasons were extreme. Weather could be extreme. Also, the root-filled sod, or dirt, beneath the Plains grass was very tough. The hard work of breaking up the sod earned Plains farmers the nickname **sodbusters**.

In the 1890s western Plains farmers began **dry farming**, a new method of farming that shifted the focus away from water-dependent crops such as corn. Instead, farmers grew more hardy crops like red wheat. In addition, by the 1880s mechanical farming was becoming common. By using machinery, farmers could work much more quickly on large fields with fewer workers. Farmers shipped their harvest east by train. From there, crops were shipped overseas. The Great Plains soon became known as the breadbasket of the world.

LETTER
Letter from the Plains, 1863

In a letter to her family in Norway, immigrant Gro Svendsen describes her new life as a farmer on the plains of Iowa.

"I remember I used to wonder when I heard that it would be impossible to keep the milk here as we did at home. Now I have learned that it is indeed impossible because of the heat here in the summertime . . . It's difficult, too, to preserve the butter. One must pour brine [salt water] over it or salt it.

The thunderstorms are so violent that one might think it was the end of the world . . . Quite often the lightning strikes down both cattle and people, damages property, and splinters sturdy oak trees into many pieces."

—quoted in *Sources in American History*

ANALYSIS SKILL **ANALYZING PRIMARY SOURCES**

What might be some of the differences between Norway and Svendsen's new home in Iowa?

Pioneers like this family often lived in houses made of sod because there were few trees for lumber on the Plains.

Building Communities

Women were an important force in the settlement of the frontier. They joined in the hard work of farming and ranching and helped build communities out of the widely spaced farms and small towns. Their role in founding communities **facilitated** a strong voice in public affairs. Wyoming women, for example, were granted the vote in the new state's constitution, which was approved in 1869. **Annie Bidwell**, one of the founders of Chico, California, used her influence to support a variety of moral and social causes such as women's suffrage and temperance.

Many early settlers found life on their remote farms to be extremely difficult. Farmers formed communities so that they could assist one another in times of need. One of the first things that many pioneer communities did was establish a local church and school.

Children helped with many chores around the farm. Author Laura Ingalls Wilder was one of four children in a pioneer family. Wilder's books about settlers' lives on the prairie are still popular today.

READING CHECK Comparing and Contrasting How were settlers' lives alike and different from their lives in the East?

ACADEMIC VOCABULARY
facilitate to make easier

Farmers' Political Groups

From 1860 to 1900, the U.S. population more than doubled. To feed this growing population, the number of farms tripled. With modern machines, farmers in 1900 could harvest a bushel of wheat almost 20 times faster than they could in 1830.

Farm Incomes Fall

The combination of more farms and greater productivity, however, led to overproduction. Overproduction resulted in lower prices for crops. As their incomes decreased, many farmers found it difficult to pay bills. Farmers who could not make their mortgage payments lost their farms and homes. Many of these homeless farmers became tenant farmers who worked land owned by others. By 1880 one-fourth of all farms were rented by tenants, and the number continued to grow.

The National Grange

Many farmers blamed businesspeople— wholesalers, brokers, grain buyers, and especially railroad owners—for making money at their expense. As economic conditions worsened, farmers began to follow the example of other workers. They formed associations to protect and help their interests.

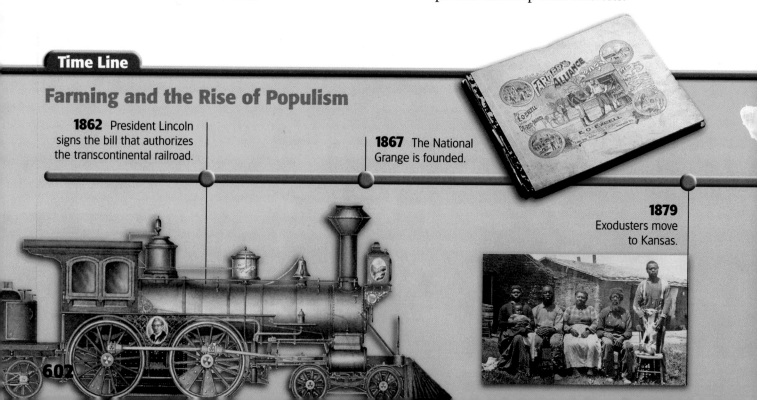

Time Line

Farming and the Rise of Populism

1862 President Lincoln signs the bill that authorizes the transcontinental railroad.

1867 The National Grange is founded.

1879 Exodusters move to Kansas.

602

One such organization was founded by Oliver Hudson Kelley, who toured the South in 1866 for the U.S. Department of Agriculture. Kelley saw firsthand how the country's farmers suffered. Afterward, Kelley and several government clerks formed the National Grange of the Patrons of Husbandry in 1867. The **National Grange** was a social and educational organization for farmers. (*Grange* is an old word for granary.) Local chapters were quickly founded, and membership grew rapidly.

The Grange campaigned for political candidates who supported farmers' goals. The organization also called for laws that regulated rates charged by railroads. The U.S. Supreme Court ruled in 1877 that the government could regulate railroads because they affected the public interest. In 1886 the Court said that the federal government could only regulate companies doing business across state lines. Rate regulation for railroad lines within states fell to the state governments.

In February 1887 Congress passed the Interstate Commerce Act, providing national regulations over trade between states and creating the Interstate Commerce Commission to ensure fair railroad rates. However, the commission lacked power to enforce its regulations.

Agricultural Supply and Demand

CONNECT TO ECONOMICS

Supply is the amount of a good that is available.
Demand is the amount of a good that people want to buy.
When supply exceeds demand, prices fall.

What happened to the price of wheat as the supply increased?

Wheat Production, 1866–1880

Wheat (in millions of bushels)

Wheat Prices, 1866–1880

Cost ($ per bushel of wheat)

1887 The Interstate Commerce Commission is formed to regulate railroad prices.

W. McKINLEY.

1896 The Populist Party backs William Jennings Bryan as the Democratic presidential candidate.

1892 The national Populist Party is formed.

ANALYSIS SKILL **READING TIME LINES**

How many years after the authorization of the transcontinental railroad was the Interstate Commerce Commission created?

Free Silver Debate

Money issues also caused problems for farmers. Many farmers hoped that help would come from new laws affecting the money supply.

Since 1873 the United States had been on the gold standard, meaning that all paper money had to be backed by gold in the treasury. As a result, the money supply grow more slowly than the nation's population and led to **deflation**—a decrease in the money supply and overall lower prices. One solution was to allow the unlimited coining of silver and to back paper currency with silver. This was the position of those in the Free Silver movement.

During the late 1870s, there was a great deal of support for the Free Silver movement. Many farmers began backing political candidates who favored free silver coinage. One such candidate was **William Jennings Bryan** of Nebraska.

The two major political parties, however, largely ignored the money issue. After the election of 1888, the Republican-controlled Congress passed the Sherman Silver Purchase Act. The act increased the amount of silver purchased for coinage. However, this did not help farmers as much as they had hoped.

BIOGRAPHY

William Jennings Bryan
1860–1925

William Jennings Bryan was born in Illinois but moved to Nebraska when he finished law school. He was elected Nebraska's first Democratic Congress member in 1890. Through his political campaigns and work as a newspaper editor, he became one of the best-known supporters of Populist ideas. After a dramatic speech at the 1896 Democratic National Convention, Bryan was nominated for the presidency. He was the youngest presidential candidate up to that time. Although he lost the election, he continued to be an influential speaker.

Making Inferences Why was Bryan's support of Populist ideas important?

Populist Party

To have greater power, many farmers organized to elect candidates that would help them. These political organizations became known as the Farmers' Alliances.

In the 1890 elections the Alliances were a strong political force. State and local wins raised farmers' political hopes. At a conference in Cincinnati, Ohio, in 1891, Alliance leaders met with labor and reform groups. Then, at a convention in St. Louis in February 1892, the Alliances formed a new national political party.

The new party was called the **Populist Party**, and it called for the government to own railroads and telephone and telegraph systems. It also favored the "free and unlimited coinage of silver." To gain the votes of workers, the Populists backed an eight-hour workday and limits on immigration.

The concerns of the Populists were soon put in the national spotlight. During the Panic of 1893, the U.S. economy experienced a crisis that some critics blamed on the shortage of gold. The failure of several major railroad companies also contributed to the economic problems.

The Panic of 1893 led more people to back the Populist call for economic reform. In 1896 the Republicans nominated William McKinley for president. McKinley was firmly against free coinage of silver. The Democrats nominated William Jennings Bryan, who favored free coinage.

The Populists had to decide between running their own candidate, and thus splitting the silver vote, or supporting Bryan. They decided to support Bryan. The Republicans had a well-financed campaign, and they won the election. McKinley's victory in 1896 marked the end of both the Populist Party and the Farmers' Alliances.

READING CHECK Summarizing Why did farmers, laborers, and reformers join to form the Populist Party?

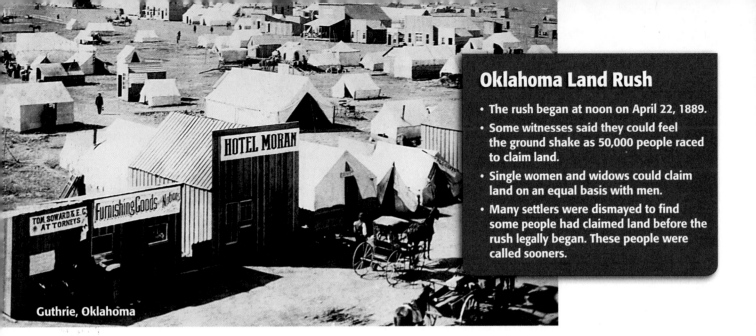

Oklahoma Land Rush

- The rush began at noon on April 22, 1889.
- Some witnesses said they could feel the ground shake as 50,000 people raced to claim land.
- Single women and widows could claim land on an equal basis with men.
- Many settlers were dismayed to find some people had claimed land before the rush legally began. These people were called sooners.

Guthrie, Oklahoma

HOTEL MORAN

TOM SOWARD & E.G. AT TORNEYS

Furnishing Goods

End of the Frontier

By 1870 only small portions of the Great Plains remained unsettled. For most of the next two decades, this land remained open range.

In March 1889, government officials announced that homesteaders could file claims on land in what is now the state of Oklahoma. This land had belonged to Creek and Seminole Indians. Within a month, about 50,000 people rushed to Oklahoma to stake their claims.

In all, settlers claimed more than 11 million acres of former Indian land in the famous Oklahoma land rush. This huge wave of pioneers was the last chapter of the westward movement. By the early 1890s, the frontier had ceased to exist in the United States.

READING CHECK Finding Main Ideas
What event signaled the closing of the frontier?

SUMMARY AND PREVIEW In this section you read about the challenges settlers faced. In the next chapter you will read about the growth of America's industrial power and how that growth affected American lives.

go.hrw.com
Online Quiz
KEYWORD: SB7 HP18

Section 3 Assessment

Reviewing Ideas, Terms, and People

1. **a. Describe** What groups settled in the Great Plains?
   b. Explain How did the U.S. government make lands available to western settlers?
   c. Elaborate Would you have chosen to settle on the frontier? Why or why not?
2. **a. Recall** What was the goal of the **National Grange**?
   b. Make Inferences Why did the **Populist Party** want the government to own railroads and telegraph and telephone systems?
   c. Evaluate Do you think farmers were successful in bringing about economic and political change? Explain.
3. **a. Recall** What was the Oklahoma land rush?
   b. Explain Why did the frontier cease to exist in the United States?

Critical Thinking

4. **Comparing and Contrasting** Look back over your notes about the rise of populism. Use them to explain why Populists sought the changes they did in a chart like the one below.

Change sought	Reason why

FOCUS ON WRITING

5. **Farming the Great Plains** As you read this section, take notes on the growth of farming on the Great Plains. How did farmers interact with the railroads? What changes might have been apparent to a railroad worker?

Social Studies Skills

Analysis | Critical Thinking | Civic Participation | Study

Comparing Migration Maps

Define the Skill

One of the best ways of using geography to learn history is by comparing maps. This skill allows you to see changes over time. It also helps you see relationships between one factor, such as population growth, and another factor, such as transportation routes or economic activities in an area.

Learn the Skill

Follow these steps to compare information on maps.

1. Apply basic map skills by reading the title and studying the legend and symbols for each map.

2. Note the date of each map and the area it covers. Maps compared for changes over time should include the same areas. Those used to look for relationships should have similar dates.

3. Note similarities or differences. Closely examine and compare each map's patterns and symbols.

4. Apply critical thinking skills. Make generalizations and draw conclusions about the relationships you find.

Practice the Skill

Use the maps below to answer the following questions.

1. What present-day state was unsettled by Americans in 1850 and almost completely settled in 1890?

2. Which other two present-day states show the most settlement by Americans from 1850 to 1890?

3. Why do you think the West coast was settled before the interior of the United States?

4. According to the maps, how might rivers have shaped the settlement of the West?

Chapter Review

HOLT
History's Impact
▸ video series
Review the video to answer the closing question:
How was a cowboy's job essential to the American economy?

Visual Summary

QUICK FACTS

Use the visual summary below to help you review the main ideas of the chapter.

The American West

As settlers moved West, they came into conflict with American Indians. The U.S. government defeated Indian resistance and moved many tribes to reservations.

The completion of the transcontinental railroad in 1869 opened the West to more settlement. Gold and silver strikes also drew people hoping to get rich.

The railroads helped make the rise of the Cattle Kingdom possible. Cowboys drove huge herds of cattle from ranches to railway stations to be shipped to the East.

Farmers settled the Great Plains in large numbers. They overcame many hardships to make the Plains the breadbasket of America.

Reviewing Vocabulary, Terms, and People

1. Who was the leader of the 7th Cavalry in the Battle of the Little Bighorn?
   - **a.** Cyrus McCormick
   - **c.** William Jennings Bryan
   - **b.** Leland Stanford
   - **d.** George Armstrong Custer

2. What act gave millions of acres of federal lands to the states, which were to sell them and use those funds to build agricultural and engineering colleges?
   - **a.** Morrill Act
   - **c.** Pacific Railway Act
   - **b.** Sherman Act
   - **d.** Interstate Commerce Act

3. Which frontier woman was instrumental in supporting reform efforts in the West?
   - **a.** Sarah Winnemucca
   - **c.** Annie Bidwell
   - **b.** Laura Ingalls Wilder
   - **d.** Lucretia Mott

Comprehension and Critical Thinking

SECTION 1 *(Pages 586–592)*

4. **a. Recall** Why were many Americans eager to move to the western frontier?

   b. Analyze How did railroads and ranching change the landscape of the West?

   c. Elaborate In your opinion, which made the greatest changes to the West—mining, ranching, or railroads? Explain your answer.

SECTION 2 *(Pages 593–598)*

5. **a. Describe** What was life like for the Plains Indians before and after the arrival of large numbers of American settlers?

   b. Draw Conclusions Why did the spread of the Ghost Dance movement cause concern for U.S. officials?

   c. Elaborate What do you think about the reservation system established by the United States?

6. a. Identify What political organizations did western farmers create? Why did farmers create these organizations?

b. Analyze How did women participate in the settling of the American frontier?

c. Predict How might the end of the frontier in the United States affect the nation?

Reviewing Themes

7. Geography What geographic obstacles did miners, ranchers, and railroad workers face in the West?

8. Science and Technology What types of technology did farmers on the Great Plains use, and how did it benefit them?

Using the Internet
go.hrw.com
KEYWORD: SB7 CH18

9. Activity: Creating a Presentation Our view of the settlement of the West is heavily influenced by popular culture. Writers, painters, and illustrators provided a steady flow of words and images that sensationalized life in the American West. Later, film makers and television producers also contributed to the myth of the Wild West. "When legend becomes fact," said one actor in the classic western movie *The Man Who Shot Liberty Valance,* "print the legend." How does legend affect our view of this part of our history? Enter the activity keyword. Analyze the myths and realities of the West and the ways in which they shaped our view of that time period. Then create a visual display or PowerPoint presentation to present your research.

Reading Skills

Understanding Through Questioning *Use the Reading Skills taught in this chapter to answer the question about the reading selection below.*

> For survival, Plains Indians depended on two animals—the horse and the buffalo. The Spanish brought horses to America in the 1500s. Plains Indians learned to ride horses, and hunters used them to follow buffalo herds year-round. *(p. 594)*

10. Write two or three questions you have about the information in the passage above. Remember to use the five W's—Who? What? When? Where? and Why?

Social Studies Skills

Comparing Migration Maps *Use the Social Studies Skills taught in this chapter to answer the questions about the map below.*

11. According to the map above, for what reasons did settlers migrate to the West?

a. for mining, ranching, and farming

b. for jobs in manufacturing

c. for the homes in the major cities there

d. for the fishing industry

FOCUS ON WRITING

12. Writing Your Letter Review your notes. Then write a letter to your sister back in Ireland about your experiences on the Great Plains. Describe all the changes you have seen. Use colorful language and precise details to make your sister feel as though she were there.

DIRECTIONS: Read each question and write the letter of the best response.

1

- Government ownership of railroads
- Free and unlimited coinage of silver
- An eight-hour day for industrial workers
- Strict limits on foreign immigration
- Election of officials who will help farmers

Which of the following intended to accomplish the changes listed above in American society?

A the Morrill Act

B the Populist Party

C the National Grange

D the Homestead Act

2 The goal of many reformers who wanted to help Native Americans in the late 1800s was to

A get Indians to adopt the ways of white people.

B return to Indians all the land that had been taken from them.

C relocate all the nations to create an American Indian state in Oklahoma.

D negotiate treaties to bring peace to the frontier.

3 What played the *most* important part in the growth of the West's population and economy between 1865 and 1900?

A the mining industry

B the Cattle Kingdom

C the Populist Party

D the railroad

4 In general, the policy of the United States government toward Native Americans in the West was to

A send the army to track them down and engage them in battle.

B move them onto reservations and open their homelands to white settlers.

C kill all the buffalo so that they could not continue their traditional way of life.

D drive them into Canada or Mexico to settle.

5 The biggest problem facing western farmers in the late 1800s was

A a scarcity of good, cheap land to farm.

B their lack of organization to achieve change.

C overproduction and low crop prices.

D the threat of attacks by Native Americans.

6 Read the following speech from Comanche chief Ten Bears and use it to answer the question below.

"You said that you wanted to put us upon a reservation, to build us houses and make us medicine lodges [places of religious practice]. I do not want them. I was born upon the prairie, where the wind blew free and there was nothing to break the light of the sun. I was born where there were no enclosures and where everything drew a free breath. I want to die there and not within walls."

—Ten Bears, quoted in *Eyewitnesses and Others*

Document-Based Question **Why does Ten Bears not want to move to a reservation?**

The Industrial Age

 Virginia Standards of Learning

USII.2 The student will use maps, globes, photographs, pictures, or tables for

b) explaining relationships among natural resources, transportation, and industrial development after 1865;

c) locating the 50 states and the cities most significant to the historical development of the United States

USII.4 The student will demonstrate knowledge of how life changed after the Civil War by

d) explaining the impact of new inventions, the rise of big business, the growth of industry, and life on American farms

USII.6 The student will demonstrate knowledge of the social, economic, and technological changes of the early twentieth century by

a) explaining how developments in factory and labor productivity and transportation (including the use of the automobile), communication, and rural electrification changed American life; **b)** describing the social and economic changes that took place, including prohibition, and the Great Migration north and west

FOCUS ON WRITING

A Business Plan You are an inventor in the late 1800s, and you want to start a business to sell your new inventions. Write a business plan for investors that will encourage them to lend you money to start your business. As you read this chapter, gather information about the new business practices that you can use to run your business. Then write your plan. Include information about what you will sell, how you will make it, and how you can avoid conflicts with the workers who make your product.

UNITED STATES

1879
Thomas Edison invents the first lightbulb.

1870

 WORLD

1876
German engineer Nikolaus A. Otto perfects a gasoline-powered engine.

What You Will Learn...

In this chapter you will learn about how the United States became an industrial power in the late 1800s. A new wave of immigrants provided the labor, and the combination of industry and immigration led to increased urbanization of the country. Cities like San Francisco, shown here, began to take the shape that they still have today. In fact, much of what we know as modern America developed during this important period.

1886
The American Federation of Labor is formed on December 8.

1890
Congress passes the Sherman Antitrust Act.

1892
On June 29 the Homestead strike begins. Carnegie Steel Company refuses to negotiate with the union.

1880

1883 The island volcano of Krakatau in the Pacific Ocean erupts in one of the world's greatest natural disasters.

1889
The Eiffel Tower is built in Paris.

1890

1900

1898 French scientists Pierre and Marie Curie discover radium.

Reading Social Studies

by Kylene Beers

Economics | Geography | Politics | Society and Culture | Science and Technology

Focus on Themes In this chapter, you will read about the advancements in transportation and communication made during what is called the Second Industrial Revolution. You will learn about the rise of powerful corporations. You will also read about the workers who organized in the late 1800s and will see what happened as unions began demanding better treatment for workers. Throughout the chapter, you will see how **society** was affected by the changing **economy**.

Organization of Facts and Information

Focus on Reading How are clothes organized in a department store? How are files arranged in a file cabinet? Clear organization helps us find the product we need, and it also helps us find facts and information.

Understanding Structural Patterns Writers use structural patterns to organize information in sentences or paragraphs. What's a structural pattern? It's simply a way of organizing information. Learning to recognize those patterns will make it easier for you to read and understand social studies texts.

Patterns of Organization		
Pattern	**Clue Words**	**Graphic Organizer**
Cause-effect shows how one thing leads to another.	as a result, therefore, because, this led to	Cause → Effect → Effect / Effect
Chronological order shows the sequence of events or actions.	after, before, first, then, not long after, finally	First → Next → Last
Comparison-contrast points out similarities and/or differences.	although, but, however, on the other hand, similarly, also	Differences / Similarities
Listing presents information in categories such as size, location, or importance.	also, most important, for example, in fact	Category • Fact • Fact • Fact

To use text structure to improve your understanding, follow these steps:

1. Look for the main idea of the passage you are reading.
2. Then look for clues that signal a specific pattern.
3. Look for other important ideas and think about how the ideas connect. Is there any obvious pattern?
4. Use a graphic organizer to map the relationships among the facts and details.

You Try It!

The following passages are from the chapter you are about to read. As you read each set of sentences, ask yourself what structural pattern the writer used to organize the information.

Recognizing Structural Patterns

(A) Great advances in communication technologies took place in the late 1800s. By 1861, telegraph wires connected the East and West coasts. Five years later, a telegraph cable on the floor of the Atlantic Ocean connected the United States and Great Britain. *(p. 617)*

(B) Many business leaders justified their business methods through their belief in social Darwinism . . . Other business leaders, however, believed that the rich had a duty to aid the poor. *(p. 621)*

(C) During the late 1800s, several factors led to a decline in the quality of working conditions. Machines run by unskilled workers were eliminating the jobs of many skilled craftspeople. These low-paid workers could be replaced easily. *(p. 624)*

After you read the passages, answer the questions below:

1. Reread passage A. What structural pattern did the writer use to organize this information? How can you tell?

2. Reread passage B. What structural pattern did the writer use to organize this information? How can you tell? Why do you think the writer chose this pattern?

3. Reread passage C. What structural pattern did the writer use to organize this information? How can you tell? Why do you think the writer chose this pattern?

As you read Chapter 19, think about the organization of the ideas. Ask yourself why the writer chose to organize the information in this way.

Key Terms and People

Chapter 19

Section 1
Second Industrial Revolution *(p. 615)*
Bessemer process *(p. 615)*
Thomas Edison *(p. 616)*
patents *(p. 616)*
Alexander Graham Bell *(p. 617)*
Henry Ford *(p. 617)*
Wilbur and Orville Wright *(p. 618)*

Section 2
corporations *(p. 619)*
Andrew Carnegie *(p. 620)*
vertical integration *(p. 620)*
John D. Rockefeller *(p. 620)*
horizontal integration *(p. 621)*
trust *(p. 621)*
Leland Stanford *(p. 621)*
social Darwinism *(p. 621)*
monopoly *(p. 622)*
Sherman Antitrust Act *(p. 622)*

Section 3
Frederick W. Taylor *(p. 624)*
Knights of Labor *(p. 625)*
Terence V. Powderly *(p. 625)*
American Federation of Labor *(p. 625)*
Samuel Gompers *(p. 625)*
collective bargaining *(p. 626)*
Mary Harris Jones *(p. 626)*
Haymarket Riot *(p. 626)*
Homestead strike *(p. 627)*
Pullman strike *(p. 627)*

Academic Vocabulary
In this chapter, you will learn the following academic words:
implement *(p. 617)*
acquire *(p. 620)*

Virginia Standards of Learning USII.1a, USII.1b, USII.1c, USII.2b, USII.4d, USII.6a

What You Will Learn...

Main Ideas

1. Breakthroughs in steel processing led to a boom in railroad construction.
2. Advances in the use of oil and electricity improved communications and transportation.
3. A rush of inventions changed Americans' lives.

The Big Idea

The Second Industrial Revolution led to new sources of power and advances in transportation and communication.

Key Terms and People

Second Industrial Revolution, *p. 615*
Bessemer process, *p. 615*
Thomas Edison, *p. 616*
patents, *p. 616*
Alexander Graham Bell, *p. 617*
Henry Ford, *p. 617*
Wilbur and Orville Wright, *p. 618*

TAKING NOTES As you read this section, take notes on the inventors of the Second Industrial Revolution. Organize your notes in a table like the one below.

Inventor

The Second Industrial Revolution

If YOU were there...

You live in a small town but are visiting an aunt in the city in the 1890s. You are amazed when your aunt pushes a button on the wall to turn on electric lights. At home you still use kerosene lamps. You hear a clatter outside and see an electric streetcar traveling down the street. You are shocked when a telephone rings, and your aunt speaks to someone miles away!

Which of these inventions would you find most amazing?

BUILDING BACKGROUND The first Industrial Revolution in America began in the early 1800s. It changed the way products were made, from handwork to machines. It moved the workplace from cottages to factories. Later, it brought advances in transportation and communication. The Second Industrial Revolution built on these changes, introducing new technology and new sources of power.

Breakthroughs in Steel Processing

Technological advances were important to the **Second Industrial Revolution**, a period of rapid growth in U.S. manufacturing in the late 1800s. By the mid-1890s, the United States had become the world's industrial leader.

The Steel Industry

Some of the most important advances in technology happened in the steel industry. Steel is iron that has been made stronger by heat and the addition of other metals. In the mid-1850s Henry Bessemer invented the **Bessemer process**, a way to manufacture steel quickly and cheaply by blasting hot air through melted iron to quickly remove impurities. Before, turning several tons of iron ore into steel took a day or more. The Bessemer process took only 10 to 20 minutes.

The Bessemer process helped increase steel production. U.S. mills had produced 77,000 tons of steel in 1870. By 1879 production had risen to more than 1 million tons in one year.

Riding the Rails

As steel dropped in price, so did the cost of building railroads. Companies built thousands of miles of new steel track. The design of elegant passenger and sleeping cars improved passenger service. Manufacturers and farmers sent products to market faster than ever by rail in newly invented refrigerated shipping cars. Cities where major rail lines crossed, such as Chicago, grew rapidly. Railroads also increased western growth by offering free tickets to settlers. Finally, as rail travel and shipping increased, railroads and related industries began employing more people.

READING CHECK **Identifying Cause and Effect** How did steel processing change in the 1850s, and how did this affect the United States?

Factors Affecting Industrial Growth
- Greater ability to use natural resources
- A growing population
- Transportation advances
- Rising immigration
- Inventions and innovations
- Increasing business investment
- Government policies assisting business, such as protective tariffs

Homestead Steel Mill

Steel mills like this one in Homestead, Pennsylvania, were the center of the new steel industry that led to advancements in rail travel. Workers used the Bessemer process to make steel more quickly.

How do you think mills like this one affected the surrounding area?

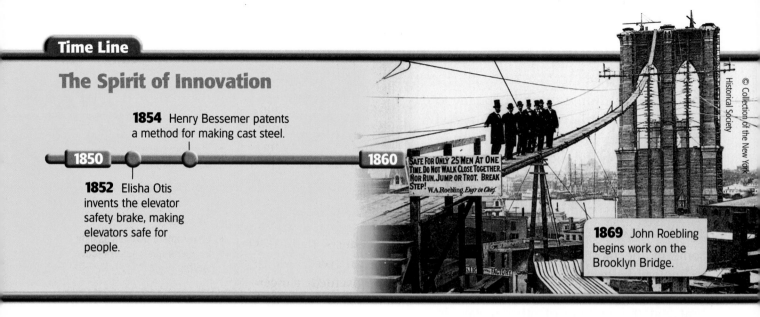

The Spirit of Innovation

1854 Henry Bessemer patents a method for making cast steel.

1850

1852 Elisha Otis invents the elevator safety brake, making elevators safe for people.

1860

SAFE FOR ONLY 25 MEN AT ONE TIME. DO NOT WALK CLOSE TOGETHER, NOR RUN, JUMP, OR TROT. BREAK STEP! W.A.Roebling, Eng'r in Chief.

1869 John Roebling begins work on the Brooklyn Bridge.

© Collection of the New York Historical Society

Use of Oil and Electricity

The Second Industrial Revolution was characterized by dramatic developments in the use and distribution of oil and electricity. These power sources fueled other changes.

Oil as a Power Source

An important technological breakthrough in the late 1800s was the use of petroleum, or oil, as a power source. People had known about oil for many years but had discovered few ways to use it. However, in the 1850s, chemists invented a way to convert crude, or unprocessed, oil into a fuel called kerosene. Kerosene could be used for cooking, heating, and lighting. Suddenly there was a demand for oil.

FOCUS ON READING

How does this paragraph show the cause and effect structure?

As demand grew, people began searching for a reliable source for oil. In 1859 Edwin L. Drake proved that it was possible to pump crude oil from the ground. Soon, wildcatters, or oil prospectors, drilled for oil in Ohio, Pennsylvania, and West Virginia. Oil became a big business as these states began producing millions of barrels per year. Oil companies built refineries to turn the crude oil into finished products like kerosene. One oil company supervisor referred to oil workers as "men who are supplying light for the world."

Electricity Spreads

In addition to kerosene, electricity became a critical source of light and power during the Second Industrial Revolution. The possible uses of electricity interested inventors like **Thomas Edison**. His research center in Menlo Park, New Jersey, was called an invention factory. Edison explained his practical approach to science.

❝I do not regard myself as a pure scientist, as so many persons have insisted that I am. I do not search for the laws of nature … for the purpose of learning truth. I am only a professional inventor … with the object [goal] of inventing that which will have commercial utility [use].❞

—Thomas Edison, quoted in *American Made*, by Harold C. Livesay

Edison eventually held more than 1,000 **patents**, exclusive rights to make or sell inventions. Patents allowed inventors to protect their inventions from being manufactured by others.

In 1878 Edison announced that he would soon invent a practical electric light. By the end of 1879 Edison and his team of inventors had created the electric lightbulb. The public was excited. However, Edison had a problem. At the time, few homes or businesses could get electricity. Edison therefore built a power plant that began supplying electricity to dozens of New York City buildings in

1872 Elijah McCoy receives the patent for his device that oiled machine engines.

1876 Alexander Graham Bell invents the telephone.

1879 Thomas Edison creates a durable electric lightbulb.

1887 Harriet Strong receives a patent for her advances in dam and reservoir construction.

1893 J. Frank and Charles Duryea successfully test their first gasoline-powered automobile.

1870   1880   1890

September 1882. The *New York Times* reported that with electric lighting in the newspaper offices, "it seemed almost like writing by daylight." However, Edison's equipment could not send electricity over long distances. As a result, his power company, Edison Electric, provided electricity mainly to central cities.

In the late 1880s, George Westinghouse built a power system that could send electricity across many miles. As Edison and Westinghouse competed, the use of electricity spread rapidly in the nation's cities. After a while, electricity soon lit homes and businesses and powered city factories. Electricity also was used to power streetcars in cities across the nation.

READING CHECK Drawing Conclusions
Why did people begin to pump oil from the ground?

Rush of Inventions

In the late 1800s, inventors focused on finding solutions to practical problems. Communication and transportation took the lead.

Advances in Communication

Great advances in communication technologies took place in the late 1800s. By 1861, telegraph wires connected the East and West coasts. Five years later, a telegraph cable on the floor of the Atlantic Ocean connected the United States and Great Britain.

However, the telegraph carried only written messages and was difficult for untrained people to use. These problems were solved in March 1876, when inventor **Alexander Graham Bell** patented the telephone. Bell was a Scottish-born speech teacher who studied the science of sound. He called the telephone a "talking telegraph."

Telephone companies raced to lay thousands of miles of phone lines. By 1880 there were about 55,000 telephones in the United States, and by 1900 there were almost 1.5 million.

Automobiles and Planes

In 1876 a German engineer invented an engine powered by gasoline, another fuel made from oil. In 1893 Charles and J. Frank Duryea used a gasoline engine to build the first practical motorcar in the United States. By the early 1900s, thousands of cars were being built in the United States.

At first, only the wealthy could buy these early cars. **Henry Ford** introduced the Model T in 1908. Ford was the first to **implement** the moving assembly line in manufacturing, a process that greatly reduced the cost of building a product, thus making cars more affordable.

THE IMPACT TODAY

AT&T Corporation is a direct descendant of Bell's original company. AT&T pioneered the use of telephone cables across the oceans, satellite communications, and a radar system for the U.S. Defense Department.

ACADEMIC VOCABULARY

implement
to put in place

The Spirit of Innovation

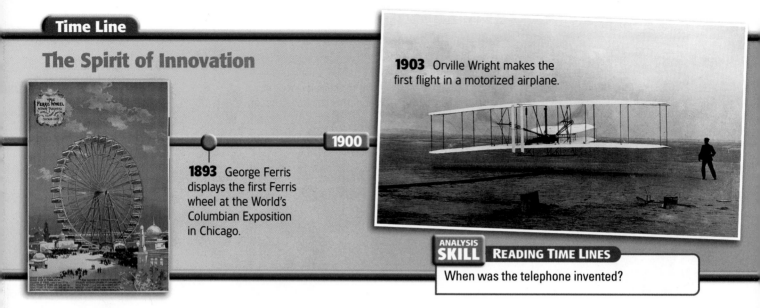

1903 Orville Wright makes the first flight in a motorized airplane.

1893 George Ferris displays the first Ferris wheel at the World's Columbian Exposition in Chicago.

1900

ANALYSIS SKILL **READING TIME LINES**

When was the telephone invented?

New engine technology helped make another breakthrough in transportation possible—air flight. Brothers **Wilbur and Orville Wright** built a lightweight airplane that used a small, gas-powered engine. In Kitty Hawk, North Carolina, Orville Wright made the first piloted flight in a gas-powered plane on December 17, 1903. This invention would change the way that many Americans traveled in the future and would increase the demand for oil production.

READING CHECK **Comparing** What new inventions excited the public in the 1800s, and how were they used?

SUMMARY AND PREVIEW The Second Industrial Revolution led to advances in energy sources, communication, and transportation. In the next section you will learn about the growth of big business.

Section 1 Assessment

go.hrw.com
Online Quiz
KEYWORD: SB7 HP19

Reviewing Ideas, Terms, and People

1. **a. Describe** What was the **Bessemer process**?
   b. Summarize How did improvements to railroads affect the economy and transportation in the United States?
   c. Elaborate What do you think was the most important effect of the Bessemer process? Why?
2. **a. Identify** What is kerosene, and for what could it be used?
   b. Explain What problem did **Thomas Edison** face regarding the use of electricity, and how did he solve it?
3. **a. Recall** What contribution did **Wilbur and Orville Wright** make to transportation?
   b. Draw Conclusions How did **Alexander Graham Bell**'s invention improve life in the United States?
   c. Elaborate Why do you think there was a rush of inventions in the late 1800s?

Critical Thinking

4. **Analyzing** Look over your notes on inventors. Use them to complete a table like the one below about inventors and their inventions.

Inventor	Invention

FOCUS ON WRITING

5. **Information on a Product** In your notes, list what kinds of new products became available at this time. What do you think would be a good thing to make and sell during the late 1800s?

Big Business

If YOU were there...

It is 1895, and your town is home to a large corporation. The company's founder and owner, a wealthy man, lives in a mansion on a hill. He is a fair employer but not especially generous. Many townspeople work in his factory. You and other town leaders feel that he should contribute more to local charities and community organizations.

How could this business leader help the town more?

BUILDING BACKGROUND Advanced technology along with the use of oil and electric power helped American businesses grow. Soon the shape of the American economy changed. Some companies grew so large that they began to dominate entire industries.

Dominance of Big Business

In the late 1800s many entrepreneurs formed their businesses as **corporations**, or businesses that sell portions of ownership called stock shares. The leaders of these corporations were some of the most widely respected members of American society in the late 1800s. Political leaders praised prosperous businesspeople as examples of American hard work, talent, and success.

New sales techniques like those taught by John H. Patterson helped change business practices.

Virginia Standards of Learning USII.1a, USII.1d, USII.2b, USII.4d, USII.6b

What You Will Learn...

Main Ideas

1. The rise of corporations and powerful business leaders led to the dominance of big business in the United States.
2. People and the government began to question the methods of big business.

The Big Idea

The growth of big business in the late 1800s led to the creation of monopolies.

Key Terms and People

corporations, *p. 619*
Andrew Carnegie, *p. 620*
vertical integration, *p. 620*
John D. Rockefeller, *p. 620*
horizontal integration, *p. 621*
trust, *p. 621*
Leland Stanford, *p. 621*
social Darwinism, *p. 621*
monopoly, *p. 622*
Sherman Antitrust Act, *p. 622*

TAKING NOTES As you read this section, take notes on the new business practices you learn about. Keep them organized in a chart like the one below.

New Business Practice

Corporations Generate Wealth

Successful corporations reward not only the people who found them but also investors who hold stock. Stockholders in a corporation typically get a percentage of profits based on the amount of stock they own. Although stockholders actually own the corporation, they do not run its day-to-day business. Instead, they elect a board of directors that chooses the corporation's main leaders, such as the president.

ACADEMIC VOCABULARY
acquire to get

Corporations provided several important advantages over earlier business forms. Stockholders in a corporation are not responsible for business debts. If a corporation fails financially, the stockholders lose only the money that they invested. Stockholders are also usually free to sell their stock to whomever they want, whenever they want. As a result, corporations encouraged more investment in businesses. By 1900 more than 100 million shares per year were being traded on the New York Stock Exchange.

Business Leaders

Countless business leaders became wealthy, powerful, and famous because of the business boom. **Andrew Carnegie** was one of the most admired businesspeople of the time. Born in Scotland, Carnegie came to the United States as a poor immigrant. As a teenager he took a job with a railroad company and quickly worked his way up to the position of railroad superintendent.

In 1873 he focused his efforts on steelmaking. Carnegie expanded his business by buying out competitors when steel prices were low. By 1901 Carnegie's mills were producing more steel than all of Great Britain's mills combined. Carnegie's businesses succeeded largely through **vertical integration**, or ownership of businesses involved in each step of a manufacturing process. For example, to lower production costs, Carnegie **acquired** the iron ore mines, coalfields, and railroads needed to supply and support his steel mills.

John D. Rockefeller was also successful in consolidating, or combining, businesses. By age 21, while a partner in a wholesale business, he decided to start an oil-refining company. In only 10 years Rockefeller's Standard Oil Company was the country's largest oil refiner. Like Carnegie, Rockefeller used ver-

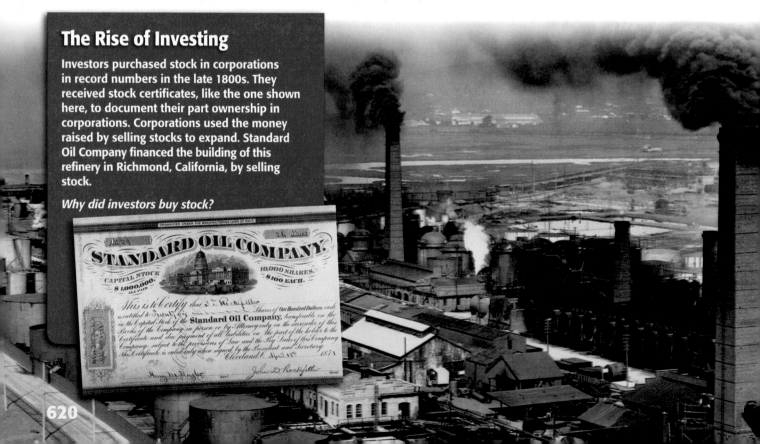

The Rise of Investing

Investors purchased stock in corporations in record numbers in the late 1800s. They received stock certificates, like the one shown here, to document their part ownership in corporations. Corporations used the money raised by selling stocks to expand. Standard Oil Company financed the building of this refinery in Richmond, California, by selling stock.

Why did investors buy stock?

POLITICAL CARTOON
Trusts

The wealth and size of trusts such as Standard Oil made many Americans fear the influence of business leaders over government.

What do you think the smokestacks on the Capitol building represent?

What does the position of the White House suggest?

ANALYSIS SKILL **ANALYZING PRIMARY SOURCES**
How does the cartoonist show Rockefeller's power?

tical integration. For example, the company controlled most of the pipelines it used.

Rockefeller's company also developed **horizontal integration**, or owning all businesses in a certain field. By 1880 Rockefeller's companies controlled about 90 percent of the oil refining business in the United States. Rockefeller also formed a **trust**, a legal arrangement grouping together a number of companies under a single board of directors. To earn more money, trusts often tried to get rid of competition and to control production.

Leland Stanford was another important business leader of the late 1800s. He made a fortune selling equipment to miners. While governor of California, he became one of the founders of the state's Central Pacific railroad. Stanford also founded Stanford University.

Late in life, Stanford argued that industries should be owned and managed cooperatively by workers. He believed this would be the fulfillment of democracy.

READING CHECK Comparing and Contrasting
Why did Andrew Carnegie use vertical integration?

Questioning the Methods of Big Business

By the late 1800s, people and the government were becoming uncomfortable with child labor, low wages, and poor working conditions. They began to view big business as a problem.

Social Darwinism

Many business leaders justified their business methods through their belief in **social Darwinism**, a view of society based on scientist Charles Darwin's theory of natural selection. Social Darwinists thought that Darwin's "survival of the fittest" theory decided which human beings would succeed in business and in life in general.

Other business leaders, however, believed that the rich had a duty to aid the poor. These leaders tried to help the less fortunate through philanthropy, or giving money to charities. Carnegie, Rockefeller, Stanford, and other business leaders gave away large sums. Carnegie gave away more than $350 million to charities, about $60 million of which went to fund public libraries to expand access to books. By the late 1800s, various charities had received millions of dollars from philanthropists.

The Antitrust Movement

Critics of big business said that many business leaders earned their fortunes through unfair business practices. These criticisms grew stronger in the 1880s as corporations became more powerful. Large corporations often used their size and strength to drive smaller competitors out of business. Carnegie and Rockefeller, for example, pressured railroads to charge their companies lower shipping rates. Powerful trusts also arranged to sell goods and services below market value. Smaller competitors went out of business trying to match those prices. Then the trusts raised prices again.

Some people became concerned when a trust gained a **monopoly**, or total ownership of a product or service. Critics argued that monopolies reduced necessary competition. Competition, they believed, kept prices low and the quality of goods and services high.

Some Americans also worried about the political power of wealthy trusts. Union leader John W. Hayes called trusts "the common enemy of society." Many citizens and small businesses wanted the government to help control monopolies and trusts. People who favored trusts responded that trusts were more efficient and gave the consumer dependable products or services.

Many members of Congress favored big business. However, elected officials could not ignore the concerns of voters. In July 1890 Congress passed the **Sherman Antitrust Act**, a law that made it illegal to create monopolies or trusts that restrained trade. It stated that any "attempt to monopolize . . . any part of the trade or commerce among the several States" was a crime. However, the act did not clearly define a trust in legal terms. The antitrust laws were therefore difficult to enforce. Corporations and trusts kept growing in size and power.

READING CHECK **Analyzing** How did concerns about trusts lead to the Sherman Antitrust Act?

SUMMARY AND PREVIEW In the late 1800s some corporations became monopolies that dominated industries such as oil. In the next section you will learn about how industrial workers organized to improve working conditions.

Section 2 Assessment

go.hrw.com
Online Quiz
KEYWORD: SB7 HP19

Reviewing Ideas, Terms, and People

1. **a. Identify** What are **horizontal** and **vertical integration**?
   b. Explain What are the benefits of investing in **corporations**?
   c. Evaluate What do you think about the business methods of **Carnegie**, **Rockefeller**, and **Stanford**?
2. **a. Describe** What is **social Darwinism**?
   b. Summarize What concerns did critics of big business have regarding **trusts**?
   c. Evaluate Was the **Sherman Antitrust Act** successful? Why or why not?

Critical Thinking

3. **Contrasting** Look back over your notes about new business practices. Find examples of the new business practices. Use them to complete a graphic organizer like the one below.

New Practices	Example

FOCUS ON WRITING

4. **Gathering Information on Business** Look back over your notes and determine what new practices helped businesses expand during this time. Which practices could you use to start your business? Where would you try to sell your product?

Andrew Carnegie, John D. Rockefeller, and Leland Stanford

How would you go about building an industry?

Andrew Carnegie (1835–1919) Born in Scotland, Carnegie rose to become a multibillionaire in the steel industry. He brought new technologies to his steel mills and made them extremely efficient. In 1901 he sold Carnegie Steel Company for $250 billion, making him the richest man in the world.

John D. Rockefeller (1839–1937) Rockefeller got his start in the oil business in Cleveland, Ohio. Rockefeller's Standard Oil Company quickly bought out its competitors throughout the United States. To better control oil production and delivery, Rockefeller also bought railroad rights, terminals, and pipelines.

Leland Stanford (1825–1893) Leland Stanford was born to a New York farming family that sent him to excellent private schools. After practicing law in Wisconsin, he made his career in California. Stanford was instrumental in building the western section of the transcontinental railroad. He then plunged into politics, serving one term as governor. His political connections helped him obtain huge state land grants and other benefits for his railroad companies. As president of Central Pacific and Southern Pacific, he oversaw the laying of thousands of miles of track throughout the West.

Why are they so important? Carnegie, Rockefeller, and Stanford helped make America the world's greatest industrial power by the end of the 1800s. They built giant industries that made goods cheaply by keeping workers' wages low. They also engaged in ruthless business practices to defeat their competition and create monopolies. The Sherman Antitrust Act was passed in reaction to the Standard Oil monopoly. Later in life, all three men became philanthropists, people devoted to charity work. Rockefeller's philanthropies gave out $500 million in his lifetime. Carnegie spent $350 million, funding educational grants, concert halls, and nearly 3,000 public libraries. Stanford founded Stanford University in 1884.

Finding Main Ideas
Why are these three men important figures in U.S. history?

Carnegie

Rockefeller Stanford

623

Industrial Workers

Virginia Standards of Learning USII.1b, USII.1i, USII.2b, USII.2c, USII.4d, USII.6a, USII.6b

What You Will Learn...

Main Ideas

1. The desire to maximize profits and become more efficient led to poor working conditions.
2. Workers began to organize and demand improvements in working conditions and pay.
3. Labor strikes often turned violent and failed to accomplish their goals.

The Big Idea

Changes in the workplace led to a rise in labor unions and workers' strikes.

Key Terms and People

Frederick W. Taylor, *p. 624*
Knights of Labor, *p. 625*
Terence V. Powderly, *p. 625*
American Federation of Labor, *p. 625*
Samuel Gompers, *p. 625*
collective bargaining, *p. 626*
Mary Harris Jones, *p. 626*
Haymarket Riot, *p. 626*
Homestead strike, *p. 627*
Pullman strike, *p. 627*

TAKING NOTES As you read this section, take notes about the problems workers faced in the new economy. Organize your notes in a chart like the one below.

Problems of Workers

If YOU were there...

You run a button machine in a clothing factory in the 1890s. You work from 7:00 in the morning until 6:00 at night, every day except Sunday. Your only break is 15 minutes for lunch. Now you hear about a movement to start a workers' union to bargain with your employer. Union members will ask for an eight-hour workday. But you think your employer might fire you if you join.

Would you join the union?

BUILDING BACKGROUND The rise of corporations and the establishment of monopolies gave big business a great deal of power. An antitrust movement arose to try to limit the power of trusts. Workers themselves began to organize and take action against bad working conditions and other problems.

Maximizing Profits and Efficiency

During the late 1800s, several factors led to a decline in the quality of working conditions. Machines run by unskilled workers were eliminating the jobs of many skilled craftspeople. These low-paid workers could be replaced easily. Factories began to focus on specialization, or workers repeating a single step again and again. Specialization brought costs down and caused production to rise. But it also made workers tired, bored, and more likely to be injured. Specialization allowed for Henry Ford's idea of a moving assembly line to speed production. Ford's use of the moving assembly line allowed automobiles to be made more quickly and cheaply. Automobiles soon became available to a wider segment of the population than ever before.

In 1909 **Frederick W. Taylor**, an efficiency engineer, published a popular book called *The Principles of Scientific Management*. He encouraged managers to view workers as interchangeable parts of the production process. In factories, managers influenced by Taylor paid less attention to working conditions. Injuries increased, and as conditions grew worse, workers looked for ways to bring about change.

READING CHECK **Identifying Cause and Effect** Why did companies begin to use scientific management, and how did it affect workers?

Poor Working Conditions

Small, crowded rooms. Stuffy air. Unsafe workplaces. Long hours. Low pay. No job security. These were the facts of working life for millions of Americans during the Second Industrial Revolution.

How did workers respond to these conditions?

Workers Organize

Workers formed labor unions to get better wages and working conditions for all workers in a factory or industry. The first national labor union, the **Knights of Labor**, was founded in the 1870s. It pushed for an eight-hour workday, equal pay for equal work, and an end to child labor. Union members also wanted the government to regulate trusts. Unlike most unions at the time, the Knights included both skilled and unskilled workers. The Knights of Labor was originally organized much like a secret society. In 1879 **Terence V. Powderly** became leader of the Knights. He ended all secrecy, creating the first truly national labor union in the United States.

Another early labor union was the **American Federation of Labor (AFL)**, led by **Samuel Gompers**. Unlike the Knights, the American Federation of Labor organized individual national unions, such as the mineworkers' and steelworkers' unions. The AFL

BIOGRAPHY

Samuel Gompers
1850–1924

Samuel Gompers was born in London. He came to the United States with his parents in 1863 at age 13. He worked as a cigar maker and joined a local union, eventually becoming its president. The Cigarmakers Union was reorganized and later joined the American Federation of Labor. Gompers became the AFL's first president and remained so, except for the year 1895, until his death. He campaigned for basic trade-union rights, such as the right to picket and to organize boycotts and strikes. His efforts on behalf of workers helped organized labor to gain respect.

Summarizing How did Samuel Gompers help the labor-union movement?

Interactive Map

Major Labor Strikes, Late 1800s

CANADA

Union Membership, 1880–1900

(Haymarket Riot) (Pullman Strike)

- Knights of Labor
- American Railway Union
- AFL (Organized in 1886)

1. **Haymarket Riot** In May 1886 the Haymarket Riot erupted between protesters and police in Chicago. It resulted in the decline of the Knights of Labor.

2. **Homestead Strike** In 1892 a strike occurred at Carnegie Steel Company in Homestead, Pennsylvania. The resulting fight left workers and Pinkerton guards dead.

3. **Colorado Miners' Strike** In the summer of 1893, gold miners at Cripple Creek, Colorado, went on strike for higher wages and a shorter workday.

4. **Pullman Strike** The Pullman strike of 1894 began with workers who made Pullman train cars. It soon spread to workers who worked on trains pulling the sleeper cars.

5. **California Railroad Strike** In 1894 railroad workers in Oakland went on strike in the Bay Area's first major strike. Supporting Chicago Pullman workers, they halted passenger, freight, and mail trains for months.

go.hrw.com
Interactive Map
KEYWORD: SB7 CH19

ANALYSIS SKILL **ANALYZING INFORMATION**

How did conflicts between striking workers and authorities affect union membership?

also limited its membership to skilled workers. This gave the union great bargaining power but left out most workers. The AFL tried to get better wages, hours, and working conditions for laborers. By 1890 the AFL's membership was larger than that of the Knights. With **collective bargaining**—all workers acting collectively, or together—workers had a much greater chance of success in negotiating with management. Most employers opposed collective bargaining. One company president said, "I shall never give in. I would rather go out of business."

Many women took active roles in unions. For example, **Mary Harris Jones**, an Irish immigrant, worked for better conditions for miners. A fiery speaker, she organized strikes and helped educate workers.

READING CHECK **Contrasting** How did the Knights of Labor and the AFL differ?

THE IMPACT TODAY

In 1955 the AFL merged with the Congress of Industrial Organizations to become the AFL-CIO. Today the organization has more than 10 million members.

Labor Strikes

By the late 1800s, other unions were gaining strength. Major workers' strikes swept the country and included miners in Colorado, steel workers in Pennsylvania, and railroad workers in Illinois and California. The first major labor strike began in 1886 in Chicago.

In May 1886, thousands of union members in Chicago went on strike because they wanted an eight-hour workday. Two strikers were killed in a fight with police. The next night, workers met at Haymarket Square to protest the killings. In what became known as the **Haymarket Riot**, someone threw a bomb that wounded many police officers and killed eight. The police fired into the crowd, killing several people and wounding 100 others.

Eight people, some of whom were not at the riot, were arrested and convicted of conspiracy. One of them had a Knights of Labor membership card. Though Knights leadership had not supported the strike, several local chapters had. Membership in the Knights fell quickly.

Sometimes, business owners succeeded in breaking up unions. In 1892 a violent strike called the **Homestead strike** took place at Andrew Carnegie's Homestead steel factory in Pennsylvania. Union members there protested a plan to buy new machinery and cut jobs. The company refused to negotiate with the union and locked workers out of the plant. The workers responded by seizing control of the plant. Gunfire erupted on July 6, when Pinkerton detectives—hired by the company to break the union—tried to enter the plant. A fierce battle raged for 14 hours, leaving 16 people dead. The governor called out the state militia to restore order. Continuing for four more months, the union was eventually defeated.

Another major strike happened at George Pullman's Pullman Palace Car Company in the company town of Pullman, Illinois. Most of the company workers lived there, paying high rents. During a financial depression that began in 1893, Pullman laid off about half of the workers and cut pay for those that were left, without lowering their rents. On May 11, 1894, workers began the **Pullman strike**, which stopped traffic on many railroad lines until federal courts ordered the workers to return to their jobs. President Grover Cleveland sent federal troops to Chicago to stop the strike. Such defeats seriously damaged the labor movement for years.

READING CHECK **Analyzing** What were the effects of early major strikes on workers?

SUMMARY AND PREVIEW Workers formed unions to fight for better conditions and to keep their jobs. In the next section, you will learn about a new wave of immigrants in the late 1800s.

go.hrw.com
Online Quiz
KEYWORD: SB7 HP19

Section 3 Assessment

Reviewing Ideas, Terms, and People

1. **a. Recall** Why did conditions in factories begin to decline?
   b. Draw Conclusions How were workers affected by specialization and scientific management?
   c. Evaluate Do you think scientific management made businesses more successful? Explain.
2. **a. Identify** What role did **Mary Harris Jones** play in the labor movement?
   b. Analyze Why did workers demand **collective bargaining**, and why did business owners oppose it?
   c. Elaborate Do you think the demands made by labor unions were reasonable? Explain your answer.
3. **a. Describe** What major labor strikes took place in the late 1800s?
   b. Evaluate Do you think President Cleveland was right to use federal troops to end the **Pullman strike**? Explain.

Critical Thinking

4. **Analyzing** Review your notes about the problems workers faced. Use them to complete a table like the one below about how workers tried to solve the problems they faced.

Problem	Solution

FOCUS ON WRITING

5. **Taking Notes on Working Conditions** In your notebook, list some reasons why industrial workers were unhappy with working conditions. Can you think of ways to run your business so that you can avoid the problem of strikes?

Social Studies Skills

Analysis | Critical Thinking | Civic Participation | Study

Analyzing Costs and Benefits

Define the Skill

Everything you do has both costs and benefits connected to it. *Benefits* are things that you gain from something. *Costs* are what you give up to obtain benefits. For example, if you buy a video game, the benefits of your action include the game itself and the enjoyment of playing it. The most clear cost is what you pay for the game. However, there are other costs that do not involve money. One is the time you spend playing the game. This is a cost because you give up something else, such as doing your homework or watching a TV show, when you choose to play the game.

The ability to analyze costs and benefits is a valuable life skill as well as a useful tool in the study of history. Weighing an action's benefits against its costs can help you decide whether or not to take it.

Learn the Skill

Analyzing the costs and benefits of historical events will help you to better understand and evaluate them. Follow these guidelines to do a cost-benefit analysis of an action or decision in history.

1. First determine what the action or decision was trying to accomplish. This step is needed in order to determine which of its effects were benefits and which were costs.

2. Then look for the positive or successful results of the action or decision. These are its benefits.

3. Consider the negative or unsuccessful effects of the action or decision. Also think about what positive things would have happened if it had *not* occurred. All these things are its costs.

4. Making a chart of the costs and benefits can be useful. By comparing the list of benefits to the list of costs you can better understand the action or decision and evaluate it.

For example, you learned in Chapter 19 about the Second Industrial Revolution and its effects on the American economy. A cost-benefit analysis of the changes in American businesses might produce a chart like this one:

Benefits	Costs
New inventions made life easier.	New business methods ran smaller companies out of business.
Communication became easier with new technologies.	Workers received lower wages.
Efficient management reduced costs of products.	Strikes resulted in violence and deaths.
Workers began to organize for better conditions.	

Based on this chart, one might conclude that the Second Industrial Revolution was beneficial to the nation's economy.

Practice the Skill

Among the changes that occurred in the early 1900s was an increase in specialization and efficiency in the workplace. Use information from the chapter and the guidelines above to do a cost-benefit analysis of this development. Then write a paragraph explaining whether or not it was a wise one.

Chapter Review

HOLT

History's Impact
▶ video series
Review the video to answer the closing question:
What advantages and disadvantages did the assembly line create? Do you think assembly lines still exist today?

Visual Summary

Use the visual summary below to help you review the main ideas of the chapter.

Inventions
• Bessemer process
• Lightbulb
• Automobile

Big Business
• Growth of corporations
• Wealthy business owners
• Antitrust movements

Labor Movement
• Knights of Labor
• American Federation of Labor
• Haymarket Riot
• Homestead Strike

Reviewing Vocabulary, Terms, and People

Identify the descriptions below with the correct term or person from the chapter.

1. Labor organization that represented both skilled and unskilled laborers and was the first national labor union in the United States

2. Inventor who patented the telephone in 1876

3. A way of making steel quickly and cheaply by blasting hot air through melted iron to quickly remove waste

4. A system of business in which one company owns businesses in each step of the manufacturing process

5. Powerful business leader who helped to found the Central Pacific Railroad

6. Union speaker who worked to better the lives of mine workers

7. A method of negotiating for better wages or working conditions in which all workers act together to ensure a better chance for success

Comprehension and Critical Thinking

SECTION 1 *(Pages 614–618)*

8. **a. Identify** What was the Second Industrial Revolution?

   b. Draw Conclusions Why were advances in transportation and communication important to the Second Industrial Revolution?

   c. Elaborate Which invention do you think had the greatest effect on people's lives in the late 1800s? Explain your answer.

SECTION 2 *(Pages 619–622)*

9. **a. Recall** What criticisms were made of business leaders and trusts?

   b. Analyze How did the rise of corporations and powerful business leaders lead to the growth of big business?

   c. Evaluate Do you think the growth of big business helped or hurt ordinary Americans? Explain your answer.

SECTION 3 *(Pages 624–627)*

10. a. Recall What led to poor working conditions in factories during the Second Industrial Revolution?

b. Make Inferences Why did labor unions have a better chance of improving working conditions than laborers did on their own?

c. Evaluate Did the strikes of the 1880s and 1890s hurt or help the labor movement in the long run? Explain your answer.

Reviewing Themes

11. Economics How did the rise of big business affect consumers in the United States?

12. Society and Culture What changes in society were brought about by the organization of labor?

Using the Internet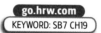

go.hrw.com
KEYWORD: SB7 CH19

13. Activity: Creating a Time Line Technology in some sense has been part of human history since we began to write history. All tools are, in a sense, technology. In this chapter you read about new scientific discoveries that had positive and negative effects. Enter the activity keyword. Then choose one technological innovation mentioned in the chapter and trace its development to the present day. Create an illustrated time line to present your research.

Reading Skills

Organization of Facts and Information *Use the Reading Skills taught in this chapter to answer the question about the reading selection below.*

> Corporations provided several important advantages over earlier business forms. Stockholders in a corporation are not responsible for business debts. If a corporation fails financially, the stockholders lose only the money that they invested. Stockholders are also usually free to sell their stock to whomever they want, whenever they want. *(p. 620)*

14. By which structural pattern is the above passage organized?

a. Listing

b. Cause-effect

c. Chronological order

d. Comparison-contrast

Social Studies Skills

Analyzing Costs and Benefits *Use the Social Studies Skills taught in this chapter to answer the question below.*

15. Write two costs and two benefits of the Pullman strike from the point of view of the workers who participated.

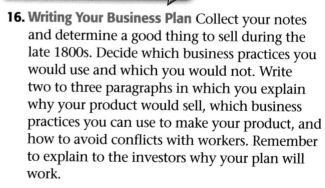

FOCUS ON WRITING

16. Writing Your Business Plan Collect your notes and determine a good thing to sell during the late 1800s. Decide which business practices you would use and which you would not. Write two to three paragraphs in which you explain why your product would sell, which business practices you can use to make your product, and how to avoid conflicts with workers. Remember to explain to the investors why your plan will work.

DIRECTIONS: Read each question and write the letter of the best response. Use the map below to answer question 1.

1

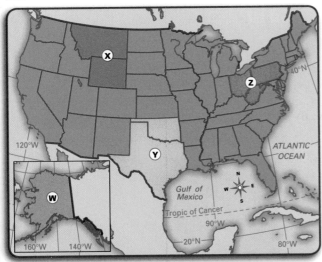

Which area on the map provided the petroleum for the oil-refining industry that arose in the United States in the mid- to late 1800s?

A the area labeled W

B the area labeled X

C the area labeled Y

D the area labeled Z

2 **The person *most* responsible for making the steel industry a big business in the United States is**

A John D. Rockefeller.

B Andrew Carnegie.

C Henry Bessemer.

D Leland Stanford.

3 **The exclusive right to make or sell an invention or product is called**

A a corporation.

B a patent.

C vertical integration.

D a trust.

4 **The development of corporations in America was helped by**

A suburbs.

B vertical integration.

C the Sherman Antitrust Act.

D social Darwinism.

5 **Which of the following was an inventor of the late 1800s?**

A Andrew Carnegie

B Thomas Edison

C Leland Stanford

D John D. Rockefeller

6 **One cause of labor strikes in the late 1800s was that workers sought**

A shorter workdays.

B vertical integration.

C social Darwinism.

D lower wages.

7 **Read the following excerpt from the 1889 book *Recent Economic Changes* and use it to answer the question below.**

> *"Machinery is now recognized as essential to cheap production. Nobody can produce effectively and economically without it, and what was formerly known as domestic manfacture is now almost obsolete. But machinery is one of the most expensive of all products, and its extensive purchase and use require an amount of capital far beyond the capacity [ability] of the ordinary individual to furnish."*
>
> —David Wells, quoted in *Voices of the American Past*

Document-Based Question **How might the large amounts of money needed for machinery affect the future of business?**

Immigrants and Urban Life

Virginia Standards of Learning

USII.1 The student will demonstrate skills for historical and geographical analysis, and responsible citizenship, including the ability to

  a) analyze and interpret primary and secondary source documents to increase understanding of events and life in United States history from 1865 to the present; **b)** make connections between past and present; **c)** sequence events in United States history from 1865 to the present; **d)** interpret ideas and events from different historical perspectives; **e)** evaluate and debate issues orally and in writing

USII.4 The student will demonstrate knowledge of how life changed after the Civil War by

  b) explaining the reasons for the increase in immigration, growth of cities, new inventions, and challenges arising from this expansion

USII.6 The student will demonstrate knowledge of the social, economic, and technological changes of the early twentieth century by

  b) describing the social and economic changes that took place, including prohibition, and the Great Migration north and west

FOCUS ON WRITING

A Memo You are a writer at a television network, and you have an idea for a TV drama series set in the late 1800s. Draft a memo telling your boss about your story idea. As you read this chapter, gather information about the people, places, and events of this time period. Tell about the cast of characters, the setting, and the basic plot of your series.

UNITED STATES

1873 Olmsted designs the U.S. Capitol grounds.

1876 The Centennial Exposition opens in Philadelphia.

1870

WORLD

1878 Electric streetlights are introduced in London.

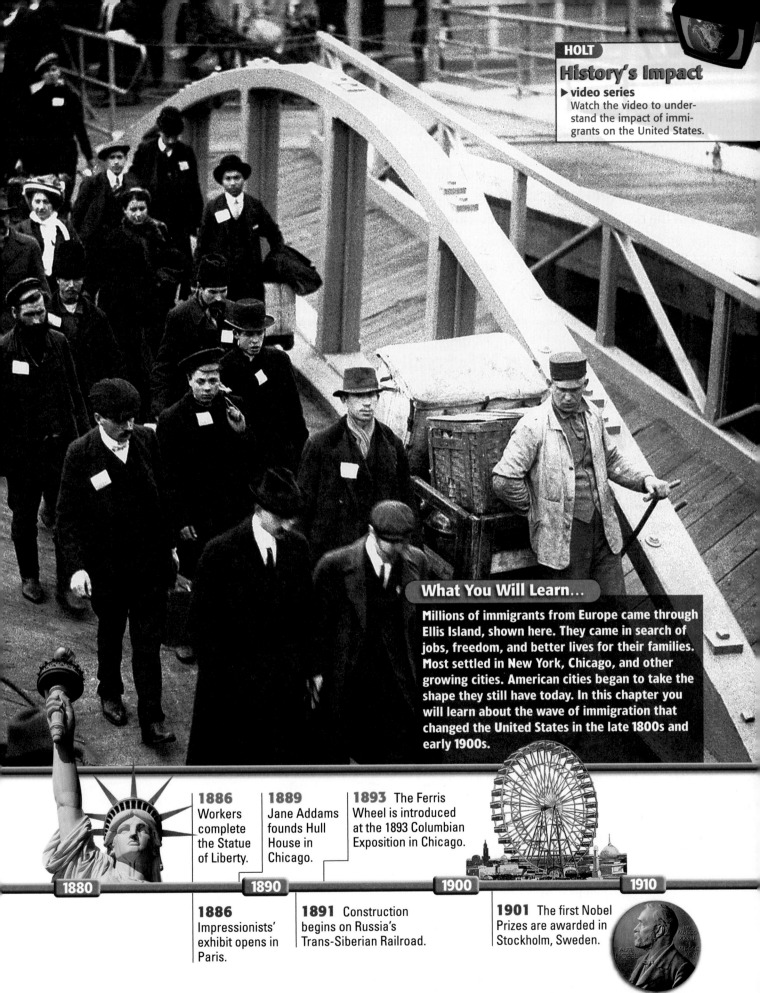

What You Will Learn...

Millions of immigrants from Europe came through Ellis Island, shown here. They came in search of jobs, freedom, and better lives for their families. Most settled in New York, Chicago, and other growing cities. American cities began to take the shape they still have today. In this chapter you will learn about the wave of immigration that changed the United States in the late 1800s and early 1900s.

1886 Workers complete the Statue of Liberty.

1889 Jane Addams founds Hull House in Chicago.

1893 The Ferris Wheel is introduced at the 1893 Columbian Exposition in Chicago.

1880

1890

1900

1910

1886 Impressionists' exhibit opens in Paris.

1891 Construction begins on Russia's Trans-Siberian Railroad.

1901 The first Nobel Prizes are awarded in Stockholm, Sweden.

Reading Social Studies

Economics	Geography	Politics	Society and Culture	Science and Technology

Focus on Themes In this chapter, you will read about the changes in **society and culture** in the late 1800s. Among these changes was an increase in immigration. New immigrants to America found a society full of **economic** opportunities and hardships. Immigration and technology combined to change the way of life in cities.

Understanding Historical Fact versus Historical Fiction

Focus on Reading When you read a book like *The Red Badge of Courage* or see a movie about World War II, do you ever wonder how much is fiction and how much is fact?

Distinguishing Fact from Fiction Historical fiction gives readers a chance to meet real historical people and real historical events in the framework of a made-up story. Some of what you read in historical fiction could be verified in an encyclopedia, but other parts existed only in the author's mind until he or she put it on paper. As a good reader of history, you should know the difference between facts, which can be proved or verified, and fiction.

Notice how one reader determined which details could be verified or proved.

That was a *woman filling her pail by the hydrant* you just bumped against. The *sinks are in the hallway,* that all the tenants may have access—and all be poisoned alike by their summer stenches. Hear the pump squeak! It is the lullaby of tenement house babes. In summer, when *a thousand thirsty throats pant for a cooling drink in this block,* it is worked in vain ...
— From *How the Other Half Lives,* by Jacob Riis

> The woman filling her pail isn't a fact I can check. He's just using her as an example of what women did.

> We could probably check city records to see whether the buildings really had sinks in the hallways.

> The writer is generalizing here. We probably can't prove 1,000 thirsty throats. We could find out whether the city's water pumps actually went dry in the summer. That's verifiable.

VA **Virginia Standards of Learning**

Reading 7.6d Identify the source, viewpoint, and purpose of texts.

Key Terms and People

Chapter 20

Section 1

old immigrants *(p. 636)*
new immigrants *(p. 636)*
steerage *(p. 637)*
benevolent societies *(p. 639)*
tenements *(p. 639)*
sweatshops *(p. 640)*
Chinese Exclusion Act *(p. 641)*

Section 2

mass transit *(p. 644)*
suburbs *(p. 644)*
mass culture *(p. 644)*
Joseph Pulitzer *(p. 645)*
William Randolph Hearst *(p. 645)*
department stores *(p. 645)*
Frederick Law Olmsted *(p. 645)*

Section 3

Jacob Riis *(p. 646)*
settlement houses *(p. 648)*
Jane Addams *(p. 648)*
Hull House *(p. 648)*
Florence Kelley *(p. 648)*

Academic Vocabulary

advocate *(p. 641)*
factor *(p. 643)*

You Try It!

The following passage is from *Bread Givers* by Anzia Yezierska, a young immigrant to New York. After you read it, answer the questions below.

> Mashah [Anzia's sister] came home with stories that in rich people's homes they had silver knives and forks, separate, for each person. And new-ironed tablecloths and napkins every time they ate on them. And rich people had marble bathtubs in their own houses, with running hot and cold water all day and night long so they could take a bath any time they felt like it, instead of having to stand on a line before the public bath-house, as we had to do when we wanted a bath for the holidays. But these millionaire things were so far over our heads that they were like fairy tales.
>
> That time when Mashah had work hemming towels in an uptown house, she came home with another new-rich idea, another money-spending thing, which she said she had to have. She told us that by those Americans, everybody in the family had a toothbrush and a separate towel for himself.
>
> —Anzia Yezierska, *Bread Givers*

1. Which facts from the paragraph above can be confirmed?

2. What sources might you check to confirm some of these facts?

3. List two things from the passage that could not be confirmed.

4. Why are these two things not able to be confirmed?

As you read Chapter 20, notice which facts you could easily confirm.

IMMIGRANTS AND URBAN LIFE **635**

A New Wave of Immigration

 Virginia Standards of Learning USII.1a, USII.1b, USII.4b, USII.6b

What You Will Learn...

Main Ideas

1. U.S. immigration patterns changed during the late 1800s as new immigrants arrived from Europe, Asia, and Mexico.
2. Immigrants worked hard to adjust to life in the United States.
3. Some Americans opposed immigration and worked to restrict it.

The Big Idea

A new wave of immigration in the late 1800s brought large numbers of immigrants to the United States.

Key Terms and People

old immigrants, *p. 636*
new immigrants, *p. 636*
steerage, *p. 637*
benevolent societies, *p. 639*
tenements, *p. 639*
sweatshops, *p. 640*
Chinese Exclusion Act, *p. 641*

TAKING NOTES As you read, look for information about new immigrants' lives in the United States. Take notes on the benefits and challenges immigrants found. Use a diagram like the one below.

Benefits   Challenges

If YOU were there...

You live with your family on a small farm in Italy in the 1890s. You want to earn some money to help your parents, but there are not many jobs nearby. You have heard that jobs are easy to find in the booming factories of the United States. But you speak no English and know no one in America.

Would you travel to the United States in search of new opportunities?

BUILDING BACKGROUND From its beginnings, America has attracted people from many parts of the world. They came for many reasons, including land, religious freedom, and the chance to start new lives. In the late 1800s, jobs created by the rapid growth of the U.S. economy drew millions of new immigrants.

Changing Patterns of Immigration

Millions of immigrants came to the United States from northern Europe in the mid-1800s. They came mainly from Great Britain, Germany, Ireland, and the countries of Scandinavia. Except for the Irish, who were Roman Catholics, most were Protestants. Many were skilled workers. Others settled in rural areas and became farmers. By the late 1800s immigrants from northern Europe were known as **old immigrants**. A newer and larger wave of immigration—from different parts of the world—was arriving in the United States.

New Immigrants

During the 1880s more than 5 million immigrants arrived in the United States—about the same number of people as had arrived during the six decades from 1800 to 1860 combined. The majority of these **new immigrants** were from southern and eastern Europe. Thousands of Czechs, Greeks, Hungarians, Italians, Poles, Russians, and Slovaks came to the United States to find new opportunities and better lives. A young woman from Russia spoke for many of her fellow immigrants when she said she hoped "for all manner of miracles in a strange, wonderful land!"

New immigrants came from many different cultural and religious backgrounds. They included Orthodox Christians, Roman Catholics, and Jews. Some were escaping political or religious persecution. They were eager for the job opportunities created by the U.S. industrial boom of the late 1800s.

Arriving in a New Land

Immigrants usually faced a difficult journey by ship to America. Most traveled in **steerage**— an area below a ship's deck where steering mechanisms were located. Steerage tickets were inexpensive, but the cabins were hot, cramped, and foul-smelling. Many passengers were seasick for the entire journey. Some even died of diseases contracted along the way.

Once in the United States, new arrivals were processed through government-run immigration centers. The busiest center on the East Coast was Ellis Island, which opened in New York Harbor in 1892. The first immigrant processed through Ellis Island was Annie Moore Schayer, a 14 year old from Ireland. Over the next 40 years, millions of European immigrants came through Ellis Island.

At immigration centers officials interviewed and examined immigrants to decide whether to let them enter the country. People with contagious diseases or legal problems could be turned away. "There was this terrible anxiety that one of us might be rejected," remembered one immigrant traveling with his family. "And if one of us was, what would the rest of the family do?" This rarely happened, however. Less than 2 percent of the people who arrived at Ellis Island were not allowed into the country.

On the West Coast, many Chinese immigrants entered the United States through Angel Island, which opened near San Francisco in 1910. Because laws limited immigration from China, only people whose fathers were

U.S. citizens were allowed into the country. Chinese immigrants were often kept at Angel Island for weeks or months while officials investigated their families.

Mexican immigrants also came to the United States in large numbers in the late 1800s. The main processing center for immigrants from Mexico was in El Paso, Texas. Most settled in the Southwest. They found work in construction, steel mills, and mines, and on large commercial farms.

READING CHECK **Contrasting** How was the experience of immigrants at Ellis Island different from that of immigrants at Angel Island?

THE IMPACT TODAY

Almost half of all Americans today are related to someone who passed through Ellis Island. Visitors can now research their family origins at the Ellis Island Immigration Museum.

ASIA

NORTH AMERICA

PACIFIC OCEAN

40°N

San Francisco

New York City

El Paso

Equator

160°W

SOUTH AMERICA

In this photo, Japanese men and Chinese women leave the detention center on Angel Island in San Francisco Bay. Angel Island was the processing center for many immigrants from Asia.

Augustin and Maria Lozano and their two children are shown after moving from Mexico to California. Many Mexican immigrants moved into the Southwest.

Adjusting to a New Life

Once they entered the United States, immigrants began the hard work of adjusting to life in a new country. They needed to find homes and jobs. They had to learn a new language and get used to new customs. This was all part of building a new life.

FOCUS ON READING

How could you verify the facts in this paragraph?

Immigrant Neighborhoods

Many immigrants moved into neighborhoods with others from the same country. In these neighborhoods, they could speak their native language and eat foods that reminded them of home. Immigrants could also practice the customs that their families had passed down from generation to generation. An Italian immigrant remembered that in his new neighborhood, "cheeses from Italy, sausage, salamis were all hanging in the window."

In their newly adopted neighborhoods, many immigrant groups published newspapers in their own languages. They founded schools, clubs, and places of worship to help preserve their customs. In New York City, for example, Jewish immigrants founded a theater that gave performances in Yiddish—the language spoken by Jews from central and eastern Europe.

Immigrants often opened local shops and small neighborhood banks. Business owners helped new arrivals by offering credit and giving small loans. Such aid was important for newcomers because there were few commercial banks in immigrant neighborhoods. In 1904 Italian immigrant Amadeo Peter Giannini started the Bank of Italy in San Francisco. This bank later grew and became the Bank of America.

Shifting Patterns of Immigration

Where Immigrants Came From, 1840–1860
1%
1%
2%
3%
93%

Where Immigrants Came From, 1880–1900
.5%
1.5%
6%
61%
31%

- ■ Northern and western Europe
- ■ Eastern and southern Europe
- ■ North and South America
- ■ Asia
- ■ All other areas

EUROPE

AFRICA

Swedish immigrant Swan August Swanson followed his father to Wisconsin to help with the family farm. Like many new Americans, he married within the immigrant community.

The son of Italian immigrants, Amadeo Peter Giannini founded the Bank of Italy in San Francisco in 1904. Due to his guidance and perseverance, it became the largest privately owned bank in the world.

During the late 1800s the places people came from began to change. The charts above show the percentages of people who moved from different places. The total number of immigrants reached a peak in the 1880s, when about 5 million people came to the United States.

By how much did the percentage of immigrants from northern and western Europe change from 1840 to 1900?

Some immigrant communities formed **benevolent societies**. These aid organizations offered immigrants help in cases of sickness, unemployment, or death. At that time, few national government agencies provided such aid.

Even with neighborhood support, however, immigrants often found city life difficult. Many immigrants lived in **tenements**—poorly built, overcrowded apartment buildings. One young woman in New York City described the difference between her hopes and reality in the new land:

" [I dreamed] of the golden stairs leading to the top of the American palace where father was supposed to live. [I] went 'home' to … an ugly old tenement in the heart of the Lower East Side. There were stairs to climb but they were not golden."
– Miriam Shomer Zusner, *Yesterday: A Memoir of a Russian Jewish Family*

Immigrants worked hard to adjust to their new country. Children often learned American customs more quickly than their parents. In public schools immigrant children learned English from McGuffey's Readers—illustrated textbooks that taught reading and writing.

Finding Work

Many new immigrants had worked on farms in their homelands. Few could afford to buy land in the United States, however. Instead, they found jobs in cities, where most of the country's manufacturing took place.

Having come from rural areas, few new immigrants were skilled in modern manufacturing or industrial work. They often had no choice but to take low-paying, unskilled jobs in garment factories, steel mills, or construction. Long hours were common.

Not all industrial labor took place in large factories. Some immigrants worked for little pay in small shops or mills located in their own neighborhoods. Often associated with the clothing industry, these workplaces were called **sweatshops** because of long hours and hot, unhealthy working conditions. One young immigrant worker remembered:

"When the shirtwaists were finished at the machine ... we were given scissors to cut the threads off. It wasn't heavy work, but it was monotonous [boring], because you did the same thing from seven-thirty in the morning till nine at night."

– Pauline Newman, quoted in *American Mosaic: The Immigrant Experience in the Words of Those Who Lived It*, by Joan Morrison and Charlotte Fox Zabusky

Immigrants with skills that were in demand sometimes found work outside factories and sweatshops. For example, some immigrants worked as bakers, carpenters, masons, or skilled machinists. Others saved or borrowed money to open small businesses such as laundries, barbershops, or street vending carts. New immigrants often opened the same types of businesses in which other immigrants from the same country were already succeeding. They worked hard for long hours to become successful themselves.

READING CHECK **Summarizing** How did new immigrants help themselves and others to try to make successful lives in the United States?

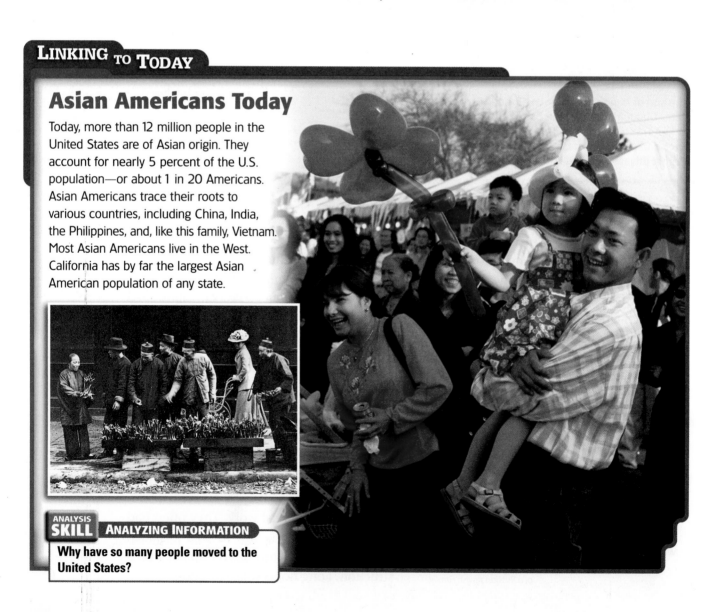

LINKING TO TODAY

Asian Americans Today

Today, more than 12 million people in the United States are of Asian origin. They account for nearly 5 percent of the U.S. population—or about 1 in 20 Americans. Asian Americans trace their roots to various countries, including China, India, the Philippines, and, like this family, Vietnam. Most Asian Americans live in the West. California has by far the largest Asian American population of any state.

ANALYSIS SKILL **ANALYZING INFORMATION**

Why have so many people moved to the United States?

Opposition to Immigration

Some Americans welcomed new immigrants. Many business leaders, for example, wanted immigrant workers who were willing to work for low pay. In general, however, anti-immigrant feelings grew along with the rise in immigration in the late 1800s. Some labor unions opposed immigration because their members believed immigrants would take jobs away from native-born Americans.

Other Americans called nativists also feared that too many new immigrants were being allowed into the country. Many nativists held racial and ethnic prejudices. They thought that the new immigrants would not learn American customs, which might harm American society.

Some nativists were violent toward immigrants. Others **advocated** laws to stop or limit immigration. For example, in 1880 about 105,000 Chinese immigrants lived in the United States. Two years later, Congress passed the **Chinese Exclusion Act**, banning Chinese people from immigrating to the United States for 10 years. This law marked the first time a nationality was banned from entering the country. Although the law violated treaties with China, Congress continued to renew the law for decades to come. In 1892 another law was passed restricting convicts, immigrants with certain diseases, and those likely to need public assistance from entering the country.

Despite such opposition immigrants continued to arrive in large numbers. They worked for low pay in factories and built buildings, highways, and railroads. Their labor helped power the continuing industrial growth of the late 1800s and early 1900s. Although they did not always achieve their dreams as quickly as they had hoped, most immigrants were still confident about the future for themselves and their families in the United States. An immigrant from Russia named Abraham Hyman expressed this idea, saying, "Your feeling is that a better time is coming, if not for yourself, for your families, for your children."

READING CHECK **Analyzing** Why did nativists oppose immigration?

ACADEMIC VOCABULARY
advocate to plead in favor of

SUMMARY AND PREVIEW Immigrants helped build the nation's economy and cities, but they met resistance from some native-born Americans. In the next section you will learn about what life was like in urban America.

Section 1 Assessment

go.hrw.com
Online Quiz
KEYWORD: SB7 HP20

Reviewing Ideas, Terms, and People

1. a. **Identify** What was Ellis Island?
   b. **Contrast** What differences existed between the **old immigrants** and the **new immigrants**?
2. a. **Identify** What job opportunities were available to new immigrants?
   b. **Summarize** How did immigrants attempt to adapt to their new lives in the United States?
   c. **Elaborate** Why do you think many immigrants tolerated difficult living and working conditions?
3. a. **Recall** What was the purpose of the **Chinese Exclusion Act**?
   b. **Explain** Why did some labor unions oppose immigration?
   c. **Predict** How might the growing opposition to immigration lead to problems in the United States?

Critical Thinking

4. **Categorizing** Review your notes on the benefits and challenges new U.S. immigrants faced. Then use the following graphic organizer to categorize the challenges into different areas of life.

Education:

Challenges faced by new immigrants

Culture:

Work:

Living Conditions:

FOCUS ON WRITING

5. **Writing about Immigrants and Their Lives** Make a list of potential characters for your TV series, and be sure to include new immigrants. Take notes about what life was like for them.

The Growth of Cities

Virginia Standards of Learning USII.1a, USII.1b, USII.4b, USII.6b

What You Will Learn...

Main Ideas

1. Both immigrants and native-born Americans moved to growing urban areas in record numbers in the late 1800s and early 1900s.
2. New technology and ideas helped cities change and adapt to rapid population growth.

The Big Idea

American cities experienced dramatic expansion and change in the late 1800s.

Key Terms and People

mass transit, *p. 644*
suburbs, *p. 644*
mass culture, *p. 644*
Joseph Pulitzer, *p. 645*
William Randolph Hearst, *p. 645*
department stores, *p. 645*
Frederick Law Olmsted, *p. 645*

TAKING NOTES As you read, take notes on the causes of the growth of cities.

Causes → Growth of Cities

If YOU were there...

The year is 1905 and you have just come to the city of Chicago from the small town where you grew up. People rush past as you stop to stare up at the skyscrapers. Elevated trains roar overhead, and electric streetcars clatter along streets already crowded with pushcarts and horse-drawn wagons.

Will you stay and look for work in this big city?

BUILDING BACKGROUND Industrial growth and a new wave of immigration swelled the populations of American cities in the late 1800s. Cities changed quickly to accommodate so many new people, offering urban residents excitement and new kinds of entertainment.

Growth of Urban Areas

In 1850 New York City was the only U.S. city with a population of more than 500,000. By 1900 New York City, Chicago, Philadelphia, St. Louis, Boston, and Baltimore all had more than half a million residents. More than 35 U.S. cities had populations greater than 100,000. About 40 percent of Americans now lived in urban areas.

As you have read, new immigrants were responsible for a lot of this urban growth. So were families from rural areas in the United States. As farm equipment replaced workers in the countryside, large numbers of rural residents moved to the cities in search of work. African Americans from the rural South also began moving to northern cities in the 1890s. They hoped to escape discrimination and find better educational and economic opportunities. Cities such as Chicago; Cleveland, Ohio; Detroit, Michigan; and New York saw large increases in their African American populations during the late 1800s and early 1900s.

Perhaps the most dramatic example of urban growth was the rise of Chicago. The city's population exploded from 30,000 in 1850 to 1.7 million in 1900. Chicago passed St. Louis as the

POSTCARD
Chicago, 1900

Postcards like this one were one way people shared the experience of visiting or living in a big city like Chicago. This scene shows a bustling street corner at which modern transportation like streetcars mingle with horse-drawn carts.

Streetcars move large numbers of people through the crowded cities.

ANALYSIS SKILL **ANALYZING PRIMARY SOURCES**

What changes does this picture show taking place in cities at the time?

Population Growth of Chicago, 1870–1900

biggest city in the Midwest. Along with the large numbers of African Americans moving to the city, many of Chicago's new residents were immigrants from southern and eastern Europe. In 1900 immigrants and their children made up three quarters of Chicago's population.

Chicago's location was another **factor** in its rapid growth. Many of the new railroad lines connecting the East and West coasts ran through Chicago. This put Chicago at the heart of the nation's trade in lumber, grain, and meat. Thousands of new Chicago residents found work in the city's huge slaughterhouses and meatpacking plants. Here, meat from the West and Midwest was packed into refrigerated train cars and shipped to the growing cities of the East, where it could be sold in shops to customers.

READING CHECK Identifying Cause and Effect

What factors led to massive population growth in urban areas during the late 1800s and early 1900s?

Changing Cities

American cities such as Chicago were ill-prepared for the rapid urban growth of the late 1800s and early 1900s. Where was everyone going to live? How were people going to get from home to work on crowded city streets? Several new technologies helped cities meet these challenges. These technologies forever changed the look and function of U.S. cities.

Building Skyscrapers

With so many people moving to urban areas, cities quickly ran out of building space in downtown areas. One solution would be to build taller buildings. Typical city buildings in the mid-1800s were only five stories tall, but taller structures were impossible to construct because the building materials available were either too weak or too heavy.

This changed with the rise of the American steel industry in the late 1800s.

ACADEMIC VOCABULARY

factor cause

Mills began producing tons of strong and inexpensive steel. Soon, architects such as Louis Sullivan of Chicago began designing multistory buildings called skyscrapers. Architects used steel beams to make sturdy frames that could support the weight of tall buildings. This allowed builders to use limited city space more efficiently.

The safety elevator, patented by Elisha Otis in the 1850s, helped make skyscrapers practical. Previous elevators had been unsafe because they would crash to the ground if the elevator cable snapped. Otis's safety elevator included a device to hold the elevator in place if the cable broke.

Getting Around

Taller buildings made it possible for more people to live and work in city centers. This increased the need for **mass transit**, or public transportation designed to move many people. By the late 1860s New York City had elevated trains running on tracks above the streets. Chicago followed in the 1890s.

Some cities built underground railroads, known as subways. In 1897 the first subway in the United States opened in Boston. In 1904 the first line of the New York City subway system began operation. Cable cars and electric trolleys also became common. These streetcars cheaply and quickly carried people in the cities to and from work.

Many Americans who could afford it moved to **suburbs**, residential neighborhoods outside of downtown areas that had begun springing up before the Civil War. Mass transit networks made such moves possible. People could live in the suburbs and take trolleys, subways, or trains into the cities.

New Ideas

In the late 1800s the United States also began to develop forms of **mass culture**, or leisure and cultural activities shared by many people. One factor contributing to mass culture was a boom in publishing. The invention of the Linotype, an automatic typesetting machine, greatly reduced the time and cost of printing. In 1850

Frederick Law Olmsted

Olmsted intentionally placed the pond near busy streets, hoping that it would attract walkers.

People can walk, ride, or roller skate on the many trails through Central Park.

CONNECT TO THE ARTS

Frederick Law Olmsted designed Central Park to serve as a place where New York City residents could relax, exercise, and enjoy nature. Olmsted included areas for horseback riding, ice-skating, boating, and baseball. The Children's District was designed as a place where parents could bring children to stay cool in the summer.

Why do you think a city dweller might be attracted to Central Park?

there were fewer than 300 daily newspapers in the country. Because of the use of Linotype machines, by 1900 there were more than 2,000 newspapers.

Big cities often had many newspapers, so publishers had to compete for readers. In 1896 **Joseph Pulitzer** added a color comic to his *New York World* newspaper. More people started buying Pulitzer's paper. **William Randolph Hearst**, publisher of the *New York Journal*, saw that comics helped sell newspapers. So he added a color comic strip to the *Journal*. Soon, newspapers across the country were adding comic strips.

Mass culture affected how people shopped as well. Giant retail shops, or **department stores**, appeared in some cities during the late 1800s. One of the earliest was Marshall Field in Chicago, which offered low prices and large quantities of products. It also was the first department store to offer its customers a restaurant where they could eat while shopping. Newspaper advertising was used to bring in customers. The public was also attracted by fancy window displays.

World fairs were another example of mass culture. Fairs brought merchants together, which sometimes resulted in new ideas and products. At the 1904 St. Louis World's Fair, for example, a Syrian food vendor began making cones for a nearby ice cream vendor who had run out of dishes. Ice cream cones became popular throughout the country.

The demand for public entertainment also led to the creation of amusement parks, such as New York's Coney Island. The inexpensive entry tickets made Coney Island a favorite destination for children and families. For a nickel, visitors could ride a new invention called the Switchback Railway—the country's first roller coaster.

As cities grew, people became aware of the need for open public space. Landscape architect **Frederick Law Olmsted** became nationally famous. He designed Central Park in New York City, as well as many state and national parks. Some of his other well-known projects include Prospect Park in Brooklyn, New York, and the U.S. Capitol grounds, which he worked on between 1874 and 1895.

READING CHECK **Summarizing** What forms of mass culture were available in urban areas?

SUMMARY AND PREVIEW Immigration and new technology helped cities grow in the late 1800s. In the next section you will learn about some of the problems caused by rapid urban growth.

Section 2 Assessment

go.hrw.com
Online Quiz
KEYWORD: SB7 HP20

Reviewing Ideas, Terms, and People

1. **a. Identify** What groups of people began moving to cities in the late 1800s?
   b. Explain Why did African Americans begin to move to northern cities in the 1890s?
   c. Predict Do you think cities such as Chicago continued to grow in the 1900s? Why or why not?
2. **a. Define** What is **mass transit**? What made mass transit necessary?
   b. Explain How did new inventions make it possible for people to build skyscrapers?
   c. Evaluate Which improvement to urban living do you think had the greatest impact on people's lives? Explain your answer.

Critical Thinking

3. **Identifying Cause and Effect** Review your notes on the causes for the growth of cities. Then copy the following graphic organizer and use it to identify the effects of city growth. You may need to add more circles.

FOCUS ON WRITING

4. **Describing Setting** A city like those you have read about could serve as the setting of your TV series. How could you describe the city?

City Life

Virginia Standards of Learning USII.1a, USII.1b, USII.4b, USII.6b

What You Will Learn...

Main Ideas

1. Crowded urban areas faced a variety of social problems.
2. People worked to improve the quality of life in U.S. cities.

The Big Idea

The rapid growth of cities in the late 1800s created both challenges and opportunities.

Key Terms and People

Jacob Riis, *p. 646*
settlement houses, *p. 648*
Jane Addams, *p. 648*
Hull House, *p. 648*
Florence Kelley, *p. 648*

TAKING NOTES As you read, take notes on problems facing city residents. You can organize your notes in a table like this one.

Urban Problems

If YOU were there...

You live in a fast-growing city in 1895. When you walk the streets, you meet families that are packed into run-down apartments in crowded, filthy neighborhoods. You meet immigrants who want to study English but have no money for classes. You are determined to help these city residents improve their lives.

What would you do to help improve life in your city?

BUILDING BACKGROUND Despite the new public parks, skyscrapers, and mass transit systems, many cities were not ready for the rapid population growth that began taking place in the late 1800s. Overcrowding and poor living conditions forced people to search for solutions to these problems.

Urban Problems

In the late 1800s and early 1900s, shortages of affordable housing forced many poor families to squeeze into tiny tenement apartments, which were frequently unsafe and unsanitary. Journalist and photographer **Jacob Riis** became famous for exposing the horrible conditions in New York City tenements. Riis wrote about one typical tenement family:

" There were nine in the family: husband, wife, an aged grandmother, and six children ... All nine lived in two rooms, one about ten feet square that served as parlor, bedroom, and eating-room, the other a small hall-room made into a kitchen. "

— Jacob Riis, *How the Other Half Lives*

This kind of overcrowding caused sanitation problems. Most cities did not have a good system for collecting trash, so garbage often piled up outside apartment buildings. An article in the *New York Tribune* described the garbage in front of one tenement as a "mass of air poisoning, death-breeding filth, reeking in the fierce sunshine."

Unsafe conditions were also common in tenements. Before 1900 most cities did not have laws requiring landlords to fix their tenements or to maintain safety standards. A fire on one floor could easily spread, and fire escapes were often blocked or broken.

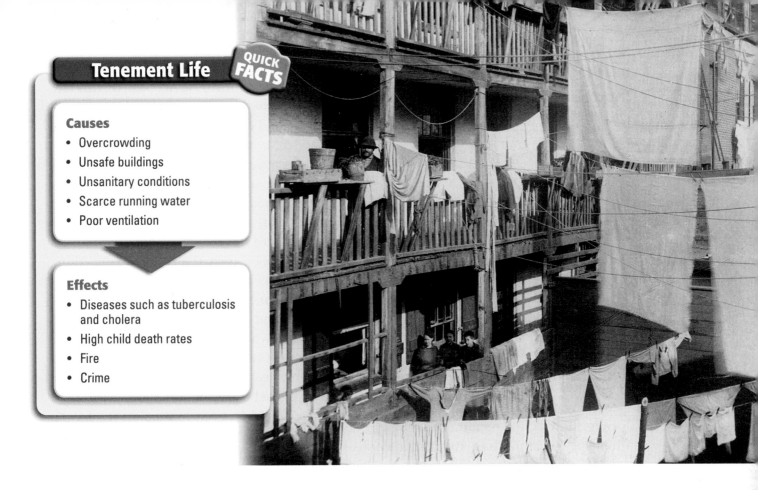

Tenement Life — QUICK FACTS

Causes
- Overcrowding
- Unsafe buildings
- Unsanitary conditions
- Scarce running water
- Poor ventilation

Effects
- Diseases such as tuberculosis and cholera
- High child death rates
- Fire
- Crime

Tenement rooms had few or no windows to let in fresh air and sunshine. Comfort was also scarce, with so many people crowded into such small spaces. Running water and indoor plumbing were also scarce. So was clean water—cities often dumped garbage into local rivers that were used for drinking water.

Disease-causing bacteria grew easily in these conditions. Diseases such as cholera, typhoid, influenza, and tuberculosis spread quickly in crowded neighborhoods. Children were the most vulnerable to these diseases. For example, babies born in Chicago in 1870 had only a 50 percent chance of living to the age of five.

Air pollution was also a serious problem in many growing cities. This was a time when many business leaders were building huge oil refineries, steel mills, and other factories. The steel mills of Andrew Carnegie, for example, helped make Pittsburgh the nation's steel-making center in the late 1800s. Steel mills brought jobs and wealth to Pittsburgh, but they also caused some of the nation's worst air pollution. "Every street appears to end in a huge, black cloud," said one writer. "Pittsburgh is smoke, smoke, smoke—everywhere smoke." The air was so polluted at times that the city had to turn on outdoor lighting during the day.

The work of many city governments slowly helped to lessen some of these urban problems. By the late 1800s new sewage and water purification systems improved city sanitation. Many major cities also were hiring full-time firefighters and police officers. Police officers in cities were typically placed in one neighborhood. They knew the local residents and were frequently involved in local activities. They could spot local problems and, in many cases, provide help to immigrants.

THE IMPACT TODAY

Like many industrial cities, Pittsburgh has made great progress in cleaning its air and water. Today, Pittsburgh is ranked as one of the cleanest American cities.

READING CHECK Summarizing What challenges did many city residents face in the late 1800s?

Improving City Life

Jacob Riis hoped his book *How the Other Half Lives* would shock many Americans—and it did. A reformer named Lawrence Veiller helped lead the effort to improve conditions in tenements. Describing the effects of tenement living on children, he wrote:

> " A child living its early years in dark rooms, without sunlight or fresh air, does not grow up to be a normal, healthy person … It is not of such material that strong nations are made. "
> – Lawrence Veiller, quoted in *Readings in American History, Vol. 2*

Veiller worked with an organization called the Charity Organization Society (COS) to get changes made to New York laws. In 1900 he and the COS sponsored an exhibit of photographs and maps graphically showing the conditions of New York tenements. More than 10,000 people visited the exhibit, and they were shocked by what they saw. The work of Veiller and the COS helped to get the 1901 New York State Tenement House Act passed. This law required new buildings to have better ventilation and running water. The act became a model for housing reform in other states.

Because there was little government aid available in the 1800s, private organizations generally took on the task of helping the urban poor. Some individuals set up **settlement houses**, or neighborhood centers in poor areas that offered education, recreation, and social activities.

Settlement houses were staffed by professionals and volunteers. Many were educated women who came from wealthy families. In 1886 Charles B. Stover and Stanton Coit established the first settlement house in the United States. It was called Neighborhood Guild and was located on the Lower East Side in New York City. In 1889 **Jane Addams** and Ellen Gates Starr moved into a run-down building in a poor Chicago neighborhood and turned it into **Hull House**, the most famous settlement house of the period.

The Hull House staff focused on the needs of immigrant families, and by 1893 Hull House was serving 2,000 people a week. It provided services such as English classes, day care, and cooking and sewing classes. Children and adults came to take part in club meetings, art classes, plays, and sports.

Jane Addams and the staff at Hull House also worked for reforms. They studied the problems facing immigrants and poor city dwellers, then searched for ways to improve conditions. **Florence Kelley** was one important reformer at Hull House. She visited sweatshops and wrote about the problems there. Her work helped convince lawmakers to take action. Illinois passed a law in 1893 to limit working hours for women and to prevent child labor.

Kelley became the state's chief factory inspector and helped enforce the law. Although she believed more reforms were needed, she did report some improvements:

Hull House

Neighborhood children attended kindergarten at Hull House. Their parents typically had low-paying jobs, and many were children of immigrants. Children like these had few other options for education.

How did Hull House try to improve the lives of children?

"Previous to the passage of the factory law of 1893, it was the rule of [a candy] factory to work the children ...from 7 A.M. to 9 P.M., with twenty minutes for lunch, and no supper, a working week of eighty-two hours ...Since the enactment of the factory law, their working week has consisted of six days of eight hours each, a reduction of thirty-four hours a week."

– Florence Kelley and Alzina P. Stevens, from *Hull House Maps and Papers*

As Hull House gained recognition, the settlement house movement spread to other cities. Most settlement houses continued to provide programs and services for city dwellers through the early 1900s. Some, such as Germantown Settlement in Pennsylvania, remain active today.

READING CHECK **Drawing Conclusions**
How did Hull House help improve city life?

SUMMARY AND PREVIEW Reformers in the late 1800s worked to solve urban problems. In the next chapter you will learn how Progressives pushed for further reforms.

BIOGRAPHY

Jane Addams
1860–1935

Jane Addams was born in Cedarville, Illinois. Like many upper-class women of the era, she received a college education but found few jobs open to her. In 1888, on a visit to England with classmate Ellen Gates Starr, she visited a London settlement house. On their return to the United States, Addams and Starr opened a settlement house in Chicago. They started a kindergarten and a public playground. Addams also became involved in housing safety and sanitation issues, factory inspection, and immigrants' rights. In 1931 she shared the Nobel Peace Prize for her work with the Women's International League for Peace and Freedom.

Summarizing How did Jane Addams try to improve the lives of workers?

go.hrw.com
Online Quiz
KEYWORD: SB7 HP20

Section 3 Assessment

Reviewing Ideas, Terms, and People

1. **a. Describe** What were conditions like in tenements?
   b. Summarize What problems resulted from the rapid growth of cities?
   c. Draw Conclusions Why do you think people lived in tenements?
2. **a. Define** What is a **settlement house**?
   b. Explain How did settlement houses help city dwellers?
   c. Evaluate Do you think settlement houses were successful? Why or why not?

Critical Thinking

3. **Categorizing** Review your notes on urban problems. Then copy the chart to the right onto your own sheet of paper and use it to identify the responses to those problems.

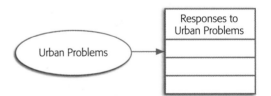

FOCUS ON WRITING

4. **Writing about Urban Problems** Finding solutions to problems is an important part of the plot of many stories. Take notes on scenes you could include in your TV series in which characters deal with the problems of urban life.

Social Studies Skills

Analysis | **Critical Thinking** | Civic Participation | Study

Making Comparisons

Define the Skill

Understanding similarities is important when studying history. Comparing two or more people, things, events, or ideas highlights the similarities between them. Making comparisons can help clarify larger historical issues. This is true when comparing different time periods or when comparing different things from the same time period. Making comparisons is important in identifying historical connections.

Learn the Skill

When you encounter similar people, things, events, or ideas in history, use the following guidelines to make comparisons.

1 Identify who or what you are going to compare.

2 Look for similarities between them. Find examples of what makes them alike. Note any differences as well.

3 Use comparison words such as "like," "both," and "similar" to point out similarities.

In this chapter, you have learned about several reformers, including Lawrence Veiller and Florence Kelley. Veiller helped lead the effort to improve conditions in tenements. Kelley was a reformer who worked at Hull House.

Lawrence Veiller and Florence Kelley were alike in many ways. Although Veiller focused on tenements and Kelley concentrated on factory work, both were concerned with problems that affected children. Both did research about their issues. Both then wrote about the poor conditions they found.

Both Veiller and Kelley worked successfully for laws that would improve those conditions. Kelley's work helped convince Illinois lawmakers to pass a law to limit child labor. Similarly, Veiller helped to get the 1901 New York State Tenement House Act passed.

Practice the Skill

Review the chapter to find two people, things, events, or ideas that are similar. Then apply the guidelines to answer the following questions.

1 Which people, events, or ideas will you compare? Why is each of them important?

2 How are they alike? How are they different?

Chapter Review

HOLT

History's Impact
▶ **video series**
Review the video to answer the closing question:

Why do you think the United States had stricter immigration regulations for Asian immigrants?

Visual Summary

QUICK FACTS

Use the visual summary below to help you review the main ideas of the chapter.

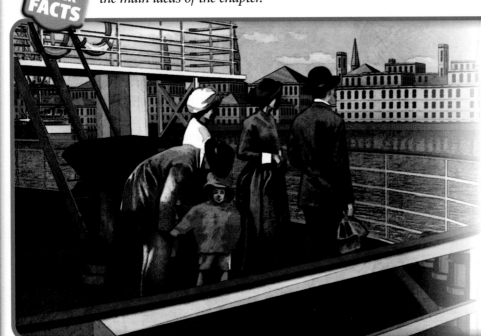

People Arrived
• New immigrants, mostly from southern and eastern Europe
• Came for new opportunities and better lives
• Mostly found jobs in cities
• Faced opposition from some Americans

Cities Grew
• Massive urban growth
• New technologies emerged—skyscrapers and mass transit
• New urban culture

Problems Developed
• Overcrowded tenements
• Unsanitary conditions

Reviewing Vocabulary, Terms, and People

Identify the descriptions below with the correct term or person from the chapter.

1. Public transportation systems built to move many people and ease traffic in crowded cities

2. Founded Hull House with Ellen Gates Starr in 1889

3. Organizations created by immigrants to help each other in times of sickness, unemployment, or other troubles

4. Law banning Chinese people from moving to the United States

5. Neighborhood centers in poor urban areas that offered education, recreation, and social activities

6. Landscape architect who designed New York City's Central Park

7. Small shops or mills where immigrants worked for long hours in hot, unhealthy conditions

Comprehension and Critical Thinking

SECTION 1 *(Pages 636–641)*

8. **a. Identify** From what parts of the world did the wave of new immigrants come?

   b. Analyze In what ways did immigration patterns in the United States change in the late 1800s?

   c. Elaborate In your opinion, were the difficulties that immigrants faced worth the benefits of life in the United States? Explain.

SECTION 2 *(Pages 642–645)*

9. **a. Recall** Why did U.S. cities experience such rapid growth in the late 1800s?

   b. Analyze How did new technologies help cities deal with population growth?

   c. Elaborate Would you have preferred to live in a city or in a suburb? Why?

10. **a. Recall** What were conditions like in tenements in the late 1800s?

b. Make Inferences Why did rapid population growth cause problems in cities?

c. Elaborate Why do you think the settlement house movement grew in the late 1800s and early 1900s?

Reviewing Themes

11. **Economics** What role did economics play in the growth of cities?

12. **Society and Culture** How did the lives of city dwellers change with the rise of mass culture?

Reading Skills

Understanding Historical Fact versus Historical Fiction *Use the Reading Skills taught in this chapter to answer the question about the reading selection below.*

> Mass culture affected how people shopped as well. Giant retail shops, or department stores, appeared in some cities during the late 1800s. One of the earliest was Marshall Field in Chicago, which offered low prices and large quantities of products. It also was the first department store to offer its customers a restaurant where they could eat while shopping. Newspaper advertising was used to bring in customers. The public was also attracted by fancy window displays. *(p. 645)*

13. Which facts above can be verified? Where would you look to verify them?

Social Studies Skills

Making Comparisons *Use the Social Studies Skills taught in this chapter to answer the question below.*

14. Choose two reforms that were discussed in this chapter. Make a comparison between the two.

Using the Internet

go.hrw.com
KEYWORD: SB7 CH20

15. **Activity: Investigating Culture** Mass culture developed in the late 1800s and early 1900s as a result of new and broader forms of communication taking root. Enter the activity keyword and explore some of the early influences on mass culture. Then research the ways in which modern culture is influenced by the media, the Internet, and other forms of mass communication. How does today's society experience mass culture? Create a visual display or computer-based presentation that compares mass culture then and now.

FOCUS ON WRITING

16. **Writing Your Memo** Look back over your notes about the people, places, and events of the late 1800s. Decide which of these you will include in your television drama series. Then draft a one- to two-paragraph memo to your boss describing the series. Remember to describe the basic plot, setting, and characters.

DIRECTIONS: *Read each question and write the letter of the best response.*

1 Which of the following is associated with providing a better life for urban immigrants in the late 1800s and early 1900s?

A the department store

B the suburb

C the tenement

D the settlement house

2 Immigrants to the United States in the late 1800s and early 1900s came *mainly* from

A southern and eastern Europe.

B Japan, China, and the rest of Asia.

C Mexico and Central America.

D northern and western Europe.

3 Ellis Island and Angel Island were both

A locations of settlement houses.

B immigration processing centers.

C centers of shipping and industry.

D amusement parks.

4 Which of the following is an example of mass culture?

A newspaper comics

B immigrant neighborhoods

C Yiddish-language theaters

D subways

5 The *main* goal of Hull House was to

A provide jobs for wealthy women.

B pass the Tenement House Act of 1901.

C help poor immigrants.

D oppose the Chinese Exclusion Act.

6 Anti-immigrant feeling resulted in

A benevolent societies.

B the Chinese Exclusion Act.

C tenements.

D the Tenement House Act.

7 Which of the following groups moved from the southern United States to the North in large numbers during the 1890s?

A Chinese immigrants

B Mexican Americans

C African Americans

D Irish immigrants

8 Read this 1896 newspaper article describing poor conditions faced by many people and use it to answer the question below.

> "lack of family privacy … lack of light and air, and of sanitary accommodations, insuring a large death rate, and danger from fire … [These places are] infested with vermin [insects] and infected with disease germs, they are a disgrace to humanity and a menace, not only to the health of the unfortunate residents therein, but to the health of the whole community."
>
> —*The New York Times*, 1896

Document-Based Question Based on this description, to what was this article most likely referring?

Assignment

Write a persuasive essay either for or against one of these statements.

1. New laws should have limited immigration in the late 1800s.
2. The government should have done more to improve conditions in tenements.

TIP **Using Order of Importance**

How do you know whether to start or end with your most important or most convincing reason? If you are worried about getting your readers to read your entire paper, you might try to catch their attention by starting with the most convincing reason. If you are concerned that your readers remember one point after they finish reading, you may want to place that point, or reason, at the end of your paper.

Persuasion and History

You have probably heard people disagree about current political events—perhaps a new law or a government leader. People also disagree about events of the past. When we disagree about historical events, those of the past or those of the present, we can use persuasive arguments to convince others to agree with our opinion.

1. Prewrite

Stating Your Opinion

Persuasion starts with an opinion or a position on a topic. Choose one of the statements in the assignment and decide on your opinion, either for or against. Write your opinion in a statement: it will be the big idea of your persuasive paper. For example, here is an opinion statement about the first topic:

The government should not have limited immigration in the late 1800s.

Building and Organizing a Logical Argument

A strong persuasive essay includes a logical argument, sound reasoning, and proof in support of an opinion. Reasons tell *why* you have an opinion. Proof, or evidence, includes facts, examples, or expert opinions.

- **Opinion:** *Reformers' work improved Americans' lives.*
- **Reason:** *Reforms improved life in cities.*
- **Evidence:** *Lawrence Veiller influenced the passage of the 1901 New York State Tenement House Act.*

Persuasive writing is usually organized by order of importance.

2. Write

Here is a framework to help you write your first draft.

A Writer's Framework

Introduction
- Start with an interesting opener, such as a quotation or a surprising fact.
- Include your opinion statement, or big idea, for the paper.

Body
- Present one reason and its supporting evidence in each body paragraph.
- Address your reasons by order of importance.

Conclusion
- Restate your opinion in different words.
- Summarize your reasons.
- Make a connection to a current event.

3. Evaluate and Revise

Evaluating

Use these questions to discover ways to improve your draft.

Evaluation Questions for a Persuasive Essay

- Does your introduction include a clear statement of your opinion on the topic?
- Do you present your reasons by order of importance in the body paragraphs?
- Do you provide at least three reasons to support your opinion?

- Do you include facts, examples, or expert opinions to support each reason?
- Do you restate your opinion in different words in your conclusion?
- Does your conclusion include a summary of the reasons that support your opinion?

TIP **Fact vs. Opinion** Knowing the difference between a fact and an opinion is important for both writers and readers of persuasive essays.

- **Facts** are statements that can be proven true or false. *Jane Addams founded Hull House in 1889.*

- **Opinions** are statements of personal belief and cannot be proven. *Jane Addams was the greatest American woman of her time.*

Revising

Your essay will be more forceful if you write in the active voice.

Passive voice: *New parks were designed by Frederick Law Olmsted.*

Active voice: *Frederick Law Olmsted designed new parks.*

Active voice is more forceful, and often clearer, because it makes a stronger connection between the action and the actor. However, we may use passive voice because we do not know, or do not want to say, who the actor is or was.

Example: *New parks were designed in the late 1800s.*

4. Proofread and Publish

Proofreading

If you are writing your paper on a computer, you should use the spell-check feature to look for spelling errors. However, the spell-check feature will not help much if you have used the wrong word. Here are some examples to look for: *their/they're, its/it's, accept/except, affect/effect, advice/advise, altar/alter, capitol/capital.* When you spot one of these words in your paper, check your dictionary to make sure you have used the correct word.

Publishing

Share your essay with a classmate who took an opinion opposed to yours. Review each other's reasons. Can one of you persuade the other?

5. Practice and Apply

Use the steps and strategies in this workshop to write a persuasive essay.

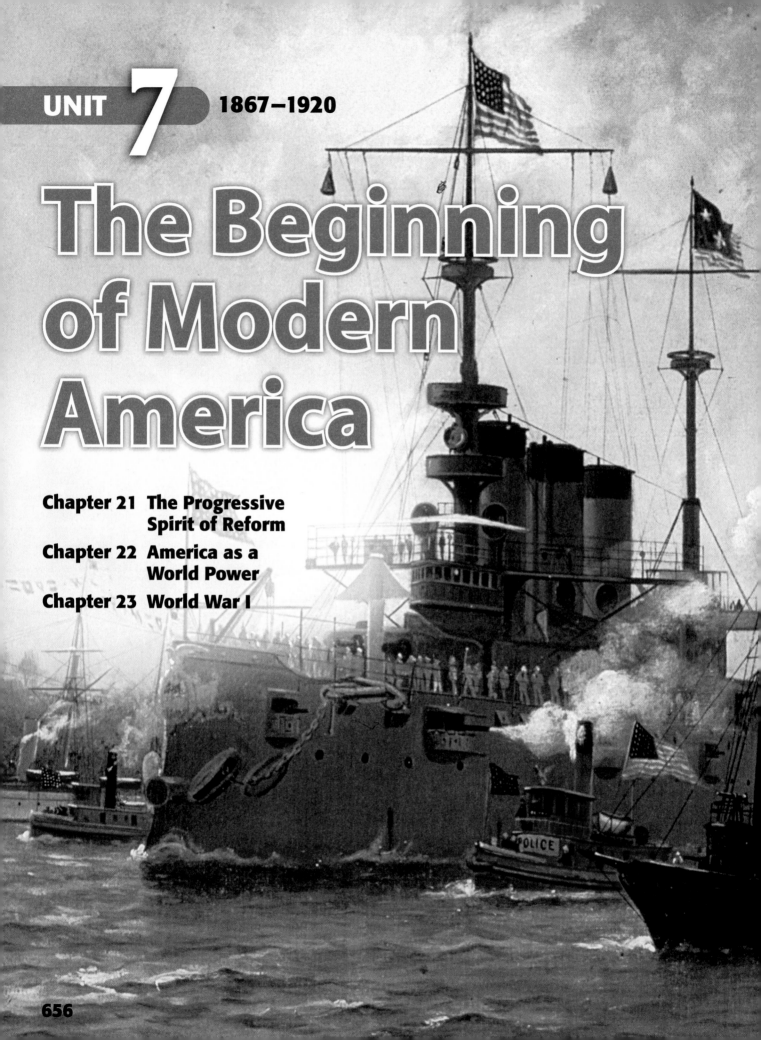

The Beginning of Modern America

What You Will Learn…

As cities in the United States became more prosperous, people began to examine the inequalities in American society. A progressive spirit emerged that led to changes in American culture. The United States also began to expand its influence overseas.

Presidents were called upon to deal with many domestic and foreign challenges, including two wars that changed the landscape of international politics. During the Spanish-American War, the United States acquired overseas territories. During World War I, Americans fought in Europe for the first time.

Explore the Art

This painting shows the Great White Fleet, a group of U.S. ships that toured the world from 1907 to 1909. How might a tour of American ships affect foreign views of the United States?

The Progressive Spirit of Reform

Virginia Standards of Learning

USII.1 The student will demonstrate skills for historical and geographical analysis, and responsible citizenship, including the ability to

a) analyze and interpret primary and secondary source documents to increase understanding of events and life in United States history from 1865 to the present; **b)** make connections between past and present; **c)** sequence events in United States history from 1865 to the present; **d)** interpret ideas and events from different historical perspectives

USII.4 The student will demonstrate knowledge of how life changed after the Civil War by

c) describing racial segregation, the rise of "Jim Crow," and other constraints faced by African Americans and other groups in the post-Reconstruction South; **e)** describing the impact of the Progressive Movement on child labor, working conditions, the rise of organized labor, women's suffrage, and the temperance movement

USII.6 The student will demonstrate knowledge of the social, economic, and technological changes of the early twentieth century by

b) describing the social and economic changes that took place, including prohibition, and the Great Migration north and west

FOCUS ON SPEAKING

Campaign Promises In this chapter you will read about the political corruption of the Gilded Age and the reform movements that followed. Serious problems face the nation, and you must convince voters that you should be the one to tackle those problems. Create and present a list of campaign promises that you would make if you were a politician running for office in the United States in the late 1800s or early 1900s.

UNITED STATES

WORLD

1868
Ulysses S. Grant is elected president.

| 1865 | 1870 |

1871 The British Parliament legalizes labor unions.

HOLT
History's Impact
▶ **video series**
Watch the video to understand the impact of women's suffrage.

What You Will Learn...

In this chapter you will learn about how reform movements swept across the United States in the late 1800s and early 1900s. These movements had a variety of aims, from ending government corruption to abolishing child labor. Ordinary citizens, like these women calling for their right to vote, participated in the movements.

1881 Charles Guiteau, a frustrated federal job seeker, assassinates President James A. Garfield.

1901 President William McKinley is assassinated, and Vice President Theodore Roosevelt becomes president.

1920 Congress declares the Nineteenth Amendment ratified, giving women the right to vote.

| 1880 | 1890 | 1900 | 1910 | 1920 |

1888 Brazil officially ends slavery.

1912 The British luxury liner *Titanic* sinks after hitting an iceberg during its first voyage. About 1,500 passengers die.

1917 Mexico adopts a new constitution.

THE PROGRESSIVE SPIRIT OF REFORM **659**

Reading Social Studies

by Kylene Beers

Economics | Geography | **Politics** | **Society and Culture** | Science and Technology

Focus on Themes In this chapter, you will read about the corrupt **politics** of the Gilded Age, a time marked by attempts at reform. You will learn how **society and culture** reacted and responded to the problems of corruption and inequality. Finally, you will read about several presidents of the early 1900s who supported ideas and initiatives that promoted social reform.

Evaluating Sources

Focus on Reading Historical texts and current history books are good sources of information about the past. However, some sources can be more reliable than others to learn the truth.

Evaluating Texts Sometimes people write texts with a specific purpose or viewpoint in mind. Determining what the author's goal was in writing a passage can help you evaluate whether to believe all of the text, or merely some of it. Knowing which parts you can believe and which you cannot will help you understand what really happened in history.

Notice how one reader evaluated the source below.

> The man, therefore, who as the owner of newspapers, <u>would corrupt public opinion is the most dangerous enemy of the State.</u> We may talk about the perils incident [dangers attached] to the <u>concentration of wealth,</u> about the perils flowing from a <u>disregard of fiduciary [financial] responsibility,</u> about <u>abuses of privilege,</u> about <u>exploiting the government for private advantage</u>; but all of these menaces, great as they are, are nothing compared with a deliberate, persistent, artful, purchased endeavor to [change and direct] the public judgment.
>
> —*Harper's Weekly*, October 20, 1906, quoted in *Yellow Journalism* by W. Joseph Campbell

The author is using strong words to describe his viewpoint. Maybe he isn't being as objective as he should be.

The article lists several ideas that the author seems to think are bad. Are these things really bad? Can that help me determine the author's viewpoint?

This magazine was widely read when the article appeared. I think that makes the article a good source for some viewpoints of the time.

You Try It!

Read the passage below and evaluate whether you would use it as a source for a paper.

> Space is no intervention now between communication. [N]ot only do the wires of copper bind the world together in closer communication, but with the telephone it is possible to converse [talk] with friends a thousand miles away, hearing distinctly every word and recognizing the individual voice. Closer acquaintance has thus wrought [created] vast changes in public opinions and policies. The entire civilized world has been drawn more closely together, old ideas and prejudices have been wiped out.
>
> –*Cincinnati Times-Star*, January 1, 1900, quoted in *Yellow Journalism* by W. Joseph Campbell

1. What viewpoint of new technology is the author taking in this article? How can you tell?

2. Do you believe that the telephone brought about "changes in public opinions and policies"? Why or why not? Why might the author say this?

3. Can you trust the author when he says that "old ideas and prejudices have been wiped out"? Why or why not? Why might the author say this?

4. Did this article appear in a well-known newspaper? Does this make it more trustworthy or less?

5. Would you use this article as a source for writing a paper about how new inventions affected life in the early 1900s? Explain your answer.

As you read **Chapter 21**, evaluate the primary sources for their usefulness in understanding history.

Key Terms and People

Chapter 21

Section 1
political machines *(p. 662)*
Progressives *(p. 664)*
muckrakers *(p. 664)*
Seventeenth Amendment *(p. 666)*
recall *(p. 666)*
initiative *(p. 666)*
referendum *(p. 666)*
Robert M. La Follette *(p. 667)*

Section 2
Triangle Shirtwaist Fire *(p. 673)*
workers' compensation laws *(p. 673)*
capitalism *(p. 674)*
socialism *(p. 674)*
William "Big Bill" Haywood *(p. 674)*
Industrial Workers of the World *(p. 674)*

Section 3
Eighteenth Amendment *(p. 676)*
National American Woman Suffrage Association *(p. 676)*
Alice Paul *(p. 677)*
Nineteenth Amendment *(p. 677)*
Booker T. Washington *(p. 677)*
Ida B. Wells *(p. 677)*
W. E. B. Du Bois *(p. 678)*
National Association for the Advancement of Colored People *(p. 678)*

Section 4
Theodore Roosevelt *(p. 680)*
Pure Food and Drug Act *(p. 681)*
conservation *(p. 681)*
William Howard Taft *(p. 682)*
Progressive Party *(p. 682)*
Woodrow Wilson *(p. 682)*
Sixteenth Amendment *(p. 683)*

Academic Vocabulary

In this chapter you will learn the following academic words:

motive *(p. 666)*
various *(p. 682)*

The Gilded Age and the Progressive Movement

Virginia Standards of Learning USII.1a, USII.1b, USII.1d, USII.4e, USII.6b

What You Will Learn...

Main Ideas

1. Political corruption was common during the Gilded Age.
2. Progressives pushed for reforms to improve living conditions.
3. Progressive reforms expanded the voting power of citizens.

The Big Idea

From the late 1800s through the early 1900s, the Progressive movement addressed problems in American society.

Key Terms and People

political machines, *p. 662*
Progressives, *p. 664*
muckrakers, *p. 664*
Seventeenth Amendment, *p. 666*
recall, *p. 666*
initiative, *p. 666*
referendum, *p. 666*
Robert M. La Follette, *p. 667*

TAKING NOTES As you read, take notes on progressive reforms and the problems they addressed. Organize your notes in a chart like the one below.

Progressive reform	Problem it addressed

If YOU were there...

You live in a big-city neighborhood in the 1890s. You and your brother are both looking for jobs. You know that the man down the street is the "ward boss." He can always get city jobs for his friends and neighbors. But in return you'll have to promise to vote the way he tells you to in the upcoming election.

Would you ask the ward boss for a job? Why or why not?

BUILDING BACKGROUND The late 1800s were a time of contrasts in American life. Great wealth created through business ventures existed alongside poverty and the difficulties of tenement life. In politics, money led to corruption and dishonesty. Reacting to these conditions, reformers worked to improve many areas of American life.

Political Corruption

The late 1800s in the United States are often called the Gilded Age. The term came from a novel by that name. *The Gilded Age* highlights the inequality between wealthy business owners, who profited from the Industrial Revolution, and workers, who often labored under terrible conditions for little pay. Many people began to believe that the government should help fix this inequality. The first step was to get rid of corruption in politics.

Political Machines

In the late 1800s city and county politics were dominated by **political machines**—powerful organizations that used both legal and illegal methods to get their candidates elected to public office. For example, members of political machines sometimes stuffed ballot boxes with extra votes for their candidates. They also paid people to vote a certain way and then bribed vote counters. Through such actions, political machines could control local governments.

POLITICAL CARTOON
The Tammany Ring

This political cartoon shows a ring of corrupt politicians known as Tammany Hall. The cartoonist shows how each person blames the one next to him for the corruption in government. As a result of political machines like Tammany Hall, many Americans began demanding political reforms.

The men have labels on their backs that show they represent different interests.

The Granger Collection, New York

ANALYSIS SKILL   ANALYZING PRIMARY SOURCES

Why are the men shown standing in a circle?

Political machines were run by leaders called bosses. The machine's boss frequently traded favors for votes. For example, the boss might hand out city jobs to unqualified people or allow an illegal business to operate. The bosses drew much of their support from immigrants. They became popular among poor families because of the services they provided, including jobs and social services such as a fire brigade. A Boston politician said that the role of the machine boss was "to be . . . somebody that any bloke [man] can come to . . . and get help."

New York City's political machine, Tammany Hall, was one of the most notorious. After winning city elections in 1888, members of Tammany Hall rewarded their supporters with about 12,000 jobs. As boss of Tammany Hall, William Marcy Tweed may have stolen up to $200 million from the city. One man remembered how Tammany Hall stayed in power by intimidating voters:

"Father used to say, 'They know how you're voting. You can't fool them.' He was a Republican at heart, but he had to vote Democratic in order that they didn't find out and make it difficult for him."

—Henry Fenner, quoted in *You Must Remember This,*
edited by Jeff Kisseloff

Cleaning Up Political Corruption

Corruption was also a problem in the federal government. Many people thought that the corruption extended to the presidential administration of Ulysses S. Grant. During Grant's second term, federal officials were jailed for taking bribes from whiskey makers in exchange for allowing them to avoid paying taxes. Another scandal involved members of Congress who had taken bribes to allow the Union Pacific Railway to receive government funds. These scandals and others caused many Americans to question the honesty of national leaders.

In response, Americans began calling for changes in the civil service, the government job system. They disliked the spoils system, the practice of giving jobs to the winning candidates' supporters. Thomas Jefferson was the first to reward supporters with jobs. After his administration, each time a new party took power, it replaced many government officials. Many new employees were unqualified and untrained.

By the late 1800s government corruption was so widespread that reformers demanded that only qualified people be given government jobs. In response, President Rutherford B. Hayes

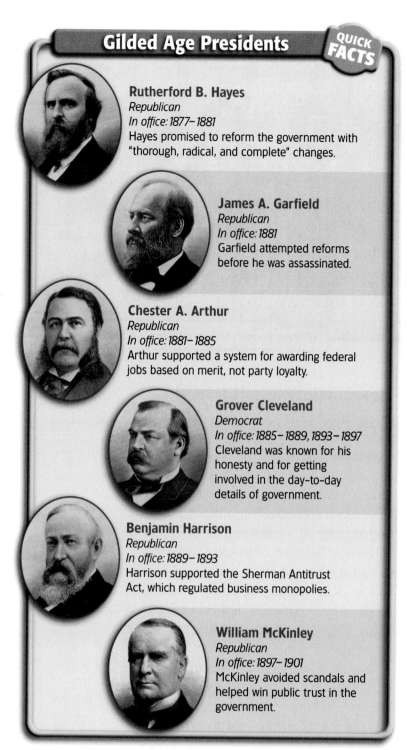

Rutherford B. Hayes
Republican
In office: 1877–1881
Hayes promised to reform the government with "thorough, radical, and complete" changes.

James A. Garfield
Republican
In office: 1881
Garfield attempted reforms before he was assassinated.

Chester A. Arthur
Republican
In office: 1881–1885
Arthur supported a system for awarding federal jobs based on merit, not party loyalty.

Grover Cleveland
Democrat
In office: 1885–1889, 1893–1897
Cleveland was known for his honesty and for getting involved in the day-to-day details of government.

Benjamin Harrison
Republican
In office: 1889–1893
Harrison supported the Sherman Antitrust Act, which regulated business monopolies.

William McKinley
Republican
In office: 1897–1901
McKinley avoided scandals and helped win public trust in the government.

THE IMPACT TODAY

Tests are still required for many federal jobs, including secretarial positions, air traffic control, and law enforcement.

made minor reforms, such as firing a powerful member of the New York Republican political machine. President James A. Garfield also attempted reforms. But on July 2, 1881, Garfield was attacked and shot twice by a mentally unstable federal job seeker named Charles Guiteau. The president later died from his wounds, and Vice President Chester A. Arthur became president.

Arthur continued the push for reforms by backing the Pendleton Civil Service Act, which was passed in 1883. This law set up a merit system for awarding federal jobs. Under the Pendleton Act, more than 10 percent of government job applicants had to pass an exam before they could be hired. It was a start to reforming other government practices.

READING CHECK **Analyzing** What factors led to civil-service reform?

Progressives Push for Reforms

A group of reformers known as **Progressives** were also working to improve society in the late 1800s. Progressives tried to solve problems caused by rapid industrial and urban growth. Their goals were to eliminate the causes of problems such as crime, disease, and poverty. They fought for reforms ranging from better working conditions to education programs in poor neighborhoods.

Muckrakers at Work

Some journalists urged Progressives to action by writing stories that vividly described problems in U.S. society. These journalists were nicknamed **muckrakers** because they "raked up" and exposed the muck, or filth, of society. Muckrakers wrote about troubling issues such as child labor, racial discrimination, slum housing, and corruption in business and politics.

In 1902 and 1903 Lincoln Steffens wrote a series of articles in *McClure's Magazine* exposing corruption in city government. In one article, he described how government officials in St. Louis, Missouri, used their positions to earn extra money illegally:

" Men empowered to issue peddlers' licenses and permits to citizens who wished to erect awnings or use a portion of the sidewalk for storage purposes charged an amount in excess of the prices stipulated [set] by law, and pocketed the difference. "
—Lincoln Steffens, *The Shame of the Cities*

PHOTOGRAPH
The Other Half

In 1890 Jacob Riis published How the Other Half Lives. *The book was a collection of photographs of residents and workers in New York City tenement buildings, including families and immigrants. The conditions of life that Riis showed in his photographs, like this one, shocked many wealthier Americans.*

Sweatshops turned out large amounts of clothing at low prices.

Sweatshops were located in tenements to avoid the labor laws that affected factories. Workers crowded into the small, stuffy spaces.

This 12-year-old boy said he was 16 in order to keep his job of pulling threads.

ANALYSIS SKILL **ANALYZING PRIMARY SOURCES**

How might this photograph encourage people to become reformers?

Another muckraker, Ida B. Tarbell, wrote articles criticizing the unfair business practices of the Standard Oil Company. Upton Sinclair exposed unsanitary practices in the meat-processing industry in his novel *The Jungle.*

Although such writing angered many politicians and business leaders, it also helped to unite Progressives. Muckrakers influenced voters, causing them to pressure politicians into backing reforms.

Reform Successes

A major goal of Progressive reformers was to help the urban poor. You have read about the work of housing reformers, which led to the 1901 New York State Tenement House Act. Other Progressives started settlement houses similar to Jane Addams's Hull House. People usually started settlement houses in poor areas in order to improve education, housing, and sanitation there.

The movement for urban reform also led to new professions, such as city planning and civil engineering. City planners helped design safer building codes and opened new public parks. Civil engineers improved transportation by paving streets and building bridges. Sanitation engineers tried to solve problems concerning pollution, waste disposal, and impure water supplies. Death rates dropped dramatically in areas where planners and engineers addressed these problems.

Progressives also believed that improving education would lead to a better society. In response to their demands for reform, states passed laws requiring all children to attend school. Some Progressives started kindergarten programs to help young city children learn basic social skills. In 1873 reformer Susan Blow opened the first American public kindergarten in St. Louis. By 1898 more than 4,000 kindergartens had opened in the United States.

Philosopher John Dewey was a key supporter of early childhood education. His motive was to help children learn problem-solving skills, not just memorize facts. This, he thought, would help them in everyday life. Dewey's teaching methods became a model for progressive education across the country.

Progressives also worked to improve the education of medical professionals. In the late 1800s the United States lacked a ready supply of well-trained and professionally organized doctors. Researchers knew the causes of diseases such as pneumonia and tuberculosis. However, there were few medical organizations that could help spread this knowledge.

Under the leadership of Joseph McCormack, the American Medical Association (AMA) brought together local medical organizations in 1901. The AMA supported laws designed to protect public health and showed how Progressives could organize to help improve society. Other organizations followed the AMA's lead.

READING CHECK Finding Main Ideas How did progressive reforms improve society?

BIOGRAPHY

Robert M. La Follette
1855–1925

Born in rural Wisconsin, Robert M. La Follette began his political career at a young age. He was elected to the U.S. House of Representatives in 1884, becoming the youngest member of Congress. He soon earned the nickname "Fighting Bob" for his energetic speaking style and his active support for progressive reforms.

After serving as Wisconsin's governor and as U.S. senator, La Follette ran for president as the Progressive Party candidate in 1924. He won his home state and received about 16 percent of the popular vote.

Drawing Conclusions Why might La Follette have been proud of the nickname "Fighting Bob"?

Expansion of Voting Power

Some Progressives worked to change state and local governments in order to reduce the power of political machines. In many places, reformers replaced corrupt ballots that listed only one party's candidates with government-prepared ballots that listed all candidates. Under pressure from reformers, many states adopted secret ballots, a measure that ensured the privacy of every voter.

Voting Reforms

Reformers also hoped to expand voting power. For example, they favored the **Seventeenth Amendment**, which allowed Americans to vote directly for U.S. senators. Before the constitutional amendment was passed in 1913, state legislatures had elected senators. Reformers also favored the direct primary, in which voters choose candidates for public office directly. Previously, party leaders had selected which candidates would run for office.

Other reform measures allowed voters to take action against corrupt politicians. Some states and cities gave unhappy voters the right to sign a petition asking for a special vote. The purpose of that vote was to **recall**, or remove, an official before the end of his or her term. If enough voters signed the petition, the vote took place. The official could then be removed from office if there was a majority of recall votes.

In California, Oregon, and states in the Midwest, Progressives worked on reforms to give voters direct influence over new laws. A procedure called the **initiative** allowed voters to propose a new law by collecting signatures on a petition. If enough signatures were collected, the proposed law was voted on at the next election. Another measure, called the **referendum**, permitted voters to approve or reject a law that had already been proposed or passed by a government body. This process gave voters a chance to overrule laws that they opposed.

Government Reforms

In addition to working for greater voter participation, Progressives attempted to change the way city government operated. Some reformers wanted city government to be run like a business. As a result of their efforts, several cities changed to council-manager governments. Under this system, voters elect a city council. The council then appoints a professional manager to run the city. Other business-minded reformers supported the commission form of government. Under this system, the city is headed by a group of elected officials. Each official manages a major city agency, such as housing or transportation.

One of the leaders of the effort to reform state government was Wisconsin's Republican governor **Robert M. La Follette**. La Follette decreased the power of political machines and used university professors and other experts to help write new laws and work in state agencies. He also made available to the public information on how politicians voted. That way, voters would know if leaders had

QUICK FACTS

Expanding Democracy

Direct Primaries	Voters choose candidates.
Recall	Voters can remove an official from office.
Initiatives	Voters can propose laws by petition.
Referendum	Voters can overrule a law.
17th Amendment	Senators are elected directly by voters.

kept their campaign promises. Called the Wisconsin Idea, La Follette's plan became a model for progressive reforms in other states.

READING CHECK **Evaluating** How did Progressives work to change voting procedures?

SUMMARY AND PREVIEW Progressives worked to reform government and improve city life. In the next section you will learn about reforms in working conditions.

Section 1 Assessment

go.hrw.com
Online Quiz
KEYWORD: SB7 HP21

Reviewing Ideas, Terms, and People

1. **a. Recall** What was the main goal of **political machines** during the Gilded Age?
   b. Draw Conclusions Why do you think some immigrants supported political machines?
   c. Predict Do you think the system of testing created by the Pendleton Civil Service Act would work to reduce corruption in the spoils system? Why or why not?
2. **a. Identify** Who were **muckrakers**, and what effect did they have on reform?
   b. Explain How did **Progressives** try to improve education?
   c. Evaluate Which progressive reform do you think was most important? Why?
3. **a. Describe** What new ideas and practices were introduced to give voters more power?
   b. Draw Conclusions How did progressive reforms limit the power of political machines?

Critical Thinking

4. **Categorizing** Review your notes on the problems that progressive reforms addressed. Then copy the chart below and use it to categorize the various progressive reforms.

Progressive Reforms		
Social	Political	Urban

FOCUS ON SPEAKING

5. **Addressing Political and Social Problems** How would you address the problems of political corruption and urban growth during the late 1800s? Jot down notes about campaign promises you might make to assure voters that you would make the necessary reforms.

Reform
Literature

from *How the Other Half Lives*
by Jacob Riis (1849–1914)

About the Reading How the Other Half Lives *describes the tenement houses where immigrants lived in New York City. Its author, Jacob Riis, was a newspaper reporter. His nonfiction book made Americans aware of the extremes of poverty suffered by working people. Riis believed that every human being deserved a decent, safe place to live.* How the Other Half Lives *led to reforms and new laws that improved housing conditions.*

AS YOU READ Look for details that help you see, hear, and smell Cherry Street.

Cherry Street. Be a little careful, please! ❶ The hall is dark and you might stumble over the children pitching pennies back there. Not that it would hurt them; kicks and cuffs are their daily diet. They have little else. Here where the hall turns and dives into utter darkness is a step, and another, another. A flight of stairs. You can feel your way, if you cannot see it. Close? Yes! What would you have? All the fresh air that ever enters these stairs comes from the hall door that is forever slamming, and from the windows of dark bedrooms that in turn receive from the stairs their sole supply of the elements God meant to be free . . . That was a woman filling her pail by the hydrant you just bumped against. The sinks are in the hallway, that all the tenants may have access—and all be poisoned alike by their summer stenches. Hear the pump squeak! It is the lullaby of tenement house babes. In summer, when a thousand thirsty throats pant for a cooling drink in this block, it is worked in vain . . . ❷

The sea of a mighty population, held in galling fetters, heaves uneasily in the tenements . . . If it rise once more, no human power may avail to check it. The gap between the classes in which it surges, unseen, unsuspected by the thoughtless, is widening day by day . . . I know of but one bridge that will carry us over safe, a bridge founded upon justice and built of human hearts.

GUIDED READING

WORD HELP

cuffs punches

utter complete

close stuffy

sole only

access right to use

stenches bad smells

in vain without success

galling causing pain; irritating

fetters chains

heaves rises and falls

avail help

❶ *The writer wants you to imagine that he is taking you on a tour of the building. Why do you think he chooses this way to describe the place?*

❷ *Find one detail that appeals to each sense: sight, sound, smell, taste, and touch. How would you sum up, in one sentence, the place that Riis describes?*

from *The Jungle*

by Upton Sinclair (1878–1968)

About the Reading *The Jungle focused the nation's attention on immigrant workers in the meatpacking industry. Upton Sinclair's novel showed bosses forcing human beings to live and work like animals. He also described, in shocking detail, how meat was handled. Sinclair published his book in 1906. Later that same year, the U.S. government passed the Pure Food and Drug Act and the Meat Inspection Act. Many Americans even gave up eating meat for a while.*

AS YOU READ Look for details that create one overwhelming effect.

There was never the least attention paid to what was cut up for sausage; there would come back from Europe old sausage that had been rejected, and that was mouldy and white—it would be dosed with borax and glycerine, and dumped into hoppers, and made over again for home consumption. There would be meat that had tumbled out on the floor, in the dirt and sawdust, where the workers had tramped and spit uncounted billions of consumption germs. ❶ There would be meat stored in great piles in rooms and the water from leaky roofs would drip over it, and thousands of rats would race about on it. It was too dark in these storage places to see well, but a man would run his hand over these piles of meat and sweep off handfuls of the dried dung of rats. ❷ These rats were nuisances, and the packers would put poisoned bread out for them; they would die, and then rats, bread, and meat would go into the hoppers together . . . ❸ There was no place for the men to wash their hands before they ate their dinner, and so they made a practice of washing them in the water that was to be ladled into the sausage. ❹

GUIDED READING

WORD HELP

borax white powder used in manufacturing and cleaning
glycerine sweet, sticky liquid
hoppers containers
consumption to eat or drink
consumption tuberculosis, a lung disease that was fatal at that time
ladled added with a large spoon

❶ *What overall effect or mood does Sinclair create?*

❷ *Based on the details in this passage, what were the packers most concerned about?*

❸ *Why do you think rats were considered nuisances?*

❹ *Find details that reveal how one improvement in working conditions might have resulted in healthier sausage.*

CONNECTING LITERATURE TO HISTORY

1. **Identify Cause and Effect** Jacob Riis and Upton Sinclair were both muckraking journalists. Why do you think so much muck existed in the tenements and in the meatpacking business? Why had people ignored those conditions for so long?
2. **Identify Cause and Effect** Both Riis and Sinclair believed that improving conditions for immigrants would benefit all of society. Explain how one specific change in the tenements might have a favorable effect on everyone. Then explain how one specific change in meat handling might affect everyone.
3. **Compare and Contrast** Both *How the Other Half Lives* and *The Jungle* inspired Progressives to work for reform. Which work do you think had the greater effect on its readers? Use details from each passage to explain your answer.

Reforming the Workplace

Virginia Standards
of Learning USII.4e, USII.6b

What You Will Learn...

Main Ideas

1. Reformers attempted to improve conditions for child laborers.
2. Unions and reformers took steps to improve safety in the workplace and to limit working hours.

The Big Idea

In the early 1900s, Progressives and other reformers focused on improving conditions for American workers.

Key Terms and People

Triangle Shirtwaist Fire, *p. 673*
workers' compensation laws, *p. 673*
capitalism, *p. 674*
socialism, *p. 674*
William "Big Bill" Haywood, *p. 674*
Industrial Workers of the World, *p. 674*

TAKING NOTES As you read, take notes on important labor problems and the workers they affected. You can organize your notes in a table like this one.

Problems in the Workplace

If YOU were there...

You have been working in a hat factory since 1900, when you were eight years old. Now you are experienced enough to run one of the sewing machines. You don't earn as much as older workers, but your family needs every penny you bring home. Still, the long hours make you very tired. One day you hear that people are trying to stop children from doing factory work. They think that children should be at school or playing.

Would you be for or against this social reform? Why?

BUILDING BACKGROUND Since the Second Industrial Revolution, more and more people were working long hours in difficult conditions. With adult workers earning low wages, many children had to work full time to help support their families. Progressive reformers began to focus on these problems.

Improving Conditions for Children

In the early 1900s a reformer named Marie Van Vorst took a series of jobs in factories and clothing mills around the country. She wanted to investigate working conditions for children by living and working alongside them. In a South Carolina textile mill, Van Vorst met children as young as seven years old. She described working with one young child:

"Through the looms I catch sight of ... my landlord's little child. She is seven; so small that they have a box for her to stand on ... I can see only her fingers as they clutch at the flying spools."
– Marie Van Vorst, quoted in *A History of Women in America,* edited by Carol Hymowitz

This girl—and other children like her—provided cheap labor for manufacturers. Some children were paid as little as 40 cents per day. Marie Van Vorst helped focus attention on the problem of child labor. Eliminating the problems of child labor became a major issue for Progressives and other reformers.

Children at Work

Children did many jobs in the late 1800s. Boys sold newspapers and shined shoes on the streets. Girls often cooked or cleaned for boarders staying with their families. Girls also worked at home with their mothers, sewing clothes or making handicrafts.

Like the child Van Vorst encountered, many children worked in industry. In 1900 more than 1.75 million children age 15 and under worked in factories, mines, and mills, earning very low wages.

Calls for Reform

As reporters published shocking accounts of working conditions for children, more people became aware of the problem. Progressives began to call for new reforms. You have read about Florence Kelley's work against child labor in Illinois. Kelley also served as a board member of the National Consumers' League, the major lobbying group for women's and children's labor issues. A lobbying group works to influence legislators in favor of a cause.

During the early 1900s, reformers finally succeeded in getting some laws passed to ease the conditions of child laborers. In 1912 the state of Massachusetts passed the first minimum wage law, and a commission was created to establish rates for child workers.

In 1916 and 1919 Congress passed federal child labor laws. The laws banned products made with child labor from being shipped from one state to another. The Supreme Court, however, ruled that the laws were unconstitutional. The Court argued that the laws went beyond the federal government's legal power to regulate interstate commerce.

In any case, laws alone could not end child labor. Some parents ignored child labor laws so that their children could continue contributing to the family income. Children were often instructed to lie about their age to government inspectors and tell them they were older than they really were.

FOCUS ON READING

What do you think the author's goal is in this paragraph?

READING CHECK **Finding Main Ideas** How did reformers try to improve child labor conditions?

Child Labor

Young children did much of the work in the American factories of the late 1800s. They were paid less than adult workers.

Why did some parents want their children to work?

Working Conditions for Children, Early 1900s

This illustration shows some of the jobs that children did in glass factories in the early 1900s. You can see that there were many ways for young workers to be injured on the job.

Hot air blew from the glass ovens into the working space.

Adult workers closely supervised child workers.

Workers wore no protection against the fires and machinery.

Temperatures in the ovens used to make glass were more than 2,000° Fahrenheit.

Bending and lifting often left young workers tired and sore after their long day's work.

ANALYSIS SKILL **ANALYZING VISUALS**

Using the illustration, what can you tell about the life and work of these boys?

Safety and Working Conditions

Child labor reform was only part of the progressive effort to help American workers. Many Progressives also favored laws to ensure workers' safety, limit working hours, and protect workers' rights.

Workplace Safety

Workplace accidents were common in the 1800s and early 1900s. In 1900 some 35,000 people were killed in industrial accidents. About 500,000 suffered injuries. One child described how her sister was injured using a machine in a string factory. "You see you mustn't talk or look off a minute," she explained. "My sister was like me. She forgot and talked, and just that minute her finger was off, and she didn't even cry till she picked it up."

Accidents like this were not big news in the early 1900s, but in 1911 a much greater workplace tragedy shocked the nation. It took place at the Triangle Shirtwaist Company, a New York City clothing factory that employed mostly teenage immigrant women. On the afternoon of March 25, a fire started on the eighth floor of the factory. Workers tried to escape, but factory owners had locked the exit doors—to reduce theft of materials, they said.

By the time firefighters brought the fire under control, 146 workers had died. At a memorial service for the victims, union leader Rose Schneiderman called for action. "It is up to the working people to save themselves," she said. The **Triangle Shirtwaist Fire** and similar accidents led to the passage of laws improving factory safety standards.

Labor leaders and reformers also fought for **workers' compensation laws**, which guaranteed a portion of lost wages to workers injured on the job. In 1902 Maryland became the first state to pass such a law. However, new laws were not always strictly enforced. Working conditions remained poor in many places.

TRIAL TRANSCRIPT
Triangle Shirtwaist Fire

Ethel Monick was one of the teenage factory workers at the Triangle Shirtwaist Company. In the trial that followed the disaster, she described her experience in the fire. Rose Freedman, pictured, was the longest living survivor of the fire. She died in 2001.

I seen the fire and then I seen all the girls rushing down to the place to escape. So I tried to go through the Greene Street door, and there were quick girls there and I seen I can't get out there, so I went to the elevator, and then I heard the elevator fall down, so I ran through to the Washington Place side . . . I tried the door and I could not open it, so I thought I was not strong enough to open it, so I hollered girls here is a door, and they all rushed over and they tried to open it, but it was locked and they hollered "the door is locked and we can't open it!"

—Testimony of Ethel Monick, age 16

ANALYSIS SKILL ANALYZING PRIMARY SOURCES

According to Monick, what is the feeling in the factory?

The Courts and Labor

Not everyone supported the new workplace regulations. Some business leaders believed that the economy should operate without any government interference. They went to court to block new labor laws.

One important case began in New York in 1897, after the state passed a law limiting bakers to a 10-hour workday. Joseph Lochner, a bakery owner, challenged the law. The case eventually went to the U.S. Supreme Court in 1905. In *Lochner* v. *New York*, the Court ruled that states could not restrict the rights of employers and workers to enter into any type of labor agreement. The New York law was declared unconstitutional.

The Supreme Court did uphold some limits on working hours for women and children. In the 1908 *Muller* v. *Oregon* case, the Court upheld laws restricting women's work hours. The justices stated that such laws protected women's health, which was of public concern.

Labor Organizations

Labor unions were also a strong force for improving working conditions. Union membership rose from about 800,000 in 1900 to about 5 million in 1920. Led by Samuel Gompers, the American Federation of Labor (AFL) remained one of the strongest labor unions. The AFL focused on better working conditions and pay for skilled workers. Gompers supported the American system of **capitalism**, an economic system in which private businesses run most industries and competition determines the price of goods.

Some union members, however, believed in **socialism**—a system in which the government owns and operates a country's means of production. Socialists, led by Eugene V. Debs, hoped that the government would protect workers.

In 1905 a group of socialists and union leaders founded a union that welcomed immigrants, women, African Americans, and others not welcome in the AFL. Led by **William "Big Bill" Haywood**, this socialist union was called the **Industrial Workers of the World** (IWW). Its goal was to organize all workers into one large union that would overthrow capitalism. Staging strikes across the country, the IWW frightened many Americans with its aggressive tactics. Strong opposition led to its decline by 1920.

READING CHECK Analyzing How did reforms change the workplace?

SUMMARY AND PREVIEW Progressive reformers fought to improve working conditions. In the next section you will learn about how women and minorities struggled for their rights.

Section 2 Assessment

go.hrw.com
Online Quiz
KEYWORD: SB7 HP21

Reviewing Ideas, Terms, and People

1. **a. Recall** What jobs did child laborers often hold?
   b. Explain Why did businesses employ children in factories?
   c. Elaborate Why do you think reformers began to demand improvements to child labor conditions?
2. **a. Identify** What events led to the movement to improve workplace safety?
   b. Make Inferences Why did the **Industrial Workers of the World** frighten some people?
   c. Predict What conflicts might arise between supporters of **capitalism** and **socialism**?

Critical Thinking

3. **Analyzing** Review your notes on labor reforms and workers. Then copy the graphic organizer shown below. Use it to give specific examples of how Progressives tried to reform child labor, women's labor, and workplace conditions.

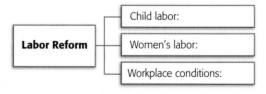

```
                 ┌─ Child labor:

Labor Reform ────┼─ Women's labor:

                 └─ Workplace conditions:
```

FOCUS ON SPEAKING

4. **Addressing Problems in the Workplace** How would you address problems in the workplace? Make notes on campaign promises you might make to assure voters that you would address issues of child labor and workplace safety.

The Rights of Women and Minorities

VA Virginia Standards of Learning USII.1a, USII.1c, USII.1d, USII.4c, USII.4e, USII.6b

What You Will Learn...

Main Ideas
1. Women fought for temperance and the right to vote.
2. African American reformers challenged discrimination and called for equality.
3. Progressive reforms failed to benefit all minorities.

The Big Idea
The Progressive movement made advances for the rights of women and some minorities.

Key Terms and People
Eighteenth Amendment, *p. 676*
National American Woman Suffrage Association, *p. 676*
Alice Paul, *p. 677*
Nineteenth Amendment, *p. 677*
Booker T. Washington, *p. 677*
Ida B. Wells, *p. 677*
W. E. B. Du Bois, *p. 678*
National Association for the Advancement of Colored People, *p. 678*

If YOU were there...

You are a member of the graduating class of 1912 from an excellent women's college. You have always been interested in science, especially biology. You would like to be a doctor, but you know that medical schools accept very few women. One career path for you is to go into social work. Yet that's not what you really want to do.

How would you want to use your education?

BUILDING BACKGROUND The Progressives had a wide variety of goals. Besides attacking social problems such as child labor, they worked to reform government and make it more democratic. Changes in women's education affected the movement, as college-educated women often became leaders in working for reforms.

Women Fight for Temperance and Voting Rights

New educational opportunities drew more women into the Progressive movement. In the late 1800s, women began attending women's colleges, such as Smith College in Massachusetts and Vassar College in New York, in record numbers. In 1870 only about 20 percent of college students were women. By 1910 that number had doubled. The goal of female students was "to develop as fully as may be the powers of womanhood," said Sophia Smith, founder of Smith College.

Many women graduates entered fields such as social work and teaching. They found it much harder to enter professions such as law and medicine, which were dominated by men. Denied access to such professions, women often put their education to use by becoming active in reform. Women's clubs campaigned for causes such as temperance, women's suffrage, child welfare, and political reform.

TAKING NOTES As you read, take notes on the causes supported by different groups of progressive reformers. In each circle of a diagram like the one below, fill in details about one cause or goal. You may need to add more circles.

Progressive Reforms

The Temperance Movement

In the mid-1800s many of these reformers blamed social problems such as family violence and criminal behavior on a number of factors, including urbanization and immigration. They also blamed problems on alcohol consumption. As a result, many groups took up the cause of temperance, or avoidance of alcohol.

In 1874, reformers from many different backgrounds formed the Woman's Christian Temperance Union (WCTU), which fought for adoption of local and state laws restricting the sale of alcohol. Under the leadership of Frances Willard, the organization started 10,000 branches. More than 1,000 saloons were forced to shut down as a result of temperance supporters' efforts.

One especially radical temperance fighter chose more aggressive methods to fight for her cause. In the 1890s Carry Nation became famous for storming into saloons with a hatchet and smashing liquor bottles. Nation described destroying a Kansas saloon with bricks and rocks:

"I threw as hard, and as fast as I could, smashing mirrors and bottles and glasses and it was astonishing how quickly this was done."
—Carry Nation, quoted in *Witnessing America: The Library of Congress Book of Firsthand Accounts of Life in America, 1600–1900*

In 1919 many years of temperance efforts led to the passage of the **Eighteenth Amendment**, banning the production, sale, and transportation of alcoholic beverages throughout the United States.

The Right to Vote

Women reformers also fought for suffrage, or the right to vote. Many people at this time opposed giving women the vote. Political bosses, for instance, worried about the anti-corruption efforts of women. Some business leaders worried that women voters would support minimum wage and child labor laws. Other people believed that women should only be homemakers and mothers and not politically active citizens.

In spite of such opposition, the women's suffrage movement began to gain national support in the 1890s. Elizabeth Cady Stanton and Susan B. Anthony founded the **National American Woman Suffrage Association** (NAWSA) in 1890 to promote the cause of women's suffrage. That same year, women

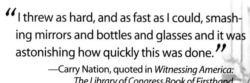

Time Line

The Nineteenth Amendment

Women had been seeking the right to vote since 1776. Finally, in 1920 they achieved success with the passage of the Nineteenth Amendment.

1919

May 21, 1919 The House of Representatives passes the Nineteenth Amendment by a vote of 304 to 89.

June 4, 1919 The Senate passes the Nineteenth Amendment by a vote of 56 to 25.

June 10, 1919 Illinois, Michigan, and Wisconsin become the first states to ratify the Nineteenth Amendment.

won the right to vote in Wyoming. Colorado, Idaho, and Utah followed.

Carrie Chapman Catt became president of the NAWSA in 1900. Catt mobilized more than 1 million volunteers for the movement. She argued that women should have a voice in creating laws that affected them. "We women demand an equal voice," she said. "We shall accept nothing less."

Some women believed that NAWSA did not go far enough. In 1913 **Alice Paul** founded what would become the National Woman's Party (NWP). The NWP used parades, public demonstrations, picketing, hunger strikes, and other means to draw attention to the suffrage cause. Paul even organized picketing in front of the White House. Paul and other NWP leaders were jailed for their actions.

Suffragists finally succeeded in gaining the vote. In 1919 the U.S. Congress passed the **Nineteenth Amendment**, granting American women the right to vote. The Nineteenth Amendment was ratified by the states the following year, making it law.

READING CHECK **Analyzing** How did reformers draw attention to the temperance and women's suffrage movements?

African Americans Challenge Discrimination

White reformers often overlooked issues such as racial discrimination and segregation. African American reformers took the lead in addressing these problems.

One of the most important African American leaders was **Booker T. Washington**. Born into slavery, he became a respected educator while in his twenties. Washington's strategy was not to fight discrimination directly. Instead, he encouraged African Americans to improve their educational and economic well-being. This, he believed, would eventually lead to the end of discrimination.

Other African Americans spoke out more directly against discrimination. Journalist **Ida B. Wells** wrote articles about the unequal education available to African American children. In her Memphis newspaper *Free Speech*, Wells also drew attention to the lynching of African Americans. During lynchings people were murdered by mobs instead of receiving a trial after being accused of a crime, or even for breaking social codes. More than 3,000 African Americans were lynched between 1885 and 1915.

Although death threats forced Wells to move to the North, she continued campaigning against lynching. In 1900 she wrote:

*"Our country's national crime is *lynching* ... In fact, for all kinds of offenses—and, for no offenses— from murders to misdemeanors, men and women are put to death without judge or jury."*
—Ida B. Wells, from her article "Lynch Law in America"

August 26, 1920 The secretary of state officially declares the Nineteenth Amendment ratified by three-fourths of the states, making it law.

1920

August 18, 1920 Tennessee becomes the thirty-sixth state to ratify the Nineteenth Amendment.

November 2, 1920 The first national election in which all women can vote is held.

1921

Like Wells, **W. E. B. Du Bois** took a direct approach to fighting racial injustice. Born in Massachusetts, Du Bois was a college graduate who earned a doctorate from Harvard University. As part of his research, he studied and publicized cases of racial prejudice. Du Bois believed that African Americans should protest unjust treatment and demand equal rights.

In 1909 Du Bois and other reformers founded the **National Association for the Advancement of Colored People** (NAACP), an organization that called for economic and educational equality for African Americans. The NAACP attacked discrimination by using the courts. In 1915 it won the important case of *Guinn* v. *United States,* which made grandfather clauses illegal. These laws were used in the South to keep African Americans from voting. Grandfather clauses imposed strict qualifications on voters unless their grandfathers had been allowed to vote. Many white voters met this requirement and were therefore automatically permitted to vote in elections. However, most African Americans' grandfathers had been enslaved and could not vote.

Another important organization, the National Urban League, was formed in 1911 by Dr. George Edmund Haynes. This organization aided many African Americans moving from the South by helping them find jobs and housing in northern cities. The League addressed many of the same problems faced by other Progressives, such as health, sanitation, and education.

READING CHECK **Finding Main Ideas** What was the purpose of the NAACP?

THE IMPACT TODAY

Today the NAACP has around 2,200 adult branches and 1,700 branches for young people.

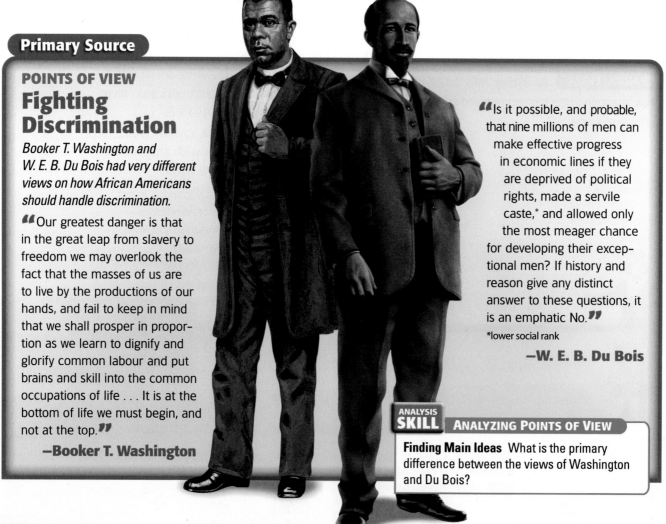

Primary Source

POINTS OF VIEW

Fighting Discrimination

Booker T. Washington and W. E. B. Du Bois had very different views on how African Americans should handle discrimination.

❝Our greatest danger is that in the great leap from slavery to freedom we may overlook the fact that the masses of us are to live by the productions of our hands, and fail to keep in mind that we shall prosper in proportion as we learn to dignify and glorify common labour and put brains and skill into the common occupations of life . . . It is at the bottom of life we must begin, and not at the top.❞

—Booker T. Washington

❝Is it possible, and probable, that nine millions of men can make effective progress in economic lines if they are deprived of political rights, made a servile caste,* and allowed only the most meager chance for developing their exceptional men? If history and reason give any distinct answer to these questions, it is an emphatic No.❞

*lower social rank

—W. E. B. Du Bois

ANALYSIS SKILL **ANALYZING POINTS OF VIEW**

Finding Main Ideas What is the primary difference between the views of Washington and Du Bois?

Failures of Reform

Other minority groups felt left behind by the Progressive movement. Although some reformers tried to aid such groups, the aim of many was to encourage other ethnicities to adopt the ways of European society. The Society of American Indians, formed in 1911, was one such attempt. Started by Native American doctors Carlos Montezuma and Charles Eastman, the society believed that integration into white society would end Native American poverty. Many Native Americans, however, wanted to preserve their traditional culture. They resisted the movement toward adopting white culture.

Immigrant groups from non-European countries also formed groups to help support their members. Chinese immigrants, for example, organized neighborhood associations in the communities in which they lived. District associations, cultural groups, churches, and temples provided public services that white reformers ignored. Such groups provided the money for building San Francisco's Chinese hospital in 1925. Chinese immigration dropped, however, due in part to anti-Chinese riots that occurred in some western towns and cities.

While fewer Chinese immigrants came to the United States, the number of Mexican immigrants increased. The northern and southern borders between the United States and its neighbors were fairly easy to cross in this period. Many Mexican immigrants moved to the South and Southwest, where they became an important part of the societies and economies of these regions. Many Mexican immigrants found jobs in the mining and railroad industries. Others began farms or became migrant workers. Progressive labor laws and factory reforms did nothing to improve the poor living and working conditions of migrant farm workers.

READING CHECK Summarizing What were the limitations of progressive reforms?

SUMMARY AND PREVIEW Many U.S. citizens worked for progressive reforms. In the next section you will read about presidents who also worked for progressive goals.

go.hrw.com
Online Quiz
KEYWORD: SB7 HP21

Section 3 Assessment

Reviewing Ideas, Terms, and People

1. **a. Identify** What did the **Eighteenth** and **Nineteenth Amendments** accomplish?
   b. Summarize How did **Alice Paul** and the National Woman's Party try to draw attention to the issue of women's suffrage?
2. **a. Identify** What role did **Ida B. Wells** play in reform efforts for African Americans?
   b. Contrast How did **Booker T. Washington** differ from other African American leaders?
   c. Evaluate Do you think the **National Association for the Advancement of Colored People** was successful in fighting discrimination? Explain.
3. **a. Describe** What discrimination did Chinese Americans face?
   b. Summarize How were some minority groups overlooked by the Progressive movement?

Critical Thinking

4. **Analyzing** Review your notes on Progressives' causes. Then copy the diagram shown and use it to identify the progressive reforms introduced by the temperance movement, the women's suffrage movement, and African Americans.

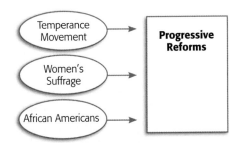

FOCUS ON SPEAKING

5. **Addressing the Rights of Women and Minorities** Review this section's material on education for women, women's suffrage, temperance, racial discrimination, and segregation. As a politician, what promises would you make regarding these issues? Think about how you would make your ideas acceptable to the American public. Would you be willing to compromise your ideals?

The Progressive Presidents

Virginia Standards of Learning USII.1b, USII.1c, USII.2c, USII.4e, USII.6b

What You Will Learn...

Main Ideas

1. Theodore Roosevelt's progressive reforms tried to balance the interests of business, consumers, and laborers.
2. William Howard Taft angered Progressives with his cautious reforms, while Woodrow Wilson enacted far-reaching banking and antitrust reforms.

The Big Idea

American presidents in the early 1900s did a great deal to promote progressive reforms.

Key Terms and People

Theodore Roosevelt, *p. 680*
Pure Food and Drug Act, *p. 681*
conservation, *p. 681*
William Howard Taft, *p. 682*
Progressive Party, *p. 682*
Woodrow Wilson, *p. 682*
Sixteenth Amendment, *p. 683*

TAKING NOTES As you read, take notes on the achievements of each of the progressive presidents. Use a table like the one below to organize your notes.

Roosevelt	Taft	Wilson

If YOU were there...

It is 1912 and you're voting in your first presidential election. This election is unusual—there are three major candidates. One is the popular former president Theodore Roosevelt, who is running as a third-party candidate. He thinks the Republican candidate will not make enough progressive reforms. But the Democratic candidate is a progressive reformer too.

How will you decide which candidate to support?

BUILDING BACKGROUND Political corruption was one early target of the progressive reformers. Some politicians who joined them believed that government—local, state, and national—should play an active role in improving society and people's lives.

Roosevelt's Progressive Reforms

During a summer tour after his second inauguration in 1901, President William McKinley met a friendly crowd in Buffalo, New York. Suddenly, anarchist Leon Czolgosz stepped forward and shot the president. A little more than a week later, McKinley died. Vice President **Theodore Roosevelt** took office.

Roosevelt's Square Deal

Roosevelt believed that the interests of businesspeople, laborers, and consumers should be balanced for the public good. He called this policy the Square Deal. He put the policy to the test in 1902 when faced by a coal miners' strike. Roosevelt knew the strike might leave the country without heating fuel for the coming winter. He threatened to take over the mines unless managers and strikers agreed to arbitration—a formal process to settle disputes. He felt this was the only fair way to protect Americans.

"The labor unions shall have a square deal, and the corporations shall have a square deal, and in addition all private citizens shall have a square deal."

—President Theodore Roosevelt, quoted in *The Presidency of Theodore Roosevelt,* by Lewis L. Gould

The National Park System

In 1872 Yellowstone National Park, located mostly in Wyoming, became the first national park in the United States—and the world. Today there are 55 national parks in the United States. They are managed by the National Park Service (NPS), an agency of the federal government established in 1916. The National Park Service administers almost 84 million acres (133,000 square miles) of land.

President Theodore Roosevelt and conservationist John Muir in Yosemite National Park in California

Cathedral Rocks, Yosemite National Park

Regulating Big Business

Roosevelt made regulating big business a top goal of his administration. Muckrakers helped build support for this regulation. The public was shocked, for instance, after reading Upton Sinclair's description of the meatpacking industry in *The Jungle.* Roosevelt opened an investigation and later convinced Congress to pass a meat inspection law.

In 1906 Congress passed the **Pure Food and Drug Act**. This law prohibited the manufacture, sale, and transport of mislabeled or contaminated food and drugs. Roosevelt also was the first president to successfully use the 1890 Sherman Antitrust Act to break up a monopoly. He persuaded Congress to regulate railroad shipping rates. The public largely supported this expansion of federal regulatory powers.

Conservation

Roosevelt's love of the outdoors inspired him to join other Progressives in supporting **conservation**, or the protection of nature and its resources. Roosevelt was the first president to consider conservation an important national priority.

People believed in conservation for various reasons. Preservationists such as John Muir thought that nature should be left untouched so that people could enjoy its beauty:

"Thousands of tired, nerve-shaken, over-civilized people are beginning to find out that going to the mountains is going home; that wildness is a necessity; and that mountain parks and reservations are useful not only as fountains of timber and irrigating rivers, but as fountains of life."
—John Muir, *Our National Parks*

Other conservationists wanted to make sure the nation used its natural resources efficiently. Gifford Pinchot, the first head of the newly created Forest Service, valued forests for the resources they provided to build "prosperous homes." The disagreement between the two ideals of conservation eventually widened.

While Roosevelt was in office, the Forest Service gained control of nearly 150 million acres of public land. Roosevelt doubled the number of national parks, created 18 national monuments, and started 51 bird sanctuaries.

READING CHECK Summarizing What reforms did Roosevelt support?

Reforms of Taft and Wilson

Theodore Roosevelt hoped that his secretary of war, **William Howard Taft**, would take his place as president in 1908. Like Roosevelt, Taft favored business regulation and opposed socialism. With Roosevelt's assistance, Taft defeated William Jennings Bryan in the election of 1908.

Taft Angers Progressives

Despite their friendship, Roosevelt and Taft held different ideas about how a president should act. Taft thought Roosevelt had claimed more power than a president was constitutionally allowed.

ACADEMIC VOCABULARY

various
of many types

As president, therefore, Taft chose to move cautiously toward reform and regulation. This upset Roosevelt and **various** Progressives, who supported stricter regulation of big business. Although Taft's administration started twice as many antitrust lawsuits as Roosevelt's had, Progressives were not satisfied.

Taft angered Progressives further by signing the Payne-Aldrich Tariff of 1909. This tariff reduced some rates on imported goods, but it raised others. Progressives wanted all tariffs to be lowered, in order to lower prices for consumers.

Furious with Taft, Roosevelt decided to run for president again in 1912. After Taft won the Republican nomination, Roosevelt and his followers formed the **Progressive Party**. It was nicknamed the Bull Moose Party because Roosevelt said he was "as strong as a bull moose." The split between Taft and Roosevelt divided the Republican vote, and Democratic candidate **Woodrow Wilson** won the electoral vote by a wide margin.

Wilson's Reforms

In his inaugural address, Wilson spoke of the terrible social conditions under which many working-class Americans lived. "We have been proud of our industrial achievements," he said, "but we have not hitherto [yet] stopped thoughtfully enough to count the human cost." Passing reform legislation was Wilson's top goal. He pushed for two measures soon after taking office: tariff revision and banking reform.

Wilson backed the Underwood Tariff Act of 1913, which lowered tariffs. The act also introduced a version of the modern

The Election of 1912

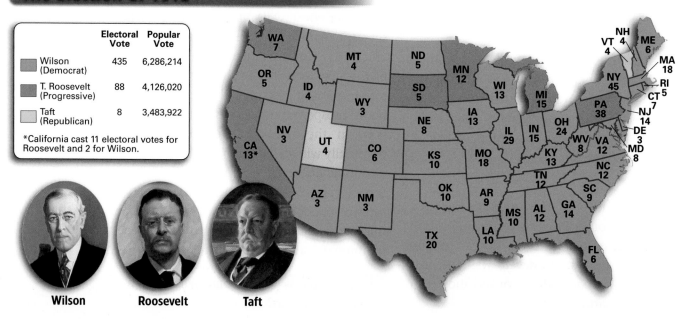

	Electoral Vote	Popular Vote
Wilson (Democrat)	435	6,286,214
T. Roosevelt (Progressive)	88	4,126,020
Taft (Republican)	8	3,483,922

*California cast 11 electoral votes for Roosevelt and 2 for Wilson.

WA 7
OR 5
ID 4
MT 4
WY 3
NV 3
UT 4
CA 13*
AZ 3
NM 3
CO 6
ND 5
SD 5
NE 8
KS 10
OK 10
TX 20
MN 12
IA 13
MO 18
AR 9
LA 10
WI 13
IL 29
MS 10
MI 15
IN 15
KY 13
TN 12
AL 12
GA 14
OH 24
WV 8
VA 12
NC 12
SC 9
FL 6
PA 38
NY 45
MD 8
DE 3
NJ 14
CT 7
RI 5
MA 18
NH 4
VT 4
ME 6

Wilson   **Roosevelt**   **Taft**

The Progressive Amendments, 1909–1920

QUICK FACTS

Number	Description	Proposed by Congress	Ratified by States
16th	Federal income tax	1909	1913
17th	Senators elected by people rather than state legislatures	1912	1913
18th	Manufacture, sale, and transport of alcohol prohibited	1917	1919
19th	Women's suffrage	1919	1920

income tax. The new tax was made possible in 1913 by the ratification of the **Sixteenth Amendment**. This amendment allows the federal government to impose direct taxes on citizens' incomes.

President Wilson next addressed banking reform with the 1913 Federal Reserve Act. This law created a national banking system called the Federal Reserve to regulate the economy.

Wilson also pushed for laws to regulate big business. The Clayton Antitrust Act of 1914 strengthened federal laws against monopolies. The Federal Trade Commission, created in 1914, had the power to investigate and punish unfair trade practices. Wilson's success in guiding reform programs through Congress helped him to win re-election in 1916.

READING CHECK **Analyzing** Why did Wilson win the election of 1912?

SUMMARY AND PREVIEW The progressive presidents tried to change American society for the better. In the next chapter you will learn how they also helped the United States become a world power.

Section 4 Assessment

go.hrw.com
Online Quiz
KEYWORD: SB7 HP21

Reviewing Ideas, Terms, and People

1. **a. Describe** How did **Theodore Roosevelt** support progressive reforms?

   b. Analyze Why did many Americans support **conservation**?

   c. Evaluate Do you think Roosevelt's reforms benefited the nation? Why or why not?

2. **a. Identify** What was the **Progressive Party**? Why was it created?

   b. Compare and Contrast How were the administrations of **William Howard Taft** and Roosevelt similar, and how were they different?

   c. Evaluate Which president do you think had the biggest influence on progressive reform—Roosevelt, Taft, or **Woodrow Wilson**? Explain your choice.

Critical Thinking

3. **Comparing and Contrasting** Review your notes on the progressive presidents. Then copy the diagram below and use it to compare and contrast the reforms of the progressive presidents.

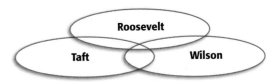

Roosevelt

Taft   Wilson

FOCUS ON SPEAKING

4. **The Ideas of Roosevelt, Taft, and Wilson** Do you agree or disagree with Presidents Roosevelt, Taft, and Wilson? Take notes on any of their ideas that you would include in your campaign promises.

Social Studies Skills

Short- and Long-term Causal Relationships

Define the Skill

Most historical events are the result of other events. When something happens as a result of other things that occur, it is an effect of those things. Some events take place soon after the things that cause them. Such events are called *short-term effects*. In contrast, *long-term effects* can occur years, decades, or even hundreds of years after the events that caused them. Being able to recognize short-term and long-term cause-and-effect relationships will help you to better understand historical events.

Learn the Skill

Clue words can sometimes reveal a cause-and-effect relationship between events. Often, however, such language clues may not be present. Therefore, when you study history, you should always look for other clues that might explain why an action or event occurred.

Short-term effects are usually fairly easy to identify. In historical writing they are often closely linked to the event that caused them. For example, consider this passage from Chapter 21.

" Some Progressives worked to change state and local governments in order to reduce the power of political machines. In many places, reformers replaced corrupt ballots that listed only one party's candidates with government-prepared ballots that listed all candidates. Under pressure from reformers, many states adopted secret ballots, giving every voter a private vote. "

This passage contains no clue words. Yet it is clear that cause-and-effect relationships exist. The power of political machines created corrupt voting practices. Reformers wanted to change this. One effect of this situation was the government-prepared ballot, and another was the secret ballot.

Recognizing long-term causal relationships is often more difficult. Since long-term effects take place well after the event that caused them, they may not be discussed at the same time as their cause. This is why you should always question why an event occurred as you learn about it. For example, in 1971 Congress passed the first federal law to protect the health and safety of all workers. This law was a long-term result of efforts begun years earlier by the progressives you read about in this chapter.

Many long-term effects result from major forces running through history that make things happen. They include economics, science and technology, expansion, conflict and cooperation among people, cultural clashes and differences, and moral and religious issues. Ask yourself if one of these forces is involved in the event being studied. If so, the event may have long-term effects that you should be on the lookout for when studying later events.

Practice and Apply the Skill

Review the information in Chapter 21 and answer these questions to practice recognizing short- and long-term causal relationships.

1. All packaged food today must have its contents listed on the container. This requirement is a long-term effect of what progressive reform?

2. Write a paragraph explaining the effects of the muckrakers on the news media today.

Chapter Review

Visual Summary

QUICK FACTS

Use the visual summary below to help you review the main ideas of the chapter.

Progressives hoped to improve society through reform. Their goals included

- Temperance
- Women's suffrage
- Big business regulation
- Conservation
- Tariff and banking reform

PROSPERITY

Reviewing Vocabulary, Terms, and People

Complete each sentence by filling in the blank with the correct term or person from the chapter.

1. Some Americans supported a _____ system, which proposed government ownership of the country's means of production.

2. Republican _____ began a program to reform state politics in Wisconsin.

3. The _____ granted women in the United States the right to vote.

4. The _____ prohibited the manufacture, sale, and transport of mislabeled or contaminated food and drugs.

5. During the Gilded Age, _____ often dominated local politics and used corruption to get their candidates elected.

6. _____ were journalists who wrote about troubling issues such as child labor, tenement housing, and political corruption.

Comprehension and Critical Thinking

SECTION 1 *(Pages 662–667)*

7. **a. Describe** What tactics did bosses and political machines use to gain control of local governments?

   b. Analyze What changes did Progressives make to city life?

   c. Elaborate Which progressive reform do you think had the greatest effect on Americans?

SECTION 2 *(Pages 670–674)*

8. **a. Identify** What reforms were made to improve working conditions, and who was affected by these reforms?

   b. Contrast What are the differences between capitalism and socialism?

   c. Elaborate If you were a business owner, would you have supported the progressive workplace reforms? Explain your answer.

9. a. Recall What minority groups were overlooked by progressive reform efforts?

b. Analyze How did women's involvement in the Progressive movement lead to constitutional change?

c. Elaborate Do you agree with Booker T. Washington's approach to improving life for African Americans? Explain your answer.

SECTION 4 *(Pages 680–683)*

10. a. Describe How did William Howard Taft disappoint Progressives?

b. Compare In what ways were the reforms of Presidents Roosevelt, Taft, and Wilson similar?

c. Elaborate Would you have supported Wilson's progressive reforms? Explain your answer.

Reviewing Themes

11. Politics What role did political machines play in local politics during the Gilded Age?

12. Society and Culture How were children affected by the movement for workplace reforms?

Reading Skills

Evaluating Sources *Use the Reading Skills taught in this chapter to answer the question about the reading selection below.*

> The next day Rose went to town [Chicago] alone. The wind had veered [turned] to the south, the dust blew, and the whole terrifying panorama [view] of life in the street seemed some way blurred together, and forms of men and animals were like figures in tapestry. The grind and clang and clatter and hiss and howl of the traffic was all about her . . .
>
> —Hamlin Garland, from his novel *Rose of Dutcher's Coolly*, 1895

13. Is this a good source for understanding the experiences of Chicago in the late 1800s? Why or why not?

Social Studies Skills

Short- and Long-Term Causal Relationships *Use the Social Studies Skills taught in this chapter to answer the question about the reading selection below.*

> Despite their friendship, Roosevelt and Taft held different ideas about how a president should act. Taft thought Roosevelt had claimed more power than a president was constitutionally allowed.
>
> As president, therefore, Taft chose to move cautiously toward reform and regulation.
> *(p. 682)*

14. According to the passage above, what was a long-term cause of Taft's cautious reforms?

Using the Internet

go.hrw.com
KEYWORD: SB7 CH21

15. Activity: Researching Progressives Rapid industrial and urban growth in America in the late 1800s resulted in a number of problems. Progressives worked to address these issues in many ways, including efforts to clean up political corruption, improve working conditions, and enact social reforms. Enter the activity keyword and explore the lives of some of the leaders of the Progressive movement. Then write a profile of a Progressive leader that outlines his or her life and impact on American reform.

FOCUS ON SPEAKING

16. Share Your Campaign Promises Review your notes about possible campaign promises. Which promises will be most helpful in getting you elected? Look at your promises to see whether they focus on issues important to voters. Then write a speech including your campaign promises that you can deliver to your class.

DIRECTIONS: Read each question and write the letter of the best response.

1

The people in this photograph would probably have been *most* interested in which of the following reforms?

A secret ballots

B the Pure Food and Drug Act

C child labor laws

D elimination of political machines

2 One direct result of immigration and urban growth was the rise of

A political machines.

B the civil-service system.

C the spoils system.

D primary elections.

3 What was the *main* idea behind the creation of the civil-service system in the late 1800s?

A Government jobs should be awarded to people who support the party in power.

B Government workers should be required to support the elected officials who hire them.

C Government employees should be qualified to do the jobs for which they were hired.

D Government jobs should not be filled with employees who serve in those jobs for life.

4 The Nineteenth Amendment to the Constitution increased democracy in the United States by

A granting women the right to vote.

B allowing the people of each state to elect their senators.

C establishing direct primary elections.

D enabling voters to remove elected officials from office before the end of their terms.

5 Earlier in the book you learned how Frederick Douglass wrote and spoke against slavery and unfair treatment of African Americans. What later reformer also spoke out for equal rights for African Americans?

A John Dewey

B W. E. B. Du Bois

C William Howard Taft

D Upton Sinclair

6 Read the following excerpt from an interview with a boss at Tammany Hall and use it to answer the question below.

There's only one way to hold a district: you must study human nature and act accordin' . . . To learn real human nature you have to go among the people, see them and be seen. I know every man, woman, and child in the Fifteenth District, except them that's been born this summer—and I know some of them, too. I know what they like and what they don't like, what they are strong at and what they are weak in, and I reach them by approachin' at the right side.

—George Washington Plunkitt, quoted in *Eyewitnesses and Others*

Document-Based Question How did Plunkitt say he kept his position in the political machine?

America Becomes a World Power

Virginia Standards of Learning

USII.1 The student will demonstrate skills for historical and geographical analysis, and responsible citizenship, including the ability to

a) analyze and interpret primary and secondary source documents to increase understanding of events and life in United States history from 1865 to the present; **b)** make connections between past and present; **c)** sequence events in United States history from 1865 to the present; **d)** interpret ideas and events from different historical perspectives; **e)** evaluate and debate issues orally and in writing; **f)** analyze and interpret maps that include major physical features; **h)** interpret patriotic slogans and excerpts from notable speeches and documents

USII.5 The student will demonstrate knowledge of the changing role of the United States from the late nineteenth century through World War I by

a) explaining the reasons for and results of the Spanish American War; **b)** describing Theodore Roosevelt's impact on the foreign policy of the United States

FOCUS ON WRITING

A List of Pros and Cons In the last half of the 1800s, the United States became more involved in international affairs. As you read this chapter, you will analyze the nation's new role and use the results of your analysis to guide U.S. policy in the future. In order to analyze the advantages and disadvantages of an aggressive foreign policy, you will need to create a list of the pros and cons of U.S. involvement with other nations in the late 1800s and early 1900s. As you create your list, note which items are facts and which are opinions—either yours or someone else's.

UNITED STATES

1867 The United States buys Alaska.

1867

WORLD

1868 Japan begins a time of modernization known as the Meiji Restoration.

What You Will Learn...

In this chapter you will learn about how the United States became a global power in the late 1800s and early 1900s. Through a combination of economic strength, military might, and aggressive foreign policy, America made its presence known in many parts of the world. One such place was Panama, where the United States built the Panama Canal, shown here. The United States has remained a powerful force on the international stage to this day.

1890 Congress passes the McKinley Tariff, which gives a subsidy to U.S. sugar producers.

1898 The United States wins the Spanish-American War, gaining the Philippine Islands and Puerto Rico.

1914 The Panama Canal officially opens.

1880   1890   1900   1910   1920

1885 The Indian National Congress is formed in British-controlled India.

1895 Cubans rebel against Spanish rule.

1900 The Boxer Rebellion erupts in China.

1903 Panama declares itself an independent nation.

1910 The Mexican Revolution begins.

AMERICA AS A WORLD POWER   **689**

Reading Social Studies

by Kylene Beers

Economics | Geography | Politics | Society and Culture | Science and Technology

Focus on Themes In this chapter, you will learn about how the physical **geography** of the United States changed as it acquired overseas territories. You will also read about how national and international **politics** affected foreign policy and brought new responsibilities to the government of the United States.

Comparing Historical Texts

Focus on Reading A good way to learn what people in the past thought is to read what they wrote. However, most documents will only tell you one side of the story. By comparing writings by different people, you can learn a great deal about various sides of a historical issue or debate.

Comparing Texts When you compare historical texts, you should consider two things: who wrote the documents and what the documents were meant to achieve. To do this, you need to find the writers' main point or points.

Document 1

"We have cherished the policy of non-interference with affairs of foreign governments wisely inaugurated [begun] by Washington, keeping ourselves free from entanglement, either as allies or foes, content to leave undisturbed with them the settlement of their own domestic concerns."

–President William McKinley, First Inaugural Address, 1897

Document 2

"Therefore, Mr. President, here is a war with terrible characteristics flagrant [obvious] at our very doors [in Cuba]. We have the power to bring it to an end. I believe that the whole American people would welcome steps in that direction."

–Senator Henry Cabot Lodge, Speech in Congress, 1896

Document 1	Document 2
Writer	
President William McKinley	Senator Henry Cabot Lodge
Main point	
The United States should not involve itself in the affairs of other countries.	The United States should go to war in Cuba.
Both Sides of the Issue	
Americans were torn over the war in Cuba. Some thought the United States should remain uninvolved as it always had. Others thought it was time for a change in foreign policy.	

You Try It!

Read the following passages, both taken from presidential addresses to Congress. As you read, look for the main point each president makes in his address.

Foreign Policy

In treating of our foreign policy and of the attitude that this great Nation should assume in the world at large, it is absolutely necessary to consider the Army and the Navy, and the Congress, through which the thought of the Nation finds its expression, should keep ever vividly in mind the fundamental fact that it is impossible to treat our foreign policy, whether this policy takes shape in the effort to secure justice for others or justice for ourselves, save as conditioned upon the attitude we are willing to take toward our Army, and especially toward our Navy.

—*President Theodore Roosevelt,*
Message to Congress, 1904

The diplomacy of the present administration has sought to respond to modern ideas of commercial intercourse [involvement]. This policy has been characterized as substituting dollars for bullets. It is one that appeals alike to idealistic humanitarian sentiments [feelings], to the dictates [rules] of sound policy and strategy, and to legitimate [make real] commercial aims.

—*President William Howard Taft,*
Message to Congress, 1912

After you read the passages, answer the following questions.

1. What was the main point Roosevelt made in his address?

2. What was the main point Taft made in his address?

3. How can a comparison of Roosevelt's and Taft's addresses to Congress help you understand the issues that shaped U.S. foreign policy in the early 1900s?

As you read Chapter 22, organize your notes to help you point out the similarities and differences among events or policies.

What You Will Learn...

Main Ideas

1. The United States ended its policy of isolationism.
2. Hawaii became a U.S. territory in 1898.
3. The United States sought trade with Japan and China.

The Big Idea

In the last half of the 1800s, the United States joined the race for control of overseas territories.

Key Terms and People

imperialism, *p. 692*
isolationism, *p. 693*
William H. Seward, *p. 693*
Liliuokalani, *p. 694*
spheres of influence, *p. 695*
Open Door Policy, *p. 695*
Boxer Rebellion, *p. 695*

TAKING NOTES As you read, make a list of examples of U.S. expansion in a chart like this one.

Areas or Trade Rights Gained

The United States Gains Overseas Territories

If YOU were there...

You are a Hawaiian living on Maui, one of the Hawaiian Islands, in 1890. Your parents work in a sugar mill owned by American planters. Although the mill supplies jobs, you don't trust the sugar planters. They have already made your king sign a treaty that gives them a lot of power in the islands. You are afraid they will take over the government.

What would you do if the planters took over your islands?

BUILDING BACKGROUND In the mid-1800s, most Americans had little interest in being involved with the rest of the world diplomatically. The Civil War and Reconstruction kept their focus on challenges at home. In the meantime, though, European nations were busily acquiring overseas territories. The United States would soon join them.

End of Isolation

In the 1800s powerful Western nations were busy building naval bases to protect their shipping routes around the world. This was an aspect of **imperialism**—building an empire by founding colonies or conquering other nations. Between 1870 and 1914, Europeans extended their colonial empires until they controlled most of Africa and Southeast Asia.

Roots of Imperialism

Several forces drove this wave of European imperialism. Countries wanted sources of raw materials—such as copper, rubber, and tin—to fuel industrial growth. Businesspeople wanted new markets for their manufactured goods. And many

Europeans saw colonies as a source of power and national pride.

In contrast, the United States followed a limited policy of **isolationism**—avoiding involvement in the affairs of other countries. In 1789 President George Washington had warned Americans "to steer clear of permanent alliances" with other countries. American leaders tried to follow this advice by staying out of overseas conflicts.

By the late 1800s, however, some Americans believed the United States needed to expand to keep its economy strong. In his 1890 book *The Influence of Sea Power upon History,* Alfred T. Mahan argued that the United States needed a strong navy to protect its economic interests. Mahan also explained that a strong navy needed overseas bases and coaling stations—places for ships to take on coal for fuel.

Seward's Folly

In 1867 the United States greatly expanded its North American territory when Secretary of State **William H. Seward** arranged the purchase of Alaska from Russia for $7.2 million. Some people thought Alaska was a frozen wasteland, calling the deal "Seward's Folly" [foolish act]. But Seward had purchased an area more than twice the size of Texas for two cents an acre. And as he had hoped, Alaska became a source of valuable natural resources such as fur, timber, and minerals. Gold was found in Alaska in the 1890s, bringing miners and settlers to the area.

Based on Seward's belief that the United States "must continue to move on westward," the nation also annexed the Midway Islands in 1867. The islands' location about halfway between the U.S. West Coast and Japan made Midway an excellent coaling station for the U.S. Navy.

The United States wanted the island group of Samoa for similar reasons. The United States and Germany agreed to divide Samoa in 1899.

READING CHECK **Analyzing** Why did U.S. leaders end isolationist policies in the late 1800s?

THE IMPACT TODAY

The United States still has hundreds of military bases in foreign countries.

U.S. Territories in the Pacific, 1856–1899

United States and possessions

1898 Date of acquisition

0   1,000   2,000 Miles

0   1,000   2,000 Kilometers

RUSSIA

Sea of Okhotsk

Bering Sea

ALASKA 1867

Boundary disputed until 1903

CANADA

Beijing

KOREA   JAPAN

Tokyo

CHINA

TAIWAN

PHILIPPINES 1898

Manila

MIDWAY 1867

PACIFIC OCEAN

UNITED STATES

MEXICO

60°W

40°N

Tropic of Cancer

GUAM 1898

WAKE ISLAND 1898

Honolulu   HAWAII 1898

JOHNSTON ISLAND 1858

0° Equator

HOWLAND ISLAND 1856

DUTCH EAST INDIES

Pago Pago

AMERICAN SAMOA 1899

AUSTRALIA

Tropic of Capricorn

100°E   140°E   180°

GEOGRAPHY SKILLS **INTERPRETING MAPS**

Between 1856 and 1898, Alaska and many Pacific islands, including Hawaii, became U.S. territories.
1. What U.S. territory was located below the equator?
2. In what year did the United States acquire the most territories?

40°S

Hawaii Becomes a Territory

Even more appealing than Samoa were the Hawaiian Islands. Hawaiians first saw Europeans in 1778. Trading and whaling ships in the Pacific soon began stopping in Hawaii. In the early 1800s American missionaries came and attempted to convert Hawaiians to Christianity. Missionaries opened businesses and raised crops, such as sugarcane. Some Americans became rich sugar planters.

By the 1840s most shops and shipyards in Hawaii were owned by Americans. Sugar became a leading export of the Hawaiian economy. An 1875 treaty allowed Hawaiian sugar to be shipped duty-free to the United States. (A duty is a tax on imported items.) This agreement helped the Hawaiian sugar industry prosper.

The planters used their power to force the Hawaiian king to sign a new constitution in 1887. It became known as the Bayonet Constitution because the king was forced to sign it at gunpoint. The constitution granted more power to the planter-controlled legislature. Many Hawaiians feared the foreigners' increase in power.

THE IMPACT TODAY

Today, sugarcane is Hawaii's most valuable crop.

In 1891 the king died, and his sister, **Liliuokalani** (li-LEE-uh-woh-kuh-LAHN-ee), became queen. She proposed a new constitution that would return power to the monarchy. The planters revolted. John L. Stevens, U.S. minister to Hawaii, called 150 marines ashore to support the revolt, and it succeeded without a battle. The planters formed a new government. Congress voted to annex the Hawaiian Islands in 1898.

READING CHECK **Identifying Cause and Effect** What effect did the growing power of the planters have on the Hawaiian monarchy?

United States Seeks Trade with Japan and China

Economic interest also drew the United States to Japan and China. The United States wanted to open and secure trade markets in both Asian countries.

Opening Trade with Japan

By the mid-1800s European powers had formed strong trade ties with most East Asian countries. However, the island nation of Japan had isolated itself from the rest of the world for hundreds of years.

The United States wanted to open up trade with Japan before Europeans arrived. President Millard Fillmore sent Commodore Matthew Perry to Japan to secure "friendship, commerce, [and] a supply of coal and provisions." Perry attempted a peaceful alliance in 1853, but he was not successful.

Perry returned to Japan in 1854 with seven warships. He gave Japanese leaders gifts and tried to show some of the benefits that Japanese-American trade would have. For instance, Perry presented them with a telegraph transmitter and a model train. This effort—and the presence of U.S. naval power—persuaded Japanese officials to open trade with the United States. The two countries signed a trade agreement in 1858.

BIOGRAPHY

Liliuokalani
(1838–1917)
Born in Honolulu, Queen Liliuokalani was proud of Hawaiian traditions. Even after being driven from power in 1883, she continued speaking out on behalf of native-born Hawaiians. In 1887 she traveled to Washington, D.C., meeting with President Grover Cleveland to argue against the annexation of Hawaii by the United States. Until her death, Liliuokalani served as a symbol of Hawaiian pride and a reminder of the islands' history as an independent nation.

Drawing Conclusions Why do you think Liliuokalani was a symbol of Hawaiian pride?

Perry Arrives in Japan

How might the Japanese have felt seeing these ships arrive?

CONNECT TO THE ARTS

This painting from 1854 shows Commodore Perry landing at Yokohama, Japan. He staged a parade to disembark and meet the imperial commissioners that represented the emperor. This meeting was the first official meeting between an agent of the United States and officials from Japan.

How does this picture show U.S. imperialism and its effects on Japan?

Some Japanese leaders welcomed trade with the United States. In 1868 people who favored the industrialization **process** came to power in Japan, beginning a 40-year period of modernization. By the 1890s Japan was becoming a major imperial power. It defeated China in the Sino-Japanese War from 1894 to 1895. As a result, Japan gained new territory and enjoyed the same trading privileges in China as European countries. In 1904 Japan attacked Russian forces stationed in China. President Theodore Roosevelt helped to negotiate a peace treaty to end the Russo-Japanese War a year later. Japan gained control of Korea, a lease on Port Arthur in China, and other rights. Japan had become a world power.

Foreign Powers in China

After Japan defeated China, other countries took advantage of China's weakness by seizing **spheres of influence**—areas where foreign nations controlled resources. Germany, Great Britain, France, Japan, and Russia all took control of areas within China.

Some U.S. leaders feared that the United States would be closed out of Chinese markets. In 1899 Secretary of State John Hay sent notes to Japan and many European countries announcing the **Open Door Policy**. This policy stated that all nations should have equal access to trade in China. The policy was neither rejected nor accepted by European powers and Japan but made U.S. intentions clear.

Meanwhile, many Chinese resented the power and control held by foreign nations. This hostility sparked the **Boxer Rebellion**. The Boxers were Chinese nationalists who were angered by foreign involvement in China. In their language, the group was called the Fists of Righteous Harmony. Westerners called them Boxers because they used a clenched fist as their symbol. Although officially denounced, they were secretly supported by the Chinese government.

In June 1900 the Boxers took to the streets of Beijing, China's capital, and laid siege to the walled settlement where foreigners lived. They killed more than 200 people.

ACADEMIC VOCABULARY

process a series of steps by which a task is accomplished

The siege continued for two months. Foreign military forces, including United States Marines, fought their way from the port of Tianjin to Beijing, where they invaded the Forbidden City. The Boxers were soon defeated. China was forced to make a cash payment of $333 million to foreign governments, $25 million of which went to the United States. Secretary of State Hay then sent another Open Door note to Japan and the European nations. The Open Door Policy remained in effect until World War II again closed China's borders to foreign influence.

READING CHECK **Identifying Cause and Effect** What factors led to the Boxer Rebellion, and what was the result?

SUMMARY AND PREVIEW The United States greatly expanded its territory and influence in the Pacific. In the next section, you will learn about the causes and effects of the Spanish-American War.

Chinese nationalists attack the foreigners' compound in Beijing in this illustration of China's Boxer Rebellion.

Section 1 Assessment

go.hrw.com
Online Quiz
KEYWORD: SB7 HP22

Reviewing Ideas, Terms, and People

1. **a. Describe** What policy had the United States followed regarding other countries before the late 1800s?
   b. Analyze Why did the United States expand to Alaska and to islands in the Pacific?
   c. Evaluate Do you think **William H. Seward**'s purchase of Alaska was a good decision? Explain.

2. **a. Recall** What became Hawaii's leading export?
   b. Sequence What events led to Hawaii's annexation as a U.S. territory?
   c. Elaborate What do you think about the planters' revolt against Queen **Liliuokalani**?

3. **a. Describe** How did the United States persuade Japanese leaders to sign a trade treaty?
   b. Contrast How was the U.S. experience establishing trade with China different from U.S. attempts to open trade with Japan?
   c. Evaluate Do you think Japan made the right decision in agreeing to open trade with the United States? Explain your answer.

Critical Thinking

4. **Generalizing** Review your notes on the areas or trade rights gained by the United States. Then use the chart below to identify the benefits of these areas and trade rights.

American Expansion

Areas or Trade Rights Gained	Benefits for United States

FOCUS ON WRITING

5. **Identifying Pros and Cons of U.S. Involvement Overseas** What did the United States gain from its involvement in these areas of the world? What were the disadvantages? As you read this section, identify pros and cons to add to your list.

The Spanish-American War

Virginia Standards of Learning USII.1b, USII.5a, USII.5b

If YOU were there...

You live in New York City in 1898. Newspaper headlines are screaming about the start of war in Cuba. You hear that Theodore Roosevelt wants volunteers for a cavalry troop called the Rough Riders. You know how to ride a horse, and you've admired Roosevelt ever since he was New York's police commissioner. You know it will be dangerous, but it also sounds like a great adventure.

Would you join the Rough Riders? Why?

BUILDING BACKGROUND While the United States, Japan, and several European powers were gaining colonies, Spain's empire was declining. By the late 1800s Spain's once-extensive American empire was reduced to two island colonies—Cuba and Puerto Rico. Eager for independence, some Cubans revolted against Spanish rule. Many Americans sympathized with Cuba's fight for independence.

War with Spain

You read earlier that newspaper publishers Joseph Pulitzer and William Randolph Hearst were in a fierce competition for readers. In the late 1890s their newspapers published stories from Cuba, where Cuban rebels were fighting for independence from Spain. To attract readers, Pulitzer and Hearst printed sensational, often exaggerated news stories. This technique is called **yellow journalism**. Vivid stories about Spanish brutality in Cuba convinced many Americans that the U.S. military should support the Cuban rebels.

What You Will Learn...

Main Ideas
1. In 1898 the United States went to war with Spain in the Spanish-American War.
2. The United States gained territories in the Caribbean and Pacific.

The Big Idea
The United States expanded into new parts of the world as a result of the Spanish-American War.

Key Terms and People
yellow journalism, *p. 697*
Teller Amendment, *p. 698*
Emilio Aguinaldo, *p. 699*
Anti-Imperialist League, *p. 700*
Platt Amendment, *p. 701*

TAKING NOTES As you read, use a graphic organizer like this one to list the results of the Spanish-American War.

Spanish-American War

Results

$50,000 REWARD.—WHO DESTROYED THE MAINE?—$50,000 REWARD.

NEW YORK JOURNAL
AND ADVERTISER

DESTRUCTION OF THE WAR SHIP MAINE WAS THE WORK OF AN ENEMY.

$50,000!
$50,000 REWARD!
For the Detection of the Perpetrator of the Maine Outrage!

Assistant Secretary Roosevelt Convinced the Explosion of the War Ship Was Not an Accident.

$50,000!
$50,000 REWARD!
For the Detection of the Perpetrator of the Maine Outrage!

Newspapers such as this one encouraged Americans to seek war with Spain.

Despite growing support for military action in Cuba, President Grover Cleveland was opposed to U.S. involvement. In 1896 William McKinley, a supporter of Cuban independence, was elected president. Several events soon led to war.

In February 1898 Hearst's newspaper published a letter written by the Spanish minister to the United States, Enrique Dupuy de Lôme. In it, de Lôme called McKinley "weak and a bidder for the admiration of the crowd." Many Americans were outraged.

In January 1898, even before de Lôme's letter became public, the United States sent the battleship USS *Maine* to Havana Harbor. The *Maine*'s mission was to protect U.S. citizens and economic interests in Cuba. On February 15 the *Maine* exploded and

sank, with a loss of 266 men. Although the cause of the explosion was unclear, the American press immediately blamed Spain. "Remember the *Maine*!" became a rallying cry for angry Americans.

President McKinley requested $50 million to prepare for war. Congress approved the money. Although Cuba was not a U.S. territory, Congress issued a resolution on April 20 declaring Cuba independent and demanding that Spain leave the island within three days. Attached to the resolution was the **Teller Amendment**, which stated that the United States had no interest in taking control of Cuba. In response to the resolution, Spain declared war on the United States. The next day, Congress passed, and McKinley signed, a declaration of war against Spain.

"Remember the *Maine*!"

Most of the men aboard the USS *Maine* were sleeping when a terrible explosion demolished the forward third of the ship at 9:40 P.M. on February 15, 1898. The rest of the ship sank quickly. Some 266 men were killed.

Who did the United States blame for the explosion?

War in the Philippines

While attention was focused on Cuba, the U.S. Navy won a quick victory nearly halfway around the world in the Philippines, a Spanish colony in the Pacific. Filipinos, like Cubans, were rebelling against Spanish rule.

As soon as the Spanish-American War began, American commodore George Dewey raced to the Philippines with four large warships and two small gunboats. On May 1, ignoring reports that mines beneath the water barred his way, he sailed into Manila Bay and destroyed the Spanish Pacific fleet stationed there. Dewey's forces sank or captured 10 ships. The Spanish lost 381 lives, but none of Dewey's men were killed.

Dewey had defeated the Spanish, but he did not have enough troops to occupy and secure the Philippines. Troops eventually arrived, and on August 13, U.S. troops and Filipino rebels led by **Emilio Aguinaldo** (ahg-ee-NAHL-doh) took control of the Philippine capital, Manila.

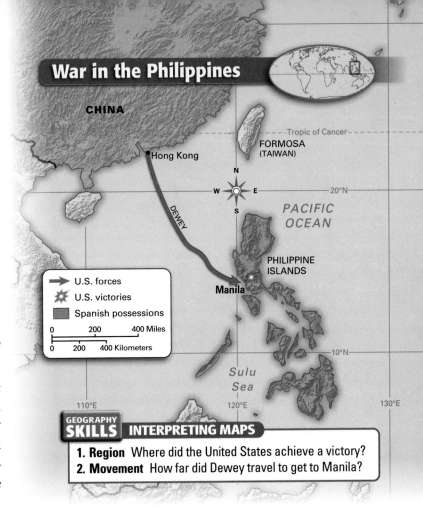

War in the Philippines

CHINA

Hong Kong

FORMOSA (TAIWAN)

--Tropic of Cancer--

DEWEY

20°N

PACIFIC OCEAN

PHILIPPINE ISLANDS

Manila

→ U.S. forces
★ U.S. victories
■ Spanish possessions

0   200   400 Miles
0   200   400 Kilometers

Sulu Sea

110°E   120°E   130°E

10°N

GEOGRAPHY SKILLS   **INTERPRETING MAPS**

1. **Region** Where did the United States achieve a victory?
2. **Movement** How far did Dewey travel to get to Manila?

War in the Caribbean

In contrast to the navy, the U.S. Army was unprepared for war. At the start of the conflict, the entire U.S. Army had only 28,000 soldiers. New volunteers quickly raised that figure to more than 280,000. The army did not have enough rifles or bullets for these soldiers. It did not even have appropriate clothing for the troops. Many soldiers received warm woolen uniforms to wear in Cuba's tropical heat.

The soldiers faced harsh living conditions in Cuba. They ate canned meat that one general called "embalmed beef," and many were stricken with yellow fever and other deadly diseases. More than 2,000 Americans died from diseases they contracted in Cuba. Fewer than 400 were killed in battle.

The most colorful group of soldiers was the Rough Riders. Second in command of this group was Lieutenant Colonel Theodore Roosevelt. Roosevelt had organized the Rough Riders to fight in Cuba. Volunteers included Native Americans, college athletes, cowboys, miners, and ranchers. Newspaper stories of their heroism earned the Rough Riders Americans' admiration. Four privates of the African American 10th Cavalry, who served with the Rough Riders, received the Congressional Medal of Honor.

Landing on June 22, 1898, the U.S. troops captured the hills around the main Spanish forces at Santiago. At the village of El Caney on July 1, some 7,000 U.S. soldiers, aided by Cuban rebels, overwhelmed about 600 Spanish defenders.

The main U.S. force then attacked and captured San Juan Hill. The Rough Riders and the African American 9th and 10th cavalries captured nearby Kettle Hill. The many accounts of the battle became popular with the American public back home. A journalist on the scene described the soldiers' charge:

FOCUS ON READING

How might accounts of the war written by these various soldiers have been different?

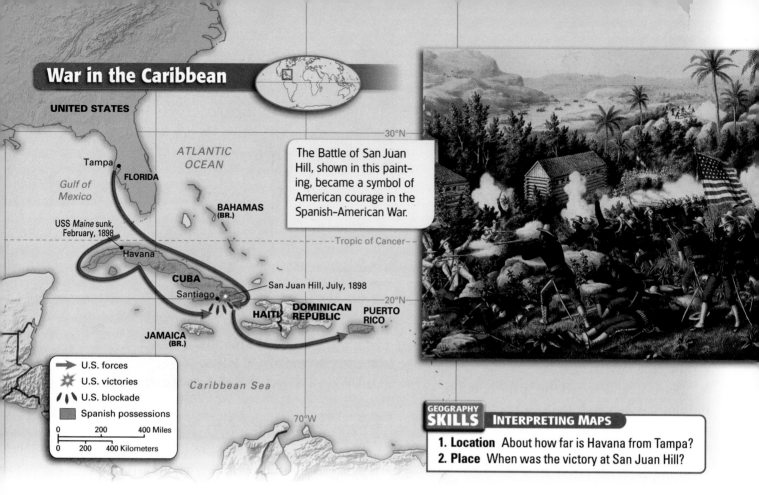

War in the Caribbean

UNITED STATES

Tampa

FLORIDA

Gulf of Mexico

ATLANTIC OCEAN

30°N

BAHAMAS (BR.)

USS *Maine* sunk, February, 1898

Havana

Tropic of Cancer

CUBA

Santiago

San Juan Hill, July, 1898

20°N

HAITI

DOMINICAN REPUBLIC

PUERTO RICO

JAMAICA (BR.)

Caribbean Sea

70°W

U.S. forces
U.S. victories
U.S. blockade
Spanish possessions

0   200   400 Miles
0 200 400 Kilometers

The Battle of San Juan Hill, shown in this painting, became a symbol of American courage in the Spanish–American War.

GEOGRAPHY SKILLS | **INTERPRETING MAPS**

1. **Location** About how far is Havana from Tampa?
2. **Place** When was the victory at San Juan Hill?

"It was a miracle of self-sacrifice, a triumph of bulldog courage … The fire of the Spanish riflemen … doubled and trebled [tripled] in fierceness, the crests of the hills crackled and burst in amazed roars and rippled with waves of tiny flame. But the blue line [of United States soldiers] crept steadily up and on."

—Richard Harding Davis, quoted in *The American Reader*, edited by Paul M. Angle

On July 3 the commander of the Spanish fleet decided to try breaking through the U.S. blockade. Though every Spanish ship was destroyed in the battle, American forces suffered only two casualties. Santiago surrendered two weeks later. President McKinley began peace negotiations with Spain, which was assured of defeat. A few days later, U.S. troops invaded Spanish-held Puerto Rico, which surrendered with little resistance. Spain signed a cease-fire agreement on August 12, 1898.

READING CHECK **Comparing** How was fighting in the Pacific and the Caribbean similar?

United States Gains Territories

The peace treaty placed Cuba, Guam, Puerto Rico, and the Philippines under U.S. control. In reaction, some Americans formed the **Anti-Imperialist League**, a group that opposed the treaty and the creation of an American colonial empire. They argued that the treaty threatened democracy because it denied self-government to the people living in the newly acquired territories. The Senate approved the peace treaty by a vote of 57 to 27—just one vote more than the two-thirds majority needed to ratify treaties.

Cuba

The Teller Amendment had declared that the United States would not annex Cuba. However, McKinley wanted to create stability and increase U.S. economic activity there, so he set up a military government. He appointed Leonard Wood, who had commanded the Rough Riders during the war, as governor.

Wood quickly began building schools and a sanitation system.

Even with the new sanitation system, disease remained a major problem. Dr. Walter Reed, head of the army's Yellow Fever Commission, was sent to Cuba in 1900 to help fight the disease. He and his volunteers conducted experiments, including allowing themselves to be bitten by infected insects. They soon proved that yellow fever was transmitted by mosquitoes. Getting rid of the standing water where mosquitoes lived helped health officials to control the disease.

Governor Wood also oversaw the writing of a Cuban constitution. The document included the **Platt Amendment**, which limited Cuba's right to make treaties and allowed the United States to intervene in Cuban affairs. It also required Cuba to sell or lease land to the United States. Cuban leaders compared the Platt Amendment to "handing over the keys to our house so that they [the Americans] can enter it at any time, whenever the desire seizes them." The Cubans reluctantly accepted the amendment, and U.S. troops withdrew. The amendment remained in force until 1934, and the U.S. government stayed actively involved in Cuban affairs until the late 1950s.

Puerto Rico

Like Cubans, Puerto Ricans had hoped for independence after the war. Instead, the U.S. government made the island a territory. On April 12, 1900, the Foraker Act established a civil government in Puerto Rico. It was headed by a governor and included a two-house legislature.

A debate over the new territory soon arose. People who lived in Puerto Rico were

LINKING TO TODAY

Puerto Ricans Today

Today about 3.7 million Puerto Ricans live on the mainland United States. This is the second-largest Hispanic population in the country, behind people of Mexican descent. Puerto Ricans live throughout the United States, but about one-third live in New York State.

Puerto Rican culture is very strong in New York—the National Puerto Rican Day Parade in New York City is one of the largest parades for any ethnic group in the city.

Puerto Ricans in the Mainland United States

Puerto Rican Population (in millions)

Year: 1970, 1980, 1990, 2000

ANALYSIS SKILL **ANALYZING INFORMATION**

How are the people in the picture showing support for Puerto Rican culture?

considered citizens of the island but not of the United States. In 1917 the Jones Act gave Puerto Ricans U.S. citizenship and made both houses of the legislature elective. However, another 30 years passed before Puerto Ricans could elect their own governor. Today the island has its own constitution and elected officials but remains associated with the United States as what is known as a commonwealth.

The Philippines

Spain had surrendered the Philippines in return for a $20 million payment from the United States. Many Americans agreed with President McKinley, who said that the United States would benefit from the islands' naval and commercial value and that annexing the islands would keep Europeans from seizing them.

Filipino rebels, however, had expected to gain independence after the war. They had helped U.S. forces to capture Manila. When the United States decided instead to keep the islands, rebels led by Emilio Aguinaldo started a guerrilla war against the American forces. More than 4,200 U.S. soldiers and hundreds of thousands of Filipinos died before the conflict ended in 1902.

That same year, Congress passed the Philippine Government Act. It provided that an appointed governor and a two-house legislature would rule the Philippines. In 1946 the United States granted full independence to the Philippines.

READING CHECK **Summarizing** What areas did the United States control as a result of the war?

SUMMARY AND PREVIEW The United States fought a war with Spain and gained new territories in the Pacific and Caribbean regions. In the next section you will learn about U.S. interests in Latin America.

Section 2 Assessment

go.hrw.com
Online Quiz
KEYWORD: SB7 HP22

Reviewing Ideas, Terms, and People

1. a. **Recall** What was the cause of the conflict between Cuba and Spain?
   b. **Analyze** How did **yellow journalism** affect public support for U.S. military action in Cuba?
   c. **Elaborate** Why do you think the United States was so successful in defeating Spain? Explain your answer.
2. a. **Identify** What territories did the United States gain as a result of the war?
   b. **Analyze** Why did some Americans oppose the annexation of the Philippines?

Critical Thinking

3. **Categorizing** Review your notes on the results of the Spanish-American War. Then copy the graphic organizer to the right. Use your notes to identify arguments for and against taking control of foreign territories.

Arguments for Imperialism		Arguments against Imperialism
	VS.	

FOCUS ON WRITING

4. **Identifying Pros and Cons of the Spanish-American War** As you read this section, add to your pros and cons list by identifying American losses and gains as a result of the Spanish-American War. What were the costs in human lives? What were the gains in territory? Can you identify any other losses and gains? For example, how did the United States handle the issues of self-rule involved in the war?

Theodore Roosevelt

What would you do to reform your country and make it stronger?

When did he live? 1858–1919

Where did he live? Theodore Roosevelt was born into a wealthy family in New York City. He spent two years on a ranch in the Dakota Territory, where he became an avid hunter and conservationist. His political career then took him to Albany, New York, where he served as state governor, and Washington, D.C., where he served as vice president and president.

What did he do? Roosevelt became a national hero while leading the Rough Riders in the Spanish-American War. After serving less than a year as vice president, the 42-year-old Roosevelt became the youngest president in U.S. history when President William McKinley was killed in 1901. As president, Roosevelt fought for progressive reforms and set aside millions of acres as national parks and forests. Roosevelt's aggressive foreign policy expanded American power in the world.

Why is he so important? "I believe in a strong executive," Roosevelt once declared. "While president, I have been president, emphatically [forcefully]; I have used every ounce of power there was in the office." As this quote suggests, Roosevelt was a strong leader who set a precedent for a more active and powerful presidency.

Drawing Conclusions What characteristics made Theodore Roosevelt a successful leader?

President Theodore Roosevelt and the Rough Riders

KEY EVENTS

1882
Elected to the New York State Assembly at age 23

1898
Becomes a hero in the Spanish-American War; elected governor of New York

1900
Elected vice president

1901
Becomes president when McKinley is assassinated

1903
Gains Panama Canal Zone for the United States

1906
Visits Panama, becoming the first president to travel outside the country while in office

1919
Dies at home in New York

The United States and Latin America

Virginia Standards of Learning USII.1b, USII.1c, USII.1d, USII.1f, USII.5b

What You Will Learn...

Main Ideas

1. The United States built the Panama Canal in the early 1900s.
2. Theodore Roosevelt changed U.S. policy toward Latin America.
3. Presidents Taft and Wilson promoted U.S. interests in Latin America.

The Big Idea

The United States expanded its role in Latin America in the early 1900s.

Key Terms and People

Panama Canal, *p. 705*
Roosevelt Corollary, *p. 707*
dollar diplomacy, *p. 708*
Mexican Revolution, *p. 708*
John J. Pershing, *p. 709*
Francisco "Pancho" Villa, *p. 709*

TAKING NOTES As you read, take notes on changing U.S. policies toward Latin America. List each policy in an outer circle of a web like this one.

U.S. policies toward Latin America

If YOU were there...

You are an engineer, and you've been working on the Panama Canal for almost eight years. Your work crews used huge steam shovels to slice through a ridge of mountains and built a huge artificial lake. You planned a system to move ships through different water levels. Now your work is done. You can watch massive ships travel from the Atlantic to the Pacific.

Which part of the work on the canal was the most challenging?

BUILDING BACKGROUND When the Spanish-American War began in 1898, the U.S. battleship *Oregon* set out from Washington State to join the fighting in Cuba. The approximately 12,000-mile trip around the southern tip of South America took more than two months. This delay convinced many U.S. leaders that the United States needed to build a canal linking the Atlantic and Pacific oceans.

Building the Panama Canal

A canal across the narrow neck of Central America would link the Atlantic and Pacific oceans and cut some 8,000 miles off the voyage by ship from the West to the East coasts of the United States. It would also allow the U.S. Navy to link its Atlantic and Pacific naval fleets quickly.

Revolution in Panama

No one was a stronger supporter of a Central American canal than President Theodore Roosevelt. Roosevelt knew that the best spot for the canal was the Isthmus of Panama, which at the time was part of the nation of Colombia. But he was unable to convince the Colombian senate to lease a strip of land across Panama to the United States.

Roosevelt considered other ways to gain control of the land. He learned that Panamanian revolutionaries were planning a revolt against Colombia. On November 2, 1903, a U.S. warship arrived outside Colón, Panama. The next day the revolt began. Blocked by the U.S. warship, Colombian forces could not reach Panama to stop the rebellion. Panama declared itself an independent country. The United States then recognized the new nation.

The new government of Panama supported the idea of a canal across its land. The United States agreed to pay Panama $10 million plus $250,000 a year for a 99-year lease on a 10-mile-wide strip of land across the isthmus.

Building the Canal

Canal construction began in 1904. The first obstacle to overcome was tropical disease. The canal route ran through 51 miles of forests and swamps filled with mosquitoes, many of which carried the deadly diseases malaria and yellow fever.

Dr. William C. Gorgas, who had helped Dr. Walter Reed stamp out yellow fever in Cuba, organized a successful effort to rid the canal route of disease-carrying mosquitoes. If Gorgas had not been successful, the canal's construction would have taken much longer. It also would have cost much more in terms of both lives and money.

Even with the reduced risk of disease, the work was very dangerous. Most of the canal had to be blasted out of solid rock with explosives. Workers used dozens of steam shovels to cut a narrow, eight-mile-long channel through the mountains of central Panama. Sometimes workers died when their shovels struck explosive charges. "The flesh of men flew in the air like birds every day," recalled one worker from the West Indies.

Some 6,000 lives were lost during the American construction of the **Panama Canal**. It was finally opened to ships on August 15, 1914, linking the Atlantic and Pacific oceans. An opening ceremony was held the next year. It had taken 10 years to complete, and the cost was $375 million. In the end, however, the world had its "highway between the oceans."

READING CHECK **Drawing Conclusions** Why did building the canal cost so many lives?

THE IMPACT TODAY

Today the Panama Canal Zone is threatened by deforestation and erosion because of heavy use. Decreased rainfall is also hurting the canal.

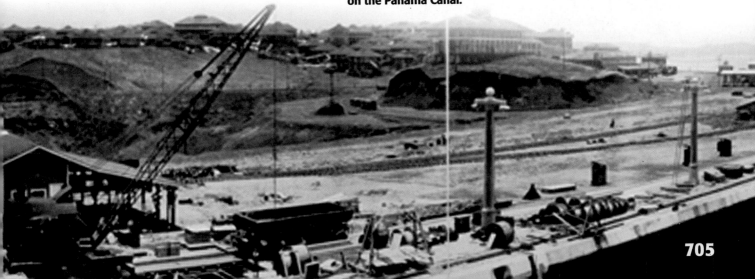

The massive Gatun Locks, shown here under construction in 1914, raise ships 85 feet onto Gatun Lake, an inland waterway on the Panama Canal.

NORTH AMERICA

UNITED STATES

San Francisco

Gulf of Mexico

Caribbean Sea

CENTRAL AMERICA

5,200 Miles (8,370 Kilometers)

13,000 Miles (20,900 Kilometers)

PACIFIC OCEAN

New York City

ATLANTIC OCEAN

Tropic of Cancer

Panama Canal

SOUTH AMERICA

0° Equator

Tropic of Capricorn

CONNECT TO ECONOMICS

Increasing Exports The Panama Canal did not just increase trade between the East and West coasts of the United States. By shortening the trip from many U.S. ports to other parts of the world, the canal also led to increased exports of agricultural and manufactured goods.

By how many miles did the Panama Canal shorten the shipping distance between New York City and San Francisco?

Inset map

Canal zone
Canal route
Railroad
Locks

0   10   20 Miles
0   10   20 Kilometers

Caribbean Sea

Colón
Cristobal
Gatun Locks
Gatun Lake

Gaillard Cut

Pedro Miguel Locks
Miraflores Locks
Balboa
Panama City
Bay of Panama

PANAMA

go.hrw.com
Interactive Map
KEYWORD: SB7 CH22

GEOGRAPHY SKILLS **INTERPRETING MAPS**

1. **Place** Why was Panama chosen as the site for a canal?
2. **Movement** How many locks did ships have to travel through from Balboa to Colón?

0   400   800 Miles
0   400   800 Kilometers

U.S. Policy Toward Latin America

As president, Theodore Roosevelt actively pursued progressive reforms at home. He also believed the United States should play a more active role in the Western Hemisphere. In 1900 Roosevelt said, "I have always been fond of the West African proverb: 'Speak softly and carry a big stick; you will go far.'" Roosevelt wanted everyone to know he would use a "big stick"—meaning U.S. military force—to protect U.S. interests in Latin America.

This was a change from the policies of previous presidents. In the 1823 Monroe Doctrine, President James Monroe had warned European nations not to interfere in the Western Hemisphere. And while the Monroe Doctrine became a major principle of U.S. foreign policy, the United States did not have the military strength to enforce it. By the time Roosevelt became president, however, this situation was changing. The United States was growing stronger and expanding its influence. The United States was becoming a world power.

How should the United States use its new power in Latin America? This question came up often in the early 1900s. European banks had made loans to a number of Latin American countries. Venezuela, for example, fell deeply in debt to British and German investors. Venezuela refused to repay these debts in 1902. A similar situation arose in the Caribbean nation of the Dominican Republic in 1904. European powers prepared to use military force to collect the debts.

Roosevelt insisted the countries must repay their debts. But he did not want to allow Europeans to intervene in Latin America. The presence of European forces there would violate the Monroe Doctrine and threaten U.S. power in the region.

Roosevelt knew that U.S. officials would have to force debtor nations to repay their loans in order to keep European nations from directly intervening in Latin America. In December 1904 he announced what became known as the **Roosevelt Corollary** to the Monroe Doctrine. This addition warned that in cases of "wrongdoing" by Latin American countries, the United States might exercise "international police power."

The Roosevelt Corollary asserted a new **role** for the United States as an "international police power" in the Western Hemisphere. Roosevelt actively enforced the corollary throughout the rest of his presidency.

ACADEMIC VOCABULARY
role assigned behavior

READING CHECK **Finding Main Ideas** Why did Roosevelt announce the Roosevelt Corollary?

Primary Source

POLITICAL CARTOON
Roosevelt's Imperialism

Theodore Roosevelt's foreign policy is shown visually in this cartoon. Roosevelt is the giant leading a group of ships that represent debt collection. The U.S. president is patrolling the Caribbean Sea and Latin American countries, trying to enforce the payment of debts to European countries.

What do you think this stick represents?

Why are these vessels warships?

ANALYSIS SKILL **ANALYZING PRIMARY SOURCES**

Analyzing How does the cartoonist portray the parts of the Roosevelt Corollary?

The United States in Latin America

Interactive Map

Guantánamo Bay
The United States maintains a naval base on the island of Cuba.

Puerto Rico
The island remains a commonwealth of the United States.

Panama Canal
The United States turned the canal over to Panama in 1979 but kept the right to defend it.

Legend:
- United States and possessions
- U.S. protectorates
- Bombarded by U.S. forces
- 1898 Date of bombardment or occupation
- Route of Pershing's U.S. Expeditionary Force
- Boundary line negotiated by United States

0   300   600 Miles
0   300   600 Kilometers

GEOGRAPHY SKILLS   INTERPRETING MAPS

go.hrw.com
Interactive Map
KEYWORD: SB7 CH22

1. **Region** What parts of this region does the United States still control?
2. **Place** Which country was a U.S. protectorate for the longest period of time?

U.S. Interests in Latin America

William Howard Taft, who became president in 1909, also acted to protect U.S. interests in Latin America. Taft used a policy called **dollar diplomacy**—influencing governments through economic, not military, intervention.

President Taft described dollar diplomacy as "substituting dollars for bullets. It is . . . directed to the increase of American trade." He wanted to encourage stability and keep Europeans out of Latin America by expanding U.S. business interests there.

For example, in 1911 Nicaragua failed to repay a loan from British investors. American bankers lent Nicaragua $1.5 billion in return

for control of the National Bank of Nicaragua and the government-owned railway. When local anger over this deal led to revolt in Nicaragua, Taft sent U.S. Marines to protect American interests.

When President Woodrow Wilson took office in 1913, he rejected Taft's dollar diplomacy. He believed the United States had a moral obligation to promote democracy in Latin America. Like Roosevelt, Wilson was willing to use military force to protect U.S. interests in the region.

In 1910 many Mexicans revolted against the harsh rule of Mexican dictator Porfirio Díaz. This was the start of the **Mexican Revolution**, a long, violent struggle for power in Mexico. The war affected U.S. interests

Departing from the example set by the nation's first president, George Washington, future presidents increased U.S. involvement around the world, particularly in Latin America.

Washington's Farewell Address
The United States will not become involved in European affairs.

Monroe Doctrine
The United States will defend its interests in the Western Hemisphere and keep European powers out.

Roosevelt Corollary
The United States will police wrongdoing by nations in the Western Hemisphere.

Taft's Dollar Diplomacy
The United States will use economic means to aid its interests in Latin America.

Wilson and Democracy
The United States will promote and protect democracy in the Western Hemisphere.

---

because Americans had invested more than $1 billion in Mexican land, mining, oil, and railways. American business leaders feared they would lose their investments.

In 1914 President Wilson learned that a German ship carrying weapons was headed to the port of Veracruz, Mexico. To keep the weapons from reaching the rebels, Wilson ordered the navy to seize Veracruz. Wilson acted again in 1916, sending General **John J. Pershing** and 15,000 U.S. soldiers into Mexico. Pershing's mission was to catch the rebel leader **Francisco "Pancho" Villa**, who had killed 17 Americans in New Mexico. Pershing failed to capture Villa, and Wilson recalled the troops.

In 1917 a new constitution began to bring order to Mexico. The violence caused more than 120,000 Mexicans to flee to the United States between 1905 and 1915.

READING CHECK **Summarizing** How did Wilson respond to events in Mexico?

SUMMARY AND PREVIEW The United States and Latin America established relationships through both conflicts and agreements. In the next chapter, you will learn how the United States became involved in conflict in Europe.

Reviewing Ideas, Terms, and People

1. **a. Recall** Why did the United States want to build a canal?
   b. Analyze What challenges did the builders of the **Panama Canal** face, and how did they overcome them?
   c. Elaborate Defend or criticize the U.S. decision to support the revolution in Panama.
2. **a. Describe** What problem was causing conflict between European and Latin American nations?
   b. Summarize How and why did Theodore Roosevelt change U.S. policy toward Latin America?
3. **a. Recall** What did Woodrow Wilson believe was the United States's obligation to Latin America?
   b. Compare and Contrast How were the policies of Taft and Wilson toward Latin America similar, and how were they different?

Critical Thinking

4. **Categorizing** Review your notes on U.S. policies toward Latin America. Then copy the web diagram below. Use it to identify American policies toward Latin America.

Roosevelt ← U.S. Policy → Wilson
Taft

FOCUS ON WRITING

5. **Identifying Pros and Cons of U.S. Intervention**
   What were the pros and cons of the construction of the Panama Canal and interventionist U.S. policies toward Latin America? Take notes for your list as you read this section.

America's Global Influence 1900

By 1900 most of the current boundaries of the United States had been established. But the world had become a much smaller place. American inventions were spreading, changing daily life in countries around the world. In addition, U.S. troops stationed in China were displaying the increasing importance of the United States in global affairs.

ASIA

PACIFIC OCEAN

On July 5, 1900, William Jennings Bryan spoke out against U.S. involvement in China, saying, "Imperialism is the most dangerous of the evils now menacing [threatening] our country."

Asia Before 1898, U.S. troops had never been sent outside the Western Hemisphere. But in 1900, some 5,000 troops were in Asia, fighting alongside European troops.

Paris The Paris Exposition of 1900 showcased many U.S. inventions. One British writer claimed the exposition displayed "the Americanization of the world."

London In August 1900, English farmers protested in London against new farm equipment introduced from the United States that they feared would cause farmers to lose their jobs.

EUROPE

London

Paris

UNITED STATES

New York

ATLANTIC OCEAN

New York City Nearly 500,000 people immigrated to the United States in 1900. By 1920 more than 16 million had come. Many arrived in New York City.

AFRICA

SOUTH AMERICA

GEOGRAPHY SKILLS **INTERPRETING MAPS**

1. **Region** By 1900, what role was the U.S. military playing in China?
2. **Movement** In what ways did the U.S. influence other countries?

Social Studies Skills

Analysis | Critical Thinking | Civic Participation | Study

Continuity and Change in History

Define the Skill

A well-known saying claims that "the more things change, the more they stay the same." Nowhere does this observation apply better than to the study of history. Any examination of the past will show many changes—nations expanding or shrinking, empires rising and falling, changes in leadership, or people on the move, for example.

The reasons for change have not changed, however. The same general forces have driven the actions of people and nations across time. These forces are the threads that run through history and give it continuity, or connectedness. They are the "sameness" in a world of continuous change.

Learn the Skill

You can find the causes of all events of the past in one or more of these major forces or themes that connect all history.

1. **Cooperation and Conflict** Throughout time, people and groups have worked together to achieve goals. They have also opposed others who stood in the way of their goals.

2. **Cultural Invention and Interaction** The values and ideas expressed in peoples' art, literature, customs, and religion have enriched the world. But the spread of cultures and their contact with other cultures have produced conflict as well.

3. **Geography and Environment** Physical environment and natural resources have shaped how people live. Efforts to gain, protect, or make good use of land and resources have been major causes of cooperation and conflict in history.

4. **Science and Technology** *Technology,* or the development and use of tools, has helped humans across time make better use of their environment. Science has changed their knowledge of the world, and changed their lives, too.

5. **Economic Opportunity and Development** From hunting and gathering to herding, farming, manufacturing, and trade, people have tried to make the most of their resources. The desire for a better life has also been a major reason people have moved from one place to another.

6. **The Impact of Individuals** Political, religious, military, business, and other leaders have been a major influence in history. The actions of many ordinary people have also shaped history

7. **Nationalism and Imperialism** *Nationalism* is the desire of a people to have their own country. *Imperialism* is the desire of a nation to influence or control other nations. Both have existed across time.

8. **Political and Social Systems** People have always been part of groups—families, villages, nations, or religious groups, for example. The groups to which people belong shape how they relate to others around them.

Practice the Skill

Check your understanding of continuity and change in history by answering the following questions.

1. What forces of history are illustrated by the events in Chapter 22? Explain with examples.

2. How do the events in this chapter show continuity with earlier periods in U.S. history?

Chapter Review

Visual Summary

QUICK FACTS

Use the visual summary below to help you review the main ideas of the chapter.

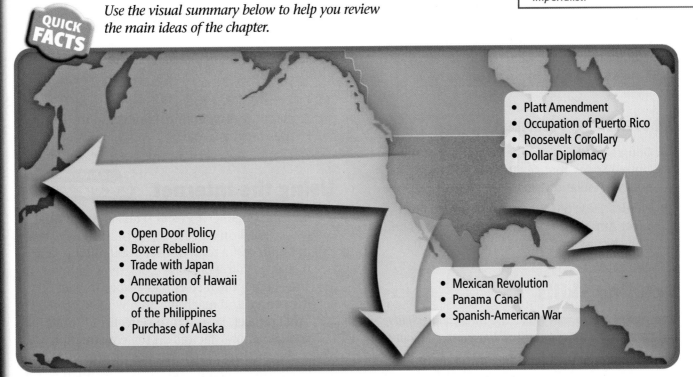

- Platt Amendment
- Occupation of Puerto Rico
- Roosevelt Corollary
- Dollar Diplomacy

- Open Door Policy
- Boxer Rebellion
- Trade with Japan
- Annexation of Hawaii
- Occupation of the Philippines
- Purchase of Alaska

- Mexican Revolution
- Panama Canal
- Spanish-American War

Reviewing Vocabulary, Terms, and People

1. In which of the following did the United States declare that it had no interest in taking control of Cuba?
   - **a.** Roosevelt Corollary
   - **b.** Monroe Doctrine
   - **c.** Open Door Policy
   - **d.** Teller Amendment

2. Which leader upset sugar planters in Hawaii by proposing a plan to return power to the monarchy?
   - **a.** Liliuokalani
   - **b.** John L. Stevens
   - **c.** Millard Fillmore
   - **d.** Woodrow Wilson

3. Which president supported Panama's revolt against Colombia in 1903?
   - **a.** Woodrow Wilson
   - **b.** William McKinley
   - **c.** William Howard Taft
   - **d.** Theodore Roosevelt

4. Who led U.S. forces into Mexico after attacks against U.S. citizens by Mexican rebels?
   - **a.** John Hay
   - **b.** William H. Seward
   - **c.** John J. Pershing
   - **d.** Theodore Roosevelt

Comprehension and Critical Thinking

SECTION 1 *(Pages 692–696)*

5. **a. Identify** Into what areas did the United States expand in the late 1800s?

   b. Draw Conclusions How did the United States benefit from contact with foreign nations and territories?

   c. Elaborate Which policy would you have supported—isolationism or imperialism? Explain your answer.

SECTION 2 *(Pages 697–702)*

6. **a. Describe** What events led the United States to declare war on Spain?

   b. Analyze How did the United States benefit from the Spanish-American War?

   c. Predict How might foreign countries view the actions of the United States in the Spanish-American War?

7. a. Identify In what ways did the United States become involved in Latin American affairs?

b. Draw Conclusions Why did the United States expand its role in Latin America in the early 1900s?

c. Elaborate Do you think the United States should have been as actively involved in Latin America as it was? Explain your answer.

Reviewing Themes

8. Geography How did the geography of the United States change after the end of its policy of isolationism?

9. Politics How did the policy of imperialism affect American politics in the late 1800s and early 1900s?

Reading Skills

Comparing Historical Texts *Use the Reading Skills taught in this chapter to answer the question about the reading selections below.*

A. "Sad to say, this most precious and sublime feature of the Yosemite National Park (Hetch Hetchy Valley), one of the greatest of all our natural resources for the uplifting joy and peace and health of the people, is in danger of being dammed and made into a reservoir to help supply San Francisco with water and light . . ."

—John Muir, *The Yosemite*, 1912

B. "As we all know, there is no use of water that is higher than the domestic use. Then, if there is, as the engineers tell us, no other source of supply that is anything like so reasonably available as this one; if this is the best, and, within reasonable limits of cost, the only means of supplying San Francisco with water, we come straight to the question of whether the advantage of leaving this valley in a state of nature is greater than the advantage of using it for the benefit of the city of San Francisco."

—Gifford Pinchot, address to Congress, 1913

10. How do the two men quoted above differ on the issue of building a dam in the Hetch Hetchy Valley?

Social Studies Skills

Continuity and Change in History *Use the Social Studies Skills taught in this chapter to answer the question below.*

11. Pick three of the themes listed on page 712. Explain how the themes connect to the history of the Panama Canal.

Using the Internet

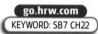
go.hrw.com
KEYWORD: SB7 CH22

12. Activity: Creating a Poster The Panama Canal was opened on August 15, 1914. It took 10 years to build, cost a total of over $600 million, and had a death toll of some 6,000 lives. Human and geographic factors had a huge impact on the people and machines that worked on the canal project. Research the effects of human and geographic factors on the construction of the Panama Canal. Physical factors include landforms, climate, and weather. Human factors should focus on the use of technology and the reasons humans modified the environment, along with the hazards they faced. Then create a poster about the canal, highlighting the most important details.

FOCUS ON WRITING

13. Writing Your List of Pros and Cons Review your notes and choose the pros and cons to include in your final list. Decide whether you want to include only facts, only opinions, or some of each. How can your analysis of history help guide U.S. foreign policy in the future? When you have finished your list, use it as the basis for a paragraph recommending either that the United States continue to involve itself in the affairs of other nations or that it pull back from such involvement.

DIRECTIONS: Read each question and write the letter of the best response. Use the map below to answer question 1.

1

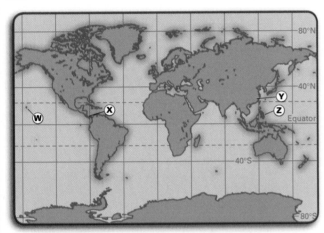

The only area in which the United States did not control territory in the late 1800s and early 1900s is shown on the map by which letter?

A W

B X

C Y

D Z

2 The practice of using U.S. businesses and economic aid to influence foreign governments and achieve U.S. goals in Latin America is known as

A imperialism.

B dollar diplomacy.

C isolationism.

D the big stick.

3 During the Mexican Revolution, President Wilson sent U.S. forces to Veracruz, Mexico. Which U.S. policy did this act best express?

A Roosevelt Corollary

B dollar diplomacy

C Teller Amendment

D isolationism

4 Which two nations did the United States hope to trade with rather than annex in the late 1800s?

A Hawaii and Japan

B Japan and China

C China and Cuba

D Cuba and Hawaii

5 How did American newspapers respond to the explosion of the USS *Maine* in Havana Harbor?

A They refused to report the story.

B They reported that the explosion was an accident.

C They blamed the explosion on Spain.

D They blamed the explosion on Cuban rebels.

6 In his book *The Influence of Sea Power upon History,* Alfred T. Mahan argued that the United States should

A avoid foreign conflicts.

B sell its naval bases.

C build a strong navy.

D remain isolationist.

7 Read the following passage from a letter from President Fillmore and use it to answer the question below.

> "I am desirous that our two countries should trade with each other, for the benefit of both Japan and the United States. We know that the ancient laws of your imperial majesty's government do not allow of foreign trade, except with the Chinese and the Dutch; but as the state of the world changes . . . it seems to be wise, from time to time, to make new laws."
>
> —Letter from U.S. President Millard Fillmore to Japan, 1852

Document-Based Question What is President Fillmore asking the Japanese to do?

World War I

Virginia Standards of Learning

USII.1 The student will demonstrate skills for historical and geographical analysis, and responsible citizenship, including the ability to

a) analyze and interpret primary and secondary source documents to increase understanding of events and life in United States history from 1865 to the present; **b)** make connections between past and present; **c)** sequence events in United States history from 1865 to the present; **d)** interpret ideas and events from different historical perspectives; **e)** evaluate and debate issues orally and in writing; **h)** interpret patriotic slogans and excerpts from notable speeches and documents

USII.5 The student will demonstrate knowledge of the changing role of the United States from the late nineteenth century through World War I by

c) explaining the reasons for the United States' involvement in World War I and its international leadership role at the conclusion of the war

FOCUS ON SPEAKING

Persuasive Speech Before the United States entered World War I in 1917, Americans heatedly debated joining the fight. Many were torn between either helping Britain and France or remaining isolated from world conflict. In this chapter, you will read about U.S. involvement in World War I. Then you will make a speech presenting your point of view on whether the United States should have entered the war.

UNITED STATES

1914 President Wilson issues a proclamation of neutrality in the European war.

1914

WORLD

1914 Archduke Francis Ferdinand is assassinated.

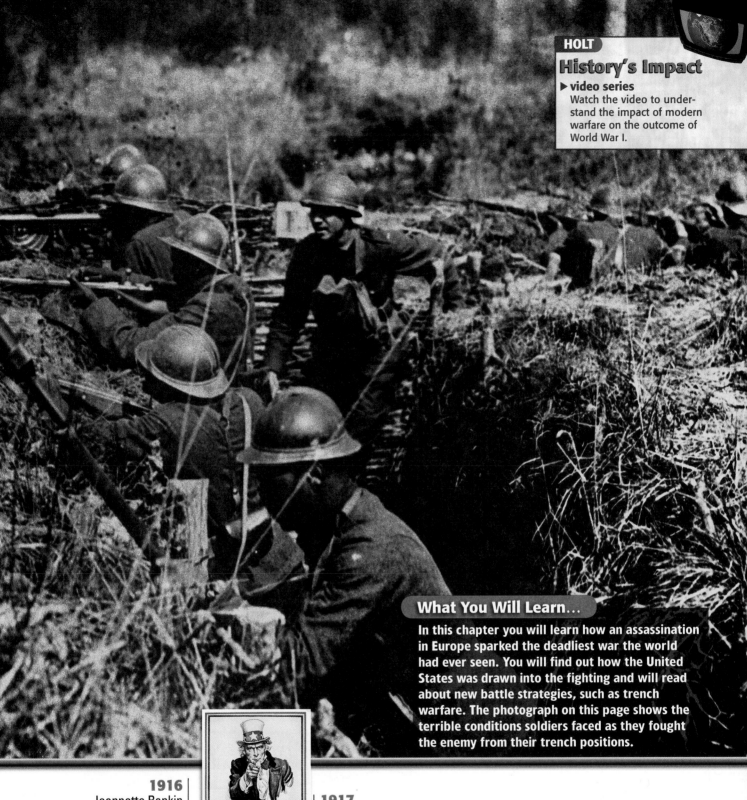

HOLT

History's Impact

▶ **video series**
Watch the video to understand the impact of modern warfare on the outcome of World War I.

What You Will Learn...

In this chapter you will learn how an assassination in Europe sparked the deadliest war the world had ever seen. You will find out how the United States was drawn into the fighting and will read about new battle strategies, such as trench warfare. The photograph on this page shows the terrible conditions soldiers faced as they fought the enemy from their trench positions.

1916
Jeannette Rankin becomes the first woman elected to Congress.

I WANT **YOU** FOR U.S. ARMY
NEAREST RECRUITING STATION

1917
The Selective Service Act is passed, introducing the draft.

1918 President Wilson announces the Fourteen Points.

1919 The U.S. Senate refuses to approve the Treaty of Versailles.

1916

1918

1920

1915 A German U-boat sinks the *Lusitania.*

CUNARD
EUROPE via LIVERPOOL
LUSITANIA

1917 The United States declares war on Germany.

1918 Germany agrees to an armistice, ending World War I.

Reading Social Studies

by Kylene Beers

Economics | **Geography** | **Politics** | **Society and Culture** | **Science and Technology**

Focus on Themes In this chapter, you will read about World War I and the changes it brought to the United States and the world. Many of the **political** tensions that led to the war were caused by the rise of nationalism in European countries. You will read about how the war devastated European **economies**, and how peace affected European countries.

Recognizing Fallacies in Reasoning

Focus on Reading As part of evaluating a historical argument, you can judge whether the reasoning is sound. A *fallacy* is a false or mistaken idea.

Recognizing Fallacies As you identify a main idea, judge its soundness. Look for cause-and-effect relationships that support the idea. Decide whether you think the argument is logical.

Notice how a reader explained the logical reasoning behind the main idea in the following paragraph.

Three main factors led to a shortage of labor in the United States during the war. First, American factories were working nonstop to produce weapons and supplies for the Allied forces. Factories needed new workers to meet this huge demand. Second, the war almost completely cut off immigration. As you know, immigrants had provided a steady source of labor to American industry. And third, many of the young men who would normally take factory jobs were off fighting in Europe.

From Chapter 23, p. 728

If factories were working overtime, they would need more workers. This supports the main idea of a labor shortage.

If factories were used to having immigrants to hire, and there were fewer immigrants, it would make sense that there was a labor shortage.

Here's a third reason for a labor shortage: many men became soldiers. It makes sense that there was a labor shortage during the war.

Virginia Standards of Learning

Reading 8.6b Analyze the author's credentials, view-point and impact.

You Try It!

The man who assassinated Archduke Francis Ferdinand was a Serb.

All Serbians wanted war with Austria-Hungary.

Wilson wanted to establish the League of Nations

because he thought it would help ensure peace.

Trench warfare was a new kind of warfare.

Therefore, trench warfare was more horrible than any other kind of warfare.

1. Is the first conclusion reasonable? Why or why not? How can you tell?

2. Do you think the second conclusion is logical or illogical? What makes you think so?

3. Is the third conclusion a fallacy of reason? What reasonable conclusions can you draw from the statement?

Key Terms and People

Chapter 23

Section 1
militarism *(p. 721)*
Archduke Francis Ferdinand *(p. 721)*
mobilize *(p. 721)*
Central Powers *(p. 721)*
Allied Powers *(p. 721)*
trench warfare *(p. 722)*
stalemate *(p. 723)*
U-boats *(p. 724)*

Section 2
Lusitania (p. 726)
Zimmermann Note *(p. 726)*
Selective Service Act *(p. 727)*
Liberty bonds *(p. 727)*
National War Labor Board *(p. 729)*

Section 3
American Expeditionary Force *(p. 730)*
Communists *(p. 731)*
armistice *(p. 734)*

Section 4
League of Nations *(p. 737)*
reparations *(p. 737)*
Treaty of Versailles *(p. 738)*
Henry Cabot Lodge *(p. 738)*

Academic Vocabulary

In this chapter, you will learn the following academic words:

neutral *(p. 724)*
strategy *(p. 733)*

As you read Chapter 23, notice how the authors use logical reasoning to support their main ideas.

The Road to War

Virginia Standards of Learning USII.1b, USII.5c

What You Will Learn...

Main Ideas

1. Many factors contributed to the outbreak of World War I.
2. European nations suffered massive casualties in the war's early battles.

The Big Idea

In 1914 tensions in Europe exploded into the deadliest war the world had ever seen.

Key Terms and People

militarism, *p. 721*
Archduke Francis Ferdinand, *p. 721*
mobilize, *p. 721*
Central Powers, *p. 721*
Allied Powers, *p. 721*
trench warfare, *p. 722*
stalemate, *p. 723*
U-boats, *p. 724*

TAKING NOTES As you read, identify the major battles of the beginning of World War I. In a chart like the one below, list the battles and where they were fought.

Battle	Location

If YOU were there...

You are walking past a newspaper stand when a headline catches your eye: "Austria-Hungary's Archduke Francis Ferdinand Assassinated in Sarajevo." Your first thought is, "Who's he?" You pick up the paper and read about the archduke and about the rising tensions in Europe related to his death. The article makes it sound like Europe is about to explode into war.

At this point, do you think the assassination will affect the United States? Why or why not?

BUILDING BACKGROUND European nations had not been involved in a major war in the region since the 1870s. Rising political tensions during the early 1900s threatened this peace, however, and nations began to build up their military forces. Even a small incident might trigger a major war.

Outbreak of War

Though Europe was at peace in the early 1900s, relations between European nations were not necessarily friendly. In fact, feelings of fear and distrust were growing among European powers such as Germany, France, Great Britain, Russia, and Austria-Hungary. This dangerous tension had several important causes.

Tensions in Europe

One cause of tension was the rise of nationalism in the 1800s. Nationalism is a strong sense of pride and loyalty to one's nation or culture. Nationalism inspired people who shared a language or culture to want to unite politically. In 1871, for example, Chancellor Otto von Bismarck and Kaiser Wilhelm I brought together several German states to form the nation of Germany.

While nationalism helped bring stability to Germany, it caused instability in other places. The empire of Austria-Hungary included people from many different cultural groups. One of these groups was the Slavs. Slavic nationalists wanted to break away from Austria-Hungary and join the independent Slavic country of Serbia on the

Balkan Peninsula. Leaders of Austria-Hungary reacted angrily, seeing this movement as a threat to their empire.

Another source of tension in Europe was imperialism. Britain's huge empire, stretching from Africa to Asia, brought it wealth and power. Eager to share in such benefits, other European powers competed for control of overseas territories. Fierce competition for territory took place within Europe as well. For example, Germany had taken the Alsace-Lorraine region from France in the Franco-Prussian War in 1871. France wanted it back.

In this competitive atmosphere, nations focused their resources on **militarism**—the aggressive strengthening of armed forces. European nations raced to build armies and navies that were larger than ever before.

As nations became more powerful, they sought to protect themselves by forming new alliances. Germany formed an alliance with Austria-Hungary in 1879. Each promised to defend the other in case of enemy attack. Concerned with Germany's growing power, France and Russia created their own alliance in 1893. Britain joined France and Russia in 1907.

The Spark

With so much hostility dividing the nations of Europe, a German general felt that "a European war is bound to come sooner or later." All that was needed was a spark to set Europe on fire. That spark flew from the Balkan province of Bosnia and Herzegovina.

Bosnia and Herzegovina had gained independence from Turkish rule in 1878. In 1908, however, Austria-Hungary annexed the province. Slavic nationalists resisted violently—they wanted the region to be part of Serbia.

On June 28, 1914, **Archduke Francis Ferdinand**, heir to the throne of Austria-Hungary, visited the province's capital of Sarajevo with his wife, Sophie. While riding through the streets, they were shot and killed by a 19-year-old Serb nationalist named Gavrilo Princip.

An End to Peace

The assassination of Archduke Francis Ferdinand and his wife, Sophie, by a Serb nationalist sparked the beginning of World War I.

How did the murder of the archduke bring war to Europe?

The assassination shattered Europe's fragile peace. Determined to crush Serbia and the Slavic nationalists, Austria-Hungary declared war on Serbia. Very quickly, other countries were pulled into the fighting. Russia had promised to support Serbia in case of war. It began to **mobilize**, or prepare its military for war. On August 1 Germany, Austria-Hungary's ally, declared war on Russia. Two days later, Germany also declared war on France, Russia's ally. To reach France quickly, the German army marched into Belgium on August 4. Britain, which had promised to support Belgium, then declared war on Germany.

As the fighting started, the alliance between Austria-Hungary and Germany came to be known as the **Central Powers**. Bulgaria and the Ottoman Empire later sided with the Central Powers. France, Russia, and Britain were known as the **Allied Powers**. Italy joined them in 1915. Over the next several years, soldiers from 30 nations and six continents would fight in what was then called the Great War. The conflict later became known as World War I.

READING CHECK Identifying Cause and Effect
How did nationalism contribute to political tensions in Europe?

Early Battles of the War

FOCUS ON READING
What mistake did the German leaders make in their reasoning?

Both sides expected the war to be over in a few months. German leaders planned to defeat France quickly, before Russia could join the fighting. But as the Germans marched toward France, they met fierce resistance from Belgian soldiers. This gave Britain and France time to mobilize their own troops.

The First Battle of the Marne

Belgian resistance slowed the German advance but could not stop it. On September 3 the German army was just 25 miles from Paris, the capital of France. The French army blocked the German advance at the Marne River, east of Paris. The First Battle of the Marne raged for several days before the Germans were pushed back.

By mid-September French and German troops faced each other along a long battle line called the western front. The western front stretched from the North Sea all the way to Switzerland. Meanwhile, the Russian and German armies were struggling back and forth along the eastern front, which reached from the Black Sea to the Baltic Sea. It quickly became clear that this war would be longer and deadlier than anyone had expected.

A New Kind of War

Part of what made World War I so long and deadly was a new technique called **trench warfare**—defending a position by fighting from the protection of deep ditches. When the French defeated the Germans in the First Battle of the Marne, the Germans did not retreat far. Instead, they dug trenches nearby. Opposite them, the French dug their own trenches. A 400-mile-long network of trenches soon stretched across the western front.

Soldiers fought in these cold, wet, and muddy ditches, sometimes for months at a time. The filthy trenches were perfect breeding

History Close-up
Trench Warfare

A series of trenches at the back was used to deliver food, ammunition, and mail to soldiers on the front lines.

Trenches were dug in a zigzag pattern so that the enemy could not stand at one end and fire down the length of a trench.

Some trenches served as first-aid posts where wounded soldiers were cared for until they could be evacuated.

grounds for germs, and soldiers on both sides died from disease. An American in the French army described life in the trenches:

"The impossibility of the simplest kind of personal cleanliness makes vermin [bugs] a universal ill, against which there is no remedy. Cold, dirt, discomfort, are the ever present conditions, and the soldier's life comes to mean ... the most misery that the human organism [body] can support."

—Alan Seeger, *Letters and Diary of Alan Seeger*

The empty patch of ground between enemy trenches came to be known as "no-man's-land." This area was quickly stripped of trees and blasted full of holes by artillery shells. Anyone who ventured into no-man's-land was likely to be killed by enemy fire.

Another factor that made World War I deadlier than previous wars was the use of modern technology. New machine guns, for example, could fire 400 to 600 bullets a minute. Enormous artillery guns fired shells over the trenches, where they exploded and sent speeding scraps of metal onto the soldiers below. Other shells spread poisonous gases. If soldiers were not wearing gas masks, the gas destroyed their lungs, causing slow, painful deaths. Poisonous gases were originally banned but came into use by both sides by the end of the war.

Other new weapons included tanks and airplanes. Tanks are armored combat vehicles that can cause heavy damage but cannot be destroyed easily. Airplanes were used to fire down on soldiers in trenches and to gather information about enemy locations. Airplanes also battled each other in fights called "dogfights."

Land and Sea Battles

After a year of vicious fighting, the war had become a **stalemate**—a situation in which neither side can win a decisive victory. Determined to break the stalemate, both sides launched massive attacks in 1916. In February 1916 the Germans attacked the French city of Verdun, at the southern end of the western front. That summer, the Allies staged an attack along the Somme River, in northeastern

THE IMPACT TODAY

Many of the weapons first used in World War I, such as tanks and airplanes, are still used in warfare today. The use of poison gas, however, has been outlawed by international treaties.

Airplanes could scout enemy positions and drop bombs into trenches.

Because tanks were not damaged by either machine-gun or rifle fire, their use marked the beginning of the end for trench warfare.

No-man's land was the name given to the area between opposing trenches. It was usually about 250 yards wide and full of barbed wire and abandoned military equipment.

ANALYSIS SKILL ANALYZING INFORMATION

How does this picture help you understand why World War I was so deadly for soldiers?

German U-boats

Germany developed small submarines called U-boats as part of its war strategy. U-boats could strike Allied ships without being seen. They destroyed around 10 million tons of Allied and neutral ships and cargo from 1914 to 1918.

Why might U-boats have been so effective against the Allies?

go.hrw.com
Online Quiz
KEYWORD: SB7 HP23

France. Both battles raged for months, as the armies attacked and counterattacked.

By the end of the year, the Germans had failed to take Verdun. At the Somme River, the Allies had advanced just seven miles. Almost nothing had changed on the western front. But nearly 1 million men had been killed at Verdun and the Somme River.

As the stalemate on land dragged on, sea battles in the Atlantic Ocean and the North Sea became even more important. The powerful British navy blockaded the ports of the Central Powers and laid explosive mines in the North Sea. These could blow a huge hole in a ship, sinking it in minutes. The tactic effectively stopped ships from reaching German ports with needed supplies.

ACADEMIC VOCABULARY

neutral unbiased, not favoring either side in a conflict

The Germans responded by using submarines called **U-boats**. U-boats launched torpedoes against Allied supply ships, causing heavy losses. The Germans also attacked ships belonging to **neutral** countries they believed were helping the Allies. This would soon pull the United States into World War I.

READING CHECK **Categorizing** What new technologies did armies in World War I use?

SUMMARY AND PREVIEW World War I became a stalemate by 1916 as countries battled for control. In the next section you will find out why the United States decided to join the fighting.

Section 1 Assessment

Reviewing Ideas, Terms, and People

1. a. Describe What factors contributed to the outbreak of World War I?
b. Contrast How did nationalism affect Germany and Austria-Hungary differently?
c. Predict What might have happened if Russia had not honored its agreement to defend Serbia?
2. a. Identify What were the outcomes of the early battles of the war?
b. Explain How did Belgian resistance affect the German war plan?
c. Evaluate How successful was **trench warfare** as a strategy?

Critical Thinking

3. Identifying Cause and Effect Review your notes on the major battles of World War I. Then copy the graphic organizer below and use it to show the outcomes of these early battles and how they affected the war.

Battle	Outcome	Results

FOCUS ON SPEAKING

4. Analyzing Rising Tensions Start a list of ways that World War I might affect the United States. Was there sufficient reason for the United States to join the conflict at this time?

Americans Prepare for War

Virginia Standards of Learning USII.1b, USII.5c

If YOU were there...

Everywhere you go people are talking about the war in Europe. The United States has just joined the fighting on the side of the Allied Powers. Many young men you know are volunteering to fight. Women are signing up to drive ambulances or work as nurses. You know that the situation in Europe is dangerous, but you want to serve your country.

Will you volunteer for service in World War I?

BUILDING BACKGROUND When World War I began, the United States had a long history of avoiding involvement in European conflicts. Most Americans wanted the United States to remain neutral in this war as well. But as tensions with Germany increased, it became clear that distance from Europe would not keep Americans out of battle.

The United States Enters World War I

Millions of Americans at this time were immigrants or children of immigrants. Many came from countries belonging to the Allied or Central Powers. They naturally sympathized with their former homelands. This did not change the fact that most Americans viewed World War I as a European conflict. They did not want American soldiers sent to the bloody battlefields of Europe. Shortly after World War I began, President Woodrow Wilson announced that the United States would remain neutral. Most Americans agreed that America should stay out of the war.

American Neutrality Threatened

Although the United States had a policy of neutrality, its merchants continued to trade with European nations. American ships carried supplies and war materials to the Allies. U.S. banks invested $2 billion in European war bonds, nearly all of it in Allied countries.

The Germans used U-boat attacks to try to stop supplies from reaching the Allies. Sometimes they attacked ships without

---

What You Will Learn...

Main Ideas

1. The United States entered the war after repeated crises with Germany.
2. The United States mobilized for war by training troops and stepping up production of supplies.
3. Labor shortages created new wartime opportunities for women and other Americans.

The Big Idea

After entering World War I in 1917, Americans began the massive effort of preparing for war.

Key Terms and People

Lusitania, p. 726
Zimmermann Note, *p. 726*
Selective Service Act, *p. 727*
Liberty bonds, *p. 727*
National War Labor Board, *p. 729*

TAKING NOTES As you read, take notes on the new laws and government programs created to prepare for World War I. In each outer circle of this web, name one new law or program. You may need to add more circles.

New laws and government programs

---

warning. In May 1915 a German U-boat sank the **Lusitania**, a British passenger liner. Nearly 1,200 people, including 128 Americans, were killed. The incident fueled anti-German feeling in the United States. Throughout the coming war, German Americans faced nativist attacks, including anti-German speeches, discrimination, and physical attacks.

Secretary of State William Jennings Bryan resigned over President Wilson's handling of the affair. Bryan thought that Wilson's protest note to the Germans was designed to bring the United States into the war.

In March 1916 a U-boat attacked the *Sussex*, a French passenger ship. Several of the 80 casualties were Americans. Wilson demanded that the Germans stop attacking nonmilitary ships. German leaders responded with the *Sussex* pledge, agreeing not to attack merchant ships without warning.

Congress Declares War

When Wilson ran for reelection in 1916, the promise to remain neutral helped him win the election. Nearly a year after the *Sussex* pledge, however, the Germans again began launching attacks on ships, including American vessels. In response, Wilson broke off diplomatic relations with Germany.

The United States stepped closer to war when Americans found out about the **Zimmermann Note**. This secret telegram to Mexico sent by the German foreign minister, Arthur Zimmermann, was decoded and then published by American newspapers in March 1917. In the note, Zimmermann proposed an alliance against the United States. He promised that Germany would help Mexico recapture areas that Mexico had lost during the Mexican-American War.

The American public was outraged by the telegram. President Wilson asked Congress to declare war on Germany. "The world must be made safe for democracy," he proclaimed. Congress declared war on April 6, 1917.

READING CHECK **Finding Main Ideas** What events challenged U.S. neutrality?

Primary Source

NEWSPAPER ARTICLE
Sinking of the *Lusitania*

In 1915 German U-boats sank the Lusitania, *an event that pushed the United States toward entry into World War I. Newspapers quickly spread news of the disaster.*

The accounts which have so far been received are fragmentary, and give no clear idea of the disaster. There is, however, no doubt that two torpedoes were fired without warning into the starboard side of the ship soon after 2 o'clock yesterday afternoon. There were conflicting accounts of the period during which the *Lusitania* remained afloat, but the Cunard Company states that she sunk 40 minutes after being struck.

—*The Register*, quoted in the *Times of London*

The ship was treated as an enemy warship.

The ship sank before enough rescue ships could arrive.

ANALYSIS SKILL **ANALYZING PRIMARY SOURCES**

How might this disaster draw the United States into war with Germany?

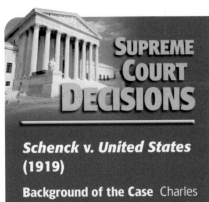

SUPREME COURT DECISIONS

Schenck v. United States (1919)

Background of the Case Charles Schenck was arrested for violating the Espionage Act. He had printed and distributed pamphlets urging resistance to the draft. Schenck argued that the First Amendment, which guarantees freedom of speech and freedom of the press, gave him the right to criticize the government.

The Court's Ruling

The Supreme Court ruled that the pamphlet was not protected by the First Amendment and that the Espionage Act was constitutional.

The Court's Reasoning

The Supreme Court decided that under certain circumstances, such as a state of war, Congress could limit free speech. The Court created a test to distinguish between protected and unprotected speech. Unprotected speech would have to present "a clear and present danger" to national security. For example, the First Amendment would not protect a person who created a panic by yelling "Fire!" in a crowded theater.

Why It Matters

Schenck v. *United States* was important because it was the first case in which the Supreme Court interpreted the First Amendment. The Court concluded that certain constitutional rights, such as free speech, could be limited under extraordinary conditions, such as war. Later rulings by the Court narrowed the test of "clear and present danger" to speech advocating violence. The nonviolent expression of ideas and opinions—however unpopular—was thereby protected.

ANALYSIS SKILL **ANALYZING INFORMATION**

1. According to the Supreme Court, when could free speech be limited?
2. How do you think this case affected other people who opposed the war?

Mobilizing for War

In order to persuade the public to support the war effort, President Wilson formed the Committee on Public Information (CPI). The CPI organized rallies and parades and published posters and pamphlets. Speakers known as "four-minute men" gave short patriotic speeches in movie theaters and churches.

The U.S. government's war effort also involved limiting some freedoms in the United States. The Espionage Act of 1917 and the Sedition Act of 1918 restricted free speech and allowed the government to arrest opponents of the war. Antiwar mail was prohibited and seized. About 900 opponents of the war were jailed for violating these laws. The Sedition Act was later repealed, but the Espionage Act is still in effect today.

To prepare the U.S. military, Congress passed the **Selective Service Act** in 1917. The act required men between the ages of 21 and 30 to register to be drafted. Almost 3 million Americans were drafted into service in World War I. A number of the draftees were African Americans. Altogether, about 400,000 African Americans served in the war. Their units were segregated from white forces and were commanded by white officers. Eventually, African Americans were trained as officers. During World War I, however, they were never placed in command of white troops.

Preparations for war were very expensive. Troops had to be trained, supplied, transported, and fed. Ships and airplanes had to be built and fueled. The government raised taxes and issued war bonds. Money from the sale of these **Liberty bonds** provided billions of dollars in loans to the Allies.

The government took other actions to supply the troops. The War Industries Board (WIB) oversaw the production and distribution of steel, copper, cement, and rubber. The Food Administration worked to increase food supplies for the troops. It guaranteed farmers high prices for their crops. To conserve food at home, citizens were encouraged to practice "meatless Mondays" and "wheatless Wednesdays." Many people also grew their own vegetables in "victory gardens" at home.

THE IMPACT TODAY

To conserve fuel used for lighting for the war effort, daylight saving time was first introduced in March 1918. The plan is still in effect today.

READING CHECK **Analyzing** How did the U.S. government gain public support for the war?

Women on the Battlefield

The role of women in World War I was much like their roles in previous wars—providing support for male troops. Women drove ambulances and entered the battlefield as nurses and medics. Red Cross volunteers were often responsible for the first stage of treatment of the wounded. Today, women may also serve in the military as soldiers. They are not allowed to fight in ground combat, but they do serve as guards and pilots, and in the navy.

Red Cross volunteers in World War I

Soldier on duty in Iraq

ANALYSIS SKILL **ANALYZING INFORMATION**

How have wartime roles for women changed since World War I?

New Wartime Opportunities

Three main factors led to a shortage of labor in the United States during the war. First, American factories were working nonstop to produce weapons and supplies for the Allied forces. Factories needed new workers to meet this huge demand. Second, the war almost completely cut off immigration. As you know, immigrants had provided a steady source of labor to American industry. And third, many of the young men who would normally take factory jobs were off fighting in Europe.

Women's War Efforts

This labor shortage created new opportunities for many workers. American women took on new roles to help the war effort. Some 1 million women joined the U.S. workforce during the war years. For many, this was their first experience working outside the home.

Women also worked for the war effort in Europe. About 25,000 American women volunteered as nurses, telephone operators, signalers, typists, and interpreters in France. Women were not given jobs in combat, but they braved gunfire at the front lines as nurses and ambulance drivers. One female driver described her World War I experiences:

" We had our first air-raid work last night. I was the night driver on duty … Some bombs fell very near just as I got to the [hospital] … when shrapnel [metal fragments] whizzed past my head and there was a tremendous crash close beside … Then an ambulance call came and I tore off. "

—Mrs. Guy Napier-Martin, quoted in *The Overseas War Record of the Winsor School, 1914–1919*

Other women, meanwhile, spoke out against U.S. participation in the war. Social reformer Jane Addams was against U.S. entry into the war. Jeannette Rankin of Montana, the first female member of Congress, was one of 50 House members to cast a vote against declaring war in 1917. "I want to stand by my country," she said, "but I cannot vote for war."

Labor and the War

Even with so many women joining the work-force, factories needed additional workers. New job opportunities encouraged Mexican Americans from the West and African Americans from the South to move to northern industrial cities.

Because labor was scarce, workers were in a good position to demand better wages and conditions. Union membership increased. More than 4 million unionized workers went on strike during the war. Because factory owners could not easily replace workers, they often agreed to demands.

President Wilson set up the **National War Labor Board** in April 1918. The board helped workers and management avoid strikes and reach agreements. The board settled more than 1,000 labor disputes. Its members were generally sympathetic to workers. They helped establish a minimum wage and limited work hours. They also required fair pay for women.

READING CHECK **Finding Main Ideas** How did war mobilization benefit American workers?

Patriotic Posters

Posters like this one encouraged American citizens to participate in the effort to provide weapons and food to soldiers fighting in World War I.

How does this poster inspire patriotism?

TEAMWORK WINS
UNITED STATES SHIPPING BOARD EMERGENCY FLEET CORPORATION

SUMMARY AND PREVIEW The war effort created new opportunities for women and other Americans. In the next section you will learn about what life was like for soldiers overseas.

Section 2 Assessment

Reviewing Ideas, Terms, and People

1. a. Explain Why did the United States enter World War I?
b. Evaluate Do you think the United States was right to stay neutral for so long? Why or why not?
2. a. Explain How did the United States prepare for war?
b. Recall What was the purpose of the Committee on Public Information?
c. Summarize How did the government exercise control over the economy during the war?
3. a. Describe How did women help the war effort abroad?
b. Predict How do you think the end of the war affected labor unions? Explain your answer.

Critical Thinking

4. Problem Solving Review your notes on new laws and government programs during World War I.

Then copy the graphic organizer below and use it to identify the challenges the United States faced when mobilizing for World War I. List which new laws, government programs, and other changes responded to those challenges.

Challenges → Responses

FOCUS ON SPEAKING

5. Analyzing Wilson's Policies Add to your list examples of causes of growing tension between Germany and the United States. What events led President Wilson to support war with Germany? Do you agree with his view? Why or why not?

Virginia Standards of Learning USII.1h, USII.5c

What You Will Learn...

Main Ideas

1. American soldiers started to arrive in Europe in 1917.
2. The Americans helped the Allies win the war.
3. Germany agreed to an armistice after suffering heavy losses.

The Big Idea

American troops helped the Allies achieve victory in World War I.

Key Terms and People

American Expeditionary Force, *p. 730*
Communists, *p. 731*
armistice, *p. 734*

TAKING NOTES As you read, take notes on the achievements and victories of the American Expeditionary Force (AEF). Organize your notes in a chart like this one.

Achievements of the AEF

Americans in World War I

If YOU were there...

It is April 1918. You are marching into Paris with your army unit on your way to the front lines. Women and children throw flowers from windows and balconies as you pass through the city. You want to do whatever it takes to defend this city and its residents. You know that defeating Germany will be difficult and very dangerous.

Do you think American forces can help the Allies win the war?

BUILDING BACKGROUND Preparations for war helped make the United States a strong military power. By 1918 nearly 5 million Americans were serving in the army, navy, and marine corps. While this huge armed force was being trained, however, the fighting in Europe was going badly for the Allies. French and British leaders were eager for help from America.

American Soldiers Arrive

By the time U.S. troops started to arrive in Europe in 1917, the Allies were dangerously near defeat. German forces were advancing in France, once again driving toward Paris. The German navy was destroying Allied ships at sea. And on the eastern front, the Russians were desperately struggling to hold back the Germans.

Joining the Fight

French and British generals called for immediate help on the front lines. They wanted the U.S. troops, known as the **American Expeditionary Force** (AEF), to join French and British units. But General John J. Pershing, leader of the American troops, insisted that the Americans join the fight as a separate force. He refused to have the AEF "scattered among the Allied forces where it will not be an American army at all."

Pershing also demanded that his troops be thoroughly trained for combat before rushing to the front lines. The AEF included many well-trained regular army and National Guard troops. But it also included a large number of inexperienced volunteers and draftees. Pershing gave the men three months of intense training in army discipline and trench warfare. He believed that taking the time to train his soldiers would help the Allies achieve victory.

Russia Leaves the War

While Pershing trained his troops, the Allies' position became even more dangerous. In November 1917 a group of Russians called the Bolsheviks overthrew the Russian government and seized power. The Bolsheviks were **Communists**—people who favor the equal distribution of wealth and the end of all forms of private property.

Led by Vladimir Lenin, the new Russian government faced a desperate situation. Around 8 million Russians had been killed or wounded during the war. Soldiers were deserting from the eastern front, and sailors were leaving naval bases. Food riots raged in the cities. The Russians could not keep fighting under these conditions. In March 1918 Russia signed the Treaty of Brest-Litovsk, a peace agreement with the Central Powers. A civil war then broke out in Russia between the Communists and forces loyal to the czar (ZAHR), Russia's emperor. The United States and other Allied countries sent aid to the czarist forces. Russia, however, one of the main Allied Powers, was out of World War I.

READING CHECK Drawing Inferences Why do you think General Pershing refused to put American troops in foreign units?

Winning the War

With Russia out of the fighting, German generals saw a chance to win the war. In the spring of 1918 Germany transferred many of its divisions of troops from the eastern front to the western front. Germany planned to smash the stalemate.

World War I U.S. Soldier

The appearance of the Springfield rifles fooled the Germans into thinking the Americans had machine guns.

Soldiers carried a pack called a haversack, which held food, personal items, and extra socks.

Gas masks were carried in a pouch around the neck.

A wool tunic was worn over a wool shirt and wool breeches.

A blanket could be carried at the bottom of the haversack with a special attachment.

Wool cloth strips called puttees were wrapped around the legs and tops of shoes for protection.

ANALYSIS SKILL **ANALYZING VISUALS**
How did clothing and supplies help a U.S. soldier in the battlefield?

The Final Battles

At the same time, American soldiers arrived. Even training had not prepared them for the realities of war. The troops lived on dried beef, hard biscuits, and canned emergency rations. The men shared the trenches with rats, lice, and sometimes the bodies of dead soldiers. A soldiers' song of the time described the situation:

"Sing me to sleep where bullets fall,
Let me forget the war and all;
Damp is my dug-out [trench], cold my feet,
Nothing but bully [canned meat] and biscuits to eat."

—Quoted in *Great Push: An Episode of the Great War*, by Patrick MacGill

World War I, 1914–1918

Interactive Map ✶

Legend

- Allied Powers, 1916
- Central Powers, 1916
- Neutral Countries
- Allied Powers troop movements
- Central Powers troop movements
- British naval blockade
- Farthest Russian advance (1914)
- Farthest Central Powers advance
- Trench line, western front
- Armistice line, Nov. 11, 1918
- ✶ Allied victory
- ✶ Central Powers victory
- ✶ Undecided battle
- German submarine activity

0   200   400 Miles
0   200   400 Kilometers

ATLANTIC OCEAN

NORWAY

SWEDEN

FINLAND

Petrograd

GREAT BRITAIN

Lusitania sunk May 1915

London

North Sea

DENMARK

RUSSIA

Berlin

Stebark Aug. 1914

EASTERN FRONT DEC. 1917

NETHERLANDS

Ypres Oct.–Nov. 1914 Apr.–May 1915

BELGIUM

GERMANY

English Channel

Sussex torpedoed March 1916

Somme July–Nov. 1916

LUXEMBOURG

Paris

Battle of the Marne Sept. 1914, July 1918

Château-Thierry June 1918

Argonne Forest Sept.–Oct. 1918

Verdun Feb.–Dec. 1916

ALSACE-LORRAINE

WESTERN FRONT

SWITZERLAND

Vienna

AUSTRIA-HUNGARY

Budapest

Bay of Biscay

FRANCE

Kobarid Oct.–Nov. 1917

BOSNIA and HERZEGOVINA

Sarajevo

SERBIA

ROMANIA

Black Sea

PORTUGAL

SPAIN

Adriatic Sea

ITALY

Rome

MONTENEGRO

ALBANIA

BALKANS

BULGARIA

Bosporus

Constantinople

GREECE (Joined Allied Powers 1917)

Gallipoli April 1915–Jan. 1916

Dardanelles

OTTOMAN EMPIRE

Mediterranean Sea

go.hrw.com
Interactive Map
KEYWORD: SB7 CH23

GEOGRAPHY SKILLS · **INTERPRETING MAPS**

1. **Human-Environment Interaction** Why was the British naval blockade located where it was?
2. **Location** In which country were the most battles fought, according to this map?

On March 21, 1918, the Germans began blasting more than 6,000 heavy guns at Allied troops along the Somme River in northern France. German forces drove 40 miles into Allied lines before the advance stalled. Some 250,000 Germans had been killed or wounded. British and French casualties totaled 133,000.

The Germans then attacked farther south, advancing to the Marne River and pushing the French line back toward Paris. At this critical moment, General Pershing promised Allied commander Ferdinand Foch: "Infantry, artillery, aviation—all that we have . . . The American people would be proud to be engaged in the greatest battle of history." Two divisions of the AEF joined French forces.

The Germans were unprepared for the fresh energy and fighting skills of the Americans. The U.S. soldiers succeeded in stopping the German advance less than 50 miles from Paris. Then, at Belleau Wood, the Allies attacked and gradually drove the Germans back.

German generals became desperate. In July 1918 they launched their final offensive—one last attempt to cross the Marne River. Terrible losses on the German side stopped the German offensive and protected Paris from invasion. Although they suffered about 12,000 casualties, American troops had helped force a major turning point in the war.

Driving the Germans Back

Now the Allies drove toward victory. There were more than 1 million U.S. troops in France, and they played a key role in the later battles of the war. In September 1918 Allied forces attacked and defeated the Germans at the town of Saint-Mihiel on the border of France and Germany. Along the Meuse River and in the Argonne Forest, near the French-Belgian border, American and Allied troops again attacked German forces.

Among the many heroes of these battles was a young man from Tennessee named Alvin York. In October 1918 York killed 25 German gunners and captured 132 prisoners. His heroism earned him fame and many awards, including the Congressional Medal of Honor. His life story even became the basis for a popular movie in 1941.

Also among the brave American troops were the African American soldiers of the 369th Infantry. Known as the Harlem Hellfighters, the 369th spent more time in combat than any other American unit. Its members were the first to reach the Rhine River on the German border. France awarded them the prized Croix de Guerre (Cross of War) medal for their bravery.

The Allies were also winning the war at sea. Allied war planners used a new **strategy** called the convoy system to protect their ships. This meant that destroyers capable of sinking U-boats escorted and protected groups of Allied merchant ships.

By November 1918, American soldiers were making rapid advances toward Germany. "For the first time the enemy lines were completely broken through," reported General Pershing.

READING CHECK Sequencing Identify significant events leading to the turning of the tide in the war.

ACADEMIC VOCABULARY
strategy a plan for fighting a battle or war

Armistice

At home and on the battlefield, Germans were tired of war. Food was so scarce in Germany that more than 800 German civilians were dying of starvation every day. In Germany and other nations of the Central Powers, food riots and strikes occurred. Germany was also running out of soldiers. In addition to those killed or wounded in 1918, one quarter of Germany's fighting men had been captured by the Allies.

Germany's allies were also eager to end the war. Bulgaria and the Ottoman Empire quit the war in the fall of 1918. Austria-Hungary reached a peace agreement with the Allies on November 3. Seeing that his country was beaten, the German leader, Kaiser Wilhelm II, gave up his throne and fled to the Netherlands.

The 369th Infantry

The 369th Infantry spent 191 days in combat, longer than any other American force sent to Europe during World War I. Its members aided French forces at Château-Thierry and Belleau Wood, receiving the Croix de Guerre for their bravery. The "Harlem Hellfighters" became famous throughout Europe and America for their valor.

The Croix de Guerre was created by France in 1915 to reward bravery by members of the Allied armed forces—French citizens and foreigners alike.

The Germans then agreed to a cease-fire. The Allies demanded that Germany pull back from all its conquered territory. They insisted that Germany destroy its aircraft, tanks, and big guns, and surrender its U-boats. The Germans had no choice but to accept these demands to disarm. The **armistice**, or truce, went into effect on the 11th hour of the 11th day of the 11th month of 1918. "At eleven o'clock everything got so quiet that the silence was nearly unbearable," remembered an American soldier. Then the silence was broken with shouts like "I've lived through the war!"

READING CHECK Analyzing How did Allied troops break the stalemate with Germany?

SUMMARY AND PREVIEW America's entry into World War I helped the Allies achieve victory. In the next section, you will learn about the effort to work out a permanent peace agreement.

Section 3 Assessment

go.hrw.com
Online Quiz
KEYWORD: SB7 HP23

Reviewing Ideas, Terms, and People

1. **a. Define** What was the **American Expeditionary Force**?
   b. Analyze How did the Russian Revolution change the course of the war?
   c. Evaluate Why did Russia leave the war?
2. **a. Analyze** How did U.S. troops make a difference in the final battles of the war?
   b. Recall How was the Second Battle of the Marne a turning point in the war?
3. **a. Describe** What was Germany required to surrender in the **armistice**?
   b. Interpret Were the terms of the armistice fair? Explain your answer.

Critical Thinking

4. **Categorizing** Review your notes on the victories of the American Expeditionary Force. Then copy the graphic organizer below and use it to list challenges the Allies faced from 1917 to 1918. List the Allies' achievements during the same time period.

Allied Challenges	
Allied Achievements	

FOCUS ON SPEAKING

5. **Analyzing the War's Effects on Soldiers** What examples from this section could you add to your list of how World War I events affected the United States? How did American soldiers contribute to the Allied war effort? What were conditions like for American soldiers? Do you think U.S. involvement was justified?

Establishing Peace

If YOU were there...

Your older brother was drafted in 1917 and sent to fight on the western front in Europe. He has written home about the terrible conditions in the trenches and the horror of seeing men killed in battle. Now the war is over. You read in the newspaper that a peace treaty is being negotiated in Paris, France.

What do you hope the peace treaty will say?

> **BUILDING BACKGROUND** After World War I, many questions about the future remained. Who would pay for the huge costs of the war? How should defeated powers' territories be divided? How could countries work together to avoid another world war? Leaders began discussing and debating these questions.

The Costs of War

While soldiers and civilians around the world celebrated the end of World War I in November 1918, the tragedy of war was never far from people's minds. When asked what the armistice meant, one British soldier simply said, "Time to bury the dead."

War Dead

The number of soldiers killed in World War I was beyond anything the world had ever experienced. About 5 million Allied soldiers and 3.5 million soldiers from the Central Powers died in combat. More than 20 million soldiers on both sides were wounded. The war devastated an entire generation of young men in many European nations. In France, for example, 90 percent of the healthy young men had served in World War I. More than 7 out of 10 of these men were killed or wounded. While the United States escaped this extreme level of devastation, American forces did suffer heavy losses. Some 116,000 U.S. troops died, and about 200,000 were wounded.

Financial Losses

Along with the shocking human losses, the war brought financial disaster to many parts of Europe. Factories and farms were left in ruins. "For mile after mile nothing was left," said one British visitor

Virginia Standards of Learning USII.1b, USII.5c

What You Will Learn...

Main Ideas

1. The costs of war included millions of human lives as well as financial burdens.
2. President Woodrow Wilson and European leaders met to work out a peace agreement.
3. The U.S. Senate rejected the Treaty of Versailles.

The Big Idea

The United States and the victorious Allied Powers clashed over postwar plans.

Key Terms and People

League of Nations, *p. 737*
reparations, *p. 737*
Treaty of Versailles, *p. 738*
Henry Cabot Lodge, *p. 738*

TAKING NOTES As you read, take notes on the provisions of the Treaty of Versailles. You can use a graphic organizer like the one below to keep track of your notes.

Treaty of Versailles

about the French countryside. "No building was habitable [livable] and no field fit for the plow." With farmers unable to raise crops, severe food shortages occurred.

The overall economic cost of the war was huge. Property worth $30 billion had been destroyed. The Allies had spent $145 billion on the war effort, and the Central Powers had spent $63 billion. France and Britain had borrowed large amounts of money to fight the war, and now they were deeply in debt to American banks. Germany was also in debt, and its people faced starvation.

The Influenza Epidemic

The world was in for another shock in 1918 when a worldwide epidemic of influenza, or flu, broke out. The virus was extremely contagious and deadly. Over the next two years, it spread around the world, killing approximately 30 million people—even more than the war itself.

The epidemic started in an army training camp in Kansas. Because the flu is transmitted through the air, it spread rapidly. American soldiers unknowingly spread the disease to other army camps, to American civilians, and eventually to soldiers and civilians in Europe. One American doctor said that seeing stacks of bodies at an army camp in Massachusetts "beats any sight they ever had in France after a battle." Half of the Americans who died during this period died from influenza.

The epidemic changed life everywhere in the United States. In Chicago, for example, the flu more than doubled the normal death rate in the fall of 1918. Many of those killed were young and strong. State and local governments took measures to prevent the spread of the disease. Kearney, Nebraska, imposed a quarantine, forbidding people who were ill from leaving their homes. Many cities banned public gatherings, including school classes. A man named Dan Tonkel remembered what life was like for children in his hometown of Goldsboro, North Carolina:

> "I felt like I was walking on eggshells. I was afraid to go out, to play with my playmates, my classmates, my neighbors … I remember I was actually afraid to breathe. People were afraid to talk to each other. It was like—don't breathe in my face, don't even look at me, because you might give me germs that will kill me."
>
> —Dan Tonkel, quoted in *Influenza 1918: The Worst Epidemic in American History*, by Lynette Lezzoni

Although there was no cure for the flu, people would try anything. One woman surrounded her daughter with raw onions. Another remembered, "We hung bags of . . . garlic about our necks. We smelled awful, but it was okay, because everyone smelled bad." By the time the influenza epidemic ended in 1919, it had killed 800,000 Americans at home and abroad.

READING CHECK **Finding Main Ideas** What made the influenza epidemic of 1918 so deadly?

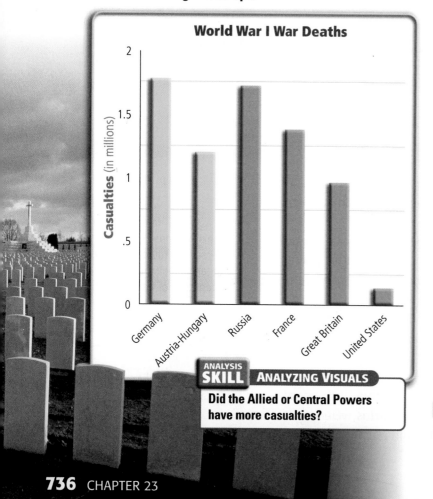

Memorials to soldiers killed in World War I, like this one at Somme, France, are located throughout Europe.

World War I War Deaths

Casualties (in millions)

Germany · Austria-Hungary · Russia · France · Great Britain · United States

ANALYSIS SKILL **ANALYZING VISUALS**
Did the Allied or Central Powers have more casualties?

The Peace Agreement

Even before the United States entered World War I, President Woodrow Wilson began making plans for a peace agreement. He was determined to do everything possible to prevent another world war. On January 8, 1918, Wilson outlined his vision for the postwar world in a plan known as the Fourteen Points.

Wilson's Fourteen Points

Wilson's Fourteen Points were a list of specific proposals for postwar peace. Several of the points would settle national border disputes. Others called for military cutbacks, proposed lower tariffs, and banned secret agreements between nations. Another proposed settlements for colonial peoples who wished to be independent. This reflected Wilson's strong belief in self-determination—the right of people to choose their own political status. The final point called for the creation of an international assembly of nations called the **League of Nations**. The League's mission would be to work to settle international disputes and encourage democracy.

European leaders disagreed with Wilson's vision for the peace settlement, wanting it to clearly punish Germany for its role in the war. They wanted to prevent Germany from ever again becoming a world power.

The Treaty of Versailles

President Wilson traveled to Europe to attend the Paris Peace Conference, which was held at the palace of Versailles (ver-SY), outside of Paris. Wilson felt it was his duty to "play my full part in making good what [our soldiers] offered their lives to obtain."

The leaders, called the Big Four—President Wilson, British prime minister David Lloyd George, French premier Georges Clemenceau, and Italian prime minister Vittorio Orlando—took control of the conference. No representatives from Russia or the Central Powers attended.

Key Goals of the Fourteen Points
QUICK FACTS

- End secret alliances
- Encourage free shipping
- Remove barriers to trade
- Reduce armies and navies
- Resolve colonial claims
- Support the right of people to choose their own government
- Settle border disputes
- Establish the League of Nations

Many Allied leaders defended their own country's interests and insisted on severe punishment for Germany. They wanted Germany to accept complete blame for the war and pay for the damage it had caused. These **reparations**, or payments for war damages, were set at $33 billion. France and the other Allies also wanted to take control of large parts of German territory.

Europe after World War I

Legend:
- Countries created after World War I
- Occupied by Allies
- British mandate
- French mandate
- Lost by Austria–Hungary
- Lost by Bulgaria
- Lost by Germany
- Lost by Ottoman Empire
- Lost by Russia
- Area unchanged

*Becomes Republic of Turkey, 1923
**Becomes U.S.S.R., 1922

0   250   500 Miles
0   250   500 Kilometers

GEOGRAPHY SKILLS INTERPRETING MAPS

1. **Location** Poland was created from territories lost by which countries?
2. **Human-Environment Interaction** How did World War I change the map of Europe?

Wilson reluctantly agreed to the **Treaty of Versailles**, the peace settlement of World War I. In it, the League of Nations was established. Estonia, Finland, Latvia, Lithuania, Czechoslovakia, and Yugoslavia became independent countries. Poland was restored as a nation. The Central Powers turned over their colonies to the League of Nations, which assigned other European powers to rule. Though the Treaty of Versailles did not give Wilson everything he wanted, he hoped the League of Nations would solve remaining problems.

READING CHECK Identifying Points of View
Why did Allied leaders object to Wilson's plan?

Versailles Treaty Rejected

The U.S. Constitution states that treaties must be ratified by at least two-thirds of the members of the Senate. Wilson knew he was going to have a hard time convincing some senators to vote to ratify the Versailles Treaty. Republican senator **Henry Cabot Lodge** declared: "No peace that satisfied Germany in any degree can ever satisfy us." Lodge wanted the winners to set the terms of the peace.

Republicans insisted on changes to the treaty before they would ratify it. Their main objection was the League of Nations' power to use military force. They were worried that as a member of the League, the United States could be forced to send troops to war based on decisions made by the League of Nations. This, they argued, conflicted with Congress's constitutional power to declare war.

Wilson refused to compromise. He insisted that the treaty be ratified exactly as it was written. He traveled around the country, trying to convince the public to pressure Republican senators to vote for the treaty. Before he completed his tour, however, Wilson was weakened by a stroke.

Lodge announced that he was prepared to accept most of the treaty, though he still wanted to limit U.S. military commitment to the League of Nations. Wilson demanded that Democrats in the Senate refuse to change the treaty. When the vote was taken on November 19, 1919, neither the Democrats nor the Republicans would compromise. The Treaty of Versailles was defeated in the Senate.

It was a bitter disappointment for President Wilson. The United States signed separate peace treaties with Austria, Hungary, and Germany and never joined the League of Nations.

Causes and Effects of World War I

QUICK FACTS

Causes
- Nationalism
- Militarism
- Competition for territory
- Alliance system in Europe

Effects
- U.S. entry into the war in 1917
- Millions of deaths and widespread destruction in Europe
- Treaty of Versailles
- Creation of several new nations
- League of Nations

READING CHECK Supporting a Point of View
Do you think Wilson should have compromised with Republicans in the Senate on the Treaty of Versailles? Why or why not?

SUMMARY AND PREVIEW World War I changed the world map and affected the lives of millions. In the next chapter you will learn about American social, political, and economic conditions after the war.

go.hrw.com
Online Quiz
KEYWORD: SB7 HP23

Section 4 Assessment

Reviewing Ideas, Terms, and People

1. **a. Recall** Approximately how many soldiers were killed or wounded in World War I?
   b. Draw Conclusions How did the war affect the European economy?
   c. Summarize How did Americans try to fight the influenza epidemic of 1918?
2. **a. Define** What was the **League of Nations**?
   b. Explain How did the **Treaty of Versailles** change the map of Europe?
   c. Elaborate Which countries did not attend the Paris Peace Conference? How do you think this affected the outcome?
3. **a. Identify** Who was **Henry Cabot Lodge**?
   b. Predict How might Wilson have ensured that the U.S. Senate would ratify the Treaty of Versailles?

Critical Thinking

4. **Identifying Points of View** Review your notes on the Treaty of Versailles. Then copy the graphic

organizer below and use it to compare the positions of Woodrow Wilson, Allied leaders, and Senate Republicans. Fill in the results of each person's or group's goals.

	Goals	Results
Woodrow Wilson		
Allied Leaders		
Senate Republicans		

FOCUS ON SPEAKING

5. **Analyzing the Peace** Add to your list ways the United States was affected by World War I. How many American lives were lost? What were the results of the war? Do you think U.S. involvement in the war could have been avoided? Should the United States have joined the League of Nations?

Social Studies Skills

Using Visual Resources

Define the Skill

A major part of history is understanding the events and ideas of the past. Visual resources are often good sources of information about the past. Visual resources include paintings, drawings, cartoons, posters, and photographs. The symbols and images in these resources tell us about the ideas and values of a time period. They often provide different information and points of view than do written documents.

Learn the Skill

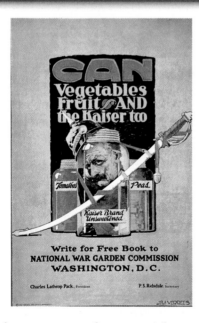

Visual resources can have special purposes. For example, the poster above was produced by the U.S. government to inspire patriotism and encourage support for the war effort. It uses symbols and images to suggest that all Americans can contribute to the war effort.

You know from reading the chapter that conserving food to provide supplies for troops was an important part of the war effort. This poster encourages Americans to can fruits and vegetables. The pictures show canned tomatoes and peas in glass jars.

The poster also shows the German kaiser in a jar. He cannot reach his sword, which is outside the jar. He is helpless. This suggests that, by canning fruit and vegetables, Americans can help defeat the German leader.

Practice the Skill

Study the World War I poster below. Like the poster above, it was produced by the U.S. government to encourage support for the war effort. Write a paragraph describing the poster. Your paragraph should include the specific purpose of the poster, the symbols it uses, and whether it conveys its message effectively. You can use the text above as a model.

Chapter Review

Visual Summary

QUICK FACTS

Use the visual summary below to help you review the main ideas of the chapter.

The assassination of Archduke Francis Ferdinand threw Europe into a state of war.

Brutal fighting took place across Europe.

President Wilson thought a League of Nations would prevent future wars.

Reviewing Vocabulary, Terms, and People

Identify the descriptions below with the correct term or person from the chapter.

1. International assembly of nations designed to settle international disputes and encourage democracy

2. Strategy of defending a position by fighting from the protection of deep ditches

3. American fighting force trained and led by General John J. Pershing

4. Law that required men between the ages of 21 and 30 to register to be drafted into the armed forces

5. Senate leader who opposed the Treaty of Versailles

6. Truce between warring nations

7. Telegram from the German foreign minister proposing an alliance between Germany and Mexico against the United States

Comprehension and Critical Thinking

SECTION 1 *(Pages 720–724)*

8. **a. Identify** What event sparked World War I?

   b. Explain How did tensions in Europe lead to war?

   c. Draw Conclusions Why did the war in Europe become a stalemate?

SECTION 2 *(Pages 725–729)*

9. **a. Recall** What happened to the *Lusitania*? How did the American public react?

   b. Analyze How did the country's mobilization for war affect American women?

   c. Evaluate Do you think U.S. efforts to prepare for war were successful? Why or why not?

SECTION 3 *(Pages 730–734)*

10. a. Define How did the American Expeditionary Force prepare for war?

b. Contrast How was the Second Battle of the Marne different from the First Battle of the Marne?

c. Draw Conclusions Do you think the Allies would have won World War I without American help? Explain your answer.

SECTION 4 *(Pages 735–739)*

11. a. Recall Which nations' leaders dominated the Paris Peace Conference?

b. Summarize What were the main ideas of Wilson's Fourteen Points?

c. Predict How effective do you think the League of Nations was? Why?

Using the Internet
go.hrw.com
KEYWORD: SB7 CH23

12. Activity: Researching the Technology of War Many new technologies were introduced in World War I. The introduction of new weapons, like poison gas and machine guns, and combat vehicles, such as tanks and aircraft, made this war deadlier than any previous one. Enter the activity keyword. Research new battlefield technologies in World War I. Then write three journal entries from the point of view of a soldier in the trenches. Your entries should describe what the soldier who experienced these technologies and inventions for the first time saw, felt, and thought. Remember to use facts from your research in your journal entries.

Reviewing Themes

13. Economics How did World War I affect the economy of the United States?

14. Politics What lasting political changes were brought about by World War I?

Social Studies Skills

Using Visual Resources *Use the Social Studies Skills taught in this chapter to answer the question below.*

15. What parts of the U.S. war effort are shown in this poster?

Reading Skills

Recognizing Fallacies in Reasoning *Use the Reading Skills taught in this chapter to answer the question about the reading selection below.*

> The number of soldiers killed in World War I was beyond anything the world had ever experienced. About 5 million Allied soldiers and 3.5 million soldiers from the Central Powers died in combat. More than 20 million soldiers on both sides were wounded. *(p. 735)*

16. Which of the following is an example of a false conclusion drawn from the selection above?

a. More soldiers were killed in World War I than in any war up to that point.

b. World War I devastated the European population.

c. Europe would never recover from World War I.

d. The number of soldiers wounded was more than two times the number of soldiers killed.

FOCUS ON SPEAKING

17. Presenting Your Persuasive Speech Review your notes and form an opinion on whether the United States should have entered World War I. You will have about five minutes to present your point of view. Use note cards to organize your ideas. Begin by writing a one-sentence introduction clearly stating your opinion. Then write several sentences with details and examples from the chapter that support your point of view. Conclude your speech with a sentence that summarizes your ideas. Practice your speech and then present it to the class.

DIRECTIONS: Read each question and write the letter of the best response.

1 Which of the following was made up of Germany, Austria-Hungary, the Ottoman Empire, and Bulgaria?

A Central Powers

B Allied Powers

C League of Nations

D Big Four

2 The Communist takeover of the Russian government caused

A the armistice to go into effect.

B a German victory at the Second Battle of the Marne.

C the United States to remain neutral.

D Russia to leave the war.

3 During the war, many African Americans

A gained equal rights because of their military service.

B served in segregated units in the military.

C were removed from jobs in war industries and the military.

D volunteered to serve in the military without pay.

4 One reason the United States entered World War I was Germany's violation of

A the Treaty of Versailles.

B the Zimmermann Note.

C the *Sussex* pledge.

D Wilson's Fourteen Points.

5 A major opponent of the Treaty of Versailles was

A Otto von Bismarck.

B Woodrow Wilson.

C Henry Cabot Lodge.

D John J. Pershing.

6 Which of the following technologies was important to warfare at sea during World War I?

A U-boats

B bayonets

C ironclads

D poison gas

7 Examine the fourth of Woodrow Wilson's Fourteen Points and use it to answer the question below:

> " Adequate guarantees given and taken that national armaments [weapons] will be reduced to the lowest point consistent with domestic safety."
>
> —Woodrow Wilson, Fourteen Points

Document-Based Question Why do you think Wilson wanted to reduce the amount of weapons in nations around the world?

Assignment

Find a primary source from World War I and write an analysis of it.

Analyzing a Primary Source

Primary sources are often the best sources of information available to historians. Primary sources provide answers to questions about the past. They also provide a unique point of view from the past. Analyzing a primary source allows you to share that information.

1. Prewrite

Locating Primary Sources

Many primary sources are available in libraries and on the Internet. Letters, diaries, autobiographies, memoirs, newspaper articles, public speeches, and legal documents are good examples of primary sources.

Reading the Primary Source

Take notes on these questions to better understand the document.

- Who wrote the document?
- What kind of document is it?
- When was it written? Where did it originally appear?
- What was the author's point of view? What was his or her experience during the war?
- Why did the author write the document?

As you read the primary source, take notes on these questions.

- Why is the document important? The answer to this question will be the main idea of your essay.
- What questions about World War I does it answer? Answering this question will help you write your body paragraphs.

2. Write

You can use this framework to help you write your first draft.

TIP **Using the Internet** If you find a primary source on the Internet, make sure it is accurate. You should be able to identify the person or institution that runs the Web site and make sure that person or institution is trustworthy. The Web site should include basic information about the source, such as its author, when it was written, and where it first appeared. University and library Web sites are excellent places to find primary sources.

A Writer's Framework

Introduction	Body	Conclusion
■ Introduce your primary source and its main purpose. ■ Introduce the author of the source and include the date it was written. ■ State your main idea, explaining why this source is important.	■ Explain how the source answers at least two questions about World War I. ■ Include examples from the document.	■ Summarize the information in the source. ■ Restate why the document is important for historians.

3. Evaluate and Revise

Evaluating

Use these questions to discover ways to improve your paper.

Evaluation Questions for Analyzing a Primary Source

- Do you introduce your primary source with its main purpose?
- Do you introduce the author of the source and the document's date?
- Do you state a main idea explaining why this source is important?

- Do you explain how the source answers at least two questions about World War I?
- Do you include examples from the document?
- Do you summarize the information in the source?

Revising

Make sure each paragraph has a topic sentence at the beginning. Then check the information in the paragraph. It should all relate to the topic sentence. If it does not, there are several ways to fix the paragraph. First, you can remove unrelated information. If the information is related but not clearly explained, add a more detailed explanation. You can also change the topic sentence to include all the information in the paragraph.

4. Proofread and Publish

Proofreading

Reread your paper carefully to make sure all the verbs are in the same tense. The past tense is usually best for history writing. Summaries of primary sources should also be in the past tense. A direct quotation from a primary source, however, should remain in its original tense.

Publishing

Share your paper with a classmate. Read each other's papers. Then write a one-paragraph summary of the new information you each learned.

5. Practice and Apply

Use the steps and strategies in this workshop to analyze your primary source.

TIP **Using Pronouns Effectively**
Use pronouns such as *he, she,* and *it* to replace frequently used nouns and proper nouns. This will help you vary your sentences. Make sure that the person or thing to which each pronoun refers is clear. If it is not, repeat the original noun or name.

EXAMPLE
Woodrow Wilson proposed a peace plan called the Fourteen Points. He wanted to make sure the postwar peace would last.

Boom Times and Challenges

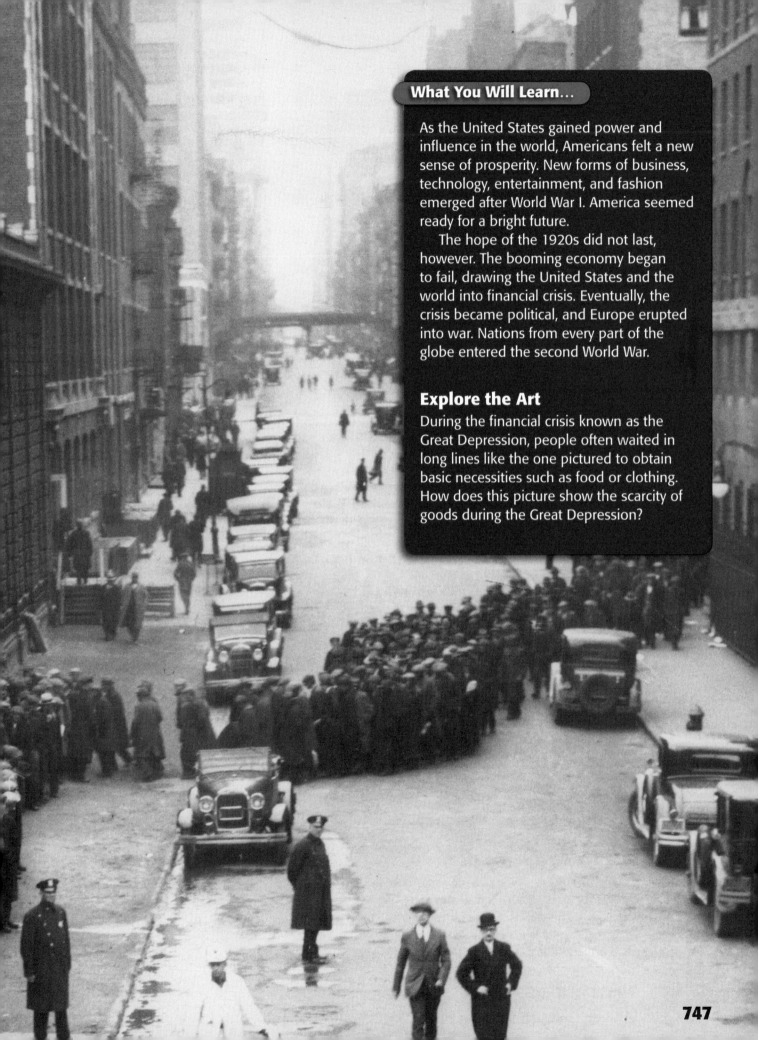

What You Will Learn...

As the United States gained power and influence in the world, Americans felt a new sense of prosperity. New forms of business, technology, entertainment, and fashion emerged after World War I. America seemed ready for a bright future.

The hope of the 1920s did not last, however. The booming economy began to fail, drawing the United States and the world into financial crisis. Eventually, the crisis became political, and Europe erupted into war. Nations from every part of the globe entered the second World War.

Explore the Art

During the financial crisis known as the Great Depression, people often waited in long lines like the one pictured to obtain basic necessities such as food or clothing. How does this picture show the scarcity of goods during the Great Depression?

The Roaring Twenties

Virginia Standards of Learning

USII.1 The student will demonstrate skills for historical and geographical analysis, and responsible citizenship, including the ability to

a) analyze and interpret primary and secondary source documents to increase understanding of events and life in United States history from 1865 to the present **b)** make connections between past and present; **c)** sequence events in United States history form 1865 to the present

USII.6 The student will demonstrate knowledge of the social, economic, and technological changes of the early twentieth century by

a) explaining how developments in factory and labor productivity and transportation (including the use of the automobile), communication, and rural electrification changed American life; **b)** describing the social and economic changes that took place, including prohibition, and the Great Migration north and west; **c)** examining art, literature, and music from the 1920s and 1930s, emphasizing Langston Hughes, Duke Ellington, Georgia O'Keeffe, and the Harlem Renaissance

USII.9 The student will demonstrate knowledge of the key domestic and international issues during the second half of the twentieth century by

c) identifying how individual citizens from the time period influenced America scientifically, culturally, academically, and economically

FOCUS ON WRITING

Radio Advertisement Radio stations began to air regular broadcasts in the 1920s. Radios linked Americans from coast to coast, allowing them to hear the same programs—and the same advertisements. In the 1920s Americans with means had new choices in entertainment, travel, fashion, and convenience. In this chapter, you will read about these new choices. You will then write a radio advertisement for a new product or form of entertainment of the 1920s.

UNITED STATES

1920
Warren Harding wins the presidency in a landslide victory.

1920

WORLD

1920
The League of Nations is established.

HOLT
History's Impact
▶ **video series**
Watch the video to understand the impact of younger generations on national culture.

What You Will Learn...

In this chapter you will learn about the ways that American life changed in the decade following World War I. With a booming economy, many people had money to spend on exciting new forms of entertainment. People flocked to bustling city centers like New York City's Times Square, shown in this painting.

1924 Native Americans are granted the right of U.S. citizenship.

1926 Ernest Hemingway publishes *The Sun Also Rises.*

THE SUN ALSO RISES
ERNEST HEMINGWAY

1929 Construction begins on the Empire State Building.

| 1922 | 1924 | 1926 | 1928 | 1930 |

1922 The tomb of King Tutankhamen is discovered.

1924 Joseph Stalin becomes dictator of Communist Russia.

1926 Prince Hirohito becomes emperor of Japan.

1928 Alexander Fleming discovers penicillin.

749

Reading Social Studies

by Kylene Beers

Economics | Geography | Politics | Society and Culture | Science and Technology

Focus on Themes In this chapter, you will learn about the decade of the 1920s, a period called the Roaring Twenties. During this time, many in **society** thought that the Great War would be the last major war and that the future was bright. Also during this time, **science and technology** made leaps forward that would make life easier for millions of Americans.

Synthesizing Information

Focus on Reading Learning about history means synthesizing, or combining, many different sources about the past. When you read this textbook, you are reading a synthesis of other sources, accounts, and ideas about history.

Synthesizing Once you have identified the subject you are studying, you should try to read as many different accounts of the story as you can. Be sure to investigate the author of a source to learn what his or her goals might be. Compare and contrast the different sources and evaluate which ones you believe. Finally, use all the various stories you have read to form your own interpretation of what happened in history.

Key Terms and People

You Try It!

Read these varying accounts of the assassination of Archduke Francis Ferdinand and his wife, Sophie. Then write your own version of the story.

> "Two bullets fired on a Sarajevo street on a sunny June morning in 1914 set in motion a series of events that shaped the world we live in today. World War One, World War Two, the Cold War and its conclusion all trace their origins to the gunshots that interrupted that summer day."
>
> —Anonymous

> "As the car came abreast he stepped forward from the curb, drew his automatic pistol from his coat and fired two shots. The first struck the wife of the Archduke, the Archduchess Sofia, in the abdomen . . . She died instantly. The second bullet struck the Archduke close to the heart. He uttered only one word, 'Sofia'—a call to his stricken wife. Then his head fell back and he collapsed. He died almost instantly."
>
> —conspirator Borijove Jevtic

> "As I was pulling out my handkerchief to wipe the blood away from his mouth, the duchess cried out to him, 'In Heaven's name, what has happened to you?' At that she slid off the seat and lay on the floor of the car ... I had no idea that she too was hit and thought she had simply fainted with fright. Then I heard His Imperial Highness say, "Sopherl, Sopherl, don't die. Stay alive for the children!"
>
> —guard Count Franz von Harrach,
> quoted in "Assassination of an Archduke," *Eyewitness to History*

1. What differences do you notice between accounts?

2. Why might these different authors have a different view of the assassination?

3. How can you tell what each author's viewpoint is?

4. Write your own version of what might have happened. Use details that you believe from the sources above.

As you read Chapter 24, notice any differing views from different sources.

Boom Times

Virginia Standards of Learning USII.1a, USII.1b, USII.1d, USII.1h, USII.6a, USII.6b, USII.9c

What You Will Learn...

Main Ideas

1. President Harding promised a return to peace and prosperity.
2. Calvin Coolidge supported a probusiness agenda.
3. American business boomed in the 1920s.
4. In 1928, Americans elected Herbert Hoover, hoping he would help good financial times continue.

The Big Idea

American industries boomed in the 1920s, changing many Americans' way of life.

Key Terms and People

Warren G. Harding, *p. 752*
Calvin Coolidge, *p. 752*
Teapot Dome scandal, *p. 753*
Kellogg-Briand Pact, *p. 754*
Model T, *p. 755*
moving assembly line, *p. 755*
Herbert Hoover, *p. 757*

TAKING NOTES As you read, take notes on the presidents of the 1920s. Record your notes in a chart like this one.

President	Year Elected	Political Party

If YOU were there...

You have been working in a car factory for years, and now you have finally bought a car of your own—a shiny new 1920 Ford Model T. As you set out on your first drive, the car rattles and bounces over unpaved roads that were designed for horse-and-buggy travel. But you don't mind the rough ride. You now have the freedom to drive anywhere you want to go!

How will owning a car change your life?

BUILDING BACKGROUND The American economy boomed during World War I, as industries raced to produce weapons and supplies for the Allied armies. With more than 4 million men serving in the armed forces, there was a shortage of workers in American factories, and many people found jobs. When the war ended, however, conditions changed quickly, and the economy faced a difficult adjustment.

Return to Peace and Prosperity

The end of World War I had an immediate impact on the American economy. Because the government no longer needed war supplies, it canceled billions of dollars' worth of contracts with American factories. This meant that factories cut back on production at the very moment that millions of soldiers left the military and began looking for jobs. The result was a sharp rise in unemployment. Meanwhile, many people who did have jobs rushed to buy products they could not buy during the war. This caused prices to soar. Wages could not keep up with the rising prices, and thus workers could no longer afford to buy the goods they needed and wanted. Many went on strike for higher wages—more than 4 million in 1919 alone.

As the 1920 presidential election approached, the economic difficulties were bad news for the party in power, Woodrow Wilson's Democratic Party. Many voters blamed the Democrats for the hard times. Sensing the public's anger, the Republicans looked for a candidate who would offer new hope for American voters. They chose **Warren G. Harding**, a senator from Ohio. Harding picked Governor **Calvin Coolidge** of Massachusetts as his running mate.

POLITICAL CARTOON
Teapot Dome

During the Teapot Dome scandal, people began to question the judgment and honesty of government leaders. This cartoon, called "Juggernaut," was published in 1924 to show how harmful the scandal had been. A juggernaut is an indestructible force that crushes everything in its path.

How do the images in the cartoon illustrate the destructive force of the scandal?

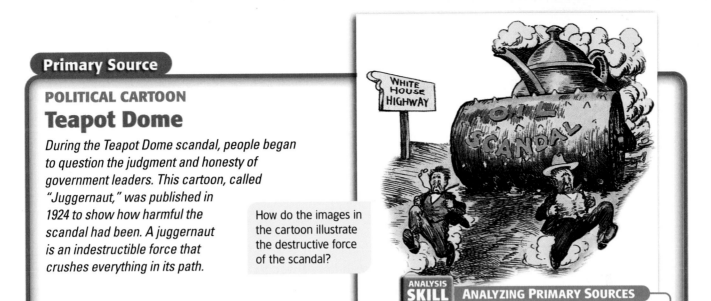

ANALYSIS SKILL **ANALYZING PRIMARY SOURCES**

Why do you think the artist called this cartoon "Juggernaut"?

Harding based his campaign strategy on a promise to return the country to stability and prosperity, what he called "normalcy." His conservative policies contrasted with the reform-minded policies of the Progressive Era. Harding summed up his ideas in a campaign speech:

" America's present need is not heroics, but healing; not nostrums [uncertain cures] but normalcy [normal times]; not revolution, but restoration. "

—Warren G. Harding, 1920

Democrats believed there was still support for Wilson's ideas for reform. They ran Ohio governor James M. Cox for president, and New York's Franklin D. Roosevelt for vice president. But Harding's promise of a return to normalcy captured the public's mood in 1920. Harding won a landslide victory with about 60 percent of the popular vote.

Harding worked quickly to help strengthen the economy. He put together a cabinet of experts who believed in reducing money owed by the government and limiting government involvement in the economy. Secretary of the Treasury Andrew Mellon pushed for tax cuts for wealthy Americans. Mellon believed that this policy would give the wealthy an **incentive** to invest in new businesses and create new jobs for other Americans. Mellon's opponents called

this idea the trickle-down theory, arguing that money would only "trickle down" in small drops to less-well-off Americans.

While Harding was president, businesses did in fact bounce back from the postwar recession. The economy created new, better-paying jobs, leading to an economic boom that lasted for most of the decade.

Harding faced problems in other areas, however. He had appointed many of his trusted friends to high positions. Some of these men used their positions to gain wealth through illegal means. "I have no trouble with my enemies," Harding once said. "But my . . . friends . . . keep me walking the floor nights."

What came to be known as the the **Teapot Dome scandal** involved Secretary of the Interior Albert Fall, who accepted large sums of money and valuable gifts from private oil companies. In exchange, Fall allowed the companies to control government oil reserves in Elk Hills, California, and Teapot Dome, Wyoming. The U.S. Senate soon began investigating Fall, who was convicted of accepting bribes. He was the first cabinet member ever to be convicted of a crime for his actions while in office.

READING CHECK **Summarizing** What did Harding mean when he promised a return to normalcy?

ACADEMIC VOCABULARY

incentive something that encourages people to behave a certain way

Coolidge's Probusiness Administration

Just before details of the Teapot Dome scandal became public, President Harding died of a heart attack. In August 1923 Vice President Calvin Coolidge took charge. Coolidge had a strong reputation as an honest and trustworthy leader. These qualities helped him restore confidence in the government.

Coolidge acted quickly to fire all officials who had been involved in the bribery scandals of Harding's administration. This helped him win the presidential election in 1924. He received nearly twice as many votes as the Democratic candidate, John W. Davis.

Coolidge proved to be even more pro-business than Harding had been. He once declared that "the business of America is business." He expanded the policies started under Harding, such as tax cuts for wealthier citizens. He also supported raising tariffs on foreign goods to decrease competition with domestic products. Despite higher tariffs, trade with other countries actually increased under Coolidge. This was mainly because many nations depended on trade with the United States to rebuild their economies after World War I. Not everyone profited from Coolidge's efforts, however. Coolidge vetoed congressional attempts to provide aid to farmers through the regulation of prices.

Like the United States, European nations wanted a return to prosperity. Europeans also wanted to avoid another devastating war. In 1928 the United States and 14 other nations signed the **Kellogg-Briand Pact**, an agreement that outlawed war. Eventually 62 nations accepted the pact. There was no way to enforce the pact, however. One U.S. senator complained that the treaty would be "as effective to keep down war as a carpet would be to smother an earthquake." Still, it was a sign that most countries wanted to prevent another global conflict.

READING CHECK **Comparing and Contrasting** How were Harding and Coolidge similar, and how were they different?

THE IMPACT TODAY

Countries still try to prevent wars with international agreements. More than 180 nations have signed the Treaty on the Non-Proliferation of Nuclear Weapons, an agreement to prevent the spread of nuclear weapons.

The Model T Assembly Line

CONNECT TO SCIENCE AND TECHNOLOGY

Early assembly lines involved workers moving down a line of parts. On a moving assembly line, workers along the line specialize in one or two simple assembly tasks that they perform as parts move past them. The moving assembly line greatly increases the efficiency of mass production.

These workers are attaching the leather seat covers to the carriage and are stuffing them with horsehair.

Business Booms

The 1920s were years of rapid economic growth in the United States. Between 1921 and 1929, U.S. manufacturing nearly doubled. As jobs and wages increased, so did people's ability to buy new products. Some of these products changed the way Americans lived.

Ford's Model T

Today we think of cars as a major part of American life. In the early 1900s, though, cars were seen as luxury items that only the wealthy could afford. Henry Ford, an inventor and business leader from Detroit, helped to change this. Ford dreamed of building a car that most Americans could afford:

" I will build a motor car for the great multitude [most of the people]. It will be large enough for the family but small enough for the individual to run and care for. It … will be so low in price that no man making a good salary will be unable to own one. "

—Henry Ford, quoted in *Daily Life in the United States, 1920–1940*, by David E. Kyvig

Ford achieved his goal by building a sturdy and reliable car called the **Model T**, nicknamed the Tin Lizzie. In 1908 the Model T sold for $850. By 1925 it cost just $290. Ford was able to make his car affordable by cutting costs of production. For example, every car looked the same. The Model T came only in black for many years.

To decrease the time it took to make the cars, Ford also began using a **moving assembly line**. This system used conveyer belts to move parts and partly assembled cars from one group of workers to another. The workers stood in one place and did a specialized job.

The chassis, or frame, and the engine are assembled on separate lines. Workers on a third line then attach them.

The assembled chassis is then connected to the body of the car.

> Workers use large amounts of leather to upholster the interiors of the carriages.

> A foreman ensures that the line continues to run smoothly.

From the Collections of Henry Ford Museum and Greenfield Village

ANALYSIS SKILL | ANALYZING VISUALS

How does the moving assembly line reduce the time it takes to build a car?

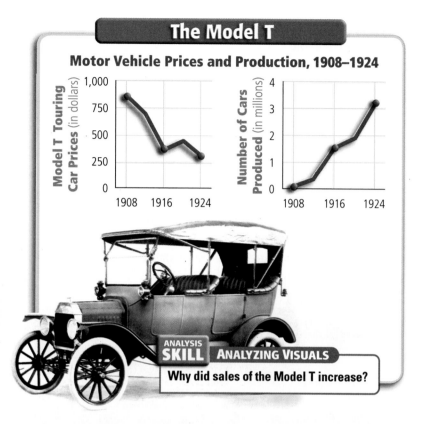

The Model T

Motor Vehicle Prices and Production, 1908–1924

ANALYSIS SKILL · **ANALYZING VISUALS**

Why did sales of the Model T increase?

In 1914 Ford raised the wages for his factory workers to $5 a day. This was good pay, compared with the $2 or $3 per day offered by many other factories. Ford believed the wage increase would keep his employees from quitting. He also lowered the workday to eight hours and employed people that other factories would not hire, such as African Americans and people with disabilities.

Even with the good wages, many workers had a hard time adjusting to the fast-paced and repetitive work on Ford's assembly line. One wife of an autoworker wrote to Ford saying, "My husband has come home and thrown himself down and won't eat his supper—so done out [tired]! . . . That $5 a day is a blessing—a bigger one than you know, but oh they earn it."

To help make his cars more affordable, Ford allowed customers to buy cars using an installment plan. Most people were used to saving up for years to buy items. Installment plans let people pay a small amount of the cost every month until the entire car was paid for. Ford's competitors also allowed customers to pay with installment plans. For a slightly higher price than the Model T, companies such as General Motors offered cars in a variety of colors and with more power.

The automobile changed the way Americans lived. They could now go on long drives or take jobs farther away from where they lived. Cars gave people a sense of freedom and adventure. As *Motor Car* magazine told drivers, "You are your master, the road is ahead . . . your freedom is complete."

Growing Industries

The rise of the automobile affected the entire American economy. Millions of Americans found work making steel for car bodies, rubber for tires, or glass for windows. To improve road safety, the government spent millions of dollars paving highways and building new bridges. People opened roadside businesses to serve travelers, such as gas stations, restaurants, and motels. The rising number of cars also created a demand for car repair shops and car insurance.

Following Ford's example, other manufacturers began using assembly lines and allowing customers to pay on installment plans. Many companies also took advantage of the increasing number of homes with electricity. By 1929 about 85 percent of all Americans living in towns or cities had electricity. Companies responded by building new electrical appliances designed to make household chores easier, such as washing machines, vacuum cleaners, and refrigerators.

As companies competed to sell these new goods, the advertising industry boomed. Companies advertised in magazines and on the radio to convince people that their lives would be improved if they owned a certain product. Many advertisers targeted women, hoping to convince them that they needed the newest labor-saving products. For example, one advertisement for an electric dishwasher called its product "the greatest gift of electricity to the modern housewife."

READING CHECK **Identifying Cause and Effect**
How did the automobile change society?

FOCUS ON READING

How is this paragraph an example of synthesized information?

Hoover Elected

With the economy booming, public support for the Republican Party remained strong. When President Coolidge decided not to run for reelection in 1928, the party chose his secretary of commerce, **Herbert Hoover**, as its nominee. The Democrats nominated New York governor Alfred E. Smith.

Hoover told voters that he was the right choice to maintain economic prosperity. Hoover boldly claimed that "we in America today are nearer to the final triumph over poverty than ever before in the history of any land."

Smith's campaign focused mainly on issues facing city dwellers. This concerned some rural voters. Smith's religious faith also became an issue. He was the first Catholic to run for president. His opponents stirred up fears that Smith would be controlled by the pope and other church officials. In the end, Hoover won easily, gaining 58 percent of the popular vote.

READING CHECK Drawing Conclusions What helped Herbert Hoover win the presidency in 1928?

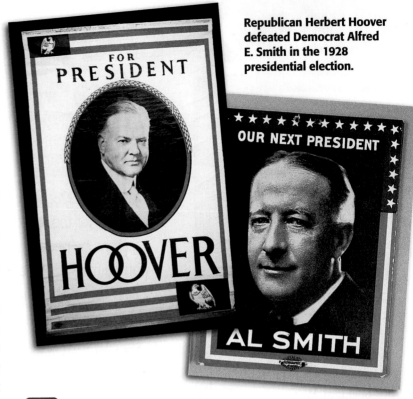

Republican Herbert Hoover defeated Democrat Alfred E. Smith in the 1928 presidential election.

SUMMARY AND PREVIEW In this section you learned about politics and the economy in the 1920s. In the next section you will learn more about how society changed during the decade.

Section 1 Assessment

Reviewing Ideas, Terms, and People

1. a. Describe What was the result of the 1920 presidential election, and why?
b. Summarize What did the **Teapot Dome scandal** reveal about **Warren G. Harding**'s administration?

2. a. Identify Who succeeded Harding as president, and what were his main policies?
b. Analyze What was the main weakness of the **Kellogg-Briand Pact**?

3. a. Recall Why did American businesses grow during the 1920s?
b. Explain Why were Model T prices low?

4. a. Recall Why was **Herbert Hoover** elected?
b. Elaborate Who would you have voted for in the 1928 election? Explain your answer.

Critical Thinking

5. Summarizing Review your notes on the presidents from the 1920s. Then copy the graphic organizer below and expand on your notes by summarizing the main ideas or achievements of each president.

President	Ideas/ Achievements

FOCUS ON WRITING

6. Taking Notes on Consumer Goods Make a list of new products people had access to in this decade, including cheaper automobiles and appliances for the home. Be sure to note how these products improved the lives of Americans. Use the information about advertising in this section to help you with ideas for your radio advertisement.

Life during the 1920s

Virginia Standards of Learning USII.1b, USII.6b

What You Will Learn...

Main Ideas

1. In the 1920s many young people found new independence in a changing society.
2. Postwar tensions occasionally led to fear and violence.
3. Competing ideals caused conflict between Americans with traditional beliefs and those with modern views.
4. Following the war, minority groups organized to demand their civil rights.

The Big Idea

Americans faced new opportunities, challenges, and fears as major changes swept the country in the 1920s.

Key Terms and People

flappers, *p. 759*
Red Scare, *p. 760*
Twenty-first Amendment, *p. 761*
fundamentalism, *p. 762*
Scopes trial, *p. 762*
Great Migration, *p. 763*
Marcus Garvey, *p. 763*

TAKING NOTES As you read, look for changes that affected American life in the 1920s. Record your notes in a diagram like this one.

If YOU were there...

The year is 1925. You have just finished school and you are visiting a big city for the first time. You and your friends go to a club and watch young people dancing energetically to popular music. The women have short hair and wear makeup, trying to copy the glamorous style of movie stars. Some of your friends start talking about finding an apartment and looking for jobs in the city.

Would you want to move to a big city in 1925? Why?

BUILDING BACKGROUND The United States enjoyed nearly a decade of economic expansion during the 1920s. American society changed rapidly during this period. Although many people welcomed the new opportunities, others felt their traditional beliefs were being challenged. Conflicts between competing ideals and different groups of people ruffled the surface of America's peace and prosperity.

A Changing Society

The experience of living through World War I changed the way many young people saw the world around them. Young men returning from Europe had visited far-off countries and learned about other cultures. Many of them came home with a desire to continue expanding their horizons. The title of one popular song in 1919 asked, "How 'Ya Gonna Keep 'em Down on the Farm after They've Seen Paree [Paris]"?

Many young people moved away from farms and small towns to cities. By 1920, for the first time in American history, more than half of the country's population lived in urban areas. Young people took advantage of the economic opportunities of the 1920s to gain independence. In the past most young people had lived and worked at home until they got married. Now more young adults were experiencing a time of freedom before settling down. A new youth culture developed, which included going to parties and dance clubs, listening to popular music, and driving fast cars.

For many young Americans, access to education was an important part of this new independence. High school attendance doubled during the decade. The percentage of students going on to college was higher in the United States than in any other country. This included women, who were attending college in higher numbers than ever before.

The number of women in the workforce continued to grow as well. Women with college degrees worked as nurses, teachers, librarians, and social workers. Women were also finding new opportunities in politics. In 1925 Nellie Tayloe Ross (Wyoming) and Miriam "Ma" Ferguson (Texas) became the first women to serve as governors in the United States. Three years later, there were 145 women serving in state legislatures. Five women had won terms in the U.S. House of Representatives.

Women were still discouraged from pursuing fields such as medicine, law, and architecture, however. By the end of the 1920s, less than 5 percent of the country's doctors, lawyers, and architects were women. The percentage was small—but it was beginning to rise.

Some young women found other ways to express their freedom. Young women known as **flappers** cut their hair short and wore makeup and short dresses, openly challenging traditional ideas of how women were supposed to behave. Many older Americans considered this behavior scandalous. One 1920s writer expressed her admiration for flappers, saying:

> "I want my girl to do what she pleases, be what she pleases ...I want [my daughter] to be a flapper, because flappers are brave."
> —Zelda Fitzgerald, quoted in *Zelda*, by Nancy Milford

Fashion magazines, Hollywood movies, and advertising helped promote these new images and ideas of youthful freedom.

READING CHECK **Generalizing** How did women in the 1920s express their independence?

Focus on Women

In 1923 suffrage leader Alice Paul introduced the Equal Rights Amendment to Congress, calling for equality of rights regardless of a person's gender. The U.S. Senate passed the amendment 49 years later, but it was never ratified by the states.

Bryn Mawr and other colleges provided education to women in new fields.

Bessie Coleman became the first African American woman to obtain her international pilot's license. She traveled the United States, performing stunts under the name "Brave Bessie."

Flappers challenged many of society's ideas about womanhood. They established new rules of speech, dress, and behavior.

ANALYSIS SKILL **ANALYZING VISUALS**

How do these images reflect new roles for women during the 1920s?

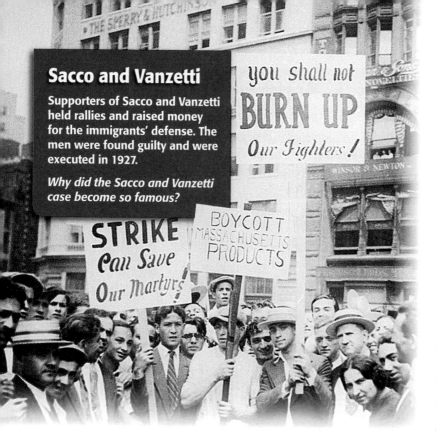

YOU SHALL NOT **BURN UP** *Our Fighters!*

STRIKE *Can Save Our Martyrs*

BOYCOTT MASSACHUSETTS PRODUCTS

Fear and Violence

Not all social changes during the 1920s were peaceful. You have read about the hard times that hit the U.S. economy after World War I—unemployment, inflation, and labor disputes that resulted in large strikes. These troubles worried many Americans. In this atmosphere, suspicion of foreigners and radicals, or people who believe in an extreme change in government, sometimes led to violence.

The Red Scare

After the Communists took power in Russia in 1917, many Americans began to fear Communist ideas. They worried that Communists would soon try to gain power in the United States. This fear increased when millions of American workers went on strike in 1919. Many Americans blamed Communists and radicals for the upheaval.

These attitudes led to a **Red Scare**, a time of fear of Communists, or Reds. The Red Scare began in April 1919, when U.S. postal workers found bombs hidden in several packages addressed to famous Americans. Officials never found out who sent the bombs, but they suspected members of the Communist Party.

In June a bomb exploded outside the home of Attorney General A. Mitchell Palmer. Palmer responded by organizing police raids to break up Communist and other groups. In what became known as the Palmer raids, government agents arrested thousands of suspected radicals, often without evidence. Palmer frightened the public by warning that radicals were planning a revolution.

The Red Scare led to one of the best-known criminal cases in American history. In 1920 police arrested Italian-born anarchists Nicola Sacco and Bartolomeo Vanzetti for the robbery and murder of a factory paymaster and his guard. (Anarchists are people opposed to organized government.) Though both men declared themselves innocent of the crime, Sacco and Vanzetti were found guilty. The American Civil Liberties Union (ACLU), founded in 1920 to defend people's civil rights, tried unsuccessfully to get the verdict overturned. Sacco and Vanzetti were convicted. They were executed in 1927.

Restricting Immigration

Some people thought the Sacco and Vanzetti case was influenced by a general fear of foreigners. Many recent immigrants were poor and did not speak English. Some Americans saw them as a threat to their jobs and culture. Immigrants "fill places that belong to the loyal wage-earning citizens of America," said Alabama senator James Thomas Heflin.

The government responded to these concerns with new laws. The Emergency Quota Act of 1921 limited the total number of immigrants allowed into the country. It also favored immigrants from western Europe. The National Origins Act of 1924 banned immigration from East Asia entirely and further reduced the number of immigrants allowed to enter the country. These laws caused a dramatic drop in immigration to the United States.

READING CHECK **Drawing Conclusions** Why were new immigration laws passed in the 1920s?

Competing Ideals

Fear of radical ideas and foreigners was part of a larger clash over ideals and values in America. Differences were growing between older, rural traditions and the beliefs and practices of modern urban society. Americans had very different ideas about what was best for the country's future.

Prohibition

An issue that highlighted this conflict was prohibition. The Eighteenth Amendment—which outlawed the manufacture, sale, and transportation of alcoholic beverages—went into effect in 1920. Support for prohibition was strongest in rural areas, while opposition was strongest in cities.

Government officials found it nearly impossible to enforce prohibition. Congress passed the Volstead Act, which set fines and punishments for disobeying prohibition. Even respectable citizens, however, broke the law. Many people found ways to make alcohol at home using household products. Others bought alcohol at speakeasies, or illegal bars.

Organized criminals called bootleggers quickly seized control of the illegal alcohol business. They made their own alcohol or smuggled it in from Canada or Mexico. Gangsters were able to avoid arrest by bribing local police and politicians. Competition between gangs often led to violent fighting. In Chicago gangster Al "Scarface" Capone gained control of the alcohol trade by murdering his rivals. By 1927 Capone was earning more than $60 million a year from his illegal businesses.

By the end of the decade, the nation was weary of the effects of prohibition. The law had reduced alcohol consumption but had not stopped Americans from drinking. Prohibition had also created new ways for criminals to grow rich. Without government supervision of alcohol production, much of the alcohol consumed in speakeasies was more dangerous than what had been produced before prohibition. Many people came to believe that it would be better to have a legal alcohol trade that could be monitored by the government. In 1933 state and federal governments responded with the **Twenty-first Amendment**, which ended prohibition.

THE IMPACT TODAY

The Twenty-first Amendment made the manufacture and sale of alcohol legal again, but laws today still regulate drinking. The National Minimum Drinking Age Act of 1984 raised the minimum drinking age from 18 to 21 in every state.

Primary Source

PHOTOGRAPH
Prohibition

Agents of federal and state governments tried to enforce the Eighteenth Amendment against great odds. They usually destroyed any liquor that they found. This photograph shows an illegal barrel of beer being broken with an axe. More illegal beer and liquor would soon turn up, however. Faced with a lack of public support and an impossible task of enforcing the ban on alcohol, prohibition was repealed with the Twenty-first Amendment in 1933.

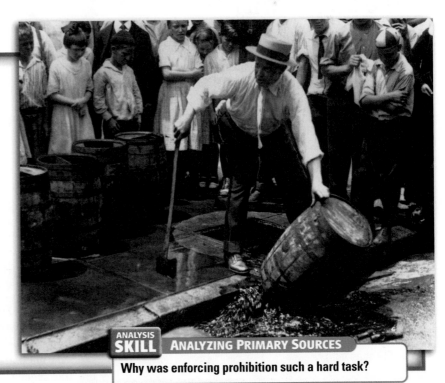

ANALYSIS SKILL **ANALYZING PRIMARY SOURCES**

Why was enforcing prohibition such a hard task?

Religious Ideals

ACADEMIC VOCABULARY

traditional
customary, time-honored

Youth culture of the 1920s and prohibition's failure concerned many religious leaders. They saw these changes as movements away from **traditional** values. This led to a Protestant religious movement known as **fundamentalism**—characterized by the belief in a literal, or word-for-word, interpretation of the Bible. Popular preachers like Aimee Semple McPherson used the radio and modern marketing tools to draw followers. Fundamentalism was especially strong in rural areas and small towns, where people often blamed society's problems on the culture of urban areas.

Many fundamentalists believed that modern scientific theories, such as Charles Darwin's theory of evolution, conflicted with the teachings of the Bible. Darwin's theory states that species evolve over time by adapting to their environment. To fundamentalists, this contradicted the biblical account of how the world was made. They opposed the teaching of evolution in public schools. Many cities and states passed laws to prevent the teaching of evolution.

In May 1925 a Dayton, Tennessee, high school science teacher named John T. Scopes was put on trial for teaching evolution in what became known as the **Scopes trial**. National interest in the event was heightened by the fact that famous Americans represented each side. Criminal attorney Clarence Darrow led the ACLU defense team. Three-time presidential candidate William Jennings Bryan assisted the prosecution.

Over live radio, Darrow and Bryan attacked each other's ideas. After more than a week on trial, Scopes was convicted and fined $100 for breaking the law. The state supreme court later overturned his conviction, but the debate over evolution continued.

READING CHECK **Evaluating** What cultural conflict did the Scopes trial represent?

Primary Source

POINTS OF VIEW
The Scopes Trial

Although the focus of the Scopes trial was whether or not John Scopes had broken the law, prosecution witness William Jennings Bryan saw the conflict as one between science and faith.

"Science is a magnificent force, but it is not a teacher of morals. It can perfect machinery, but it adds no moral restraints to protect society from the misuse of the machine . . . The [Scopes] case has assumed the proportions of a battle-royal [a struggle involving many people] between unbelief that attempts to speak through so-called science and the defenders of the Christian faith."

Clarence Darrow saw the conflict as a battle over free speech.

"If today you can take a thing like evolution and make it a crime to teach it in the public school, tomorrow you can make it a crime to teach it in the private schools, and the next year you can make it a crime to teach it . . . in the church. At the next session you may ban books and the newspapers. Soon you may set Catholic against Protestant and Protestant against Protestant, and try to foist [force] your own religion upon the minds of men."

ANALYSIS SKILL **ANALYZING POINTS OF VIEW**

Why did Darrow believe the Scopes trial was about free speech?

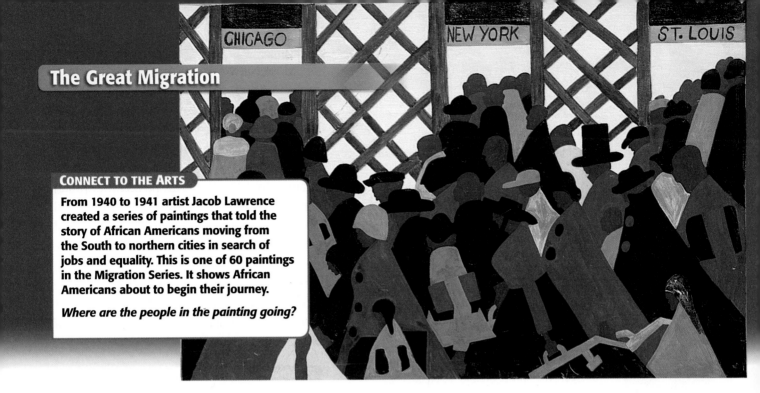

CONNECT TO THE ARTS

From 1940 to 1941 artist Jacob Lawrence created a series of paintings that told the story of African Americans moving from the South to northern cities in search of jobs and equality. This is one of 60 paintings in the Migration Series. It shows African Americans about to begin their journey.

Where are the people in the painting going?

Minority Rights

During World War I large numbers of African Americans began leaving the South to take jobs in northern factories. This movement, called the **Great Migration**, continued during the economic boom of the 1920s. While African Americans found jobs in the North, they did not escape racism.

Racial Tensions

The economic recession that followed the war led to increased racial tensions. Many white laborers feared the competition for jobs. Several race riots broke out in 1919, including one in Chicago that left 38 dead.

Racial tensions and fear of foreigners helped give rise to a new form of the Ku Klux Klan, the racist group that had terrorized African Americans during Reconstruction. The new Klan harassed Catholics, Jews, and immigrants, as well as African Americans. It also worked against urbanization, women's rights, and modern technology. By the mid-1920s the Klan had become an influential force in American politics, with more than 5 million members. Its influence then began to decline as news of financial corruption became public.

Protecting Rights

People who were the targets of the Klan's hatred found new ways to protect their rights. In 1922, for example, the NAACP began placing advertisements in newspapers that presented the harsh facts about the large number of lynchings taking place across the South.

Another way minorities attempted to protect their rights was to strengthen their culture. During the 1910s and 1920s, **Marcus Garvey** encouraged black people around the world to express pride in their culture. Garvey argued that black people should establish economic independence by building their own businesses and communities. These ideas were the basis of a movement known as black nationalism. The New York *Amsterdam News* praised Garvey's work, saying he "made black people proud of their race."

Hispanic Americans also organized to fight prejudice and promote civil rights. In 1929 Mexican American leaders met in Corpus Christi, Texas, to form the League of United Latin American Citizens (LULAC). This group worked to end unfair treatment such as segregation in schools and voting restrictions.

Marcus Garvey
1887–1940

Marcus Garvey grew up in Jamaica and moved to the United States in 1916. A talented speaker, he quickly became one of the country's most famous and controversial black leaders. His newspaper *Negro World* promoted the idea of building an independent black economy. To encourage worldwide trade among black people, he created the Black Star Steamship Line. Some black leaders, including W. E. B. Du Bois, considered Garvey's ideas dangerous and extremist. After a series of legal problems related to his steamship company, Garvey was arrested in 1922 and was later deported.

Drawing Inferences How did Marcus Garvey try to help African Americans?

Most Native Americans lacked the legal protections of citizenship and the right to vote because they were not citizens of the United States. The fact that thousands of Native Americans had performed military service in World War I helped bring about change. In 1924 Congress passed the Indian Citizenship Act, granting citizenship to all Native Americans. However, the federal government also attempted to buy or take back some of the reservation lands. Native Americans successfully organized to stop these attempts, which were part of a larger effort to encourage Indians to adopt the culture of white Americans.

READING CHECK **Finding Main Ideas** How did minorities react to discrimination in the 1920s?

SUMMARY AND PREVIEW Americans saw many conflicts as their culture changed. In the next section you will learn about entertainment and the arts in the 1920s.

Section 2 Assessment

go.hrw.com
Online Quiz
KEYWORD: SB7 HP24

Reviewing Ideas, Terms, and People

1. **a. Recall** How did **flappers** express their freedom?
   b. Elaborate How were young people of the 1920s more independent than their parents?
2. **a. Identify** What caused the **Red Scare**, and what was its result?
   b. Explain Describe the results of the immigration laws of the 1920s.
3. **a. Recall** What kinds of social conflicts developed during the 1920s?
   b. Describe What did the **Twenty-first Amendment** accomplish?
   c. Analyze How did **fundamentalism** influence the **Scopes trial**?
4. **a. Identify** How did minorities fight for their rights in the 1920s?
   b. Define What was the **Great Migration**?
   c. Draw Conclusions Why did **Marcus Garvey** call for black people to build their own businesses?

Critical Thinking

5. **Identifying Cause and Effect** Review your notes on social changes that took place in the 1920s. Then copy the graphic organizer below and use it to identify the causes and effects of several changes in American society.

Cause		Effect
	→	
	→	
	→	

FOCUS ON WRITING

6. **Taking Notes on New Fashions** In the 1920s many women wore fashions that reflected their new independence. Look back at the example of flapper fashion on page 759. Think of how a radio advertisement could describe clothing like this to an audience that cannot see it.

The Jazz Age

If YOU were there...

The year is 1924, and the New York Giants are playing the Washington Senators in the World Series. You just bought your first radio, and you are listening to an announcer describe the tense action as the seventh and deciding game goes into extra innings. You used to have to wait to read about the games in the newspaper. Now you can follow your favorite team pitch by pitch!

What other forms of entertainment could the radio bring to you?

BUILDING BACKGROUND You read earlier about the rise of mass culture in the United States in the late 1800s. Newspapers, department stores, and world's fairs allowed millions of Americans to share the same cultural activities. In the 1920s technologies such as radio broadcasts and movies helped the rise of mass culture continue.

A National Culture

On November 2, 1920, KDKA, the first commercial radio station, announced that Warren Harding had won the presidential election held that day. Just one year later, stations broadcast the action from the 1921 World Series. One newspaper writer predicted, "It might not be too long before farmers at the four corners of the Union may sit in their own houses and hear the president of the United States." Such an event seemed amazing to Americans in the early 1900s. But it quickly became a reality, as hundreds of radio stations began broadcasting all over the United States.

National radio networks, such as the National Broadcasting Company (NBC) and Columbia Broadcasting System (CBS), allowed people all over the country to listen to the same programs. People suddenly had access to music, news, weather reports, children's bedtime stories, sports broadcasts, and political speeches without leaving their homes. Business owners loved this technology because it allowed their advertisements to reach millions of listeners. Radio helped build a new national culture by allowing Americans everywhere to share common experiences.

Virginia Standards of Learning USII.1c, USII.6c

What You Will Learn...

Main Ideas

1. Radio and movies linked the country in a national culture.
2. Jazz and blues music became popular nationwide.
3. Writers and artists introduced new styles and artistic ideas.

The Big Idea

Musicians, artists, actors, and writers contributed to American popular culture in the 1920s.

Key Terms and People

talkie, *p. 766*
Jazz Age, *p. 767*
Harlem Renaissance, *p. 768*
Langston Hughes, *p. 768*
Lost Generation, *p. 768*
expatriates, *p. 768*
Georgia O'Keeffe, *p. 769*

TAKING NOTES As you read, look for examples of popular culture in the 1920s. Record your notes in a diagram like this.

> **1920s Popular Culture**
> 1.
> 2.
> 3.
> 4.

Movies also became a major national passion in the 1920s. Though early motion pictures had no sound, they opened a new world of exciting adventures for audiences. People packed theaters to see Westerns, romances, and stories about bootlegging gangsters. Movie fans were even more thrilled by the 1927 movie *The Jazz Singer*, in which actor Al Jolson shouted the line "You ain't heard nothin' yet!" This was the first **talkie**, or motion picture with sound.

The movies quickly became big business. By the end of the decade, Americans were buying 95 million movie tickets each week, an amazing figure considering that the U.S. population was only 123 million. Young movie fans copied hair and clothing styles of movie stars. Fans felt a personal connection to stars like Douglas Fairbanks, Charlie Chaplin, and Mary Pickford, who was known as "America's Sweetheart." Few fans at the time realized that Pickford was also a smart businesswoman. She was one of the highest paid actors in Hollywood and a founder of United Artists, one of the nation's most successful film companies.

Movie stars were not the only national heroes. Fans packed baseball stadiums to watch the great players of the 1920s, especially George Herman "Babe" Ruth. Ruth shattered home-run records, drawing thousands of new fans to the sport. Because baseball was segregated, African American players and business leaders started their own league. Negro League stars such as Satchel Paige and Josh Gibson are considered to be among the best baseball players in history.

Fans always loved to see athletes break records. In 1926 American swimmer Gertrude Ederle became the first woman to swim the English Channel between England and France, beating the men's world record by almost two hours.

Pilots also became national heroes in the 1920s. Charles Lindbergh dominated the national news in 1927 when he completed the first nonstop solo flight across the Atlantic Ocean, traveling from New York to Paris. A few years later, Amelia Earhart became the first woman to fly solo across the Atlantic.

New ideas like psychoanalysis became more popular. Developed by psychologist Sigmund Freud, psychoanalysis is a method for examining human behavior to find out why people behave the way they do.

READING CHECK **Summarizing** How did American culture change during the 1920s?

Time Line

Popular Culture of the 1920s

1920 Babe Ruth begins playing for the New York Yankees.

1920

1924 First Negro-League World Series is played.

AMERICAN NEGRO LEAGUE

Popular Music

With a booming economy and exciting forms of entertainment, the 1920s became known as the Roaring Twenties. An explosion in the popularity of jazz music gave the decade another nickname — the **Jazz Age**.

Jazz developed in New Orleans, where African American musicians blended spirituals with European harmonies and West African rhythms. When blacks moved north during the Great Migration, they brought their music with them.

As with many new forms of popular culture, jazz sparked arguments between older and younger generations. "When my grandmother found out that I was playing jazz music . . . she told me that I had disgraced the family," remembered "Jelly Roll" Morton, an early jazz composer. But young Americans loved the music and the wild, fast-paced dances that went along with it. Dance crazes sweeping the nation included the Charleston, the Toddle, and the Shimmy. New magazines arose that taught dance steps to subscribers.

Jazz musicians such as Louis Armstrong experimented with various sounds and rhythms to create a new kind of music. Armstrong, who played the trumpet, was known for his solo numbers. His method of stepping out from the band to perform a solo was an **innovation** that is still copied by musicians today. Another major figure of the Jazz Age was conductor and composer Edward "Duke" Ellington. His "big band" sound blended many instruments together in songs such as "Take the A Train." Ellington described the exciting life of Jazz Age musicians in New York City:

> "A lot of guys liked to play so much that in spite of being on a regular job, they'd still hire out to work matinees, or breakfast dances . . . Nobody went to bed at nights and round three or four in the mornings you'd find everyone making the rounds bringing their horns with them."
>
> — Duke Ellington, quoted in *Reminiscing in Tempo*, by Stuart Nicholson

Blues music, which came from the rural South of the Mississippi Delta, also gained national popularity in the 1920s. Blues began as an expression of the suffering of African Americans during slavery. One of the leading blues singers of the 1920s was Bessie Smith, nicknamed the Empress of the Blues. "She had music in her soul," said Louis Armstrong.

READING CHECK **Finding Main Ideas** Where did jazz originate, and what musical styles influenced it?

ACADEMIC VOCABULARY

innovation
a new idea or way of doing something

1925 F. Scott Fitzgerald's *The Great Gatsby* is published.

1925 Louis Armstrong begins recording with his band, the Hot Five.

1926 Gertrude Ederle becomes the first woman to swim across the English Channel.

1926 NBC, the first national radio network, begins broadcasting.

1927 Charles Lindbergh completes the first non-stop solo flight across the Atlantic Ocean.

1927 *The Jazz Singer,* the first full-length talkie, is released.

1928

ANALYSIS SKILL **READING TIME LINES**

Which events reflected people's interest in breaking records?

THE ROARING TWENTIES **767**

Writers and Artists

While musicians were creating new forms of music, writers and artists were also reshaping American culture. Many creative works of the 1920s are still admired today.

The Harlem Renaissance

Many of the African Americans who came north in the Great Migration built a thriving community in the Harlem neighborhood of New York City. This community became the center of the **Harlem Renaissance**, a period of African American artistic accomplishment.

Primary Source

POEM
"I, Too"

In one of his most celebrated poems, Langston Hughes expressed both pride in being African American and faith in the American dream.

❝ I, Too

I, too, sing America.
I am the darker brother.
They send me to eat in the kitchen
When company comes,
But I laugh,
And eat well,
And grow strong.

Tomorrow,
I'll be at the table
When company comes.
Nobody'll dare
Say to me,
'Eat in the kitchen,'
Then.

Besides,
They'll see how beautiful I am
And be ashamed—
I, too, am America. ❞

ANALYSIS SKILL | **ANALYZING PRIMARY SOURCES**

Analyzing Who do you think Hughes is referring to when he speaks of "they"?

Harlem Renaissance writers included **Langston Hughes** and Claude McKay. Hughes produced poems, plays, and novels about African American life. His works often incorporated African American slang and jazz rhythms. McKay was a poet and activist who spoke out against racial discrimination and called on African Americans to stand up against lynchings and other violence.

Another important writer of the Harlem Renaissance was Zora Neale Hurston. Her novels, such as *Their Eyes Were Watching God,* reflected the experiences of African American women.

The Lost Generation

Other Americans also wrote of their experiences living in the United States and in places around the world. Soon after he graduated from high school in Illinois, Ernest Hemingway volunteered as an ambulance driver in World War I. Hemingway called the war "the most colossal, murderous, mismanaged butchery that had ever taken place on earth." He began writing short stories and novels, and soon he gained fame for his powerful and direct writing style. Hemingway was among a group of young American writers who expressed feelings of disillusionment in the American society that they felt denied them a voice in their own futures. Author Gertrude Stein called these writers "a lost generation." Writers who criticized American society in the 1920s thus became known as the **Lost Generation**.

Many members of the Lost Generation moved to Paris in the 1920s and formed a community of **expatriates**—people who leave their home country to live elsewhere. Hemingway wrote about the expatriate community in his best-selling novel *The Sun Also Rises.* Another Lost Generation writer was F. Scott Fitzgerald. His novel *The Great Gatsby* focused on what he saw as the loss of morality behind the seemingly fun and free-spirited times of the Jazz Age. Criticizing a glamorous couple, Fitzgerald wrote:

> "They were careless people ...they smashed up things and creatures and then retreated back into their money or their vast carelessness or whatever it was that kept them together, and let other people clean up the mess they had made."
>
> —F. Scott Fitzgerald, *The Great Gatsby*

Another writer of the time, Sinclair Lewis, became the first American to receive the Nobel Prize in literature.

New Directions in Art

Painters were also experimenting with new artistic styles in the 1920s. Edward Hopper painted images of the loneliness of modern urban life. **Georgia O'Keeffe** was well known for her detailed paintings of flowers and of the Southwest.

Architects of the 1920s embraced a style they called art deco. Buildings constructed in this style had clean, sharp lines that resembled machines. Today art deco skyscrapers still stand out in American city skylines.

READING CHECK **Comparing and Contrasting** How were the artists of the Harlem Renaissance and the Lost Generation similar and different?

BIOGRAPHY

Georgia O'Keeffe
1887–1986

Georgia O'Keeffe grew up in Wisconsin and studied art in Chicago and New York. While teaching art at a college in Canyon, Texas, she would sometimes hike in Palo Duro Canyon, where she sketched scenes of amazing colors and rock formations. This was the start of a lifelong fascination with the beauty of the desert landscape. O'Keeffe lived much of her life in rural New Mexico, where many of her paintings were created. Animal bones, rocks, and desert flowers fill her works. She would often paint these objects in close-up view, showing tiny details. O'Keeffe said, "Most people in the city rush around so, they have no time to look at a flower. I want them to see it whether they want to or not."

Finding Main Ideas How did Georgia O'Keeffe's life influence her painting?

SUMMARY AND PREVIEW Americans became interested in new forms of entertainment and art in the 1920s. In the next chapter you will learn about how life changed in the 1930s.

Section 3 Assessment

go.hrw.com
Online Quiz
KEYWORD: SB7 HP24

Reviewing Ideas, Terms, and People

1. **a. Recall** What new forms of entertainment dominated American society during the 1920s?
   b. Identify What was the first **talkie**?
2. **a. Explain** Why were the 1920s called the **Jazz Age**?
   b. Make Inferences Why do you think jazz music became so popular?
3. **a. Recall** How did writers and artists express new ideas during the 1920s?
   b. Describe What did the **Lost Generation** writers express in their works?
   c. Predict How might the artists of the **Harlem Renaissance** influence African American artists of later generations?

Critical Thinking

4. **Categorizing** Review your notes on examples of popular culture in the 1920s. Then copy the graphic organizer below. Use it to categorize examples of popular culture in the 1920s.

FOCUS ON WRITING

5. **Taking Notes on Entertainment** Make a list of popular forms of entertainment in the 1920s. How would you persuade people to attend a sports event, a talkie, or a jazz club? Begin to think about which product or form of entertainment you will choose for your radio advertisement.

Social Studies Skills

Analysis	Critical Thinking	Civic Participation	Study

Comparing Graphs

Define the Skill

Graphs are often a very useful way to organize historical information. They can present a large amount of detailed information clearly. Graphs can be an especially good way of showing how something like population or average income changed over time.

When information is organized in a graph, it is often easy to see patterns. Looking at two related graphs, you can compare patterns and make conclusions. For example, you can ask yourself, "Do the numbers in the graphs go up or down for the same reasons? What are the causes behind the changes shown by these graphs?"

Learn the Skill

These guidelines will help you to compare information in two or more graphs.

1. Use your basic graph-interpreting skills. Identify each graph's subject, purpose, and type. Study its parts and categories.

2. Analyze the data in each graph. Then compare any increases, decreases, changes, or patterns you find.

3. Finally, draw conclusions about the relationship between the information in each graph. Think about what could cause such relationships. It will probably help you to review what you know about related events at the same time.

Practice the Skill

Compare the graphs below to answer the following questions.

1. What are the topics of these graphs?

2. What percentage of American households had electricity in 1922? What was the first year when more than half of American households had electricity?

3. Based on the information in the graphs, draw a conclusion about how electricity changed American households.

Households with Electricity, 1920–1928

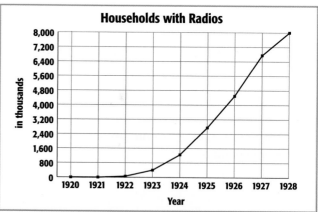
Households with Radios

Source: *Historical Atlas of the United States*

Chapter Review

HOLT
History's Impact
▶video series
Review the video to answer the closing question:
How did the post–World War I economy have an impact on film, literature, and music?

Visual Summary

QUICK FACTS

Use the visual summary below to help you review the main ideas of the chapter.

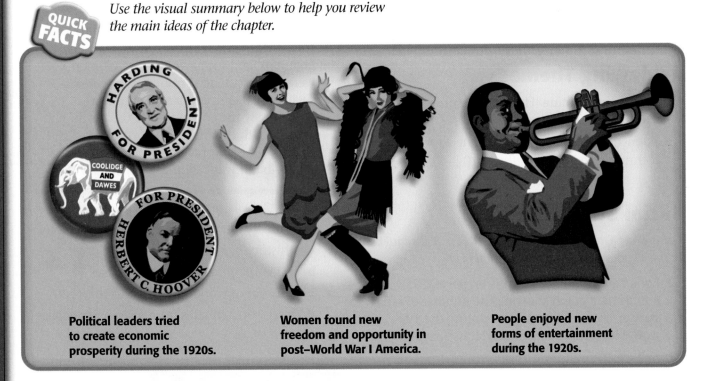

Political leaders tried to create economic prosperity during the 1920s.

Women found new freedom and opportunity in post–World War I America.

People enjoyed new forms of entertainment during the 1920s.

Reviewing Vocabulary, Terms, and People

Complete each sentence by filling in the blank with the correct term or person from the chapter.

1. Harlem Renaissance writer _____ wrote poems, plays, and novels about African American life.

2. The United States and other nations signed the _____, which outlawed war.

3. In the _____, Clarence Darrow defended a high school teacher tried for teaching evolution.

4. The _____ repealed prohibition.

5. Writers who criticized American culture during the 1920s were known as the _____.

6. African Americans moved north for jobs during the _____.

Comprehension and Critical Thinking

SECTION 1 *(Pages 752–757)*

7. **a. Describe** What was President Warren Harding's plan for strengthening the U.S. economy?

b. Explain What methods did Henry Ford's competitors use to attract customers?

c. Elaborate What do you think might have made the Kellogg-Briand Pact more effective?

SECTION 2 *(Pages 758–764)*

8. **a. Recall** What was the Red Scare?

b. Analyze What are some reasons women had more opportunities in the 1920s?

c. Evaluate Would you have become involved in the youth culture if you had lived during the 1920s? Why or why not?

9. a. Identify What were talkies?

b. Explain How did African Americans play an important role in Jazz Age culture?

c. Predict How do you think new aspects of American culture affected life after the 1920s?

Reviewing Themes

10. Society and Culture How did the prosperity of the 1920s change American culture?

11. Science and Technology What new forms of technology emerged in the 1920s?

Social Studies Skills

Comparing Graphs *Use the Social Studies Skills taught in this chapter to answer the question below.*

12. Look back at the line graphs on page 770. Do you think a graph showing the number of radio stations in the United States during the 1920s would look similar to these graphs? Explain your answer.

Using the Internet

go.hrw.com
KEYWORD: SB7 CH24

13. Activity: Experiencing the Jazz Age The arts flourished in America during the 1920s. There were amazing developments in the literary and visual arts, and new forms of performing arts, like blues and jazz, became popular. Enter the activity keyword. Use the Internet links provided to research some of the most influential writers, artists, and musicians of the 1920s. Choose one and conduct an imaginary interview with that person about his or her work and impact on American culture. Document your conversation by creating an audio recording or by writing a transcript.

Reading Skills

Synthesizing Information *Use the Reading Skills taught in this chapter to answer the question below.*

The number of women in the workforce continued to grow as well. Women with college degrees worked as nurses, teachers, librarians, and social workers . . . Women were still discouraged from pursuing fields such as medicine, law, and architecture, however. By the end of the 1920s, less than 5 percent of the country's doctors, lawyers, and architects were women. The percentage was small—but it was beginning to rise. *(p. 759)*

14. Which of the following sources might have been used to synthesize the information above?

a. a history of architecture

b. an instructional manual for nurses

c. a history of working women in the 1920s

d. the list of graduates from a women's college in 1910

FOCUS ON WRITING

15. Writing Your Radio Advertisement Look over your notes and choose one product that was popular in the 1920s. Think about these questions as you design your radio ad: Who is your audience? How will this product improve people's lives? What words or sounds will best describe your product? Write the dialogue for your ad, including directions for the actors. Also, include information about music or sound effects you want to use.

DIRECTIONS: Read each question and write the letter of the best response.

1 **President Warren Harding's secretary of the interior was convicted and jailed for his participation in the**

A Scopes trial.

B Teapot Dome scandal.

C Red Scare.

D Kellogg-Briand Pact.

2 **Marcus Garvey was a leader in which of the following movements?**

A black nationalism

B fundamentalism

C socialism

D communism

3 **Which of the following is a reason why consumers bought more manufactured products in the 1920s?**

A More Americans had electricity in their homes, so they could use new electric appliances.

B Radio and print advertising made it easier to buy products.

C Immigrants came to the United States in record numbers and bought new goods.

D The Lost Generation felt separated from American culture.

4 **Which of the following was a famous jazz musician and composer?**

A Zora Neale Hurston

B Mary Pickford

C Charles Lindbergh

D Edward "Duke" Ellington

5 **One effect of the Red Scare was**

A the election of Herbert Hoover in 1928.

B the trial and execution of Nicola Sacco and Bartolomeo Vanzetti.

C new opportunities for women, immigrants, and minorities.

D the Scopes trail.

6 **Which of the following quotes is attributed to Calvin Coolidge?**

A "The business of America is business."

B "I will build a motor car for the great multitude."

C "I want my girl to be a flapper, because flappers are brave."

D "America's present need is not heroics, but healing; not nostrums but normalcy."

7 **Read the following excerpt from a 1928 campaign speech by Herbert Hoover and use it to answer the question below.**

> *"We in America today are nearer to the final triumph over poverty than ever before in the history of any land . . . We have not yet reached the goal, but given a chance to go forward with the policies of the last eight years, we shall soon with the help of God be in sight of the day when poverty will be banished from this nation."*
>
> — Herbert Hoover, 1928 inaugural speech

Document-Based Question **What did Hoover believe about poverty in the United States?**

The Great Depression

Virginia Standards of Learning

USII.1 The student will demonstrate skills for historical and geographical analysis, and responsible citizenship, including the ability to

a) analyze and interpret primary and secondary source documents to increase understanding of events and life in United States history from 1865 to the present; **b)** make connections between past and present; **c)** sequence events in United States history from 1865 to the present; **d)** interpret ideas and events from different historical perspectives; **e)** evaluate and debate issues orally and in writing; **f)** analyze and interpret maps that include major physical features

USII.2 The student will use maps, globes, photographs, pictures, or tables for

c) locating the 50 states and the cities most significant to the historical development of the United States

USII.6 The student will demonstrate knowledge of the social, economic, and technological changes of the early twentieth century by

d) identifying the causes of the Great Depression, its impact on Americans, and the major features of Franklin D. Roosevelt's New Deal

FOCUS ON WRITING

Journal Entry We know a lot about life during the Great Depression because many Americans described their experiences in journals and letters. In this chapter you will read about how people struggled through hard times in the 1930s. Read the chapter and then write a one-page journal entry as if you were a person living during the Depression. You may choose to write from the point of view of a student, artist, farmer, or other individual. As you read, think about how the events in the 1930s may have affected this person.

WALL ST. LAYS AN EGG

 UNITED STATES

1929 The U.S. stock market crashes on Black Tuesday.

1930

 WORLD

1930 Mahatma Gandhi and a group of followers begin the Salt March.

HOLT

History's Impact
▶ **video series**
Watch the video to understand the impact of the 1929 stock market crash.

$100. WILL BUY THIS CAR. MUST HAVE CASH. LOST ALL ON THE STOCK MARKET

What You Will Learn...

The prosperity of the Roaring Twenties came crashing to an end in October 1929. Americans who had been dreaming of growing rich were suddenly forced to focus on day-to-day survival. Many Americans, like the man in this photo, had to sell prized possessions just to eat. In this chapter you will learn how Americans coped with the economic difficulties of the 1930s.

SWEEPING THE DEPRESSION OUT

1932 Franklin D. Roosevelt wins his first presidential election, beating Herbert Hoover.

1935 The CIO is organized.

1937 The first Social Security payments are made.

1939 The film *The Wizard of Oz* is released.

1932

1934

1936

1938

1940

1932 At least 30 million people worldwide are unemployed.

1933 Adolf Hitler becomes chancellor of Germany.

1936 Jesse Owens wins four gold medals at the Berlin Olympics.

1937 War officially begins between Japan and China.

1938 Violence against German Jews erupts into Kristallnacht ("night of broken glass").

THE GREAT DEPRESSION **775**

Reading Social Studies

by Kylene Beers

Economics	Geography	Politics	Society and Culture	Science and Technology

Focus on Themes In this chapter, you will learn about the Great Depression, one of the most serious **economic** crises in America's history. You will also learn about the **politics** that arose to try to deal with this crisis. Finally, you will read about how the Depression affected the global economy and how world leaders responded to it.

Recognizing Implied Main Ideas

Focus on Reading When you read, you will notice that not every paragraph has a main idea sentence. Sometimes the main idea is implied.

Implied Main Ideas While main ideas give a basic structure to a paragraph, supporting details help convince the reader of the author's point. Main ideas can be presented in a sentence, or simply implied. Usually, a paragraph without a main idea sentence will still have an implied main idea that ties the sentences together.

Notice how one reader found the main idea of the following paragraph.

During the boom years of the 1920s, one General Motors executive boldly declared: "Anyone not only can be rich, but ought to be rich." For almost all of the Roaring Twenties, the stock market was a bull market, or one with rising stock values. It seemed easy to make money by investing in stocks. For example, you could have bought shares in the Radio Corporation of America for $85 each at the beginning of 1928. You could have sold them a year later for $549 each. *(p. 778)*

This quote is about making money and being rich. Maybe the main idea is about money or economics.

This sentence is about making money through the stock market. I guess the main idea has to do with investing.

Here is a great example of how easy it was to make money in the late 1920s. I think the main idea is something like "The stock market provided an easy way for many to become rich in the 1920s."

Key Terms and People

Academic Vocabulary

In this chapter you will learn the following academic words:
implement *(p. 781)*
authority *(p. 786)*

You Try It!

Read the following paragraph and then answer the questions below.

The action began when Roosevelt called Congress into a special session. Known as the Hundred Days, the session started just after the inauguration and lasted until the middle of June. During the Hundred Days, Roosevelt and Congress worked together to create new programs to battle the Depression and aid economic recovery. These programs became known as the New Deal.

From Chapter 25, p. 784

1. List two ideas that this paragraph discusses.

2. How are these two ideas related to each other?

3. Write an example of the main idea of this paragraph.

4. Which details support your main idea?

As you read Chapter 25, think of a main idea for any paragraph that does not have a main idea sentence.

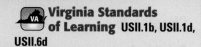
What You Will Learn...

Main Ideas

1. The U.S. stock market crashed in 1929.
2. The economy collapsed after the stock market crash.
3. Many Americans were dissatisfied with Hoover's reaction to economic conditions.
4. Roosevelt defeated Hoover in the election of 1932.

The Big Idea

The collapse of the stock market in 1929 helped lead to the start of the Great Depression.

Key Terms and People

buying on margin, *p. 778*
Black Tuesday, *p. 779*
business cycle, *p. 780*
Great Depression, *p. 780*
Bonus Army, *p. 781*
Franklin D. Roosevelt, *p. 782*

TAKING NOTES As you read, look for information about the American economy in the 1920s and 1930s. Take notes about your findings in a diagram like the one shown.

The End of Prosperity

If YOU were there...

For almost a year you've been working part-time at a neighborhood store. You earn money for your family and still have time to go to school. But when you arrive at work today, your boss says business has been so bad that he can't afford to pay you anymore. With your father out of work, your family had been counting on your income from this job.

How can you continue earning money to help your family?

BUILDING BACKGROUND By the late 1920s many Americans were used to year after year of economic expansion. It was easy to believe that the prosperity of the 1920s would last forever. But the U.S. economy historically has experienced periods of prosperity followed by periods of economic downturn. This cycle would continue in a way that shocked Americans in the 1930s.

The Stock Market Crashes

During the boom years of the 1920s, one General Motors executive boldly declared: "Anyone not only can be rich, but ought to be rich." For almost all of the Roaring Twenties, the stock market was a bull market, or one with rising stock values. It seemed easy to make money by investing in stocks. For example, you could have bought shares in the Radio Corporation of America for $85 each at the beginning of 1928. You could have sold them a year later for $549 each.

The chance to make huge profits from small investments encouraged many people to buy stocks. Some who could not afford the stocks' full price began **buying on margin**—purchasing stocks on credit, or with borrowed money. These stockholders planned to sell the stocks at a higher price, pay back the loan, and keep what remained as profit. But this plan only worked if stock values went up. Few considered what would happen if the bull market turned into a bear market, or one with declining stock prices.

Black Tuesday

More than 16 million shares were traded on Wall Street on Black Tuesday, a record that stood for 39 years. Just weeks later, roughly one-third of the value of the stock market had disappeared.

How are the events of Black Tuesday shown on the chart?

Stock Prices, March 1929–January 1930

Average opening price / Month

Black Tuesday (October 29)

Stock prices peaked in the late summer of 1929. Then prices started to drop. Frightened investors who had bought stocks on margin rushed to sell their stocks in order to pay off their loans. On Thursday, October 24, panic hit the stock market. Within three hours the market had lost $11 billion in value. The following Monday, prices dropped again. On Tuesday, October 29—a day that became known as **Black Tuesday**—the stock market crashed. So many people wanted to sell their stocks, and so few wanted to buy, that stock prices collapsed. One journalist described the nightmare:

"The wires to other cities were jammed with frantic orders to sell [stock]. So were the cables, radio, and telephones to Europe and the rest of the world. Buyers were few, sometimes wholly absent ...This was real panic ...When the closing bell rang, the great bull market was dead and buried."
—Jonathan Norton Leonard, from *Three Years Down*

In September 1929 the total value of all stocks was $87 billion. Less than two months later, more than $30 billion in stock value had disappeared.

READING CHECK Analyzing Information Why was buying on margin risky?

The Economy Collapses

President Herbert Hoover tried to calm public fears by assuring Americans that the economy was still strong. "The fundamental business of the country . . . is on a sound and prosperous basis," he said. But this was just the beginning of more than 10 years of economic hard times.

The Banking Crisis

One immediate effect of the stock market crash was a banking crisis. Banks had invested heavily in the stock market, so they lost heavily when the market crashed. Banks had also lent their customers money to buy stocks on margin. Now those customers were unable to pay back their loans. Some banks went out of business. People who had deposited their life savings in those banks lost everything.

This created a panic all over the country, as customers rushed to their banks to withdraw their money. But since banks usually do not keep enough cash on hand to cover all deposits, the banks soon ran out of money. Many had to close their doors. In 1931 alone, more than 2,200 banks closed. The banking crisis contributed to a business crisis. Some businesses lost their savings in failed banks and had to close. Others were forced to cut back production, which meant they needed fewer workers. In the last three months of 1929, U.S. unemployment soared from under half a million workers to more than 4 million.

The Causes

Throughout the history of the United States, the economy has followed a pattern of ups and downs. When businesses produce more than they can sell, unsold goods pile up. Businesses then cut back on their production and lay off workers. People who have lost their jobs, and others who are afraid they might soon lose their jobs, buy fewer goods. This causes more businesses to fail. This economic event is called a recession. Deep and long-lasting recessions are known as depressions.

As time passes, an economy will tend to bounce back. Consumers buy surplus goods, and companies increase production to meet the demand. Soon more workers are hired and unemployment drops. This up-and-down pattern is known as the **business cycle**.

The United States had experienced recessions and depressions before 1929. Each time, the economy followed the business cycle and recovered. But the economy did not recover quickly from the downturn that began in 1929. Because of its severity and length, it was called the **Great Depression**.

Historians and economists still debate the exact causes of the Great Depression. Some believe that the government's monetary policy was a cause. Most agree that a major factor was the overproduction of goods at a time when the market for those goods was shrinking. Companies built millions of cars and appliances during the 1920s. By the late 1920s, however, most people who could afford these products already had them. That meant that American businesses were producing far more goods than people were consuming.

Uneven distribution of wealth made this problem worse. In 1929 the wealthiest 5 percent of Americans earned one-third of all income, while the bottom 40 percent earned only one-eighth of all income. Millions of Americans simply did not earn enough money to buy expensive new products.

Declining world trade also hurt American manufacturers. Europeans were still recovering from World War I and could not afford many American goods. At the same time, high tariffs made it difficult for European nations to sell products to the United States. As a result, Europeans had even less money to buy American goods.

READING CHECK Making Predictions Do you think the Great Depression could have been avoided? How?

Unemployment during the Depression

CONNECT TO ECONOMICS

People are considered unemployed if they are trying to find work but do not have a job. High rates of unemployment hurt the economy because unemployed people cannot buy many goods and services. This causes businesses to lose money.

During what year was unemployment the highest?

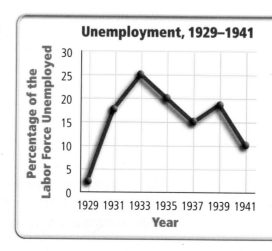

Unemployment, 1929–1941

Percentage of the Labor Force Unemployed

30
25
20
15
10
5
0

1929 1931 1933 1935 1937 1939 1941

Year

POLITICAL CARTOON
"Blame It on Hoover"

Presidents can affect the economy to some degree through their policies. During the Great Depression, President Hoover was blamed for the financial crisis. Political cartoons like this one gave voice to those Americans who thought Hoover could have prevented the crisis or could have brought it to an end quickly through government programs.

How does the cartoonist show Hoover reacting to the crisis?

What kind of people are blaming Hoover?

ANALYSIS SKILL **ANALYZING PRIMARY SOURCES**

Why is this cartoon useful for showing the feelings of the American public during the Great Depression?

A Most Vicious Circle
—Costello in the Albany "News."

Hoover's Reaction

As unemployment skyrocketed, more and more Americans struggled just to feed themselves and their families. Hungry people searched city dumps for scraps of food. One woman remembered taking off her glasses when she cooked so she could not see the maggots in the meat her family was about to eat. Private charities, as well as state and local governments, set up soup kitchens and bread lines. But the need far exceeded the available resources. Many people turned to President Herbert Hoover and the federal government to lead the relief effort.

Hoover knew that many Americans needed help. He did not believe, however, that it was the federal government's role to provide direct relief to Americans. Hoover felt it was up to private individuals and institutions, not the government, to offer relief. Despite this belief, Hoover did **implement** some new government programs. In 1932 he created the Reconstruction Finance Corporation (RFC). That year, the RFC loaned $1.2 billion to 5,000 different financial institutions, including banks and farm mortgage companies. Hoover continued to resist giving direct assistance to individuals.

This angered Americans who believed the president should do more to fix the economy. People bitterly referred to empty pockets turned inside out as Hoover flags. Groups of tin and cardboard shacks built by homeless families were nicknamed Hoovervilles.

In 1932 a new Hooverville was built in Washington, D.C. Its more than 17,000 residents were World War I veterans, some with their families. Called the **Bonus Army**, they had come to the capital to demand early payment of a military bonus. After the government denied the payment, most of the veterans returned home. About 2,000, however, stayed in their shantytown.

President Hoover authorized General Douglas MacArthur to use U.S. troops to evict the Bonus Army. MacArthur used force, including tear gas and tanks, to scatter the veterans. Several veterans were killed. The public reacted with outrage to the government's treatment of war veterans. Americans would have a chance to express this frustration in the upcoming election.

READING CHECK **Making Generalizations**
How would you describe President Hoover's response to the Depression?

ACADEMIC VOCABULARY
implement
put in place

Election of 1932

The Republican Party nominated Herbert Hoover again for president in 1932, but few people believed he could win. Regarding his chances of re-election, even Hoover realized that "the prospects are dark." Still, he began campaigning hard for a second term.

He called the election "a contest between two philosophies of government." He warned that the government aid programs Democrats were promising would weaken Americans' spirit of self-reliance.

By 1932, however, much of the public had lost confidence in Hoover. Many even blamed him for the Depression. In contrast, as governor of New York during the first years of the Depression, **Franklin D. Roosevelt** had taken active steps to provide aid. He directed the state government to provide relief for the state's citizens, especially farmers. He also helped establish the Temporary Emergency Relief Administration, which gave unemployment assistance to many out-of-work New Yorkers.

Roosevelt's confident and optimistic personality appealed to many voters. At the Democratic Party convention, Roosevelt declared to Americans: "I pledge you, I pledge myself, to a new deal for the American people." Voters responded overwhelmingly to this message of hope. Roosevelt won the 1932 election in a landslide. In addition, the Democrats won strong majorities in both houses of Congress.

READING CHECK Analyzing Information How did Franklin D. Roosevelt win the 1932 presidential election?

SUMMARY AND PREVIEW After the stock market crash and the start of the Great Depression, Franklin Roosevelt offered hope for the future. In the next section you will learn about his programs for relief.

Section 1 Assessment

Reviewing Ideas, Terms, and People

1. **a. Recall** Why did the stock market crash in 1929?
   b. Compare How is **buying on margin** similar to buying on an installment plan?
2. **a. Recall** What happened to the economy as a result of the stock market crash?
   b. Explain Why did many banks close in the late 1920s and early 1930s?
   c. Draw Conclusions What do you think was the goal of U.S. tariffs?
3. **a. Make Inferences** Why did many Americans blame President Hoover for the Depression?
   b. Describe What did the **Bonus Army** want?
   c. Elaborate Do you think Americans were justified in blaming Hoover for the hard times?
4. **a. Identify** Which party was more successful in the 1932 elections?
   b. Make Inferences Why do you think voters did not listen to Hoover's ideas about government?
   c. Elaborate How do you think **Franklin D. Roosevelt**'s experiences as governor of New York helped him appeal to voters?

Critical Thinking

5. **Identifying Cause and Effect** Review your notes on the American economy in the 1920s and 1930s. Then copy the graphic organizer below and use it to identify the economic causes of the Depression and their effects.

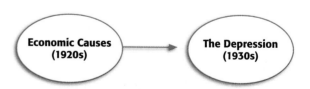

Economic Causes (1920s) → The Depression (1930s)

FOCUS ON WRITING

6. **Taking Notes on the End of Prosperity** To begin thinking about creating a character for your journal entry, answer the question at the end of the "If YOU Were There" on page 778. Then make some notes on the stock market crash, the banking crisis, and rising unemployment. Decide how your character would feel about these developments.

Franklin Delano Roosevelt

How would you try to lead your country through times of national crisis?

When did he live? 1882–1945

Where did he live? Roosevelt lived much of his life in New York State, where he served in the state senate and as governor. He also lived in Washington, D.C., while he was serving as assistant secretary of the navy and later as president. He had a second home in Warm Springs, Georgia.

What did he do? He began the New Deal, a set of government programs designed to help the country survive and recover from the Great Depression. He gave many Americans hope for the future when he spoke to them in his fireside chats. Roosevelt also led the country through World War II. His support for strong ties between the Allied countries helped the Allies achieve victory.

Why is he so important? Roosevelt led the United States during two of the most serious crises that our country has ever faced: the Great Depression and World War II. He served as president for 12 years, longer than any other. Many of the programs he began in the 1930s expanded the role of government in American life.

Making Predictions How do you think Franklin Roosevelt's experience as president during the Depression might have helped him lead the country during World War II?

> "*The only thing we* **have to fear** *is fear itself, nameless, unreasoning, unjustified terror.*"

Franklin Roosevelt, 1933 inaugural address

KEY EVENTS

1905
Marries Eleanor Roosevelt

1921
Stricken with polio; unable to walk without leg braces and canes for the rest of his life

1928
Elected governor of New York

1932
Elected president; reelected in 1936, 1940, and 1944

1941
U.S. entry into World War II

1945
Dies at his home in Warm Springs, Georgia

783

Roosevelt's New Deal

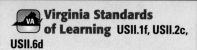
Virginia Standards of Learning USII.1f, USII.2c, USII.6d

What You Will Learn...

Main Ideas

1. Congress approved many new programs during the Hundred Days.
2. Critics expressed concerns about the New Deal.
3. New Deal programs continued through Roosevelt's first term in what became known as the Second New Deal.
4. Roosevelt clashed with the Supreme Court over the New Deal.

The Big Idea

Franklin Roosevelt's New Deal included government programs designed to relieve unemployment and help the economy recover.

Key Terms and People

New Deal, *p. 784*
fireside chats, *p. 785*
Tennessee Valley Authority, *p. 785*
Frances Perkins, *p. 785*
Eleanor Roosevelt, *p. 787*
Social Security Act, *p. 787*
Congress of Industrial Organizations, *p. 788*
sit-down strike, *p. 788*

TAKING NOTES As you read, take notes on the challenges the nation and President Roosevelt faced during the Great Depression in a chart like the one below.

The Nation	President Roosevelt

If YOU were there...

It has been five months since you lost your job. One of your friends has found work in a new government program that is hiring young people to work in national parks and forests. The pay is low, and you would have to leave home, but you would have enough food, a place to live, and a little money to send back to your family every month.

Would you take a job with the Civilian Conservation Corps? Why or why not?

BUILDING BACKGROUND When he ran for president in 1932, Franklin D. Roosevelt promised to provide relief to people suffering from the Depression. Even before he took office, Roosevelt began making plans with his Brain Trust, a group of expert advisers. People endured the harsh winter of 1932–1933, looking forward to Roosevelt's inauguration.

The Hundred Days

Immediately after taking the oath of office in March 1933, President Franklin Roosevelt spoke to the nation. In his first inaugural address, Roosevelt told nervous Americans that economic recovery was possible. "The only thing we have to fear is fear itself," he said, "nameless, unreasoning, unjustified terror." It was only fear of the future, he argued, that could keep America from moving forward. Roosevelt spoke openly of the severe problems facing the American people—unemployment, failing banks, and products with no markets. He promised that the government would help. "This nation asks for action," he said, "and action now."

The action began when Roosevelt called Congress into a special session. Known as the Hundred Days, the session started just after the inauguration and lasted until the middle of June. During the Hundred Days, Roosevelt and Congress worked together to create new programs to battle the Depression and aid economic recovery. These programs became known as the **New Deal**.

Tennessee Valley Authority, 1933–1945

Tennessee Valley Authority
- Major dams
△ Steam power plants

0   300   600 Miles
0   300   600 Kilometers

GEOGRAPHY SKILLS | **INTERPRETING MAPS**

1. **Human-Environment Interaction** What changes were made to the environment by the TVA?
2. **Place** Where were most of the dams built?

Restoring Confidence

One of Roosevelt's first goals was to restore confidence in American banks. The day after his inauguration, Roosevelt announced a "bank holiday," ordering all banks to close temporarily. Three days later, Congress's special session began. Congress quickly passed the Emergency Banking Relief Act, and President Roosevelt signed it into law.

That Sunday, President Roosevelt gave the first of his **fireside chats**—radio addresses in which he spoke directly to the American people. In this first fireside chat, he explained the new bank relief law. The government would inspect the finances of every bank and allow only healthy banks to reopen. The new bank law and Roosevelt's fireside chat helped Americans trust banks with their money again. As banks reopened, there were no rushes to withdraw money. Over the next month, Americans deposited almost $1 billion in banks.

Relief and Recovery

Roosevelt next turned his attention to other serious problems. In 1933 some 13 million Americans—about 25 percent of the nation's workforce—were unemployed. New Deal programs helped to get Americans back to work. The Civil Works Administration (CWA) employed more than 4 million Americans, building roads and airports. One grateful CWA worker expressed the feelings of many when he said, "I was working, and I could again hold my head up when I met people." The Civilian Conservation Corps (CCC) provided jobs for hundreds of thousands of people through projects such as planting trees and improving national parks.

Another federal project, the **Tennessee Valley Authority** (TVA), hired people to build dams and generators, bringing electricity and jobs to communities in the Tennessee River valley. The New Deal also included programs to help farmers. The Farm Credit Administration (FCA) helped farmers refinance their mortgages so they could keep their farms. The Agricultural Adjustment Act (AAA) helped stabilize agricultural prices.

The National Industrial Recovery Act (NIRA) addressed business concerns by eliminating unfair competition among companies. This law was passed with support from Secretary of Labor **Frances Perkins**, the nation's first woman cabinet member.

FOCUS ON READING
What is the main idea of this paragraph?

READING CHECK **Categorizing** Which New Deal programs employed people to build public projects?

RADIO BROADCAST
Fireside Chats

An American family sits around the radio listening to President Roosevelt answer his critics in his first fireside chat.

❝There is an element in . . . our financial system more important than currency [money], more important than gold, and that is the confidence of the people. Confidence and courage are the essentials of success in carrying out our plan. You people must have faith; you must not be stampeded by rumors or guesses. Let us unite in banishing [driving away] fear. We have provided the machinery to restore our financial system; it is up to you to support and make it work. It is your problem no less than it is mine. Together we cannot fail.❞

ANALYSIS SKILL **ANALYZING PRIMARY SOURCES**

According to Roosevelt, how should the American people help the government deal with the banking crisis?

New Deal Critics

While many Americans approved of the New Deal, others criticized President Roosevelt's programs. New Deal critics fell into two main groups—those who believed the New Deal went too far, and those who believed it did not go far enough.

Those who felt the New Deal went too far criticized the enormous expansion of the federal government. For example, members of the American Liberty League said that New Deal laws gave the president too much **authority**. Many business leaders were concerned that the high cost of new government programs would lead to new taxes. As one writer explained:

ACADEMIC VOCABULARY

authority power, right to rule

❝It's simple arithmetic to figure that taxpayers must pay the bills for current billions of emergency expenditures. The question is, Which taxpayers? Under this administration the answering finger points pretty much in the direction of business interests. Thus higher taxes of the future will eat into profits.❞

—W. H. Kiplinger, quoted in *The New Deal and the American People,* edited by Frank Freidel

One critic who thought the New Deal did not go far enough was a U.S. senator from Louisiana, Huey Long. Long proposed a program called "Share Our Wealth," which would tax rich Americans and use the money to help the poor. Every family would be guaranteed an annual income of $5,000. As Long prepared to challenge Roosevelt in the 1936 election, he announced his goal "to break up the swollen fortunes of America and to spread the wealth among all our people." Long's White House dreams ended when an assassin shot him in 1935.

Another fierce critic of Roosevelt's New Deal was Father Charles Edward Coughlin. Coughlin was a Roman Catholic priest in Detroit who developed a large following by broadcasting sermons over the radio. Although he initially supported Roosevelt and his programs, Coughlin eventually decided that the New Deal helped only business interests. Coughlin wanted the government to nationalize, or take over, all of the country's wealth and natural resources.

READING CHECK **Supporting a Point of View**
Do you agree with any of the New Deal critics? Why or why not?

The New Deal Continues

Despite criticism of the New Deal, Democrats increased their majorities in both houses of Congress in the 1934 election. With this show of support from the American people, Roosevelt continued to introduce additional New Deal legislation. These later laws were known as the Second New Deal.

The Second New Deal

After the Civil Works Administration ended in 1934, Congress formed a new agency to provide jobs for unemployed Americans. Between 1935 and 1943, the Works Progress Administration (WPA) employed some 8.5 million people on tens of thousands of projects all over the country. WPA employees built more than 650,000 miles of roads; 75,000 bridges; 8,000 parks; and 800 airports. WPA workers also built the Grand Coulee Dam in Washington and New York City's Lincoln Tunnel, as well as prisons, swimming pools, hospitals, and courthouses nationwide.

First Lady **Eleanor Roosevelt** was an active supporter of New Deal programs. She was concerned, however, that the WPA was not solving the problem of unemployment among young Americans in their teens and early twenties. "I live in real terror when I think we may be losing this generation," she said. "We have got to bring these young people into the active life of the community and make them feel that they are necessary." The first lady helped convince the president to create the National Youth Administration (NYA). The NYA gave part-time jobs to many students. These jobs allowed young workers to stay in school and help their families. One NYA worker said, "I tell you, the first time I walked through the front door with my paycheck, I was somebody!"

President Roosevelt also wanted to help those who were "unable . . . to maintain themselves independently . . . through no fault of their own." The **Social Security Act**, passed in 1935, provided some financial security for the elderly, the disabled, children, and the unemployed. To help pay for these programs, the law placed a new tax on workers and employers. The passage of the Social Security Act marked the first time the federal government took direct responsibility

THE IMPACT TODAY

Social Security today is a matter of great debate. Some Americans support the continuation of the program, while others believe that the government spends too much on the program and it should be privatized.

QUICK FACTS

Selected New Deal Programs

Program	Purpose
Emergency Banking Relief Act	Gave the executive branch the right to regulate banks
Farm Credit Act (FCA)	Refinanced loans to keep farmers from losing their land
Civilian Conservation Corps (CCC)	Created jobs for single, unemployed young men
Agricultural Adjustment Act (AAA)	Paid farmers to grow less (declared unconstitutional)
Tennessee Valley Authority (TVA)	Built dams and power plants in the Tennessee Valley
Federal Deposit Insurance Corporation (FDIC)	Guaranteed deposits in individual bank accounts
National Industrial Recovery Act (NIRA)	Established fair competition laws (declared unconstitutional)
Civil Works Administration (CWA)	Provided jobs for the unemployed
Works Progress Administration (WPA)	Created jobs in construction, research, and the arts
National Youth Administration (NYA)	Provided part-time jobs to students
National Labor Relations Act (Wagner Act)	Recognized unions' right to bargain collectively
Social Security Act	Provided government aid to the retired and unemployed

for many citizens' economic well-being. In a national radio address, Secretary of Labor Perkins told Americans she believed Social Security was "a most significant step in our national development, a milestone in our progress toward the better-ordered society."

New Deal Labor Programs

The National Industrial Recovery Act of 1933 helped regulate business by requiring minimum wage and allowing collective bargaining. In 1935, however, the Supreme Court declared the NIRA unconstitutional.

In response to this setback, Congress passed the National Labor Relations Act (NLRA). This law is sometimes called the Wagner Act after its sponsor, Senator Robert F. Wagner of New York. This law allowed workers to join labor unions and take part in collective bargaining. It also established the National Labor Relations Board to oversee union activities. Union membership grew after the passage of the Wagner Act. Organized labor became a powerful political force.

At the start of the Depression, many skilled workers belonged to craft unions. Such unions were often associated with the American Federation of Labor, which had existed since the 1880s. Unskilled workers, however, such as those who worked on assembly lines, did not qualify to belong to AFL unions. In 1935 a new union called the **Congress of Industrial Organizations** (CIO) organized workers into unions based on industry, not skill level. For example, all workers in the automobile industry would belong to the same union. The CIO also welcomed African American and Hispanic members, as well as women and immigrants.

Unions led a number of major strikes during the Depression. On New Year's Eve 1936, the CIO went on strike against General Motors for 44 days. Instead of leaving the buildings as strikers usually did, workers stayed in the factories so they could not be replaced by new workers. This strategy became known as the **sit-down strike**. The success of the General Motors strike attracted more workers to CIO unions.

READING CHECK Comparing and Contrasting How were the WPA and the Social Security Act similar, and how were they different?

National Youth Administration

A New Deal program called the National Youth Administration (NYA) helped thousands of young people continue their education while working to support their families. Eleanor Roosevelt was a strong supporter of the program, which aimed to teach young people the skills they would need to remain part of the workforce.

How did the NYA demonstrate the ideals of the New Deal?

Clashes with the Court

Roosevelt won re-election by a huge margin in 1936, carrying every state but Maine and Vermont. Democrats expanded their dominant control of Congress. But Roosevelt and the Democrats in Congress could not control the Supreme Court.

In 1935 the Supreme Court issued a series of rulings declaring several New Deal programs, including the AAA, unconstitutional. Roosevelt and his advisers felt that the entire New Deal was in danger. "Mr. President, they mean to destroy us," said Attorney General Homer Cummings.

Roosevelt decided to propose a plan for reorganizing the federal judiciary that was soon to be labeled the "court-packing" bill. This bill would allow the president to appoint a new Supreme Court justice for every justice who was 70 years old or older. Roosevelt would be able to appoint six new justices immediately.

Roosevelt's judiciary plan drew harsh criticism from Congress and the public. Critics charged that Roosevelt was trying to change the balance of power so carefully defined in the U.S. Constitution. After a heated debate, Congress rejected the bill. The Supreme Court, however, did not overturn any more New Deal legislation. Roosevelt eventually had the opportunity to nominate nine new Supreme Court justices to replace those who had retired or died.

READING CHECK **Analyzing Information** Why did Roosevelt try to alter the Supreme Court?

SUMMARY AND PREVIEW Roosevelt's New Deal programs brought economic relief to many Americans. In the next section you will read about how the country continued to suffer the effects of the Depression.

Section 2 Assessment

Reviewing Ideas, Terms, and People

1. a. **Recall** What were the Hundred Days?
   b. **Make Inferences** What was the purpose of the bank holiday Roosevelt declared?
   c. **Evaluate** Which of the **New Deal** programs that passed during the Hundred Days was most effective? Why?
2. a. **Describe** Who were some of the critics of the New Deal?
   b. **Contrast** How were the ideas of Huey Long and the American Liberty League different?
   c. **Elaborate** Why do you think people supported New Deal critics such as Huey Long and Father Coughlin?
3. a. **Identify** What programs were part of the Second New Deal?
   b. **Make Inferences** Why did the Wagner Act encourage people to join unions?
4. a. **Recall** What happened to some of the New Deal programs when they were challenged in court?
   b. **Make Inferences** What was the purpose of Roosevelt's judiciary reorganization bill?

Critical Thinking

5. **Problem Solving** Review your notes on the challenges faced by the nation and the president during the Depression. Then copy the graphic organizer below and use it to identify Depression problems and New Deal solutions.

Problems	New Deal solutions

FOCUS ON WRITING

6. **Thinking about New Deal Programs** Take notes on the New Deal programs. Think about how your character might be affected by one or more of the programs. For instance, how do you think he or she would feel about getting a construction job with the Works Progress Administration?

Virginia Standards of Learning USII.1a, USII.1b, USII.1d, USII.1e, USII.1f, USII.1i, USII.2c, USII.6d

What You Will Learn...

Main Ideas

1. Parts of the Great Plains came to be known as the Dust Bowl as severe drought destroyed farms there.
2. Families all over the United States faced hard times.
3. Depression-era culture helped lift people's spirits.
4. The New Deal had lasting effects on American society.

The Big Idea

All over the country, Americans struggled to survive the Great Depression.

Key Terms and People

Dust Bowl, *p. 790*
Mary McLeod Bethune, *p. 792*
John Steinbeck, *p. 793*
Woody Guthrie, *p. 793*

TAKING NOTES As you read, take notes on people's lives during the Depression. In each circle of a diagram like the one below, fill in details about their challenges, struggles, and culture.

Life during the Depression

Americans Face Hard Times

If YOU were there...

You own a wheat farm on the Great Plains, where you and your family live and work. Wheat prices have been low for years, and you have managed to get by only by borrowing thousands of dollars. Now the region is suffering through a terrible drought. Without water, you have been unable to grow any wheat at all. But if you do not start paying your debts, you will lose your farm.

Would you stay on your farm or leave and start a new life somewhere else?

BUILDING BACKGROUND The New Deal provided jobs and relieved suffering for many Americans, but it did not end the Great Depression. Unemployment fell to about 14 percent in 1937 but then rose again to about 17 percent in 1939. All over the country, people still struggled to survive.

The Dust Bowl

For American farmers, hard times began well before the start of the Great Depression. Despite the widespread prosperity of the 1920s, prices for farm products remained low. The Depression worsened this already bad situation. Conditions worsened again when a severe drought hit the Great Plains in the early 1930s and lasted most of the decade. From North Dakota to Texas, crops withered away. With no roots to hold it in place, topsoil began to blow away.

Massive dust storms swept the region, turning parts of the Great Plains into the **Dust Bowl**. "These storms were like rolling black smoke," recalled one Texas schoolboy. "We had to keep the lights on all day. We went to school with the headlights on, and with dust masks on." A woman from Kansas remembered dust storms "covering everything—including ourselves—in a thick, brownish gray blanket . . . Our faces were as dirty as if we had rolled in the dirt; our hair was gray and stiff and we ground dirt between our teeth."

Unable to raise crops, farmers in the Dust Bowl region could not pay their mortgages. Many lost their farms. Several New Deal programs tried to assist farmers by offering loans and by working to stabilize prices for farm products. Scientists also began thinking of ways to prevent dust storms during future droughts. Soil conservation experts encouraged farmers to adopt new farming methods to protect the soil. Grass was planted to hold soil in place, and rows of trees were planted to help break the wind. These changes have helped prevent another Dust Bowl in the years since the Great Depression.

For many farmers in the 1930s, however, the new programs came too late. After losing their crops and livestock to dust storms, about 2.5 million people left the area. Many packed up whatever they could fit in the family car or truck and drove to California to look for any kind of work they could find. Once there, they often found that there were already more workers than available jobs.

READING CHECK **Identifying Cause and Effect** How did the Dust Bowl affect farmers?

Hard Times

The Great Depression took a heavy toll on families all over the United States. Many families were forced to split up, as individual members roamed the country in search of work. To help their families buy food, children often had to drop out of school and take very low-paying jobs. Others left home

Primary Source

PERSONAL ACCOUNT
The Dust Bowl

Lawrence Svobida was a Kansas wheat farmer who saw his life's work destroyed in the 1930s.

"When I knew that my crop was irrevocably [forever] gone I experienced a deathly feeling which, I hope, can affect a man only once in a lifetime. My dreams and ambitions . . . and my shattered ideals seemed gone forever. The very desire to make a success of my life was gone, the spirit and urge to strive were dead within me. Fate had dealt me a cruel blow above which I felt utterly unable to rise."

ANALYSIS SKILL **ANALYZING PRIMARY SOURCES**
How did Svobida feel after his crop was destroyed?

★ Interactive Map
The Dust Bowl

CANADA

MT, ND, SD, WY, NE, IL Chicago, MO St. Louis, CO, Liberal KS, Dodge City, Pueblo, NV, CA, Boise City, OK, Oklahoma City, Los Angeles, AZ, Amarillo, NM, TX, MEXICO

Great Plains

120°W
PACIFIC OCEAN
ATLANTIC OCEAN
30°N
Gulf of Mexico
80°W

go.hrw.com
Interactive Map
KEYWORD: SB7 CH25

Dust Bowl
Other areas with severe wind erosion
Migration routes

0   300   600 Miles
0   300   600 Kilometers

Severe drought during the 1930s destroyed the livelihood of many Great Plains farmers. Here, a black cloud of dust rages toward the outbuildings of a farm.

ANALYSIS SKILL **ANALYZING VISUALS**
Which part of the United States was affected by wind erosion?

to fend for themselves. One boy wrote this diary entry in 1932:

"Slept in paper box. Bummed swell breakfast three eggs and four pieces meat ...Rode freight [train] to Roessville. Small burg [town], but got dinner. Walked Bronson ...Couple a houses. Rode to Sidell ...Hit homes for meals and turned down. Had to buy supper 20 cents. Raining."
—Anonymous, quoted in *The Great Depression*, by Thomas Minehan

The Great Depression was especially hard on minority groups. As white families moved west in search of jobs, Mexican Americans found it harder to get work. In California local leaders and unions convinced the government to deport many Mexican-born workers. Some of the workers' children were American-born, which made them U.S. citizens, but they were deported anyway.

African Americans also faced discrimination. Many lost jobs to unemployed white workers. One man recalled traveling around Michigan in search of work. He went into a factory that was hiring workers:

"They didn't hire me because I didn't belong to the right kind of race. Another time I went into Saginaw, it was two white fellas and myself made three. The fella there hired the two men and didn't hire me. I was back out on the streets. That hurt me pretty bad, the race part."
—Louis Banks, quoted in *Hard Times: An Oral History of the Great Depression,* by Studs Terkel

In spite of this type of discrimination, hundreds of thousands of African Americans were able to find work though relief programs such as the CCC and WPA. President Roosevelt also consulted with African American leaders, including educator **Mary McLeod Bethune**. Bethune was one of several African Americans who Roosevelt appointed to his administration. Other members included Walter White and William Henry Hastie. These advisers became known as the Black Cabinet. Their role was to advance the concerns of African Americans in the Roosevelt White House.

First Lady Eleanor Roosevelt was a strong supporter of equal rights. She encouraged the president to include African Americans in his recovery programs. In 1939 the Daughters of the American Revolution (DAR) refused to rent their auditorium to the African American singer Marian Anderson. In protest, Eleanor Roosevelt resigned her membership in the DAR. She then helped Anderson arrange a concert at the base of the Lincoln Memorial. Some 75,000 people attended.

READING CHECK Drawing Inferences What weakened families during the Depression?

Primary Source

PHOTOGRAPH
"Migrant Mother"

Photographer Dorothea Lange gained fame in the 1930s for documenting the conditions of the poor during the Depression. Lange took this famous photograph of a widowed migrant worker and two of her seven children. The woman worked in the pea fields of Nipomo, California. Her family survived by eating frozen peas and birds the children caught. The woman had just sold her car's tires for money to buy food.

ANALYSIS SKILL ANALYZING PRIMARY SOURCES

How would you describe the expression on the face of the woman in the photograph?

Depression-Era Culture

Starting in 1935, new Works Progress Administration projects began to put the country's painters, sculptors, writers, and actors to work. When he was criticized for hiring artists, WPA director Henry Hopkins said, "They've got to eat just like other people."

Some of the work done by WPA artists has become an important part of American culture. For example, WPA musicians went into the nation's rural areas to record cowboy ballads, folk songs, and African American spirituals. This music might have been lost without these recordings. Artists employed by the WPA made more than 2,500 murals and 17,000 pieces of sculpture for public spaces. WPA writers created a permanent record of American life by interviewing Americans of many different backgrounds about their lives and memories.

Like many people at the time, author **John Steinbeck** was deeply affected by the Great Depression. Depression life became a main theme of Steinbeck's most famous novel, *The Grapes of Wrath*. The novel tells the story of the Joads, a family of farmers that is forced to move to California for work.

Some of the music of the day expressed themes similar to Steinbeck's. Oklahoma-born folk singer **Woody Guthrie** crisscrossed the country singing his songs of loss and struggle. One contained the line, "All along your green valley I'll work till I die"—a grim reality for some Americans.

Swing music, meanwhile, became popular for a different reason. Instead of focusing on the sadness of the Depression, swing helped people forget their troubles. Big-band leaders such as Duke Ellington, Benny Goodman, and Count Basie helped make swing wildly popular in the 1930s. People tuned into swing music shows on inexpensive radios and danced to the fast-paced rhythms. Radios provided people with other forms of entertainment as well. Every week millions of Americans put aside their

worries to listen to radio shows such as *Little Orphan Annie* and *The Lone Ranger*.

Movies offered Americans another welcome escape from reality. One boy remembered how he and his friends would save their pennies for movie tickets. "[It] was two for a nickel," he said. "You'd come to the movie in the summer like 8:30 in the mornin' and you'd see about 200 kids." For 25 cents or less, adults, too, could forget their troubles as they watched historical dramas, gangster films, comedies, and musicals.

READING CHECK Evaluating How was the work of writers and musicians affected by the Great Depression?

Escape to the Movies

Weekly Movie Attendance, 1929–1939

ANALYSIS SKILL **ANALYZING INFORMATION**

How many Americans attended movies in 1930?

THE IMPACT TODAY

Today many of the thousands of interviews conducted by WPA writers are available on the Internet. You can read the stories of former slaves, pioneers, Native American leaders, and others in their own words.

Causes and Effects of the New Deal

QUICK FACTS

Causes
- Stock market crash
- Banking crisis
- Soaring unemployment
- Farmers' troubles
- Widespread poverty

Effects
- Expanded role of federal government
- Created major programs such as Social Security and the FDIC
- Provided hope and relief to many Americans but did not end the Great Depression

that the New Deal gave Americans help and hope in a time of severe economic crisis.

People today do agree that the New Deal greatly expanded the role of the federal government. Some of the programs and agencies created as part of the New Deal, such as Social Security and the Federal Deposit Insurance Corporation (FDIC), remain part of our lives. Social Security still provides economic relief to the elderly, children, and those with disabilities. The FDIC protects the savings of bank customers.

READING CHECK **Finding the Main Idea** What are some current government programs that began during the New Deal?

SUMMARY AND PREVIEW The New Deal helped Americans but did not end the Great Depression. The Depression finally ended after the United States entered World War II, which you will learn about in the next chapter.

Effects of the New Deal

People are still debating the effects of the New Deal today. New Deal critics point out that Roosevelt's programs did not end the Great Depression. Full recovery occurred in the early 1940s, after the United States entered World War II. Roosevelt's supporters, however, believe

Section 3 Assessment

go.hrw.com
Online Quiz
KEYWORD: SB7 HP25

Reviewing Ideas, Terms, and People

1. **a. Identify** What was the **Dust Bowl**?
   b. Explain What factors contributed to farmers' difficulties in the 1920s and 1930s?
2. **a. Recall** What were some of the problems people faced during the Depression?
   b. Compare How was the experience of African Americans and Mexican Americans in the Depression similar?
   c. Evaluate Do you think President Roosevelt did enough to help African Americans? Explain your answer.
3. **a. Draw Conclusions** Why do you think swing music, radio shows, and movies were popular during the Great Depression?
   b. Identify How did the WPA help the arts?
4. **a. Recall** What are the different viewpoints on the success of the New Deal?
   b. Elaborate How are Social Security and the FDIC still important today?

Critical Thinking

5. **Categorizing** Review your notes on life during the Great Depression. Then copy the graphic organizer below and use it to identify challenges people faced during the Depression and the ways they coped.

Challenges people faced	Ways people coped with challenges

FOCUS ON WRITING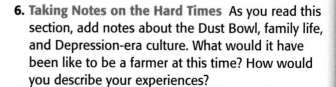

6. **Taking Notes on the Hard Times** As you read this section, add notes about the Dust Bowl, family life, and Depression-era culture. What would it have been like to be a farmer at this time? How would you describe your experiences?

Depression-Era Literature

from *The Grapes of Wrath*

by John Steinbeck (1902–1968)

About the Reading *Published in 1939,* The Grapes of Wrath *described the impact of the Great Depression on the nation. In this passage, Steinbeck describes a journey of Dust Bowl families to California.*

AS YOU READ **Look for details that appeal to the five senses.**

GUIDED READING

WORD HELP

migrant a person who moves regularly

Divide The Continental Divide separates rivers that flow east from those that flow west.

tributary stream that feeds into a larger river or lake (Steinbeck applies the word to the road system.)

❶ *From what are people on Highway 66 fleeing?*

❷ *How does Steinbeck describe what people are running from?*

Highway 66 is the main migrant road. 66—the long, concrete path across the country, waving gently up and down the map, from the Mississippi [River] to Bakersfield [California]—over the red lands and the gray lands, twisting up into the mountains, crossing the Divide and down into the bright and terrible desert to the mountains again, and into the rich California valleys.

66 is the path of people in flight,❶ refugees from dust and shrinking land, from the thunder of tractors and shrinking ownership, from the desert's slow northward invasion, from the twisting winds that howl up out of Texas, from the floods that bring no richness to the land and steal what little richness is there.❷ From all of these the people are in flight, and they come into 66 from the tributary side roads, from the wagon tracks and the rutted country roads. 66 is the mother road, the road of flight.

CONNECTING LITERATURE TO HISTORY

1. **Steinbeck describes in vivid detail the fear that people on the road felt.** According to this passage, why might driving between towns be a terror? What does this tell you about the migrants?

2. *The Grapes of Wrath* **became a favorite among readers for its honest portrayal of the realities of the Depression.** Based on Steinbeck's description and on what you already know, how might people traveling on Route 66 have felt? Why?

Social Studies Skills

Analysis | Critical Thinking | Civic Participation | Study

Having a Debate

Define the Skill

The First Amendment to the United States Constitution guarantees freedom of speech, assembly, and the press. These freedoms have become a key part of American democracy. They guarantee that both government officials and citizens can express their opinions. People also have the right to express disagreement with leaders or the government.

The ability to discuss opposing points of views is key to a democratic society. In the United States, citizens vote for their leaders. Having access to different points of view helps people decide which candidates to support in elections.

One way to express opposing points of view is to have a debate. Debates are organized to present two sides of an issue. Debate rules make sure that both sides are treated fairly. By learning about the strengths and weaknesses of two positions on an issue, people can decide which position is more convincing.

Learn the Skill

Think about the opposition President Franklin D. Roosevelt faced when he tried to begin new programs during the Great Depression. He had to convince people to support his ideas. Roosevelt and members of his administration used radio programs and newspaper articles to promote their point of view and answer questions from their critics.

In a debate, it is important to make your point of view clear. Explain why you support a certain position, or give specific reasons why you oppose it. The more detailed the argument, the more persuasive it will be. When you are in a debate, make sure to prepare plenty of evidence and examples to support your case.

Debaters have the chance not only to present a case but also to argue against the opposite point of view. One way to get ready for this is to think of possible arguments against your position. Prepare responses to each of these arguments in advance. Having good answers to criticism makes your position stronger.

In a debate, it is important to follow any rules that have been set up. Not all debates have the same rules. They do share some basic guidelines, however. Only one person is allowed to speak at once, and speaking time is limited. The two sides take turns presenting their arguments. Debates may have additional rules as well.

Practice the Skill

Suppose that your class is the Senate in 1933. President Roosevelt has already begun several new government programs. Now he is asking you to pass more new laws, which he believes will help the economy. Follow the guidelines above to have a debate about the New Deal. One group should support expanding the New Deal, and one group should oppose it. When the debate is over, answer the following questions.

1. Did your group make its point of view clear? Did it explain the reasons for taking that position? What do you think was your group's most persuasive supporting detail or example?

2. Did your group prepare arguments against the other side in advance? Were any of these arguments particularly effective?

HOLT
History's Impact
▶ video series
Review the video to answer the closing question:
How did some of Roosevelt's programs lessen the damage caused by the recessions of 1987 and the early 2000s?

Visual Summary

QUICK FACTS

Use the visual summary below to help you review the main ideas of the chapter.

Stock Prices Plunge

The economy began to decline when the stock market crashed in 1929.

Many farmers from the Great Plains moved elsewhere to escape the devastation of the Dust Bowl.

President Roosevelt and Congress tried to end the financial crisis.

Reviewing Vocabulary, Terms, and People

Read each question and write the letter of the best response.

1. Which of the following refers to a severe economic downturn that lasted for more than 10 years?
   a. the Bonus Army   **c.** the bull market
   b. the Great Depression **d.** the business cycle

2. Who was Franklin Roosevelt's secretary of labor and the first woman Cabinet member?
   a. Frances Perkins   **c.** Eleanor Roosevelt
   b. Mary McLeod Bethune **d.** Dorothea Lange

3. Parts of the Great Plains where a severe drought struck were known as the
   a. Tennessee Valley.   **c.** Dust Bowl.
   b. New Deal.   **d.** Hoovervilles.

4. Which of the following means purchasing stocks on credit with a loan?
   a. the installment plan **c.** the banking crisis
   b. buying on margin   **d.** bear market

Comprehension and Critical Thinking

SECTION 1 *(Pages 778–782)*

5. **a. Describe** What happened on Black Tuesday—October 29, 1929?

   b. Summarize How did President Hoover respond to the Depression?

   c. Elaborate Why do you think Americans were so unprepared for difficult times?

SECTION 2 *(Pages 784–789)*

6. **a. Recall** What New Deal programs did lawmakers create during the Hundred Days?

   b. Explain How did the Works Progress Administration help Americans?

   c. Evaluate Do you think the New Deal was successful? Explain your answer.

7. a. Recall How did the Great Depression affect Mexican Americans?

b. Contrast How did Depression-era culture show both hope and the difficulties of everyday life?

c. Draw Conclusions Why do you think many African Americans supported President Roosevelt, even though they continued to face discrimination and segregation?

Reviewing Themes

8. Economics How did the economy of the country change during the Great Depression?

9. Politics What role did politics play in easing the Great Depression?

Reading Skills

Recognizing Implied Main Ideas *Use the Reading Skills taught in this chapter to answer the question about the reading selection below.*

> Banks had invested heavily in the stock market, so they lost heavily when the market crashed. Banks had also lent their customers money to buy stocks on margin. Now those customers were unable to pay back their loans. Some banks went out of business. People who had deposited their life savings in those banks lost everything. *(p. 779)*

10. Write a main idea for the paragraph above.

Using the Internet

go.hrw.com
KEYWORD: SB7 CH25

11. Activity: Writing an Article During the 1930s, part of the Great Plains region of the United States became known as the Dust Bowl. The troubled region earned its nickname from the dust storms that swept through the dry, drought-stricken area. Enter the activity keyword. Research accounts of the Dust Bowl and write a magazine feature article about it. Your article should include references to your research and quotations from accounts of the Depression, and it should have correct spelling, punctuation, and grammar.

Social Studies Skills

Having a Debate *Use the Social Studies Skills taught in this chapter to answer the question below.*

12. Suppose you have been invited to participate in a debate on Franklin Roosevelt's plan to "pack" the Supreme Court by adding extra justices. First decide on your position. Then prepare several supporting arguments. Summarize the main points of your argument in a paragraph.

FOCUS ON WRITING

13. Writing Your Journal Entry Review your notes. Then decide on a fictional character and a set of circumstances for your character. Choose one or more events from the Great Depression for your character to talk about. Write a one-page journal entry about the life of this person. Begin by placing a date from the 1930s at the top of the page. Think about what life would have been like for this person. Remember to describe how the character feels about his or her experiences. What are your character's hopes and fears for the future?

DIRECTIONS: Read each question and write the letter of the best response.

1 **President Roosevelt successfully used his fireside chats to**

A promote the American movie industry.

B hold negotiations between labor unions and business owners.

C persuade many Americans to vote for him in the election of 1932.

D convince people that it was safe to keep their money in reopened banks.

2 **Dorothea Lange contributed to our understanding of Depression life by**

A writing novels about Dust Bowl farmers.

B singing songs about loss and hardship.

C photographing migrant workers.

D making movies that helped people forget their troubles.

3 **How did the National Labor Relations Act affect organized labor?**

A It increased the power of labor unions and helped them grow.

B It banned all strikes and increased the power of big business.

C It created new government jobs but did not affect labor unions.

D It gave relief money directly to labor unions to help unemployed workers.

4 **What part of the business cycle contributes to a depression?**

A Consumers begin buying more and companies increase production.

B Businesses produce more than they can sell and manufacturing slows.

C The stock market is a bull market and investors make large profits.

D People are buying products with cash.

5 **Which of the following was a part of the New Deal?**

A nationalizing businesses

B relieving unemployment

C guaranteeing every family an income of at least $5,000

D discouraging negotiations between labor unions and business owners

6 **Which of the following was a way many families coped with the Depression?**

A They bought stocks on margin.

B They sent their children to boarding schools in California.

C They moved to the Dust Bowl looking for farm jobs.

D They separated to look for work.

7 **Read the excerpt from John Steinbeck's *The Grapes of Wrath* and use it to answer the question below.**

> *"66 is the path of people in flight, refugees from dust and shrinking land, from the thunder of tractors and shrinking ownership, from the desert's slow northward invasion, from the twisting winds that howl up out of Texas, from the floods that bring no richness to the land and steal what little richness is there."*
>
> —John Steinbeck, *The Grapes of Wrath*

Document-Based Question Why did people travel on Highway 66, according to Steinbeck?

World War II

Virginia Standards of Learning

USII.1 The student will demonstrate skills for historical and geographical analysis, and responsible citizenship, including the ability to

a) analyze and interpret primary and secondary source documents to increase understanding of events and life in United States history from 1865 to the present; **b)** make connections between past and present; **c)** sequence events in United States history from 1865 to the present; **d)** interpret ideas and events from different historical perspectives; **e)** evaluate and debate issues orally and in writing

USII.2 The student will use maps, globes, photographs, pictures, or tables for

c) locating the 50 states and the cities most significant to the historical development of the United States

USII.7 The student will demonstrate knowledge of the major causes and effects of American involvement in World War II by

a) identifying the causes and events that led to American involvement in the war, including the attack on Pearl Harbor; **b)** locating and describing the major events and turning points of the war in Europe and the Pacific; **c)** describing the impact of World War II on the homefront

FOCUS ON WRITING

A Radio News Broadcast During World War II, millions of Americans had relatives fighting overseas. They relied on radio broadcasts for up-to-date news from the battlefronts around the world. In this chapter, you will read about American involvement in World War II. Then you will write a radio news broadcast about an event from the war.

UNITED STATES

1938 Orson Welles broadcasts "War of the Worlds."

1938

WORLD

HOLT
History's Impact
► **video series**
Watch the video to understand the impact of the GI Bill.

What You Will Learn...

In this chapter, you will learn how the United States prepared for and fought in World War II. Life changed at home, as U.S. industries worked around the clock to supply the Allied armies. Life also changed for the 16 million Americans who served in the military around the world, like these soldiers who took part in the D-Day invasion of Normandy, France.

1941 On December 7, the Japanese attack the U.S. fleet at Pearl Harbor, Hawaii.

1942 German submarines begin attacking the United States.

1944 U.S. forces participate in the D-Day invasion.

1945 The United States drops atomic bombs on Hiroshima and Nagasaki, Japan.

1940

1942

1944

1946

1940 Alan Turing devises a way to break the code of the German Enigma machine.

1943 Mussolini is overthrown and executed in Italy.

1944 The Allies enter Paris.

1945 Hideki Tojo, prime minister of Japan, attempts suicide after atomic bombs are dropped on Japan.

Reading Social Studies

by Kylene Beers

Economics | Geography | Politics | Society and Culture | Science and Technology

Focus on Themes In this chapter, you will read about the causes and consequences of World War II. You will learn about how **geography** played an important role in the fighting of the war. You will also read about how **society and culture** reacted to the Second World War.

Categorizing

Focus on Reading Have you ever read a schoolbook and been overwhelmed by the amount of information it contained? Categorizing events, people, and ideas can help you make sense of the facts you learn in this book.

Understanding Categorizing Ideas, people, events, and things can all be categorized in many different ways. For the study of history, some of the most useful ways are by time period and by similarity between events. Categorizing events by the people involved can also be helpful. Within a category, you can make subcategories to further organize the information.

People involved in WWII	Events of WWII
• Winston Churchill	• Key battles
• Franklin D. Roosevelt	• Treaties
• Adolf Hitler	• Invasions
• Benito Mussolini	⬇
• Hideki Tojo	**Invasions**
• Soldiers	• China
• Civilians	• Rhineland
	• Czechoslovakia
	• Poland
	• Dunkirk
	• French Indochina
	• D-Day

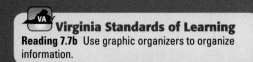
You Try It!

The following passage is from the chapter you are getting ready to read. As you read the passage, look for ways to organize the information.

Japan Advances

American and Filipino forces under the command of American general Douglas MacArthur could not stop Japan's advance in the Philippines. MacArthur left the islands in March 1942, vowing to return. More than 70,000 American and Filipino soldiers surrendered to the Japanese. The exhausted soldiers were forced to march 63 miles up the Bataan Peninsula to prison camps. Many prisoners were starved and beaten by Japanese soldiers. More than 600 Americans and about 10,000 Filipinos died in the Bataan Death March.

From Chapter 26, p. 820

After you read the passage, answer the following questions.

1. What are two categories you could use to organize the information in this passage?

2. How many different kinds of people are mentioned in this passage?

3. What different places are mentioned in this passage?

4. Complete the chart below using the information from the passage above.

People involved	Countries involved	Places mentioned

As you read Chapter 26, remember to look for categories that can help you organize the information you read.

Key Terms and People

Chapter 26

Section 1
totalitarianism (p. 804)
Benito Mussolini (p. 804)
fascism (p. 804)
Adolf Hitler (p. 805)
Nazis (p. 805)
Joseph Stalin (p. 805)
Axis Powers (p. 806)
appeasement (p. 806)
Winston Churchill (p. 806)
Allied Powers (p. 806)
Lend-Lease Act (p. 808)
Pearl Harbor (p. 808)

Section 2
War Production Board (p. 810)
A. Philip Randolph (p. 812)
Tuskegee Airmen (p. 812)
Benjamin O. Davis Jr. (p. 812)
zoot-suit riots (p. 813)
internment (p. 813)

Section 3
Battle of El Alamein (p. 816)
Dwight D. Eisenhower (p. 816)
Battle of Stalingrad (p. 817)
D-Day (p. 819)

Section 4
Douglas MacArthur (p. 820)
Bataan Death March (p. 820)
Chester Nimitz (p. 821)
Battle of the Coral Sea (p. 821)
Battle of Midway (p. 821)
island hopping (p. 822)
Battle of Leyte Gulf (p. 822)
kamikaze (p. 822)

Section 5
Battle of the Bulge (p. 826)
Harry S. Truman (p. 826)
Holocaust (p. 827)
genocide (p. 827)
Manhattan Project (p. 828)
atomic bomb (p. 828)

Academic Vocabulary
In this chapter, you will learn the following academic word:
execute (p. 822)

The War Begins

Virginia Standards of Learning USII.1a, USII.1b, USII.2c, USII.7a, USII.7b, USII.7c

What You Will Learn...

Main Ideas

1. During the 1930s, totalitarian governments rose to power in Europe and Japan.
2. German expansion led to the start of World War II in Europe in 1939.
3. The United States joined the war after Japan attacked Pearl Harbor in 1941.

The Big Idea

The rise of aggressive totalitarian governments led to the start of World War II.

Key Terms and People

totalitarianism, p. 804
Benito Mussolini, p. 804
fascism, p. 804
Adolf Hitler, p. 805
Nazis, p. 805
Joseph Stalin, p. 805
Axis Powers, p. 806
appeasement, p. 806
Winston Churchill, p. 806
Allied Powers, p. 806
Lend-Lease Act, p. 808
Pearl Harbor, p. 808

TAKING NOTES As you read, take notes on the countries in which totalitarian governments gained power before World War II. Use a graphic organizer like the one below.

Totalitarianism before WW II	
Country	Leader

If YOU were there...

The year is 1933 and your family is struggling through the Great Depression along with millions of others. Sometimes your parents wonder if they should have left Italy to come to the United States. But conditions in Italy are far from ideal. A dictator rules the country, and the people have little personal freedom.

What would you say to your parents?

BUILDING BACKGROUND The devastating effects of the Great Depression reached well beyond the United States. In Europe, war debt and the huge costs of rebuilding after World War I made economic recovery even more difficult.

The Rise of Totalitarianism

Desperate to end the hard times, many people were willing to give up their individual rights to leaders who promised to deliver prosperity and national glory. As a result, in the 1920s and 1930s, several European countries moved toward **totalitarianism**, a political system in which the government controls every aspect of citizens' lives.

Italy

In the years after World War I, the people of Italy suffered through economic depression, unemployment, strikes, and riots. Many Italians looked for a strong leader who could bring stability to the country. They found such a leader in **Benito Mussolini**, who gained complete control of Italy in 1922. Mussolini's rule was based on **fascism**, a political system in which the "state"—or government—is seen as more important than individuals. Fascist systems are typically militaristic and headed by a strong leader.

Mussolini restored order to Italy and improved the economy through public works projects. But the fascist government violently crushed all opposition, destroying basic individual rights such as freedom of speech. In 1935 Mussolini tried to expand Italy's territory by attacking the nation of Ethiopia, making it a colony. Haile Selassie, Ethiopia's overthrown emperor, warned the world, "It is us today. It will be you tomorrow."

Germany

Germany was also suffering the effects of the global depression. In addition, many Germans were furious about the Treaty of Versailles, which forced Germany to make crippling reparation payments for its role in World War I. Politician and World War I veteran **Adolf Hitler** took advantage of public anger to gain power. A fiery speaker, he inspired huge audiences by vowing to restore Germany to prosperity and a position of international power.

Hitler also offered Germans a scapegoat, or someone to blame for their problems. He accused intellectuals, Communists, and especially Jews of causing Germany's defeat in World War I and its economic problems after the war. Only by ridding itself of Jews, Hitler declared, would Germany again rise to greatness. Hitler's National Socialist Party, or **Nazis**, gained a large following. Hitler became chancellor in 1933 and quickly seized all government power.

The Soviet Union

Hitler spoke with fury of his hatred of communism. But he had something in common with the Communist ruler of the Soviet Union—both ruled as ruthless dictators. By 1928 **Joseph Stalin** had become dictator of the Soviet Union. In the 1930s Stalin terrorized those he saw as political enemies, killing or imprisoning millions of Soviet citizens. As one Soviet artist put it, "There isn't a single thinking adult in this country who hasn't thought that he might get shot."

Japan

Though Japan never had one single dictator, a group of military leaders slowly gained complete control over the government during the early 1900s. By the early 1930s this group had more influence than the Japanese emperor. The military leaders wanted to build a large Japanese empire in East Asia. In 1931 Japan invaded and conquered a region in northern China and called it Manchukuo. From 1937 to 1938, at least 360,000 Chinese were killed by the invading Japanese in the fall of Nanjing. The United States protested the invasion. Fearful of another world war, however, most Americans opposed using force to help China.

READING CHECK **Comparing and Contrasting**
What did the leaders of totalitarian governments have in common?

Germany Expands

Hitler dreamed of avenging Germany's defeat in World War I. "The lost land will never be won back by solemn appeals to God," he told Germans, "nor by hopes in any League of Nations, but only by force of arms." Hitler wanted to build an empire, uniting all German-speaking people in Europe. He also wanted "living space" for the growing German population.

In violation of the Treaty of Versailles, Hitler began to rebuild the German military. In 1936 Nazi troops invaded the Rhineland, a former German territory lost during World War I. That year he also signed an alliance with Mussolini, forming the **Axis Powers**. Japan later joined this pact. In 1938 Hitler forced Austria to unite with Germany. Then he demanded control of the Sudetenland, a region in Czechoslovakia where many Germans lived. When the Czechs refused, Hitler threatened war.

Nazi planes bombed London from September 1940 to May 1941. During that time, residents of London sought shelter wherever they could, including subway stations. Here, a relief effort passes out food to Londoners who have lost their homes.

Appeasement Fails

Czech leaders looked to their allies in France and Great Britain for help. But neither country wanted to be pulled into an armed conflict. British prime minister Neville Chamberlain organized a meeting with Hitler to work out a peaceful solution. At the 1938 Munich Conference, Germany was given control over the Sudetenland in return for a promise not to demand more land. This approach was known as **appeasement**—a policy of avoiding war with an aggressive nation by giving in to its demands. British admiral **Winston Churchill** was convinced that this strategy would not stop Hitler. "The government had to choose between shame and war," Churchill warned. "They have chosen shame. They will get war."

Churchill was right. In March 1939, German troops seized the rest of Czechoslovakia and began demanding territory from Poland. Great Britain and France pledged to defend Poland if Hitler attacked. To keep the Soviets out of the conflict, Hitler signed a nonaggression pact with Joseph Stalin in August 1939. In addition to promising not to attack each other, the two countries secretly agreed to divide Poland between them.

On September 1, 1939, Hitler's troops and tanks rushed into Poland. This was the start of World War II. Two days later, Britain and France, known as the **Allied Powers**, declared war on Germany. Neville Chamberlain spoke bitterly of the failure of appeasement, saying, "Everything that I believed in during my public life has crashed into ruins."

Hitler Moves West

The Allied Powers had little time to organize their forces to protect Poland. Using a strategy called *blitzkrieg,* or "lightning war," German tanks and airplanes broke through Polish defenses. As German forces drove into Poland from the west, the Soviets attacked from the east. Within a month, the two powers had taken control of Poland.

With Poland secure, Hitler turned toward western Europe. In the spring of 1940, Germany quickly conquered Denmark, Norway,

World War II in Europe, 1939–1941

Interactive Map

Axis Powers
Axis control
Allied Powers
Allied control
Neutral countries
Area of the Battle of Britain
Farthest Soviet advance, 1940
Axis advances
Maginot Line

0   100   200 Miles
0   100   200 Kilometers

GEOGRAPHY SKILLS **INTERPRETING MAPS**

go.hrw.com
Interactive Map
KEYWORD: SB7 CH26

1. **Place** Which countries shown on the map remained neutral during World War II?
2. **Human-Environment Interaction** What major British city was affected by the Battle of Britain?

Belgium, Luxembourg, and the Netherlands. German troops then invaded France, trapping hundreds of thousands of Belgian, British, and French soldiers in the French port city of Dunkirk. British ships raced to Dunkirk and carried the soldiers across the English Channel to safety in Britain.

German forces, meanwhile, continued their march through France. As the Germans approached the French capital of Paris, Italy declared war on the Allied powers. France surrendered to Germany on June 22, 1940. Many of the French soldiers who had escaped at Dunkirk, however, continued to resist Germany's occupation of France. In London, French general Charles de Gaulle organized a "Free French" army to fight alongside the Allies. "France has lost a battle," de Gaulle declared. "But France has not lost the war!"

The Battle of Britain

Great Britain now stood alone against Hitler's war machine. "The final German victory over

England is now only a question of time," said German general Alfred Jodl. Hitler prepared to invade Britain. To safely move troops and equipment across the English Channel, Germany first had to defeat the British Royal Air Force (RAF). In July 1940 the Luftwaffe, or German air force, began attacking British planes and airfields in what became known as the Battle of Britain.

In August Hitler ordered the Luftwaffe to begin bombing British cities in the hope of crushing British morale. But Winston Churchill, the new prime minister, refused to give in. "We shall fight on the beaches," he vowed. "We shall fight in the fields and in the streets, we shall never surrender." Using the new technology of radar, the RAF was able to detect and destroy some 2,300 of the Luftwaffe's aircraft. Hitler canceled the invasion of Britain.

READING CHECK **Sequencing** What event sparked World War II?

The United States Joins the War

Most Americans opposed Hitler's actions, but they did not want to join the war. When President Franklin Roosevelt ran for re-election in 1940, he told voters that "your boys are not going to be sent into any foreign wars." Privately, however, Roosevelt was convinced that the United States would soon be at war.

Helping the Allies

In 1941 Roosevelt proposed new programs to assist the Allies. "We must be the great arsenal [arms supply] of democracy," he told Congress. In March 1941 Congress passed the **Lend-Lease Act**, allowing the president to aid any nation believed vital to U.S. defense. Under Lend-Lease, the United States sent billions of dollars' worth of aid in the form of weapons, tanks, airplanes, and food to Great Britain, the Nationalists in China, and other Allied countries. In June 1941 Hitler violated his nonaggression pact with Stalin and invaded the Soviet Union. The Soviets then joined the Allies in the fight against Germany. In November the United States extended the Lend-Lease program to the Soviet Union, though many Americans worried about giving aid to a Communist country.

Japan Attacks Pearl Harbor

Like Germany and Italy, Japan was quickly building an empire. After conquering much of China in the 1930s, Japanese forces moved into Southeast Asia. Japan's leaders wanted control of oil and other resources there.

When Japanese forces captured French Indochina in July 1941, Roosevelt protested. He demanded that Japan withdraw. Then the United States froze Japanese funds in its banks and cut off exports to Japan.

Japanese military leaders had already begun planning a large-scale attack to destroy the U.S. naval fleet stationed at **Pearl Harbor**, in Hawaii. This would give Japan time to secure control of East Asia before the U.S. military could respond.

Pearl Harbor, 1941 — Interactive Map

Japanese forces bombarded the American naval fleet for several hours in the attack on Pearl Harbor. Eighteen ships were hit, and more than 2,400 Americans were killed.

The first Japanese aircraft take off at 6 a.m. on December 7.

Japanese submarines deployed December 6.

Japanese territory

Route of Japanese aircraft carriers

0   500   1,000 Miles
0   500   1,000 Kilometers

November 26 — 2,900 miles — December 3 — 800 miles — 3,300 miles — December 16 — 1,000 miles — December 6 — 700 miles — December 7 — December 8 — Wake Island — December 23 — 2,400 miles — Midway Islands — Pearl Harbor — Oahu — HAWAII

Sea of Okhotsk — Kuril Islands — PACIFIC OCEAN — Bering Sea — Aleutian Islands — International Date Line — ALASKA

MANCHUKUO — Sea of Japan — KOREA — JAPAN — Tokyo — 30°N — Tropic of Cancer — 180° — 150°W

GEOGRAPHY SKILLS   INTERPRETING MAPS

go.hrw.com
Interactive Map
KEYWORD: SB7 CH26

1. **Place** How many miles is it from Pearl Harbor to Tokyo?
2. **Movement** From where did the Japanese fleet leave on November 26?

At 7:55 A.M. on Sunday, December 7, 1941, Japanese airplanes dove from the sky and attacked Pearl Harbor. An American sailor aboard the USS *Arizona* remembered how quickly his battleship was hit and destroyed:

"I began to realize there were dead men all around me . . . it was obvious the ship was doomed. I made my way to the side of the ship, which by this time was sinking fast, and jumped off."

—George D. Phraner, quoted in *World War II,* by H. P. Willmott

In just a few hours, the Japanese sank or damaged all of the battleships anchored at Pearl Harbor. More than 2,400 Americans were killed. Almost 200 airplanes were destroyed.

Speaking to Congress the next day, President Roosevelt called December 7, 1941, "a date which will live in infamy [disgrace]." Congress voted to declare war on Japan. Germany then declared war on the United States. Less than 25 years after entering World War I, the United States joined the Allies in another global war. This one would be even more devastating.

BIOGRAPHY

Daniel Inouye
1924–

Daniel Inouye was born in Honolulu, Hawaii, to Japanese parents. When the Japanese attacked Pearl Harbor, the 17-year-old Inouye used his medical aid training to help treat victims. He joined the army the next year, winning several medals for bravery in combat. In an attack in Italy, Inouye was shot three times, and his right arm had to be amputated. After the war, Inouye studied law and entered politics. In 1959 he became Hawaii's first representative in Congress, as well as the first Japanese American to serve in Congress. He was elected to the U.S. Senate in 1962 and became an important figure in U.S. politics.

Drawing Conclusions Why do you think Inouye went into politics?

READING CHECK **Identifying Cause and Effect** What did Japan hope to gain by attacking Pearl Harbor?

SUMMARY AND PREVIEW Military aggression in Europe and Asia drew the United States into war. In the next section you will learn how the war affected the home front.

Section 1 Assessment

go.hrw.com
Online Quiz
KEYWORD: SB7 HP26

Reviewing Ideas, Terms, and People

1. **a. Identify** What types of leaders came to power in Italy, Germany, and the Soviet Union before World War II?
   b. Explain Why did some Europeans have faith in these leaders?
2. **a. Summarize** What did **Adolf Hitler** promise the German people, and how did he act on this promise?
   b. Recall Which countries formed the **Axis Powers** and the **Allied Powers**?
   c. Elaborate Do you think **Winston Churchill** was a good choice for Britain's prime minister? Explain your answer.
3. **a. Explain** What event brought the United States into World War II?
   b. Describe How did the **Lend-Lease Act** help the Allies?

Critical Thinking

4. **Identifying Cause and Effect** Review your notes on totalitarian countries and their leaders prior to World War II. Then copy the graphic organizer below and use it to give details on the causes of World War II.

Causes of WWII

FOCUS ON WRITING

5. **Taking Notes on Pearl Harbor** Look back at what you have read about the attack on Pearl Harbor. Take notes on who attacked Pearl Harbor, where the attack took place, and when. What were the results of the attack?

The Home Front

What You Will Learn...

Main Ideas

1. Businesses, soldiers, and citizens worked to prepare the United States for war.
2. The war brought new opportunities for many women and minorities.
3. Japanese Americans faced internment during the war.

The Big Idea

American involvement in World War II helped the U.S. economy and changed the lives of many Americans.

Key Terms and People

War Production Board, *p. 810*
A. Philip Randolph, *p. 812*
Tuskegee Airmen, *p. 812*
Benjamin O. Davis Jr., *p. 812*
zoot-suit riots, *p. 813*
internment, *p. 813*

TAKING NOTES As you read, look for information about how the war brought both opportunities and challenges to minorities. Record your notes in a graphic organizer like the one below.

Opportunities   Challenges

If YOU were there...

Shopping for food has become a whole new experience since the United States entered World War II. When your mother sends you to the grocery store these days, she gives you government-issued ration stamps. These stamps limit the amount of sugar, butter, and meat each family can buy. The sacrifice is difficult, but you know it will help the soldiers fighting overseas.

In what other ways can you help the war effort?

BUILDING BACKGROUND As World War II raged in 1940 and 1941, the Allies relied on war supplies and food from the United States. President Roosevelt and Congress also increased defense spending at home, believing that the United States would soon join the fighting. The increased spending boosted the U.S. economy.

Preparing for War

The United States was still experiencing the effects of the Great Depression when the Japanese attacked Pearl Harbor in December 1941. The enormous effort of mobilizing for war finally brought the Depression to an end. Factories ran 24 hours a day, producing ships, tanks, jeeps, guns, and ammunition. Americans turned their knowledge of mass production toward the production of war supplies. One remarkable example was the building of Liberty ships—transport vessels for troops and supplies. Workers could build an entire 441-foot-long Liberty ship in as little as four days.

American workers were soon doubling the war production of Germany, Japan, and all other Axis Power countries combined. Unemployment fell to 1 percent in 1944. Agricultural production increased as well, as farmers sent food overseas to feed Allied soldiers. To organize the war effort, the government created the **War Production Board** (WPB) to oversee the conversion of factories to war production. In 1942, for example, the WPB banned the production of cars so that auto plants could produce military equipment.

The United States also needed millions of soldiers. Congress had begun to prepare for war by passing the Selective Training and Service Act in 1940. This was the first peacetime draft in the country's history.

Men from the ages of 21 to 35 (later 18 to 38) were required to register for the draft. More than 16 million Americans served during the war.

To finance the war effort, the government increased taxes and sold war bonds. War bonds were essentially loans that people made to the government. People who bought war bonds in 1942, for example, would get their money back 10 years later, with interest.

Americans also contributed to the war effort by collecting scrap metal that could be used in weapons factories. People learned to adjust to government rations limiting the supply of gasoline, rubber, shoes, and some foods. Posters urged Americans to "Use it up, wear it out, make it do, or do without."

READING CHECK **Identifying Cause and Effect**
How did the war affect the U.S. economy?

Wartime Opportunities

You read that wartime production during World War I created new opportunities for many women and minorities. The same thing happened on an even larger scale during World War II.

New Roles for Women

With so many men leaving home to fight in World War II, factories badly needed new workers. The government urged women to fill these positions. Women found themselves doing work that had traditionally been considered "unladylike." One female riveter (a person who fastens parts on a machine) recalled her experiences building airplanes:

" [I] learned to use an electric drill . . . and I soon became an outstanding riveter . . . The war really created opportunities for women. It was the first time we got a chance to show that we could do a lot of things that only men had done before."

—Winona Espinosa, quoted in *Ordinary Americans*, edited by Linda Monk

Women also filled new roles in military service. About 300,000 women served in the armed forces through special divisions such as the Women's Auxiliary Army Corps (WAAC) and Women's Airforce Service Pilots (WASP). WASP pilots flew test flights and ferried planes between factories and air bases. Army and navy nurses served in combat areas.

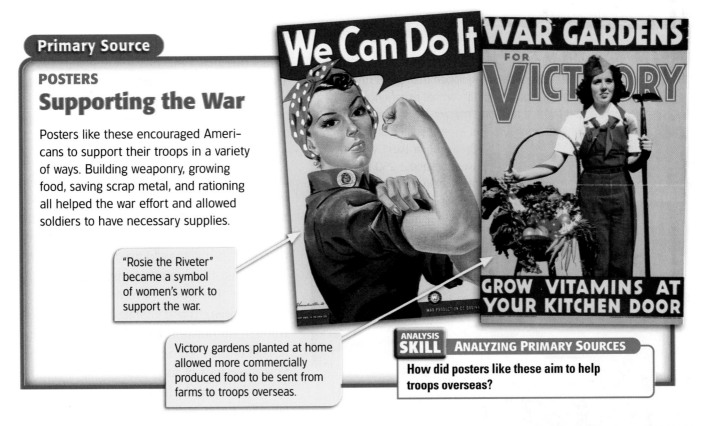

Primary Source

POSTERS
Supporting the War

Posters like these encouraged Americans to support their troops in a variety of ways. Building weaponry, growing food, saving scrap metal, and rationing all helped the war effort and allowed soldiers to have necessary supplies.

"Rosie the Riveter" became a symbol of women's work to support the war.

Victory gardens planted at home allowed more commercially produced food to be sent from farms to troops overseas.

ANALYSIS SKILL **ANALYZING PRIMARY SOURCES**
How did posters like these aim to help troops overseas?

African Americans

The Great Migration that began during World War I continued as African Americans moved to northern cities to find factory jobs. In most cases, however, black workers received lower pay than did white workers. They also were restricted in what kinds of jobs they were hired to perform.

To protest this unfair treatment, African American labor leader **A. Philip Randolph** began to organize a march to Washington, D.C., in 1941. "If freedom and equality are not [granted for] the peoples of color, the war for democracy will not be won," he argued. Randolph canceled the march, however, after President Roosevelt issued an order prohibiting racial discrimination in the government and in companies producing war goods.

FOR COLORED ONLY

Primary Source

AUTOBIOGRAPHY
Tuskegee Airmen

Benjamin O. Davis was a graduate of West Point who became the first African American Air Force officer to achieve the rank of general. During World War II he led the first African American flying unit, the 99th Fighting Squadron. These men had been trained at the Tuskegee Institute in Alabama.

"While no AAF [American Air Force] unit had gone into combat better trained or better equipped than the 99th Fighter Squadron, we lacked actual combat experience. So as we approached our first missions, my own inexperience and that of my flight commanders was a major source of concern. On the other hand, we had averaged about 250 hours per man in a P-40 (quite a lot for pilots who had not yet flown their first missions), and we possessed an unusually strong sense of purpose and solidarity."

—Benjamin O. Davis,
*Benjamin O. Davis,
American: An Autobiography*

ANALYSIS SKILL **ANALYZING PRIMARY SOURCES**

What advantages did the Tuskegee airmen bring to battle?

About 1 million African Americans served in the armed forces during the war, mostly in segregated units. In the Navy, African Americans were assigned only to support positions and denied the right to participate in combat. Despite this, many black soldiers became national heroes during the war, including Dorie Miller. Leaving his post as ship's cook, Miller manned a machine gun on the deck of the USS *West Virginia* until he was ordered to abandon the ship because it was sinking.

The **Tuskegee Airmen** were African American pilots who trained at the Tuskegee Army Air Field in Alabama. **Benjamin O. Davis Jr.**, who later became the first African American general in the U.S. Air Force, led the group. Davis and his pilots had to overcome prejudice in the military as well as the hazards of war. He later described the pilots as "outstanding Americans who served their country unselfishly. Despite treatment that would have demoralized men of lesser strength and character, they persisted through humiliations and dangers to earn the respect of their fellows." The Tuskegee Airmen flew thousands of successful combat missions in North Africa and Italy.

Japanese American Internment

- Not interned 6%
- Japanese citizens living in America interned 37%
- American citizens of Japanese descent interned 57%

Mexican Americans

About 300,000 Mexican Americans served in the military during the war. Many Mexican Americans also found wartime jobs on the West Coast and in the Midwest. Because of a shortage of farm workers, the federal government asked Mexico to provide agricultural workers. The workers, called *braceros*, were guaranteed a minimum wage, food, shelter, and clean living conditions. About 200,000 Mexicans worked in the *bracero* program.

Young Mexican Americans of the time created their own culture by blending different music styles and clothing styles. Some men wore zoot suits—fancy, loose-fitting outfits with oversized hats. Despite their aiding of the war effort, many faced discrimination. In Los Angeles in June 1943, groups of sailors attacked Mexican Americans wearing zoot suits, beginning the **zoot-suit riots**. During the 10-day period, white mobs attacked many Mexican Americans.

READING CHECK **Evaluating** How did the war create both opportunities and challenges for minorities?

Japanese American Internment

Japanese Americans faced a different form of prejudice during World War II. After the Japanese attack on Pearl Harbor, some Americans began to look at Americans of Japanese descent with fear and suspicion. Most Japanese Americans lived on the West Coast at this time. It was feared that they would serve as secret agents for Japan and help Japan prepare an invasion of the West Coast or try to sabotage U.S. war efforts.

The U.S. government had no evidence to support these fears. In spite of this fact, President Roosevelt issued Executive Order 9066. This order allowed the government to begin the process of **internment**, or forced relocation and imprisonment, of Japanese Americans. About 115,000 Japanese Americans were evacuated from their homes and held in isolated internment camps. Half of those held in the camps were children. A smaller number of Americans of German and Italian ancestry were also held in internment camps during the war.

THE IMPACT TODAY

Congress passed the Civil Liberties Act of 1988 to compensate victims of internment. Each living Japanese American who had been interned—60,000 in all—received $20,000 and a formal apology signed by President Ronald Reagan.

At this time, some Japanese Americans were *Issei*, or immigrants born in Japan. But most were *Nisei*, American citizens born in the United States to Japanese immigrant parents. Whether they were U.S. citizens or not, Japanese Americans lost their jobs, homes, and belongings when they were forced to move to internment camps. A farm owner named Yuri Tateishi spoke of feeling betrayed by his government. "You hurt," he said. "You give up everything that you worked for that far, and I think everybody was at the point of just having gotten out of the Depression and was just getting on his feet. And then all that happens! You have to throw everything away."

After the Pearl Harbor attack, the government banned young Japanese American men from serving in the military. But Roosevelt reversed this policy in 1943. Daniel Inouye remembered the excitement he and his fellow Japanese Americans in Hawaii felt when they heard that the government was going to form an all-*Nisei* combat team. An army recruiter had prepared a pep talk for the young Japanese Americans, but this proved to be unnecessary:

"As soon as he said that we were now eligible to volunteer, that room exploded into a fury of yells and motion. We went bursting out of there and ran—ran!—the three miles to the draft board ... jostling for position, like a bunch of marathoners gone berserk."

—Daniel Inouye, quoted in *Only What We Could Carry*, edited by Lawson Fusao Inada

Inouye was one of about 33,000 *Nisei* who served in World War II. The Japanese American 100th/442nd Regimental Combat Team received more than 18,000 decorations for bravery—more than any other unit of its size in U.S. military history. Many of the soldiers of the 100th/442nd served while their families were held in internment camps back home.

READING CHECK **Evaluating** Why were Japanese Americans interned?

SUMMARY AND PREVIEW The war effort changed life on the home front. In the next section you will learn about the fighting in Europe and North Africa.

Section 2 Assessment

go.hrw.com
Online Quiz
KEYWORD: SB7 HP26

Reviewing Ideas, Terms, and People

1. **a. Describe** How did people on the home front support the war effort?
   b. Identify What government agency oversaw factory production during the war?
2. **a. Recall** What were the WAAC and the WASP?
   b. Explain Why did **A. Philip Randolph** organize a march on Washington and then cancel it?
   c. Elaborate How did the *bracero* program benefit both Mexicans and Americans?
3. **a. Define** What was the **internment** program?
   b. Contrast How did the U.S. government change its policy toward Japanese Americans serving in the military? How did many respond?

Critical Thinking

4. **Categorizing** Review your notes on challenges and opportunities for different groups of people in America during World War II. Then copy the graphic organizer below and use it to list opportunities that women, African Americans, and Mexican Americans found during the war.

Wartime Opportunities

Women	African Americans	Mexican Americans

FOCUS ON WRITING

5. **Taking Notes on the Home Front** Radio broadcasts often reminded Americans to "Do your part" in winning World War II. Take notes on the ways ordinary citizens helped the troops by supporting the war effort on the home front. How might you convince someone to support the effort?

War in Europe and North Africa

If YOU were there...

The year is 1943 and you are a senior in high school. You know that you will be drafted into the armed forces as soon as you graduate. Every day after school you listen to radio reports about the battles being fought around the world. Your future, and the future of the whole world, seems so uncertain.

How do you feel about fighting in this war?

BUILDING BACKGROUND By the time the United States entered the war, the Allies were in trouble. The Axis Powers controlled much of western Europe and were advancing in North Africa and the Soviet Union. German submarine attacks on Allied ships were making it difficult to get American supplies to the British.

The Allies Fight Back

In December 1941, soon after the United States entered the war, President Roosevelt met with British prime minister Winston Churchill to work out a plan to defeat the Axis Powers. Roosevelt agreed that the United States would place "Europe first" in its plans to defeat the Axis, while still aiding China in the fight against Japan in the Pacific. In addition, Roosevelt and Churchill agreed on two initial strategies: a buildup of troops in Great Britain to be used to invade France, and an assault on German forces in North Africa.

Meanwhile, the Soviets had been demanding Allied help on the eastern front, where they had borne the brunt of the European war for months after Hitler's invasion. Stalin wanted the Allies to attack

The Allies began using sonar to destroy German U-boats, shown here in a German harbor.

What You Will Learn...

Main Ideas
1. The Allies fought back against the Axis Powers in North Africa and Europe.
2. Key Allied victories halted the German advance.
3. In the D-Day invasion, Allied forces attacked German-controlled France.

The Big Idea
After fierce fighting in North Africa and Europe, the Allies stopped the German advance and slowly began driving back German forces.

Key Terms and People
Battle of El Alamein, *p. 816*
Dwight D. Eisenhower, *p. 816*
Battle of Stalingrad, *p. 817*
D-Day, *p. 819*

TAKING NOTES As you read, make a list of the major battles and campaigns in different areas of the world. You may want to organize your list in a table like this one.

North Africa	Italy	Eastern Europe	Western Europe

in Europe immediately, to take some of the pressure off of the Soviet forces in the east. In July 1942, however, the Allies decided to put a European invasion on hold and launch an initial offensive in North Africa. Stalin was angry. The Soviets would have to continue to fight the war on the eastern front without a western European assault to distract the Germans.

FOCUS ON READING
What categories could you use to organize the information in this paragraph?

As they prepared their battle plans, the Allies faced many obstacles. One major threat the Allies had to combat was U-boat attacks. In 1942 alone German U-boats sank more than 6,000,000 tons of Allied materials. To prevent further damage, the Allies used the convoy system of multiple ships traveling at once, along with new sonar technology. Sonar, which uses sound waves to detect objects underwater, helped Allied ships find and destroy German U-boats. In addition, new long-range Allied planes protected the convoys from the air. Long-range planes could also fly into German territory to drop bombs on factories, railroads, and cities, inflicting tremendous damage on German targets.

 READING CHECK **Explaining** What battle plan did the Allies agree to pursue after American entry into the war?

BIOGRAPHY
Dwight D. Eisenhower
1890–1969

Dwight D. Eisenhower was born in Denison, Texas. "Ike," as his friends called him, attended the U.S. Military Academy at West Point and trained soldiers for tank warfare during World War I. With a strong ability to organize and plan strategies, as well as a persuasive and optimistic personality, Eisenhower rose to the rank of general during World War II. He was named supreme commander of Allied forces in western Europe in 1943. His standing as a war hero helped him win the presidential elections of 1952 and 1956.

Drawing Inferences What were some of Eisenhower's strengths?

Halting the German Advance

Churchill predicted that the road to victory would be long and difficult. By winning several key battles, however, Allied forces finally stopped the German advance.

North Africa and Italy

As you have read, a main focus for the Allies when the United States entered the war was North Africa. The Germans and British were battling for control there because Axis leaders wanted to grab control of the Suez Canal, a crucial supply route in Egypt. Germany's Afrika Korps was led by General Erwin Rommel, nicknamed the Desert Fox for his bold, surprise attacks.

In the summer of 1942, Rommel began an offensive to take Egypt. General Bernard Montgomery led the British forces to stop the Germans. The British stopped the Afrika Korps in July at the **Battle of El Alamein**. At the same time, U.S. and British troops, led by American general **Dwight D. Eisenhower**, came ashore in Morocco and Algeria, west of Egypt. Caught between two Allied forces, the Afrika Korps surrendered in May 1943.

With North Africa under their control, the Allies prepared to attack the Axis Powers in Europe. Churchill identified Italy as the "soft underbelly" of the Axis. Allied forces invaded the island of Sicily in July 1943 and moved from there to the Italian mainland. Italian leaders overthrew Mussolini and surrendered to the Allies. But Hitler refused to recognize the Axis defeat. He sent German troops to Italy to block the Allied advance.

In January 1944, Allied forces tried to get behind the Germans with a surprise attack at Anzio, on the western coast of Italy. American and British troops landed at Anzio but were pinned down on the beach for several months. The "soft underbelly" proved to be much tougher than expected. Finally, the Allied forces in southern Italy battled north to Anzio. The combined forces captured Rome, the capital of Italy, in June

Winston Churchill
Prime Minister of
Great Britain

Franklin Roosevelt
President of
the United States

Joseph Stalin
Premier of
the Soviet Union

Adolf Hitler
Chancellor of
Germany

Benito Mussolini
Prime Minister
of Italy

1944. Early in 1945, German forces were driven out of Italy. Italian freedom fighters executed Mussolini.

The Battle of Stalingrad

Meanwhile, massive German and Soviet armies were battling on the eastern front. By the middle of 1942, Axis armies had driven deep into Soviet territory. Millions of Soviet soldiers had been killed or captured.

German forces then advanced to the key industrial city of Stalingrad. German firebombs set much of the city on fire. But Soviet leader Joseph Stalin was determined to hold on to Stalingrad at all costs. Savage street fighting dragged on for months. Soviet snipers used the ruined buildings to their advantage, firing at German soldiers from behind piles of stone and brick.

German supplies began to run desperately low as the harsh Russian winter began. Hitler remained obsessed with capturing Stalingrad, however. He ordered his troops to keep fighting, though he did not send enough new supplies or soldiers. Thousands of Germans froze or starved to death. In late January 1943 the German commander at Stalingrad defied Hitler and surrendered to save his remaining troops. The **Battle of Stalingrad** thus became a key turning point of the war.

The Soviet victory came at an enormous cost—more than 1 million Soviet soldiers died at Stalingrad. About 800,000 Axis soldiers were killed. After Stalingrad, the Soviets won another victory in the city of Kursk, in the biggest tank battle ever fought. The Axis Powers now began to retreat from the Soviet Union. The tide of the war in the east had turned.

READING CHECK **Sequencing** What events led to the Allied victories in Italy and Russia?

The D-Day Invasion

After hard-fought victories in North Africa and Italy, the Allies were ready for an even tougher task—the invasion of German-occupied France. This was the first step toward the goal of liberating Europe and forcing Hitler to surrender.

World War II in Europe, 1942–1945

Interactive Map

Legend:
- Axis controlled, June 1944
- Allied controlled, June 1944
- Neutral country
- Farthest Axis advance, 1942
- Allied advance
- Major battle
- Allied air attack

0   150   300 Miles
0   150   300 Kilometers

Tanks thundered across Europe, destroying much of what lay in their paths.

Airplanes dropped millions of bombs on opposing forces. They were also used for moving troops and for spying on the enemy.

**Map labels:**
FINLAND · Leningrad · NORWAY · SWEDEN · DENMARK · North Sea · Baltic Sea · GREAT BRITAIN · London · Antwerp · English Channel · BELGIUM · NETHERLANDS · Elbe River · Berlin Apr.–May 1945 · Oder River · Vistula River · SOVIET UNION · Stalingrad Nov. 1942–Feb. 1943 · D-Day June 1944 · Paris · Battle of the Bulge Dec, 1944 · GERMANY · Rhine River · Danube River · SLOVAKIA · HUNGARY · ROMANIA · ATLANTIC OCEAN · FRANCE · SWITZERLAND · AUSTRIA · AUG. 1944 · VICHY FRANCE · CROATIA · SERBIA · BULGARIA · MONTENEGRO · ALBANIA · PORTUGAL · SPAIN · Corsica · Rome · Anzio Jan. 1944 · ITALY · Adriatic Sea · GREECE · Aegean Sea · GIBRALTAR (BR) · Sardinia · NOV. 1942 · SPANISH MOROCCO · NOV. 1942 · Sicily · SEPT. 1943 · Malta · Mediterranean Sea · Crete · MOROCCO · ALGERIA · TUNISIA · JULY 1943 · LIBYA · El Alamein Oct.–Nov. 1942 · EGYPT

go.hrw.com
Interactive Map
KEYWORD: SB7 CH26

1942

July 1942
Allies win the Battle of El Alamein.

February 1943
Final German troops surrender at Stalingrad.

May 1943
Axis forces in North Africa surrender.

July 1943
Allies begin an invasion of Sicily.

Dwight Eisenhower was in charge of planning what would be the largest sea-to-land invasion ever attempted. Eisenhower knew that German forces were expecting an invasion of France. The Germans had planted mines and stretched barbed wire along the French coastline. Heavily armed German soldiers waited on the beaches in bombproof bunkers. Eisenhower warned his troops of the danger but expressed confidence in their ability to succeed. "The hopes and prayers of liberty-loving people everywhere march with you," he told them.

American, British, and Canadian troops invaded France on June 6, 1944—known as **D-Day**, or "designated day." They crossed the choppy waters of the English Channel and landed on five beaches in Normandy. More than 6,000 ships, 11,000 planes, and 156,000 men were part of the invasion. Soldiers jumped from boats and waded ashore, often under heavy fire.

The Americans landed on two beaches, codenamed Utah and Omaha. Fighting was especially fierce on Omaha Beach, where almost 3,000 men were killed or wounded. "The entire beach was strewn with mines," wrote one U.S. soldier to his wife. "With a stream of lead coming towards us, we were at the mercy of the Germans."

By the end of D-Day, all five beaches were secured. The Allies then began driving east through French villages and countryside toward Germany.

READING CHECK Summarizing What was the goal of the D-Day invasion?

SUMMARY AND PREVIEW Allied victories led to the D-Day invasion. In the next section you will read about the Pacific war.

June 5, 1944 Allies capture Rome.

June 6, 1944 Allied forces invade France on D-Day.

1945

American soldiers landed on the beaches of Normandy during the D-Day invasion.

go.hrw.com

Section 3 Assessment

Online Quiz KEYWORD: SB7 HP26

Reviewing Ideas, Terms, and People

1. a. **Describe** What new strategies did the Allies use in the fight in Europe and North Africa?
   b. **Draw Conclusions** Why was it important for no individual Allied Power to make peace with the Axis countries?
2. a. **Recall** What role did **Dwight D. Eisenhower** play in the North Africa campaign?
   b. **Analyze** Why did the Allies decide to invade North Africa and Italy?
   c. **Evaluate** Why do you think people call the **Battle of Stalingrad** a turning point in the war?
3. a. **Define** What was **D-Day**?
   b. **Elaborate** What did Eisenhower mean when he said, "The hopes and prayers of liberty-loving people everywhere march with you"?

Critical Thinking

4. **Categorizing** Review your list of the major battles and campaigns in different areas of the world. Then copy the graphic organizer below and use it to explain the significance of each event shown.

Event	Significance
Battle of El Alamein	
Capture of Rome	
Battle of Stalingrad	
D-Day invasion	

FOCUS ON WRITING

5. **Taking Notes on the Progress of the War** Take notes on the major battles involving American soldiers. How did American leaders, strategies, and individual soldiers contribute to victories in Europe and North Africa?

War in the Pacific

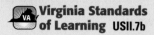
Virginia Standards of Learning USII.7b

What You Will Learn...

Main Ideas

1. The Japanese continued advancing across the Pacific in 1942.
2. The Allies stopped Japan's advance with key victories over the Japanese navy.
3. The Allies began battling toward Japan.

The Big Idea

Allied forces reversed Japan's expansion in the Pacific and battled toward the main Japanese islands.

Key Terms and People

Douglas MacArthur, *p. 820*
Bataan Death March, *p. 820*
Chester Nimitz, *p. 821*
Battle of the Coral Sea, *p. 821*
Battle of Midway, *p. 821*
island hopping, *p. 822*
Battle of Leyte Gulf, *p. 822*
kamikaze, *p. 822*

TAKING NOTES As you read, take notes on the main events of the war in the Pacific. You may want to organize your list in a chart like this one.

Pacific War
1.
2.
3.
4.

If YOU were there...

It is spring 1945, and your older brother is fighting the Japanese in the Pacific. You've been following the news reports closely and you know that fighting in the Pacific is terribly fierce. You hear that the Japanese soldiers often refuse to surrender, fighting to the death instead. Your brother reveals in his letters that he is lonely and suffering many hardships. Now you are writing to him.

What would you say to encourage him?

BUILDING BACKGROUND Japan attacked China in the early 1930s, leading to all-out war between Japan and China in 1937. Japanese forces captured key Chinese cities, including Nanjing, where they killed up to 300,000 civilians. Under the command of General Hideki Tojo, Japanese forces continued to expand the Japanese empire in Asia.

Japan Advances

Japan's attack on Pearl Harbor left the U.S. Pacific Fleet so weakened that it could not immediately respond to the Japanese advance. While the United States recovered from Pearl Harbor, Japan conquered Thailand, Burma, the British colonies of Hong Kong and Singapore, and the U.S. territories of Guam and Wake Island. The same day as the attack on Pearl Harbor, Japan invaded Hong Kong. British, Canadian, and Indian forces attempting to stop the invasion were outnumbered. Japan attacked the American-controlled Philippines the same day.

American and Filipino forces under the command of American general **Douglas MacArthur** could not stop Japan's advance in the Philippines. MacArthur left the islands in March 1942, vowing to return. More than 70,000 American and Filipino soldiers surrendered to the Japanese. The exhausted soldiers were forced to march 63 miles up the Bataan Peninsula to prison camps. Many prisoners were starved and beaten by Japanese soldiers. More than 600 Americans and about 10,000 Filipinos died in the **Bataan Death March**.

READING CHECK **Identifying Cause and Effect** Why could the U.S. Pacific Fleet not immediately stop the Japanese advance?

Code Talkers

More than 40,000 Native Americans served in the U.S. armed forces during the war. About 400 Navajo Native Americans served as "Code Talkers", relaying coded messages based on the complex Navajo language. Japan's expert code breakers were never able to crack the Navajo code.

Why might the Japanese have been unable to break the Navajo code?

Key Allied Victories

The Allies feared the Japanese might next attack India, Australia, or even the United States mainland. Admiral **Chester Nimitz** led the U.S. Pacific Fleet. Nimitz was determined to stop the Japanese advance, and he had an important advantage—the ability to crack secret Japanese codes.

American code breakers helped the Allies in two key naval battles in the Pacific. Nimitz learned that the Japanese were planning an attack on Port Moresby, New Guinea, an island just north of Australia. If the Japanese took New Guinea, they would have a base from which to invade Australia. In May 1942 Nimitz sent Allied forces to stop the Japanese fleet. American and Japanese aircraft carriers and fighter planes clashed in the **Battle of the Coral Sea**. Neither side won a clear victory, but the Japanese assault on Port Moresby was stopped.

Allied leaders then learned that the Japanese planned a surprise attack on the Midway Islands. Nimitz was prepared. The **Battle of Midway** began on June 4, 1942, when Japan started bombing the islands.

American aircraft carriers launched their planes, catching the Japanese aircraft carriers while many of their planes were refueling on deck. American dive bombers destroyed four of Japan's aircraft carriers, severely weakening Japanese naval power. "Pearl Harbor has now been partially avenged," said Nimitz.

The Allies then began the enormous and difficult task of recapturing territory from Japan. In August 1942 American Marines invaded Guadalcanal, one of the Solomon Islands northeast of Australia. Intense fighting raged for nearly six months. Marine Louis Ortega remembered that enemy bombs and bullets were only part of the danger in the hot, rainy jungles of Guadalcanal. Soldiers also suffered from diseases, such as malaria, and from hunger due to lack of supplies. "I had gone to Guadalcanal weighing about 150," Ortega said. "I left weighing about 110." American forces finally took control of the island in February 1943.

READING CHECK **Drawing Conclusions** How did the Allied victory at Midway change the course of the war in the Pacific?

Battling toward Japan

Allied victories at Midway and Guadalcanal helped change the course of the war in the Pacific. The Allies now saw their chance to go on the offensive, with the goal of reaching Japan itself.

Island Hopping

To fight their way toward Japan, Allied war planners developed a strategy called **island hopping**, where Allied forces took only the most strategically important islands, instead of each Japanese-held island. They could use each captured island as a base for the next attack, while isolating the Japanese forces on the bypassed islands.

ACADEMIC VOCABULARY

execute perform, carry out

Island hopping proved to be a successful strategy, though very costly to **execute**. Japanese forces fortified key islands and fought fiercely to hold on to them. In November 1943, U.S. Marines leapt off their boats and waded toward Tarawa, one of the Gilbert Islands. They advanced into ferocious fire from Japanese machine guns. "The water seemed never clear of . . . men," one Marine said. "They kept falling, falling, falling." Both sides sustained heavy casualties at Tarawa, but the Marines captured the island. The Allies won similar victories in the Marshall, Mariana, Volcano, and Bonin islands.

In October 1944 General MacArthur led a mission to retake the Philippines. The Japanese navy confronted the Allies at the **Battle of Leyte Gulf**, the largest naval battle in history. The Allies crushed the Japanese fleet, crippling Japan's naval power for the remainder of the war. It also gave the Allies a base from which to attack the main shipping routes that supplied Japan. After splashing ashore on Leyte, MacArthur proudly declared: "People of the Philippines: I have returned." Securing the Philippines took many more months of fighting. Allied forces and Filipino guerrillas finally drove out or captured all of the Japanese defenders by the summer of 1945.

Final Battles

With key islands close to Japan secured, Allied planes began bombing targets in Japan in November 1944. American B-29 bombers, able to carry 20,000 pounds of explosives each, led bombing raids on more than 60 major Japanese cities. A March 1945 raid set Japan's capital city of Tokyo on fire, leaving 1 million people homeless. Japanese factories were destroyed, and food became so scarce that many people neared starvation. Still, Japan refused to surrender.

Two of the war's fiercest battles occurred on Japan's outer islands early in 1945. In February U.S. Marines stormed the beaches of Iwo Jima, now known as Iwo To. Japanese defenders were dug into caves, with orders to fight to the death. "On Iwo, we hardly ever saw the enemy," recalled one marine. After the Marines raised the American flag on Iwo Jima, a month of bloody fighting followed. Of more than 20,000 Japanese defenders on Iwo Jima, about a thousand were taken prisoner—the rest were killed or wounded in battle. Around 6,800 Americans had died.

Beginning in April an even deadlier battle was fought for the island of Okinawa. There were an estimated 100,000 Japanese soldiers on the island when U.S. forces began their attack. One U.S. Marine officer described the hard fighting at the Battle of Okinawa:

> "We poured a tremendous amount of metal in on those positions ... It seemed nothing could possibly be living in that churning mass where the shells were falling and roaring but when we next advanced, [Japanese troops] would still be there and madder than ever."
> —Colonel Wilburt S. Brown, quoted in *The Final Campaign: Marines in the Victory on Okinawa* by Colonel Joseph H. Alexander

In the waters near the island, Japanese planes struck U.S. ships with the tactic of **kamikaze**—purposely crashing piloted planes into enemy ships. In wave after wave, kamikaze pilots flew planes loaded with explosives straight down onto the decks of Allied ships. An American sailor who was on the deck of an aircraft carrier when a kami-

War in the Pacific, 1941–1945

Interactive Map

ALASKA

SOVIET UNION

60°N

Bering Sea

MONGOLIA

MANCHUKUO

1945

45°N

Aleutian Islands
1943

Beijing

KOREA

Hiroshima
Aug. 6,
1945

1945

JAPAN
Tokyo

*PACIFIC
OCEAN*

CHINA

1944

Chengdu

Nagasaki
Aug. 9,
1945

1944–1945

30°N

Midway
June 1942

*Midway
Islands*

1943

Okinawa
April–
June,
1945

*Volcano
Islands*

1945

Hawaiian Islands

Iwo Jima (Iwo To)
Feb.–Mar. 1945

Taiwan

1945

1945

Japanese attack
Pearl Harbor
Dec. 7, 1941

15°N

BURMA

Hong
Kong

*Mariana
Islands*

Tinian

NIMITZ
1944

*Marshall
Islands*

*BATAAN
PENINSULA*

**PHILIPPINE
ISLANDS**

Guam

FRENCH
INDOCHINA

Philippine Sea
June 1944

THAILAND

Leyte Gulf
Oct. 1944

1945

MALAYA

1944

0° Equator

*Gilbert
Islands*

1943

MACARTHUR

DUTCH EAST INDIES

Bismarck Sea
March 1943

Guadalcanal
Aug. 1942–
Feb. 1943

*Solomon
Islands*

Port Moresby

1942–1943

Coral Sea
May 1942

150°E

▨ Japan (Axis Power)	✦ Major battle
▢ Controlled by Japan, July 1942	← Allied advance
▨ Allied	◄- - Allied air attack
▨ Allied control	☂ Atomic bombing

0   500   1,000 Miles

0   500   1,000 Kilometers

AUSTRALIA

135°E

Kamikaze pilots as young as
17 flew their airplanes directly
into enemy targets, committing
suicide to fulfill their duty.

go.hrw.com
Interactive Map
KEYWORD: SB7 CH26

GEOGRAPHY
SKILLS **INTERPRETING MAPS**

1. **Location** Did the area controlled by Japan by July
   1942 include the Hawaiian Islands? How can you tell?
2. **Human-Environment Interaction** Which major
   battles occurred south of the equator?

WORLD WAR II **823**

Six Marines are shown raising the American flag atop Mt. Suribachi on the island of Iwo Jima after an important battle there. They were instructed to raise the flag on the highest point of the island so that all the men still fighting could see it.

The plane "cartwheeled the length of the carrier and plowed into the planes we had on the [flight deck]. We were burning bow to stern . . . All the guys manning the guns were dead. Standing up. Pointing their guns. They never left their posts."

More than 2,500 kamikaze missions were flown, killing more than 4,000 Allied sailors. The fighting on Okinawa lasted nearly three months and led to terrible casualties. By the time the island was secure, some 12,000 Allied troops were dead and 36,000 wounded. The Japanese losses were staggering—some 110,000 troops and 80,000 civilians had been killed.

After their victories at Iwo Jima and Okinawa, the Allies were one step closer to final victory. Allied leaders began to plan for an all-out assault on the main Japanese islands.

READING CHECK **Analyzing** How did the Allied strategy in the Pacific change starting in 1943?

SUMMARY AND PREVIEW The Allies made major gains in the Pacific war, moving closer to Japan. In the next section, you will learn how the Allies achieved full victory.

Section 4 Assessment

go.hrw.com
Online Quiz
KEYWORD: SB7 HP26

Reviewing Ideas, Terms, and People

1. **a. Identify** Why were the Japanese able to advance in the Pacific in 1942?
   b. Explain Why did so many prisoners die on the **Bataan Death March**?
2. **a. Recall** What Allied victories halted Japan's advance?
   b. Analyze Why was the **Battle of the Coral Sea** important?
   c. Elaborate How do you think the war might have been different if the Allies had lost at Midway?
3. **a. Define** What was **island hopping**?
   b. Sequence What event led to the retaking of the Philippines?
   c. Evaluate Why do you think someone would serve as a **kamikaze** pilot?

Critical Thinking

4. **Sequencing** Review your notes on the main events of the Pacific war. Then copy the graphic organizer below and use it to put the events in the correct sequence.

| 1942 | → | 1943 | → | 1944 | → | 1945 |

FOCUS ON WRITING

5. **Taking Notes on Military Achievements** Take notes on the challenges U.S. soldiers faced in the Pacific. How was fighting in the Pacific different from and similar to fighting in Africa and Europe? How might you describe a Pacific battle to someone?

Victory and Consequences

Virginia Standards of Learning USII.1a, USII.1b, USII.1c, USII.1d, USII.7b

What You Will Learn...

Main Ideas

1. The Allies gained victory in Europe with Germany's surrender.
2. Nazis murdered millions of Jews and other people in the Holocaust.
3. Victory in the Pacific came after the United States dropped atomic bombs on Japan.

The Big Idea

The Allies won World War II, the most devastating war in world history.

Key Terms and People

Battle of the Bulge, *p. 826*
Harry S. Truman, *p. 826*
Holocaust, *p. 827*
genocide, *p. 827*
Manhattan Project, *p. 828*
atomic bomb, *p. 828*

If YOU were there...

It is August 1944. You are an American soldier in France. You have seen the horrors of battle up close, but today is a day to rejoice. You and other Allied soldiers are marching through the streets of Paris, celebrating its liberation from Nazi control. It seems as if the whole city has come out to greet the Americans. People rush up to shake your hand. Children cheer and hand you flowers.

How does it feel to be part of this moment in history?

BUILDING BACKGROUND By late 1944 Allied forces were advancing in Europe and Asia. But Germany and Japan were both resisting, showing no signs of being willing to surrender. Allied leaders knew there was much more fighting still to be done.

Germany Surrenders

In the weeks after the successful D-Day invasion, hundreds of thousands of Allied troops landed in France. Led by American general Omar Bradley, Allied forces began fighting their way across France toward Germany. At the same time, the Soviets were closing in on Germany from the east. Although Germany's defeat seemed certain to the Allies, Hitler refused to surrender.

In July 1944 Allied tank forces led by American general George Patton broke through German lines on the western front. While Patton drove forward, more Allied forces invaded southern France. Both groups of Allied forces fought their way toward Paris. Encouraged by the Allies' success, the citizens of Paris rebelled against the German occupying force. By the end of August, General Bradley was leading Allied troops through the streets of the freed city. "All Paris surged out to meet the Allied columns and welcome their liberators," remembered one witness. After securing Paris, the Allies continued driving through Belgium and Luxembourg, making their way toward Germany. Hitler drafted every able-bodied German man from the age of 16 to 60 and planned one last desperate attack.

TAKING NOTES As you read, take notes on the final days of the war in both Europe and the Pacific. You may want to use a graphic organizer like the one below.

Europe	Pacific

Hitler's goal was for German forces to drive through a weak spot in the Allied lines and capture the city of Antwerp, Belgium. On December 16 the Germans seized a moment when Allied planes were grounded due to bad weather. In heavy snow some 25 German divisions attacked the Ardennes (ahr-DEN), a densely forested region defended by just a few American divisions. The Germans quickly pushed the Allied forces back about 65 miles, creating a huge bulge in the Allied lines. This gave the battle its name—the **Battle of the Bulge**.

Allied forces recovered rapidly and stopped the German advance. When the skies cleared in late December, Allied planes began pounding German troops. In early January 1945 the Germans began to retreat. American losses were heavy—between 70,000 and 81,000 casualties. Germany's losses were even greater, and Hitler's ability to wage offensive war was now completely crushed.

In the final months of the war, Allied bombing raids devastated major German cities such as Berlin and Hamburg. Both sides in World War II had used these kinds of bombing raids against the enemy's cities. German raids, for instance, killed about 30,000 civilians in the British capital of London. In February 1945 Allied bombers attacked the German city of Dresden, igniting a firestorm that destroyed the city and killed more than 35,000 civilians. "Dresden was an inferno," recalled one U.S. soldier. "I have nightmares, even today."

As Allied forces surrounded Berlin, Hitler retreated to an underground bunker in the heart of the ruined city. On April 30, as Soviet troops entered Berlin, Hitler committed suicide. A week later, the Germans surrendered. The war in Europe had finally come to an end. The Allies celebrated May 8, 1945, as V-E (Victory in Europe) Day.

President Franklin Roosevelt, who had led the United States throughout World War II, did not live to see V-E Day. He died of a stroke on April 12. **Harry S. Truman** became president and immediately faced the challenge of winning the war in the Pacific.

READING CHECK **Sequencing** What events led to Germany's surrender?

INTERVIEW TRANSCRIPT
Battle of the Bulge

In the Battle of the Bulge, American soldiers faced a strong German attack in snowy forests during the coldest winter northern Europe had seen in 40 years. Private Dave Nutt described the long, tense nights on the front lines:

❝The cold, the snow, and the darkness were enough to set young nerves on edge. The thud of something as innocuous [harmless] as snow plopping to the ground from a tree branch could be terrifying. Was it snow? Was it maybe a German patrol? Should you fire at the sound and risk giving away your position, or worse, hitting one of your own men? But did the Germans have us surrounded?❞

—Dave Nutt, quoted in *Citizen Soldiers*, by Stephen Ambrose

ANALYSIS SKILL **ANALYZING PRIMARY SOURCES**

What factors made the Battle of the Bulge especially hard on soldiers?

Horrors of the Holocaust

When Allied forces liberated Europe, they uncovered evidence of horrifying Nazi crimes against humanity. In a program of mass murder that became known as the **Holocaust**, Hitler and the Nazis had attempted to exterminate the entire Jewish population of Europe.

The Final Solution

Soon after gaining power in Germany, Hitler began his campaign of terror against the Jews. The Nazis stripped German Jews of their citizenship and seized their property. Many Jews who did not escape the country were imprisoned in concentration camps such as Dachau (DAH-kow), near Munich.

When Germany conquered huge sections of Europe and the Soviet Union early in World War II, nearly 10 million Jews came under Hitler's control. The Nazis forced many Jews into urban centers called ghettos. Others were sent to concentration camps and used as slave labor for German industries. Many laborers died from hunger or disease. The Nazis also formed special killing squads that rounded up groups of Jews, shot them, and buried them in mass graves. When the Germans invaded the Soviet Union, these squads murdered more than 33,000 Soviet Jews near Kiev in just three days. By the end of 1941, the death squads had executed nearly 1 million people.

The Death Camps

In January 1942 senior Nazi officials met to plan what they called "a final solution to the Jewish question." Hitler's "final solution" was **genocide**, or the extermination of an entire group of people. The Nazi plan was to kill the Jews in specially built death camps, mainly in German-occupied Poland. The camps were equipped with gas chambers designed to kill large numbers of people, and furnaces were used to cremate the bodies of victims.

By mid-1942 the Nazis had begun to ship Jews from throughout German-occupied Europe to the camps. Several hundred thousand Jews, for example, were transported by train from the ghetto in the Polish capital of Warsaw to a death camp called Treblinka. In April 1943 Jews in the Warsaw ghetto staged a violent uprising, attacking the Germans with guns and homemade bombs. It took German troops nearly a month to crush the revolt. Survivors were sent to Treblinka.

THE IMPACT TODAY

There are more than 50 museums in the world that honor victims of the Holocaust. The United States Holocaust Memorial Museum in Washington, D.C., displays historical film footage and artifacts from the Holocaust.

At the death camps most children, the elderly, and the sick were immediately executed. Those strong enough to work were used as laborers. When they became too weak to work, they too were sent to the gas chambers. Moritz Vegh was 13 when his family was sent from Czechoslovakia to Auschwitz, one of the most notorious of the death camps. He later described what happened to his mother and sister:

"When we got off the cattle truck, they ordered, 'Men, right; women, left.'...I went with my father. My little sister, Esther, she went with my mother. Esther was only eleven. She was holding my mother's hand. When they made a selection of the women, Esther clung to my mother. My mother wouldn't give her up ...They went straight to the gas chamber."

—Moritz Vegh, quoted in *The Boys: Triumph over Adversity*

Moritz survived the war, working as a laborer at Auschwitz.

The Allied soldiers who liberated the death camps were horrified by what they found. About 6 million Jews—some two-thirds of Europe's prewar Jewish population—had been killed in the Holocaust. The Nazis had also murdered millions of others, including Gypsies, Slavs, political opponents, and people with physical or mental disabilities.

READING CHECK **Summarizing** What was the purpose of the Nazis' "final solution"?

Victory in the Pacific

In the Pacific Allied war planners prepared for an invasion of Japan. They estimated that the invasion could result in more than 1 million Allied casualties.

The Allies had another option. Since 1942 Allied scientists had been working on a secret program known as the **Manhattan Project**. The goal was to develop an **atomic bomb**, a weapon that produces tremendous power by splitting atoms. On July 16, 1945, the Allies successfully tested the first atomic bomb in the New Mexico desert. The massive explosion melted the desert sand into glass for 800 yards in all directions.

When Japanese leaders refused the Allies' demand for an unconditional surrender, President Truman gave the order to use the atomic bomb. On August 6, 1945, the B-29 bomber *Enola Gay* dropped an atomic bomb above the city of Hiroshima. "When I saw a very strong light, a flash, I put my arms over my face unconsciously," said one Japanese survivor. "Almost instantly I felt my face was inflating . . . I saw people looking for water and they died soon after they drank it . . . The whole city was destroyed and burning. There was no place to go." The explosion killed almost 80,000 people instantly. Thousands more died later from burns and radiation poisoning.

The atomic blast over Hiroshima destroyed the city. Over 80,000 people were killed instantly, and thousands more died later from the effects of radiation.

Japanese leaders still refused to surrender. On August 9 U.S. forces dropped a second atomic bomb on the city of Nagasaki. About one-third of the city was destroyed, and approximately 22,000 people died immediately. The Japanese announced their surrender on August 15, 1945.

After six years, World War II was finally over. More than 50 million people had been killed—more than half of them civilians. National economies in Europe and Asia were devastated, and millions of people were left without food, water, or shelter. Since the war had been fought far from American soil, the United States escaped this level of destruction. As the strongest power left in the world, much of the responsibility for postwar rebuilding fell to the United States.

READING CHECK **Drawing Conclusions** Why did Japan surrender?

SUMMARY AND PREVIEW In this section you learned how World War II ended. In the next chapter you will learn how the world recovered from the war and worked to prevent such wars in the future.

Causes and Effects of World War II

QUICK FACTS

Causes
- Global and local economic problems
- Totalitarian governments
- Germany's aggression in Europe
- Japanese aggression in Asia and the Pacific

Effects
- Millions of deaths worldwide
- Widespread destruction of cities and industries
- The Holocaust
- Rise of the United States as the leading world power

Section 5 Assessment

go.hrw.com
Online Quiz
KEYWORD: SB7 HP26

Reviewing Ideas, Terms, and People

1. **a. Identify** What was the last major battle of the war in Europe?
   b. Evaluate What was the biggest task facing **Harry S. Truman** when he became president?
2. **a. Define** What was the **Holocaust**?
   b. Elaborate How did the oppression of Jews increase during the war?
3. **a. Recall** What was the purpose of the **Manhattan Project**, and how did it result in the end of the war against Japan?
   b. Explain What was the status of the United States after the war?
   c. Predict How do you think the invention of the **atomic bomb** changed people's views of war?

Critical Thinking

4. **Identifying Causes** Review your notes on the final days of the war in both Europe and the Pacific. Then copy the graphic organizer below and use it to show the short-term causes of Germany's and Japan's surrenders.

FOCUS ON WRITING

5. **Taking Notes on the Impact of the War** Take notes on the last days of World War II. How did the Allies finally win the war? What impact did the war have on people and countries around the world?

Literature of the
Holocaust

from *Diary of Anne Frank*

by Anne Frank (1929–1945)

About the Reading *Anne Frank was a Jewish teenager in Amsterdam who experienced the Nazi occupation of the Netherlands firsthand. Frank and her family hid for more than two years in the sealed-off back room of an office. The family was betrayed to the Gestapo in 1944. Frank and her family members were sent to concentration camps in Germany. Frank died in 1945 at the Bergen-Belsen concentration camp.*

AS YOU READ   Notice how Frank describes the oppression of Jews.

19th November, 1942

Mr. Dussel has told us much about the outside world we've missed for so long. He had sad news. Countless friends and acquaintances have been taken off to a dreadful fate. ❶ Night after night, green and grey military vehicles cruise the streets. They knock on every door, asking whether any Jews live there. If so, the whole family is immediately taken away. If not, they proceed to the next house. It's impossible to escape their clutches unless you go into hiding. They often go around with lists, knocking only on those doors where they know there's a big haul to be made... In the evenings when it's dark, I often see long lines of good, innocent people, accompanied by crying children, walking on and on, ordered about by a handful of men who bully and beat them until they nearly drop. No one is spared. The sick, the elderly, children, babies and pregnant women—all are marched to their death. ❷

9th October, 1942

Our many Jewish friends and acquaintances are being taken away in droves. The Gestapo is treating them very roughly and transporting them in cattle-trucks to Westerbork, the big camp in Drenthe to which they're sending all the Jews. ❸

GUIDED READING

WORD HELP

Mr. Dussel a friend of Anne's father

droves large numbers

Gestapo German military police

Westerbork a concentration camp on the Dutch-German border

Drenthe a province of the Netherlands

❶ *Jews in hiding knew that they would be sent to concentration camps if discovered.*

❷ *Anne cannot hide her feelings at seeing innocent victims of the Germans being treated poorly.*

❸ *Jews suffered harsh treatment before and after arrest.*

from *Night*

by Elie Wiesel (1928–), translated by Stella Rodway

About the Reading *Elie Wiesel was taken to Auschwitz when he was age 15. Though he survived the camp, not all of his family did. Years after the war, Wiesel wrote about his time spent imprisoned at Auschwitz.*

AS YOU READ Look for ways that Wiesel describes the trauma of being taken away.

GUIDED READING

WORD HELP

molten melted

phylacteries wooden prayer devices

ghetto neighborhood set aside for Jews

truncheons sticks

indiscriminately without care

invalids people who are ill

convoy military escort

❶ *The Hungarian police used physical force to gather people together.*

By eight o'clock in the morning, a weariness like molten lead began to settle in the veins, the limbs, the brain. I was in the midst of my prayers when suddenly there were shouts in the street. I tore myself from my phylacteries and ran to the window. Hungarian police had entered the ghetto and were shouting in the neighboring street:

"All Jews outside! Hurry!"

Some Jewish police went into the houses, saying in broken voices:

"The time's come now . . . you've got to leave all this . . . "

The Hungarian police struck out with truncheons and rifle butts, to right and left, without reason, indiscriminately, their blows falling upon old men and women, children and invalids alike. ❶

One by one the houses emptied, and the street filled with people and bundles. By ten o'clock, all the condemned were outside. The police took a roll call, once, twice, twenty times. The heat was intense. Sweat streamed from faces and bodies.

Children cried for water.

Water? There was plenty, close at hand, in the houses, in the yards, but they were forbidden to break the ranks. "Water! Mummy! Water!"

The Jewish police from the ghetto were able to go and fill a few jugs secretly. Since my sisters and I were destined for the last convoy and we were still allowed to move about, we helped them as well as we could.

CONNECTING LITERATURE TO HISTORY

1. **The Nazi oppression of Jews eventually led to the Gestapo taking Jews from their homes.** How does Frank describe the job that the Gestapo did?

2. **The oppression soon changed to removal.** How does Wiesel describe the removal of the Jews from his hometown?

3. **Jews were treated with physical violence by Nazi supporters.** Give two examples of violence against Jews found in these passages.

Social Studies Skills

Analysis   Critical Thinking   Civic Participation   Study

Constructing Time Lines

Define the Skill

Time lines are a good way to organize historical information. Time lines clearly show a sequence of historical events over a certain period of time. Many time lines focus on a specific theme within a time period.

When you construct a time line, it often makes the sequence of events easier to follow. Time lines show events in the order they happened and the amount of time between events. Constructing a time line can therefore help you better understand events' context. For example, organizing events on a time line can help you determine their causes and effects.

Learn the Skill

When you construct a time line, you need to make some basic decisions. First, the time line needs a topic. This topic can be general or specific. One example of a general topic is the 1940s. A more specific topic might be major battles of World War II. The time line should cover a time period that includes the main events related to the topic. For example, it would make sense for a time line on American battles in World War II to cover the period 1941 to 1945.

The next step in constructing a time line is gathering information. This includes taking notes on events from the chosen time period related to the topic. It is important to write down the date when each event happened. Putting the events in order

before making the time line is often helpful. If there are too many events, it is a good idea to include only the most important ones.

The first step in actually constructing the time line is to draw a straight line using a ruler. The next step is to mark even intervals on the line. Intervals are dates that divide the time line into smaller, equal time periods. For example, a time line of the 1940s might include two-year intervals: 1940, 1942, 1944, and so on. Then add events in the correct places on the time line. The beginning and end of the time line, each interval, and each event should be labeled with dates. The finished time line should include at least six events. As a final touch, the time line needs a title. The title tells what the entries in the time line are about and may include the dates the time line covers.

Practice the Skill

Follow these instructions to construct a time line.

1. Using your textbook, choose a topic related to World War II for your time line. Decide on the dates your time line will need to cover.

2. Use your textbook to take notes on events to include in your time line and their dates. Put the events in order.

3. Following the steps described above, construct your time line. The finished time line should include clearly labeled dates, at least six events, and a title.

Chapter Review

History's Impact
▶ **video series**
Review the video to answer the closing question:
Why do you think the United States made the GI Bill of Rights a permanent policy?

Visual Summary

QUICK FACTS

Use the visual summary below to help you review the main ideas of the chapter.

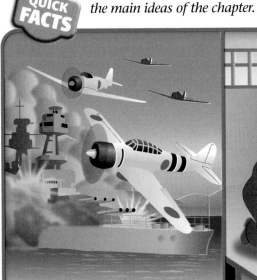

The bombing of Pearl Harbor drew the United States into World War II.

To help supply the troops, women worked in jobs usually held by men.

American soldiers helped defeat the Axis Powers in Europe and the Pacific.

Reviewing Vocabulary, Terms, and People

Identify the term or person from the chapter that best fits each of the following descriptions.

1. The first African American flying unit in the U.S. military

2. American general who retreated from and then retook the Philippines

3. The dictator of the Soviet Union

4. A weapon that produces a massive explosion by splitting atoms

5. Battle at which British troops stopped the German *Afrika Korps*

6. Policy of avoiding war with an aggressive nation by giving in to its demands

7. Extermination of an entire group of people

Comprehension and Critical Thinking

SECTION 1 *(Pages 804–809)*

8. **a. Define** What is fascism?

   b. Make Inferences Before Pearl Harbor, what U.S. policies suggested that the United States would join the Allies?

   c. Evaluate How well did the policy of appeasement work? Explain your answer.

SECTION 2 *(Pages 810–814)*

9. **a. Recall** What happened during the zoot-suit riots?

   b. Analyze Why was the War Production Board important to the war effort?

   c. Elaborate How do you think Japanese Americans felt about internment?

SECTION 3 (Pages 815–819)

10. a. Identify What led the Axis powers to retreat from the Soviet Union?

b. Summarize In which regions and countries did the Allies win major victories against Germany?

c. Draw Conclusions Why do you think D-Day succeeded?

SECTION 4 (Pages 820–824)

11. a. Describe What did kamikaze pilots do?

b. Explain How did cracking Japanese codes help the Allies in the Pacific?

c. Draw Conclusions Why do you think Japan was determined to continue fighting?

SECTION 5 (Pages 825–829)

12. a. Recall What were the effects of the atomic bombs on Hiroshima and Nagasaki?

b. Contrast How was the Holocaust different from other wartime tragedies?

c. Evaluate Do you think the strategy of bombing civilian centers was fair? Why or why not?

Reviewing Themes

13. Geography How did geography affect the course of World War II?

14. Society and Culture What changes in society did World War II bring about?

Using the Internet

go.hrw.com
KEYWORD: SB7 CH26

15. Activity: Understanding Code Talkers Guns and bombs were not the only weapons of World War II. Cryptography, or the use of secret codes, was also an important tool for the Allied forces. Some Native Americans in the U.S. military used their own language as a form of cryptography. They spoke Navajo, a complex language, and adapted it for battlefield communications and to transmit secret information by radio and telephone. Soldiers who could speak it became known as "code talkers." Enter the activity keyword. Research the Navajo code talkers of World War II and then create a poster to present your findings.

Reading Skills

Categorizing *Use the Reading Skills taught in this chapter to answer the question from the reading selection below.*

> American, British, and Canadian troops invaded France on June 6, 1944—known as D-Day or "designated day." They crossed the choppy waters of the English Channel and landed on five beaches in Normandy. More than 6,000 ships, 11,000 planes, and 156,000 men were part of the invasion. Soldiers jumped from boats and waded ashore, often under heavy fire. (*p. 819*)

16. Which of the following general categories could help you organize this information?

a. generals of the American forces

b. types of ammunition used

c. resources of invading forces

d. leaders of Allied nations

Social Studies Skills

Constructing Time Lines *Use the Social Studies Skills taught in this chapter to answer the question below.*

17. Make a time line about the end of World War II, covering the events of 1945.

FOCUS ON WRITING

18. Writing Your Radio News Broadcast Review your notes. Choose one event or story from World War II as the focus of your radio broadcast. You can include quotes from soldiers or national leaders. Remember that people cannot see your broadcast, so use descriptive language. Be sure to answer the following questions: *Who? What? Where? When? Why?* and *How?*

DIRECTIONS: *Read each question and write the letter of the best response. Use the map below to answer question 1.*

1

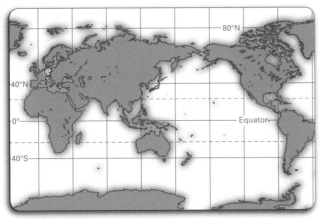

The yellow countries above represent the

A Central Powers.

B Allied Powers.

C Axis Powers.

D Big Three.

2 Which one of the following battles took place in the Pacific?

A Battle of Omaha Beach

B Battle of El Alamein

C Battle of Stalingrad

D Battle of Midway

3 During the war, many American women

A did work that traditionally had been done by men.

B served in battlefront combat positions in the military.

C worked as *braceros*.

D participated in labor strikes.

4 The Allies' successful 1944 invasion of France is known as

A D-Day.

B the Desert Fox.

C sonar.

D the Battle of Britain.

5 Who became president when Franklin D. Roosevelt died in 1945?

A Eleanor Roosevelt

B Harry S. Truman

C Winston Churchill

D Douglas MacArthur

6 The majority of Holocaust victims were

A Slavs.

B Japanese.

C disabled people.

D Jews.

7 Read the following excerpt from the diary of Anne Frank, a Dutch Jew who died in the Holocaust, and use it to answer the question below.

July 15, 1944

"It's a wonder I haven't abandoned all my ideals, they seem so absurd and impractical. Yet I cling to them because I still believe, in spite of everything, that people are truly good at heart."

—Anne Frank, *The Diary of Anne Frank*

Document-Based Question Why does Frank call her ideals "absurd and impractical"?

Assignment

Write an essay describing either Hoovervilles or the Dust Bowl during the Great Depression.

A Descriptive Essay

Vivid descriptions of a place and time can help us understand history. Primary sources often provide such descriptions from one person's point of view. Historians provide a different point of view in descriptions based on many primary and secondary sources.

TIP **Using Visual Images** Look at visual images such as photographs from the 1930s. What do they show about Hoovervilles or the Dust Bowl and the people who lived there? Use this information in your description.

1. Prewrite

Getting Started

Descriptive essays depend on details that will help the reader create a mental picture. The quotes about the Dust Bowl on page 790 are examples of vivid descriptions. The passage from *The Grapes of Wrath* on page 795 is another good example. For your description, review Chapter 25 and look in the encyclopedia and other sources. Collect as many details as you can about Hoovervilles or the Dust Bowl. Try to find details that involve all of the five senses (sight, sound, smell, touch, and taste). Good description depends on strong details.

Organizing Information

Make one generalization that sums up all your details. This will be your main idea. Then organize the details and examples you have found into two, three, or four categories. These will become the body paragraphs of the essay. All of these categories should support the main idea.

For example, the main idea of an essay could be that the name *Dust Bowl* was an accurate description of the area. One detail might be that the gritty dirt often became caught in people's skin, hair, and clothing. This detail could fit into the category of people in the Dust Bowl.

2. Write

You can use this framework to help you write your first draft.

A Writer's Framework

Introduction	Body	Conclusion
■ Make a generalization about your topic.	■ Separate details into paragraphs by category.	■ Summarize your information.
■ List the categories that will be included in the body paragraphs.	■ Use vivid details that involve the five senses.	■ Explain how your topic is related to larger issues.
	■ Use details from different sources.	

3. Evaluate and Revise

Evaluating

Use these questions to discover ways to improve your essay.

Evaluation Questions for a Descriptive Essay

- Do you begin with a generalization about your topic?
- Do you separate details into separate paragraphs by category?
- Do you use vivid details that involve the five senses?

- Do you use details from different sources?
- Do you explain how your topic is related to larger issues?

TIP **Show, Don't Tell** Writers are often advised, "Show, don't tell." This phrase means that writers should use strong words, details, and examples to make a point. Choose vivid, clear examples for your description. They should not need much explanation.

Revising

When you revise your essay, make examples and details as specific as possible. This will make your description more vivid.

General: *People built flimsy houses in Hoovervilles.*
Specific: *In Hoovervilles, people built shelters out of scraps of lumber, tin, and cardboard.*

4. Proofread and Publish

Proofreading

Check your sentences for fragments and run-ons. A fragment is an incomplete sentence. Adding a subject or a verb can often make a fragment into a complete sentence. A run-on has too many subjects and verbs for one sentence. It usually needs to be broken into two or more separate sentences.

Publishing

Share your essay with one or more classmates. Make illustrations based on the descriptions in each other's essays.

5. Practice and Apply

Use the steps and strategies in this workshop to write your descriptive essay.

Postwar America

After the end of World War II, Americans became concerned with the global spread of communism. The government began taking steps to defend the nation against possible aggression from Communist nations. At home, many Americans enjoyed the economic prosperity of 1950s society. Not everyone benefited, however. Some Americans spoke out against American society and a government that did not guarantee equality to all citizens.

During the civil rights movement many Americans demanded equal rights for minority groups. Despite sometimes violent opposition, many successes were achieved. Differing viewpoints within society were further exposed, however, by reactions to the Vietnam War, a war fought in Southeast Asia over Communist expansion.

Explore the Art

The movies of the 1950s often portrayed American life as prosperous and content, although this was not true for everyone. What does this image suggest about the prosperity of postwar America?

839

Early Years of the Cold War

 Virginia Standards of Learning

USII.8 The student will demonstrate knowledge of the economic, social, and political transformation of the United States and the world between the end of World War II and the present by

a) describing the rebuilding of Europe and Japan after World War II, the emergence of the United States as a superpower, and the establishment of the United Nations; **b)** describing the conversion from a wartime to a peacetime economy; **c)** identifying the role of America's military and veterans in defending freedom during the Cold War, including the wars in Korea and Vietnam, the Cuban missile crisis, the collapse of communism in Europe, and the rise of new challenges; **d)** describing the changing patterns of society, including expanded educational and economic opportunities for military veterans, women, and minorities

USII.9 The student will demonstrate knowledge of the key domestic and international issues during the second half of the twentieth century by

b) describing the development of new technologies in communication, entertainment, and business and their impact on American life; **c)** identifying how individual citizens from the time period influenced America scientifically, culturally, academically, and economically

FOCUS ON WRITING

Song Lyrics The end of World War II brought economic prosperity to the United States, along with new fears and challenges. Americans adjusted to changes in their everyday lives and the new threat of nuclear war. In this chapter you will read about life at the beginning of the Cold War. Then you will write the words to a song that reflects some aspect of American life in the 1950s.

 UNITED STATES

1945 After Roosevelt's death, Harry S. Truman becomes president.

1945

 WORLD

1946 Winston Churchill declares an "iron curtain" between Western powers and the Soviet Union.

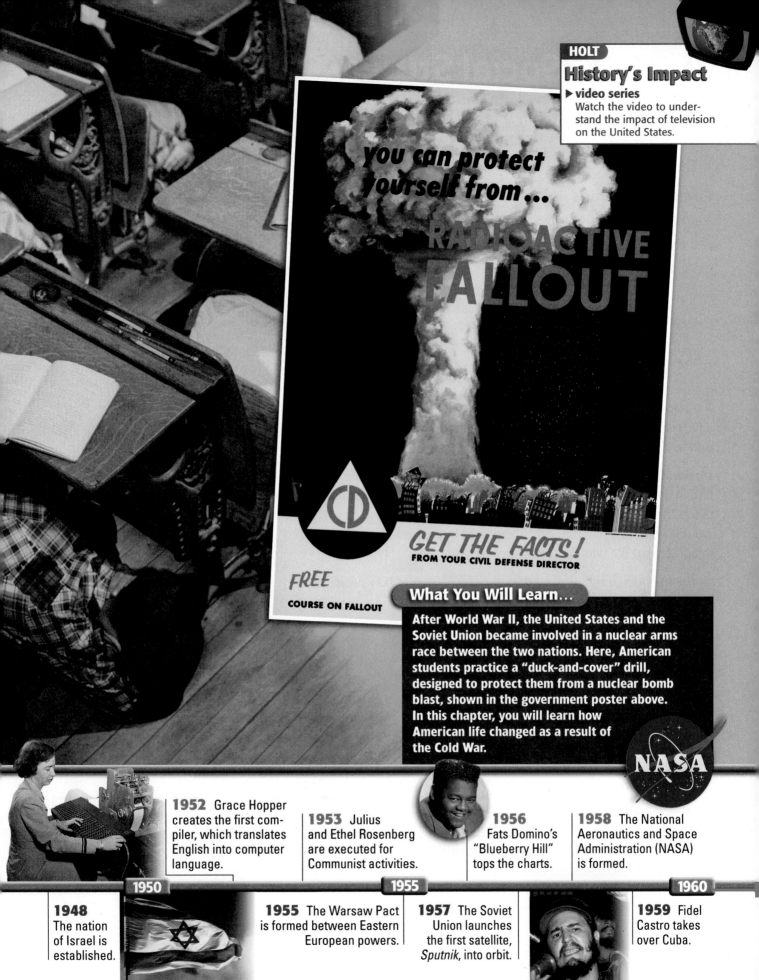

you can protect
yourself from...

RADIOACTIVE
FALLOUT

CD

GET THE FACTS!
FROM YOUR CIVIL DEFENSE DIRECTOR

FREE
COURSE ON FALLOUT

What You Will Learn...

After World War II, the United States and the Soviet Union became involved in a nuclear arms race between the two nations. Here, American students practice a "duck-and-cover" drill, designed to protect them from a nuclear bomb blast, shown in the government poster above. In this chapter, you will learn how American life changed as a result of the Cold War.

NASA

1952 Grace Hopper creates the first compiler, which translates English into computer language.

1953 Julius and Ethel Rosenberg are executed for Communist activities.

1956 Fats Domino's "Blueberry Hill" tops the charts.

1958 The National Aeronautics and Space Administration (NASA) is formed.

1950

1955

1960

1948 The nation of Israel is established.

1955 The Warsaw Pact is formed between Eastern European powers.

1957 The Soviet Union launches the first satellite, *Sputnik*, into orbit.

1959 Fidel Castro takes over Cuba.

Reading Social Studies

by Kylene Beers

Economics | Geography | **Politics** | Society and Culture | **Science and Technology**

Focus on Themes In this chapter, you will learn about the Cold War between the United States and the Soviet Union. This war was unlike other wars in that it was often fought between **politicians** instead of soldiers. Each country used developments in **science and technology** to declare itself superior. You will also read about U.S. society and its reaction to the Cold War.

Visualizing

Focus on Reading Visualizing how your life might have been different if you had been alive during a period in history can help you understand life at that time.

Understanding Visualizing Using clues about everyday life that you find in a history book like this one can help you imagine what life was like in the past. You can imagine yourself and your life, and how life would have been different if you had lived in the past. Or you can try to imagine what life was like for the people alive then.

Notice the clues in this passage that give you an idea of how people felt living during the Cold War.

> All the time, in the homely [plain], cluttered rooms of our private lives the television displayed the continuing spectacle of public life— all of it still going on in the windless places on the other side of the screen. Presidents and First Secretaries trod [climbed] down the metal staircases from the bellies of great aircraft to shake hands on the tarmac [runway] and climb into big black cars. Tanks wheeled down blind streets and across muddy fields. Rolls of heavy wire netting were unwound and veered [turned] upwards against a dawn sky.
>
> — From *The Cruel Peace*, by Fred Inglis

The author is using description to inform the reader about the feeling of watching the Cold War unfold on television.

Here the author uses frightening images to help the reader understand the fear of the Cold War.

VA **Virginia Standards of Learning**
Reading 6.4c Describe the images created by language.

You Try It!

The following passage is from the chapter you are getting ready to read. As you read the passage, look for details that help you visualize the past.

In 1946 Winston Churchill described how Soviet control cut these countries off from the Western world. "An iron curtain has descended [fallen] across the [European] Continent," he said. The term *iron curtain* thus came to be used to describe this division. Presidential adviser Bernard Baruch warned of the seriousness of the Soviet threat, saying, "Let us not be deceived—we are today in the midst of a cold war." The phrase *Cold War* came to be used often to describe the long struggle for global power between the United States and the Soviet Union.

From Chapter 27, p. 846

After you read the passage, answer the following questions.

1. Which details help you understand the attitude existing between the United States and the Soviet Union?

2. How does the quote by Winston Churchill help you visualize the political atmosphere of the time?

3. How does the phrase *Cold War* help you visualize the political atmosphere of the time?

Key Terms and People

Chapter 27

Section 1
Yalta Conference *(p. 844)*
Nuremberg trials *(p. 845)*
United Nations *(p. 846)*
Cold War *(p. 846)*
containment *(p. 847)*
Truman Doctrine *(p. 847)*
Marshall Plan *(p. 847)*
North Atlantic Treaty Organization *(p. 848)*
GI Bill of Rights *(p. 848)*
Fair Deal *(p. 850)*

Section 2
Mao Zedong *(p. 852)*
38th parallel *(p. 852)*
Joseph McCarthy *(p. 855)*
hydrogen bomb *(p. 856)*
arms race *(p. 856)*
Sputnik (p. 856)
brinkmanship *(p. 856)*

Section 3
baby boom *(p. 858)*
Sun Belt *(p. 858)*
urban renewal *(p. 859)*
beats *(p. 861)*

Academic Vocabulary
In this chapter, you will learn the following academic words:
concrete *(p. 855)*

As you read Chapter 27, look for details that help you visualize the past.

Adjusting to Peace

Virginia Standards of Learning USII.1b, USII.8a, USII.8b, USII.8c, USII.8d

What You Will Learn...

Main Ideas

1. As World War II ended, leaders began planning the future of the postwar world.
2. The United States and the Soviet Union went from being allies to enemies after World War II.
3. Americans adjusted to postwar life.

The Big Idea

After World War II, Americans adjusted to new challenges both at home and around the world.

Key Terms and People

Yalta Conference, *p. 844*
Nuremberg trials, *p. 845*
United Nations, *p. 846*
Cold War, *p. 846*
containment, *p. 847*
Truman Doctrine, *p. 847*
Marshall Plan, *p. 847*
North Atlantic Treaty Organization, *p. 848*
GI Bill of Rights, *p. 848*
Fair Deal, *p. 850*

TAKING NOTES As you read, take notes on the results of the end of World War II. Organize your notes in a diagram like this one.

If YOU were there...

You are an adviser to President Harry S. Truman in July 1945. You have traveled with him to Potsdam, outside the ruined city of Berlin, where Allied leaders are discussing postwar plans. Everyone agrees that steps must be taken to prevent another world war. But you are worried that Soviet leader Joseph Stalin cannot be trusted.

What advice would you give to President Truman?

BUILDING BACKGROUND U.S. leaders had mistrusted the Soviet government before World War II. The goals of the totalitarian, Communist Soviet state conflicted with American democratic, capitalistic ideals. In addition, Soviet dictator Joseph Stalin used brutal tactics, including murder, to maintain power and control political opposition. During the war, the rivals put aside their differences to defeat Germany. After the war, however, old tensions resurfaced.

The Future of the Postwar World

As 1945 began, it was becoming clear that the Allies were going to win World War II. In February Allied leaders known as the Big Three—Franklin D. Roosevelt of the United States, Winston Churchill of Great Britain, and Joseph Stalin of the Soviet Union—met in the Soviet city of Yalta to discuss plans for peace.

At the **Yalta Conference**, the three leaders made important decisions about the future of European governments. They expressed support for the creation of an international peacekeeping organization. They also agreed that nations freed from Germany should have the right "to create democratic institutions of their own choice." Stalin promised to allow free elections in the Soviet-occupied countries in Eastern Europe. However, after driving German troops out of Poland, Soviet forces set up a pro–Soviet Communist government.

In July 1945 President Truman met with British and Soviet leaders near Berlin, Germany, at the Potsdam Conference. The Allied leaders divided conquered Germany into four zones. Britain, France, the United States, and the Soviet Union would each occupy one zone. The capital city of Berlin—located deep inside the Soviet zone—was also divided into four zones.

War Crimes Trials

After World War II, Allied leaders formed a special court, called the International Military Tribunal, to try Axis leaders accused of war crimes. In November 1945 the tribunal put high-ranking Nazis on trial in the German city of Nuremberg in what became known as the **Nuremberg trials**. U.S. Supreme Court justice Robert H. Jackson served as the chief American attorney. In his opening statement, Jackson explained the importance of the trials:

"The wrongs which we seek to condemn and punish have been so calculated [well planned], so malignant [evil] and devastating, that civilization cannot tolerate their being ignored because it cannot survive their being repeated."
—Robert H. Jackson, quoted in *The Nuremberg Trial,* edited by Mitchell Bard

The court charged Nazi officials with "crimes against humanity." One defendant was Hermann Goering, a key planner of Hitler's "final solution." Another was Hans Frank, Poland's wartime governor, who had organized the killing of hundreds of thousands of Poles and Polish Jews. The tribunal found 19 Nazi leaders guilty. Of these, 12, including Goering and Frank, were sentenced to death.

The International Military Tribunal for the Far East held trials in Japan. Japan's wartime leader Hideki Tojo was convicted and executed. Seven other Japanese leaders were also sentenced to death. The trials in Germany and Japan helped establish the principle that individuals must be held responsible for committing war crimes, even when acting on behalf of a government.

The United Nations

During the war, President Roosevelt had spoken of the need for a new international organization to promote world peace. Roosevelt did not believe the United States alone could bring peace to the whole world. "The structure of world peace," he said, "must be a peace which rests on the cooperative effort of the whole world."

FOCUS ON READING

How does the quote from Robert H. Jackson help you visualize the atmosphere of the Nuremberg trials?

Yalta Conference, February 1945

Who attended?
- Franklin Roosevelt, United States
- Winston Churchill, Great Britain
- Joseph Stalin, Soviet Union

What was the outcome?
- Free elections for countries liberated from German control
- Strong support for creation of an international peacekeeping organization

Winston Churchill, Franklin Roosevelt, and Joseph Stalin (seated left to right) met at Yalta in 1945.

Potsdam Conference, July 1945

Who attended?
- Harry S. Truman, United States
- Winston Churchill and Clement Attlee, Great Britain
- Joseph Stalin, Soviet Union

What was the outcome?
- Germany and the city of Berlin would be divided into four zones. Britain, France, the United States, and the Soviet Union would each control one zone.

Clement Attlee, Harry Truman, and Joseph Stalin (seated left to right) met at Potsdam in 1945.

The United Nations

Written in 1945, the United Nations Charter declared the organization's commitment "to unite our strength to maintain international peace and security." Since 1945 the UN has grown from 51 member nations to more than 190. In addition to working to prevent war, the United Nations today works to provide disaster relief, prevent hunger and disease, and combat international terrorism.

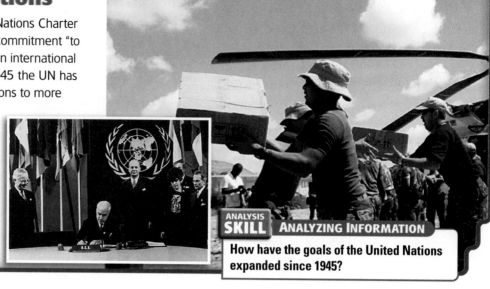

ANALYSIS SKILL ANALYZING INFORMATION

How have the goals of the United Nations expanded since 1945?

In 1944 American, British, Soviet, and Chinese representatives met to draft a plan for the **United Nations** (UN)—an organization dedicated to resolving international conflicts. In 1945, representatives from 50 countries met to write the UN Charter. President Truman appointed Eleanor Roosevelt as one of the first U.S. delegates to the UN.

One of the UN's first actions concerned Palestine, occupied by the British after World War I. The UN General Assembly voted to divide the area into separate Arab and Jewish states. Jews had begun moving to Palestine, an area important to the Jewish, Christian, and Islamic religions, after World War I. Many more moved there before and during World War II. On May 14, 1948, Jewish leaders announced the creation of the nation of Israel.

The United States quickly recognized the new Jewish state. Arab leaders refused to do so and claimed the land as their own. Armies from five Arab states attacked Israel. Israeli forces drove them back, and the two sides reached a truce in 1949. Israel then joined the UN. But tensions remained high.

READING CHECK Finding Main Ideas What steps did world leaders take to establish peace?

From Allies to Enemies

During World War II, the United States and the Soviet Union cooperated to win the war. Afterward, the differences between the two nations led to new hostility. The Soviet Union hoped to spread communism around the world. Americans remained committed to capitalism and democracy.

The Iron Curtain

After Stalin created a Communist government in Poland, the Soviet Union expanded its control over Eastern Europe by creating "satellite states"—countries under complete Soviet control. In 1946 Winston Churchill described how Soviet control cut these countries off from the Western world. "An iron curtain has descended [fallen] across the [European] Continent," he said. The term *iron curtain* thus came to be used to describe this division. Presidential adviser Bernard Baruch warned of the seriousness of the Soviet threat, saying, "Let us not be deceived—we are today in the midst of a cold war." The phrase **Cold War** came to be used to describe the struggle for global power between the United States and the Soviet Union.

Cold War Policies

The United States quickly developed a new foreign policy to deal with the Cold War. It was based on the goal of **containment**, or preventing the Soviet Union from expanding its influence around the world.

In 1945 the Soviet Union began demanding control over areas in the Mediterranean Sea that were under Turkish authority. In 1946 Communist rebels in Greece threatened to topple the Greek monarchy. At Truman's request, Congress passed an aid package worth millions of dollars for Greece and Turkey. The money, the president said, would "support free peoples who are resisting attempted subjugation [conquest] by armed minorities or outside pressures." U.S. aid helped the Greek army defeat the Communist rebels and protected Turkey from Soviet expansion. This policy of providing aid to help foreign countries fight communism became known as the **Truman Doctrine**.

The nations of Europe, meanwhile, were still devastated from World War II. American secretary of state George C. Marshall saw this as a threat both to stability in Europe and to the U.S. economy, which depended on trade with Europe. Marshall called on European leaders to develop plans for economic recovery, which the United States would help fund. Under the **Marshall Plan**, Western Europe received more than $13 billion in U.S. loans and grants for European economic recovery between 1948 and 1952. Soviet leaders rejected Marshall Plan aid. They also kept Eastern European nations from participating.

Cold War tensions rose further in 1948 when France, Britain, and the United States

This cartoon shows Czechoslovakia's freedom being crushed by the Soviet Union.

Cold War Europe, 1955

NATO member, 1955
Warsaw Pact member, 1955
Nonaligned Communist nation
Nonaligned nation

The United States, Canada, and Iceland were also NATO members.

0   200   400 Miles
0   200   400 Kilometers

GEOGRAPHY SKILLS INTERPRETING MAPS

1. **Place** Which countries remained non-aligned during the Cold War?
2. **Location** What is the northernmost NATO member country shown on the map?

decided to join their occupation zones of Germany into one unit. The Soviet Union had good reason to fear the creation of a strong West German state. On June 24, the Soviet Union suddenly blocked all rail, highway, and water traffic between western Germany and the city of Berlin. West Berlin's 2 million residents were trapped behind the iron curtain.

To respond to this crisis without using military force, U.S. and British planes began airlifting supplies into West Berlin. For more than a year, planes delivered lifesaving food, fuel, and machinery to West Berliners. The Soviet Union made no determined effort to stop the airlift, fearing a war. It then lifted the blockade in May 1949.

That same year, the United States joined nine Western European countries, along with Iceland and Canada, to form the **North Atlantic Treaty Organization** (NATO). NATO members promised to defend each other if attacked. In 1955 the Soviet Union created the Warsaw Pact, which provided a unified system of military command between the Soviet Union and its Eastern European satellite countries for their mutual defense.

THE IMPACT TODAY

When the Cold War ended, many former Warsaw Pact nations joined NATO. Today NATO has 26 member nations.

READING CHECK Comparing How were NATO and the Warsaw Pact similar?

BIOGRAPHY

Harry S. Truman
1884–1972

Harry S. Truman grew up in Independence, Missouri. He was an artillery officer in France during World War I, then returned to Missouri and later became active in politics. He was elected to the U.S. Senate in 1934, where he served until becoming vice president in 1945. When President Roosevelt died, Truman was sworn in as president of the United States. "I felt like the moon, the stars, and all the planets had fallen on me," he said. Truman later called his first year in office a "year of decisions," as he led the country through the end of World War II and the start of the Cold War.

Analyzing Information What made Truman's first year as president especially challenging?

Postwar America

You have read about the economic depression that followed the end of World War I. As World War II ended, President Truman was worried about a similar downturn. More than 16 million Americans had served in the armed forces during the war. Now they were coming home, and most would be looking for work.

The Postwar Economy

To provide jobs for returning veterans, the government urged the millions of women who had gone to work during the war to give up their jobs. New laws also eased the transition for returning soldiers. The Servicemen's Readjustment Act, or **GI Bill of Rights**, offered veterans money for school, as well as loans for houses, farms, and businesses. The GI Bill's home loans enabled veterans to buy about 20 percent of the new houses built right after the war. Some 8 million veterans used the GI Bill's educational benefits to attend colleges and technical schools. Bob Dole, former U.S. senator from Kansas, described how the GI Bill changed his life:

❝In my case, I went from a couple of nondescript [ordinary] years in college before the war, and came back and made excellent grades. I went on to law school and got involved in politics. None of that would have happened without the GI Bill.❞

—Bob Dole, quoted in *GI Bill: The Law That Changed America*, by Milton Greenberg

Another major postwar change was Truman's decision to end the rationing of scarce products. Prices skyrocketed as people rushed to buy gasoline and other products that had been limited during the war. The inflation rate in 1946 rose above 18 percent. The U.S. economy remained strong, however.

Labor Unrest

More than 35 percent of all nonfarm workers were members of unions in 1946, more than ever before. With prices rising quickly,

Jackie Robinson

On April 15, 1947, Jackie Robinson played his first game for the Brooklyn Dodgers. Robinson became a hero to millions by ending segregation in major league baseball. He went on to be a Hall of Fame player—and an outspoken supporter of equal rights. "The right of every American to first-class citizenship is the most important issue of our time," Robinson said.

How did Robinson show his support for equal rights for all Americans?

JACKIE ROBINSON 3b of BROOKLYN DODGERS

workers went on strike to demand higher wages. In 1946 alone, 4.5 million workers participated in nearly 5,000 strikes.

The strikes became a major political problem for President Truman. Many people began to wonder if he could handle the presidency. In April 1946 the 400,000-member United Mine Workers Union went on strike. When Truman was unable to negotiate a settlement, he placed the mines under government control. In May Truman ended a railroad strike by threatening to draft all the striking workers into the army.

To reduce the power of labor unions, Congress passed the Taft-Hartley Act in 1947. This act outlawed closed shops—businesses that could hire only union members. It also allowed the president to order an 80-day "cooling-off" period before a strike began. In addition, union leaders had to swear they were not Communists. In spite of his clashes with unions, Truman thought this bill went too far to weaken unions. He vetoed the bill, but Congress overrode his veto.

Civil Rights

After serving their country in World War II, many African Americans faced prejudice and segregation at home. "Black servicemen were

overseas dying for this country," said civil rights lawyer Constance Baker Motley. "And . . . they would be coming home to a situation that said, in effect, You're a second-class citizen." African American veterans helped lead a major effort to gain equal rights.

Truman responded in 1946 by appointing the Committee on Civil Rights to investigate discrimination and suggest solutions. As a result of the committee's report, Truman recommended that Congress pass anti-lynching laws, outlaw segregation, and protect civil rights. Congress failed to act on Truman's ideas. But in 1948, under pressure from African American groups, Truman issued an executive order ending segregation in the armed forces. He also banned discrimination in the hiring of federal employees.

The Election of 1948

As the election of 1948 drew near, President Truman's chances of reelection looked bleak. The Republicans had gained control of Congress in 1946. They felt confident that their presidential candidate, New York governor Thomas Dewey, could beat Truman.

Truman faced challenges from within the Democratic Party as well. Some southern Democrats protested Truman's support for civil rights laws by walking out of the 1948 Democratic National Convention. Many joined the States' Rights Party, or Dixiecrats, which favored racial segregation. The Dixiecrats nominated their own presidential candidate—South Carolina governor Strom Thurmond.

Truman took his case for re-election directly to the American people. He traveled more than 30,000 miles by train and delivered hundreds of speeches. He attacked what he called the "do-nothing, good-for-nothing" Congress for refusing to pass his legislation.

"I spoke I believe altogether to between fifteen and twenty million people," he later said. "I met them face to face, and I convinced them, and they voted for me." Truman won a surprise victory. The Democratic Party also regained control of both houses of Congress.

In his 1949 State of the Union Address, Truman urged Congress to support his plans for the nation. Truman's domestic program, called the **Fair Deal**, included a higher minimum wage, the creation of a national health insurance plan for all Americans, and expanded Social Security benefits for the elderly. It also asked for federal protection of civil rights and an end to racial discrimination in hiring.

Congress approved some parts of the Fair Deal, such as a higher minimum wage and expanded Social Security benefits. Congress rejected other Fair Deal proposals. These included civil rights legislation that would have created a permanent Fair Employment Practices Committee.

READING CHECK **Analyzing** How did the GI Bill help returning soldiers?

SUMMARY AND PREVIEW The United States faced a series of new challenges after World War II. In the next section you will learn how the fear of communism grew in the 1950s.

QUICK FACTS

The Fair Deal

The Fair Deal included
- National health insurance
- Expanded social security
- Higher minimum wage
- Public housing
- Civil rights legislation
- Federal aid to education

Section 1 Assessment

go.hrw.com
Online Quiz
KEYWORD: SB7 HP27

Reviewing Ideas, Terms, and People

1. **a. Describe** How did the Allies divide Germany at the Potsdam Conference?
   b. Explain Why were the **Nuremberg trials** important?
   c. Predict Based on its founding and early years, do you think the **United Nations** would be an effective organization?

2. **a. Define** What was the **Truman Doctrine**?
   b. Analyze How did the **Marshall Plan** help stabilize Western Europe?
   c. Elaborate Why do you think the United States and Western European countries were concerned about Soviet expansion?

3. **a. Recall** What kinds of programs were included in President Truman's **Fair Deal**?
   b. Explain What was the purpose of the Taft-Hartley Act?
   c. Evaluate Do you think President Truman did enough to promote civil rights? Why or why not?

Critical Thinking

4. **Categorizing** Review your notes on the results of World War II. Then copy the graphic organizer below and use it to identify the effects of the war's end on the United States and the world.

Results of World War II	
In the United States	In the World

FOCUS ON WRITING

5. **The Postwar World** Take notes on postwar developments in the United States and the world. Which events might have given Americans hope? Which might have made them concerned? If you had lived during the 1950s, which issue would have been of the most interest to you?

Eleanor Roosevelt

How would you work for human rights for all?

When did she live? 1884–1962

Where did she live? She lived much of her life in New York, where she married Franklin D. Roosevelt in 1905. She also lived in Washington, D.C., when her husband was assistant secretary of the navy and, later, president.

What did she do? During the Great Depression, Eleanor Roosevelt acted as President Roosevelt's "eyes and ears" by traveling around the United States to study conditions among the people. She investigated New Deal programs and reported on their effectiveness. She also worked for equal rights for African Americans. Serving on the UN Commission on Human Rights from 1946 to 1951, she helped write the Universal Declaration of Human Rights, which the UN adopted in 1948. In 1961 President John F. Kennedy chose her to chair his Commission on the Status of Women.

Why is she so important? She changed the role of first lady by acting as a public figure. She held her own press conferences, made speeches, and wrote newspaper columns. She was a leading figure in the movements to promote human rights, children's welfare, and equal rights for women and minorities.

Making Inferences How did Eleanor Roosevelt's different jobs and activities reflect her values and beliefs?

KEY EVENTS

1905
Marries Franklin D. Roosevelt

1921
Becomes active in politics

1936
Begins writing daily newspaper columns; holds press conferences for women correspondents

1945
Appointed delegate to the UN

1946
Becomes chair of the UN Commission on Human Rights

1961
Appointed chair of the Commission on the Status of Women

1962
Dies in New York City

War in Korea and a New Red Scare

What You Will Learn...

Main Ideas

1. The United States fought Communist North Korea in the Korean War.
2. Fear of Communists led to a new Red Scare at home.
3. President Eisenhower faced Cold War crises around the world.

The Big Idea

During the Cold War, the U.S. government confronted communism globally and within the United States.

Key Terms and People

Mao Zedong, *p. 852*
38th parallel, *p. 852*
Joseph McCarthy, *p. 855*
hydrogen bomb, *p. 856*
arms race, *p. 856*
Sputnik, p. 856
brinkmanship, *p. 856*

TAKING NOTES As you read, take notes on Cold War conflicts and crises. In each circle of a diagram like the one below, describe one conflict or crisis. You may need to add more circles.

Cold War Conflicts and Crises

If YOU were there...

A radio broadcast on June 26, 1950, delivers a shocking announcement. Communist forces from North Korea have just invaded South Korea. President Truman has demanded that the North Koreans halt their invasion, but they seem to be ignoring this demand. Now Truman has to decide whether to use American military force to stop the North Koreans.

Do you think the United States should send troops to Korea? Why or why not?

BUILDING BACKGROUND The earliest Cold War conflicts were in Central and Eastern Europe, where countries were divided by the Iron Curtain. But the Truman Doctrine committed the United States to containing communism on a wider scale. The Communist takeover of China in 1949 soon focused Cold War fears on Asia.

The Korean War

The Cold War began in Europe but quickly spread to the Asian nations of China and Korea. In China, the Communist Party and the Nationalist Party had been struggling for control of the country since the early 1900s. The two rivals joined forces against Japan during World War II but then resumed their civil war after Japan's defeat. The United States, as part of its commitment to stop the spread of communism, backed the Nationalists. The Nationalists were defeated, however, and were forced to flee to the island of Taiwan. Led by **Mao Zedong**, the Communists officially established the People's Republic of China on October 1, 1949. Many Americans saw this as a disastrous failure of U.S. foreign policy. They feared that all of Asia might soon fall to communism.

These fears were heightened by a crisis in Korea. Japan had controlled Korea from 1910 to the end of World War II. After the war, the Allies divided Korea at the **38th parallel**. The Soviet Union

The Korean War

Legend:
- Farthest advance of Communist forces, Sept. 1950
- Farthest advance of UN forces, Nov. 1950
- Farthest advance of Chinese/North Korean forces, Jan. 1951
- Armistice line, July 1953
- Demilitarized Zone, boundary set by Allies after World War II

0 75 150 Miles
0 75 150 Kilometers

CHINA
Yalu River
Pyongyang
Sea of Japan
130°E
38°N
Seoul
Inchon
125°E
Yellow Sea
Pusan

GEOGRAPHY SKILLS INTERPRETING MAPS

1. **Location** Why do you think the Demilitarized Zone is located where it is?
2. **Movement** Which two forces advanced into South Korea?

BIOGRAPHY

Douglas MacArthur
1880–1964

Douglas MacArthur grew up on a series of military bases, where his father served in the U.S. Army. "It was here I learned to ride and shoot even before I could read or write," he later said. After graduating first in his class at West Point, MacArthur began an army career that would last more than 50 years. He reached the rank of general in 1918 and commanded troops in World War I, World War II, and the Korean War. "When I joined the Army," he told Congress in 1951, "it was the fulfillment of all my boyhood hopes and dreams."

Drawing Inferences How can you tell how MacArthur felt about the U.S. Army?

controlled the northern part of Korea, and the United States occupied the south. Both sides set up governments, neither of which recognized the other as legitimate.

Fighting in Korea

On June 25, 1950, North Korea's Soviet-trained and equipped army stormed across the 38th parallel and invaded South Korea. The United Nations called for a cease-fire. But the North Koreans continued their attack.

President Truman had to make an immediate decision: Should the United States use force to try to stop the North Korean invasion? On June 27 Truman announced: "I have ordered United States air and sea forces to give the [South] Korean government troops cover and support." That same day, the UN decided to help South Korea "to repel the armed attack." American general Douglas MacArthur was put in command of the UN forces, which included troops from the United States and 15 other countries. The majority of the troops were from the United States and South Korea.

In the early battles, MacArthur's forces were driven back to the southeastern tip of the Korean Peninsula, near the city of Pusan. Fierce fighting raged for six weeks before the UN troops turned the tide of the war with a surprise attack. Landing at the port city of Inchon on September 15, UN forces attacked the North Koreans from behind. About a month later, MacArthur's troops captured Pyongyang, North Korea's capital. They then advanced north to the Yalu River, the border between North Korea and China. MacArthur told Truman he would "have the boys home by Christmas."

Then China suddenly sent hundreds of thousands of soldiers across the border to join the North Koreans. They drove UN forces south again, back below the 38th parallel. MacArthur suggested air strikes on Chinese cities and an attack on mainland China. Truman refused permission. He was determined to contain the war in Korea.

When MacArthur publicly criticized the president's strategy, Truman relieved the general of command. "I fired General MacArthur because he wouldn't respect the authority of the president," Truman said. This was a very unpopular decision with the American public. MacArthur came home to a hero's welcome.

The War Ends

By the spring of 1951 the fighting in Korea settled into a violent stalemate. The UN forces had driven the North Koreans and Chinese back across the 38th parallel. But neither side seemed able to win the war.

Americans' frustration with the war dominated the 1952 presidential election. The Republicans nominated war hero Dwight D. Eisenhower. He promised to end the increasingly unpopular conflict, saying, "The first task of a new administration will be to . . . bring the Korean War to an early and honorable end."

This promise helped Eisenhower win the election. Eisenhower visited Korea, but the conflict dragged on. A cease-fire finally ended the fighting on July 27, 1953. After three years of fighting, North and South Korea were again divided near the 38th parallel. More than 130,000 Americans had been killed or wounded. Korean and Chinese casualties topped 2 million.

READING CHECK **Summarizing** What were the effects of the Korean War?

POLITICAL CARTOON
Fear of Communism

In the 1950s the fear of communism caused some government leaders to ignore the civil liberties of suspected Communists. Some critics, like this cartoonist, believed these tactics threatened the freedom of all Americans. Here, a frightened man climbs the arm of the Statue of Liberty to put out her torch.

The Statue of Liberty's burning torch symbolizes freedom.

Hysteria means "senseless excitement."

The frightened man carries water to put out the fire.

"FIRE!" from *Herblock: A Cartoonist's Life* (Times Books 1998)

ANALYSIS SKILL **ANALYZING PRIMARY SOURCES**

Why is the man shown to be putting out Liberty's torch?

A New Red Scare

The first Red Scare swept America after the Russian Revolution in 1917. Cold War fears led to another Red Scare in the late 1940s and 1950s. Attorney General J. Howard McGrath summed up these fears when he said, "There are today many Communists in America. They are everywhere—in factories, offices, butcher shops, on street corners."

Fear of Communists

A congressional committee called the House Un-American Activities Committee (HUAC) investigated Communist influence in America. In 1947 HUAC launched a series of hearings to expose what it believed was Communist influence in the Hollywood movie industry. The committee branded as "red," or Communist, actors and writers who would not answer questions or who refused to reveal the names of suspected Communists. People suspected of Communist sympathies were often blacklisted, or denied work. Some of these people never worked in movies again.

POINTS OF VIEW
McCarthyism

Journalist Edward R. Murrow frequently criticized Senator McCarthy's tactics. This drew a furious response from McCarthy.

❝ If none of us ever read a book that was 'dangerous', nor had a friend who was 'different', or never joined an organization that advocated 'change', we would all be just the kind of people Joe McCarthy wants. Whose fault is that? Not really [McCarthy's]. He didn't create this situation of fear. He merely exploited [took advantage of] it, and rather successfully. **❞**

—Edward R. Murrow

❝ Murrow is a symbol—the leader and the cleverest of the jackal [wild dog] pack which is always found at the throat of anyone who dares to expose individual Communists and traitors. I am compelled by the facts to say to you that Mr. Edward R. Murrow, as far back as twenty years ago, was engaged in propaganda for Communist causes. **❞**

—Joseph McCarthy

ANALYSIS SKILL **ANALYZING POINTS OF VIEW**

How would you describe Murrow's criticism of McCarthy's ideas?

Explosive spy cases also fed the fears that Communists were at work in the United States. In 1950 a German-born physicist was convicted of providing the Soviets information about the atomic bomb project at Los Alamos, New Mexico, that allowed them to develop an atomic bomb at least one year earlier than they would have. In 1951 Julius and Ethel Rosenberg also were tried for providing Soviet spies with secret details about atomic bomb design. The Rosenbergs denied the charges but were found guilty and executed in 1953.

The Rise of McCarthy

Wisconsin senator **Joseph McCarthy** contributed to fears in the early 1950s by charging that Communists were working inside the State Department. He claimed to have the names of fifty-seven people who were "either card-carrying members or certainly loyal to the Communist Party."

McCarthy produced no **concrete** proof of crimes. When challenged, he made up new charges, labeling those who questioned him as "soft on communism." This method of making aggressive accusations without proof became known as McCarthyism.

McCarthy finally went too far in 1954. In televised Senate hearings, he charged that there were Communists in the U.S. Army. For five weeks, Americans watched McCarthy's bullying tactics. At one point, McCarthy tried to discredit Joseph Welch, the army's attorney, by attacking a young assistant in Welch's law firm. This shocked Welch—and the nation. "Let us not assassinate this lad further, Senator," Welsh said. "Have you left no sense of decency?" A later Senate vote condemned McCarthy's actions, but it came too late for those whose careers had been ruined by his attacks.

ACADEMIC VOCABULARY

concrete
specific, real

READING CHECK **Comparing** How were HUAC's and McCarthy's actions similar?

Eisenhower and the Cold War

Cold War tensions increased around the world during the presidency of Dwight Eisenhower. In this hostile atmosphere, Americans adjusted to the reality of living with the constant threat of nuclear war.

The Arms Race

In 1950 President Truman approved work on the **hydrogen bomb**, a weapon far more powerful than the atomic bombs used in World War II. American scientists tested the first hydrogen bomb in the South Pacific in 1952. "The fireball expanded to three miles in diameter," said a test observer. He soon saw that the entire island on which the bomb exploded "had vanished, vaporized."

The Soviet Union tested its first atomic bomb in 1949 and its first hydrogen bomb in 1953. In what became a nuclear **arms race**, both the United States and the Soviet Union rushed to build more and more weapons. American school children practiced "duck and cover" drills, in which they were taught to crouch under their desks in case of nuclear attack. Some families built underground bomb shelters in their backyards.

In October 1957 the Soviets launched **Sputnik,** the world's first artificial satellite. Americans feared that if the Soviet Union could launch a satellite, it could launch missiles to attack the United States. In January 1958 the United States responded by launching its own satellite. Later that year, the U.S. government established the National Aeronautics and Space Administration (NASA) to conduct space research.

Cold War Crises

President Eisenhower modified Truman's policy of containment. He and Secretary of State John Foster Dulles supported **brinkmanship**—a willingness to go to the brink of war to oppose communism. "The ability to get to the verge [edge] without getting into war is the necessary art," Dulles explained. The president and Dulles also

History Close-up

Inside a Bomb Shelter

Many families built personal bomb shelters for use in a nuclear emergency. The shelters were stocked with essentials like food and water and were often located in the family's backyard.

underground shelter

entrance

beds

food

water

threatened the Soviet Union with "massive retaliation" against Soviet advances.

As part of his effort, Eisenhower used covert, or secret, operations around the world. In 1953, for example, the Central Intelligence Agency (CIA) helped overthrow the premier of Iran. American officials had feared he was a Communist. In 1954 the CIA helped organize the removal of the Guatemalan president for similar reasons.

In 1956 a crisis in Egypt seemed to push the world to the brink of a third world war. Egyptian leader Gamal Abdel Nasser nationalized the Suez Canal, a vital waterway connecting the Mediterranean and Red seas in an attempt to collect tolls from the canal to finance a major dam project. Britain and France, which relied on the canal for trade, allied with Israel, a longtime enemy of Egypt, and invaded the area around the canal. The Soviet Union, an ally of Egypt, threatened to crush the invaders. This would force the United States to defend its allies. Finally, the Americans and the Soviet Union agreed to condemn the invasion, and the Suez crisis ended. After the brief moment of cooperation, the Cold War continued.

READING CHECK Analyzing How was the arms race a display of brinkmanship?

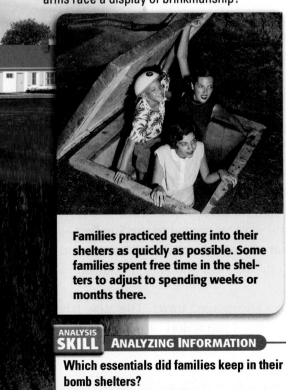

Families practiced getting into their shelters as quickly as possible. Some families spent free time in the shelters to adjust to spending weeks or months there.

SUMMARY AND PREVIEW After World War II, Americans responded to Communist threats at home and abroad. In the next section you will read about how America prospered during these challenging times.

Section 2 Assessment

go.hrw.com
Online Quiz
KEYWORD: SB7 HP27

Reviewing Ideas, Terms, and People

1. **a. Identify** What is the **38th parallel**, and why was it important in the Korean War?
   b. Analyze How did the outcome of China's civil war affect the U.S. response to North Korea's attack?
   c. Evaluate Do you think President Truman should have fired MacArthur? Explain your answer.
2. **a. Describe** Why did a second Red Scare occur in the late 1940s and 1950s?
   b. Explain How did television affect **Joseph McCarthy**'s power?
   c. Elaborate Why do you think the Red Scare lasted so long?
3. **a. Recall** How did Eisenhower deal with Cold War crises during his administration?
   b. Make Inferences How can you tell that the U.S. government took the launch of *Sputnik* seriously?
   c. Elaborate Why do you think the United States and the Soviet Union were able to cooperate during the Suez crisis?

Critical Thinking

4. **Categorizing** Review your notes on Cold War conflicts and crises. Then copy the graphic organizer below and use it to list each event under its appropriate location.

Asia	Soviet Union	United States	Other

FOCUS ON WRITING

5. **Taking Notes on Challenges at Home and Abroad** Take notes on the challenges and fears Americans faced during the Korean War, McCarthy era, and Eisenhower presidency. How did the government and individuals respond to these challenges and fears?

Virginia Standards of Learning USII.8b, USII.8d, USII.9b

What You Will Learn...

Main Ideas

1. America's economy boomed in the 1950s.
2. Americans enjoyed new forms of popular culture.
3. Social critics found fault with 1950s society.

The Big Idea

An expanding economy led to new ways of life for many Americans in the 1950s.

Key Terms and People

baby boom, *p. 858*
Sun Belt, *p. 858*
urban renewal, *p. 859*
beats, *p. 861*

TAKING NOTES As you read, take notes on the suburban lifestyle and culture of the 1950s. You can organize your notes in a table like this one.

Suburban Life and Culture

The Nation Prospers

If YOU were there...

You live with your parents in an apartment building in 1954. You have grown up in the city, and you are used to walking or taking the subway everywhere you need to go. But your parents are talking about moving out to the suburbs. They like the idea of having a house of their own, with a driveway and a backyard. They ask what you think about moving to the suburbs.

How would you respond?

BUILDING BACKGROUND A long economic boom after World War II led to a rapid rise in the income of many Americans. By the mid-1950s nearly 60 percent of the U.S. population qualified as middle class, with annual incomes between $3,000 and $10,000. The prosperity of the 1950s brought many changes to American life.

America's Economy in the 1950s

The American economy boomed during the 1950s. Millions of Americans earned more money than ever before and, therefore, had more money to spend on homes, cars, vacations, and large appliances. Feeling better off than they had during the Depression and World War II, many young Americans were getting married and starting families. This led to a **baby boom**, or a significant increase in the number of babies born.

A Nation on the Move

Americans were also on the move in the 1950s, as people relocated to new parts of the country to take jobs and improve the quality of their lives. Many businesses and workers moved to the **Sun Belt**— southern and western states that offered a warm climate year-round and low tax rates. As a result, the region's population doubled in the 30 years after World War II.

The 1956 Highway Act also encouraged travel. This new law provided billions of dollars for the construction of a 41,000-mile

New Housing Construction

Amount Spent (in billions)

$40
$30
$20
$10
$0

1945   1960

Live Births

Births (in millions)

50

40

30

20

1945   1960

Personal Income

Total (in billions)

$450
$350
$250
$150
$50

1945   1960

Many American families used their newfound wealth to buy consumer products like houses, automobiles, and appliances. Advertisements like this one used an idealized version of an American family to sell products.

ANALYSIS SKILL ANALYZING VISUALS

How did rising wealth affect families in the 1950s?

interstate highway system. New highways helped to greatly increase both business and personal travel between cities throughout the country. The roads also made it easier for people to move to suburbs and commute to jobs in cities.

Suburbs and Cities

The rising demand for homes in the suburbs encouraged developers to build new suburban neighborhoods. On Long Island, New York, William Levitt created Levittown, one of the nation's first preplanned suburbs. Between 1946 and 1951, Levitt built more than 17,000 low-priced, mass-produced houses. Like Henry Ford's Model-T, Levitt's homes were designed to be simple and affordable. By the mid-1950s, builders were constructing similar suburban homes all over the country. By 1970 more Americans lived in suburbs than in cities.

Many families welcomed the comfort and convenience of suburban living. Suburban homes usually had driveways, large lawns, and labor-saving appliances. Suburban children could participate in a wide variety of sports and other activities. Many mothers spent so much

time driving their children from one activity to another that one commentator referred to the task as "motherhood on wheels."

Some critics of suburbs complained that suburban life was too heavily based on consumer culture. They also criticized the suburbs for encouraging conformity, or sameness. Most of the people living in the suburbs were white and middle-class. In fact, some communities—including Levittown—refused to sell homes to black families.

As middle-class families moved to the suburbs, cities collected fewer tax dollars. This led to a decline in city services. Those who were unable to afford a move to the suburbs lived in increasingly decaying urban areas. As conditions worsened, the federal government began an **urban renewal** program—a plan to improve life in cities. Urban renewal projects focused on improving city services and urban housing. In reality, however, the programs sometimes led to more problems for urban residents.

READING CHECK **Contrasting** How was life different in suburbs and cities?

Life in the 1950s

Life for the average citizen in the United States changed dramatically in the prosperous years after World War II. More money was available to buy a wider variety of products, and technological advances made life safer and easier for many.

In 1952 Dr. Jonas Salk developed a vaccine for the paralyzing disease of polio.

Ralph Ellison began his writing career with the Federal Writers' Project during the Great Depression. He eventually became famous for writing about discrimination against African Americans.

Teenagers enjoyed the music of Elvis Presley and other rock 'n' roll stars.

Drive-in movie theaters became increasingly popular during the 1950s. Movies were shown on large outdoor screens as patrons watched from their cars. The largest drive-ins could accommodate 3,000 cars.

DRIVE-IN
RAIN OR SHINE
GREGORY PECK & ANNE BAXTER
YELLOW SKY
MY LITTLE CHICKADEE
MAE WEST & W C FIELDS
EXIT

American Pop Culture

American life was changing quickly in the 1950s as new technology developed. Many people began shopping in malls and eating at new fast-food restaurants. By the end of the decade, nearly 90 percent of all American families owned at least one television set. On average, American families watched about six hours of television a day.

Americans all over the country shared the experience of watching the same news, comedies, and sports programs. Many shows, such as *The Lone Ranger*, were versions of shows that began on the radio. Early hits included Milton Berle's variety show *Texaco Star Theater* and the Western drama *Gunsmoke*. But the most popular show was *I Love Lucy*, a situation comedy (or sitcom) starring Lucille Ball and her real-life husband, Cuban American bandleader Desi Arnaz. About 44 million Americans tuned in to one episode of *I Love Lucy* in 1953 to see the birth of their son—twice the number that watched President Eisenhower's inauguration the next day.

New styles of music also helped reshape American culture in the 1950s. African American jazz greats Charlie Parker and Dizzy Gillespie became known as the Fathers of Bebop, a complex jazz style often played at a rapid pace. Meanwhile, musicians like Elvis Presley, Buddy Holly, Chuck Berry, and Little Richard helped rock 'n' roll sweep the nation. Teenage music fans powered the rock 'n' roll revolution, buying more than 70 percent of all records sold in the late 1950s. Just like jazz in the 1920s, rock music drew criticism from some adults. One journalist even labeled rock 'n' roll "a menace to morals." An Arizona teenager responded to this type of criticism by saying, "Man, I believe the older generation just doesn't want the younger generation to have any fun."

READING CHECK Finding Main Ideas What changes took place in American pop culture during the 1950s?

Social Critics

Though the postwar years were happy and productive for many Americans, not everyone was happy with American society in the 1950s. Some women, for instance, were frustrated that they could only find work in a limited number of fields such as teaching, nursing, or office work. Others were discouraged by the expectation that they would give up their jobs when they got married. One woman recalled,

" There was always the assumption, even when I was getting my graduate degree in education, that any work I did was temporary, something to do until I assumed [began] my principal role in life which was to be the perfect wife and mother, supported by my husband. "

—Sally Ann Carter, quoted in *The Fifties: A Women's Oral History*, by Brett Harvey

Many writers commented on 1950s society in their work. In 1951 J. D. Salinger published *The Catcher in the Rye*. The novel's teenage narrator, Holden Caulfield, criticizes the "phoniness" of the adults around him, who he believed loved only money and wanted everyone to be the same. In his 1952 novel *Invisible Man*, Ralph Ellison wrote about how African Americans felt left out by American society. "I am an invisible man," Ellison wrote. "I am invisible, understand, simply because people refuse to see me."

Young people known as beatniks, or **beats**, criticized society with unusual writing styles and rebellious behavior. The works of beat poet Allen Ginsberg and novelist Jack Kerouac inspired many young people to question the rules of mainstream American society. Many young people also identified with rebellious characters in popular movies of the 1950s. In the 1953 film *The Wild One*, actor Marlon Brando plays Johnny, a wild biker who challenges the rules of society. When asked, "Hey Johnny, what are you rebelling against?" Johnny replies, "Whadda ya got?"

READING CHECK **Finding Main Ideas** Why did people criticize 1950s society?

SUMMARY AND PREVIEW In the 1950s, suburban life, television, and pop culture changed American society. In the next chapter you will learn how the civil rights movement affected the United States.

Section 3 Assessment

go.hrw.com
Online Quiz
KEYWORD: SB7 HP27

Reviewing Ideas, Terms, and People

1. **a. Recall** How did a booming economy affect life in the United States in the 1950s?
   b. Explain How did the growth of suburbs affect cities?
   c. Elaborate How do you think the **baby boom** affected 1950s society?

2. **a. Identify** How did American pop culture change in the 1950s?
   b. Make Inferences Based on what you have read, how was teenage culture in the 1950s different from adult culture?

3. **a. Describe** What was *Invisible Man* about?
   b. Compare What did J. D. Salinger and Jack Kerouac have in common?
   c. Predict How do you think some women in the 1950s might have wanted to change their lives?

Critical Thinking

4. **Analyzing Information** Review your notes on 1950s suburban life and culture. Then copy the graphic organizer below and use it to list the benefits and challenges of suburban life and culture.

Benefits   Challenges

FOCUS ON WRITING

5. **Taking Notes on Daily Life and Culture** Take notes on daily life and pop culture during the 1950s. What did Americans want, and what was important to them? What kind of music would be appropriate for a song about the 1950s?

Social Studies Skills

Analysis   Critical Thinking   Civic Participation   Study

Interpreting Battle Maps

Define the Skill

Battle maps show events during a battle or war. They may show army movements or locations of battles. A single battle map often shows events that occurred at different times. Reading the map key is very important when you interpret battle maps. Battle maps usually include many different symbols. The map key explains the symbols used on the map.

Learn the Skill

Follow these steps to interpret battle maps.

1 Read the title to determine what the map is about.

2 Study the map key to understand what the symbols on the map mean. Locate the symbols from the key on the map.

3 Look for labels and other information on the map. Use what you already know about the time period to determine the importance of these features.

4 Use the map to make a generalization about a battle or war, such as which side won.

Practice the Skill

1. What is this map about?

2. What does the solid blue line on this map represent? What does the solid red line represent?

3. What does the green line on the 38th parallel show? Why is this important?

Based on this map, make a generalization about the Korean War.

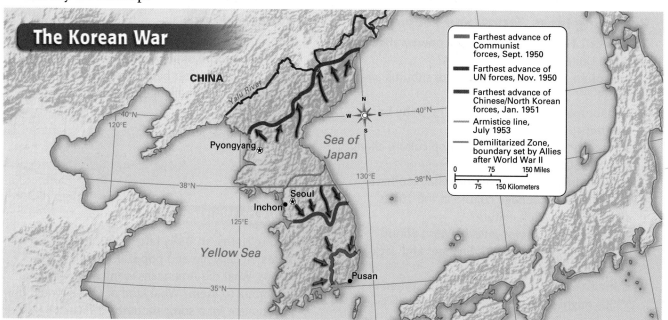

The Korean War

Map key:
- Farthest advance of Communist forces, Sept. 1950
- Farthest advance of UN forces, Nov. 1950
- Farthest advance of Chinese/North Korean forces, Jan. 1951
- Armistice line, July 1953
- Demilitarized Zone, boundary set by Allies after World War II

0 75 150 Miles
0 75 150 Kilometers

CHINA

Yalu River

Pyongyang

Sea of Japan

Seoul

Inchon

Yellow Sea

Pusan

Chapter Review

Visual Summary

QUICK FACTS

Use the visual summary below to help you review the main ideas of the chapter.

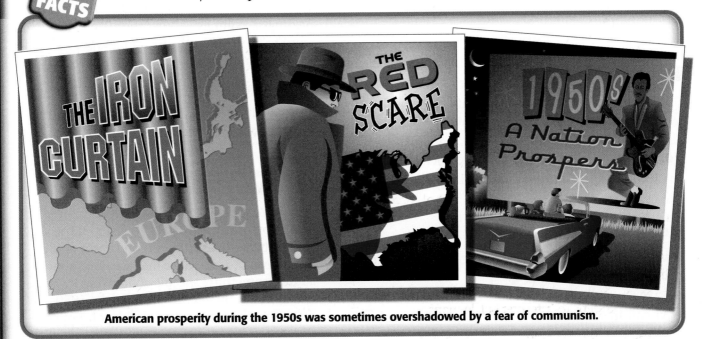

American prosperity during the 1950s was sometimes overshadowed by a fear of communism.

Reviewing Vocabulary, Terms, and People

Match the numbered person or term with the correct lettered definition.

1. GI Bill of Rights
2. Yalta Conference
3. Truman Doctrine
4. Joseph McCarthy
5. Fair Deal

a. U.S. senator who unfairly accused many citizens of being Communists

b. meeting at which Franklin Roosevelt, Winston Churchill, and Joseph Stalin discussed strategy for postwar peace

c. package of domestic reforms proposed by President Truman

d. U.S. policy of containing communism through economic aid

e. program that offered veterans money for school after World War II

Comprehension and Critical Thinking

SECTION 1 *(Pages 844–850)*

6. a. Recall What is the United Nations?

b. Explain Why did Franklin Roosevelt support the formation of the UN?

c. Elaborate Would you have supported the policy of containment? Why or why not?

SECTION 2 *(Pages 852–857)*

7. a. Identify How did the United States battle communism in Asia in the 1950s?

b. Explain What effect did the launch of *Sputnik* have on the United States?

c. Evaluate What were some risks and advantages of the strategy of brinkmanship?

SECTION 3 (Pages 858–861)

8. a. Describe How did life in the United States change in the 1950s?

b. Summarize Why were some women frustrated with 1950s society?

c. Elaborate How has American popular culture changed since the 1950s? How has it stayed the same?

Reviewing Themes

9. Politics How did the Cold War affect political relations between the United States and the Soviet Union?

10. Science and Technology How did science and technology advance during the 1950s?

Reading Skills

Visualizing *Use the Reading Skills taught in this chapter to answer the question below.*

> Wisconsin senator Joseph McCarthy contributed to fears in the early 1950s by charging that Communists were working inside the State Department. "I have in my hand," he said, "fifty-seven cases of individuals who would appear to be either card-carrying members or certainly loyal to the Communist Party, but who nevertheless are still helping to shape our foreign policy." *(p. 855)*

11. What elements of the selection above help you visualize the feelings created by the Red Scare?

Social Studies Skills

Interpreting Battle Maps *Use the Social Studies Skills taught in this chapter to answer the question below.*

12. Look back at the battle map on page 853. In what year did North Korean forces make their farthest advance?

Using the Internet

go.hrw.com KEYWORD: SB7 CH27

13. Activity: Researching the Second Red Scare Fear of communism and spies grew during the late 1940s and 1950s. What were Americans' fears? How did Senator Joseph McCarthy and congressional hearings affect the lives of those accused of Communist activities? What did the hearings accomplish? Enter the activity keyword to learn about the second Red Scare. Then write a journal entry from the point of view of Senator McCarthy, a blacklisted writer, or Joseph Welch, attorney for the U.S. Army. Your journal entry should include direct references to your research.

FOCUS ON WRITING

14. Writing Your Song Lyrics Review your notes. Decide on a theme for your song about the 1950s. It can focus either on one event or idea, or on several. Remember that the lyrics should address something specific about what it was like to live in the United States in the 1950s. You may even want to write from the point of view of a young person living in the 1950s. What would that person think about? What would be his or her hopes and fears?

DIRECTIONS: Read each question and write the letter of the best response.

1 At the Yalta Conference, Joseph Stalin promised

A to allow free elections in the Soviet Union.

B to allow free elections in Eastern Europe.

C to prosecute Soviet war criminals.

D that the Soviet Union would join the United Nations.

2 The United Nations was formed to

A promote world peace.

B deal with problems in Palestine.

C bring Nazi leaders responsible for the Holocaust to justice.

D plan how to divide Germany among the Allies.

3 What is McCarthyism?

A denying people work

B a type of communism

C going to the brink of nuclear war

D making accusations of Communist activity without proof

4 Which president decided to use U.S. troops to help defend South Korea in 1950?

A Franklin Roosevelt

B Dwight Eisenhower

C Harry Truman

D Herbert Hoover

5 What new kind of music was popular with teenagers in the 1950s?

A suburban swing

B big band jazz

C rock 'n' roll

D beatnik

6 Which country sent hundreds of thousands of troops to fight alongside North Korean forces in the Korean War?

A Japan

B China

C the United States

D the Soviet Union

7 Social critics in the 1950s spoke out against which of the following?

A containment

B the United Nations

C Douglas MacArthur

D consumer culture

8 Read the following excerpt from a 1953 speech by President Eisenhower and use it to answer the question below.

> "Every gun that is made, every warship launched, every rocket fired signifies, in the final sense, a theft from those who hunger and are not fed, those who are cold and not clothed. This world in arms is not spending money alone. It is spending the sweat of its laborers, the genius of its scientists, the hopes of its children."
>
> —Dwight D. Eisenhower, April 16, 1953

Document-Based Question What desire do you think Eisenhower was expressing in this passage?

The Civil Rights Movement

Virginia Standards of Learning

USII.1 The student will demonstrate skills for historical and geographical analysis, and responsible citizenship, including the ability to

a) analyze and interpret primary and secondary source documents to increase understanding of events and life in United States history from 1865 to the present; **b)** make connections between past and present; **c)** sequence events in United States history from 1865 to the present; **d)** interpret ideas and events from different historical perspectives

USII.8 The student will demonstrate knowledge of the economic, social, and political transformation of the United States and the world between the end of World War II and the present by

d) describing the changing patterns of society, including expanded educational and economic opportunities for military veterans, women, and minorities

USII.9 The student will demonstrate knowledge of the key domestic and international issues during the second half of the twentieth century by

a) examining the Civil Rights Movement and the changing role of women; **c)** identifying how individual citizens from the time period influenced America scientifically, culturally, academically, and economically

WRITING JOURNAL

A Civil Rights Bill In the 1950s and 1960s, African Americans began successfully to challenge the discrimination they had faced for so many years. In this chapter, you will read about the civil rights movement and about the passage of new civil rights laws. Imagine that you are a member of Congress at this time. You will write a new civil rights bill to help people gain fair treatment under the law.

1954 Thurgood Marshall argues against segregation in the Supreme Court case *Brown* v. *Board of Education.*

UNITED STATES

1945

1953 Soviet leader Joseph Stalin dies.

WORLD

HOLT
History's Impact
▶ video series
Watch the video to under-
stand the impact of equal
rights and justice for all
Americans.

What You Will Learn...

African Americans launched a major civil rights
movement in the years following World War II.
Members of the movement organized demonstrations to protest unfair treatment, like the
March on Washington shown here. In this chapter,
you will learn about the efforts of
African Americans and others to gain
civil rights protections in the 1950s,
1960s, and 1970s.

1957 The Soviets
launch *Sputnik*, the
first human-made
satellite.

1960

1963 Lee Harvey
Oswald assas-
sinates President
John F. Kennedy.

1961 The
Berlin Wall di-
vides East and
West Berlin.

1966 The Nation-
al Organization for
Women is formed.

1966 Indira Gandhi
becomes prime
minister of India.

1970

1969 La Raza Unida
is organized to support
the rights of Mexican
Americans.

1973 The
American Indian
Movement protests
at Wounded Knee.

Reading Social Studies

by Kylene Beers

Economics   Geography   **Politics**   **Society and Culture**   Science and Technology

Focus on Themes In this chapter, you will read about the important changes in American **society** during the period called the civil rights era. You will learn about how many people came to see **politics** as a way to correct social inequalities that existed for minority groups in the United States such as African Americans, women, Mexican Americans, Native Americans, and people with disabilities. You will also read about life in the 1960s.

Using Context Clues: Synonyms

Focus on Reading Some words mean almost the same thing. Understanding the similarities can help you understand words whose meaning you may not know.

Understanding Synonyms Words that have similar meanings are called synonyms. Often, a synonym is given as a definition. The synonym will probably be a word you already understand. This will help you learn the new word through context clues.

Notice how one reader uses synonyms to understand words she does not understand.

An AIM leader described the group's goals, saying, "We don't want civil rights in the white man's society—we want our own *sovereign [self-governing]* rights."

> This is a word I don't know the meaning of.

> These brackets mean that the word inside is a synonym of the word or phrase that comes before. The word inside is a synonym of *sovereign*.

> The word *sovereign* must mean to govern on one's own.

You Try It!

The following passage is from the chapter you are getting ready to read. As you read the passage, look for synonyms in the definitions of unfamiliar words.

> On February 1, 1960, the students went into Woolworth and staged a sit-in—a demonstration in which protesters sit down and refuse to leave. They sat in the "whites-only" section of the lunch counter and ordered coffee. They were not served, but they stayed until the store closed. The next day, they returned with dozens more students to continue the sit-in. Soon, another sit-in began at the lunch counter of a nearby store.
>
> *From Chapter 28, p. 874*

After you read the passage, answer the following questions.

1. What word is a synonym of "sit-in" that is given in that word's definition?

2. What clue is given that helps you find the synonym in the above passage?

3. Can you think of another synonym for sit-in that might have been used?

Key Terms and People

Chapter 28

Section 1
Thurgood Marshall *(p. 871)*
Brown v. *Board of Education (p. 871)*
Little Rock Nine *(p. 871)*
Rosa Parks *(p. 872)*
Montgomery bus boycott *(p. 873)*
Martin Luther King Jr. *(p. 873)*
sit-in *(p. 874)*
Student Nonviolent Coordinating Committee *(p. 874)*

Section 2
John F. Kennedy *(p. 876)*
Freedom Rides *(p. 877)*
March on Washington *(p. 878)*
Lyndon B. Johnson *(p. 879)*
Civil Rights Act of 1964 *(p. 879)*
Voting Rights Act of 1965 *(p. 879)*
Great Society *(p. 880)*
Black Power *(p. 880)*
Malcolm X *(p. 880)*

Section 3
Cesar Chavez *(p. 882)*
United Farm Workers *(p. 882)*
Betty Friedan *(p. 883)*
National Organization for Women *(p. 883)*
Shirley Chisholm *(p. 883)*
Equal Rights Amendment *(p. 883)*
Phyllis Schlafly *(p. 883)*
American Indian Movement *(p. 884)*
Disabled in Action *(p. 885)*

Academic Vocabulary

In this chapter, you will learn the following academic words:
implement *(p. 871)*
consequences *(p. 883)*

As you read Chapter 28, look for synonyms that can help you define words you don't know.

The Civil Rights Movement Takes Shape

VA Virginia Standards of Learning USII.1b, USII.8d, USII.9a, USII.9c

What You Will Learn...

Main Ideas

1. Civil rights leaders battled school segregation in court.
2. The Montgomery bus boycott helped end segregation on buses.
3. Students organized sit-ins to protest segregation.

The Big Idea

Civil rights activists used legal challenges and public protests to confront segregation.

Key Terms and People

Thurgood Marshall, *p. 871*
Brown v. *Board of Education, p. 871*
Little Rock Nine, *p. 871*
Rosa Parks, *p. 872*
Montgomery bus boycott, *p. 873*
Martin Luther King Jr., *p. 873*
sit-in, *p. 874*
Student Nonviolent Coordinating Committee, *p. 874*

TAKING NOTES As you read, take notes on key events in the fight against segregation in a web diagram like the one below. In each outer circle of the web, describe one event. You may need to add more circles.

Challenges to Segregation

If YOU were there...

You are an African American student in the 1950s. You get up early every day and take a long bus ride across the city to an African American public school. There is another school just three blocks from your home, but only white students are welcome there. You have heard, however, that this school will soon be opening its doors to black students as well.

Would you want to be one of the first African Americans to attend this school? Why or why not?

BUILDING BACKGROUND African Americans continued to face segregation and discrimination after World War II. Early victories in the civil rights movement included the end of segregation in baseball in 1947 and President Truman's ban on segregation in the military in 1948. These successes were the beginning of a national movement for civil rights.

Battling School Segregation

The 1896 Supreme Court case *Plessy* v. *Ferguson* established the "separate-but-equal" doctrine. This doctrine stated that federal, state, and local governments could allow segregation as long as separate facilities were equal. One result of this ruling was that states in both the North and South maintained separate schools for white and black students. Government officials often insisted that though these schools were separate, they were equal in quality.

In fact, however, schools for black children typically received far less funding. Early civil rights leaders, led by members of the National Association for the Advancement of Colored People (NAACP), focused on ending segregation in America's public schools.

Brown v. Board of Education

The NAACP's strategy was to show that separate schools did not provide equal educational opportunities for black students. The NAACP attorney **Thurgood Marshall** led the courtroom battles against segregation. In the early 1950s, several school segregation cases came together under the title of *Brown v. Board of Education*. The "Brown" in the case title was a seven-year-old African American girl from Topeka, Kansas, named Linda Brown. Though she lived near a school for white children, Linda Brown had to travel across town to a school for black children. Linda's father and the NAACP sued to allow Linda to attend the school closer to her home.

On May 17, 1954, the Supreme Court issued a unanimous ruling on *Brown* v. *Board of Education*. The Court ruled that segregation in public schools was illegal.

The next year, the Court ordered public schools to desegregate, or integrate, "with all deliberate speed." These rulings were major turning points in the civil rights movement—but they would prove difficult to enforce.

Little Rock Nine

In the entire South, only three school districts began desegregating in 1954. Most others **implemented** gradual integration plans. In Little Rock, Arkansas, the school board decided to start by integrating one high school. It allowed nine outstanding black students to attend Central High School. These students became known as the **Little Rock Nine**. Arkansas governor Orval Faubus was determined to prevent desegregation at Central High School, however. He used National Guard troops to block the Little Rock Nine from entering the school.

On the morning of September 4, 1957, eight of the nine students arrived at the school together and were turned away by the National Guard. Then the ninth student, 15-year-old Elizabeth Eckford, arrived at the school by herself. She found the entrance blocked by the National Guard. Turning around, she faced a screaming mob. Someone began yelling, *"Lynch her! Lynch her!"* Finally, a white man and woman guided Eckford to safety.

Elizabeth Eckford and the rest of the Little Rock Nine went home. For weeks, Governor

ACADEMIC VOCABULARY

implement put in place

FOCUS ON READING

What is a synonym for *desegregate*?

THE IMPACT TODAY

In 1967 Thurgood Marshall became the first African American Supreme Court justice. Clarence Thomas became the second African American justice in 1991.

SUPREME COURT DECISIONS

Brown v. Board of Education (1954)

Background of the Case In 1896 the Supreme Court had ruled in *Plessy* v. *Ferguson* that "separate-but-equal" facilities were constitutional. In 1951 the NAACP sued the Board of Education of Topeka, Kansas. It argued that segregated schools did not give equal opportunities to black and white children. After hearing many arguments, the Court made its ruling in 1954.

The Court's Ruling
The Supreme Court overturned the *Plessy* doctrine of "separate-but-equal." It ruled that racially segregated schools were not equal and were therefore unconstitutional. All of the justices agreed to the ruling, making it unanimous.

The Court's Reasoning
The Supreme Court decided that segregation violated the Fourteenth Amendment's guarantee of "equal protection of the laws." Its opinion stated, "We conclude that, in the field of public education, the doctrine of 'separate-but-equal' has no place. Separate educational facilities are inherently [naturally] unequal."

Why It Matters
The ruling in *Brown* v. *Board of Education* led to integrated public schools. It also opened the door to other successful challenges to segregation in public places.

Linda Brown, age 9

ANALYSIS SKILL **ANALYZING INFORMATION**

1. How did the ruling in *Brown* v. *Board of Education* overturn the 1896 Supreme Court ruling in *Plessy* v. *Ferguson*?
2. How might parents of both black and white children at the time have reacted to the ruling in *Brown* v. *Board of Education*?

An Apology

The famous photograph to the right shows Elizabeth Eckford walking to Little Rock's Central High School on September 4, 1957. The young woman shouting at Eckford is Hazel Massery. Massery was later sorry for what she had done. She decided that she did not want to be, she said, the "poster child of the hate generation, trapped in the image captured in the photograph." In 1963 Massery apologized to Eckford. The two women, shown below, have since become friends and have spoken publicly together about their experiences.

Faubus refused to allow them to attend the school. The tense situation lasted until President Eisenhower sent federal troops to escort the students into the school.

The Little Rock Nine began attending classes, but resistance to integration continued. Some white students insulted, harassed, and attacked the black students. In spite of these obstacles, eight of the nine remained at the school. In May 1958 Ernest Green became the first African American student to graduate from Central High. When Green's name was called at the graduation ceremony, no one clapped. "But I figured they didn't have to," he later said. "After I got that diploma, that was it. I had accomplished what I had come there for."

READING CHECK **Summarizing** What obstacles faced supporters of desegregation?

Montgomery Bus Boycott

The victory in *Brown* v. *Board of Education* was part of a larger struggle against segregation. Most facilities in the South, including public transportation, remained segregated.

The NAACP decided to continue the battle against segregation in Montgomery, Alabama. Black passengers there were required to sit in the back of city buses. If the whites-only front section filled up, black passengers had to give up their seats.

On December 1, 1955, a seamstress and NAACP worker named **Rosa Parks** boarded a bus and sat in the front row of the section reserved for black passengers. When the bus became full, the driver told Parks and three others to give their seats to white passengers. Parks refused. The bus driver called the police, and Parks was taken to jail.

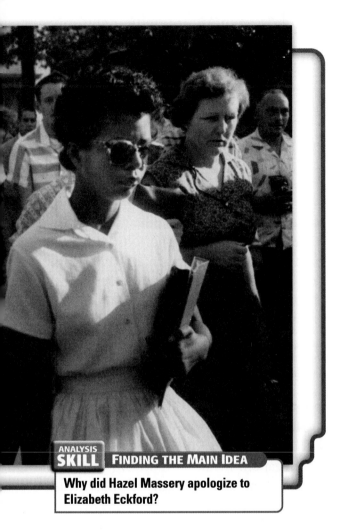

ANALYSIS SKILL **FINDING THE MAIN IDEA**

Why did Hazel Massery apologize to Elizabeth Eckford?

bicycles, and walked. Still, Montgomery's leaders refused to integrate the bus system.

As in Little Rock during the school segregation fight, many white residents were angry about the attempt to end segregation. Some people resorted to violence. King's home was bombed, and he received hate mail and phone calls threatening him and his family. The police also harassed and arrested carpool drivers. In spite of this intimidation, the boycott gained national attention, sparking similar protests in other cities.

Finally, in November 1956 the Supreme Court ruled that segregation on public transportation was illegal. The next month, King joined other black and white ministers to ride the first integrated bus in Montgomery. "It . . . makes you feel that America is a great country and we're going to do more to make it greater," remembered Jo Ann Robinson.

The Montgomery bus boycott helped make Martin Luther King Jr. a nationally known civil rights leader. He formed the Southern Christian Leadership Conference (SCLC), which led campaigns for civil rights throughout the South.

READING CHECK **Identifying Cause and Effect**
What event sparked the Montgomery bus boycott?

To protest Parks's arrest, African American professor Jo Ann Robinson organized a boycott of Montgomery buses. Local leaders formed the Montgomery Improvement Association (MIA) to help strengthen the boycott. In the **Montgomery bus boycott**, thousands of African Americans stopped riding the buses. Some white residents supported the boycott as well. Bus ridership fell by 70 percent.

To lead the MIA, African American leaders turned to **Martin Luther King Jr.**, a young Baptist minister. The 26-year-old King already had a reputation as a powerful speaker whose words could motivate and inspire listeners.

As the boycott continued, bus drivers guided nearly empty buses down the city streets. Leaders planned a carpool system that helped people find rides at more than 40 locations throughout Montgomery. For 381 days, boycotters carpooled, took taxis, rode

BIOGRAPHY

Rosa Parks
1913–2005

Rosa Parks was born in Tuskegee, Alabama, and spent most of her childhood in Montgomery. While working as a seamstress, Parks became an active member of the NAACP.

She was fired from her seamstress job for her leading role in the Montgomery bus boycott. After the boycott succeeded, she and her husband moved to Detroit, Michigan. She continued working for fair treatment for all Americans and started a program to teach children about the Underground Railroad and the civil rights movement.

Finding the Main Idea How did Rosa Parks worked for equal rights?

Sit-ins and the SNCC

Like public schools and buses, many private businesses in the South were segregated. In Greensboro, North Carolina, four students decided to challenge this form of segregation. They targeted a lunch counter at Woolworth, a popular department store. Black customers were supposed to eat standing up at one end of the counter. White customers sat down to eat at the other end.

On February 1, 1960, the students went into Woolworth and staged a **sit-in**—a demonstration in which protesters sit down and refuse to leave. They sat in the "whites-only" section of the lunch counter and ordered coffee. They were not served, but they stayed until the store closed. The next day, they returned with dozens more students to continue the sit-in. Soon, another sit-in began at the lunch counter of a nearby store.

People across the country read newspaper stories about the Greensboro sit-ins. Other black students in the South began to hold similar protests. The student protesters practiced the strategy of nonviolent resistance.

No matter how much they were insulted or threatened, they refused to respond with violence. They were inspired by Martin Luther King Jr., who was a strong supporter of nonviolent action.

Over time, some restaurants and businesses, including Woolworth, began the process of integration. To continue the struggle for civil rights, the leaders of the student protests formed the **Student Nonviolent Coordinating Committee** (SNCC) in the spring of 1960. The SNCC activists trained protesters and organized civil rights demonstrations. Bob Moses, a leader of the SNCC, helped organize sit-ins and voter registration drives.

READING CHECK **Comparing** How were sit-ins similar to other civil rights protests?

SUMMARY AND PREVIEW In the 1950s court rulings and protests challenged segregation. In the next section you will learn how the civil rights movement continued the fight against inequality.

THE IMPACT TODAY

Today Bob Moses runs the Algebra Project. Its goals include helping students in poor communities become skilled in math, get into college, and compete for jobs.

Section 1 Assessment

go.hrw.com
Online Quiz
KEYWORD: SB7 HP28

Reviewing Ideas, Terms, and People

1. **a. Summarize** How did the Supreme Court impact the desegregation of public schools?
   b. Identify Who were the **Little Rock Nine**?
2. **a. Recall** What was the purpose of the **Montgomery bus boycott**?
   b. Analyze Why was the arrest of **Rosa Parks** a turning point in the civil rights movement?
   c. Elaborate Why do you think the bus boycott lasted so long?
3. **a. Identify** What means did the **Student Nonviolent Coordinating Committee** use to protest segregation?
   b. Make Inferences What might have inspired the Greensboro students to stage a **sit-in**?
   c. Evaluate Do you think nonviolent resistance is an effective form of protest? Why or why not?

Critical Thinking

4. **Sequencing** Review your notes on events that challenged segregation. Then copy the graphic organizer below and use it to show the sequence of major events in the civil rights movement described in this section.

FOCUS ON WRITING

5. **Explaining Major Issues** Take notes on the major issues behind the civil rights movement. What were these issues? Why were they important to African Americans? What changes did the movement try to make?

Martin Luther King Jr.

How would you help lead a national movement?

When did he live? 1929–1968

Where did he live? King grew up in Atlanta, Georgia, where his father was a pastor. He studied to become a minister in Pennsylvania. He received his doctorate in Massachusetts, then became pastor of a church in Alabama. He traveled throughout the country as a civil rights leader.

What did he do? As a powerful and moving speaker, King became one of the leading voices of the civil rights movement. He was committed to achieving equality through nonviolent protest. He led a series of successful marches and protests, including the 1955 Montgomery bus boycott and the 1963 March on Washington.

Why is he so important? His leadership helped make the civil rights movement a success. His belief in and passion for nonviolence led to the boycotts, sit-ins, and marches that helped African Americans gain equal treatment. King's work helped bring an end to legal segregation and led to new laws guaranteeing equal rights for all Americans.

Evaluating Which of Martin Luther King Jr.'s contributions to the civil rights movement was most important? Why?

KEY EVENTS

- **1953** Marries Coretta Scott

- **1955** Becomes leader of the Montgomery Improvement Association

- **1957** Founds Southern Christian Leadership Conference

- **1963** Writes "Letter from Birmingham Jail"; gives the "I Have a Dream" speech at the March on Washington

- **1964** Wins the Nobel Peace Prize; Civil Rights Act of 1964 is passed

- **1968** Shot and killed in Memphis, Tennessee

- **1986** Martin Luther King Jr. Day becomes a national holiday.

" *I have a dream that my four children will one day live in a nation where they will not be judged by the color of their skin but by the content of their character.* "

—Martin Luther King Jr.,
speech at March on Washington

Kennedy, Johnson, and Civil Rights

Virginia Standards of Learning USII.1b, USII.1c, USII.2c, USII.8d, USII.9a, USII.9c

What You Will Learn...

Main Ideas

1. John F. Kennedy was elected president in 1960.
2. Civil rights leaders continued to fight for equality.
3. Lyndon B. Johnson became president when Kennedy was assassinated.
4. Changes occurred in the civil rights movement in the late 1960s.

The Big Idea

The civil rights movement made major advances during the presidencies of John F. Kennedy and Lyndon B. Johnson.

Key Terms and People

John F. Kennedy, *p. 876*
Freedom Rides, *p. 877*
March on Washington, *p. 878*
Lyndon B. Johnson, *p. 879*
Civil Rights Act of 1964, *p. 879*
Voting Rights Act of 1965, *p. 879*
Great Society, *p. 880*
Black Power, *p. 880*
Malcolm X, *p. 880*

TAKING NOTES As you read, take notes on the names of leaders who supported civil rights. Use a chart like this one for your notes on these leaders and their goals.

Leaders	Goals

If YOU were there...

You are a civil rights activist living and working in the South. It is 1960, a presidential election year. The battle for fair treatment has been difficult, and you hope that the next president will support civil rights. Both major presidential candidates will be visiting your area soon, and you might have a chance to meet them and ask some questions.

What questions would you ask the candidates?

BUILDING BACKGROUND In the 1960 presidential election Republican Richard M. Nixon, who had served as Eisenhower's vice president, ran against Democrat John F. Kennedy, a senator from Massachusetts. For the first time, presidential candidates debated each other on television. Kennedy's performance in the televised debates helped him win a very close election.

Kennedy Elected

When **John F. Kennedy** won the election of 1960, he became the youngest person ever elected president of the United States. For many Americans, Kennedy and his wife, Jacqueline, brought a sense of style and excitement to the White House. Kennedy was also the first Roman Catholic to become president.

In his inaugural address, Kennedy spoke of the opportunities and dangers facing Americans. "Man holds in his mortal hands the power to abolish all forms of human poverty and all forms of human life," he said. He encouraged all Americans to support freedom throughout the world, saying, "And so, my fellow Americans, ask not what your country can do for you—ask what you can do for your country."

As president, Kennedy pursued a set of proposals he called the New Frontier. His plan included a higher minimum wage and tax cuts to help stimulate economic growth. It called for new spending on the military and on the space program, and new programs to help

Freedom Rides, 1961

CORE route
SNCC route
★ Arrests
✦ Violence

0   100   200 Miles
0   100   200 Kilometers

Freedom Riders were attacked by white mobs, who threw stones, slashed tires, and set buses on fire. One series of rides was discontinued to protect the safety of the riders.

Washington, D.C. May 4
Richmond
Greensboro
Charlotte May 8
Rock Hill May 9
Winnsboro May 10
Nashville
Memphis
Birmingham May 14 May 17
Atlanta
Augusta
Anniston May 14
Meridian
Montgomery May 20
Selma
Jackson May 24

ATLANTIC OCEAN

Gulf of Mexico

New Orleans

go.hrw.com
Interactive Map
KEYWORD: SB7 CH28

GEOGRAPHY SKILLS | **INTERPRETING MAPS**

1. **Place** Where did the Freedom Rides attempt to travel?
2. **Location** According to this map, in which state did the Freedom Riders meet the most resistance?

---

poor and unemployed Americans. Kennedy also proposed providing greater financial help to public schools. Fearing a budget imbalance, Republicans and conservative southern Democrats blocked much of the legislation Kennedy introduced.

Kennedy also spoke of his support for the goals of the civil rights movement. This had helped convince many African Americans to vote for him in the election of 1960. As president, however, Kennedy moved slowly on civil rights legislation. He was reluctant to anger Republicans and conservative southern Democrats in Congress, whose support he needed to pass other items on his agenda. Kennedy was also busy dealing with foreign policy crises, as you will read in the next chapter.

READING CHECK **Drawing Inferences** What do you think African American voters hoped for from the new president?

The Fight for Rights Continues

Public schools and some businesses had begun to desegregate. But other facilities remained strictly segregated.

Freedom Rides

In 1947 a civil rights group called the Congress of Racial Equality (CORE) began protests in which African Americans rode in the whites-only section of interstate buses. In 1960 the Court ruled that segregation of bus stations was illegal. CORE decided to put pressure on President Kennedy to enforce this ruling.

To accomplish this, CORE organized a series of protests called the **Freedom Rides,** in which black and white bus riders traveled together to segregated bus stations in the South. White riders planned to use facilities set aside for African Americans in bus stations. Black riders would use whites-only facilities.

John F. Kennedy
1917–1963

John F. Kennedy was born to a politically powerful and wealthy family in Massachusetts. He graduated from Harvard University, then joined the U.S. Navy. He commanded a patrol boat in the South Pacific during World War II and was wounded in a sea battle. Kennedy was elected to the House of Representatives at the age of 29 and to the Senate six years later. He was elected president in 1960, bringing a youthful energy to the White House. He had served for fewer than three years when he was assassinated.

Lyndon B. Johnson
1908–1973

Lyndon B. Johnson grew up in rural Texas. After working his way through college, Johnson taught school for a year. In 1937, at the age of 29, he was elected to the House of Representatives. He was elected to the Senate in 1948. Johnson was known for his ability to guide bills through Congress by convincing members from both political parties to support them. As one fellow member of Congress said, "Lyndon got me by the lapels [jacket collar] and put his face on top of mine and he talked and talked." Johnson was elected vice president in 1960 and became president in 1963.

Contrasting How were Kennedy's and Johnson's careers similar, and how were they different?

The Freedom Rides began in May 1961, when thirteen riders boarded a bus traveling from Washington, D.C., to New Orleans, Louisiana. In one Alabama town, the riders were viciously attacked by a white mob. After more attacks, CORE leaders decided to stop the protest to protect the riders' lives.

The leaders of the SNCC decided to continue the Freedom Rides. The SNCC activists faced the same violence as the CORE riders. Arriving in Montgomery, Alabama, in late May, they were attacked by a furious mob. Many freedom riders were jailed in Jackson, Mississippi. That same month, President Kennedy ordered the Interstate Commerce Commission to enforce strict bans on segregation in interstate bus terminals.

King in Birmingham

In 1963 Martin Luther King Jr. organized marches in Birmingham, Alabama. King was arrested and jailed for marching without a permit. While jailed, he wrote "Letter from Birmingham Jail," explaining his commitment to nonviolence. "We will reach the goal of freedom in Birmingham and all over the nation, because the goal of America is freedom."

King was released from prison and led a new round of marches. In May 1963, some 2,500 demonstrators marched through downtown Birmingham. Police commissioner Eugene "Bull" Connor ordered his officers to unleash their attack dogs and blast the marchers with high-pressure water hoses. Televised images of their tactics shocked Americans.

The March on Washington

Pressure for civil rights legislation continued to grow. President Kennedy called racial discrimination "a moral crisis." In June 1963 he announced support for a sweeping civil rights bill to end racial discrimination completely.

To demonstrate support for the civil rights bill, African American leaders held the **March on Washington**—a massive demonstration for civil rights. On August 28, 1963, Martin Luther King Jr. stood at the Lincoln Memorial before a diverse crowd of more than 200,000 people. In his famous "I Have a Dream" speech, King expressed his hope for a future in which all Americans would enjoy equal rights and opportunities.

READING CHECK Summarizing How did the Birmingham marches affect public opinion?

Johnson and Civil Rights

After he became president, Lyndon Johnson promised to continue Kennedy's plans for civil rights legislation. Johnson worked with Congress and African American leaders to create and pass laws that would help ensure equality for all Americans. Here, Johnson is shown signing the Civil Rights Act of 1964 as Martin Luther King, Jr. and other leaders look on.

How did Johnson work to continue Kennedy's campaign promises?

Johnson Becomes President

In the months following the March on Washington, Congress debated Kennedy's civil rights legislation. In November 1963 Kennedy began a quick tour of Texas cities.

Kennedy Assassinated

On November 22, 1963, Kennedy rode through Dallas in a convertible, waving to supporters in the streets. Suddenly, gunshots rang out. Kennedy had been shot twice, and he died soon afterward in a Dallas hospital. Vice President **Lyndon B. Johnson** was quickly sworn in as president. Dallas police arrested an alleged assassin, Lee Harvey Oswald.

The assassination stunned Americans, who grieved the young president's death. Many of Kennedy's goals were left unfinished. Vowing to continue Kennedy's work, President Johnson urged Congress to pass a civil rights bill.

Civil Rights Laws

On July 2, 1964, President Johnson signed the **Civil Rights Act of 1964**. The act banned segregation in public places. It also outlawed discrimination in the workplace on the basis of color, gender, religion, or national origin.

That summer, activists began to push for equal voting rights for African Americans in the South. Legally, of course, African Americans had the right to vote. But in much of the South, threats and unfair election rules often kept them from the polls. During the "Freedom Summer" of 1964, hundreds of volunteers, including many white college students, came to Mississippi. Their goal was to help African Americans register to vote.

Volunteers were threatened and attacked. On June 21 three civil rights workers—James Chaney, a young black Mississippian plasterer's apprentice; Andrew Goodman, a Jewish Queens College student; and Michael Schwerner, a Jewish social worker from New York City—were murdered by members of the Ku Klux Klan. Martin Luther King, Jr. organized a voting rights march from Selma, Alabama, to Montgomery, during which many marchers were beaten and jailed. Violence against civil rights workers convinced many people to support voter registration efforts.

Congress approved the **Voting Rights Act of 1965**, which Johnson signed into law in August. This law gave the federal government new powers to protect African Americans' voting rights. Within three years, more than half of all qualified African Americans in the South registered to vote.

THE IMPACT TODAY

In June 2005 a judge in Mississippi sentenced Edgar Ray Killen to 60 years in prison for his role in the murder of the three civil rights workers. The 1967 case had ended in a deadlocked jury.

The Great Society

Great Society Legislation:

- Civil Rights Act of 1964
- Voting Rights Act of 1965
- Elementary and Secondary Education Act of 1965
- Medicare and Medicaid Bill, 1965
- Department of Housing and Urban Development Act of 1965

The Great Society

President Johnson won the election of 1964 by a huge margin. He saw this as a vote of approval for his program of domestic reforms that he called the **Great Society**. "The Great Society rests on abundance and liberty for all," Johnson said.

Congress quickly passed most of Johnson's Great Society legislation. Great Society programs included Medicare and Medicaid, which help senior citizens and low-income citizens afford health care. Another act gave local schools more than $1 billion to help students with special needs. The Department of Housing and Urban Development (HUD) was created to help low-income families get better housing. Robert Weaver served as HUD's secretary, becoming the first African American appointed to a presidential cabinet.

READING CHECK **Summarizing** How did President Johnson support civil rights?

Changes in the Rights Movement

Many young civil rights reformers found the pace of change too slow. Others entirely rejected the goal of racial integration.

New Directions

One such activist was Stokely Carmichael, who had participated in the Freedom Rides and many marches. But in the mid-1960s, he broke with the goal of nonviolence. Carmichael was a founder of the **Black Power** movement, which called for African American independence. Black Power activists believed that blacks should reject integration, focusing instead on controlling their own communities.

Malcolm X helped inspire the Black Power movement. He was a leader of the Nation of Islam, an organization that combined ideas about African American independence with the teachings of Islam. Malcolm X argued that African Americans should work for social and political independence. He believed that African Americans had the right to defend themselves, using violence if necessary.

Time Line

Civil Rights Movement, Key Events

1955 An African American tailor's assistant named Rosa Parks refused to give up her seat on a Montgomery, Alabama, bus, sparking a citywide bus boycott that would last more than a year.

1950

1960 The first sit-in at a lunch counter occurs in Greensboro, North Carolina. During these sit-ins, young African Americans sat at segregated lunch counters along with their white counterparts and asked to be served.

In 1964 Malcolm X traveled to the Muslim holy city of Mecca, where he met Muslims of many races. He began to hope that different races could coexist in peace, although he still supported freedom "by any means necessary." But in 1965 Malcolm X broke with the Nation of Islam and was killed by three of its members.

Violence in the Streets

Slow progress in the civil rights movement frustrated many members of the black community. In some U.S. cities, tensions exploded into violent, sometimes deadly, riots. One such riot occurred in August 1965 in the Watts section of Los Angeles. Twenty-four people were killed, and much of Watts was destroyed.

In April 1968 Martin Luther King Jr. was shot and killed in Memphis, Tennessee. As televised reports spread the news of King's assassination, furious rioters took to the streets in more than 100 American cities. The movement had lost its most visible leader.

1963 Four young girls die in the racially motivated bombing of a Birmingham, Alabama, church. The deaths lead to riots and civil unrest during which police attack African Americans. Televised images of the events shocked many people.

1965

1964 Civil rights leader Martin Luther King Jr. receives the Nobel Peace Prize for his work in nonviolent demonstrations against segregation.

READING CHECK **Contrasting** How did Malcolm X's goals differ from Martin Luther King Jr.'s?

SUMMARY AND PREVIEW Under Kennedy and Johnson, major civil rights legislation was passed. In the next section, you will learn how more groups began to push for equal rights.

go.hrw.com
Online Quiz
KEYWORD: SB7 HP28

Section 2 Assessment

Reviewing Ideas, Terms, and People

1. **a. Describe** How was **John F. Kennedy** different from previous presidents?
   b. Analyze Why did many African Americans vote for Kennedy?
2. **a. Identify** What were the **Freedom Rides**?
   b. Explain How did television influence public opinion about the civil rights movement?
3. **a. Recall** What happened in Dallas, Texas, on November 22, 1963?
   b. Draw Conclusions Based on Johnson's plans for the **Great Society**, what do you think he believed was the purpose of government?
4. **a. Recall** What challenges did the civil rights movement face in the late 1960s?
   b. Elaborate Why did **Malcolm X** reject the goal of racial integration?

Critical Thinking

5. **Evaluating** Review your notes on the goals and achievements of leaders who supported civil rights. Then copy the graphic organizer below and use it to evaluate the leaders discussed in the section. Tell whether or not you think the leaders' actions were effective.

Leader	Evaluation

FOCUS ON WRITING

6. **Listing Laws** List new civil rights laws passed in the 1960s. What were the goals of these laws? What problems or events did they respond to? As a member of Congress, would you have approved of these laws? Why or why not?

THE CIVIL RIGHTS MOVEMENT **881**

Rights for Other Americans

Virginia Standards of Learning USII.1b, USII.1d, USII.1e, USII.8d, USII.9a, USII.9c

What You Will Learn...

Main Ideas

1. Hispanic Americans organized for civil rights and economic opportunities.
2. The women's movement worked for equal rights.
3. Other Americans also fought for change.

The Big Idea

Encouraged by the success of the civil rights movement, many groups worked for equal rights in the 1960s.

Key Terms and People

Cesar Chavez, *p. 882*
United Farm Workers, *p. 882*
Betty Friedan, *p. 883*
National Organization for Women, *p. 883*
Shirley Chisholm, *p. 883*
Equal Rights Amendment, *p. 883*
Phyllis Schlafly, *p. 883*
American Indian Movement, *p. 884*
Disabled in Action, *p. 885*

TAKING NOTES As you read, make a list of major events that occurred as various groups worked for equal rights. You may want to organize your list in a table like this one.

Social Movements in the 1960s

If YOU were there...

Your parents came to the United States from Mexico, and you were born in California in the 1950s. You and your family work year round picking crops—the work is hard, and the pay is low. You're trying to put aside some money for school, but your family barely makes enough to get by. Some farm workers are talking about going on strike for better wages.

Would you join the strike? Why or why not?

BUILDING BACKGROUND Many Americans faced unfair treatment in the 1960s. Women were paid lower wages and had fewer job opportunities than men. Hispanic Americans had long faced discrimination as well. The victories of the civil rights movement inspired many groups to struggle for equal rights as well.

Hispanic Americans Organize for Change

The Hispanic population of the United States grew to 4 million by 1960, and to more than 10 million by 1970. Though people of Mexican descent made up the majority of this population, Hispanic Americans were a diverse group. Many people from Puerto Rico, Cuba, and other Latin American countries also lived in the United States.

The success of African Americans encouraged Hispanic Americans to fight for their own rights. **Cesar Chavez** was one of many Hispanic Americans who worked to improve conditions. In 1962 Chavez formed a union that would later become the **United Farm Workers** (UFW). This union was committed to the goal of better pay and working conditions for migrant farm workers. Chavez led the UFW in a five-year strike and boycott against California grape growers. The workers finally won better wages and benefits in 1970. The UFW became a national organization in 1976 when it merged with an eastern Puerto Rican farm workers' union.

Chavez shared the commitment to nonviolent protest. To those who complained about the slow pace of change, he replied:

> "Nonviolence takes time ... I despise exploitation [unfair gain] and I want change, but I'm willing to pay the price in terms of time. There's a Mexican saying, 'Hay más tiempo que vida'—there's more time than life. We've got all the time in the world."
>
> —Cesar Chavez, quoted in *Chávez, César: Autobiography of La Causa*

Chavez helped inspire young leaders in what became known as the Chicano movement. To fight discrimination and gain greater political influence, Chicano activists formed a political party called *La Raza Unida*, or the United Race. The Hispanic civil rights movement had important <u>consequences</u>. A 1968 amendment to the Elementary and Secondary Education Act required schools to teach students whose first language was not English in both languages until they learned English. The Voting Rights Act of 1975 required communities with large immigrant populations to print ballots in the voters' preferred language.

READING CHECK **Sequencing** What group helped inspire the Chicano movement?

The Women's Movement

Activists also brought public attention to women's position in society. In 1963 a government commission reported that women had fewer job opportunities than men and were often paid less for the same work. President Kennedy responded by ordering an end to discrimination based on gender in civil service jobs. That same year Congress passed the Equal Pay Act, which required many employers to pay men and women equal salaries for the same work. The Civil Rights Act of 1964 banned discrimination based on both gender and race.

Some women also began to question their traditional roles in society. In her 1963 book *The Feminine Mystique*, **Betty Friedan** described the dissatisfaction some women felt with their traditional roles of wife, mother, and homemaker.

BIOGRAPHY

Cesar Chavez
1927–1993

Cesar Chavez was born on a small family ranch in Arizona. After losing their land during the Great Depression, Chavez and his family began working as migrant farm workers. Moving from town to town in search of work, Chavez went to more than 30 different schools. He served in the U.S. Navy during World War II, then returned to the fields to help migrant workers fight for better pay and working conditions. The soft-spoken Chavez seemed to many an unlikely leader of a protest movement. But Chavez quickly became an influential leader, continuing to lead the struggle for farm workers' rights into the 1990s. Before his death, Chavez insisted, "It's not me who counts, it's the Movement."

Making Inferences Why do you think Chavez began the farm workers' movement?

Friedan became a leader of the modern women's rights movement. In 1966 she helped found the **National Organization for Women** (NOW) to fight for equal educational and career opportunities for women. Other women worked for change by running for public office. In 1968 **Shirley Chisholm** was elected to represent a New York City district in the House of Representatives. She was the first African American woman elected to the U.S. Congress.

In the early 1970s, NOW and other women's rights activists supported an amendment to the Constitution. The **Equal Rights Amendment** (ERA) would outlaw all discrimination based on sex. The ERA was approved by Congress in 1972.

For an amendment to go into effect, it must be ratified by three-fourths of the states—or 38 out of 50 states. The ERA was ratified by 30 state legislatures by the end of 1973. But many opponents came forward to block the ERA. **Phyllis Schlafly**, a conservative activist, founded the group STOP ERA to prevent its ratification. Schlafly and her supporters argued that the ERA would hurt

ACADEMIC VOCABULARY

consequences the effects of a particular event or events

THE IMPACT TODAY

Ninety women served in the 110th Congress, the highest total in U.S. history. In 2007, Nancy Pelosi was elected the first female Speaker of the House.

In the 1960s, women began to organize to demand equal rights. The movement became known as women's liberation. Many activists supported a woman's right to equal pay and equal protection under the law. Some opposing activists worked to maintain what they saw as women's protected status under the law.

Shirley Chisholm became the first African American woman elected to Congress in 1968.

Betty Friedan authored *The Feminine Mystique,* a book declaring that many women wanted achievements beyond those of becoming a wife and mother.

Phyllis Schlafly argued against the Equal Rights Amendment, saying it would reduce the legal rights of wives and mothers.

families by encouraging women to focus on careers rather than on motherhood. Such opposition weakened support for the ERA. In June 1982 the amendment fell three states short of ratification.

Despite this failure, the women's movement achieved many of its goals. Women found new opportunities in education and the workplace. For example, women began attending many formerly all-male universities. Increasing numbers of women pursued careers in traditionally all-male fields such as law and medicine. Many women also won political office at all levels of government.

READING CHECK Finding Main Ideas
What were some achievements of the women's movement of the 1960s?

Other Voices for Change

Other Americans also began to demand change in laws and other discriminating practices during the 1960s and 1970s. In 1974 the Asian American Legal Defense and Education Fund was founded with the purpose of building an "informed and active Asian America." The National Italian American Foundation (1975) advocates for Italian Americans. League of United Latin American Citizens, which was founded much earlier, played an important activist role for Hispanic Americans during this period as well and continues to do so today. Native Americans and people with disabilities were also inspired by the civil rights movement.

Native Americans

One major issue for Native Americans was their lack of control over tribal lands. Many worked through the National Congress of American Indians (NCAI) to gain more control over reservation lands from the federal government. They helped win passage of the Indian Civil Rights Act of 1968.

Other activists thought that groups like the NCAI worked too slowly. In November 1969 a group of young Native Americans occupied Alcatraz Island in San Francisco Bay to protest the government's takeover of Native American lands.

described the group's goals, saying, "We don't want civil rights in the white man's society—we want our own sovereign [self-governing] rights." In February 1973 AIM activists seized a trading post and church at Wounded Knee, South Dakota—the site of the U.S. Army's massacre of Sioux Indians in 1890. Federal marshals surrounded Wounded Knee, and the standoff ended with a gun battle killing two protesters and wounding one federal agent.

Such protests brought attention to issues facing Native Americans. In the early 1970s Congress began passing laws granting Native Americans greater self-government on tribal lands.

The Disability Rights Movement

In 1970 Judy Heumann and other activists created **Disabled in Action** (DIA) to make people aware of challenges facing people with disabilities. People with disabilities often lacked access to both job opportunities and to public places. The DIA's work led to the passage of new laws. The Rehabilitation Act of 1973 banned federal agencies from discriminating against people with disabili-

ties. The Education of Handicapped Children Act of 1975 required public schools to provide a quality education to children with disabilities. In 1990 the Americans with Disabilities Act (ADA) outlawed all discrimination against people with disabilities.

READING CHECK **Contrasting** How were the tactics of AIM and DIA different?

SUMMARY AND PREVIEW The fight for equal rights had far-reaching effects on American society. In the next chapter you will learn about world conflicts that also affected Americans.

Disabled in Action

Judy Heumann and other activists formed Disabled in Action in 1970. The group promotes legislation and access to independent living for people with disabilities.

What kind of rights might people with disabilities seek?

---

go.hrw.com
Online Quiz
KEYWORD: SB7 HP28

Section 3 Assessment

Reviewing Ideas, Terms, and People

1. **a. Evaluate** How did Hispanic Americans fight for civil rights?
   b. Describe Who benefited from laws like the Elementary and Secondary Education Act of 1968 and the Voting Rights Act of 1975?
2. **a. Recall** What were the goals of the women's movement?
   b. Explain What happened during the ratification process of the **Equal Rights Amendment**?
   c. Elaborate Do you think we need the ERA today? Explain your answer.
3. **a. Compare** In what way was the **American Indian Movement** similar to the Black Power movement?
   b. Identify What laws banned discrimination against people with disabilities?

Critical Thinking

4. **Categorizing** Review your notes on the achievements of groups that worked for equal rights. Then copy the graphic organizer below and use it to identify the achievements of each group.

Hispanic Americans	Women	Native Americans	People with Disabilities

FOCUS ON WRITING

5. **Describing New Movements** Describe new rights movements inspired by the success of the African American civil rights movement. What groups did these movements represent? What were their goals? What did they accomplish?

Social Studies Skills

Analysis | Critical Thinking | Civic Participation | Study

Making Speeches

Define the Skill

In a democracy, activists, government leaders, and candidates for public office often need to address people directly. Speeches allow public figures to deliver a message to many people at once. People can use speeches to make their views known. They can use speeches to try to persuade people to support their ideas or programs.

Learn the Skill

Think about the role of speeches in the civil rights movement. Speakers increased awareness of and support for the movement's goals. Civil rights leader Martin Luther King, Jr. is remembered as a powerful and effective speaker. His words moved and inspired many listeners—and continue to do so today. Here is a brief excerpt from King's famous "I Have a Dream" speech, delivered during the March on Washington on August 28, 1963:

"I have a dream that one day on the red hills of Georgia the sons of former slaves and the sons of former slaveowners will be able to sit down together at the table of brotherhood.

"I have a dream that my four little children will one day live in a nation where they will not be judged by the color of their skin but by the content of their character.

"I have a dream today."

In his speech, King followed one basic idea. He used the same words over and over to emphasize his hopes for racial equality. Every time he said "I have a dream," however, King gave a different example of equality. With these different examples on the same topic, King laid out a powerful vision for the future.

The words of the "I Have a Dream" speech are powerful, but King's delivery made the speech even stronger. King spoke with confidence in a loud, clear voice. He also looked at his audience and connected with them.

Following these steps can help you make a persuasive speech.

❶ **Write the speech.** Make sure it includes a clear main idea, good examples, and convincing language.

❷ **Practice.** Practice reading your speech out loud to a friend. You can also practice at home in front of a mirror.

❸ **Give the speech.** Remember to speak loudly and clearly and to look at your audience.

Practice the Skill

Suppose that you are a civil rights leader in the 1960s. Following the steps above, write a short speech in favor of equal rights for African Americans, Hispanic Americans, women, Native Americans, or Americans with disabilities. After you have written and practiced your speech, give the speech to the class.

CHAPTER 28

HOLT
History's Impact
▶ video series
Review the video to answer the closing question:

How did the Civil Rights Act of 1964 inspire a push for equality among other minority groups?

Chapter Review

Visual Summary

QUICK FACTS

Use the visual summary below to help you review the main ideas of the chapter.

Many groups of Americans organized to demand their civil rights during the 1960s and 1970s.

Reviewing Vocabulary, Terms, and People

Complete each sentence by filling in the blank with the correct term or person from the chapter.

1. _____ was an African American civil rights leader and minister who believed in nonviolent, direct action.

2. In 1960, black students staged a _____ at a Woolworth lunch counter in Greensboro, North Carolina.

3. The Congress of Racial Equality organized the _____ to protest segregation in bus stations throughout the South.

4. The _____ protected the voting rights of African Americans.

5. The _____ worked to get better pay and working conditions for migrant farm workers.

6. _____ was the first African American woman elected to the United States Congress.

Comprehension and Critical Thinking

SECTION 1 *(Pages 870–874)*

7. **a. Describe** What was the Court's ruling in the *Brown* v. *Board of Education* case?

   b. Explain What did the Student Nonviolent Coordinating Committee do to fight segregation?

   c. Draw Conclusions Why do you think Martin Luther King Jr. was chosen to lead the MIA?

SECTION 2 *(Pages 876–881)*

8. **a. Recall** What was the New Frontier?

   b. Contrast What roles did leaders from CORE and SNCC play in the Freedom Rides?

   c. Contrast How did Malcolm X's ideas about integration differ from those of Martin Luther King Jr.?

9. a. Identify What is the National Organization for Women?

b. Summarize How did Cesar Chavez help migrant farm workers?

c. Elaborate How did the Americans with Disabilities Act help disabled Americans?

Reviewing Themes

10. Politics How did political changes help minorities achieve their goals?

11. Society and Culture How did society change during the civil rights era?

Reading Skills

Using Content Clues: Synonyms *Use the Reading Skills taught in this chapter to answer the question below.*

> The Little Rock Nine began attending classes, but resistance to integration continued. Some white students insulted, harassed, and attacked the black students. In spite of these obstacles, eight of the nine remained at the school. *(p. 872)*

12. Which of the following would be a good synonym for the word *harassed*?

a. comforted

b. assisted

c. helped

d. insulted

Social Studies Skills

Making Speeches *Use the Social Studies Skills taught in this chapter to answer the question below.*

13. What steps should you follow to make a persuasive speech?

Using the Internet go.hrw.com
KEYWORD: SB7 CH28

14. Activity: Creating a Newspaper Even after the ruling in *Brown* v. *Board of Education*, integration was slow to take effect. Many districts began gradual integration plans, as in Little Rock, Arkansas, where local leaders chose the Little Rock Nine to start the process. Enter the activity keyword. Research the Little Rock Nine and then create a two pages of a newspaper. Make sure your newspaper articles include direct references to your research. Include quotations from the historical figures that were involved in the integration of Central High School.

FOCUS ON WRITING

15. Writing Your Bill Review your notes. Then start writing your civil rights bill. What is its goal? Explain how it will expand civil rights. Is it designed to help a certain group of people? Discuss the reasons you believe it is important to expand civil rights in this way. You may refer to problems or events the bill responds to, as well as to earlier civil rights laws and legal decisions.

DIRECTIONS: Read each question and write the letter of the best response.

1 Use the following graph to answer the question below.

Women in the Labor Force

By about how much did the percentage of women in the workforce increase between 1960 and 1980?

A 5 percent

B 25 percent

C 15 percent

D 50 percent

2 The Supreme Court case that led to the integration of public schools was called

A *Plessy* v. *Ferguson*

B *Brown* v. *Board of Education*

C *Chisholm* v. *Marshall*

D *King* v. *Alabama*

3 Leaders of the MIA organized the Montgomery Bus Boycott after

A black students staged a sit-in at a Woolworth lunch counter.

B Martin Luther King, Jr. founded the Southern Christian Leadership Conference.

C Rosa Parks was arrested for sitting in the "whites-only" section of a public bus.

D the Little Rock Nine began attending Central High School.

4 In the 1960s Cesar Chavez became

A the first Hispanic American to serve in the U.S. Congress.

B a nationally recognized Hispanic rights leader.

C a member of President Johnson's cabinet.

D a leader of the Native American rights movement.

5 In 1969 a group of activists seized Alcatraz Island to

A demand better wages and conditions for migrant farm workers.

B protest the government's takeover of Native American lands.

C demonstrate in favor of the Equal Rights Amendment.

D call attention to the needs of Americans with disabilities.

6 Read the following excerpt from Martin Luther King Jr.'s "I Have a Dream" speech and use it to answer the question below.

"When we allow freedom to ring, when we let it ring from every village and every hamlet [community], from every state and every city, we will be able to speed up that day when all of God's children, black men and white men, Jews and Gentiles [non-Jews], Protestants and Catholics, will be able to join hands and sing in the words of the old Negro spiritual, 'Free at last! Free at last! Thank God Almighty, we are free at last!'"

—Martin Luther King Jr.

Document-Based Question What is the main idea King is expressing in this passage?

The Vietnam War Years

Virginia Standards of Learning

USII.2 The student will use maps, globes, photographs, pictures, or tables for

c) locating the 50 states and the cities most significant to the historical development of the United States

USII.8 The student will demonstrate knowledge of the economic, social, and political transformation of the United States and the world between the end of World War II and the present by

c) identifying the role of America's military and veterans in defending freedom during the Cold War, including the wars in Korea and Vietnam, the Cuban missile crisis, the collapse of communism in Europe, and the rise of new challenges;

d) describing the changing patterns of society, including expanded educational and economic opportunities for military veterans, women, and minorities

USII.9 The student will demonstrate knowledge of the key domestic and international issues during the second half of the twentieth century by

b) describing the development of new technologies in communication, entertainment, and business and their impact on American life; **c)** identifying how individual citizens from the time period influenced America scientifically, culturally, academically, and economically

WRITING JOURNAL

Newscast Writing in the 1960s, Michael Arlen called the Vietnam War the first American "living room war." For the first time, Americans could sit in their homes and watch scenes from the war on TV newscasts. In this chapter, you will read about American involvement in Cold War conflicts, such as the Cuban missile crisis and the Vietnam War. Then you will present a newscast on major events of the Cold War.

UNITED STATES

1961 Kennedy sends military advisers to Vietnam.

1960

WORLD

1960 Cuba and the Soviet Union sign a trade agreement and establish diplomatic relations.

HOLT

History's Impact
▶ video series
Watch the video to understand the impact of public opinion on foreign policy.

What You Will Learn...

Tensions between the United States and the Soviet Union continued to cause conflicts in the 1960s. In this chapter you will read about the major Cold War crises of the 1960s. You will also learn how the commitment to stop the spread of communism worldwide led the United States into a long and costly war in Vietnam. Here, soldiers in the U.S. 173 Airborne are shown taking part in the Iron Triangle assault.

1968 Martin Luther King Jr. and Robert Kennedy are assassinated.

1969 Joan Baez, The Who, and Jimi Hendrix headline the Woodstock Music Festival.

1973 Last U.S. ground troops leave Vietnam.

1965

1970

1975

1965 North Vietnamese leader Ho Chi Minh refuses peace talks with President Lyndon Johnson.

1969 Ho Chi Minh dies in Hanoi.

1975 North Vietnamese troops capture Saigon.

891

Reading Social Studies

by Kylene Beers

Economics	Geography	Politics	Society and Culture	Science and Technology

Focus on Themes In this chapter, you will learn about the Vietnam War years. American soldiers faced many obstacles in Vietnam, including the country's **geography**. Jungles and mountains prevented Americans from gaining an easy victory. You will read about how the long, drawn-out conflict caused divisions between the nation's leaders and many Americans.

Setting a Purpose

Focus on Reading Setting a purpose for your reading can help you to understand the things that you read. Understanding the author's goal is often an important part of this task.

Setting a Purpose When you open this book to a page you have been assigned to read, there will be clues about what you will be learning. The information in this book is organized under headings that help explain the text. When you read a section like the one below, try to determine how the text explains the heading.

Notice how one reader used the headings to determine his purpose for reading the passage below.

Society in the 1960s

As the Vietnam War continued, growing numbers of Americans began to criticize the war . . .

From Chapter 29, p. 908

This large heading lets me know that the text below will be about everyday life during the 1960s.

Antiwar Protests

College students often took the lead in organizing antiwar protests . . .

The text below this heading might answer questions about what antiwar protests are and who took part in them.

I guess protests were frequent during the 1960s. I should read to find out what they were and why they took place.

Virginia Standards of Learning
Reading 7.6a Use knowledge of text structures to aid comprehension.

Key Terms and People

Academic Vocabulary

In this chapter, you will learn the following academic words:
aspect *(p. 896)*
values *(p. 909)*

You Try It!

The following passage is from the chapter you are getting ready to read. As you read the passage, look for information in the headings that tell you what to look for.

The Vietnam War Ends

While Nixon was running for reelection in 1972, Henry Kissinger started peace negotiations with the North Vietnamese . . .

From Chapter 29, pp. 911–912

The Impact in Southeast Asia

The war ended when North Vietnamese forces captured Saigon in April 1975 . . .

The Impact at Home

The Vietnam War carried heavy costs for the United States as well . . .

After you read the passage, answer the following questions.

1. After reading the headings, what do you think this section is going to be about?

2. What are some questions you might ask before reading this section?

3. What information do you think you will learn from the section?

As you read Chapter 29, set a purpose before you read each section.

Kennedy and Foreign Policy

Virginia Standards of Learning USII.1b, USII.8c, USII.9b, USII.9c

What You Will Learn...

Main Ideas

1. President Kennedy confronted Communist threats around the world.
2. The United States and the Soviet Union raced to send a person to the moon.
3. The Cold War conflict in Vietnam led the United States into war.

The Big Idea

The United States confronted Communist nations in Cold War conflicts around the world.

Key Terms and People

Peace Corps, *p. 894*
Fidel Castro, *p. 895*
Berlin Wall, *p. 896*
Cuban missile crisis, *p. 896*
Neil Armstrong, *p. 898*
Edwin "Buzz" Aldrin, *p. 898*
Ho Chi Minh, *p. 898*
domino theory, *p. 898*
Vietcong, *p. 899*

TAKING NOTES As you read, take notes on Cold War crises that took place during the Kennedy administration. You may want to use a graphic organizer like this one.

Bay of Pigs	Berlin Wall	Cuban Missile Crisis

If YOU were there...

You are a student in 1960. Whenever you discuss current events in class, students talk nervously about the ongoing nuclear arms race between the United States and the Soviet Union. If Cold War tensions ever spark an all-out nuclear war, entire cities and populations could be destroyed in just a matter of minutes.

Do you think Cold War tensions will lead to a nuclear war?

MEXICO

PACIFIC OCE

BUILDING BACKGROUND In the 1950s some Americans feared that the United States was falling behind the Soviet Union in missile production. The United States began using U-2 spy planes to gather information about Soviet military technology. On May 1, 1960, a U-2 plane was shot down over Soviet territory. Soviet leaders reacted angrily. Cold War tensions were running high as the Kennedy presidency began in 1961.

Kennedy Confronts Communism

As president, John F. Kennedy was committed to the Cold War policy of stopping the spread of communism worldwide. He maintained strong military forces and expanded the nation's supply of nuclear weapons. He also sought nonmilitary ways to defeat communism. For example, in a program called the Alliance for Progress, the United States pledged $20 billion in aid to countries in Latin America. This assistance did little to improve conditions in Latin America or U.S.–Latin American relations, however. Another nonmilitary program was more successful. Beginning in 1961, the **Peace Corps** sent volunteers to developing countries to help with projects such as digging wells and building schools.

Bay of Pigs

Much of Kennedy's attention, in his early days as president, involved confronting communism with U.S. military forces. The first Cold

Crises in Cuba

This map of Cuba was marked by President Kennedy during a cabinet briefing on the Cuban missile crisis.

Legend:
- U.S Navy base
- U.S. Air Force base
- U.S. blockade
- Soviet missile site

0 — 150 — 300 Miles
0 — 150 — 300 Kilometers

GEOGRAPHY SKILLS INTERPRETING MAPS

1. **Location** How far is Havana from Miami?
2. **Human-Environment Interaction** Why was the Cuban military presence so dangerous for the United States?

War crisis during his administration took place in Cuba. In the late 1950s Cuban rebel **Fidel Castro** had led a revolution against an unpopular dictator. In 1959 he overthrew the dictator and soon established a Communist government allied to the Soviet Union. Many Cubans who had opposed Castro fled to the United States.

Castro's close ties with the Soviet Union worried Kennedy, especially since Cuba is only about 90 miles from Florida. Soviet leaders could use Cuba as a base from which to attack the United States.

While president, Dwight Eisenhower had developed a plan to remove Castro from power. The Central Intelligence Agency began training Cuban exiles to invade the island and overthrow Castro. Kennedy learned of the plan when he became president. He approved the operation.

On April 17, 1961, about 1,500 Cuban exiles landed by boat at Cuba's Bay of Pigs. Castro's forces quickly responded, killing about 300 of the invaders and capturing the rest. Many Americans criticized Kennedy for the disastrous invasion attempt. His administration was off to a shaky start.

The Berlin Wall

Located behind the Iron Curtain in East Germany, the city of Berlin was the site of Kennedy's second crisis. East Berlin was part of Communist East Germany. West Berlin remained a part of democratic West Germany and stood as a model of prosperity and freedom. Desperate for freedom and better economic opportunities, about 2.5 million East Germans fled to West Berlin between 1949 and 1961. The steady loss of skilled workers alarmed Communist officials. Calling the open border between East and West Berlin a "handy escape route," Soviet premier Nikita Khrushchev demanded that the border be closed.

Khrushchev threatened to take over West Berlin. President Kennedy responded by vowing to defend the free city. "We cannot and will not permit the Communists to drive us out of Berlin," he warned. Then, on the night of August 12–13, 1961, the East German government began building the **Berlin Wall**, a barrier of concrete and barbed wire between East and West Berlin. Kennedy rushed American troops to West Berlin. But he was unwilling to go to war with the Soviet Union over the Berlin Wall. The wall stood as a symbol of the Cold War for nearly three decades.

The Cuban Missile Crisis

In October 1962 Kennedy faced yet another problem in Cuba when American U-2 spy planes discovered that the Soviets were installing nuclear missiles in Cuba. If launched, the missiles could reach, and possibly destroy, American cities within minutes.

At a press conference on October 22, Kennedy demanded that the Soviet Union remove the missiles. During the **Cuban missile crisis**, the U.S. Navy formed a blockade around Cuba to prevent Soviet ships from bringing in more weapons. As Soviet ships approached

ACADEMIC
VOCABULARY

aspect
part

the blockade, terrified Americans waited tensely for news updates. Then came some welcome news—the Soviet ships had turned back.

After the crisis ended, Khrushchev agreed to remove the nuclear missiles from Cuba. In return, Kennedy promised not to invade Cuba. He also agreed to remove some missiles in Italy and Turkey. To improve future communication, Kennedy and Khrushchev set up a telephone "hotline" so the leaders could talk directly to each other at a moment's notice. They also signed the Limited Nuclear Test Ban Treaty, which banned the testing of new nuclear weapons aboveground.

READING CHECK **Sequencing** When did Kennedy's three Cold War crises occur?

Race to the Moon

Although Kennedy and Khrushchev had taken some steps to prevent conflicts, the Cold War continued. One **aspect** of the Cold War that heated up in the 1960s was the space race—the competition between the United

Primary Source

BOOK
Thirteen Days

During the Cuban missile crisis, President Kennedy considered several options: blockade Cuba, invade the island, or bomb missile sites by air. After choosing the blockade, Kennedy and his advisers could only wait to see how Khrushchev would respond. The president's brother, Attorney General Robert F. Kennedy, later described these tense moments in the White House.

Robert Kennedy describes the doubts he and others in the room felt.

I think these few minutes were the time of gravest concern for the President. Was the world on the brink of a holocaust? Was it our error? A mistake? Was there something further that should have been done? Or not done?. . . The minutes in the Cabinet Room ticked slowly by. What could we say now—what could we do?

Then it was 10:25—a messenger brought in a note . . . 'Mr. President . . . some of the Russian ships have stopped dead in the water . . . Six ships . . . have stopped or have turned back toward the Soviet Union' . . .

Then we were back to the details. The meeting droned on. But everyone looked like a different person. For a moment the world had stood still, and now it was going around again.

—Robert F. Kennedy, from *Thirteen Days: A Memoir of the Cuban Missile Crisis*

ANALYSIS
SKILL **ANALYZING PRIMARY SOURCES**

What details from the passage show that the moment was tense?

States and the Soviet Union to explore space. The Soviet Union pulled ahead in April 1961 when Soviet cosmonaut Yuri Gagarin became the first person to travel into space, orbiting Earth once.

The United States was determined to catch up to and surpass the Soviet Union in the space race. Kennedy outlined a bold plan in a 1961 speech to Congress:

> " I believe that this nation should commit itself to achieving the goal, before this decade is out, of landing a man on the moon and returning him safely to the earth. "
> —John F. Kennedy, speech to Congress, May 25, 1961

It is difficult for us to imagine what it was like for Kennedy's audience to hear these words. Space travel seems normal to us today. But to people in the early 1960s, the idea of humans landing on the moon seemed like something out of a science fiction novel. Still, Americans supported the project. Congress provided NASA with billions of dollars to fund the development of new technology.

In May 1961 astronaut Alan Shepard Jr. became the first U.S. astronaut in space. The next year, John Glenn became the first American to orbit Earth. Then NASA pushed ahead with Project Apollo, with the goal of landing an astronaut on the moon. Even with careful planning, Apollo astronauts faced great danger. Three astronauts died in a fire during a prelaunch test in 1967.

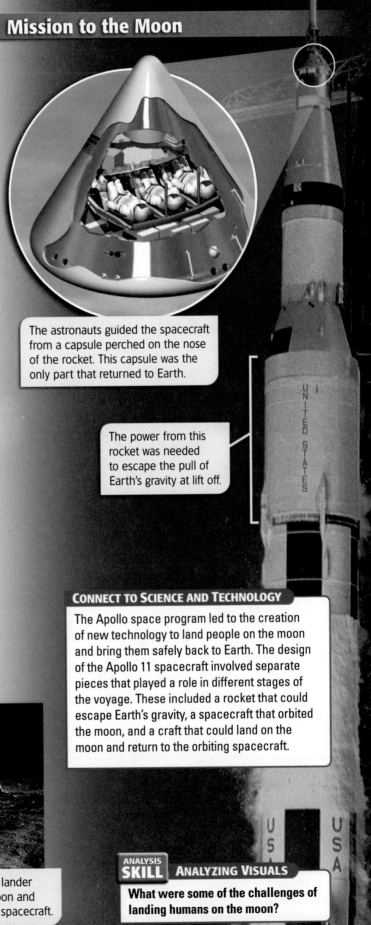

Mission to the Moon

The astronauts guided the spacecraft from a capsule perched on the nose of the rocket. This capsule was the only part that returned to Earth.

The power from this rocket was needed to escape the pull of Earth's gravity at lift off.

CONNECT TO SCIENCE AND TECHNOLOGY

The Apollo space program led to the creation of new technology to land people on the moon and bring them safely back to Earth. The design of the Apollo 11 spacecraft involved separate pieces that played a role in different stages of the voyage. These included a rocket that could escape Earth's gravity, a spacecraft that orbited the moon, and a craft that could land on the moon and return to the orbiting spacecraft.

A vehicle known as the moon lander took two astronauts to the moon and returned them to the orbiting spacecraft.

ANALYSIS SKILL **ANALYZING VISUALS**

What were some of the challenges of landing humans on the moon?

897

On July 20, 1969, while millions of people around the world watched on television, the lunar module *Eagle* landed on the surface of the moon. American astronauts **Neil Armstrong** and **Edwin "Buzz" Aldrin** climbed out and became the first people to walk on the moon. "That's one small step for [a] man, one giant leap for mankind," said Armstrong as he touched the lunar surface. Armstrong and Aldrin planted the American flag on the moon's surface and collected samples of moon rocks. The Apollo program continued, achieving five more successful moon landings by 1972.

READING CHECK **Analyzing** How did the events of July 20, 1969, fulfill the hope Kennedy had expressed in 1961?

French Indochina

0   100   200 Miles
0   100   200 Kilometers

CHINA

BURMA

Dien Bien Phu

Hanoi

Red River Delta

20°N

LAOS

Gulf of Tonkin

Hainan

Vientiane

VIETNAM

ANNAMITE MOUNTAINS

Mekong River

Hue
Da Nang

15°N

THAILAND

CAMBODIA

South China Sea

France combined its protectorates of Laos, Cambodia, and Vietnam in 1891 to create French Indochina.

Phnom Penh

100°E

Saigon

110°E

10°N

Gulf of Thailand

Mekong Delta

GEOGRAPHY SKILLS **INTERPRETING MAPS**

1. Place Which country in French Indochina is landlocked?
2. Location How far is it from Hanoi to Saigon?

Conflict in Vietnam

The most serious and deadly event of the Cold War took place in Vietnam, a country in Southeast Asia. The Vietnamese struggled against the domination of China for centuries. By the early 1880s all of Vietnam was conquered by France. The French combined Vietnam with neighboring Laos and Cambodia to create a colony called French Indochina. French leaders imposed harsh taxes and put limits on political freedoms. Vietnamese nationalists began a struggle for independence in the early 1900s.

France and Vietnam

One of the leading Vietnamese nationalists was **Ho Chi Minh**. Ho believed that only a Communist revolution could free the Vietnamese people.

During World War II, Japan drove the French out of Indochina. Ho Chi Minh did not want Vietnam to be controlled by yet another foreign power. He organized a group called the Vietminh to resist Japanese occupation. When Japan was defeated by the Allies in 1945, Ho declared Vietnamese independence. Using words echoing those of the American Declaration of Independence, he said, "All men are born equal: the Creator has given us inviolable rights, life, liberty, and happiness." In reality, Ho did not believe in the democratic principles outlined in the American document.

Vietnam was still not free of foreign rule. France insisted that Vietnam was a French colony. French forces moved to regain control of Vietnam, leading to new fighting between the two sides.

Presidents Truman and Eisenhower both supported France with military aid. They were concerned that a Vietminh victory would lead to the spread of communism in Asia. American leaders feared that if one country became Communist, nearby countries would also fall to communism. This was called the **domino theory**. Americans had already watched Communist victories in China and North Korea. They did not want Vietnam to be next.

The Vietminh had fewer weapons and supplies than the French, but they used hit-and-run guerrilla tactics to gradually weaken French forces. In May 1954 the Vietminh trapped a French army at Dien Bien Phu, where the French surrendered. In July French and Vietnamese leaders worked out an agreement called the Geneva Accords. This compromise temporarily divided Vietnam into North and South. It also called for democratic elections in July 1956 that would unite the two countries under one government.

North and South Vietnam

North Vietnam became a Communist dictatorship led by Ho Chi Minh. South Vietnam had a Western-style government led by Ngo Dinh Diem (en-GOH DIN de-EM) and supported by the United States. U.S. officials hoped Diem would win control of the country in the 1956 elections.

Diem, however, quickly proved to be a disappointing leader. He put his own family members in top government positions and used his security forces to imprison and torture his political enemies. President Eisenhower was concerned, but he and his advisers saw Diem as the only realistic alternative to a Communist Vietnam.

In North Vietnam, meanwhile, Ho Chi Minh introduced land redistribution plans. Like Diem, Ho and the Vietminh violently persecuted their opponents. During the land redistribution process, they imprisoned and killed thousands of landowners.

As the 1956 reunification elections approached, however, a growing number of South Vietnamese supported Ho and the Vietminh. Diem refused to allow South Vietnam to participate in the elections. The United States backed this decision. Diem also arrested thousands of people who supported Ho.

In 1960 members of the North Vietnamese government formed the National Liberation Front (NLF). The NLF recruited South Vietnamese who were opposed to Diem to fight against the South Vietnamese

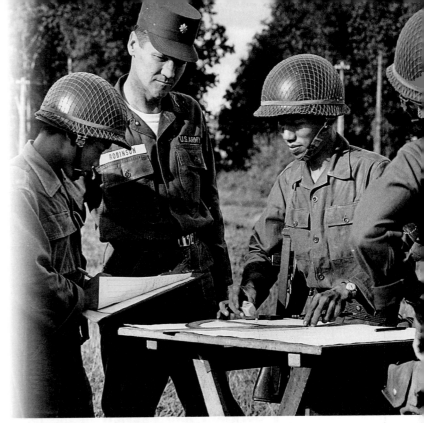

South Vietnamese soldiers plot a firing pattern under the guidance of American military personnel.

government. The NLF relied on Communist guerrilla forces called the **Vietcong** as its army, which was supplied and funded by the North Vietnamese.

American Involvement

President Eisenhower sent aid, weapons, and military advisers to South Vietnam to aid Diem. Soon after taking office in 1961, President Kennedy sent more advisers and special forces. Although they were not official combat troops, the U.S. military advisers often accompanied the South Vietnamese army on combat missions. Some were killed in action. By late 1963 about 16,000 U.S. military personnel were serving in Vietnam.

The increased U.S. support did not help Diem, who was becoming less and less popular in South Vietnam. Several attempts were made to overthrow his government, all of which failed. Diem would not hold elections, and his opponents began to consider violence as their only option. He lost more support when he ordered his troops to fire on Buddhist demonstrators.

Some Buddhist monks protested by setting themselves on fire. Horrifying images of these protests helped turn U.S. public opinion against Diem.

In November 1963 a group of South Vietnamese army officers seized power and killed Diem and his brother. Only weeks later, Kennedy was assassinated, and Vice President Lyndon Johnson became president. Johnson immediately faced tough decisions about how to handle an increasingly unstable South Vietnam.

READING CHECK **Evaluating** Why did the United States see the Vietnam conflict as a Cold War struggle?

SUMMARY AND PREVIEW In the 1950s and early 1960s, Cold War tensions caused conflicts around the world. In the next section you will read about increased U.S. involvement in Vietnam.

The Beginning of the Vietnam War
QUICK FACTS

Causes
- French lose control of Vietnam
- Cold War tensions
- Civil war in Vietnam
- Assassination of President Diem

Effects
- Eisenhower and Kennedy send military advisers
- Gulf of Tonkin Resolution

Section 1 Assessment

go.hrw.com
Online Quiz
KEYWORD: SB7 HP29

Reviewing Ideas, Terms, and People

1. a. Describe What nonmilitary tactics did President Kennedy use to confront communism?
b. Explain How was the **Cuban missile crisis** resolved?
c. Evaluate In which Cold War crisis do you think President Kennedy showed the strongest leadership? Explain your answer.

2. a. Recall How did the Soviet Union take the lead in the space race in 1961?
b. Predict How do you think the Soviet Union responded to the successful U.S. landing of a man on the moon?

3. a. Identify Who was **Ho Chi Minh**?
b. Describe According to the **domino theory**, what did U.S. leaders think might happen if Vietnam became a Communist country?
c. Analyze Do you think the United States was justified in supporting Ngo Dinh Diem? Why or why not?

Critical Thinking

4. Identifying Cause and Effect Review your notes on Cold War crises during the Kennedy administration. Then copy the graphic organizer below and use it to list the causes and effects of each crisis.

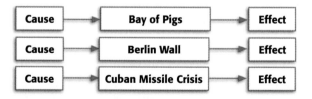

Cause	→	Bay of Pigs	→	Effect
Cause	→	Berlin Wall	→	Effect
Cause	→	Cuban Missile Crisis	→	Effect

FOCUS ON WRITING

5. Listing Cold War Conflicts List Cold War conflicts the United States faced during the 1960s. Who was involved in each conflict? How could you explain each conflict to a television audience? What could you show in your newscast to illustrate the conflicts?

Escalation in Vietnam

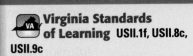
If **YOU** were there...

It is 1965, and you have just been elected to Congress. You know voters are concerned about events in Vietnam, and you are carefully following the progress of the war. No one knows what will happen if the United States gets more deeply involved in the conflict. It might turn back the tide of communism. On the other hand, thousands of young soldiers might die.

Would you support sending U.S. troops to Vietnam? Why or why not?

BUILDING BACKGROUND Lyndon Johnson had spent most of his political career focused on domestic issues. After becoming president, he dedicated himself to civil rights legislation and his Great Society programs. But Johnson also had the same goal as presidents before him—to stop the spread of communism around the world.

Johnson Commits to Victory

Lyndon Johnson was determined to prevent Communists from taking over in South Vietnam. "We have the resources and the will to follow this course as long as it may take," Johnson said. He waited for a spark that might allow him to take action.

The Tonkin Gulf Resolution

In the summer of 1964, a naval skirmish led to a rapid expansion of U.S. involvement in Vietnam. On August 2, 1964, the USS *Maddox* reportedly exchanged gunfire with North Vietnamese torpedo boats in the Gulf of Tonkin, off the North Vietnamese coast. Two days later, during a night of thunderstorms, U.S. ships reported a second attack. The captain of the *Maddox* was not sure his ship had actually been attacked, but the USS *Turner Joy* claimed to have picked up high-speed vessels on its radar. Despite the conflicting stories, President Johnson declared the incident an act of war.

What You Will Learn...

Main Ideas

1. President Johnson committed the United States to victory in Vietnam by expanding U.S. involvement.
2. American soldiers faced new challenges fighting the Vietnam War.
3. The Tet Offensive was an important turning point in the war.

The Big Idea

Johnson quickly expanded U.S. involvement in Vietnam, but American soldiers faced a determined enemy.

Key Terms and People

Tonkin Gulf Resolution, *p. 902*
Ho Chi Minh Trail, *p. 902*
escalation, *p. 902*
Willliam Westmoreland, *p. 903*
search-and-destroy missions, *p. 903*
Tet Offensive, *p. 904*
doves, *p. 904*
hawks, *p. 904*

TAKING NOTES As you read, list the events that led to the escalation of U.S. involvement in the Vietnam War. Write your notes in a table like this one.

Events that led to escalation:
1.
2.
3.
4.

Johnson asked Congress to give him the authority to take military action. Congress passed the **Tonkin Gulf Resolution**, giving the president the authority "to take all necessary measures to repel any armed attack against the forces of the United States." Johnson used the Tonkin Gulf Resolution to greatly expand the U.S. role in Vietnam.

Air Strikes Begin

Johnson sent the first U.S. combat troops to South Vietnam in March 1965. At the same time, he ordered Operation Rolling Thunder, a series of air strikes on war industries in North Vietnam. The air strikes were also designed to disrupt the **Ho Chi Minh Trail**, a supply route used by the North Vietnamese. The trail was a network of paths and tunnels that led from North Vietnam, through Laos and Cambodia, and into South Vietnam.

Because some of the Ho Chi Minh Trail was located in neutral countries, U.S. soldiers could not surround it on the ground. Instead, U.S. airplanes bombed the route, sometimes with napalm, or jellied gasoline, to kill troops and destroy supplies. Planes also released chemicals such as Agent Orange to kill the dense forests on the trail and to increase visibility from the air. American veterans and Vietnamese civilians later suffered serious health problems from exposure to these chemicals.

By late 1968 more than a million tons of explosives had been dropped on North and South Vietnam. Many Vietnamese soldiers and civilians were killed. The Communists' ability to wage war, however, was not destroyed.

READING CHECK Summarizing What authority did the Tonkin Gulf Resolution give to President Johnson?

U.S. Soldiers in Vietnam

From 1965 to 1968, President Johnson pursued a policy of **escalation**, or increased involvement, in the war. By 1968 more than 500,000 U.S. troops were serving in Vietnam. Backed by superior military technology, U.S. generals expected to win a quick victory. But the Vietnam War proved to be different from previous wars.

Strategies and Tactics

In Vietnam, there was rarely a front line where armies met face to face. Much of the war was

BIOGRAPHY

John McCain
1936–

John McCain's father and grandfather were both U.S. Navy admirals. The younger McCain also attended the Naval Academy and served in Vietnam as a combat pilot. On a bombing mission over Hanoi in 1967, his plane was shot down. McCain was held as a prisoner of war (POW) for more than five years and was often tortured and kept in solitary confinement. McCain entered politics after the war. In 2004 he was elected to his fourth term as U.S. senator from Arizona. One of his priorities as a senator was to help repair and strengthen U.S. relations with Vietnam. McCain was the Republican nominee for president in 2008.

Drawing Inferences If you were John McCain, would you want to establish good relations with Vietnam? Why or why not?

As a lieutenant, John McCain served as a flight instructor.

fought in the jungles and villages of South Vietnam. General **William Westmoreland** commanded the U.S. ground forces involved in Vietnam. He developed a strategy based on **search-and-destroy missions**, where U.S. patrols searched for hidden enemy camps, then destroyed them with massive firepower and air raids.

To make up for their disadvantage in firepower, Vietcong and North Vietnamese Army (NVA) troops used guerrilla warfare tactics. Moving quickly, they set deadly traps and land mines. They also knew the local geography, which allowed them to make quick surprise assaults on small groups of U.S. soldiers. Though the Vietcong and NVA suffered high casualty rates, they were able to match U.S. escalation by continuing to send new troops into combat. They also received supplies and weapons from Communist China and the Soviet Union.

The civilians of South Vietnam were often caught in the middle of the fighting. Vietcong forces entered villages at night and killed people they believed were cooperating with the South Vietnamese government. South Vietnamese and American troops attacked villages they suspected of assisting the Vietcong. About 4 million South Vietnamese were driven from their homes. This undermined the crucial U.S. goal of winning the support and loyalty of South Vietnamese civilians.

Soldiers' Stories

More than 2 million American soldiers served in the Vietnam War. Their average age was 18–21, several years younger than in previous American wars. About one-quarter of the soldiers were drafted, many from minority groups and poor families. College students—most of whom were white and from wealthier families—were able to get draft releases called deferments.

American troops patrolled jungles and rice paddies, carrying 75–90 pounds of equipment through 100-degree heat and rainstorms that

Primary Source

ORAL HISTORY
Vietnam War

Charley Trujillo was a soldier in the Vietnam War. He later became a writer and filmmaker, focusing on the experiences of Latinos and Chicanos in the Vietnam War. Below he describes a day in Vietnam.

"Throughout the day we received mortar and sniper fire. By that evening we had suffered more casualties. The one I remember most was a guy we called the yippie. He was totally against the war and usually tried to avoid any violence. He was even thinking, for a while, of not carrying a rifle. It didn't help him much because the dude lost his leg that afternoon.**"**

—Charley Trujillo, quoted in *Soldados: Chicanos In Việt Nam*

ANALYSIS SKILL **ANALYZING PRIMARY SOURCES**

Why might Trujillo have remembered this casualty the most?

could last for days. They never knew when they might run into enemy fire. Soldiers also faced the constant danger of land mines and booby traps. "We required this kind of instant hair-trigger alertness," said marine Philip Caputo. "You simply trusted absolutely no one. I mean, from a 5-year-old kid to a 75-year-old woman."

While American troops were often able to win individual battles, they were rarely able to control the territory they had won for long. "You were just constantly walking out over the same ground," Caputo explained. "The enemy you were supposed to be defeating statistically kept coming back for more."

READING CHECK **Comparing and Contrasting** How was Vietnam different from previous wars for U.S. soldiers?

Turning Points in Vietnam

By the end of 1967, U.S. military leaders argued that they were nearing victory in Vietnam. General Westmoreland said that he saw "a light at the end of the tunnel." But events in 1968 weakened the American public's confidence in this claim.

The Tet Offensive

On January 30, 1968, the Vietnamese celebrated their New Year, called Tet. In previous years, a cease-fire had halted fighting on this holiday. In 1968, however, Vietcong and North Vietnamese forces launched the **Tet Offensive**—surprise attacks all over South Vietnam, including an attack on the U.S. Embassy in Saigon, South Vietnam's capital.

South Vietnamese and U.S. forces successfully fought off the enemy strikes. Still, the massive size of the Tet Offensive shocked Americans. They had been told that the war would soon be over. Now they saw that the enemy was still strong and determined. Many began to wonder if government officials were being honest about the war. One poll taken after the Tet Offensive showed that only 33 percent of Americans believed that the United States was winning the war in Vietnam. About 49 percent said that the United States should never have become involved in the war.

In February 1968 Westmoreland asked for some 200,000 more troops. Many Americans questioned the wisdom of further escalation in Vietnam. President Johnson denied the general's request.

Hawks and Doves

Television reports had an important impact on public opinion about the war. Americans could watch action from the battlefield and see real images of the war's brutality on nightly news broadcasts. Many were dismayed by what they saw.

Gradually, some Americans who had been supporters of the Vietnam War began to call for an end to U.S. involvement. Opponents of the war were called **doves**—named after the birds that symbolize peace. Many doves believed that the war was draining money that should be spent on social programs at home. Supporters of the war were called **hawks**. Hawks called for increased military spending, based on the belief that winning the Cold War took priority over domestic programs.

The bitter divisions between hawks and doves deepened as the Vietnam War continued. On March 16, 1968, a company of U.S. soldiers under the command of

The Vietnam War, 1968

Interactive Map

Legend:
- Major U.S. air strikes
- Major U.S. bases
- Areas under attack in Tet Offensive, 1968
- Base areas/war zone
- Areas of prolonged fighting

0   100   200 Miles
0   100   200 Kilometers

BURMA

NORTH VIETNAM
Dien Bien Phu
Xam Nua
Hanoi
Red River
Red River Delta
20°N
Lach Chao Estuary
Gulf of Tonkin
U.S. Seventh Fleet

LAOS
Muang Ngat
Vientiane

Demilitarized Zone (DMZ)

Ho Chi Minh Trail

THAILAND

Mekong River

15°N

My Lai

South China Sea

CAMBODIA

SOUTH VIETNAM

Da Lat
Cam Rahn Bay
U.S. Seventh Fleet

Gulf of Thailand

Phnom Penh

Saigon

10°N

Ben Tre
Mekong Delta

100°E

GEOGRAPHY SKILLS — **INTERPRETING MAPS**

go.hrw.com
Interactive Map
KEYWORD: SB7 CH29

1. **Place** In which countries did major U.S. air strikes occur?
2. **Human-Environment Interaction** Which country experienced most of the fighting in the Vietnam War?

105°E   110°E

Lieutenant William Calley entered the South Vietnamese village of My Lai. Calley and his men expected to find Vietcong forces in My Lai. Their search-and-destroy mission turned into a massacre when American soldiers opened fire, killing about 500 unarmed villagers, including women and children.

At first, U.S. military officials tried to cover up news of the massacre. But former soldiers eventually made details of the events public. Lieutenant Calley was tried by the military and convicted of murder. As with the Tet Offensive, the My Lai massacre caused many Americans to question U.S. involvement in Vietnam.

READING CHECK **Summarizing** What events made some Americans oppose the war?

SUMMARY AND PREVIEW The Vietnam War escalated steadily under President Johnson. In the next section, you will learn about the final years of the war.

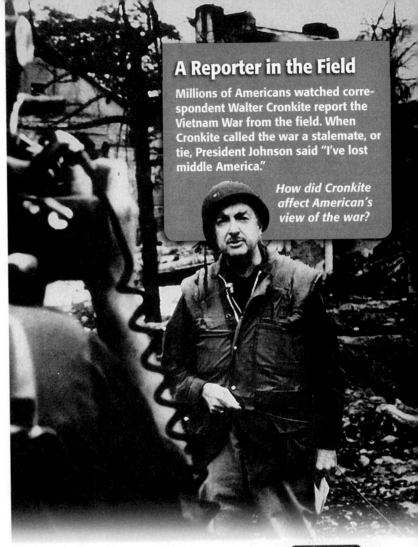

A Reporter in the Field

Millions of Americans watched correspondent Walter Cronkite report the Vietnam War from the field. When Cronkite called the war a stalemate, or tie, President Johnson said "I've lost middle America."

How did Cronkite affect American's view of the war?

go.hrw.com
Online Quiz
KEYWORD: SB7 HP29

Section 2 Assessment

Reviewing Ideas, Terms, and People

1. **a. Recall** What events led Johnson to ask Congress for authority to take military action in Vietnam?
   b. Explain Why was the **Ho Chi Minh Trail** the target of U.S. air strikes?
   c. Predict What problems might arise from giving a president powers such as those defined in the **Tonkin Gulf Resolution**?

2. **a. Define** What was **escalation**?
   b. Contrast How did strategies and tactics of U.S. troops differ from those of the NVA and Vietcong?

3. **a. Describe** What were the goals of the **doves** and the **hawks** during the Vietnam War?
   b. Analyze How did television influence public opinion during the Vietnam War?
   c. Elaborate Why was the Tet Offensive such a surprise to U.S. forces?

Critical Thinking

4. **Sequencing** Review your notes on events that led to increased U.S. involvement in the Vietnam War. Then copy the graphic organizer below and use it to put these events in the correct order.

FOCUS ON WRITING

5. **Comparing Points of View** Take notes on different people's points of view on the war. What different points of view should you present in your newscast to give a complete picture of the war in Vietnam? What kinds of people might you want to interview?

The Vietcong Tunnels

Besides knowing the geography and terrain much better than U.S. forces, the Vietcong had the advantage of an underground system of tunnels. One large system of tunnels was installed some 47 miles north of Saigon in the Cu Chi district of South Vietnam. The picture on these pages is a re-created representation of these tunnels. The tunnels provided a place from which to fight that the Americans could not attack. A tunnel complex included special rooms in which to sleep, eat, plan, store weapons and supplies, and tend wounded soldiers.

The Vietcong used the tunnel meeting rooms to plan attacks on U.S. soldiers.

Firing post

Dormitory

Hospital

Special doors were installed that could withstand bomb blasts and poisonous gases.

Generators powered by bicycles provided electricity where needed.

American soldiers had trouble finding the hidden tunnel entrances, like the one in this photograph.

Air vents

Kitchen

Some tunnels contained traps that would harm invaders.

Bomb shelter

Small tunnel complexes like this one were connected to others through longer tunnels.

Weapons storage

The Vietcong dug wells so that they could have freshwater without leaving the tunnel system.

ANALYSIS SKILL **ANALYZING VISUALS**

How did the Vietcong's tunnel system help their soldiers fight U.S. forces?

The End of the War

Virginia Standards of Learning USII.1a, USII.1b, USII.1d, USII.2c, USII.8c, USII.8d, USII.9c

What You Will Learn...

Main Ideas

1. Opinions about the Vietnam War divided American society in the 1960s.
2. The war under Nixon expanded from Vietnam to Laos and Cambodia.
3. The Vietnam War ended in 1973, but it had lasting effects on Vietnam and the United States.

The Big Idea

Growing antiwar feelings in the United States helped convince the government to end U.S. involvement in the Vietnam War.

Key Terms and People

Students for a Democratic Society, *p. 908*
hippies, *p. 909*
Richard M. Nixon, *p. 910*
Henry Kissinger, *p. 910*
Vietnamization, *p. 910*
Twenty-sixth Amendment, *p. 911*
War Powers Act, *p. 913*
Vietnam Veterans Memorial, *p. 913*

TAKING NOTES As you read, take notes on the causes of the end of the Vietnam War. Organize your notes in a graphic organizer like the one below.

Causes → End of Vietnam War

If YOU were there...

You are a high school student in 1969. You follow events in Vietnam very closely and often talk about the war with your friends. Some of your friends are active in the antiwar movement, but you also have friends who support the war. You think each group makes good points, but you are having a hard time deciding which position you support.

Would you join the antiwar protests? Why or why not?

BUILDING BACKGROUND Should the United States continue fighting in Vietnam? The debate over this question caused deep divisions in American society in the late 1960s. Antiwar demonstrators marched in cities and on college campuses. Others demonstrated in support of the war.

Society in the 1960s

As the Vietnam War continued, growing numbers of Americans began to criticize the war. "The peaceniks [war protesters] these days are legion [many]," said Charlotte Keyes, who helped organize a group called Women Strike for Peace. "They are ninety-years-old and fifteen, heads of families and housewives with babies, students, [and] young people."

Antiwar Protests

College students often took the lead in organizing antiwar protests. One of the most active protest groups was **Students for a Democratic Society** (SDS). Members of SDS protested the draft, as well as companies that made weapons used in Vietnam.

By the end of 1968, students had held antiwar demonstrations on nearly 75 percent of college campuses. Some young men protested by publicly burning their draft cards. Others avoided military service by moving to Canada. Many Americans, however, criticized the antiwar movement as anti-American. In 1970, for example, thousands of construction workers marched in New York City, shouting, "All the way with the U.S.A."

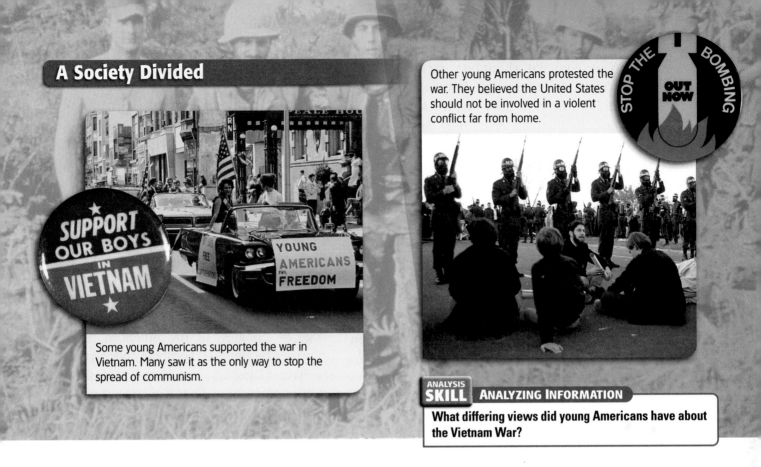

A Society Divided

Some young Americans supported the war in Vietnam. Many saw it as the only way to stop the spread of communism.

Other young Americans protested the war. They believed the United States should not be involved in a violent conflict far from home.

STOP THE BOMBING

OUT NOW

ANALYSIS SKILL **ANALYZING INFORMATION**

What differing views did young Americans have about the Vietnam War?

For some Americans, the antiwar movement was part of a rejection of traditional **values** and government authority. Some young people chose to "drop out" of mainstream society and built a counterculture—a culture with its own values and ways of behaving. Members of this counterculture, called **hippies**, emphasized individual freedom, nonviolence, and communal sharing. Hippies expressed their rejection of traditional society by growing their hair long and wearing unusual clothes. The views of hippies and war protesters upset many Americans. Commentators described a "generation gap," or division between older and younger Americans. "I know of no time in our history when the gap between the generations has been wider," said one university professor.

The Election of 1968

News of the Tet Offensive led to a sharp drop in the popularity of President Johnson. In early 1968 the percentage of Americans who approved of Johnson's performance as president fell from 48 to 36. The number of Americans who approved of the way Johnson was handling the war was even lower. As the 1968 presidential election approached, Johnson was even losing support within his own Democratic Party. On March 31 he went on live television and told Americans: "I shall not seek, and I will not accept, the nomination of my party for another term as president."

Several other candidates campaigned for the Democratic nomination. Johnson backed his vice president, Hubert Humphrey. Eugene McCarthy, a senator from Minnesota, ran as an outspoken antiwar candidate. Senator Robert F. Kennedy of New York argued that the United States should do everything possible to negotiate a quick and peaceful end to the war.

Kennedy won the California primary on June 5, 1968—an important step before the upcoming Democratic National Convention in Chicago. After giving his victory speech that night, he was assassinated by a gunman named Sirhan Sirhan.

The Democrats were badly divided going into their party's convention in Chicago.

ACADEMIC VOCABULARY

values ideas that people hold dear and try to live by

Vice President Humphrey seemed certain to win the nomination. But many delegates disliked his close ties with President Johnson and the Vietnam War. Angry debates inside the convention hall were matched by antiwar protests on the streets. When police officers moved in to stop the demonstrations, a riot broke out. Television cameras broadcast live images of the violent chaos in Chicago. More than 100 police and 100 demonstrators were injured.

Humphrey won the Democratic nomination for president, but the events in Chicago damaged his chances of victory. Republican nominee **Richard M. Nixon** promised to restore order to American society and bring "peace with honor" to Vietnam. Nixon won the election, receiving 301 electoral votes to Humphrey's 191. Southern voters gave 46 electoral votes to George Wallace, a segregationist candidate of the American Independent Party.

READING CHECK **Summarizing** Who were the candidates in the 1968 election? What was the outcome of the election?

The War under Nixon

President Nixon wanted to get U.S. troops out of Vietnam without creating the appearance of an American defeat. "I will not be the first president of the United States to lose a war," he told his fellow Republicans. With his national security adviser, **Henry Kissinger**, Nixon created a plan to pull U.S. troops from Vietnam and have the South Vietnamese Army take over all the fighting. This strategy was called **Vietnamization**.

Nixon began slowly withdrawing American troops from Vietnam. Without the knowledge of Congress or the American public, however, he approved bombing raids on Cambodia and Laos. The goal of these raids was to disrupt Vietcong supply lines. On April 30, 1970, Nixon announced that he had sent U.S. troops into Cambodia to attack Communist bases. "If, when the chips are down," he said, "the United States of America acts like a pitiful helpless giant, the forces of totalitarian anarchy will threaten free nations." Many Americans were furious. Rather than seeking peace, Nixon seemed to be expanding the war.

LINKING TO TODAY

The United States and Vietnam Today

Since the end of the Vietnam War, relations between the United States and Vietnam have slowly improved. In 1994 the United States lifted its long-standing trade embargo against Vietnam. In 1995 the former enemies officially established diplomatic relations. It became more common for American veterans and tourists to visit Vietnam.

According to the 2000 census, more than a million Vietnamese immigrants now live in the United States. Vietnamese, Laotian, and Cambodian immigrants to the United States have made significant contributions to the communities they join, many of which are along the West and Gulf coasts.

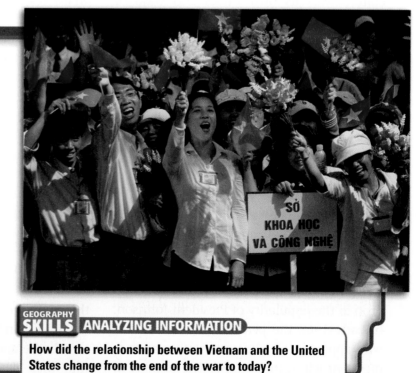

GEOGRAPHY SKILLS | **ANALYZING INFORMATION**

How did the relationship between Vietnam and the United States change from the end of the war to today?

The Election of 1972

Candidate (Political Party)	Electoral Vote	Popular Vote
■ Nixon (Republican)	520	47,165,234
■ McGovern (Democrat)	17	29,170,774

*One elector from Virginia cast his vote for John Hospers of California.

Richard M. Nixon

George McGovern

ANALYSIS SKILL **INTERPRETING CHARTS**

Location Why was the 1972 election considered a landslide victory for Nixon?

Student protests erupted on hundreds of college campuses. On May 4, at Kent State University in Ohio, the National Guard was called in to break up a demonstration. When the students refused to leave, guard troops used tear gas. Some students began throwing rocks at the National Guard. Several guard troops then opened fire into the crowd. Four students were killed. Horrified by the killings, antiwar activists expanded their protests all over the nation.

Antiwar feelings grew in June 1971 when the *New York Times* published secret government documents known as the Pentagon Papers. These documents revealed that U.S. officials had been lying to the American public about the progress of the war for years.

Public opinion was hardening against the war as the 1972 presidential race began. Democratic candidate George McGovern was an outspoken opponent of the war who promised voters an immediate U.S. troop withdrawal from Vietnam. "The doors of government will be opened, and that brutal war will be closed," he said.

McGovern hoped to appeal to young voters, many of whom would be voting for the first time. The **Twenty-sixth Amendment**, which was ratified in 1971, lowered the federal voting age from 21 to 18. McGovern did win a majority of these younger voters in 1972, but a majority of voters over 21 from both parties supported Nixon. Many of these voters feared that a McGovern victory would lead to greater disorder and protests. Nixon won by a landslide, receiving 520 electoral votes to McGovern's 17.

READING CHECK **Drawing Conclusions** Why did McGovern lose in a landslide?

The Vietnam War Ends

While Nixon was running for re-election in 1972, Henry Kissinger continued peace negotiations with the North Vietnamese. On January 27, 1973, the United States signed a cease-fire called the Paris Peace Accords with representatives of North Vietnam, South Vietnam, and the Vietcong. The United States agreed to withdraw all its troops from Vietnam. North Vietnam agreed to return all American prisoners of war. Despite the peace agreement, fighting broke out between North and South Vietnam

FOCUS ON READING

What is a purpose you can set for reading this section?

in 1974. The United States refused to send troops back to South Vietnam.

In 1975 North Vietnam invaded the South. Thousands of panic-stricken American Embassy workers and South Vietnamese scrambled to evacuate Saigon. "The city was in flames," remembered one American worker. "And the Communists had the city surrounded with missiles . . . We realized that we were down to hours if not minutes." Helicopters lifted many people to ships waiting off the coast.

THE IMPACT TODAY

Today the U.S. government is more prepared to meet the needs of veterans with post-traumatic stress disorder. It offers counseling and information to vets and their families on how to deal with symptoms of trauma.

The Impact in Southeast Asia

The war ended when North Vietnamese forces captured Saigon in April 1975. Communist leaders created the Socialist Republic of Vietnam, uniting the former countries of North and South Vietnam. Hanoi became the capital, and Saigon was renamed Ho Chi Minh City.

Life remained extremely difficult in Vietnam. Cities, villages, forests, and farms had been destroyed. Some 250,000 South Vietnamese soldiers died in the war. About 1 million North Vietnamese and Vietcong soldiers were killed. The number of civilians killed is estimated at 2 million. Hundreds of thousands of former soldiers, officials, and other professionals were forced to live in "re-education camps." Another 1.5 million Vietnamese fled the country—about half of them settling in the United States.

Communist dictators took over Laos and Cambodia in 1975. The Cambodian Communist army, the Khmer Rouge, killed about 1.5 million people in a massive campaign to destroy supposed enemies of communism.

The Impact at Home

The Vietnam War carried heavy costs for the United States as well. Some 58,000 Americans were killed, and more than 300,000 were wounded.

Returning American soldiers were not always welcomed home as heroes as other war veterans had been. Some were insulted by antiwar protesters. As veterans struggled

BIOGRAPHY

Maya Ying Lin
1959–

Ohio-born Maya Lin was a 21-year-old architecture student when she designed the Vietnam Veterans Memorial. Her design was chosen from more than 1,400 proposed memorial designs. The memorial is a V-shaped black granite wall that lists the names of more than 58,000 dead and missing Americans. Explaining the design, Lin said, "It was important to me to be extremely honest; not be concerned with the politics of war, but the results. I wanted to bring the visitor a concrete realization of the great loss." The memorial is now one of the most-visited spots in Washington, D.C. Many visitors leave letters, flowers, or other objects at the memorial to honor loved ones.

Drawing Conclusions How does Lin's design achieve the goal she describes?

to readjust to civilian life, many suffered from post-traumatic stress disorder. This condition includes symptoms such as nightmares and flashbacks to traumatic experiences.

Another effect of the war was that Americans had less trust in government officials, including the president. This led to passage in 1973 of the **War Powers Act**, which requires the president to get congressional approval before committing U.S. troops to an armed struggle.

Americans took a step toward healing the wounds of the war with the 1982 dedication of the **Vietnam Veterans Memorial**. Designed by Maya Ying Lin, the black granite memorial lists the names of dead or missing American soldiers.

READING CHECK **Summarizing** What were the long-term effects of the Vietnam War?

SUMMARY AND PREVIEW American society was deeply divided by the Vietnam War. In the next chapter, you will read about how American life changed in the 1970s and 1980s.

Causes and Effects of the Vietnam War

Long-Term Causes
- Fear of Communist expansion
- U.S. support of South Vietnam's government

Immediate Causes
- Gulf of Tonkin incident
- Communist attacks against South Vietnam

Vietnam War

Effects
- Many thousands of Americans and millions of Vietnamese killed and injured
- Vietnam united as a Communist nation
- Political divisions created in the United States
- Increased Vietnamese immigration to the United States

Section 3 Assessment

go.hrw.com
Online Quiz
KEYWORD: SB7 HP29

Reviewing Ideas, Terms, and People

1. **a. Identify** What was **Students for a Democratic Society**?
   b. Elaborate How did **hippies** express their disapproval of traditional culture?
   c. Evaluate How did the Republicans win the presidential election of 1968?
2. **a. Explain** What was **Vietnamization**?
   b. Summarize Why did the Pentagon Papers fuel antiwar feelings?
   c. Elaborate How did the **Twenty-sixth Amendment** affect the 1972 presidential election?
3. **a. Recall** How did the Vietnam War end?
   b. Describe What was the experience of veterans returning home from Vietnam?
   c. Analyze Do you think U.S. leaders made the right decision in signing the Paris Peace Accords? Why or why not?

Critical Thinking

4. **Identifying Effects** Review your notes on the causes of the end of the Vietnam War. Then copy the graphic organizer below and use it to list the effects of the end of the war.

FOCUS ON WRITING

5. **Taking Notes on the Effects of the War** Take notes on the effects of the Vietnam War. How did it affect American politics? How did it affect American culture? How did it affect the American and Vietnamese people? How will you explain these effects to television viewers?

Social Studies Skills

Analysis Critical Thinking Civic Participation Study

Using Primary Sources: Oral Histories

Define the Skill

An important part of history is understanding the lives and experiences of people in the past. Oral histories and personal memoirs are primary sources that help historians understand how people in the past acted and felt.

Oral histories are interviews in which people talk about events they participated in or witnessed. In personal memoirs, people write about their memories of such events. Both oral histories and personal memoirs are different from other kinds of primary sources because they can be written long after an event takes place. However, they both include descriptions of firsthand experiences.

Learn the Skill

Follow these guidelines to analyze oral histories and personal memoirs.

1 Identify the situation that the oral history or memoir describes.

2 Find the emotions or events that stand out in the description.

3 Make a generalization about how the individual's experience helps us understand the time period or event. Do you think other people might have had similar experiences?

In the following quotation, Diana Dwan Poole describes her experience serving in the Army Nurse Corps in Vietnam.

"One of my rules was that nurses were not allowed to cry. The wounded and dying men in our care need our strength, I told them. We couldn't indulge in the luxury of our own feelings ... I was always straight with the soldiers. I would never say, 'Oh, you're going to be just fine,' if they were on their way out. I didn't lie."

Poole was a nurse in Vietnam. In this quotation, she describes working with other nurses and with wounded and dying patients. Her strength in the face of sadness and her honesty stand out.

Other nurses might have had experiences similar to Poole's. The nurses' situation—treating the wounded and the dying—also suggests the dangers soldiers faced.

Practice the Skill

Harold Bryant was a combat engineer in Vietnam. Read the primary source quotation from Bryant below.

"Today I'm constantly thinking about the war. I walk down streets different. I look at places where individuals could hide. Maybe assault me or rob me or just harass me. I hear things that other people can't hear. My wife, she had a habit at one time of buying cheap watches and leaving them on top of the dresser. I could hear it ticking, so she would put it in a drawer. I could still hear it ticking."

1. What situation does Bryant describe?

2. Based on this description, how do you think Bryant felt at the time?

3. How can Bryant's experience help us better understand soldiers serving in Vietnam?

Chapter Review

HOLT

History's Impact
▶ video series
Review the video to answer the closing question:

How was the passing of the War Powers Act a reaction to the Vietnam War?

Visual Summary

QUICK FACTS

Use the visual summary below to help you review the main ideas of the chapter.

The spread of communism encouraged the United States to escalate the Vietnam War.

The Vietcong's superior knowledge of the geography helped them win the war.

Richard Nixon won the 1968 presidential election and pulled troops out of Vietnam.

Reviewing Vocabulary, Terms, and People

Identify the descriptions below with the correct term or person from the chapter.

1. The Cuban rebel who overthrew an unpopular dictator and established a Communist government

2. A barrier made of concrete and barbed wire that separated East Berlin and West Berlin

3. The commander of U.S. ground forces in Vietnam who developed the strategy of search-and-destroy missions

4. Supporters of the Vietnam War who believed winning the Cold War took priority over domestic reform

5. The Republican nominee who won the 1968 election for president of the United States

6. The amendment that lowered the voting age from 21 to 18

Comprehension and Critical Thinking

SECTION 1 *(Pages 894–900)*

7. a. **Recall** What is the Peace Corps?

   b. **Sequence** Describe the sequence of events that led to American astronauts landing on the moon in 1969.

   c. **Evaluate** How do you think the Cuban missile crisis would have ended had the United States pursued air strikes or an invasion of Cuba?

SECTION 2 *(Pages 901–905)*

8. a. **Define** What is guerrilla warfare?

   b. **Describe** How did the American military try to disrupt the Ho Chi Minh Trail?

   c. **Predict** Do you think Americans' opinions about the war would have been different had there been no television reporting? Explain your answer.

9. **a. Identify** What was the War Powers Act?

  b. Explain What was Henry Kissinger's role in the Vietnam War?

  c. Summarize What long-term effects did the Vietnam War have on the United States?

Reviewing Themes

10. **Geography** How did the geography of Vietnam help the Vietcong?

11. **Geography** How did the geography of Vietnam affect American forces?

Reading Skills

Setting a Purpose *Use the Reading Skills taught in this chapter to answer the question about the reading selection below.*

Johnson Commits to Victory

Lyndon B. Johnson was determined to prevent Communists from taking over in South Vietnam. "We have the resources and the will to follow this course as long as it may take," Johnson said . . . .

The Tonkin Gulf Resolution

In the summer of 1964, a naval skirmish led to a rapid expansion of U.S. involvement in Vietnam. On August 2, 1964, the USS *Maddox* reportedly-exchanged gunfire with North Vietnamese torpedo boats in the Gulf of Tonkin, off the North Vietnamese coast . . . . *(p. 901)*

12. Which of the following is an example of a purpose you could set for the passage above?

  a. Find out why the Vietnam War was fought.

  b. Find out Johnson's view of the Vietnam War.

  c. Find out when the Vietnam War ended.

  d. Find out what the Vietnam Veterans Memorial is.

Social Studies Skills

Using Primary Sources: Oral Histories *Read this passage from Marine officer Philip Caputo. Then use the Social Studies Skills taught in this chapter to answer the question below.*

"You simply trusted absolutely no one. I mean, from a 5-year-old kid to a 75-year-old woman." *(p. 901)*

13. How do you think Caputo felt about not being able to trust anyone? Do you think he felt safe? Why or why not?

Using the Internet

go.hrw.com
KEYWORD: SB7 CH29

14. **Activity: Mapping the Terrain** Geography played a very important role in the Vietnam War. American soldiers struggled to fight against enemy soldiers who knew the land and were able to use that knowledge to their advantage. Enter the activity keyword and find information about the geography of Southeast Asia. Then create a map showing the area's various geographic features. Include notes on the map that describe some of the geographical challenges American soldiers faced.

FOCUS ON WRITING

15. **Presenting Your Newscast** Review your notes and prepare your newscast. You will have about five minutes for your newscast. Include several segments on different topics from the chapter. One could be an interview with a friend in the role of a soldier back from Vietnam, a government official, or an antiwar protester. You can also use pictures to illustrate the events you are reporting. Write your script and practice reading it before your presentation.

DIRECTIONS: Read each question and write the letter of the best response.

1 The Berlin Wall separated

A Eastern Europe and Western Europe.

B East Berlin and West Berlin.

C West Germany and the Soviet Union.

D East Germany and the Soviet Union.

2 Ho Chi Minh was the leader of

A Laos.

B Cambodia.

C North Vietnam.

D South Vietnam.

3 President Johnson's policy of escalation called for

A a gradual withdrawal of U.S. troops from Vietnam.

B an immediate withdrawal of U.S. troops from Vietnam.

C a rapid buildup of U.S. forces in Vietnam.

D expanding the war into Laos and Cambodia.

4 During the war, the Vietcong and NVA fought using what tactics?

A quick surprise assaults

B air strikes

C search-and-destroy missions

D blockades

5 Who were the Democratic and Republican candidates in the 1972 election?

A Lyndon Johnson and Richard Nixon

B Eugene McCarthy and John McCain

C Robert F. Kennedy and Henry Kissinger

D George McGovern and Richard M. Nixon

6 The Pentagon Papers revealed that

A the Bay of Pigs invasion was a disaster.

B U.S. officials had been lying about the progress of the war.

C the USS *Maddox* was attacked by North Vietnamese torpedo boats.

D the 1968 election was won by Richard Nixon.

7 What was the main purpose of the War Powers Act?

A It allowed President Kennedy to blockade Cuba.

B It allowed President Johnson to expand the U.S. role in Vietnam.

C It repealed the Tonkin Gulf Resolution.

D It limited the right of any president to commit troops to an armed struggle.

8 Read the following quote from Attorney General Robert F. Kennedy and use it to answer the question below.

> "On Tuesday morning, October 16, 1962, shortly after 9:00, President Kennedy called and asked me to come to the White House. He said only that we were facing great trouble. Shortly afterward, in his office, he told me that a U-2 had just finished a photographic mission and that the Intelligence Community had become convinced that Russia was placing missiles and atomic weapons in Cuba."
>
> —Robert F. Kennedy, *Thirteen Days: A Memoir of the Cuban Missile Crisis*

Document-Based Question What clues can you read that tell you how frightening the Cuban missile crisis was for Americans?

Assignment

Write a news article about the anniversary of either (1) the Nuremberg trials, (2) the Supreme Court's *Brown* v. *Board of Education* decision, or (3) the opening of the Vietnam Veterans Memorial.

TIP **Brainstorming** Brainstorm ways to interest people in the topic of your article. Take a few minutes to review what you know about the topic. Then write down as many questions, interesting points, and examples as you can.

A News Article

You have probably read many news articles in newspapers and magazines. News articles keep people informed about events in their communities, the nation, and the world. Sometimes they also remind people about important events from the past.

1. Prewrite

Considering Purpose and Audience

Remember that you are writing for people who have a choice about what to read. Your story must keep readers interested. How will you relate the topic of your story to their lives or emotions? At the same time, your story should give people information they need. In order to share information effectively, you must choose the most important details to include in your article.

Writing a Compelling Article

Make your article vivid and compelling by including

- **A short headline** showing what the article is about.
- **A "hook"**—an interesting fact or detail—to get the reader's attention at the beginning of the article.
- **Clear descriptions** of people and events.
- **Specific examples and quotations.**
- **Reasons** why the event is important.

2. Write

You can use this framework to help you write the first draft of your article.

A Writer's Framework

Introduction
- Grab your reader's attention with a strong headline.
- Begin with a striking detail or quotation for a hook.
- Introduce the event and its importance to people today.

Body
- Describe what happened, who was involved, and where, when, and why the event took place.
- Explain the significance of the event.
- Use details to connect the event to readers' lives or emotions.

Conclusion
- Finish any incomplete thoughts.
- End with a quotation or example that sums up the main point of the article.

3. Evaluate and Revise

Evaluating

Use these questions to discover ways to improve your news article.

Evaluation Questions for a News Article

- Do you begin with a strong headline and hook?
- Do you introduce the event and its importance to people today?
- Do you describe what happened, who was involved, and where, when, and why the event took place?
- Do you explain the significance of the event?
- Do you use details to connect the event to readers' lives or emotions?
- Do you end with a quotation or example that sums up the main point of the article?

Revising

Newspapers and magazines often have limited space. News articles must express a sharply focused idea briefly. To make sure that your article does this, read each sentence carefully. Each sentence should

- Be clear and to-the-point.
- Contain no unnecessary words or phrases.
- Use only precise words. Eliminate words such as *very* unless they add meaning to the sentence.

> **TIP** **Vivid Writing** Make sentences more interesting by using vivid words and images. Use strong words that help readers create a mental picture.

4. Proofread and Publish

Proofreading

Read your essay aloud to catch any mistakes in your spelling or grammar. If something looks or sounds wrong, mark it. Come back to it later to correct the mistake. This is also a good strategy for identifying and fixing awkward sentences.

Publishing

Exchange articles with a classmate who wrote about a different topic. Did you learn from your classmate's article? Did you find it interesting? Put together a class newspaper that includes all the articles and headlines. Add pictures, and display the newspaper on a bulletin board.

5. Practice and Apply

Use the steps and strategies in this workshop to write your news article.

UNIT 10 1968–PRESENT

Modern America

Searching for Order

Virginia Standards of Learning

USII.1 The student will demonstrate skills for historical and geographical analysis, and responsible citizenship, including the ability to

a) analyze and interpret primary and secondary source documents to increase understanding of events and life in United States history from 1865 to the present

USII.8 The student will demonstrate knowledge of the economic, social, and political transformation of the United States and the world between the end of World War II and the present by

c) identifying the role of America's military and veterans in defending freedom during the Cold War, including the wars in Korea and Vietnam, the Cuban missile crisis, the collapse of communism in Europe, and the rise of new challenges

d) describing the changing patterns of society, including expanded educational and economic opportunities for military veterans, women, and minorities

USII.9 The student will demonstrate knowledge of the key domestic and international issues during the second half of the twentieth century by

a) examining the Civil Rights Movement and the changing role of women; **c)** identifying how individual citizens from the time period influenced America scientifically, culturally, academically, and economically

FOCUS ON WRITING

Historical Novel Suppose you have decided to write a historical novel set during the 1970s or 1980s. You want your story to bring one or more of the major events of this time period to life for readers. As you read this chapter, you will take notes on the important people and conflicts of this time. You will choose which historical figures and events to include in your story. Then you will write the first page of your novel.

UNITED STATES

1968 Richard Nixon is elected president.

1969

1969 Golda Meir becomes prime minister of Israel.

WORLD

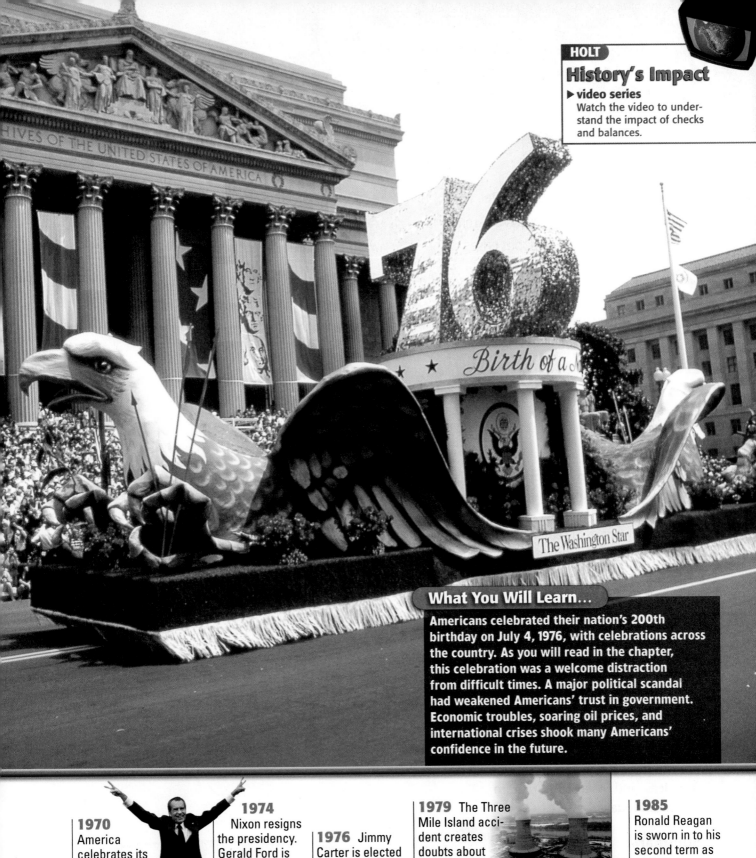

HOLT

History's Impact
▶ **video series**
Watch the video to understand the impact of checks and balances.

The Washington Star

What You Will Learn...

Americans celebrated their nation's 200th birthday on July 4, 1976, with celebrations across the country. As you will read in the chapter, this celebration was a welcome distraction from difficult times. A major political scandal had weakened Americans' trust in government. Economic troubles, soaring oil prices, and international crises shook many Americans' confidence in the future.

1970 America celebrates its first Earth Day.

1974 Nixon resigns the presidency. Gerald Ford is sworn in.

1976 Jimmy Carter is elected president.

1979 The Three Mile Island accident creates doubts about nuclear energy.

1985 Ronald Reagan is sworn in to his second term as president.

1970

1975

1980

1985

1973 Egypt and Syria attack Israel.

1975 South Vietnam surrenders to North Vietnam.

1979 The Soviet Union invades Afghanistan.

Reading Social Studies

by Kylene Beers

Economics	Geography	Politics	Society and Culture	Science and Technology

Focus on Themes In this chapter, you will learn about issues faced by several modern presidents. You will also read about crises in the **economy** and in **politics** that changed the way Americans viewed their role as a nation. Finally, you will learn about American society in the 1970s.

Summarizing

Focus on Reading After reading a large amount of information, you can summarize it into a shorter amount that is easier for you to understand.

Understanding Summarizing Using the ideas and information presented in a book can be easier if you summarize what the author is saying. When you summarize, you can use some of the key ideas and words to write your own sentences that explain the information. When you write a summary, some details can be left out.

Read the following passage and its summary. Notice which details the author chose to include and which to leave out.

The American population was changing in the 1970s. Throughout American history, most immigrants to the United States had come from Europe. Beginning in the 1970s, however, a majority of new immigrants came from the Americas and Asia. This pattern continues today.

From Chapter 30, p. 932

Summary:

The population immigrating to the United States began changing during the 1970s. Now the majority of immigrants come from Latin America and Asia.

This passage contains most of the same information but is shorter. Not all of the information is included.

Key Terms and People

You Try It!

The following passage is from the chapter you are getting ready to read. As you read the passage, look for information that is important enough to go in a summary.

> "Are you better off than you were four years ago?" That was the question Republican candidate Ronald Reagan asked voters during the 1980 presidential campaign. Millions of voters answered "No," giving Reagan an easy victory over President Carter. Reagan won 489 electoral votes to Carter's 49. On January 20, 1981—the day of Reagan's inauguration—Iran finally released the American hostages after 444 days in captivity.
>
> *From Chapter 30, p. 937*

After you read the passage, answer the following questions.

1. Do you think the campaign slogan from the passage above is essential information for a summary of the election?

2. Do you think the number of electoral votes should be included in your summary?

3. Write a two-sentence summary of the passage above.

Chapter 30

Section 1
stagflation *(p. 927)*
Organization of Petroleum Exporting Countries *(p. 927)*
realpolitik *(p. 928)*
Strategic Arms Limitation Talks *(p. 928)*
détente *(p. 928)*
Watergate *(p. 929)*
Gerald Ford *(p. 930)*
pardon *(p. 931)*

Section 2
affirmative action *(p. 933)*
Rachel Carson *(p. 933)*
Jimmy Carter *(p. 934)*
human rights *(p. 935)*
apartheid *(p. 935)*
sanctions *(p. 935)*
Camp David Accords *(p. 935)*
Iran hostage crisis *(p. 936)*

Section 3
Ronald Reagan *(p. 937)*
supply-side economics *(p. 938)*
Sandra Day O'Connor *(p. 938)*
deficit *(p. 938)*
Iran-Contra affair *(p. 939)*
Mikhail Gorbachev *(p. 940)*

Academic Vocabulary

In this chapter, you will learn the following academic words:
consequences *(p. 930)*
implications *(p. 938)*

As you read Chapter 30, practice summarizing the information from several paragraphs.

Nixon's Presidency and Watergate

Virginia Standards of Learning USII.1a, USII.1b, USII.1h, USII.8c, USII.9c

What You Will Learn...

Main Ideas

1. Americans faced domestic challenges, including an energy and economic crisis.
2. Nixon's foreign policy led to improved relations with Communist powers.
3. The Watergate scandal forced Nixon to resign.
4. Gerald Ford became president upon Nixon's resignation and faced many challenges.

The Big Idea

Richard Nixon's policies helped ease Cold War tensions before the Watergate scandal brought down his presidency.

Key Terms and People

stagflation, *p. 927*
Organization of Petroleum Exporting Countries, *p. 927*
realpolitik, *p. 928*
Strategic Arms Limitation Talks, *p. 928*
détente, *p. 928*
Watergate, *p. 929*
Gerald Ford, *p. 930*
pardon, *p. 931*

TAKING NOTES Create a concept web like the one below. Fill in the outer ovals with facts about Nixon's domestic policy, foreign policy, and the Watergate scandal.

Nixon's presidency

Foreign policy

Domestic policy

Watergate scandal

If **YOU** were there...

You experienced a decade of conflict and change in the 1960s. You were a witness to major events in the civil rights movement, and you lived through frightening Cold War crises. You saw leaders assassinated and astronauts walk on the moon. You have some friends who fought in Vietnam and others who led antiwar protests.

Do you think the United States is now headed in the right direction? Why or why not?

BUILDING BACKGROUND Protests over the Vietnam War led to bitter divisions among Americans in the 1960s. When Republican Richard Nixon ran for president in 1968, he said he would work to restore law and order to American society. Nixon won a close election over Democratic candidate Hubert Humphrey.

Domestic Challenges

As president, Richard Nixon promised to work on behalf of Americans who opposed protests and supported his plan for ending the war. Nixon called these Americans the "Silent Majority." He criticized student protesters and called on them to stop their activities. He did not believe Americans should leave Vietnam quickly.

New Federalism

Nixon also had a new plan for government. Nixon knew that his supporters blamed the federal government for setting high taxes and interfering in citizens' lives. He proposed a plan called the New Federalism, which would limit the power of the federal government. His policies represented a major shift in direction from Lyndon Johnson's Great Society ideas. Under Nixon's plan, grants of money from the federal government went directly to state and local governments, who decided how to spend the money. This plan reflected Nixon's conservatism, or a belief in limiting the involvement of government in citizens' lives.

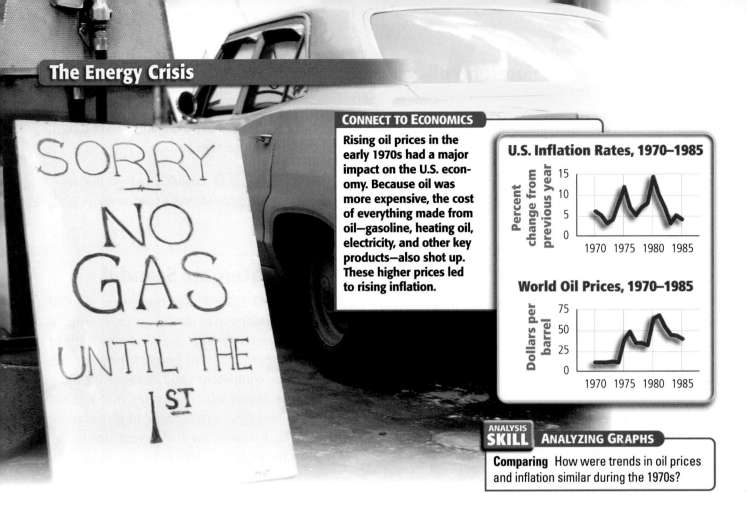

CONNECT TO ECONOMICS

Rising oil prices in the early 1970s had a major impact on the U.S. economy. Because oil was more expensive, the cost of everything made from oil—gasoline, heating oil, electricity, and other key products—also shot up. These higher prices led to rising inflation.

U.S. Inflation Rates, 1970–1985

Percent change from previous year

World Oil Prices, 1970–1985

Dollars per barrel

ANALYSIS SKILL **ANALYZING GRAPHS**

Comparing How were trends in oil prices and inflation similar during the 1970s?

President Nixon promised to reduce welfare spending and to restore law and order. He supported policies that gave more power to police and to the courts.

His political philosophy affected the Supreme Court as well. As president, he appointed four new justices. Many Court decisions soon began to reflect a more conservative point of view.

Nixon did not push for new civil rights legislation. He believed that the government had done enough in the 1960s, saying, "The laws have caught up with our consciences."

Economic Troubles

Nixon faced the difficult economic challenge of so-called **stagflation**—the economic condition of combined stagnant economic growth and high inflation. From 1967 to 1974, rising prices reduced the purchasing power of the U.S. dollar by more than 30 percent.

One cause of inflation was the rising cost of oil. By the early 1970s, the United States was importing about one-third of its oil. Much of this oil was purchased from Middle Eastern nations that were members of the **Organization of Petroleum Exporting Countries**, or OPEC. This group worked to control the production and sale of oil to keep prices high.

Most OPEC countries were Arab countries that had been opposed to the creation of the Jewish state of Israel. On October 6, 1973, the Jewish holy day of Yom Kippur, Egypt and Syria attacked Israel in what would become known as the Yom Kippur War. The United States sent military supplies to help Israel.

OPEC members responded angrily to support for Israel by declaring an embargo, or ban, on oil sales to the United States. The oil embargo and soaring oil prices caused an energy crisis. This worsened an already weak U.S. economy.

THE IMPACT TODAY

Today, about half of U.S. oil imports comes from OPEC countries.

READING CHECK **Identifying Cause and Effect**
What was one cause of inflation?

Nixon's Foreign Policy

As the energy crisis demonstrated, international events could have a serious impact on life in the United States. Henry Kissinger, a German American professor who became Nixon's senior foreign policy adviser, helped Nixon develop a new approach to foreign policy. Nixon's foreign policy decisions would be based on practical American interests, not on moral or political ideals. This approach was known as **realpolitik**, the German term meaning "actual politics." Nixon credited his realpolitik strategies with bringing an end to the Vietnam War by using political pressure from the Soviet Union and China to convince the North Vietnamese to negotiate.

Realpolitik was controversial. In several Latin American countries, for example, the United States backed harsh military governments because they were friendly to U.S. interests.

In the ongoing Cold War rivalries with China and the Soviet Union, the realpolitik approach led to important changes. American officials had long feared China and the Soviet Union would work together to spread communism. But by 1970, it was clear that these two Communist powers had become bitter rivals. Nixon believed it was in America's interest to widen this split and to improve U.S. relations with both Communist powers.

Nixon first turned his attention to China. He lifted restrictions on trade and travel, and opened negotiations with its leaders. In 1972 Nixon became the first U.S. president to make an official visit to China. Newscasts showed Nixon and Chinese leader Mao Zedong shaking hands and trading jokes.

Nixon's trip led to improved U.S.–China relations. It also caught the attention of Soviet leaders, who became more open to talks with the United States. In May 1972 Nixon flew to Moscow, where he and Soviet leader Leonid Brezhnev participated in the **Strategic Arms Limitation Talks** (SALT). These talks led to a treaty limiting each country's nuclear weapons. The SALT agreement opened a period of **détente** (day-TAHNT), or less hostile relations, between the United States and the Soviet Union. Détente brought economic benefits, as the Soviets began buying millions of tons of grain from American farmers.

READING CHECK **Supporting a Point of View**
Do you think realpolitik was a good strategy? Why or why not?

The Watergate Scandal

On June 17, 1972, five men were arrested while breaking in to the Democratic National Committee's offices at the Watergate Hotel in Washington, D.C. The burglars were carrying camera equipment and secret recording devices. Police soon discovered that some of them had ties to the Nixon administration. One had worked for the Committee to Re-elect the President (CRP).

Nixon denied that anyone in his administration was involved in the Watergate break-in. He went on to win the 1972 election in a landslide. But early in Nixon's second term,

Watergate Scandal

Microphones hidden in tubes of lip balm were used in the burglary.

On May 28, 1972, five men burglarized the Democratic National Committee headquarters in the Watergate Hotel, shown here. They took pictures of files and bugged telephones. The burglars returned for more information on June 17 and were arrested.

the seemingly minor break-in exploded into a massive political scandal that became known as **Watergate**.

Investigating the Break-in

Did Nixon administration officials have anything to do with the Watergate break-in? Reporters Bob Woodward and Carl Bernstein investigated that question in a series of articles in the *Washington Post*. Key figures in the Nixon administration refused to talk to the reporters. Then Woodward was contacted by a government official who had inside information on the Watergate investigation. To protect the identity of their source, Woodward called him by a secret codename. With the informant's information, Woodward and Bernstein began publishing stories about illegal activities by Nixon administration officials. The stories revealed that the CRP had hidden illegal campaign contributions and spread false rumors about Democratic candidates. They also presented evidence that officials in the Nixon White House were trying to cover-up the facts of the Watergate break-in.

Americans watched the Watergate drama unfold through the intense media coverage of the scandal.

A Senate committee led by Senator Sam Ervin launched its own investigation of Watergate. When the committee began televised hearings in May 1973, millions of Americans tuned in. The most damaging witness was former White House attorney John Dean, who testified that Nixon was personally involved in the Watergate cover-up. Dean could not prove this, however. Then another witness revealed that Nixon had tape-recorded almost all of his Oval Office conversations.

THE IMPACT TODAY

The identity of the *Post's* informant remained confidential for more than 30 years. In 2005 W. Mark Felt, second-in-command at the FBI during Watergate, revealed that he was the inside source for information.

Washington Post reporters soon linked the break-in to the presidential re-election campaign. A White House cover-up began.

The Senate formed a committee to investigate the break-in and possible cover-up. Its hearings (shown above) were televised.

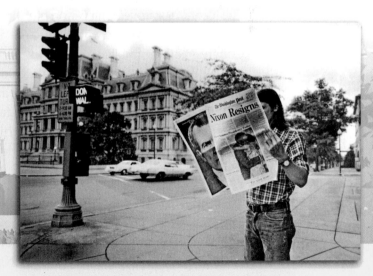

Faced with impeachment for an illegal cover-up of the break-in, Nixon resigned. He was later pardoned by President Gerald Ford.

ANALYSIS SKILL **ANALYZING INFORMATION**

Why was Nixon threatened with impeachment by the House?

SUPREME COURT DECISIONS

United States v. Nixon (1974)

Background of the Case During the Watergate investigation, a special prosecutor asked for the tapes of President Nixon's Oval Office conversations. Nixon claimed that he did not have to obey court orders to turn over the tapes because of executive privilege. On July 8, 1974, the case went before the Supreme Court.

The Court's Ruling
The Supreme Court announced its unanimous decision on July 24. It stated, "the legitimate [lawful] needs of the judicial process may outweigh presidential privilege." Nixon could not use executive privilege to avoid the subpoenas.

The Court's Reasoning
The Court decided to hear the case more quickly than most cases because of its importance to the functioning of government and the interest of the American public. The Supreme Court ruled that to claim executive privilege a president would have to show a compelling national security reason. Nixon had no such reason for refusing to hand over the tapes.

Why It Matters
The Supreme Court ruling showed that, despite their unique and important position, presidents do have to obey the law. It also showed that the government could use the powers defined in the Constitution to prevent one branch from becoming too powerful. Less than a week later, the House Judiciary Committee voted to impeach Nixon.

ANALYSIS SKILL — **ANALYZING INFORMATION**

1. How is this case an example of the checks and balances system?
2. What do you think was the most important impact of this Supreme Court decision?

Committee members asked Nixon to allow them to listen to the tapes. Nixon refused to hand the tapes over to a special prosecutor, claiming executive privilege—a president's right to keep information secret for reasons of national security. In July 1974 the Supreme Court ordered Nixon to turn over the tapes. The recordings proved that Nixon had directed the Watergate cover-up and lied about it to Congress and the public.

While this investigation was unfolding, Vice President Spiro Agnew resigned amid charges that he had taken bribes and failed to pay taxes. Nixon appointed Michigan congressman **Gerald Ford** as vice president.

Nixon Resigns

After studying the case, the House Judiciary Committee recommended impeachment. Judiciary Committee member Barbara Jordan of Texas explained why she thought Nixon should be impeached:

> "My faith in the Constitution is whole, it is complete, it is total. And I am not going to sit here and be an idle spectator to the ... destruction of the Constitution."
>
> —Barbara Jordan, in a speech before Congress, 1974

On July 27, 1974, the committee approved its first article of impeachment, charging Nixon with obstruction of justice. Within the next week, two more articles were approved by the committee, one for the abuse of power and one for contempt of Congress.

On August 8, 1974, Nixon appeared on national television and announced, "I shall resign the presidency effective at noon tomorrow." He became the first president in American history to resign from office. Gerald Ford was sworn in as president on August 9.

One of the **consequences** of Watergate was that many Americans lost faith in government officials. In a poll taken in 1974, just 36 percent of Americans said they trusted the government. Others, however, saw a more positive side of Watergate. Senator Sam Ervin viewed the hearings and Nixon's resignation as evidence that the government was able to rid itself of corruption. "Watergate ... proved our Constitution works," he said.

READING CHECK **Sequencing** What events led to Nixon's impeachment?

ACADEMIC VOCABULARY

consequences
the effects of a particular event or events

Ford as President

Vice President Gerald Ford became the first modern president to hold the office without being elected to it. Ford lost some public support when he granted Richard Nixon a **pardon**, or freedom from punishment. He declared it was best for the nation that Nixon not be tried for his crime because he would be "cruelly and excessively penalized" and "ugly passions would again be aroused [stirred]."

Adding to Ford's difficulties, oil prices and unemployment remained high, and stagflation continued. The United States also had an increasing trade deficit, an imbalance in which a country imports more than it exports.

Arguing that inflation was the main cause of the economic troubles, Ford began a campaign called Whip Inflation Now (WIN). WIN encouraged people to save money and businesses to hold down wages and prices. Ford's plan met with resistance from many members of Congress, who wanted to increase spending to help the poor and unemployed. In 1975

A U.S. Marine changes the official presidential photograph from one of Nixon to one of Ford.

Ford and Congress began to compromise. Still, inflation and unemployment remained high.

READING CHECK **Evaluating** Do you think President Ford was right to pardon Nixon?

SUMMARY AND PREVIEW Gerald Ford became president after the Watergate scandal ended Nixon's presidency. In the next section you will learn about life in the 1970s.

Section 1 Assessment

Reviewing Ideas, Terms, and People

1. **a. Describe** What challenges did the United States face during President Nixon's terms of office?
   b. Make Inferences Why do you think the **Organization of Petroleum Exporting Countries** objected to U.S. support for Israel?
2. **a. Identify** Who was Henry Kissinger?
   b. Contrast How was **realpolitik** different from other foreign policy approaches?
   c. Draw Conclusions Why do you think improved U.S.–China relations made the Soviets more open to talks with the United States?
3. **a. Recall** What was the **Watergate** scandal?
   b. Explain Why were President Nixon's tapes important?
   c. Elaborate Why do you think President Nixon decided to resign?
4. **a. Describe** How did **Gerald Ford** become president of the United States?
   b. Predict Do you think WIN was effective in helping the economy?

Critical Thinking

5. **Sequencing** Review your notes on Richard Nixon's presidency. Then copy the graphic organizer below and use it to list, in order, events in his presidency.

Event	Date

FOCUS ON WRITING

6. **Describing Major Events** Take notes on Nixon's domestic policy, Cold War strategy, and the Watergate scandal. What were the major events of this time period? Who were the major public figures involved, and what roles did they play? Which of these events and people do you find the most interesting?

Virginia Standards of Learning USII.1a, USII.2c, USII.8c, USII.8d, USII.9a, USII.9c

What You Will Learn...

Main Ideas

1. American society debated key social issues during the 1970s.
2. Jimmy Carter was elected president in 1976.
3. Carter had successes as well as failures in foreign policy during his administration.

The Big Idea

Americans faced major challenges both at home and around the world in the 1970s.

Key Terms and People

affirmative action, *p. 933*
Rachel Carson, *p. 933*
Jimmy Carter, *p. 934*
human rights, *p. 935*
apartheid, *p. 935*
sanctions, *p. 935*
Camp David Accords, *p. 935*
Iran hostage crisis, *p. 936*

TAKING NOTES As you read, take notes on new government policies in the 1970s. Write your notes in a chart like this one.

New Policies

America in the 1970s

If YOU were there...

It is July 4, 1976. Today the entire nation is celebrating the 200th anniversary of the signing of the Declaration of Independence. As you sit with your family watching a spectacular fireworks show, you think about the challenges this country has faced throughout its history. You think about the economic and foreign policy challenges facing Americans right now.

What are your hopes for the nation's future?

BUILDING BACKGROUND The celebration of the country's bicentennial, or 200th birthday, was a much-needed break from worries about political scandals, economic troubles, and Cold War dangers. This was a moment of renewal and hope—though many Americans still disagreed about how the country should move forward.

Social Issues of the 1970s

The American population was changing in the 1970s. Throughout American history, most immigrants to the United States had come from Europe. Beginning in the 1970s, however, a majority of new immigrants came from the Americas and Asia. This pattern continues today. Another change was that the birthrate, or number of births per 1,000 people, was declining. By 1970 Americans 65 and older became one of the fastest-growing population groups.

As the population grew and changed, American society faced the challenges of how to balance the views of all Americans. You read earlier that the Equal Rights Amendment caused nationwide debate in the 1970s. Although the ERA was not ratified, the women's movement did make important gains. A 1972 federal law known as Title IX banned discrimination on the basis of sex in educational programs that receive federal funds. The number of women admitted to medical and law schools climbed quickly. Title IX also opened the door for many more women to participate in college sports and earn athletic scholarships. In 1973 the Supreme Court legalized abortion in the case *Roe* v. *Wade*.

In the 1970s Americans also debated **affirmative action**, the practice of giving special consideration to nonwhites or women to make up for past discrimination. Supporters of affirmative action argued that it was needed to improve educational and job opportunities for minorities and women. Opponents insisted that any race- or gender-based preferences were unfair.

Many African Americans benefited from new opportunities in the 1970s. For example, the number of African Americans attending college in 1976 was four times higher than it had been a decade earlier. Many people credited affirmative action programs with this increase.

The environment also became a major issue in the 1970s. In her book *Silent Spring*, biologist **Rachel Carson** brought attention to the dangers of pollution. She explained how chemicals used to kills insects travelled through the food chain and affect people's health.

" Man, however much he may like to pretend the contrary, is part of nature. Can he escape a pollution that is now so thoroughly distributed throughout our world? *"*

—Rachel Carson, *Silent Spring*

First published in 1962, *Silent Spring* helped inspire a nationwide movement to improve the environment. Environmentalists in the United States celebrated the first Earth Day on April 22, 1970. "Earth Day is to remind each person of his [or her] . . . equal responsibility . . . to preserve and improve the Earth," explained activists.

Congress passed new laws to limit the release of pollutants. The Environmental Protection Agency (EPA) was established in 1970 to enforce these laws. As protections increased, debates sprung up about how to balance business interests with environmental concerns.

READING CHECK Comparing and Contrasting
How are Title IX and affirmative action similar and different?

Issues of the 1970s

Environmental protection, women's rights, and affirmative action were among the major issues of the 1970s.

Activists brought the environment to the forefront of national debate, urging legislation and individual action to help protect the Earth.

Supporters of the Equal Rights Amendment urged states to ratify the amendment they believed would ensure equal protection to women under the Constitution.

African Americans with a College Degree, 1960–2000

Percentage of African Americans / *Year*

Affirmative action helped African Americans and other minorities gain access to universities and certain jobs but also created much debate.

Carter Elected

To oppose Republican Gerald Ford in the 1976 presidential election Democrats nominated **Jimmy Carter**, a little-known former governor of Georgia. The Democrats purposely chose a candidate who was untouched by the recent scandals. Carter knew that the Vietnam War and Watergate had badly shaken American voters' trust in government. "I will never lie to you," he told voters.

Carter defeated Ford in a close election. As president, Carter wanted to show a new spirit of informality and openness at the White House. On inauguration day, he and his family broke with tradition by walking to the inauguration rather than riding in a limousine.

While Americans seemed to respond positively to his straightforward style, Carter faced serious challenges. High unemployment and inflation continued. The ongoing energy crisis also kept oil prices high. Many Americans became frustrated with the president's inability to solve these problems.

Although Democrats controlled Congress, Carter had a hard time convincing members to support his proposals. For example, Carter proposed a national energy plan that called for conservation and the use of alternative fuels such as solar energy. Congress demanded changes to the complex plan. The plan was never fully enacted.

One way Carter hoped to decrease the country's dependence on imported oil was by expanding the use of nuclear power. But an accident at the Three Mile Island nuclear power plant in Pennsylvania caused new worries about the safety of nuclear energy. On March 28, 1979, a reactor core at Three Mile Island overheated, and the plant released a small amount of radioactive gas into the air. This frightening incident damaged the nuclear power industry, and the federal government put in place a ban on building new reactors.

READING CHECK **Drawing Conclusions** How did the Three Mile Island incident affect Carter's energy plan?

Carter and Foreign Policy

President Carter rejected Nixon's realpolitik approach to foreign policy. He argued that "fairness, not force, should lie at the heart of our dealings with the nations of the world."

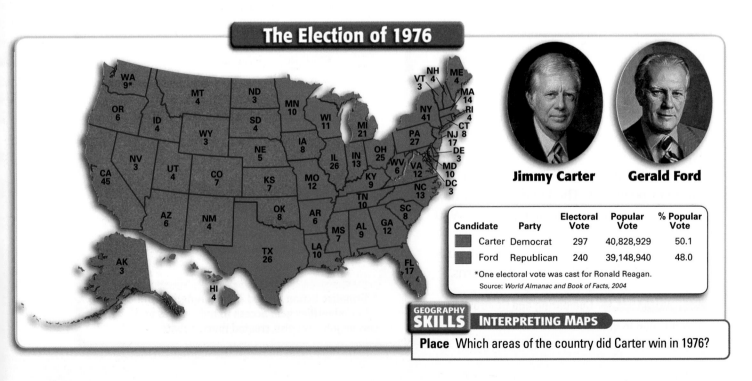

The Election of 1976

Candidate	Party	Electoral Vote	Popular Vote	% Popular Vote
Carter	Democrat	297	40,828,929	50.1
Ford	Republican	240	39,148,940	48.0

*One electoral vote was cast for Ronald Reagan.
Source: *World Almanac and Book of Facts, 2004*

Jimmy Carter   Gerald Ford

GEOGRAPHY SKILLS **INTERPRETING MAPS**

Place Which areas of the country did Carter win in 1976?

HISTORIC DOCUMENT
The Camp David Accords

During the long and often bitter Camp David negotiations, Carter worked hard to keep Israel's Menachem Begin and Egypt's Anwar el-Sadat from walking out. He later wrote about one moment when the talks nearly broke down.

❝Within a few minutes Sadat announced angrily that a stalemate [standstill] had been reached. He saw no reason for the discussions to continue. As far as he was concerned, they were over . . . They [Sadat and Begin] were moving toward the door, but I got in front of them to partially block the way. I urged them not to break off their talks, to give me another chance to use my influence and analysis, to have confidence in me. Begin agreed readily. I looked straight at Sadat; finally, he nodded his head. They left without speaking to each other.❞

Leaders Anwar el-Sadat (left), Jimmy Carter, and Menachem Begin reached a peace agreement for the Middle East in the Camp David Accords.

ANALYSIS SKILL **ANALYZING PRIMARY SOURCES**

Why do you think Begin and el-Sadat agreed to continue their negotiations?

Changing Policies

Carter favored policies that promoted **human rights**—the basic rights and freedoms of all people. He reduced U.S. aid to several former allies that committed human rights violations. In South Africa, Carter hoped to pressure the government into ending **apartheid**, a system of laws requiring racial segregation. He called for **sanctions**, or eco-nomic penalties, to encourage reform.

Carter's approach to foreign policy had effects in Latin America as well. Many Latin Americans resented previous U.S. interference in their countries. American control of the Panama Canal stood as a symbol of power in the region. In 1977 Carter signed treaties that would transfer control of the canal to Panama by the year 2000.

Carter had less success improving relations with the Soviet Union. Détente broke down when he criticized the Soviet Union for committing human rights abuses. Then in 1979 the Soviet Union invaded Afghanistan. Carter responded by breaking off arms-control talks and refusing to allow U.S. athletes to participate in the 1980 Summer Olympics in Moscow.

The Middle East

While Cold War tensions increased, Carter worked to ease tensions in the Middle East. Egypt and Israel had been at war for 30 years. In 1978 Carter invited Egyptian president Anwar el-Sadat and Israeli prime minister Menachem Begin (men-AHK-uhm BAY-guhn) to the presidential retreat at Camp David, Maryland. After 13 days of meetings, the two leaders reached a peace agreement called the **Camp David Accords**, considered by many to be Carter's greatest achievement.

Carter also experienced disaster in the Middle East. Since the 1950s, the United States had supported the pro–American shah, or king, of Iran. Many Iranians resented the shah's reform efforts and the country's shift from a traditional and agricultural society to a more urban and industrial one. The government severely punished its opponents and controlled all political participation. Many members of the opposition supported the views of Islamic spiritual leader Ruhollah Khomeini, who had been forced to leave the country because of his criticisms of the shah's policies. In 1979 Khomeini's supporters drove

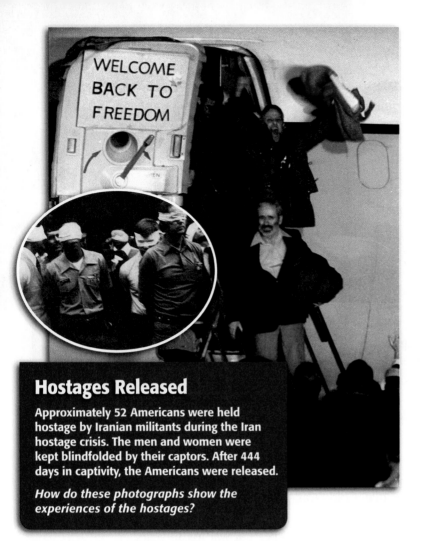

Hostages Released

Approximately 52 Americans were held hostage by Iranian militants during the Iran hostage crisis. The men and women were kept blindfolded by their captors. After 444 days in captivity, the Americans were released.

How do these photographs show the experiences of the hostages?

the shah out of Iran, and a month later, Khomeini took control of the government. On November 4, a group of Iranian students attacked the U.S. embassy in Tehran, the capital of Iran, seizing about 90 American hostages. The **Iran hostage crisis** lasted for more than a year.

In the early days of the crisis, some hostages were released. These remaining hostages were often blindfolded and beaten by their Iranian captors. Carter ended Iranian oil imports and froze Iranian assets in American banks. After a failed rescue attempt in April 1980, many Americans lost confidence in Carter's leadership.

READING CHECK **Making Generalizations**
Overall, do you think President Carter's foreign policy was effective? Why or why not?

SUMMARY AND PREVIEW President Carter's policies included both successes and failures. In the next section, you will learn about the policies of Ronald Reagan.

Section 2 Assessment

Reviewing Ideas, Terms, and People

1. **a. Define** What social issues did Americans debate during the 1970s?
   b. Contrast How had immigration patterns changed by the 1970s?
   c. Draw Conclusions Why do you think *Silent Spring* remained important in the 1970s?
2. **a. Describe** How did **Jimmy Carter** break with tradition at his inauguration?
   b. Analyze Why did Carter's promise of honesty appeal to voters?
   c. Elaborate How did the Three Mile Island accident affect the energy crisis?
3. **a. Recall** Describe the successes and failures of President Carter's foreign policy.
   b. Explain What did the treaties Carter signed about the Panama Canal promise?
   c. Draw Conclusions Why do you think many people consider the **Camp David Accords** Carter's greatest achievement?

Critical Thinking

4. **Evaluating** Review your notes on new policies in the 1970s. Then copy the graphic organizer below and use it to show President Carter's successes and failures.

Successes   Failures

FOCUS ON WRITING

5. **Identifying Important Issues** Identify important issues and challenges facing Americans during the 1970s. Which of these issues or challenges do you think you will write about? What do you know about this subject? What more would you have to learn before writing about it?

936 CHAPTER 30

The Reagan Presidency

Virginia Standards of Learning USII.1a, USII.1d, USII.8c, USII.9c

If YOU were there...

It is 1980 and you are a top adviser to the newly elected president, Ronald Reagan. You think about the challenges Reagan will face. High inflation and unemployment are plaguing the economy. Relations with the Soviet Union are falling apart. And 52 Americans are still being held hostage in Iran.

What would be your first recommendation to the president?

BUILDING BACKGROUND Many Americans blamed President Carter for the nation's economic problems and the continuing hostage crisis in Iran. These became major issues in the presidential election of 1980. Republican candidate Ronald Reagan promised to take the country in a new direction.

Reagan and Conservative Ideas

"Are you better off than you were four years ago?" That was the question Republican candidate **Ronald Reagan** asked voters during the 1980 presidential campaign. Millions of voters answered "No," giving Reagan an easy victory over President Carter. Reagan won 489 electoral votes to Carter's 49. On January 20, 1981—the day of Reagan's inauguration—Iran finally released the American hostages after 444 days in captivity.

Reagan's approach to government was based on conservative ideas. He wanted to cut taxes and reduce regulations on businesses. He promised to scale back the size of government, arguing that government involvement in business and society harmed individual ambition. "Government is not the solution to our problem; government is the problem," Reagan declared in his inaugural address.

Just two months into his presidency, Reagan was shot and severely wounded in an assassination attempt by John Hinckley Jr. Reagan was released from the hospital within two weeks, and returned to work.

What You Will Learn...

Main Ideas

1. President Reagan based his policies on conservative ideas.
2. Reagan took a tough stand against communism in his foreign policy.

The Big Idea

President Reagan enacted conservative policies at home and took a strong anti-Communist stance in the Cold War.

Key Terms and People

Ronald Reagan, *p. 937*
supply-side economics, *p. 938*
Sandra Day O'Connor, *p. 938*
deficit, *p. 938*
Iran-Contra affair, *p. 939*
Mikhail Gorbachev, *p. 940*

TAKING NOTES As you read, take notes on President Reagan's domestic and foreign policies. Organize your notes in a diagram like this one.

Domestic Policies

Foreign Policies

"Reaganomics"

Reagan's economic policies, which some called "Reaganomics," were based on a theory called **supply-side economics**. This theory calls for sharp tax cuts, with the goal of increasing the amount of money people and businesses have to invest. This investment would lead to economic growth and the creation of new jobs. Over time, the expanding economic activity would produce increased tax revenues for the government.

Though many Democrats opposed this theory, Congress approved most of Reagan's plan for large cuts in business and personal taxes. To help balance the budget, Reagan called for spending cuts as well. Congress agreed to cut the rate of the growth of spending on social programs such as school lunches, low-income housing, and food stamps.

The economy experienced a brief recession early in Reagan's presidency. Then, in 1983 the economy rebounded and began a long period of expansion. Business profits and tax revenues increased.

At the same time, spending on defense was increased dramatically, from $180 billion in 1981 to nearly $280 billion in 1985. The new spending outpaced the new tax revenues. The result was a rapidly rising **deficit**—the amount by which a government's spending exceeds its revenues.

Conservative Goals

One of Reagan's conservative goals was to reduce government regulation of key industries. Reagan hoped fewer rules would encourage expansion in those industries, thereby improving the U.S. economy. Congress responded by reducing regulations on industries such as television, airlines, and banking.

Reagan was also able to move the Supreme Court in a more conservative direction by appointing politically conservative judges. In 1981 he appointed **Sandra Day O'Connor** to the Court. She became the first woman to serve as a Supreme Court justice. Reagan later appointed two more conservative justices: Antonin Scalia and Anthony M. Kennedy.

Election of 1984

President Reagan ran for reelection in 1984 against Democratic candidate Walter Mondale, who had served as Jimmy Carter's vice president. Mondale chose Geraldine Ferraro as his running mate. Ferraro was the first woman to run for vice president on a major-party ticket. She spoke of the **implications** of her nomination:

> "By choosing an American woman to run for our nation's second-highest office, you send a powerful signal to all Americans…We will place no limits on achievement. If we can do this, we can do anything."
>
> —Geraldine Ferraro, *Ferraro: My Story*

The economy was booming as the election approached. Mondale argued that Reagan's economic policies unfairly favored the wealthy. Voters, however, gave Reagan a landslide victory. Reagan received 59 percent of the popular vote and captured 525 of the 538 electoral votes.

READING CHECK **Summarizing** What theories did "Reaganomics" include?

ACADEMIC VOCABULARY

implications effects of a decision

Reagan and Foreign Policy

President Reagan was an outspoken critic of communism and the Soviet Union, which he called an "evil empire." He saw the Cold War as a fight of "good versus evil, right versus wrong."

Conflicts in Central America

Civil wars raged in several Central American countries in the 1980s as communism spread in the area. Reagan supported anti-Communist governments in El Salvador and Guatemala with financial aid. Critics of this policy charged that the aid went to military governments that committed major human rights violations.

In Nicaragua, a revolutionary group called the Sandinistas overthrew the country's pro-American dictator in 1979. U.S. leaders became concerned when the Sandinistas formed closer ties with Communist Cuba.

Reagan cut all U.S. aid to Nicaragua and began supporting anti-Sandinista rebels known as the Contras. This led to fears that the United States could be drawn into war. In 1984 Congress passed a ban on further U.S. military aid to the Contras.

A group of Reagan administration officials secretly found a way to continue funding the Contras. One member of the group was Oliver North, a marine officer serving as a national security aide. North helped arrange the sale of U.S. missiles to Iran. In exchange, Iran released U.S. hostages that had been taken by Iranian terrorists. Profits from this secret deal were sent to the Contras, in violation of the congressional ban. The so-called **Iran-Contra affair** became a national controversy when it was exposed in 1986. Congressional hearings concluded that President Reagan was not guilty of illegal activity. Several White House officials, however, were convicted of crimes related to the affair.

Central American Conflicts in the 1980s

Legend:
- ✳ Guerrilla activity or civil war
- ■ U.S. base in continuous operation since 1903
- ▲ U.S. military presence or intervention

0   200   400 Miles
0   200   400 Kilometers

UNITED STATES

ATLANTIC OCEAN

Gulf of Mexico

Miami

THE BAHAMAS

Havana

CUBA

CAYMAN IS. (U.K.)   Guantánamo Bay

DOMINICAN REPUBLIC

PUERTO RICO (U.S.)   20°N

Mexico City

HAITI   Port-au-Prince   Santo Domingo

GUATEMALA   Belmopan   JAMAICA   Kingston

BELIZE   HONDURAS   1983, 1988

Guatemala City

EL SALVADOR   Tegucigalpa   Caribbean Sea   70°W

1981   San Salvador   NICARAGUA   GRENADA

PACIFIC OCEAN   Managua   Panama Canal   60°W

COSTA RICA   Panama   Caracas

San José   10°N

PANAMA   1989   COLOMBIA   VENEZUELA   Georgetown

GUYANA

The United States provide military aid to the Contras in Nicaragua.

GEOGRAPHY SKILLS | **INTERPRETING MAPS**

1. **Location** In which two countries did the United States intervene in 1983?
2. **Human-Environment Interaction** Why might the United States have intervened in the countries it did?

100°W   90°W   80°W

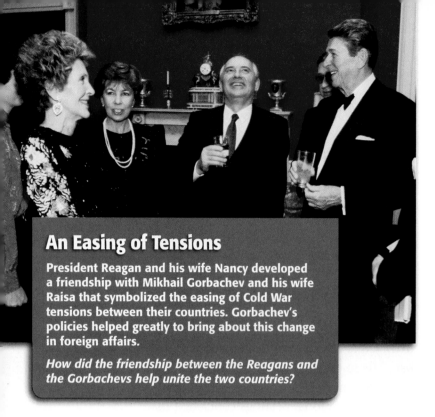

An Easing of Tensions

President Reagan and his wife Nancy developed a friendship with Mikhail Gorbachev and his wife Raisa that symbolized the easing of Cold War tensions between their countries. Gorbachev's policies helped greatly to bring about this change in foreign affairs.

How did the friendship between the Reagans and the Gorbachevs help unite the two countries?

Reagan and Gorbachev

During his first term, President Reagan took a tough stand against the Soviet Union. He halted arms negotiations and quickly expanded the U.S. military.

The Soviet Union tried to keep up with American spending in the arms race. This contributed to desperate economic times in the Soviet Union during the 1980s. In 1985

Mikhail Gorbachev became the new Soviet leader. To deal with his country's economic problems, he began a process of political and economic reforms called *perestroika*. He also adopted a new policy of political openness called *glasnost*. The newfound freedoms introduced by Gorbachev's policies threatened other leaders of the Soviet Union but were mostly supported by its citizens and by leaders in the West.

Reagan became convinced of Gorbachev's desire for change. In 1987 the two leaders signed the Intermediate-Range Nuclear Forces Treaty, eliminating all medium-range nuclear weapons in Europe. Cold War tensions were decreasing for the first time since the early 1970s.

READING CHECK Identifying Cause and Effect
Why did President Reagan change his tough stand toward the Soviet Union?

SUMMARY AND PREVIEW Conservative ideas influenced many of Ronald Reagan's policies. In the next chapter, you will learn about the policies of presidents in the 1990s.

Section 3 Assessment

go.hrw.com
Online Quiz
KEYWORD: SB7 HP30

Reviewing Ideas, Terms, and People

1. **a. Recall** What was **Ronald Reagan**'s view of government?
   b. Analyze Why did the federal budget deficit rise during Reagan's presidency?
   c. Draw Conclusions Why do you think so many Americans voted for Reagan in the 1984 election?
2. **a. Recall** What changes did **Mikhail Gorbachev** make in the Soviet Union?
   b. Explain How did Reagan administration officials violate the law in the **Iran-Contra affair**?
   c. Predict Do you think Reagan's policies were effective in fighting communism?

Critical Thinking

3. **Categorizing** Review your notes on Ronald Reagan's domestic and foreign policies. Then copy the graphic organizer below and use it to list each policy with its correct geographic focus.

United States	Central America	Soviet Union

FOCUS ON WRITING

4. **Describing Characters** How would you describe President Reagan's approach to government? What major decisions did he make during his presidency? How did these decisions influence government, politics, and foreign relations? Make notes on what you will use in your historical novel.

Ronald Reagan

How would you lead your country during the Cold War?

When did he live? 1911–2004

Where did he live? Ronald Reagan grew up in Illinois. In 1937 he moved to California, where he became a well-known movie actor. He later entered politics and was elected governor of California. After serving eight years as president, he retired to his California ranch.

What did he do? Reagan worked to reshape the American government and economy based on conservative principles. In foreign policy, he took an aggressive stand toward communism and the Soviet Union. In a famous speech at the Berlin Wall, he challenged the Soviet leader to allow freedom in Eastern Europe, saying, "Mr. Gorbachev, open this gate! Mr. Gorbachev, tear down this wall!" Reagan and Gorbachev later signed the Intermediate-Range Nuclear Forces (INF) Treaty, the first treaty reducing the number of nuclear weapons held by both countries.

Why is he so important? Nicknamed "the Great Communicator," Reagan inspired many Americans with his sense of humor and his optimistic view of America's future. Many voters credited him with restoring their confidence after the difficulties of the 1970s. Reagan's buildup of the U.S. military is believed by many to have contributed to major changes in the Cold War and the eventual fall of Communist governments in the Soviet Union and Eastern Europe.

Finding Main Ideas What was Reagan's biggest foreign policy achievement? Use evidence from the reading to support your answer.

KEY EVENTS

1937
Becomes a movie actor

1952
Marries his second wife, Nancy Davis

1966
Elected governor of California

1980
Elected president

1981
Shot by John Hinckley Jr.

1984
Elected to second term

1987
Signs INF Treaty

2004
Dies in California

Ronald Reagan used his California ranch as a retreat during his years in the White House.

Social Studies Skills

Analysis | Critical Thinking | Civic Participation | Study

Determining the Strength of An Argument

Define the Skill

Studying history often involves learning about different opinions. In order to understand these opinions, it is important to recognize strong arguments. Strong arguments are based on convincing supporting evidence. Examples and points should be true and should make sense in the context of the argument. For example, supporting points should relate to the main idea of the argument. It is also important to consider any evidence against the argument.

Many people in the past have made decisions based on the strength of an argument. Determining the strength of an argument is important for the present as well. Your judgments can help you decide whether or not to support a policy, idea, or candidate.

During the 1970s, Americans had to determine the strength of arguments during the Watergate scandal. If Nixon had not resigned, for example, members of the House of Representatives would have had to decide whether or not to vote to impeach the president. They would have had to weigh the evidence and determine the strength of arguments for and against him.

Learn the Skill

In *Silent Spring,* Rachel Carson argued that environmental pollution was harmful and had to be stopped. Here is part of her argument:

"Man, however much he may like to pretend the contrary, is part of nature. Can he escape a pollution that is now so thoroughly distributed throughout our world?"

How strong is Carson's argument? In *Silent Spring,* she gives many examples of the harmful effects of pollutants and insect poisons. This makes her argument stronger. In the quotation above, Carson points out that humans rely upon nature. As nature becomes polluted, she argues, humans will not be able to avoid the harmful health effects of that pollution.

Carson's argument was strong enough to convince the American people and Congress to take action. The environmental movement grew, and new laws were passed to protect the nation's air and water.

Practice the Skill

Suppose that you are a member of Congress during the Watergate scandal. You have to decide whether or not to impeach President Nixon. Your decision will depend on the strength of the arguments in favor of impeachment. Review the chapter and answer the following questions to help determine the strength of those arguments.

1. What is the evidence against President Nixon? How does this evidence strengthen or weaken the case against him?

2. Is there any evidence that President Nixon is innocent? How strong is this evidence?

3. Would you vote to impeach the president? Explain your answer.

Chapter Review

HOLT
History's Impact
▶ video series
Review the video to answer the closing question:

How did the Supreme Court contribute to the series of checks and balances that eventually led to President Nixon's resignation?

Visual Summary

QUICK FACTS

Use the visual summary below to help you review the main ideas of the chapter.

Positives and Negatives of the Presidencies

Richard Nixon
Positive: Nixon brought China and the United States together diplomatically.
Negative: His administration ended because of the Watergate scandal.

Jimmy Carter
Positive: Carter helped create the Camp David Accords.
Negative: He also faced the Iran hostage crisis.

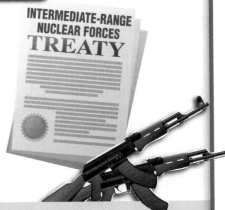

Ronald Reagan
Positive: Reagan signed a major arms treaty with several countries.
Negative: His administration was linked to the Iran-Contra affair.

Reviewing Vocabulary, Terms, and People

Read each question and write the letter of the best response.

1. Which of the following refers to a period of less hostile U.S.–Soviet relations in the 1970s?
   a. détente
   b. stagflation
   c. realpolitik
   d. *perestroika*

2. The South African government's system of official racial segregation was known as
   a. Title IX.
   b. the ERA.
   c. sanctions.
   d. apartheid.

3. Which of the following was a theory that influenced President Reagan's policies?
   a. Whip Inflation Now
   b. supply-side economics
   c. SALT
   d. *glasnost*

Comprehension and Critical Thinking

SECTION 1 *(Pages 926–931)*

4. **a. Identify** Who were the reporters who uncovered the Watergate scandal?

   b. Analyze What were some results of Nixon's visit to China?

   c. Elaborate Why do you think Nixon called his supporters the Silent Majority?

SECTION 2 *(Pages 932–936)*

5. **a. Recall** What happened at Three Mile Island?

   b. Contrast How were the foreign policies of Nixon and Carter different?

   c. Draw Conclusions Why do you think many Americans responded to *Silent Spring*?

6. a. Describe What happened in the election of 1980?

b. Summarize What were some results of Reagan's conservative policies?

c. Evaluate Do you think Congress was right to ban aid to the Contras in Nicaragua?

Reviewing Themes

7. Economics How did the energy crisis affect the economy of the United States?

8. Politics How did the politics of the presidents discussed in this chapter affect the foreign policy of the United States?

Reading Skills

Summarizing *Use the Reading Skills taught in this chapter to answer the question below.*

> Carter also experienced disaster in the Middle East. Since the 1950s, the United States had supported the pro–American shah, or king, of Iran. Many Iranians resented the shah's reform efforts and the country's shift from a traditional and agricultural society to a more urban and industrial one. The government severely punished its opponents and controlled all political participation. Many members of the opposition supported the views of Islamic spiritual leader Ruhollah Khomeini, who had been forced to leave the country because of his criticisms of the shah's policies. In 1979 Khomeini's supporters drove the shah out of Iran, and a month later, Khomeini took control of the government. On November 4, a group of Iranian students attacked the U.S. embassy in Tehran, the capital of Iran, seizing about 90 American hostages. The Iran hostage crisis lasted for more than a year. *(p. 935–936)*

9. Summarize the beginning of the Iran hostage crisis in three sentences.

Using the Internet

go.hrw.com
KEYWORD: SB7 CH30

10. Activity: Making Connections The cost of oil rose steadily in the early 1970s, and it reached a new high after OPEC nations placed an embargo on oil exports to the United States. Americans felt the impact as costs increased for all products that were made from oil, and the already weakened U.S. economy struggled to survive. Enter the activity keyword. Research the causes, effects, results, and connections between the Yom Kippur War and the OPEC oil embargo. Create a model or diagram to illustrate your research. You should label your model or diagram and be prepared to explain it to the class.

Social Studies Skills

Determining the Strength of an Argument *Use the Social Studies Skills taught in this chapter to answer the question about the selection below.*

> In this chapter, you have read about the Supreme Court case *United States v. Nixon.* Nixon argued that executive privilege, a president's right to keep information secret for reasons of national security, protected him from having to give up tapes of his official conversations.

11. In your opinion, how strong was Nixon's argument?

FOCUS ON WRITING

12. Writing Your Historical Novel Review your notes about important events and people from the 1970s and 1980s. Choose a subject that you would like to focus on in your novel. Think about the main events you will describe and main characters your story will include. Then write the first page of your novel. Be sure to describe where and when your story is taking place. Since this is a novel, you should feel free to write dialogue for historical figures who appear in your story.

DIRECTIONS: Read each question and write the letter of the best response.

1 The Camp David Accords were

A secret deals supplying Iran with weapons and the Nicaraguan Contras with money.

B the negotiations that ended the Iran hostage crisis.

C U.S.–Soviet nuclear arms reduction treaties.

D a set of peace agreements between Israel and Egypt.

2 Which of the following was a result of Reagan's economic plan?

A The deficit decreased.

B Tax rates were lowered.

C Military spending was cut.

D Unemployment and inflation rose.

3 Which president participated in the 1972 Strategic Arms Limitation Talks?

A Gerald Ford

B Richard Nixon

C Ronald Reagan

D Jimmy Carter

4 The *main* job of the Environmental Protection Agency is to

A enforce the laws that help protect air and water quality.

B raise environmental awareness through Earth Day celebrations.

C negotiate arms control agreements.

D prevent inflation and unemployment.

5 What was one aspect of Reagan's tough stance against communism?

A He dramatically increased military spending.

B He made peace agreements in the Middle East.

C He visited and established diplomatic relations with China.

D He focused on human rights.

6 How did the Watergate scandal begin?

A Government officials were caught giving information to newspaper reporters.

B Five men were caught breaking in to the Democrats' headquarters.

C Richard Nixon refused to share his tapes with Congress.

D Gerald Ford pardoned Richard Nixon.

7 How were Nixon's and Reagan's influences on the Supreme Court similar?

A Both tried to give the Supreme Court more power.

B Both denied the authority of the Supreme Court to issue subpoenas.

C Both appointed women as Supreme Court justices.

D Both appointed conservative Supreme Court justices.

8 *Stagflation* refers to the unusual economic condition of

A high oil prices but low inflation.

B stagnant economic growth and high inflation.

C low unemployment and low inflation.

D stagnant deficits and falling exports.

9 Read the following quote from a U.S. senator urging Nixon's impeachment and use it to answer the question below.

> *"What the president has done threatens to destroy our system of law. It smacks of dictatorship. Unless Congress responds in the only way provided in the Constitution for resisting such a usurpation [stealing] of authority, we endanger our country's future."*
> —Senator Edmund S. Muskie, quoted in the *Washington Post*, October 21, 1973

Document-Based Question Why did Muskie feel Nixon should be impeached?

America Looks to the Future

 Virginia Standards of Learning

USII.8 The student will demonstrate knowledge of the economic, social, and political transformation of the United States and the world between the end of World War II and the present by

c) identifying the role of America's military and veterans in defending freedom during the Cold War, including the wars in Korea and Vietnam, the Cuban missile crisis, the collapse of communism in Europe, and the rise of new challenges;
d) describing the changing patterns of society, including expanded educational and economic opportunities for military veterans, women, and minorities; **e)** describing how international trade and globalization have impacted American life

USII.9 The student will demonstrate knowledge of the key domestic and international issues during the second half of the twentieth century by

b) describing the development of new technologies in communication, entertainment, and business and their impact on American life; **c)** identifying how individual citizens from the time period influenced America scientifically, culturally, academically, and economically; **d)** examining American foreign policy, immigration, the global environment, and other emerging issues

FOCUS ON WRITING

Web Site The popularity of the Internet dramatically increased in the 1990s, changing the way we communicate and share information. The attacks of September 11, 2001, made terrorism a major concern for Americans. In this chapter you will learn about these and other important events that have taken place in your lifetime. Then you will write the text for a Web site about late twentieth century and early twenty-first century America.

UNITED STATES

1988 George H. W. Bush is elected president.

1980

WORLD

1989 Most of the Berlin Wall is dismantled.

HOLT

History's Impact
▶ **video series**
Watch the video to understand the impact of government in our daily lives.

What You Will Learn...

Young people like those pictured here are helping to shape the future of the United States. In this chapter, you will read about the amazing events that have changed our world in recent years. From the end of the Cold War to the rising terrorist threat and the development of new technology, life in the United States has been changing quickly. Today Americans are working together to face new challenges and take advantage of new opportunities.

1990 U.S. and UN forces liberate Kuwait from Iraqi control in the Persian Gulf War.

1995 Extremists bomb a federal building in Oklahoma.

2001 Terrorists attack the World Trade Center and the Pentagon on September 11.

2005 The Cassini-Huygens Mission photographs Saturn's moon Titan.

1990 | 2000 | PRESENT

1991 Nelson Mandela is elected president of South Africa.

1997 Hong Kong returns to Chinese control.

2005 Pope John Paul II dies.

Reading Social Studies

by Kylene Beers

Economics Geography Politics Society and Culture Science and Technology

Focus on Themes In this chapter, you will read about the most recent presidents and their administrations. You will learn about the changing role the United States has gained in global **politics** and the global **economy.** You will also read about September 11, 2001, and learn how that tragedy helped shape the world you live in today.

Predicting

Focus on Reading Often when you are reading, predicting what might come next can help you understand what is happening in the story of history.

Understanding Summarizing Predicting what may come next in the logical progression of a story relies on understanding what has happened in the past. You have learned many different responses to crises that have occurred throughout U.S. history. You can use this knowledge to predict what may come in the future.

Notice how one reader uses information from the past to predict what may happen

In October 2001 the United States began air strikes on Taliban targets and al Qaeda bases in Afghanistan. By December U.S. forces had driven the Taliban from power. Many of al Qaeda's members were captured, though Osama bin Laden remained at large. The United States began helping Afghanistan in the long and difficult process of establishing a democratic government and rebuilding the nation.

From Chapter 31, p. 957

Most Americans supported the use of force in Afghanistan. Disagreement soon arose, however, about how best to move forward in the war against terrorism.

After reading this section, one reader thought:

I have read about other wars in which the American public was divided over the action the country should take. In the War of 1812, there was a convention of delegates opposed to the war. During the Civil War, President Lincoln silenced antiwar Democrats by imprisoning them. In the 1960s and 1970s, many citizens publicly protested the Vietnam War, while others supported the war. What happened in these past wars that might happen in the war against terrorism?

You Try It!

The following passage is from the chapter you are getting ready to read. As you read the passage, look for the facts that can help you predict what might happen in the future.

The Internet was first developed in 1970 by scientists at the U.S. Department of Defense. Early computer networks were used mainly by government and university researchers. Then, in the 1990s, computer programmers developed the World Wide Web, enabling people to access information from computers around the world. Internet use exploded in the 1990s. Computers and the Internet made it easier and faster for people at home, work, and school to access and share information. This important development was known as the Information Revolution.

From Chapter 31, p. 961

After you read the passage, answer the following questions.

1. What other revolutions have you read about in the study of American history, and how have they affected American society?

2. Is the Information Revolution similar to any other revolution you have read about?

3. How might the Information Revolution affect American society in the future?

Key Terms and People

Chapter 31

Section 1
George H. W. Bush *(p. 950)*
Saddam Hussein *(p. 951)*
Operation Desert Storm *(p. 951)*
Colin Powell *(p. 951)*
Bill Clinton *(p. 952)*
North American Free Trade Agreement *(p. 952)*
Madeleine Albright *(p. 953)*
terrorism *(p. 953)*

Section 2
Al Gore *(p. 954)*
George W. Bush *(p. 954)*
World Trade Center *(p. 956)*
Pentagon *(p. 956)*
al Qaeda *(p. 956)*
Osama bin Laden *(p. 956)*
weapons of mass destruction *(p. 956)*

Section 3
service economy *(p. 960)*
globalization *(p. 960)*
Internet *(p. 961)*
Information Revolution *(p. 961)*
AIDS *(p. 961)*
ozone layer *(p. 962)*
global warming *(p. 962)*

Academic Vocabulary

In this chapter, you will learn the following academic words:
facilitate *(p. 961)*
ideals *(p. 963)*

As you read Chapter 31, use the information given to predict what may happen in American society in the next 10 years.

The End of the Twentieth Century

Virginia Standards of Learning USII.1a, USII.1b, USII.1d, USII.1h, USII.8c, USII.8e, USII.9c, USII.9d

What You Will Learn...

Main Ideas

1. Major global changes took place during the presidency of George H. W. Bush.
2. During Bill Clinton's presidency, the nation experienced scandal, economic growth, and the rise of terrorist threats.

The Big Idea

The United States and the world faced many new challenges at the end of the 20th century.

Key Terms and People

George H. W. Bush, *p. 950*
Saddam Hussein, *p. 951*
Operation Desert Storm, *p. 951*
Colin Powell, *p. 951*
Bill Clinton, *p. 952*
North American Free Trade Agreement, *p. 952*
Madeleine Albright, *p. 953*
terrorism, *p. 953*

TAKING NOTES As you read, look for information about key events that happened during the presidencies of George H. W. Bush and Bill Clinton. Use a diagram like the one below to help you organize your notes.

Bush	Clinton

If YOU were there...

You are visiting the city of West Berlin in 1989. Just after midnight on November 9, you see huge crowds of people pouring into the streets to celebrate. You rush outside to find out what's going on. "The wall is falling!" people shout. You run toward the Berlin Wall, and there you see East and West Germans working together to rip down the hated wall.

What might the fall of the Berlin Wall mean for the future?

BUILDING BACKGROUND Mikhail Gorbachev began a process of political and economic reforms in the Soviet Union in the late 1980s. Encouraged by these changes, people from many Eastern European countries continued to demand change as well. They were eager to break free from Soviet domination and establish their own democratic governments.

George H. W. Bush

Ronald Reagan was popular with a majority of voters as his second term as president came to an end. Republicans hoped this would help Reagan's vice president, **George H. W. Bush**, win the election of 1988. Bush's Democratic opponent was Massachusetts governor Michael Dukakis. After a hard-fought campaign, Bush won the election with 426 electoral votes to Dukakis's 111.

The Cold War Ends

As Bush began his presidency, Mikhail Gorbachev continued his reform programs in the Soviet Union. In the Soviet-controlled states of Eastern Europe, people demanded even faster change and more freedom. Prodemocracy movements in Hungary, Poland, and other nations put increasing pressure on Communist governments. This pressure produced world-changing results in 1989, as pro-Soviet governments across Eastern Europe began to fall.

In October 1989 East Germans overthrew their Communist government. The new government agreed to open the borders of East Germany—including the border with West Berlin guarded by the Berlin Wall. At midnight on November 9, a wild celebration broke out as East and West Berliners jumped onto the Berlin Wall, shouting and dancing. Some smashed through parts of the wall with hammers and chisels. The wall, which had stood as a symbol of the Cold War since 1961, began crumbling to the ground. Within a year, the two Germanys reunited as one democratic country.

Several Soviet republics soon declared independence from the Soviet regime. In a desperate attempt to hold on to power, hard-line Communists took Gorbachev hostage and tried to seize the government. Thousands of Soviets took to the streets in protest. Ignoring orders to stop the protesters, many soldiers joined the crowds. Prodemocracy leader Boris Yeltsin encouraged the protesters to stand strong. The Soviet Union soon broke apart, confirming the end of the Cold War.

The Persian Gulf War

President Bush called for all countries to work together, especially during times of crisis. A major crisis soon developed in the Middle East. In August 1990 Iraq's dictator, **Saddam Hussein**, invaded neighboring oil-rich Kuwait.

Members of the United Nations called for the immediate withdrawal of Iraqi troops. President Bush, with strong public support, began assembling a coalition of nations to drive Iraq from Kuwait by force.

When Saddam refused to withdraw from Kuwait, a U.S.-led multinational coalition launched **Operation Desert Storm** . This air offensive was led by U.S. generals Norman Schwarzkopf and **Colin Powell**—chair of the joint chiefs of staff and the highest-ranking African American ever to serve in the U.S. military. After a six-week bombing campaign, ground forces invaded Kuwait. Within days, Iraq agreed to a cease-fire.

Interactive Map

The Persian Gulf War, 1990–1991

ASIA

TURKEY

SYRIA
LEBANON
Mediterranean Sea
Haifa
ISRAEL
Jerusalem
Tel Aviv
JORDAN
EGYPT

Euphrates River
Tigris River

IRAN

Baghdad **1**

IRAQ **2**

3 KUWAIT
Kuwait City

Persian Gulf

Dhahran **2** BAHRAIN
QATAR U.A.E.
Riyadh

SAUDI ARABIA

OMAN

Red Sea

Arabian Sea

Iraqi invasion, Aug. 2, 1990
Scud missile attack
UN ground forces, Feb 23–27, 1991
UN air attacks, Jan.–Feb. 1991

0   150   300 Miles
0   150   300 Kilometers

1 Allied air strikes against targets, including Baghdad, begin January 7th.
2 Iraq launches scud missile attacks unsuccessfully against targets in Israel and Saudi Arabia.
3 Allies' ground attack begins February 24th.

go.hrw.com
Interactive Map
KEYWORD: SB7 CH31

GEOGRAPHY SKILLS INTERPRETING MAPS

1. **Place** Where did Iraqi forces invade?
2. **Location** From which country did UN ground forces attack Iraq?

About 22,300 Iraqi soldiers and civilians were killed in the Persian Gulf War. The coalition forces lost around 223 soldiers, 148 of whom were American. More than 35,000 American women served in the war, though federal laws prevented them from serving in combat.

President Bush explained the importance of the war, telling Congress:

"Now, we can see a new world coming into view. A world in which there is the very real prospect of a new world order ... A world in which freedom and respect for human rights find a home among all nations."

—George H. W. Bush, March 6, 1991

READING CHECK **Summarizing** How did the world change between 1989 and 1991?

Clinton's Presidency

An overwhelming majority of Americans supported President Bush's handling of the Gulf War. By the time of the 1992 election, however, the struggling U.S. economy had become a more important issue for most voters. The Democratic nominee, Arkansas governor **Bill Clinton**, told voters he would focus on improving the economy. Clinton won a three-way race against Bush and H. Ross Perot, who ran as an independent candidate.

Clinton and Congress

Under President Clinton's leadership, Congress passed a budget designed to reduce the deficit by cutting spending and raising taxes. He also convinced Congress to support the **North American Free Trade Agreement** (NAFTA), which eliminated trade barriers between the United States, Canada, and Mexico.

In the 1994 congressional elections, House minority leader Newt Gingrich of Georgia helped lead Republicans to an important victory. Gingrich and other Republicans promoted a set of policies called the Contract with America, promising lower taxes and smaller government. Republicans gained control of both houses of Congress for the first time since 1952.

A growing economy helped Clinton win a second term in 1996 over Senator Bob Dole of Kansas. By 1998 the U.S. government was taking in more money than it was spending. Clinton's second term, however, was dominated by questions about his personal and official conduct. Government investigators charged that the president had conducted an improper relationship with a White House intern and then lied about it under oath. In 1998 the House of Representatives voted to impeach Clinton for obstruction of justice. The Senate acquitted him of the charges in 1999. The scandal damaged Clinton's public image, though his approval ratings remained high, due in part to the booming economy.

THE IMPACT TODAY

In 2005 Congress approved a similar accord with the Central American countries of Costa Rica, El Salvador, Guatemala, Honduras, and Nicaragua. The treaty is known as CAFTA.

Primary Source

POINTS OF VIEW
NAFTA

Just before Congress voted on NAFTA in 1993, Vice President Al Gore and former presidential candidate H. Ross Perot debated the controversial issue on national television.

"If we keep shifting our manufacturing jobs across the border [to Mexico] and around the world and deindustrializing our country, we will not be able to defend this great country, and that is a risk we will never take."

—H. Ross Perot

"Everything that he [Perot] is worried about will get worse if NAFTA is defeated. We want jobs for America's working men and women. We want to get rid of the barriers that have prevented us from selling what we make in other countries. This is an historic opportunity to do that."

—Al Gore

ANALYSIS SKILL **ANALYZING POINTS OF VIEW**

According to Perot, how would NAFTA affect the United States? Why does Gore disagree?

A Dangerous World

The collapse of the Soviet Union left the United States as the world's only superpower. In 1997 President Clinton appointed **Madeleine Albright** as the first woman to be secretary of state. Albright had been born in Prague before her family moved to the United States, fleeing the Holocaust. She helped adapt U.S. foreign policy to this complex new world.

The United States worked to protect global peace and democracy. In the Balkan region of Europe, for example, the former nation of Yugoslavia broke apart. Different ethnic and religious groups fought for control of territory. U.S. diplomats helped negotiate an end to the bloody war. President Clinton then sent 20,000 U.S. troops to the region to help maintain peace.

In the 1990s **terrorism**—the use of violence by individuals or small groups to advance political goals—became a major issue. In April 1995 American terrorists bombed the Alfred P. Murrah Federal Building in Oklahoma City, killing 168 people. The United States also faced increasingly deadly attacks by extremist Islamic groups. Hundreds were killed in bomb attacks on U.S. embassies in Africa in 1998.

BIOGRAPHY

Bill Clinton
1946–

Bill Clinton was born in Hope, Arkansas. As a teenager he met and shook hands with President John Kennedy—an experience that heightened his interest in becoming a politician. He became a Rhodes scholar at Oxford after graduating from college. After graduating from Yale Law School, Clinton returned to Arkansas and was elected governor in 1978. He lost his bid for reelection in 1980 but ran again in 1982 and won, serving 10 more years as governor. Clinton was elected president in 1992 and reelected in 1996. The country experienced the longest period of continued economic growth during his presidency. In 1998, however, Clinton became only the second president in U.S. history to be impeached.

Drawing Conclusions Why might meeting President Kennedy have influenced Clinton?

READING CHECK Identifying Cause and Effect
How did the end of the Cold War change the U.S. role in the world?

SUMMARY AND PREVIEW The Cold War ended in 1990. In the next section you will learn about new world challenges.

---

go.hrw.com
Online Quiz
KEYWORD: SB7 HP31

Section 1 Assessment

Reviewing Ideas, Terms, and People

1. **a. Summarize** What were some of the major world events during **George H. W. Bush**'s presidency?
   b. Identify What was the purpose of **Operation Desert Storm**?
   c. Evaluate How did the Persian Gulf War test President Bush's vision of a new world order?
2. **a. Recall** What were some of the high points and low points of **Bill Clinton**'s presidency?
   b. Contrast How is **terrorism** different from standard warfare?
   c. Elaborate Do you think Congress was right to pass the **North American Free Trade Agreement**? Explain your answer.

Critical Thinking

3. **Sequencing** Review your notes on the presidencies of George H. W. Bush and Bill Clinton. Then copy the graphic organizer below and use it to identify major events and the year they occurred.

Year	Event

FOCUS ON WRITING

4. **Identifying Important Figures** Take notes on the main people in the chapter. Identify why each of these people was important. In what major events was each person involved? How did he or she affect the United States?

Virginia Standards of Learning USII.1a, USII.1c, USII.8c, USII.9c, USII.9d

What You Will Learn...

Main Ideas

1. George W. Bush won the disputed 2000 presidential election.
2. Americans debated the future of the War on Terror that began after terrorists attacked the United States.
3. The nation faced difficult challenges during President Bush's second term.

The Big Idea

George W. Bush led the country in response to terrorist attacks and through domestic challenges.

Key Terms and People

Al Gore, *p. 954*
George W. Bush, *p. 954*
World Trade Center, *p. 956*
Pentagon, *p. 956*
al Qaeda, *p. 956*
Osama bin Laden, *p. 956*
weapons of mass destruction, *p. 956*

TAKING NOTES As you read, take notes on the major policies of George W. Bush. Use a diagram like the one below. You may need to add more circles.

George W. Bush

George W. Bush in Office

If YOU were there...

It is the December after the presidential election between George W. Bush and Al Gore. For weeks, people have been talking about whether the votes can be recounted by hand. The race was too close to call on election night, and now the candidates are involved in a court case that will decide who the next president will be.

How would you solve the problem of recounting votes?

BUILDING BACKGROUND In the 1990s extremist Islamic groups in the Middle East vowed to attack the United States. They carried out deadly attacks on U.S. embassies in Africa and against the ship the USS *Cole*. Terrorism was not a major issue in the 2000 presidential election, but it would soon begin to dominate American politics.

The 2000 Presidential Election

The United States was at peace and enjoying economic prosperity as the 2000 presidential election neared. The Democrats chose **Al Gore**, who had served as Bill Clinton's vice president, as their nominee. The Republican candidate was Texas governor **George W. Bush**, the son of former president George H. W. Bush.

Campaign Issues

One major campaign issue was how to use the federal budget surplus, which totaled nearly $100 billion in 1999. Gore said he would use the money for education and health care and to pay off a part of the national debt. Bush promised to return the money to taxpayers in the form of tax cuts. Bush and Gore also debated the role that the United States—now the world's only superpower—should play in global affairs. Campaign polls showed that the race was very close.

On election night, the voting in some states was so close that no winner could be declared. It soon became clear that Florida's 25 electoral votes would determine the outcome of the election.

The Election of 2000

George W. Bush

Al Gore

Candidate	Party	Electoral Vote	Popular Vote	% Popular Vote
Bush	Republican	271	50,459,211	47.89
Gore	Democrat	266	51,003,894	48.41
Nader	Green		2,834,410	2.69
Other			1,062,745	1.01

*One elector from the District of Columbia abstained.

Source: *The World Almanac and Book of Facts, 2002*

ANALYSIS SKILL INTERPRETING CHARTS

Interpreting Charts By how many electoral votes did Bush win? How many more popular votes did Gore have than Bush?

The popular vote in Florida was so close that state law required the votes to be recounted. A machine recount found that Bush had received a few hundred more votes than Gore. But Gore supporters wanted the votes in four counties to be counted by hand, arguing that this would ensure all votes were counted. The Bush campaign challenged this manual recount in court.

After several weeks of suspense, the Supreme Court ruled that the manual recounts could not ensure that all votes would be counted the same way. They ordered the recount to stop. Florida's electoral votes went to Bush, making him the winner of the election. He was the first president in more than 100 years to win the electoral vote while receiving fewer popular votes than his opponent.

At his inauguration, President Bush urged Americans to come together.

"This is my solemn pledge: I will work to build a single nation of justice and opportunity … Today, we affirm a new commitment to live out our nation's promise through civility, courage, compassion, and character."

—George W. Bush, January 20, 2001

Bush's Early Days in Office

The disputed election, however, caused lingering bitterness between Democrats and Republicans. Republicans held a small majority in the House of Representatives, while the Senate was split 50–50. When votes in the Senate are tied, the vice president casts the tie-breaking vote. This gave Vice President Dick Cheney an important role in helping to pass Republican legislation.

Bush put together his cabinet, appointing Colin Powell to the key position of secretary of state. Powell became the first African American to hold this office. Bush carried through with his campaign promise to cut taxes. Six months after taking office, he signed into law a $1.35 trillion tax-cut plan. He also signed into law an education reform plan called No Child Left Behind. This act created a national set of standards for every student and every school to meet. It also raised funding for schools.

READING CHECK **Analyzing** What was unusual about the outcome of the 2000 presidential election?

Fighting Terrorism

Despite many plans for educational and economic reform, President Bush was soon faced with the challenge of confronting terrorism. His administration became focused on developing a foreign policy to protect Americans from the growing threat of terrorist attacks after the events of September 11, 2001.

September 11, 2001

On September 11, 2001, terrorists took control of four commercial airliners and used them as weapons to attack sites in Washington, D.C., and New York City. The hijackers flew an airplane into each of two towers that made up the **World Trade Center**, an important business center in New York City. The resulting fires caused the buildings, which had been the tallest in the nation, to crumble to the ground. About 2,500 people were killed in the collapsing buildings. Another airplane was flown into the **Pentagon**—the headquarters of the Department of Defense located outside of Washington, D.C. A fourth hijacked airplane crashed in a Pennsylvania field. The tragedy brought Americans together, and the nation received support from foreign leaders and citizens. One French newspaper's headline read, "WE ARE ALL AMERICANS."

President Bush promised to find and punish those responsible for the attacks.

U.S. officials determined that the hijackers were members of a fundamentalist Islamic terrorist group called **al Qaeda**, or "the Base." The group was led by a wealthy Saudi Arabian exile, **Osama bin Laden**. Bin Laden and his followers were based in Afghanistan. The Taliban, an extreme Islamic group, ruled the country. After Taliban leaders refused to turn over bin Laden, the United States took military action. In October 2001 the United States attacked Afghanistan and drove the Taliban from power but failed to find and capture bin Laden. The United States then began helping Afghanistan to rebuild and establish a democratic government.

War in Iraq

After the attack on Afghanistan, President Bush argued that Saddam Hussein, the dictator of Iraq, posed an immediate threat to U.S. security. When the Persian Gulf War ended in 1991, Saddam had agreed to give up Iraq's **weapons of mass destruction**—chemical, biological, or nuclear weapons that can kill thousands. However, Saddam failed to fully cooperate with UN weapons inspectors.

Leaders from France, Germany, and Russia argued that the UN inspectors should be

Time Line

9/11 and Beyond

2001

September 11, 2001 About 3,000 Americans are killed in terrorist attacks on the United States.

October 7, 2001 The war in Afghanistan begins.

November/December 2001 The Taliban regime is driven from power in Afghanistan.

January 2003 The Department of Homeland Security is created to oversee domestic security.

March 20, 2003 The air war in Iraq begins.

given more time to search for weapons. President Bush and British prime minister Tony Blair said force should be used to ensure Iraq was complying with the weapons ban. On March 20, 2003, the United States and a coalition of allies launched a ground attack on Iraq. Saddam's government collapsed, and Saddam was eventually captured.

As in Afghanistan, U.S. officials began working with Iraqis to establish a democratic government. Violence continued, however, with attacks on U.S. soldiers and Iraqis who were working to rebuild the country. Iraqi voters elected new government leaders and approved a new constitution in 2005. In 2006 an Iraqi court sentenced Saddam to death, and he was executed a short time later. Deep divisions among Iraqis remained an issue, however, threatening the stability of the new government.

Debates at Home

The war in Iraq caused fierce debate at home. After months of searching, no weapons of mass destruction were uncovered, and no concrete ties between Saddam and al Qaeda could be proven. Critics began to accuse the Bush administration of exaggerating the danger Saddam posed to the United States. The continuing violence between Iraqi insurgents and U.S. soldiers led many Americans to call for an end to the war. Meanwhile, growing concerns that Iraq's neighbor, Iran, was working to develop nuclear weapons caused additional tensions in the region. President Bush lost much of his support among voters, and during the elections of 2006 Democrats gained a majority in both houses of Congress. The new Congress elected Nancy Pelosi the first female speaker in the House of Representatives. In response to the outcome of the election, Secretary of Defense Donald Rumsfeld resigned and a new secretary, Robert Gates, was appointed. The newly elected Congress began calling for a plan to withdraw from Iraq.

READING CHECK **Summarizing** What led to the war in Iraq?

Domestic Issues

After the 2004 election, Secretary of State Colin Powell resigned. Bush appointed Condoleezza Rice as his replacement. She became the first African American woman to hold the office. Bush's other new cabinet appointees included Alberto Gonzales, the first Hispanic attorney general.

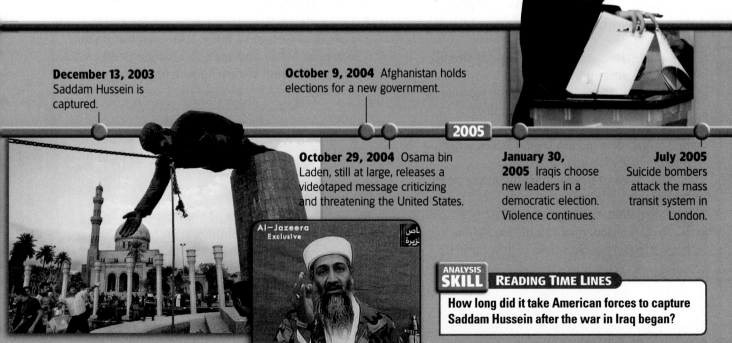

December 13, 2003 Saddam Hussein is captured.

October 9, 2004 Afghanistan holds elections for a new government.

2005

October 29, 2004 Osama bin Laden, still at large, releases a videotaped message criticizing and threatening the United States.

January 30, 2005 Iraqis choose new leaders in a democratic election. Violence continues.

July 2005 Suicide bombers attack the mass transit system in London.

Al-Jazeera Exclusive

ANALYSIS SKILL **READING TIME LINES**

How long did it take American forces to capture Saddam Hussein after the war in Iraq began?

George W. Bush

1946–

George W. Bush was born in Connecticut and grew up mainly in Texas. His family has a long history of political success—his grandfather was a U.S. senator and his father served as president from 1989 to 1993. Bush was a member of the National Guard during the Vietnam War, then attended Harvard Business School. After running unsuccessfully for Congress in 1978, he started several oil businesses in Texas and became part-owner of the Texas Rangers baseball team. He was elected governor of Texas in 1994 and reelected in 1998. In 2000 he defeated Al Gore in one of the closest presidential races in American history.

Sequencing What did George W. Bush do before he was elected president?

In late 2005 Bush nominated two new Supreme Court justices, John Roberts and Samuel Alito. The Senate investigated each thoroughly before approving them. With the confirmation of Bush's nominees, the court began making more conservative rulings.

Bush's administration faced much criticism for its response to the natural disaster of Hurricanes Katrina and Rita. Rain associated with Hurricane Katrina flooded many parts of the Gulf Coast and the city of New Orleans. The director of the Federal Emergency Management Agency (FEMA) stepped down amid criticism that the local, state, and federal governments responded inadequately to the crisis. As victims tried to rebuild their towns and cities, Hurricane Rita struck a second blow to the region. Although alone not as serious as Hurricane Katrina, the combined effects of the two storms caused many residents to move permanently from their homes along the Gulf Coast.

READING CHECK **Analyzing** What issues did Bush face in his second term?

SUMMARY AND PREVIEW Terrorism became a major concern after September 11, 2001. In the next section you will learn about other debates in America today.

Section 2 Assessment

go.hrw.com
Online Quiz
KEYWORD: SB7 HP31

Reviewing Ideas, Terms, and People

1. **a. Describe** What was the outcome of the 2000 presidential election?
   b. Explain How did **George W. Bush** promise to use the government surplus?
   c. Elaborate How do you think the election of 2000 shows the importance of voting?
2. **a. Identify** What is **al Qaeda**?
   b. Explain Why did the United States enter into the war with Iraq?
   c. Predict What do you think the future holds for the war on terror?
3. **a. Recall** Who is Condoleezza Rice?
   b. Interpret How might Hurricane Katrina have affected people's view of government?

Critical Thinking

4. **Categorizing** Review your notes on the major policies of George W. Bush. Then copy the graphic organizer below and use it to describe George W. Bush's approach to dealing with terrorism.

Fighting Terrorism

Afghanistan   Iraq

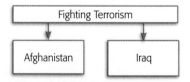
FOCUS ON WRITING

5. **Describing the Effects of September 11** Take notes on the effects of the September 11, 2001, terrorist attacks. What are your own memories of that day? How did Americans respond to the attacks? How did the attacks change the focus of the American people? How did they affect the presidency of George W. Bush?

The Road Ahead

If YOU were there...

You are a student studying American history. You have read about the dramatic impact that inventions, new industries, political changes, and wars have had on daily life over the years. In your own life, you have seen how much things can change in just a few years. Now picture yourself living in the United States 50 years from now.

What will be different about life in America?

BUILDING BACKGROUND Think of the challenges Americans have faced throughout our history. Consider how much the country has changed since it was founded and how much progress has been made. Today the United States continues to face challenges and to search for solutions.

America's Changing Economy

In public opinion polls taken in 2007, Americans listed terrorism and the continuing violence in Iraq among the most important challenges facing the United States. Other major concerns included the economy and the availability of jobs, health care costs, education, immigration, and the environment. The growing national debt was another key concern. After several years of surpluses, the government began running a deficit again in 2002. Slow economic growth, the cost of the war in Iraq, and tax cuts all contributed to the rising budget imbalance.

The American economy and job market have also experienced important ups and downs in recent years. During the 1990s the United States enjoyed the longest period of economic growth in its history. The stock market boomed and unemployment fell to its lowest level in 30 years. Much of this economic growth was powered by Internet companies and other high-tech firms. When some high-tech firms failed to earn profits, however, their stocks lost value, and many went out of business. Unemployment began rising again. "A year and a half ago, I could have gone anywhere and named a price," said one computer technology professional who lost his job in 2001. "This is definitely not the case now."

Virginia Standards of Learning USII.1a, USII.1d, USII.1e, USII.1f, USII.1i, USII.8d, USII.8e, USII.9b, USII.9c, USII.9d

What You Will Learn...

Main Ideas

1. The American economy and job market are changing.
2. Technological advances continue to solve everyday problems.
3. Americans are a diverse people united by shared ideals.

The Big Idea

The United States continues to grow and change as we move ahead in the 21st century.

Key Terms and People

service economy, *p. 960*
globalization, *p. 960*
Internet, *p. 961*
Information Revolution, *p. 961*
AIDS, *p. 961*
ozone layer, *p. 962*
global warming, *p. 962*

TAKING NOTES As you read, look for information about changes taking place in the United States. Use a diagram like the one below to help you organize your notes.

Changes		
Economy	Technology	Population

Although high-tech industries have remained a key part of the U.S. economy, other industries have declined in importance. In recent years, for example, many textile companies have closed mills and shifted their operations to countries where labor is less expensive. This is part of a larger trend in which the percentage of Americans working in manufacturing has steadily fallen. The U.S. economy has moved toward becoming a **service economy**. This means that most people have jobs providing services, such as medical care or entertainment, rather than producing goods.

By the end of the 1900s, about 75 percent of American workers were employed in service jobs. Economists predict that service industries will continue to grow in the 2000s. Health care, computer engineering, and education are expected to be among the fastest-growing fields. Such predictions are based partly on population trends. As the number of older Americans increases, for example, so will the need for nurses and other health-care professionals.

Another ongoing change in our economy is the process of **globalization**—growing connections among economies and cultures all over the world. Multinational corporations—companies that do business in more than one country—play a large part in globalization. For example, you can find American fast-food restaurants in Russia and Japanese car factories in the United States. Increasing international trade has also contributed to globalization. In 1995 more than 120 nations joined to form the World Trade Organization (WTO). The WTO's goal is to promote international trade by removing political and economic trade barriers between nations.

Americans have different opinions about how globalization will affect the United States. Supporters believe globalization will lead to increased U.S. exports and new jobs at home. Opponents worry that Americans will lose jobs as U.S. companies move their operations to countries where wages are lower. Still others insist that globalization can help our economy if it is well managed. Senator Joseph Lieberman of Connecticut said, "Only education, innovation, investment, trade, training, and hard work will give us the growth and jobs we want and need."

READING CHECK **Identifying Cause and Effect** What economic trend led to the creation of the World Trade Organization?

Life in the Twenty-First Century QUICK FACTS

New Jobs

Recent advances in technology have brought new kinds of jobs that require different skills than did jobs in the past.

New Research

Medical research has improved the lives of millions, as new medicines combat old and new diseases.

Technology Moves Forward

As you have seen throughout this book, technological changes and new inventions have dramatic effects on life in the United States and around the world. This continues to be true of our lives today. Just think about all the ways you use technology every day.

One of the new technologies that has changed everyday life is the **Internet**—a global system of computer networks through which people anywhere in the world can communicate and share information. The Internet was first developed in 1969 by scientists at the U.S. Department of Defense. Early computer networks were used mainly by government and university researchers. Then, in the 1990s, computer programmers developed the World Wide Web, enabling people to access information from computers around the world.

Internet use exploded in the 1990s. Computers and the Internet made it easier and faster for people at home, work, and school to access and share information. This important development was known as the **Information Revolution**. Bill Gates, a leader in the computer industry, described the exciting changes this revolution promised:

" We are watching something historic happening, and it will affect the world …the same way the scientific method, the invention of printing, and the arrival of the Industrial Age did. "

—Bill Gates, quoted in *Newsweek*

Excitement about the Internet and the Information Revolution helped fuel the economic boom of the 1990s. Although not all Internet companies succeeded, the Internet has changed the way we find information and communicate with each other. Internet use continues to grow rapidly around the world today.

Technology is also helping to **facilitate** new medical research. For example, researchers have made important breakthroughs in understanding connections between genetics and illness. In 2003 scientists completed the Human Genome Project, a project to identify more than 30,000 genes in human DNA. Medical researchers hope to use this information to find treatments for a wide range of diseases.

Another ongoing challenge for medical reasearchers is fighting **AIDS**—acquired immune deficiency syndrome. Caused by the human immunodeficiency virus (HIV), AIDS shuts down the body's immune system.

FOCUS ON READING

Predict how the use of the Internet might change American society.

ACADEMIC VOCABULARY

facilitate
bring about

New Technology

The further exploration of space and of other planets is possible with the use of cutting-edge technology.

New Threats

The threat of terrorism has led to the creation of new agencies to protect the borders of the United States.

New Environmental Issues

The nation and the world face the issues of environmental damage and an increase in population.

ANALYSIS SKILL **ANALYZING VISUALS**

What are some ways people are responding to the challenges of the twenty-first century?

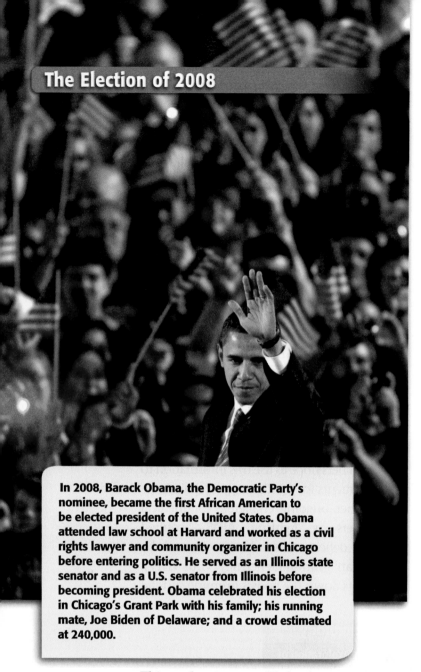

In 2008, Barack Obama, the Democratic Party's nominee, became the first African American to be elected president of the United States. Obama attended law school at Harvard and worked as a civil rights lawyer and community organizer in Chicago before entering politics. He served as an Illinois state senator and as a U.S. senator from Illinois before becoming president. Obama celebrated his election in Chicago's Grant Park with his family; his running mate, Joe Biden of Delaware; and a crowd estimated at 240,000.

This makes it more likely that people with AIDS will contract other illnesses and die. As of 2005, more than 23 million people worldwide had died from AIDS. Scientists have developed drugs that help control the HIV virus but have not yet found a cure. In 2002 leaders from around the world founded the Global Fund to Fight AIDS, Tuberculosis, and Malaria. The Global Fund provides money to treat these deadly diseases and search for cures.

Scientists are also searching for ways to help protect the environment. In our increasingly global society, environmental problems often require international solutions. In the 1980s, for example, many people became concerned about the condition of the **ozone layer**—a thin layer of gas in the upper atmosphere that blocks harmful solar rays. The United States joined with more than 100 other nations to ban the use of chemicals that were harming the ozone layer. By 2004 some scientists reported that damage to the ozone layer was slowly being repaired.

Another environmental issue facing the world is climate change, or **global warming**. The burning of fossil fuels such as gasoline and coal releases carbon dioxide into Earth's atmosphere. Many scientists warn that rising levels of carbon dioxide are causing a greenhouse effect that traps heat from the sun in Earth's atmosphere. This could cause temperatures to rise, which would have dangerous effects, including rising sea levels and more severe weather patterns. A 2001 United Nations scientific report predicted that Earth's average temperature could rise between 2 and 10 degrees by 2100.

Concerns about global warming, along with high oil prices, have encouraged the development of new kinds of transportation technology. In 2007 Americans bought record numbers of hybrid cars. These vehicles use less gas because they run partially on electricity. Scientists are also working to develop vehicles that will run entirely on hydrogen and release no pollution into the air.

Even as some scientists take on issues facing our planet, others look to the challenge of exploring space. In 2004 NASA landed two robotic vehicles on Mars. The rovers began exploring the Martian surface, sending back images that people could see on NASA's Web site. Human exploration of space continues on the International Space Station and with successful shuttle flights. NASA has faced challenges in the complicated task of sending people into space, however. In 1986 the space shuttle *Challenger* exploded, and in 2003 the *Columbia* shuttle broke apart. Fourteen astronauts were killed in these accidents.

READING CHECK Summarizing In what key areas is technology changing modern life?

The American People

The American population will continue to grow and change in the 21st century. The U.S. Census Bureau reports that our population is more ethnically diverse than ever before. In 2005 the bureau reported that Hispanics made up 14 percent of the country's total population, making them the country's largest minority group. African Americans made up just over 13 percent of the American population, and Asian Americans about 5 percent.

These changes are greatly influenced by immigration patterns. Of the more than 32.5 million foreign-born residents, 52 percent were born in Latin America and 25 percent were born in Asia. Based on these trends, the Census Bureau predicts that the country's white and nonwhite populations will be about equal by the year 2050.

Increased diversity is reflected not only in American society, but also in individual Americans. In the year 2000 the Census Bureau began allowing people to indicate in official surveys that they were of more than one race. In the 2000 census, more than 6.8 million Americans listed themselves as belonging to more than one race. In 2008, American voters chose a man of mixed race, Barack Obama, as president for the first time.

While the diversity of our population grows, Americans of all backgrounds share a belief in many basic **ideals**. Our shared commitment to the ideals of freedom, equality, and justice helps keep our nation strong. So does our shared dedication to the responsibilities of citizenship. Americans also share many of the same hopes and dreams for the future.

ACADEMIC VOCABULARY

ideals
ideas or goals that people try to live up to

READING CHECK **Predicting** How might the U.S. population change over the next 100 years?

SUMMARY The United States continues to create opportunities and face challenges. How would you like to contribute to your country's future?

Section 3 Assessment

go.hrw.com
Online Quiz
KEYWORD: SB7 HP31

Reviewing Ideas, Terms, and People

1. **a. Recall** How has the American economy changed in the past several decades?
   b. Explain What caused government deficits to rise in the early 2000s?
   c. Draw Conclusions How do you think **globalization** has changed the U.S. economy?
2. **a. Identify** What are some of the world's most recent technological advances?
   b. Explain How did the **Internet** spark an **Information Revolution**?
   c. Predict Do you think **global warming** will affect your life in the future? Why or why not?
3. **a. Describe** Describe the U.S. population today.
   b. Make Inferences Why do you think the Census Bureau started allowing people to mark more than one race?
   c. Elaborate How do you think diversity and shared ideals affect America?

Critical Thinking

4. **Categorizing** Review your notes on changes taking place in the United States. Then copy the graphic organizer below and use it to describe major technological challenges for the future.

FOCUS ON WRITING

5. **Elaborating on Key Themes** Identify key elements of American life today. In your opinion, what are some great things about life in America? What do you think are the major challenges facing Americans today? What are some possible solutions? Which subjects would you like to read more about? Think about links you could include on your Web site that would provide readers with more information about these topics.

Immigration Today

Immigrants from Asia make up about 25 percent of all foreign-born U.S. residents. Although Chinese and Japanese immigrants have been coming to the United States for generations, Southeast Asians such as the Hmong, Laotians, Vietnamese, and Cambodians are groups that have only recently begun to arrive.

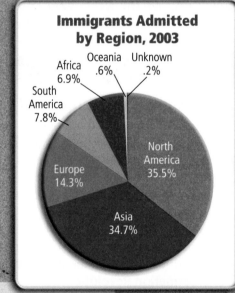

Immigrants Admitted by Region, 2003

- Africa 6.9%
- Oceania .6%
- Unknown .2%
- South America 7.8%
- Europe 14.3%
- North America 35.5%
- Asia 34.7%

America has always been a nation of immigrants. Today, people from every country move to the United States. In 2005 approximately 13 percent of the U.S. population was foreign born. Many of these people will eventually choose to become naturalized citizens. With the threat of global terrorism, however, U.S. immigration policy is becoming more strict. People from certain countries are now required to register with the Department of Homeland Security.

Many immigrants from Eastern and Western Europe come to the United States seeking a better life. They accounted for about 16 percent of the immigrants admitted in 2002.

Immigrants from around the world often choose to become naturalized U.S. citizens. The day they take the oath of American citizenship is often a day of celebration, as it was for this mother and daughter from Uganda.

Immigrants arrive in the United States searching for economic, educational, and political opportunities. Immigrants from Mexico and Central America make up about 37 percent of the foreign-born population of the United States.

GEOGRAPHY SKILLS INTERPRETING MAPS

1. **Human-Environment Interaction** From which continent does the largest number of immigrants come?
2. **Movement** How do you think immigration affects U.S. society today?

Social Studies Skills

Analysis | Critical Thinking | Civic Participation | Study

Confronting Controversial Issues

Define the Skill

The United States and the world face many challenges in the 21st century. People often have different opinions on how to deal with these challenges, which can lead to controversy. Some of the issues discussed in this book remain controversial.

As citizens of a democracy, Americans have a responsibility to confront controversial issues. This includes learning about different issues and why they are controversial. It also involves discussing the issues and forming opinions about them. Part of the democratic system is listening to other people's ideas about how to solve controversial issues and presenting your own ideas in a helpful way. In this way, everyone's ideas can be heard and discussed, so that the best course of action can be followed.

Learn the Skill

To confront controversial issues, it is important to understand them. You can start by identifying them. For example, one controversial issue in the 21st century is globalization—the process of economies and cultures becoming more closely connected. Some people think that globalization is a good way to improve the lives of all the world's citizens. Others think that globalization destroys what is unique about individual cultures.

Once the issue has been identified, you can learn more about it. Books, news reports, and articles are good sources of information on controversial issues. They can provide different points of view on an issue. Gathering different opinions about globalization, for example, can help you see why it is controversial. It can also help you determine your own point of view on the issue.

Follow these guidelines to confront other controversial issues.

1 Identify the issue.

2 Learn about the issue. Gather information on the subject from different sources. Determine why the issue is controversial.

3 Figure out your own point of view on the issue.

4 Discuss the issue with others. Because the issue is controversial and may lead to disagreements, it is important to be respectful of differences of opinion.

Practice the Skill

Follow these instructions to confront the controversial issue of how to deal with terrorism.

1. Find at least three articles showing different points of view about dealing with terrorism.

2. Read and take notes on the articles you have found. Based on what you have learned, determine your own point of view.

3. Have a class discussion about dealing with terrorism. Listen to opposing points of view. Share your own ideas and explain how you arrived at your point of view.

HOLT

History's Impact
▶ **video series**
Review the video to answer the closing question:

The National Park Service is constantly challenged to find a balance between wildlife and visitors. Why is this?

Visual Summary

QUICK FACTS

Use the visual summary below to help you review the main ideas of the chapter.

The United States today acts as a member of the global community as it faces the future.

Challenges
• Environmental issues
• Diseases
• Terrorism

Benefits
• Technology
• Political alliances

Reviewing Vocabulary, Terms, and People

Match the numbered person or term with the correct lettered definition.

1. World Trade Center
2. Colin Powell
3. Al Gore
4. global warming
5. Saddam Hussein
6. Madeleine Albright
7. AIDS
8. terrorism

a. 2000 Democratic presidential candidate
b. the rise in average temperatures around the world
c. dictator of Iraq overthrown in 2003
d. buildings attacked on September 11, 2001
e. deadly disease that shuts down the body's immune system
f. the use of violence by individuals or small groups to achieve political goals
g. the first woman secretary of state
h. the first African American secretary of state

Comprehension and Critical Thinking

SECTION 1 *(Pages 950–953)*

9. a. Recall What important Cold War symbol was destroyed in Germany in 1989?

b. Explain How did U.S. foreign policy change in the Clinton administration?

c. Evaluate Do you think NAFTA helped the U.S. economy? Why?

SECTION 2 *(Pages 954–958)*

10. a. Identify Who was responsible for the September 11, 2001, terrorist attacks on the United States?

b. Explain Why was the 2000 U.S. presidential election controversial?

c. Evaluate Do you think the United States was right to go to war with Iraq in 2003? Why?

SECTION 3 *(Pages 959–963)*

11. a. Identify What trend is responsible for increasing diversity in the United States?

b. Analyze Why are some people concerned about globalization?

c. Predict What aspects of life do you think will be most affected by new technology in the future?

Reviewing Themes

12. Economics How have changes in the economy affected American society since the 1990s?

13. Politics How have international politics changed over the course of George W. Bush's presidency?

Reading Skills

Predicting *Use the Reading Skills taught in this chapter to answer the question below.*

14. What might you predict for the future of society in the United States? What about the U.S. economy? How might American politics stay the same or change? What ideas in the chapter lead you to these conclusions?

Using the Internet

go.hrw.com
KEYWORD: SB7 CH31

15. Activity: Ending the Cold War By the 1980s, the Cold War had been going on for decades. But times were changing—communism was falling apart, and the Soviet Union would never be the same again. Enter the activity keyword. Research the factors that led to the decline of the Soviet Union's political and economic power. Then create a brochure on the fall of communism in the Soviet Union, the factors that led to this decline, and the impact on Russian society.

Social Studies Skills

Confronting Controversial Issues *Use the Social Studies Skills taught in this chapter to answer the question below.*

16. Name one controversial issue today. What are two different points of view on the issue?

FOCUS ON WRITING

17. Designing Your Web Site Review your notes and plan your Web site. Decide whether it will be just one page or multiple linked pages. Remember to include information on significant people, events, and ideas. Include ideas for photos, audio, or video you would like to place on your site. You might also want to provide links to other Web sites where viewers can find more information. Make sure your links connect to reliable Web sites, such as government sites or those for newspapers or museums. Finally, choose the Web site address you would like to use.

DIRECTIONS: Read each question and write the letter of the best response.

1 Madeleine Albright and Colin Powell both

  A conducted breakthrough medical research.

  B lost close presidential elections.

  C served as secretary of state.

  D commanded troops in Iraq.

2 One way the U.S. economy is changing is that

  A more people are working in service industries.

  B more people are working in manufacturing.

  C the health care and computer industries are shrinking.

  D textile mills are hiring thousands of new workers.

3 Saddam Hussein was

  A removed from power in Operation Desert Storm.

  B elected to the new Iraqi government in 2005.

  C killed in the September 11, 2001, attacks.

  D captured as a result of the 2003 U.S. invasion of Iraq.

4 The Cold War came to an end after

  A Communists lost power in East Germany.

  B prodemocracy movements began in Eastern Europe.

  C the Soviet Union dissolved in 1991.

  D Iraq invaded Kuwait in 1990.

5 What trend did the Internet help bring about?

  A terrorism

  B the Information Revolution

  C a service economy

  D global warming

6 Which of the following was one of Bill Clinton's achievements as president?

  A gaining the passage of the North American Free Trade Agreement

  B creating the Department of Homeland Security

  C allowing women in the military to serve in combat

  D setting new education standards in the No Child Left Behind act

7 Which state's electoral votes were contested in the election of 2000?

  A California

  B Florida

  C New York

  D Arkansas

8 Read the following speech by New York City mayor Rudolph Giuliani following the 9/11 attacks, and use it to answer the question below.

> "We're a city of immigrants unlike any other city, within a nation of immigrants. Like the victims of the World Trade Center attack, we're of every race, we're of every religion, we're of every ethnicity . . . It's the thing that renews us and revives us in every generation, our openness to new people from all over the world."
>
> —Rudolph Giuliani, quoted in *The Washington Post*

Document-Based Question What did Mayor Giuliani say was a unique strength of New York City? Why was this an important message to deliver after the attacks of September 11?

Assignment

Write an oral history, based on an interview with an adult you know, about one of the events in this chapter.

An Oral History

O ral histories can provide excellent sources of information about events in the recent past. An oral history is a report based on an interview with a person who experienced or remembers a historical event. Oral histories preserve personal experiences and memories for future generations.

1. Prewrite

Getting Started

Think about all the events you read about in this unit. Which ones interested you the most? Which ones do you think made the strongest impression on people at the time? Choose one as your subject.

Writing Questions

- Focus on finding out how the person you are interviewing experienced the event you chose.
- Write at least 10 questions.

TIP Use question words like *Who? What? When? Where? Why?* and *How?* in your interview questions.

Conducting an Interview

- Find an adult family member or friend to interview who remembers participating in or reacting to the event.
- Come prepared with your questions, paper, and something to write with.
- Take notes on the answers. Indicate direct quotations with quotation marks.
- Ask follow-up questions, even if you did not prepare them in advance.

2. Write

You can use this framework, along with your interview notes, to help you write your first draft.

A Writer's Framework

Introduction	Body	Conclusion
■ Grab your reader's attention with an interesting quote from your interview. ■ Introduce the event you chose and why it was important. ■ Explain how the event affected the person you interviewed.	■ Describe the memories and experiences of the person you interviewed about the event. ■ Summarize what you learned from the interview. ■ Use quotes from the interview.	■ Make a generalization about how people reacted to the event. ■ Draw conclusions about how people's reactions to the event affected history.

3. Evaluate and Revise

Evaluating

Use these questions to discover ways to improve your oral history.

Evaluation Questions for an Oral History

- Do you introduce the event and the person you interviewed in the first paragraph?
- Do you focus on the event from a personal point of view?
- Do you describe the memories and experiences of the person you interviewed about the event?

- Do you summarize what you learned and use quotes from the interview?
- Do you make generalizations and draw conclusions about people's reactions to the event?

Revising

When you revise your oral history, you may need to add background information. Check the material you have included from your interview. If anything is unclear, add more details about the event or time period. Make sure to explain clearly the connections between the personal experience and the event.

4. Proofread and Publish

Proofreading

In your oral history, you have been using quotations from the person you interviewed. Check the punctuation marks around these direct quotations. Also check the spelling and capitalization of all proper names, such as the name of the person you interviewed.

Publishing

Share your oral history with classmates who wrote about the same event. How were the experiences of the people you interviewed similar and different? Share your oral history with the class. The person you interviewed would probably also like to see the finished project.

5. Practice and Apply

Use the steps and strategies in this workshop to write your oral history.

TIP Using Quotations Effectively Quotations from your interview will make your oral history more interesting. Introduce quotations with a phrase or a sentence that makes it clear what they are about. Always identify the person who is quoted.

EXAMPLE
Simon remembered taking part in a demonstration in Washington, D.C., the night before President Nixon resigned. "There were thousands of people in Lafayette Park across from the White House," Simon recalled.

TIP Using Ellipses To make a quotation shorter, you can delete some words and replace them with an ellipsis—the symbol "...". Make sure the quotation still makes sense after you do this.

EXAMPLE
Original quotation: "On the morning of September 11, I woke up, brushed my teeth, ate breakfast, and did everything like any other day."
Quotation with an ellipsis: "On the morning of September 11, I ... did everything like any other day."

References

The United States of America: Political

CANADA

WASHINGTON
- Seattle
- Tacoma
- Olympia ★
- Portland
- Spokane ●

Puget Sound
Franklin D. Roosevelt Lake
Pend Oreille

OREGON
- ★ Salem
- Eugene ●

Columbia River

IDAHO
- ★ Boise
- Sun Valley ●
- Pocatello ●

Snake River
Flathead Lake

MONTANA
- Great Falls ●
- Helena ★
- Billings ●

Fort Peck Lake
Missouri River
Yellowstone River

NORTH DAKOTA
- Lake Sakakawea
- Bismarck ●

SOUTH DAKOTA
- Lake Oahe
- Pierre ★
- Rapid City ●

Yellowstone Lake

WYOMING
- Cheyenne ★

NEBRASKA

Platte River

Cape Mendocino
Goose Lake
Shasta Lake
Sacramento River
Pyramid Lake

NEVADA
- Reno ●
- ★ Carson City
Lake Tahoe

Great Salt Lake

UTAH
- Ogden ●
- ★ Salt Lake City
- Provo ●
Utah Lake
Green River

COLORADO
- Boulder ●
- Vail ●
- ★ Denver
- Aspen ●
- Colorado Springs ●
- Pueblo ●

Arkansas River

KANSAS

Berkeley ●
Oakland ●
San Francisco ●
San Francisco Bay
San Jose ●
Sacramento ●
San Joaquin River
Monterey Bay

CALIFORNIA
- Fresno ●

Santa Barbara ●
Ventura ●
Los Angeles ●
Long Beach ●
Riverside ●
Palm Springs ●
Anaheim ●
Santa Ana ●
San Diego ●
Channel Islands

Las Vegas ●
Lake Mead
Colorado River
Salton Sea

ARIZONA
- Flagstaff ●
- Phoenix ★

Lake Powell

Gila River

Casa Grande ●
Tucson ●

NEW MEXICO
- Taos ●
- Santa Fe ★
- Albuquerque ●
- Las Cruces ●
- El Paso ●

Canadian River

OKLAHOMA
- Oklahoma City ●
- Lawton ●

TEXAS
- Amarillo ●
- Lubbock ●
- Midland ●
- Odessa ●
- Abilene ●
- Fort Worth ●
- Austin ★
- San Antonio ●
- Corpus Christi ●
- Laredo ●

Brazos River
Pecos River
Colorado River
Rio Grande
Amistad Reservoir
Padre Island

PACIFIC OCEAN

Gulf of California

MEXICO

To understand the relative locations of Alaska and Hawaii, as well as the vast distances separating them from the rest of the United States, see the world map.

HAWAII
- Kauai
- Niihau
- Oahu
- Honolulu
- Molokai
- Lanai
- Maui
- Kahoolawe
- Hilo
- Hawaii

PACIFIC OCEAN

0   75   150 Miles
0   75   150 Kilometers
Projection: Mercator

22°N
19°N
160°W
155°W

ARCTIC OCEAN
Arctic Circle
Bering Strait

RUSSIA
- Nome ●

Yukon River

CANADA

St. Lawrence Island
St. Matthew Island
Nunivak Island

ALASKA
- Fairbanks ●
- Anchorage ●
- Valdez ●
- Skagway ●
- Juneau ★
Kodiak Island
Gulf of Alaska
Alexander Archipelago

Bering Sea

Attu Island

0   250   500 Miles
0   250   500 Kilometers
Projection: Albers Equal Area

55°N
50°N
170°E
180°
170°W
160°W
150°W
55°N

PACIFIC OCEAN

CANADA

MINNESOTA

Grand Forks
Red River
Fargo
Minnesota River
Duluth
Superior
Marquette
Sault Ste. Marie

Lake Superior

MICHIGAN

Lake Huron

MAINE

Augusta

Lake Champlain
Burlington
Montpelier
VT **NH**
Concord
Manchester
Portland

WISCONSIN

Green Bay

Lake Michigan

Minneapolis
St. Paul
Mississippi River
Madison
Milwaukee

Grand Rapids
Lansing
Saginaw
Detroit
Ann Arbor

Hudson R.
Connecticut R.
MA
Boston
Worcester
Providence
CT **RI**
Cape Cod

Sioux Falls

IOWA

Cedar Rapids
Rockford
Chicago
Davenport
Des Moines

Sioux City

Omaha
Lincoln

Missouri River

MISSOURI

Topeka
Kansas City
Kansas City

Wichita

Keystone Lake
Tulsa

Eufaula Lake

Lake Texoma

Gary
South Bend
Fort Wayne

Toledo

Lake Erie
Cleveland
Youngstown
Akron

OHIO

Columbus

Dayton
Cincinnati

Peoria
Springfield
ILLINOIS
Indianapolis
INDIANA

St. Louis
East St. Louis

Illinois River
Jefferson City
Lake of the Ozarks

Springfield

Louisville
Evansville

Ohio River

Frankfort
Lexington

KENTUCKY

Lake Barkley

Rochester
Syracuse
Albany
NEW YORK
Buffalo
Springfield
Hartford
Bridgeport
New Haven
Yonkers
Long Island Sound
Long Island

Lake Ontario

Susquehanna River
PENNSYLVANIA
Allentown
Harrisburg
Pittsburgh
Philadelphia
Jersey City
Newark
New York City
Trenton
Camden
NJ
Atlantic City
DE
Dover
Baltimore
MD
Washington, D.C.
Annapolis
Delaware Bay

WEST VIRGINIA
Charleston

VIRGINIA
Richmond
Newport News
Norfolk
Virginia Beach

Chesapeake Bay

ATLANTIC OCEAN

40°N
70°W
35°N

Cape Hatteras

Fayetteville

Kentucky Lake
Kentucky River

Nashville
Knoxville
Asheville
Chattanooga

TENNESSEE

Memphis
Huntsville

Mississippi River

ARKANSAS
Little Rock
Pine Bluff

Greensboro
Durham
Raleigh
Winston-Salem
NORTH CAROLINA
Charlotte

Greenville
SOUTH CAROLINA
Columbia
Charleston

Dallas
Waco
Shreveport

Toledo Bend Reservoir

Red River

LOUISIANA
Baton Rouge
Beaumont
Houston
New Orleans
Galveston

Vicksburg
Meridian
Jackson
MISSISSIPPI

Mobile
Biloxi
Chandeleur Islands

Birmingham
Montgomery
ALABAMA

Atlanta
Columbus
Macon
GEORGIA
Savannah

Chattahoochee R.
Savannah River
Sea Islands

Pensacola

Tallahassee
Gainesville
FLORIDA
Jacksonville

Cape Canaveral

Orlando
Tampa
St. Petersburg
Lake Okeechobee
Fort Myers

Cape Sable
Florida Keys

Fort Lauderdale
Miami

Straits of Florida

THE BAHAMAS

30°N
25°N
80°W
75°W

N
W E
S

Gulf of Mexico

25°N
95°W
90°W
85°W

Legend:
⊛ National capital
★ State capitals
● Other cities

0   100   200 Miles
0   100   200 Kilometers
Projection: Albers Equal Area

The United States of America: Physical

CANADA

Puget Sound

Mount Rainier
14,410 ft.
(4,392 m)

Franklin D.
Roosevelt Lake

COAST RANGES

CASCADE RANGE

Columbia River

Columbia Plateau

Flathead River

Lewis Range

Bitterroot Range

Salmon River

Salmon River Mts.

Sawtooth Mts.

Snake River

CONTINENTAL

ROCKY

Milk River

Fort Peck Lake

Yellowstone River

Missouri River

Lake Sakakawea

Klamath River

Goose Lake

Shasta Lake

Pyramid Lake

Great Salt Lake

Utah Lake

Grand Tetons

Gannett Peak
13,804 ft.
(4,207 m)

Yellowstone Lake

Wind River Range

Wind River

Uinta Mts.

Bighorn Mts.

Bighorn River

Powder River

Black Hills

Cheyenne River

White River

Niobrara River

North Platte River

GREAT INTERI

PLAINS

Cape Mendocino

San Francisco Bay

SIERRA NEVADA

Central Valley

Lake Tahoe

GREAT BASIN

Wasatch Range

MOUNTAINS

DIVIDE

Front Range

South Platte River

Platte River

Republican River

Smoky Hill River

Sacramento River

San Joaquin River

Coast Ranges

Monterey Bay

Mount Whitney
14,494 ft.
(4,419 m)

Death Valley

Mojave Desert

Colorado River

Lake Mead

Lake Powell

Grand Canyon

COLORADO PLATEAU

Painted Desert

San Juan River

Mount Elbert
14,433 ft.
(4,400 m)

Pikes Peak
14,110 ft.
(4,301 m)

San Luis Valley

Sangre De Cristo Mts.

DIVIDE

PACIFIC OCEAN

Channel Islands

Salton Sea

Imperial Valley

Sonoran Desert

Gila River

Rio Grande

CONTINENTAL

Canadian River

Pecos River

Colorado River

Amistad Reservoir

Rio Grande

Nueces River

Padre Island

Gulf of California

MEXICO

To understand the relative locations of Alaska and Hawaii, as well as the vast distances separating them from the rest of the United States, see the world map.

Kauai

Niihau

Oahu

Molokai

Lanai

Maui

Kahoolawe

HAWAII

PACIFIC OCEAN

Mauna Kea
13,796 ft.
(4,206 m)

Hawaii

| 0 | 75 | 150 Miles |
| 0 | 75 | 150 Kilometers |

Projection: Mercator

22°N

19°N

ARCTIC OCEAN

RUSSIA

Arctic Circle

Bering Strait

BROOKS RANGE

Yukon River

Tanana River

CANADA

Kuskokwim River

ALASKA RANGE

Mount McKinley
20,320 ft.
(6,194 m)

St. Lawrence Island

St. Matthew Island

Nunivak Island

Bering Sea

Attu Island

Gulf of Alaska

Kodiak Island

Alexander Archipelago

| 0 | 250 | 500 Miles |
| 0 | 250 | 500 Kilometers |

Projection: Albers Equal Area

PACIFIC OCEAN

55°N

50°N

55°N

CANADA

Red River

Mesabi Range

Isle Royale

Lake Superior

Minnesota River

Wisconsin River

Mississippi River

Lake Michigan

Lake Huron

Missouri River

Des Moines River

Illinois River

Lake Erie

Lake Ontario

St. Lawrence River

St. Lawrence Seaway

St. John River

Penobscot River

Longfellow Mts.

Lake Champlain

Adirondack Mts.

Green Mts.

White Mts.

Hudson River

Connecticut River

Cape Cod

Long Island Sound

Long Island

Catskill Mts.

Allegheny R.

PLATEAU

Susquehanna River

Delaware River

40°N

P L A I N S

OR

Kansas R.

Scioto River

Wabash River

Ohio River

ALLEGHENY

APPALACHIAN MOUNTAINS

Monongahela R.

Potomac River

Delaware Bay

ATLANTIC OCEAN

70°W

Lake of the Ozarks

OZARK PLATEAU

Keystone Lake

Eufaula Lake

Arkansas River

White River

Lake Barkley

Cumberland River

Kentucky Lake

Kanawha River

Cumberland Plateau

Great Smoky Mts.

BLUE RIDGE MOUNTAINS

James River

Roanoke River

Chesapeake Bay

Pamlico Sound

Cape Hatteras

35°N

Ouachita Mts.

Lake Texoma

Tennessee River

P I E D M O N T

Trinity River

Sabine River

Red River

Mississippi River

Pearl River

Tombigbee River

Alabama R.

Coosa River

Chattahoochee River

Oconee River

Savannah River

Altamaha River

Sea Islands

Toledo Bend Reservoir

Brazos River

GULF COASTAL PLAIN

Chandeleur Islands

Mississippi Delta

Okefenokee Swamp

FLORIDA PENINSULA

Cape Canaveral

80°W

GULF

Gulf of Mexico

Lake Okeechobee

THE BAHAMAS

25°N

The Everglades

Cape Sable

Florida Keys

Straits of Florida

75°W

95°W

90°W

25°N

85°W

ELEVATION

Feet		Meters
13,120		4,000
6,560		2,000
1,640		500
656		200
(Sea level) 0		0 (Sea level)
Below sea level		Below sea level

0 — 100 — 200 Miles

0 — 100 — 200 Kilometers

Projection: Albers Equal Area

N S E W

World: Political

ATLAS

Boundaries

⊛ National capitals

• Other cities

0   500   1,000 Miles
0   500 1,000 Kilometers
Projection: Mollweide

0   200   400 Miles
0   200   400 Kilometers
Projection: Mercator

ARCTIC OCEAN

Greenland (DENMARK)

Arctic

ICELAND

Godthåb

ALASKA (U.S.)

60N

CANADA

Aleutian Islands

Vancouver   Winnipeg

Ottawa   Montreal

40N

NORTH AMERICA

Chicago   Toronto

New York City

UNITED STATES

Washington, D.C.

Los Angeles

ATLANTIC OCEAN

Rabat

Casablanca

MOROCCO

Houston

Bermuda (U.K.)

Tropic of Cancer

20N

MEXICO

WESTERN SAHARA (Sovereignty Disputed)

MAURITANIA   MAL

Mexico City

Nouakchott

HAWAII (U.S.)

CAPE VERDE   SENEGAL

Dakar

Bamako   BURKIN FAS

Caracas

GAMBIA   GUINEA

GUINEA-BISSAU

GHAN CÔTE D'IVOIRE

SIERRA LEONE

PACIFIC OCEAN

VENEZUELA   GUYANA

Georgetown   SURINAME

LIBERIA

Bogotá   Paramaribo

FRENCH GUIANA (FRANCE)

COLOMBIA

KIRIBATI

0   Equator

Quito

N

ECUADOR

Galápagos Islands (ECUADOR)

W   E

SOUTH AMERICA

S

PERU

SAMOA   American Samoa

Lima

BRAZIL

Brasília

BOLIVIA

La Paz

Sucre

20S   TONGA

Tropic of Capricorn

PARAGUAY

Rio de Janeiro

São Paulo

CHILE

Asunción

ATLANTIC OCEAN

URUGUAY

Santiago   Buenos Aires   Montevideo

40S

ARGENTINA

Falkland Islands (U.K.)

South Georgia (U.K.)

South Sandwich Islands

60S

160W   140W   120W   100W   80W   60   40W   20W

Antarctic Circle

90W   80W

FLORIDA (U.S.)

70W

Nassau

BAHAMAS

Tropic of Cancer

60W

Havana

Turks and Caicos Is. (U.K.)

ATLANTIC   OCEAN

GULF OF MEXICO

CUBA

20N

Cayman Is. (U.K.)

HAITI   DOMINICAN REPUBLIC

Virgin Islands (U.S. and U.K.)

1

MEXICO

BELIZE

Belmopan

JAMAICA   Port-au-Prince

Kingston

Santo Domingo

Puerto Rico (U.S.)

2   Guadeloupe (FRANCE)

GUATEMALA   HONDURAS

CARIBBEAN   SEA

3

Guatemala City   Tegucigalpa

Netherlands Antilles (NETHERLANDS)

Martinique (FRANCE)

EL SALVADOR   San Salvador   NICARAGUA

N

Managua

Aruba (NETHERLANDS)

4

5   6

W   E

COSTA RICA

S

Panama City

San José

Port-of-Spain

7

PACIFIC   OCEAN

PANAMA

TRINIDAD AND TOBAGO

10N

90W

COLOMBIA

VENEZUELA

GUYANA

COUNTRY	CAPITAL
1 Antigua and Barbuda	St. Johns
2 St. Kitts and Nevis	Basseterre
3 Dominica	Roseau
4 St. Lucia	Castries
5 St. Vincent and the Grenadines	Kingstown
6 Barbados	Bridgetown
7 Grenada	St. George's

	COUNTRY	CAPITAL
1	Czech Republic	Prague
2	Slovakia	Bratislava
3	Slovenia	Ljubljana
4	Croatia	Zagreb
5	Bosnia and Herzegovina	Sarajevo
6	Macedonia	Skopje
7	Serbia	Belgrade
8	Montenegro	Podgorica
9	Lithuania	Vilnius
10	Latvia	Riga
11	Estonia	Tallinn
12	Kosovo	Pristina

North America: Political

ASIA

ARCTIC OCEAN
+ North Pole

EUROPE

ICELAND

Bering Sea
St. Lawrence Island
Nunivak Island

Point Barrow

Queen Elizabeth Islands

Ellesmere Island

Greenland (DENMARK)

Arctic Circle

ALASKA (U.S.)

Anchorage

Yukon River

Beaufort Sea

Banks Island

Baffin Bay

Cape Farewell

Denmark Strait

Gulf of Alaska
Kodiak Island
Alexander Archipelago
Juneau

Victoria Island

Great Bear Lake

Mackenzie River

Baffin Island

Davis Strait

Labrador Sea

Queen Charlotte Islands

Peace River

Great Slave Lake

Southampton Island

Hudson Strait

PACIFIC OCEAN

Vancouver Island

Edmonton

CANADA

Coats Island
Mansel Island

Hudson Bay

Anticosti Island

Newfoundland

Vancouver
Seattle
Portland

Calgary

Columbia River

Lake Winnipeg

Winnipeg

Lake Superior

St. Lawrence R.

Gulf of St. Lawrence

Prince Edward Island

Cape Breton Island

St. Pierre and Miquelon (FRANCE)

Snake River

Minneapolis

Lake Michigan

Lake Huron

Lake Ontario

Quebec
Montreal

Cape Mendocino

Missouri River

Milwaukee
Chicago

Detroit

Lake Erie

Ottawa
Toronto

Boston
Cape Cod

ATLANTIC OCEAN

San Francisco
San Jose

Great Salt Lake

Salt Lake City

Denver

Platte River

Indianapolis

Cleveland
Columbus

New York City
Philadelphia
Baltimore
Washington, D.C.

Los Angeles
San Diego
Tijuana

Colorado River

Kansas City

St. Louis

Ohio R.

Norfolk

Bermuda (U.K.)

Phoenix

UNITED STATES

Red River

Memphis

Mississippi River

Cape Hatteras

Dallas

Atlanta
Birmingham

Austin
San Antonio

Houston

New Orleans

Jacksonville

Cape Canaveral

Gulf of California

Rio Grande

MEXICO

Gulf of Mexico

Florida Keys

Miami
Nassau

THE BAHAMAS

Tropic of Cancer

Turks and Caicos Islands (U.K.)

DOMINICAN REPUBLIC

Puerto Rico (U.S.)

San Juan

ST. KITTS & NEVIS
ANTIGUA & BARBUDA
Guadeloupe (FRANCE)

DOMINICA

Guadalajara

Mexico City

Mérida

Havana

Straits of Florida

CUBA

HAITI

Santo Domingo

Virgin Is. (U.S., U.K.)

Martinique (FRANCE)

BARBADOS

ST. LUCIA

Puebla

Balsas R.

Cayman Is. (U.K.)

Kingston

Port-au-Prince

JAMAICA

ST. VINCENT AND THE GRENADINES

Netherlands Antilles (NETHERLANDS)

GRENADA

Belmopan
BELIZE

Caribbean Sea

Boundaries

National capitals

Other cities

GUATEMALA
Guatemala City
San Salvador
EL SALVADOR

HONDURAS
Tegucigalpa

NICARAGUA
Managua

Aruba (NETHERLANDS)

TRINIDAD AND TOBAGO

0   300   600 Miles
0   300   600 Kilometers
Projection: Azimuthal Equal Area

N
W   E
S

San José

COSTA RICA

Panama Canal

PANAMA

Panama City

SOUTH AMERICA

0° Equator

CENTRAL AMERICA

Caribbean Sea

Barranquilla
Cartagena
Caracas

VENEZUELA

Lake Maracaibo

Medellín
Bogotá

COLOMBIA

Cali

Orinoco River

Georgetown
Paramaribo
Cayenne

GUYANA

SURINAME
FRENCH GUIANA (FRANCE)

ATLANTIC OCEAN

Malpelo Island (COLOMBIA)

Quito

ECUADOR

Guayaquil

Río Negro

Amazon River

Amazon River

Belém

Galápagos Islands (ECUADOR)

0° Equator

Equator 0°

PERU

Marañón River

Ucayali River

BRAZIL

Recife

Trujillo

Callao
Lima

Arequipa

Lake Titicaca

La Paz

Lake Poopó

BOLIVIA

Sucre

PACIFIC OCEAN

Brasília

São Francisco River

Salvador

10°S

Belo Horizonte

20°S

PARAGUAY

Paraguay River

Campinas
São Paulo

Rio de Janeiro

Tropic of Capricorn

Asunción

Curitiba

Tropic of Capricorn

San Ambrosio Island (CHILE)

San Félix Island (CHILE)

Pôrto Alegre

CHILE

Paraná River

Uruguay River

Córdoba

Juan Fernández Islands (CHILE)

Valparaíso
Santiago

Rosario

Buenos Aires

URUGUAY

Montevideo

Río de la Plata

ATLANTIC OCEAN

30°S

ARGENTINA

Boundaries
National capitals
Other cities

0   250   500 Miles
0   250   500 Kilometers
Projection: Azimuthal Equal Area

Strait of Magellan

Falkland Islands (U.K.)

Tierra del Fuego

South Georgia Island (U.K.)

ATLAS

Europe: Political

Boundaries
⊛ National capitals
• Other cities

0   150   300 Miles
0   150   300 Kilometers
Projection: Azimuthal Equal Area

ASIA

URAL MOUNTAINS

RUSSIA

Ural River

Nizhny Novgorod

Volga River

Moscow

Don River

Caspian Sea

SOUTHWEST ASIA

Black Sea

White Sea

Barents Sea

St. Petersburg

FINLAND

Gulf of Finland

Tallinn
ESTONIA

LATVIA
Riga

LITHUANIA
Vilnius

RUSSIA

BELARUS
Minsk

Helsinki

UKRAINE
Kiev

Dnipro River

MOLDOVA
Chişinău

ROMANIA
Bucharest

Danube

BULGARIA
Sofia

Skopje
MACEDONIA

Pristina
KOSOVO

SERBIA
Belgrade

Danube River

GREECE

Aegean Sea

Athens

Rhodes

Crete

North Cape

ARCTIC OCEAN

SWEDEN

Stockholm

Göteborg

Baltic Sea

Gulf of Bothnia

POLAND
Warsaw

Krakow

SLOVAKIA
Bratislava

Budapest
HUNGARY

Vienna
AUSTRIA

CZECH REPUBLIC
Prague

Dresden

Berlin

GERMANY

Hamburg

Elbe River

CROATIA
Zagreb

Ljubljana
SLOVENIA

BOSNIA AND HERZEGOVINA
Sarajevo

MONTENEGRO
Podgorica

ALBANIA
Tirane

Adriatic Sea

NORWAY

Oslo

Bergen

North Sea

N
W   E
S

DENMARK
Copenhagen

LIECHTENSTEIN
Vaduz

SWITZERLAND
Bern

Geneva

Munich

Danube River

SAN MARINO
San Marino

ITALY
Rome

VATICAN CITY

Naples

Sicily

MALTA
Valletta

Mediterranean Sea

ICELAND
Reykjavik

Faeroe Islands
(DENMARK)

Shetland Islands

Arctic Circle

SCOTLAND
Edinburgh

NORTHERN IRELAND
Belfast

IRELAND
Dublin

UNITED KINGDOM

ENGLAND
Liverpool

WALES
London

Thames R.

British Isles

Channel Islands
(U.K.)

English Channel

THE NETHERLANDS
Amsterdam

The Hague

BELGIUM
Brussels

LUXEMBOURG
Luxembourg

Cologne
Bonn

FRANCE

Paris

Seine River

Loire River

Rhône River

Lyon

Marseille

MONACO
Monaco

Corsica
(FRANCE)

Sardinia
(ITALY)

Milan
Po River

PYRENEES

ANDORRA
Andorra la Vella

Barcelona

Balearic Islands
(SPAIN)

Bay of Biscay

PORTUGAL
Lisbon

Tagus River

SPAIN
Madrid

Valencia

Seville

Gibraltar
(U.K.)

Strait of Gibraltar

AFRICA

ATLANTIC OCEAN

Asia: Political

Boundaries
⊛ National capitals
• Other cities

0   250   500   750 Kilometers
0   250   500   750 Miles

Projection: Two-Point Equidistant

EUROPE

AFRICA

AUSTRALIA

ATLAS

PACIFIC OCEAN

INDIAN OCEAN

North Pole

Arctic Circle

Aleutian Islands

Bering Sea

Sea of Okhotsk

Kuril Islands (RUSSIA)

Sakhalin Island

Vladivostok

Sapporo

JAPAN
Tokyo
Yokohama
Nagoya
Osaka
Kyoto
Hiroshima

Yakutsk

Lena River

Angara River

Lake Baykal

Irkutsk

MONGOLIA
Ulaanbaatar

Yenisey River

Novosibirsk

Ob River

Irtysh River

URAL MOUNTAINS

Yekaterinburg

Chelyabinsk   Omsk

RUSSIA

Moscow

Barents Sea

Kara Sea

Laptev Sea

Ural River

Caspian Sea

Black Sea

KAZAKHSTAN
Astana
Lake Balkhash
Almaty

UZBEKISTAN
Tashkent

KYRGYZSTAN
Bishkek

TAJIKISTAN
Dushanbe

TURKMENISTAN
Ashgabat

AFGHANISTAN
Kabul

GEORGIA T'bilisi
ARMENIA Yerevan
AZERBAIJAN Baku

Tabriz
Mashhad

IRAN
Tehran   Isfahan
Shiraz

TURKEY
Ankara
Istanbul
Izmir

Mosul
Baghdad
Basra

Tigris River
Euphrates River

IRAQ
SYRIA Damascus
Aleppo
CYPRUS Nicosia
LEBANON Beirut
ISRAEL Tel Aviv
Jerusalem
JORDAN Amman

KUWAIT Kuwait City
BAHRAIN Manama
QATAR Doha
UNITED ARAB EMIRATES Abu Dhabi
OMAN Masqat (Muscat)

Persian Gulf

SAUDI ARABIA
Riyadh
Mecca
Jidda

Red Sea
Mediterranean Sea
Gulf of Aden

Socotra (YEMEN)

YEMEN Sanaa

CHINA
Beijing
Harbin
Changchun
Fushun
Dalian
Xi'an
Chengdu
Chongqing
Wuhan
Nanjing
Shanghai
Guangzhou
Hong Kong
Macao

Great Wall of China
Huang He (Yellow River)
Chang (Yangtze) River
Nu River

Gobi

NORTH KOREA Pyongyang
SOUTH KOREA Seoul
Pusan
Inch'on

Yellow Sea
East China Sea
Ryukyu Islands (JAPAN)

Tropic of Cancer

TAIWAN Taipei

Luzon Strait

PHILIPPINES
Manila

South China Sea

Celebes Sea

Hainan (CHINA)

VIETNAM
Hanoi
Vientiane
Ho Chi Minh City

LAOS
THAILAND Bangkok
CAMBODIA Phnom Penh
MYANMAR (BURMA) Yangon (Rangoon)
Mandalay

Gulf of Thailand

BRUNEI Bandar Seri Begawan

MALAYSIA Kuala Lumpur
SINGAPORE Singapore

INDONESIA
Jakarta
Semarang
Surabaya
Ujung Pandang
Medan
Bandung
Palembang

Java Sea
Arafura Sea
New Guinea

EAST TIMOR

NEPAL Kathmandu
BHUTAN Thimphu
BANGLADESH Dhaka
Chittagong

Brahmaputra River
Ganges River

INDIA
New Delhi
Delhi
Jaipur
Ahmadabad
Bhopal
Nagpur
Hyderabad
Kolkata (Calcutta)
Chennai (Madras)
Bangalore
Mumbai (Bombay)

Indus River

PAKISTAN
Islamabad
Lahore
Faisalabad
Karachi

Arabian Sea

Bay of Bengal

Andaman Islands (INDIA)
Nicobar Islands (INDIA)

Lakshadweep Islands (INDIA)

MALDIVES Male

SRI LANKA Colombo

R11

Africa: Political

EUROPE

SOUTHWEST ASIA

Mediterranean Sea

Azores (PORTUGAL)

Strait of Gibraltar

Madeira (PORTUGAL)

Casablanca • Rabat ⊛

Algiers Tunis

TUNISIA

Tripoli ⊛

MOROCCO

Canary Islands (SPAIN)

El Aaiún

WESTERN SAHARA (Claimed by Morocco)

Tropic of Cancer

ALGERIA

LIBYA

Alexandria •

Giza • Cairo ⊛

Suez Canal

EGYPT

Lake Nasser

Red Sea

CAPE VERDE

⊛ Praia

MAURITANIA

⊛ Nouakchott

MALI

NIGER

CHAD

Niger River

Khartoum ⊛

SUDAN

ERITREA

⊛ Asmara

Gulf of Aden

Niamey ⊛

Lake Chad

N'Djamena ⊛

DJIBOUTI

Djibouti ⊛

SENEGAL

Dakar ⊛

GAMBIA

Banjul ⊛

Bissau ⊛

Bamako ⊛

BURKINA FASO

Ouagadougou ⊛

BENIN

NIGERIA

Blue Nile

White Nile

ETHIOPIA

GUINEA-BISSAU

Conakry ⊛

GUINEA

CÔTE D'IVOIRE

GHANA

TOGO

Abuja ⊛

Addis Ababa •

Freetown ⊛

SIERRA LEONE

Yamoussoukro ⊛

Lomé ⊛

Lagos •

CENTRAL AFRICAN REPUBLIC

SOMALIA

Monrovia •

Abidjan •

Accra ⊛

Porto-Novo

Bangui ⊛

LIBERIA

Gulf of Guinea

CAMEROON

Malabo ⊛

UGANDA

KENYA

Mogadishu •

EQUATORIAL GUINEA

Yaoundé ⊛

Kampala ⊛

SÃO TOMÉ AND PRÍNCIPE

São Tomé ⊛

Congo River

REPUBLIC OF THE CONGO

Libreville ⊛

Kisangani •

RWANDA

Kigali ⊛

Nairobi •

Lake Victoria

INDIAN OCEAN

Equator 0°

Victoria ⊛

GABON

0° Equator

DEMOCRATIC REPUBLIC OF THE CONGO

Bujumbura ⊛

BURUNDI

SEYCHELLES

Brazzaville ⊛

Mombasa •

Pemba

Kinshasa ⊛

TANZANIA

Dodoma ⊛

Zanzibar •

CABINDA (ANGOLA)

Lake Tanganyika

Dar es Salaam •

Luanda ⊛

Lake Malawi (Nyasa)

COMOROS

Moroni ⊛

ATLANTIC OCEAN

10°S

Lubumbashi •

MALAWI

ANGOLA

Lilongwe ⊛

St. Helena (U.K.)

ZAMBIA

Lusaka ⊛

Zambezi River

MOZAMBIQUE

Antananarivo ⊛

MAURITIUS

Port Louis ⊛

Tropic of Capricorn

Harare ⊛

ZIMBABWE

MADAGASCAR

Réunion (FRANCE)

NAMIBIA

Bulawayo •

BOTSWANA

Tropic of Capricorn

Windhoek ⊛

Gaborone ⊛

Pretoria ⊛

Maputo ⊛

Johannesburg •

Mbabane ⊛

Bloemfontein •

SWAZILAND

Maseru ⊛

Orange River

LESOTHO

SOUTH AFRICA

Cape Town •

Boundaries

⊛ National capitals

• Other cities

0   250   500 Miles

0   250   500 Kilometers

Projection: Azimuthal Equal Area

N W E S

Australia and New Zealand: Political

NORTH
AMERICA

ASIA

NORTH PACIFIC OCEAN

SOUTH PACIFIC OCEAN

Tropic of Cancer

Tropic of Capricorn

Equator

International Date Line

Hawaiian Islands

Hawaii
(U.S.)

Midway
Island
(U.S.)

Johnston
Island
(U.S.)

Kingman Reef
(U.S.)

Palmyra Island (U.S.)

Fanning
Island

Washington
Island

Jarvis I.
(U.S.)

Howland I.
(U.S.)

Baker I. (U.S.)

Phoenix
Islands

McKean I.

Gardner

Starbuck
Island

P O L Y N E S I A

Marquesas
Islands
(FRANCE)

Tuamotu
Archipelago
(FRANCE)

French   Polynesia

Rapa Island
(FRANCE)

Tubuai Islands
(FRANCE)

Society
Islands
(FRANCE)

Tahiti
(FRANCE)

Papeete

Easter Island
(CHILE)

Pitcairn (U.K.)

Pitcairn
Island

Ducie
Island

KIRIBATI

Manihiki
Island

Cook
Islands
(NEW ZEALAND)

Rarotonga
Island

Tokelau (N.Z.)

American
Samoa

Pago
Pago

SAMOA

Apia

Niue
(N.Z.)

TONGA

Nuku'alofa

Kermadec
Islands
(N.Z.)

Chatham
Islands
(N.Z.)

Wellington

Christchurch

NEW
ZEALAND

North
Island

South
Island

Auckland

Bounty
Islands
(N.Z.)

Auckland Islands
(NEW ZEALAND)

MARSHALL ISLANDS

Eniwetok I.

Kwajalein Island

Majuro

Tarawa

Gilbert
Islands

TUVALU

Funafuti

Wallis &
Futuna (FR.)

FIJI

Suva

Port-
Vila

VANUATU

Espiritu Santo I.

Malekula I.

New
Caledonia
(FRANCE)

Loyalty
Islands
(FRANCE)

Noumea

Norfolk
Island
(AUSTRALIA)

M E L A N E S I A

Wake Island
(U.S.)

M I C R O N E S I A

Truk Is.

Palikir

Yaren

NAURU

SOLOMON
ISLANDS

Honiara

Guadalcanal I.

Bismarck
Archipelago

PAPUA
NEW GUINEA

Port
Moresby

New
Guinea

FEDERATED STATES
OF MICRONESIA

Bonin Islands
(JAPAN)

Volcano Islands
(JAPAN)

Northern
Marianas
(U.S.)

Guam
(U.S.)

Agana

PALAU

Koror

Christmas
Island
(AUSTRALIA)

Philippine
Sea

South
China
Sea

Coral
Sea

Arafura
Sea

Timor
Sea

Darwin

AUSTRALIA

Brisbane

Sydney

Canberra

Hobart

Melbourne

Adelaide

Perth

Tasman
Sea

Flinders R.

Lachlan R.

Murray R.

Darling R.

INDIAN OCEAN

N
E
S
W

Boundaries
⊛ National capitals
• Other cities

500   1,000 Miles

500   1,000 Kilometers

Projection: Mercator

Gazetteer

A

Afghanistan Landlocked country in south central Asia. Capital: Kabul. (35°N 69°E) p. 935

Africa Second-largest continent. Lies in both the northern and the southern hemispheres. p. 816

Alabama (AL) State in the southern United States. Admitted as a state in 1819. Capital: Montgomery. (33°N 87°W) p. 512

Alaska (AK) U.S. state in northwestern North America. Purchased from Russia in 1867. Became a territory in 1912. Admitted as a state in 1959. Capital: Juneau. (64°N 150°W) p. 693

Algeria Country in northwest Africa along the Mediterranean Sea. Capital: Algiers. (37°N 03°E) p. 816

Appalachian Mountains Mountain system in eastern North America that extends from Canada to central Alabama. p. 541

Arizona (AZ) State in the southwestern United States. Organized into a territory in 1863. Admitted as a state in 1912. Capital: Phoenix. (34°N 113°W) p. 525

Arkansas (AR) State in the south-central United States. Admitted as a state in 1836. Capital: Little Rock. (35°N 93°W) p. 512

Asia Largest continent. Occupies the same land mass as Europe. p. 587

Atlanta Capital of Georgia. (33°N 84°W) p. 541

Atlantic Ocean Vast body of water separating North and South America from Europe and Africa. p. 511

Australia Independent country and smallest continent. Lies between the Indian and Pacific oceans. Capital: Canberra. (35°S 149°E) p. 821

Austria-Hungary Once a major European empire, Austria declined in power. A compromise in 1867 formed the dual monarchy of Austria-Hungary. p. 720

B

Baltimore Maryland city northeast of Washington, D.C., on the Chesapeake Bay. (39°N 76°W) p. 642

Balkan Peninsula Most southeastern extension of Europe, bounded by the Black Sea, Sea of Marmara, Aegean Sea, Mediterranean Sea, Ionian Sea, and Adriatic Sea. p. 721

Baltic Sea Sea in northern Europe. Arm of the Atlantic Ocean. p. 722

Bataan Peninsula and province between Manila Bay and South China Sea in the Philippines. Capital: Balanga. (15°N 120°E) p. 820

Belgium Country bordering the North Sea in northwestern Europe. Capital: Brussels. (51°N 04°E) p. 721

Berlin Capital of Germany both before city was divided into East and West and after it was reunited. (53°N 13°E) p. 895

Bosnia and Herzegovina Mountainous country located in southeastern Europe on the Balkan Peninsula. Formerly part of Yugoslavia. Capital: Sarajevo. (44°N 18°E) p. 721

Boston Capital of Massachusetts. (42°N 71°W) p. 642

Bulgaria Mountainous country in southeastern Europe on the Balkan Peninsula bordering the Black Sea. Capital: Sofia. (43°N 23°E) p. 721

Bull Run Creek in northeastern Virginia where the Confederates won two major battles during the Civil War. p. 516

Burma Renamed Myanmar, the largest nation in southeastern Asia. Capital: Yangon. (17°N 96°E) p. 820

California (CA) State in the western United States. Admitted as a state in 1850. Capital: Sacramento. (38°N 121°W) p. 586

Cambodia Country in southeastern Asia on the Indochina Peninsula and the Gulf of Thailand. Capital: Phnom Penh. (12°N 105°E) p. 898

Camp David Presidential retreat in the middle of Catoctin Mountain National Park in Maryland. p. 935

Canada Country in northern North America. Capital: Ottawa. (50°N 100°W) p. 589

Caribbean Sea Arm of the Atlantic Ocean between North and South America. p. 510

Central America Region of land connecting North and South America. p. 587

Charleston Port city in southeastern South Carolina. Originally called Charles Town. (33°N 80°W) p. 511

Chicago Large U.S. city in northeastern Illinois on Lake Michigan. Major port. (41°N 87°W) p. 615

China Country in East Asia with the world's largest population. Capital: Beijing. (Official name: People's Republic of China) p. 637

Colombia Country in northwest South America. Capital: Bogotá. (4°N 72°W) p. 705

Colorado (CO) State in the southwestern United States. Admitted as a state in 1876. Capital: Denver. (39°N 107°W) p. 525

Connecticut (CT) State in the northeastern United States. One of the original thirteen colonies. Admitted as a state in 1788. Capital: Hartford. (41°N 73°W) p. R2

Coral Sea Home to the Great Coral Reef. Arm of southwest Pacific Ocean. p. 821

Cuba Westernmost country of the West Indies, an island republic in the northern Caribbean Sea. Capital: Havana. (23°N 82°W) p. 697

Czechoslovakia Former name of the country in central Europe that included the current Czech and Slovak republics. Capital: Prague. (15°N 14°E) p. 806

Delaware (DE) State in the eastern United States. One of the original thirteen colonies. Capital: Dover. (38°N 75°W) p. 512

Denmark Southernmost Scandinavian country in northern Europe. Peninsula and island kingdom between the North and Baltic Seas. Capital: Copenhagen. (56°N 12°E) p. 806

Detroit Largest city in Michigan. (42°N 83°W) p. 642

Dominican Republic West Indies country that occupies approximately the eastern two-thirds of Hispaniola. Capital: Santo Domingo. (19°N 71°W) p. 707

E

Egypt Middle East country in northeast Africa along the Mediterranean and Red Sea coasts. Capital: Cairo. (30°N 31°E) p. 816

El Alamein Village in northwest Egypt where Germany's Africa Korps was defeated by the Allies during World War II. (31°N 29°E) p. 816

Ellis Island New York Bay island. Part of Statue of Liberty National Monument. U.S. immigration center. Entry point for millions of people from 1892–1954. (41°N 74°W) p. 637

England Region of the United Kingdom that makes up most of the southern part of the island of Great Britain. Capital: London. (51°N 1°W) p. 513

Ethiopia Country, once known as Abyssinia, in northeastern Africa. Capital: Addis Ababa. (9°N 39°E) p. 804

Europe Continent occupying the same land mass as Asia. p. 587

F

Florida (FL) State in the southeastern United States. Organized as a territory in 1822. Admitted as a state in 1845. Capital: Tallahassee. (30°N 84°W) p. 563

Fort Sumter Fort on Charleston Harbor, South Carolina. Attack by Confederate forces here began the American Civil War. p. 511

France Country in Western Europe. Capital: Paris. (46°N 0°W) p. 510

G

Georgia (GA) State in the southeastern United States. Admitted as a state in 1788. One of the original thirteen colonies. Capital: Atlanta. (32°N 84°W) p. 513

Germany Country in Western Europe. Capital: Berlin. (51°N 8°E) p. 636

Gettysburg Town in southern Pennsylvania. (40°N 77°W) p. 537

Great Britain Country in western Europe that includes England, Scotland, and Wales. Capital: London. p. 540

Great Plains Region of central North America that lies between the Mississippi River and the Rocky Mountains. p. 586

Greece Country in southern Europe with mountains, rugged coastlines, and scenic islands; the country is called the birthplace of democracy. Capital: Athens. p. 847

Guam Unincorporated U.S. territory that is the southernmost and largest of the Mariana Islands in the west Pacific Ocean. Capital: Agana. (13°N 145°E) p. 700

Gulf of Mexico Gulf on the southeastern coast of North America, bordered by the United States, Mexico, and Cuba. p. 524

H

Harlem A neighborhood in upper Manhattan in New York City that became a political and cultural hub for many African Americans in the early 1900s. (41°N 74°W) p. 768

Hawaii Largest of group of eight large and many smaller Hawaiian Islands in the Pacific Ocean admitted to the Union in 1959 as the 50ᵗʰ state. Capital: Honolulu. (21°N 158°W) p. 694

Herzegovina *See* Bosnia-Herzegovina

Hiroshima A city in Japan where the first atomic bomb was dropped. (34°N 132°E) p. 828

Ho Chi Minh Trail Network of trails of more than 12,000 miles through eastern Laos and Cambodia into South Vietnam used by the North Vietnamese during the Vietnam War. p. 902

Hong Kong City located on this south coast of China and a special administrative zone of China. Former British colony. Capital: Victoria. (22°N 114°E) p. 820

Hungary Central European nation. Capital: Budapest. (48°N 19°E) p. 950

Idaho (ID) State in the northwestern United States. Admitted as a state in 1890. Capital: Boise. (44°N 115°W) p. R2

Illinois (IL) State in the north-central United States. Admitted as a state in 1819. Capital: Springfield. (40°N 90°W) p. R2

India Large country in southern Asia. Capital: New Delhi. (28°N 77°E) p. 821

Indiana (IN) State in the north-central United States. Admitted as a state in 1816. Capital: Indianapolis. (40°N 86°W) p. R2

Iowa (IA) State in the north-central United States. Admitted as a state in 1846. Capital: Des Moines. (42°N 94°W) p. R2

Iran Islamic country in the Persian Gulf region. Formerly Persia. Capital: Tehran. (27°N 55°E) p. 936

Iraq Persian Gulf nation known in ancient times as Mesopotamia. Capital: Baghdad. (33°N 44°E) p. 951

Ireland Island in the British Isles. Divided into Northern Ireland (Capital: Belfast), and the Republic of Ireland (Capital: Dublin). (54°N 8°W) p. 636

Israel Modern Middle Eastern country on the Mediterranean Sea formed in 1948. Capital: Jerusalem. (32°N 35°E) p. 846

Italy Country in southern Europe. Capital: Rome. (44°N 11°E) p. 804

Japan Island chain nation of East Asia. Japan in Chinese means "Land of the rising sun." Capital: Tokyo. (36°N 140°E) p. 693

Kansas (KS) State in the central United States. Organized as a territory in 1854. Admitted as a state in 1861. Capital: Topeka. (38°N 99°W) p. 525

Kentucky (KY) State in the east-central United States. Admitted as a state in 1792. Capital: Frankfort. (37°N 87°W) p. 512

Korea See North Korea and South Korea

Kuwait Persian Gulf country on the Arabian Peninsula. Capital: Al-Kuwait, also known as Kuwait City. (29°N 48°E) p. 951

Latin America Spanish-speaking countries of North and South America that were once claimed by Spain and Portugal. p. 707

Laos Landlocked country in southeast Asia. Capital (Administrative): Vientiane (18°N 103°E) Capital (Historic royal): Luang Phabang. (18°N 108°E) p. 898

Leyte Gulf Large inlet of the Philippine Sea in the Pacific Ocean. (11°N 125°E) p. 822

Little Rock Capital city in central Arkansas on the Arkansas River. (35°N 92°W) p. 871

London Capital of the United Kingdom, in England. (52°N 0°W) p. 711

Louisiana (LA) State in the southeastern United States carved out of the Louisiana Territory. Admitted as a state in 1812. Capital: Baton Rouge. (31°N 92°W) p. 522

Luxembourg Also, Grand Duchy of Luxembourg. Small European country between France, Germany, and Belgium. Capital: Luxembourg City. (50°N 6°E) p. 807

M

Maine (ME) State in the northeastern United States. Admitted as a state in 1820. Capital: Augusta. (45°N 70°W) p. R2

Maryland (MD) State in the east-central United States. One of the original thirteen colonies. Admitted as a state in 1788. Capital: Annapolis. (39°N 76°W) p. 512

Massachusetts (MA) State in the northeastern United States. One of the original thirteen colonies. Admitted as a state in 1788. Capital: Boston. (42°N 72°W) p. 560

Mexico Country in southern North America. Capital: Mexico City. (23°N 104°W) p. 510

Michigan (MI) State in the north-central United States. Admitted as a state in 1837. Capital: Lansing. (46°N 87°W) p. 553

Midway Islands Coral atoll consisting of two islands in central Pacific Ocean west of the Hawaiian chain. Site of Battle of Midway, an Allied victory during World War II. p. 693

Minnesota (MN) State in the north-central United States. Admitted as a state in 1858. Capital: St. Paul. (46°N 90°W) p. R2

Mississippi (MS) State in the southeastern United States. Admitted as a state in 1817. Capital: Jackson. (32°N 89°W) p. 523

Mississippi River River that flows from Minnesota south to the Gulf of Mexico. p. 513

Missouri (MO) State in the central United States. Admitted as a state in 1821. Capital: Jefferson City. (38°N 93°W) p. 512

Montana (MT) State in the northwestern United States. Admitted as a state in 1889. Capital: Helena. (47°N 112°W) p. 596

Montgomery Capital of Alabama. (32°N 86°W) p. 873

Morocco Country in northwest Africa bounded by western Sahara, the Mediterranean Sea, and the Atlantic Ocean. Capital: Rabat. (34°N 07°W). p. 816

N

Nebraska (NE) State in the central United States. Admitted as a state in 1867. Capital: Lincoln. (41°N 101°W) p. 590

Netherlands Country in northwestern Europe. Capital: Amsterdam. (52°N 5°E) p. 807

Nevada (NV) State in the western United States. Organized as a territory in 1861. Admitted as a state in 1864. Capital: Carson City. (39°N 117°W) p. 587

New England Northeastern section of the United States. Made up of Connecticut, Maine, Massachusetts, New Hampshire, Rhode Island, and Vermont. p. 600

New Hampshire (NH) State in the northeastern United States. One of the original thirteen colonies. Admitted as a state in 1788. Capital: Concord. (44°N 71°W) p. R2

New Jersey (NJ) State in the northeastern United States. One of the original thirteen colonies. Admitted as a state in 1787. Capital: Trenton. (40°N 75°W) p. 512

New Mexico (NM) State in the southwestern United States. Admitted as a state in 1912. Capital: Santa Fe. (34°N 107°W) p. 597

New Orleans Port city in southeastern Louisiana. (30°N 90°W) p. 523

New York (NY) State in the northeastern United States. One of the original thirteen colonies. Admitted as a state in 1788. Capital: Albany. (42°N 78°W) p. 563

New York City Largest city in the United States. (41°N 74°W) p. 532

Nicaragua Country between Caribbean Sea and Pacific Ocean in Central America. Capital: Managua. (12°N 86°W) p. 708

North Carolina (NC) State in the southeastern United States. One of the original thirteen colonies. Admitted as a state in 1789. Capital: Raleigh. p. 512

North Dakota (ND) State in north-central United States. Admitted as a state in 1889. Capital: Bismarck. (47°N 102°W) p. 790

North Korea Country in East Asia consisting of the northern half of Korean peninsula. Capital: P'yŏngyang. (39°N 126°E) p. 853

North Sea Arm of the Atlantic Ocean, between the east coast of Britain and the area northwest of the central European mainland. (Between 51°N and 62°N) p. 722

Norway Country on the northwestern part of Scandinavia in northern Europe. Capital: Oslo. (60°N 11°E) p. 806

Nuremberg Also, Nürnberg. City in southern Germany. Site of trials of German World War II war criminals. (49°N 11°E) p. 845

Ohio (OH) State in the north-central United States. Originally part of the Northwest Territory. Admitted as a state in 1803. Capital: Columbus. (40°N 83°W) p. 523

Oklahoma (OK) State in the south-central United States. Organized as a territory in 1890. Admitted as a state in 1907. Capital: Oklahoma City. (36°N 98°W) p. 594

Ottoman Empire Vast former Turkish empire that expanded to include much of southeastern Europe, the Middle East, and North Africa between the 1300s and 1900s. p. 721

Oregon (OR) State in the northwestern United States. Admitted as a state in 1859. Capital: Salem. (43°N 122°W) p. 597

Pacific Ocean Body of water extending from the Arctic Circle to Antarctica and from western North and South America to Australia, the Malay Archipelago, and East Asia. p. 586

GAZETTEER

GAZETTEER

Palestine Region between the Jordan River and the Mediterranean Sea containing modern-day Israel, the West Bank, and the Gaza Strip. Often called "The Holy Land." p. 846

Panama Country in southern Central America. Location of the Panama Canal. Capital: Panama City. (8°N 81°W) p. 705

Pearl Harbor An inlet on the Pacific island of Oahu, Hawaii. p. 808

Pennsylvania (PA) State in the eastern United States. One of the original thirteen colonies. Admitted as a state in 1787. Capital: Harrisburg. (41°N 78°W) p. 512

Persian Gulf Arm of the Arabian Sea in the Indian Ocean between the Arabian Peninsula and the Asian mainland. Called the Arabian Gulf by Arabs. p. 951

Philadelphia City in southeastern Pennsylvania. Capital of the United States from 1790 to 1800. (40°N 75°W) p. 642

Philippines Country in the western Pacific Ocean. Made up of about 7,100 islands. Capital: Manila. (14°N 125°E) p. 699

Pittsburgh Second largest city and major port in Pennsylvania. (40°N 80°W) p. 647

Poland Country in central Europe on the Baltic Sea. Capital: Warsaw. (52°N 21°E) p. 806

Puerto Rico Island east of Cuba and southeast of Florida. A U.S. territory acquired in the Spanish-American War. Capital: San Juan. (18°N 67°W) p. 700

R

Rhode Island (RI) State in the northeastern United States. One of the original thirteen colonies. Admitted as a state in 1790. Capital: Providence. (41°N 71°W) p. R2

Richmond Capital of Virginia. Capital of the Confederate States of America during the Civil War. (37°N 7°W) p. 513

Rome A city in Italy near the Mediterranean Sea; it was the capital of the Roman Empire. (42°N 13°E) p. 816

Russia Vast country that extends from Eastern Europe through northwestern Asia. Capital: Moscow. (61°N 60°E) p. 636

S

St. Louis City in Missouri on the Mississippi River. (39°N 90°W) p. 642

San Francisco City in western California on a peninsula between the Pacific Ocean and San Francisco Bay. (37°N 122°W) p. 637

San Juan Hill Hill close to the city of Santiago, Cuba. Site of a battle in the Spanish-American War. p. 699

Savannah Port city in southeastern Georgia. Founded by James Oglethorpe in 1733. (32°N 81°W) p. 541

Scandinavia Large peninsula in northern Europe. p. 636

Serbia Balkan republic. About 70 percent of former Yugoslavia. Capital: Belgrade. (45°N 21°E) p. 721

Singapore Island republic in southeast Asia. Capital: Singapore City. (1°N 104°E) p. 820

South America Continent in the southern Western Hemisphere. p. 587

South Carolina (SC) State in the southeastern United States. One of the original thirteen colonies. Admitted as a state in 1788. Capital: Columbia. (34°N 81°W) p. 511

South Dakota (SD) State in the north-central United States. Organized as part of the Dakota Territory in 1861. Admitted as a state in 1889. Capital: Pierre. (44°N 102°W) p. 597

South Korea Country in East Asia consisting of the southern half of Korean peninsula. Capital: Seoul. (38°N 127°E) p. 853

Soviet Union Former federation of republics succeeding the Russian empire. First Communist state. Full name: Union of Soviet Socialist Republics (USSR). p. 805

Spain Country in southwestern Europe that occupies the greater part of the Iberian Peninsula. Capital: Madrid. (40°N 4°W) p. 510

Stalingrad Russian city. Renamed Volgograd in 1961. (49°N 42°E) p. 817

Sun Belt Term given to the warmer climate region of southern U.S. states stretching between east and west coasts. p. 858

Switzerland Also known as Swiss Confederation. Alpine country in central Europe. Capital: Bern. (47°N 7°E) p. 722

Syria Ancient country and formerly larger region. Modern Middle East Arab country on the Mediterranean Sea. Capital: Damascus. (35°N 38°E) p. 927

Teapot Dome Rock formation rising above an oil field in Wyoming named for teapot-like shape. Known for a scandal during President Harding's administration. (43°N 116°W) p. 753

Tennessee (TN) State in the south-central United States. Admitted as a state in 1796. Capital: Nashville. (36°N 88°W) p. 512

Texas (TX) State in the south-central United States. Independent republic from 1836 to 1845. Admitted as a state in 1845. Capital: Austin. (31°N 101°W) p. 522

Thailand Country in central southeast Asia. Capital: Bangkok. (14°N 101°E) p. 820

Tonkin, Gulf of Arm of South China Sea between Vietnam and China. p. 901

Tuskegee City in Alabama. Home of Tuskegee Institute historic site. (32°N 86°W) p. 812

United States of America Country in central North America. Capital: Washington, D.C. (38°N 110°W) p. 554

Utah (UT) State in the western United States. Admitted as a state in 1896. Capital: Salt Lake City. (39°N 112°W) p. R2

Venezuela Country in South America. Capital: Caracas. (11°N 67°W) p. 707

Vermont (VT) State in the northeastern United States. Admitted as a state in 1791. Capital: Montpelier. (44°N 73°W) p. R2

Vicksburg City in western Mississippi on the bluffs above the Mississippi River. (42°N 85°W) p. 522

Vietnam Country along east coast of Southeast Asian peninsula. North and South united in 1976 after Vietnam War ended. Capital: Hanoi. (21°N 106°E) p. 898

Virginia (VA) State in the eastern United States. One of the original thirteen colonies. Admitted as a state in 1788. Capital: Richmond. (37°N 80°W) p. 512

Washington (WA) State in the northwestern United States. Admitted as a state in 1889. Capital: Olympia. (47°N 121°W) p. R2

Washington, D.C. Capital of the United States. Located on the Potomac River between Virginia and Maryland. (39°N 77°W) p. 513

West Virginia (WV) State in the east-central United States. Part of Virginia until the area refused to join the Confederacy in 1861. Admitted as a state in 1863. Capital: Charleston. (39°N 81°W) p. 512

Western Hemisphere Term given to that half of the earth's sphere that contains the Americas. p. 707

Wisconsin (WI) State in the north-central United States. Became part of the Northwest Territory in 1787. Admitted as a state in 1848. Capital: Madison. (44°N 91°W) p. 667

Wyoming (WY) State in the northwestern United States. Admitted as a state in 1890. Capital: Cheyenne. (43°N 108°W) p. 602

Yalta Ukrainian city on south shore of the Crimean peninsula by the Black Sea. Meeting place of Churchill, Roosevelt, and Stalin near end of World War II. (45°N 34°E) p. 844

Yugoslavia Former country of the Balkan peninsula in southeast Europe created in 1918 that crumbled during the late 1900s. Capital: Belgrade. (45°N 21°E) p. 953

Presidents

1 GEORGE WASHINGTON
Born: 1732   Died: 1799
Years in Office: 1789–97
Political Party: None
Home State: Virginia
Vice President: John Adams

2 JOHN ADAMS
Born: 1735   Died: 1826
Years in Office: 1797–1801
Political Party: Federalist
Home State: Massachusetts
Vice President: Thomas Jefferson

3 THOMAS JEFFERSON
Born: 1743   Died: 1826
Years in Office: 1801–09
Political Party: Republican*
Home State: Virginia
Vice Presidents: Aaron Burr,
George Clinton

4 JAMES MADISON
Born: 1751   Died: 1836
Years in Office: 1809–17
Political Party: Republican
Home State: Virginia
Vice Presidents: George Clinton,
Elbridge Gerry

5 JAMES MONROE
Born: 1758   Died: 1831
Years in Office: 1817–25
Political Party: Republican
Home State: Virginia
Vice President: Daniel D. Tompkins

6 JOHN QUINCY ADAMS
Born: 1767   Died: 1848
Years in Office: 1825–29
Political Party: Republican
Home State: Massachusetts
Vice President: John C. Calhoun

7 ANDREW JACKSON
Born: 1767   Died: 1845
Years in Office: 1829–37
Political Party: Democratic
Home State: Tennessee
Vice Presidents: John C. Calhoun,
Martin Van Buren

8 MARTIN VAN BUREN
Born: 1782   Died: 1862
Years in Office: 1837–41
Political Party: Democratic
Home State: New York
Vice President: Richard M. Johnson

* The Republican Party of the third through sixth presidents is not the party of Abraham Lincoln, which was founded in 1854.

9 WILLIAM HENRY HARRISON
Born: 1773 **Died:** 1841
Years in Office: 1841
Political Party: Whig
Home State: Ohio
Vice President: John Tyler

10 JOHN TYLER
Born: 1790 **Died:** 1862
Years in Office: 1841–45
Political Party: Whig
Home State: Virginia
Vice President: None

11 JAMES K. POLK
Born: 1795 **Died:** 1849
Years in Office: 1845–49
Political Party: Democratic
Home State: Tennessee
Vice President: George M. Dallas

12 ZACHARY TAYLOR
Born: 1784 **Died:** 1850
Years in Office: 1849–50
Political Party: Whig
Home State: Louisiana
Vice President: Millard Fillmore

13 MILLARD FILLMORE
Born: 1800 **Died:** 1874
Years in Office: 1850–53
Political Party: Whig
Home State: New York
Vice President: None

14 FRANKLIN PIERCE
Born: 1804 **Died:** 1869
Years in Office: 1853–57
Political Party: Democratic
Home State: New Hampshire
Vice President: William R. King

15 JAMES BUCHANAN
Born: 1791 **Died:** 1868
Years in Office: 1857–61
Political Party: Democratic
Home State: Pennsylvania
Vice President: John C. Breckinridge

16 ABRAHAM LINCOLN
Born: 1809 **Died:** 1865
Years in Office: 1861–65
Political Party: Republican
Home State: Illinois
Vice Presidents: Hannibal Hamlin, Andrew Johnson

17 ANDREW JOHNSON
Born: 1808 **Died:** 1875
Years in Office: 1865–69
Political Party: Democratic
Home State: Tennessee
Vice President: None

18 ULYSSES S. GRANT
Born: 1822 **Died:** 1885
Years in Office: 1869–77
Political Party: Republican
Home State: Illinois
Vice Presidents: Schuyler Colfax, Henry Wilson

19 RUTHERFORD B. HAYES
Born: 1822 **Died:** 1893
Years in Office: 1877–81
Political Party: Republican
Home State: Ohio
Vice President: William A. Wheeler

20 JAMES A. GARFIELD
Born: 1831 **Died:** 1881
Years in Office: 1881
Political Party: Republican
Home State: Ohio
Vice President: Chester A. Arthur

21 CHESTER A. ARTHUR
Born: 1829 **Died:** 1886
Years in Office: 1881–85
Political Party: Republican
Home State: New York
Vice President: None

22 GROVER CLEVELAND
Born: 1837 **Died:** 1908
Years in Office: 1885–89
Political Party: Democratic
Home State: New York
Vice President: Thomas A. Hendricks

23 BENJAMIN HARRISON
Born: 1833 **Died:** 1901
Years in Office: 1889–93
Political Party: Republican
Home State: Indiana
Vice President: Levi P. Morton

24 GROVER CLEVELAND
Born: 1837 **Died:** 1908
Years in Office: 1893–97
Political Party: Democratic
Home State: New York
Vice President: Adlai E. Stevenson

25 WILLIAM McKINLEY
Born: 1843 **Died:** 1901
Years in Office: 1897–1901
Political Party: Republican
Home State: Ohio
Vice Presidents: Garret A. Hobart, Theodore Roosevelt

26 THEODORE ROOSEVELT
Born: 1858 **Died:** 1919
Years in Office: 1901–09
Political Party: Republican
Home State: New York
Vice President: Charles W. Fairbanks

27 WILLIAM HOWARD TAFT
Born: 1857 **Died:** 1930
Years in Office: 1909–13
Political Party: Republican
Home State: Ohio
Vice President: James S. Sherman

28 WOODROW WILSON
Born: 1856 **Died:** 1924
Years in Office: 1913–21
Political Party: Democratic
Home State: New Jersey
Vice President: Thomas R. Marshall

29 WARREN G. HARDING
Born: 1865 **Died:** 1923
Years in Office: 1921–23
Political Party: Republican
Home State: Ohio
Vice President: Calvin Coolidge

30 CALVIN COOLIDGE
Born: 1872 **Died:** 1933
Years in Office: 1923–29
Political Party: Republican
Home State: Massachusetts
Vice President: Charles G. Dawes

31 HERBERT HOOVER
Born: 1874 **Died:** 1964
Years in Office: 1929–33
Political Party: Republican
Home State: California
Vice President: Charles Curtis

32 FRANKLIN D. ROOSEVELT
Born: 1882 **Died:** 1945
Years in Office: 1933–45
Political Party: Democratic
Home State: New York
Vice Presidents: John Nance Garner,
Henry Wallace, Harry S Truman

33 HARRY S TRUMAN
Born: 1884 **Died:** 1972
Years in Office: 1945–53
Political Party: Democratic
Home State: Missouri
Vice President: Alben W. Barkley

34 DWIGHT D. EISENHOWER
Born: 1890 **Died:** 1969
Years in Office: 1953–61
Political Party: Republican
Home State: Kansas
Vice President: Richard M. Nixon

35 JOHN F. KENNEDY
Born: 1917 **Died:** 1963
Years in Office: 1961–63
Political Party: Democratic
Home State: Massachusetts
Vice President: Lyndon B. Johnson

36 LYNDON B. JOHNSON
Born: 1908   Died: 1973
Years in Office: 1963–69
Political Party: Democratic
Home State: Texas
Vice President: Hubert H. Humphrey

37 RICHARD M. NIXON
Born: 1913   Died: 1994
Years in Office: 1969–74
Political Party: Republican
Home State: California
Vice Presidents: Spiro T. Agnew,
Gerald R. Ford

38 GERALD R. FORD
Born: 1913   Died: 2006
Years in Office: 1974–77
Political Party: Republican
Home State: Michigan
Vice President: Nelson A. Rockefeller

39 JIMMY CARTER
Born: 1924
Years in Office: 1977–81
Political Party: Democratic
Home State: Georgia
Vice President: Walter F. Mondale

40 RONALD REAGAN
Born: 1911   Died: 2004
Years in Office: 1981–89
Political Party: Republican
Home State: California
Vice President: George Bush

41 GEORGE BUSH
Born: 1924
Years in Office: 1989–93
Political Party: Republican
Home State: Texas
Vice President: J. Danforth Quayle

42 BILL CLINTON
Born: 1946
Years in Office: 1993–2001
Political Party: Democratic
Home State: Arkansas
Vice President: Albert Gore Jr.

43 GEORGE W. BUSH
Born: 1946
Years in Office: 2001–2009
Political Party: Republican
Home State: Texas
Vice President: Richard B. Cheney

44 BARACK OBAMA
Born: 1961
Years in Office: 2009–
Political Party: Democratic
Home State: Illinois
Vice President: Joe Biden

Facts About the States

State	Year of Statehood	2006 Population	Area (Sq. Mi.)	Population Density (Sq Mi.)	Capital
Alabama	1819	4,599,030	50,744	88.7	Montgomery
Alaska	1959	670,053	571,951	1.1	Juneau
Arizona	1912	6,166,318	113,635	49.1	Phoenix
Arkansas	1836	2,810,872	52,068	52.3	Little Rock
California	1850	36,457,549	155,959	227.5	Sacramento
Colorado	1876	4,753,377	103,718	43.9	Denver
Connecticut	1788	3,504,809	4,845	719.0	Hartford
Delaware	1787	853,476	1,954	418.4	Dover
District of Columbia	—	581,530	61	9,235.8	—
Florida	1845	18,089,888	53,927	315.6	Tallahassee
Georgia	1788	9,363,941	57,906	150.0	Atlanta
Hawaii	1959	1,285,498	6,423	195.8	Honolulu
Idaho	1890	1,466,465	82,747	16.5	Boise
Illinois	1818	12,831,970	55,584	227.6	Springfield
Indiana	1816	6,313,520	35,867	172.7	Indianapolis
Iowa	1846	2,982,085	55,869	52.7	Des Moines
Kansas	1861	2,764,075	81,815	33.3	Topeka
Kentucky	1792	4,206,074	39,728	103.7	Frankfort
Louisiana	1812	4,287,768	43,562	103.2	Baton Rouge
Maine	1820	1,321,574	30,862	42.3	Augusta
Maryland	1788	5,615,727	9,774	563.6	Annapolis
Massachusetts	1788	6,437,193	7,840	820.6	Boston
Michigan	1837	10,095,643	56,804	177.5	Lansing
Minnesota	1858	5,167,101	79,610	63.6	St. Paul

State	Year of Statehood	2006 Population	Area (Sq. Mi.)	Population Density (Sq Mi.)	Capital
Mississippi	1817	2,910,540	46,907	61.4	Jackson
Missouri	1821	5,842,713	68,886	82.8	Jefferson City
Montana	1889	944,632	145,552	6.3	Helena
Nebraska	1867	1,768,331	76,872	22.6	Lincoln
Nevada	1864	2,495,529	109,826	20.4	Carson City
New Hampshire	1788	1,314,895	8,968	143.6	Concord
New Jersey	1787	8,724,560	7,417	1,164.7	Trenton
New Mexico	1912	1,954,599	121,356	15.4	Santa Fe
New York	1788	19,306,183	47,214	406.4	Albany
North Carolina	1789	8,856,505	48,711	172.6	Raleigh
North Dakota	1889	635,867	68,976	9.2	Bismarck
Ohio	1803	11,478,006	40,948	279.3	Columbus
Oklahoma	1907	3,579,212	68,667	51.1	Oklahoma City
Oregon	1859	3,700,758	95,997	37.1	Salem
Pennsylvania	1787	12,440,621	44,817	275.9	Harrisburg
Rhode Island	1790	1,067,610	1,045	1,029.8	Providence
South Carolina	1788	4,321,249	30,109	137.7	Columbia
South Dakota	1889	781,919	75,885	10.1	Pierre
Tennessee	1796	6,038,803	41,217	141.7	Nashville
Texas	1845	23,507,783	261,797	84.5	Austin
Utah	1896	2,550,063	82,144	28.6	Salt Lake City
Vermont	1791	623,908	9,250	66.9	Montpelier
Virginia	1788	7,642,884	39,594	186.6	Richmond
Washington	1889	6,395,798	66,544	92.1	Olympia
West Virginia	1863	1,818,470	24,078	75.2	Charleston
Wisconsin	1848	5,556,506	54,310	100.8	Madison
Wyoming	1890	515,004	97,100	5.2	Cheyenne

American Flag

The American flag is a symbol of the nation. It is recognized instantly, whether as a big banner waving in the wind or a tiny emblem worn on a lapel. The flag is so important that it is a major theme of the national anthem, "The Star-Spangled Banner." One of the most popular names for the flag is the Stars and Stripes. It is also known as Old Glory.

The American flag has 13 stripes—7 red and 6 white. In the upper-left corner of the flag is the union—50 white five-pointed stars against a blue background.

The 13 stripes stand for the original 13 American states, and the 50 stars represent the states of the nation today. According to the U.S. Department of State, the colors of the flag also are symbolic:

Red stands for courage.

White symbolizes purity.

Blue is the color of vigilance, perseverance, and justice.

DISPLAYING THE FLAG

It is customary not to display the American flag in bad weather. It is also customary for the flag to be displayed outdoors only from sunrise to sunset, except on certain occasions. In a few special places, however, the flag is always flown day and night. When flown at night, the flag should be illuminated.

Near a speaker's platform, the flag should occupy the place of honor at the speaker's right. When carried in a parade with other flags, the American flag should be on the marching right or in front at the center. When flying with the flags of the 50 states, the national flag must be at the center and the highest point. In a group of national flags, all should be of equal size and all should be flown from staffs, or flagpoles, of equal height.

The flag should never touch the ground or the floor. It should not be marked with any insignia, pictures, or words. Nor should it be used in any disrespectful way—as an advertising decoration, for instance. The flag should never be dipped to honor any person or thing.

SALUTING THE FLAG

The United States, like other countries, has a flag code, or rules for displaying and honoring the flag. For example, all those present should stand at attention facing the flag and salute it when it is being raised or lowered or when it is carried past them in a parade or procession. A man wearing a hat should take it off and hold it with his right hand over his heart. All women and hatless men should stand with their right hands over their hearts to show their respect for the flag. The flag should also receive these honors during the playing of the national anthem and the reciting of the Pledge of Allegiance.

The Pledge of Allegiance was written in 1892 by Massachusetts magazine (*Youth's Companion*) editor Francis Bellamy. (Congress added the words "under God" in 1954.)

I pledge allegiance to the flag of the United States of America and to the republic for which it stands, one nation under God, indivisible, with liberty and justice for all.

Civilians should say the Pledge of Allegiance with their right hands placed over their hearts. People in the armed forces give the military salute. By saying the Pledge of Allegiance, we promise loyalty ("pledge allegiance") to the United States and its ideals.

"THE STAR-SPANGLED BANNER"

"The Star-Spangled Banner" is the national anthem of the United States. It was written by Francis Scott Key during the War of 1812. While being detained by the British aboard a ship on September 13–14, 1814, Key watched the British bombardment of Fort McHenry at Baltimore. The attack lasted 25 hours. The smoke was so thick that Key could not tell who had won. When the air cleared, Key saw the American flag that was still flying over the fort. "The Star-Spangled Banner" is sung to music written by British composer John Stafford Smith. In 1931 Congress designated "The Star-Spangled Banner" as the national anthem.

I

Oh, say, can you see, by the dawn's early light,
What so proudly we hailed at the twilight's last gleaming,
Whose broad stripes and bright stars through the perilous fight,
O'er the ramparts we watched were so gallantly streaming?
And the rockets' red glare, the bombs bursting in air,
Gave proof through the night that our flag was still there.
Oh, say, does that star-spangled banner yet wave
O'er the land of the free, and the home of the brave?

II

On the shore, dimly seen through the mists of the deep,
Where the foe's haughty host in dread silence reposes,
What is that which the breeze, o'er the towering steep,
As it fitfully blows, half conceals, half discloses?
Now it catches the gleam of the morning's first beam,
In full glory reflected, now shines on the stream.
'Tis the star-spangled banner; oh, long may it wave
O'er the land of the free, and the home of the brave!

III

And where is that band who so vauntingly swore
That the havoc of war and the battle's confusion
A home and a country should leave us no more?
Their blood has washed out their foul footsteps' pollution.
No refuge could save the hireling and slave
From the terror of flight, or the gloom of the grave:
And the star-spangled banner in triumph doth wave
O'er the land of the free, and the home of the brave!

IV

Oh! thus be it ever when freemen shall stand
Between their loved homes and the war's desolation!
Blest with victory and peace, may the heaven-rescued land
Praise the Power that hath made and preserved us a nation!
Then conquer we must, for our cause it is just,
And this be our motto: "In God is our trust!"
And the star-spangled banner in triumph shall wave,
O'er the land of the free, and the home of the brave!

Sheet music to the national anthem

"AMERICA, THE BEAUTIFUL"

One of the most beloved songs celebrating our nation is "America, the Beautiful." Katharine Lee Bates first wrote the lyrics to the song in 1893 after visiting Colorado. The version of the song we know today is set to music by Samuel A. Ward. The first and last stanzas of "America, the Beautiful" are shown below.

O beautiful for spacious skies,
For amber waves of grain,
For purple mountain majesties
Above the fruited plain!
America! America!
God shed his grace on thee
And crown thy good with brotherhood
From sea to shining sea!

O beautiful for patriot dream
That sees beyond the years
Thine alabaster cities gleam
Undimmed by human tears!
America! America!
God shed his grace on thee
And crown thy good with brotherhood
From sea to shining sea!

Supreme Court Decisions

Marbury v. Madison (1803)

Significance This ruling established the Supreme Court's power of judicial review, by which the Court decides whether laws passed by Congress are constitutional. This decision greatly increased the prestige of the Court and gave the judiciary branch a powerful check against the legislative and executive branches.

Background William Marbury and several others were commissioned as judges by Federalist president John Adams during his last days in office. This act angered the new Democratic-Republican president, Thomas Jefferson. Jefferson ordered his secretary of state, James Madison, not to deliver the commissions. Marbury took advantage of a section in the Judiciary Act of 1789 that allowed him to take his case directly to the Supreme Court. He sued Madison, demanding the commission and the judgeship.

Decision This case was decided on February 24, 1803, by a vote of 5 to 0. Chief Justice John Marshall spoke for the Court, which decided against Marbury. The court ruled that although Marbury's commission had been unfairly withheld, he could not lawfully take his case to the Supreme Court without first trying it in a lower court. Marshall said that the section of the Judiciary Act that Marbury had used was actually unconstitutional and that the Constitution must take priority over laws passed by Congress.

McCulloch v. Maryland (1819)

Significance This ruling established that Congress had the constitutional power to charter a national bank. The case also established the principle of national supremacy, which states that the Constitution and other laws of the federal government take priority over state laws. In addition, the ruling reinforced the loose-construction interpretation of the Constitution favored by many Federalists.

Background In 1816 the federal government set up the Second Bank of the United States to stabilize the economy following the War of 1812. Many states were opposed to the competition provided by the new national bank. Some of these states passed heavy taxes on the Bank. The national bank refused to pay the taxes. This led the state of Maryland to sue James McCulloch, the cashier of the Baltimore, Maryland, branch of the national bank.

Decision This case was decided on March 6, 1819, by a vote of 7 to 0. Chief Justice John Marshall spoke for the unanimous Court, which ruled that the national bank was constitutional because it helped the federal government carry out other powers granted to it by the Constitution. The Court declared that any attempt by the states to interfere with the duties of the federal government could not be permitted.

Gibbons v. Ogden (1824)

Significance This ruling was the first case to deal with the clause of the Constitution that allows Congress to regulate interstate and foreign commerce. This case was important because it reinforced both the authority of the federal government over the states and the division of powers between the federal government and the state governments.

Background Steamboat operators who wanted to travel on New York waters had to obtain a state license. Thomas Gibbons had a federal license to travel along the coast, but not a state license for New York. He wanted the freedom to compete with state-licensed Aaron Ogden for steam travel between New Jersey and the New York island of Manhattan.

Decision This case was decided on March 2, 1824, by a vote of 6 to 0. Chief Justice John Marshall spoke for the Court, which ruled in favor of Gibbons. The Court stated that the congressional statute (Gibbons's federal license) took priority over the state statute (Ogden's state-monopoly license). The ruling also defined commerce as more than simply the exchange of goods, broadening it to include the transportation of people and the use of new inventions (such as the steamboat).

Supreme Court Building, Washington, D.C.

Worcester v. Georgia (1832)

Significance This ruling made Georgia's removal of the Cherokee illegal. However, Georgia, with President Andrew Jackson's support, defied the Court's decision. By not enforcing the Court's ruling, Jackson violated his constitutional oath as president. As a result, the Cherokee and other American Indian tribes continued to be forced off of lands protected by treaties.

Background The state of Georgia wanted to remove Cherokee Indians from lands they held by treaty. Samuel Worcester, a missionary who worked with the Cherokee Nation, was arrested for failing to take an oath of allegiance to the state and to obey a Georgia militia order to leave the Cherokee's lands. Worcester sued, charging that Georgia had no legal authority on Cherokee lands.

Decision This case was decided on March 3, 1832, by a vote of 5 to 1 in favor of Worcester. Chief Justice John Marshall spoke for the Supreme Court, which ruled that the Cherokee were an independent political community. The Court decided that only the federal government, not the state of Georgia, had authority over legal matters involving the Cherokee people.

Scott v. Sandford (1857)

Significance This ruling denied enslaved African Americans U.S. citizenship and the right to sue in federal court. The decision also invalidated the Missouri Compromise, which had prevented slavery in territories north of the 36° 30′ line of latitude. The ruling increased the controversy over the expansion of slavery in new states and territories.

Background John Emerson, an army doctor, took his slave Dred Scott with him to live in Illinois and then Wisconsin Territory, both of which had banned slavery. In 1842 the two moved to Missouri, a slave state. Four years later, Scott sued for his freedom according to a Missouri legal principle of "once free, always free." The principle meant that a slave was entitled to freedom if he or she had once lived in a free state or territory.

Decision This case was decided March 6-7, 1857, by a vote of 7 to 2. Chief Justice Roger B. Taney spoke for the Court, which ruled that slaves did not have the right to sue in federal courts because they were considered property, not citizens. In addition, the Court ruled that Congress did not have the power to abolish slavery in territories because that power was not strictly defined in the Constitution. Furthermore, the Court overturned the once-free, always-free principle.

Civil Rights Cases (1883)

Significance This ruling struck down the Civil Rights Act of 1875. It allowed private businesses to discriminate based on race or color. The Court ruled that Congress could only make laws preventing states, not private individuals or companies, from discriminating.

Background Five separate cases were combined under this one decision. After the Civil Rights Act of 1875 was passed, individuals and private businesses continued to discriminate against former slaves and other African Americans. In the five separate cases, African Americans were denied the same accommodations that whites were provided.

Decision The case was decided on October 15, 1883, by a vote of 8 to 1. Justice Joseph P. Bradley wrote the opinion, which said of the 14th Amendment, "Individual invasion of individual rights is not the subject-matter of the amendment." Justice John Marshall Harlan was the lone dissenter, claiming that the 13th Amendment gave Congress the right to make the law. "The letter of the law is the body," he said. "[T]he sense and reason of the law is the soul."

Wabash, St. Louis & Pacific Railroad v. Illinois (1886)

Significance This ruling reversed an earlier decision in *Munn* v. *Illinois* and removed the power from the states to regulate railroad rates. It reasserted the authority of Congress over interstate commerce and led to the creation of the Interstate Commerce Commission.

Background The state of Illinois passed a law attempting to regulate the shipping rates of railroads that passed through the state, including the Wabash, St. Louis & Pacific line. In an attempt to operate without regulation, the railroad company sued the state.

Decision The Court struck down the Illinois law, saying that the state was able to regulate businesses that operated only within its boundaries. Businesses that operated between states were subject to regulation by the national government.

United States v. E.C. Knight Co. (1895)

Significance This ruling effectively put most monopolies out of the reach of the Sherman Antitrust Act of 1890. It declared that local manufacturing was out of the scope of the interstate-commerce regulatory power of Congress.

Background The E. C. Knight Company enjoyed a virtual monopoly of sugar refining within the United States. The federal government sued the company under the Sherman Antitrust Act in an attempt to break this monopoly and allow other companies to refine sugar.

Decision The court ruled that although the act was legal, it did not apply to manufacturing. Justice Melville Fuller said that manufacturing was not interstate commerce and could therefore not be regulated by Congress.

In Re Debs (1895)

Significance In this ruling the Court upheld the right of the federal government to halt strikes organized by union workers. After losing his case, Debs ran for president from his jail cell.

Background Railway union official Eugene V. Debs had organized a strike of union workers. The government petitioned him to halt the strike, and a court held him in contempt when he refused. Debs fought his conviction.

Decision In a unanimous decision, the Court declared that the federal government did have the power to order Debs to halt the strike. Justice David J. Brewer wrote the opinion of the Court, which stated the U.S. government "acts directly upon each citizen."

Plessy v. Ferguson (1896)

Significance This case upheld the constitutionality of racial segregation by ruling that separate facilities for different races were legal as long as those facilities were equal to one another. This case provided a legal justification for racial segregation for nearly 60 years until it was overturned by *Brown* v. *Board of Education* in 1954.

Background An 1890 Louisiana law required that all railway companies in the state use "separate-but-equal" railcars for white and African American passengers. A group of citizens in New Orleans banded together to challenge the law and chose Homer Plessy to test the law in 1892. Plessy took a seat in a whites-only coach, and when he refused to move, he was arrested. Plessy eventually sought review by the U.S. Supreme Court, claiming that the Louisiana law violated his Fourteenth Amendment right to equal protection.

Decision This case was decided on May 18, 1896, by a vote of 7 to 1. Justice Henry Billings Brown spoke for the Court, which upheld the constitutionality of the Louisiana law that segregated railcars. Justice John M. Harlan dissented, arguing that the Constitution should not be interpreted in ways that recognize class or racial distinctions.

Northern Securities Co. v. United States (1904)

Significance In this ruling the Court declared that the federal government had the right to break up companies if their formation was illegal, whether or not dissolving the company would have a harmful impact on the business community.

Background The Northern Securities Company held stock in several major railroads. Although President Theodore Roosevelt claimed the company was a trust and therefore illegal under the Sherman Antitrust Act, some disagreed that the idea of trusts extended into the realm of owning stocks.

Decision In a 5-to-4 decision, the Court ruled that the formation of the company was illegal, and that the federal government had the power to disband it. Writing for the majority, Justice John Marshall Harlan said, "every corporation created by a state is necessarily subject to the supreme law of the land," meaning the federal government.

Lochner v. New York (1905)

Significance This decision established the Supreme Court's role in overseeing state regulations. For more than 30 years, Lochner was often used as a precedent in striking down state laws such as minimum-wage laws, child labor laws, and regulations placed on the banking and transportation industries.

Background In 1895 the state of New York passed a labor law limiting bakers to working no more than 10 hours per day or 60 hours per week. The purpose of the law was to protect the health of bakers, who worked in hot and damp conditions and breathed in large quantities of flour dust. In 1902 Joseph Lochner, the owner of a small bakery in New York, claimed that the state law violated his Fourteenth Amendment rights by unfairly depriving him of the liberty to make contracts with employees. This case went to the U.S. Supreme Court.

Decision This case was decided on April 17, 1905, by a vote of 5 to 4 in favor of Lochner. The Supreme Court judged that the Fourteenth Amendment protected the right to sell and buy labor, and that any state law restricting that right was unconstitutional. The Court rejected the argument that the limited workday and workweek were necessary to protect the health of bakery workers.

Muller v. Oregon (1908)

Significance A landmark for cases involving social reform, this decision established the Court's recognition of social and economic conditions (in this case, women's health) as a factor in making laws.

Background In 1903 Oregon passed a law limiting workdays to 10 hours for female workers in laundries and factories. In 1905 Curt Muller's Grand Laundry was found guilty of breaking this law. Muller appealed, claiming that the state law violated his freedom of contract (the Supreme Court had upheld a similar claim that year in *Lochner* v. *New York*). When this case came to the Court, the National Consumers' League hired lawyer Louis D. Brandeis to present Oregon's argument. Brandeis argued that the Court had already defended the state's police power to protect its citizens' health, safety, and welfare.

Decision This case was decided on February 24, 1908, by a vote of 9 to 0 upholding the Oregon law. The Court agreed that women's well-being was in the state's public interest and that the 10-hour law was a valid way to protect their well-being.

Schechter Poultry Corporation v. United States (1935)

Significance This ruling declared that the United States could not regulate businesses that operated only within one state. It dealt a severe blow to President Franklin Roosevelt's New Deal.

Background In an attempt to lessen the effects of the Great Depression, Roosevelt encouraged Congress to pass a Recovery Act that set a minimum wage and restricted working hours. The Schechter Poultry Corporation, which operated only within New York City, maintained that the federal government did not have a constitutional right to regulate its businesses practices.

Decision In a unanimous decision, the Court upheld the Schechter Corporation's claim. Chief Justice Charles Evans Hughes wrote the opinion, which stated that the transactions in the case—wages, salaries, and working hours—were a local concern outside of the scope of federal regulation.

Korematsu v. United States (1944)

Significance This case addressed the question of whether government action that treats a racial group differently from other people violates the Equal Protection Clause of the Fourteenth Amendment. The ruling in the case held that distinctions based on race are "inherently suspect," and that laws and rules based on race must withstand "strict scrutiny" by the courts. The Court still applies the "strict scrutiny" standard today to cases involving race and other groups.

Background When the United States declared war on Japan in 1941, about 112,000 Japanese Americans lived on the West Coast. About 70,000 of these Japanese Americans were citizens. In 1942 the U.S. military was afraid that these people could not be trusted in wartime. They ordered most of the Japanese Americans to move to special camps far from their homes. Fred Korematsu, a Japanese American and an American citizen, did not go to the camps as ordered. He stayed in California and was arrested. He was sent to a camp in Utah. Korematsu then sued, claiming that the government acted illegally when it sent people of Japanese descent to camps.

Decision By a 6-to-3 margin, the Supreme Court said the orders moving the Japanese-Americans into the camps were constitutional. Justice Hugo Black wrote the opinion for the Court. He said that the unusual demands of wartime security justified the orders. However, he made it clear that distinctions based on race are "inherently suspect," and that laws based on race must withstand "strict scrutiny" by the courts. Justice Robert H. Jackson dissented; he wrote that Korematsu was "convicted of an act not commonly a crime … being present in the state [where] he is a citizen, near where he was born, and where all his life he has lived." Justice Frank Murphy, another dissenter, said the military order was based on racial prejudice.

Brown v. Board of Education (1954)

Significance This ruling reversed the Supreme Court's earlier position on segregation set by *Plessy* v. *Ferguson* (1896). The decision also inspired Congress and the federal courts to help carry out further civil rights reforms for African Americans.

Background Beginning in the 1930s, the National Association for the Advancement of Colored People (NAACP) began using the courts to challenge racial segregation in public education. In 1952 the NAACP took a number of school segregation cases to the Supreme Court. These included the Brown family's suit against the school board of Topeka, Kansas, over its "separate-but-equal" policy.

Decision This case was decided on May 17, 1954, by a vote of 9 to 0. Chief Justice Earl Warren spoke for the unanimous Court, which ruled that segregation in public education created inequality. The Court held that racial segregation in public schools was by nature unequal, even if the school facilities were equal. The Court noted that such segregation created feelings of inferiority that could not be undone. Therefore, enforced separation of the races in public education is unconstitutional.

Watkins v. United States (1957)

Significance The decision limited the inquiry powers of Congress. It was expected not to engage in law enforcement (an executive function), nor to act as a trial agency (a judicial function), but to inquire only as far as was necessary for the functioning of Congress.

Background Watkins was a labor union officer who appeared before the House Un-American Activities Committee during the 1950s Red Scare. Although he was willing to answer personal questions about himself and others whom he knew to be members of the Communist Party, he would not answer questions about past members of the Communist Party. He was therefore held in contempt of Congress.

Decision In a vote of 6 to 1 handed down on June 17, 1957, the Court threw out the charge of contempt against Watkins. Congress, it said, did not have the right to invade the private lives of individuals.

Mapp v. Ohio (1961)

Significance In this ruling the Court declared that evidence discovered in the process of an illegal search could not be used in state courts.

Background While searching for a bombing suspect, police found evidence of a separate crime in the house of Dollree Mapp. The police did not have permission to enter the home, nor did they have a search warrant. Upon conviction for the separate crime, Mapp appealed her case to the Supreme Court.

Decision In a 5-to-3 decision, the Court stated that convictions based on illegally obtained evidence must be overturned. Justice Tom Clark wrote for the majority, "all evidence obtained by searches and seizures in violation of the Constitution is … inadmissible in a state court."

Baker v. Carr (1962)

Significance Through this decision, the Court ruled that the judiciary branch may involve itself in hearing cases about political matters.

Background Voters from Tennessee sued their state in federal court, arguing that the way the state drew the boundary lines between representative districts created unequal representation within the legislature, and therefore unequal protection under the laws of the state. Tennessee argued that the federal court did not have the jurisdiction to hear the case.

Decision By a 6-to-2 margin, the Court decided that the federal court did have the right to hear the case and that the voters had the right to sue over the issue. Writing for the majority, Justice William Brennan said that the voters "are entitled to a trial and a decision" on whether they were denied equal protection.

Engel v. Vitale (1962)

Significance This case deals with the specific issue of organized prayer in schools and the broader issue of the proper relationship between government and religion under the First Amendment. The question in the case was whether a state violates the First Amendment when it composes a prayer that students must say at the beginning of each school day.

Background The state of New York recommended that public schools in the state begin the day by having students recite a prayer written by the state government. A group of parents sued to stop the official prayer, saying that it was contrary to their beliefs and their children's beliefs. They believed the law was unconstitutional because it "established" (officially supported) religion. Though students were permitted to remain silent, the parents claimed that there would always be pressure on students to pray.

Decision By a 6-to-1 margin (two justices did not take part in the case), the Court agreed with the parents. It struck down the state law. Justice Hugo Black wrote for the decision for the majority. He pointed out that the prayer was clearly religious. He said that under the First Amendment, "it is no part of the business of government to compose official prayers for any group of American people to recite as part of a religious program carried on by government." Black, referring to Jefferson and Madison, said "These men knew that the First Amendment, which tried to put an end to governmental control of religion and prayer, was not written to destroy either."

Gideon v. Wainwright (1963)

Significance This ruling was one of several key Supreme Court decisions establishing free legal help for those who cannot otherwise afford representation in court.

Background Clarence Earl Gideon was accused of robbery in Florida. Gideon could not afford a lawyer for his trial, and the judge refused to supply him with one for free. Gideon tried to defend himself and was found guilty. He eventually appealed to the U.S. Supreme Court, claiming that the lower court's denial of a court-appointed lawyer violated his Sixth and Fourteenth Amendment rights.

Decision This case was decided on March 18, 1963, by a vote of 9 to 0 in favor of Gideon. The Court agreed that the Sixth Amendment (which protects a citizen's right to have a lawyer for his or her defense) applied to the states because it fell under the due process clause of the Fourteenth Amendment. Thus, the states are required to provide legal aid to those defendants in criminal cases who cannot afford to pay for legal representation.

Heart of Atlanta Motel v. United States (1964)

Significance This ruling upheld the public accommodations clause of the Civil Rights Act of 1964. It enforced the right of African Americans to receive access to the same accommodations as whites and gave Congress judicial backing for passing more civil rights legislation.

Background The owner of the Heart of Atlanta Motel routinely discriminated against African Americans. He claimed that his business was not an interstate business and therefore not subject to regulation by congressional acts.

Decision In a unanimous decision, the Court declared that as a business that served people from across state boundaries, the Heart of Atlanta Motel was in fact an interstate business and that, therefore, congressional acts did apply.

Miranda v. Arizona (1966)

Significance This decision ruled that an accused person's Fifth Amendment rights begin at the time of arrest. The ruling caused controversy because it made the questioning of suspects and collecting evidence more difficult for law enforcement officers.

Background In 1963 Ernesto Miranda was arrested in Arizona for a kidnapping. Miranda signed a confession and was later found guilty of the crime. The arresting police officers, however, admitted that they had not told Miranda of his right to talk with an attorney before his confession. Miranda appealed his conviction on the grounds that by not informing him of his legal rights the police had violated his Fifth Amendment right against self-incrimination.

Decision This case was decided on June 13, 1966, by a vote of 5 to 4. Chief Justice Earl Warren spoke for the Court, which ruled in Miranda's favor. The Court decided that an accused person must be given four warnings after being taken into police custody: (1) the suspect has the right to remain silent, (2) anything the suspect says can and will be used against him or her, (3) the suspect has the right to consult with an attorney and to have an attorney present during questioning, and (4) if the suspect cannot afford a lawyer, one will be provided before questioning begins.

Tinker v. Des Moines Independent Community School District (1969)

Significance This ruling established the extent to which American public school students can take part in political protests in their schools. The question the case raised is whether, under the First Amendment, school officials can prohibit students from wearing armbands to symbolize political protest.

Background Students in Des Moines, Iowa, decided to wear black armbands to protest the Vietnam War. Two days before the protest, the school board created a new policy. The policy stated that any student who wore an armband to school and refused to remove it would be suspended. Three students wore armbands and were suspended. They said that their First Amendment right to freedom of speech had been violated. In 1969 the United States Supreme Court decided their case.

The Decision By a 7-to-2 margin, the Court agreed with the students. Justice Abe Fortas wrote the decision for the majority. He said that students do not "shed their constitutional rights to freedom of speech ... at the schoolhouse gate." Fortas admitted that school officials had the right to set rules. However, their rules must be consistent with the First Amendment. In this case, Des Moines school officials thought their rule was justified. They feared that the protest would disrupt learning. Fortas's opinion held that wearing an armband symbolizing political protest was a form of speech called symbolic speech. Symbolic speech is conduct that expresses an idea. Symbolic speech is protected in the same manner as the spoken word. Fortas wrote that student symbolic speech could be punished only if it disrupts the learning process. Fortas also noted that school officials allowed other political symbols, such as campaign buttons, to be worn in school.

Reed v. Reed (1971)

Significance This ruling was the first in a century of Fourteenth Amendment decisions to say that gender discrimination violated the equal protection clause. This case was later used to strike down other statutes that discriminated against women.

Background Cecil and Sally Reed were separated. When their son died without a will, the law gave preference to Cecil to be appointed the administrator of the son's estate. Sally sued Cecil for the right to administer the estate, challenging the gender preference in the law.

Decision This case was decided on November 22, 1971, by a vote of 7 to 0. Chief Justice Warren Burger spoke for the unanimous Supreme Court. Although the Court had upheld laws based on gender preference in the past, in this case it reversed its position. The Court declared that gender discrimination violated the equal protection clause of the Fourteenth Amendment and therefore could not be the basis for a law.

New York Times v. United States (1971)

Significance In this ruling the Court dismissed the idea of "prior restraint," or attempting to stop an action before it happens, by the government as unconstitutional. The ruling allowed the *New York Times* to continue publishing documents that were critical of the government's handling of the Vietnam War.

Background The *New York Times* began publishing a series of papers called the Pentagon Papers that were critical of the government. The government attempted to stop publication of the papers with a court order, citing national security. Because of the national importance of the case, the Supreme Court agreed to hear the case quickly.

Decision In a 6-to-3 decision, the Court declared that the government could not stop publication of the Pentagon Papers. Although the government did have the right to stop publication if it could prove the danger to national security, the Court said that in this case the government had not met the burden of proof.

Roe v. Wade (1973)

Significance This ruling made abortions available to women during their first trimester of pregnancy, even when their health was not in danger.

Background The case was brought in the name of Jane Roe against the restrictive abortion laws of Texas. Until this case, states had widely varying laws about the availability of abortions, some restricting them altogether.

Decision With a 7 to 2 decision, the Court said that elective abortions must be available to any woman in her first three months of pregnancy. Because of the variety of moral opinions about when life begins, the court ruled that a fetus does not have the same rights as an infant.

United States v. Nixon (1974)

Significance This ruling forced President Nixon to turn over tapes of White House conversations to the congressional committee investigating his wrongdoing in the Watergate break-in. Nixon resigned shortly after.

Background Nixon had been secretly taping every conversation that took place in the Oval Office. After the president was implicated in the cover-up of the Watergate Hotel break in, Congress wanted to hear these tapes. Nixon refused to hand them over, claiming "executive privilege" to keep some information secret.

Decision In a unanimous decision, the Court ruled that Nixon must turn the tapes over to the prosecution as requested. Writing for the court, Chief Justice Warren Burger stated that finding the truth requires that courts have all the evidence they need, even if it includes presidential communication.

New Jersey v. TLO (1985)

Significance In this ruling, the Court declared that searches of juveniles on school grounds are not subject to the same standards of "reasonableness" and "probable cause" that protect other citizens.

Background T. L. O. was a fourteen year old who was caught smoking in the girls' bathroom of her school. A principal at the school questioned the girl and searched her purse, finding marijuana and other drug paraphernalia.

Decision In a 7 to 2 decision, the Court ruled that the suspension of the rules of "reasonable" search and seizure as defined by the Fourth Amendment and later court rulings applied only to school officials and not to law enforcement officers.

Texas v. Johnson (1989)

Significance This ruling answered the question of whether the First Amendment protects burning the U.S. flag as a form of symbolic speech. It deals with the limits of symbolic speech. This case is particularly important because it involves burning the flag, one of our national symbols.

Background At the 1984 Republican National Convention in Texas, Gregory Lee Johnson doused a U.S. flag with kerosene. He did this during a demonstration, as a form of protest. Johnson was convicted of violating a Texas law that made it a crime to desecrate [treat disrespectfully] the national flag. He was sentenced to one year in prison and fined $2,000. The Texas Court of Criminal Appeals reversed the conviction because, it said, Johnson's burning of the flag was a form of symbolic speech protected by the First Amendment. Texas then appealed to the U.S. Supreme Court.

Decision The Court ruled for Johnson, five to four. Justice William Brennan wrote for the majority. He said that Johnson was within his constitutional rights when he burned the U.S. flag in protest. As in Tinker v. Des Moines Independent Community School District (1969), the Court looked at the First Amendment and "symbolic speech." Brennan concluded that Johnson's burning the flag was a form of symbolic speech—like the students wearing armbands in Des Moines—is protected by the First Amendment. According to Brennan, "Government may not prohibit the expression of an idea [because it is] offensive." Chief Justice Rehnquist dissented. He said the flag is "the visible symbol embodying our Nation. It does not represent the views of any particular political party, and it does not represent any particular political philosophy. The flag is not simply another 'idea' or 'point of view' competing for recognition in the marketplace of ideas." Since this decision, several amendments banning flag burning have been proposed in Congress, but so far all have failed.

Cruzan v. Director, Missouri Department of Health (1990)

Significance This ruling helped define who may refuse medical treatment. Although the issue is still undecided, this case began a series of efforts to provide legislative and judicial guidelines for the "right to die."

Background The parents of comatose patient Nancy Cruzan wanted to remove her life support system. The Department of Health ruled that Cruzan had not previously made clear her desire to refuse medical treatment in the event of brain damage.

Decision By a 5-to-4 margin, the Court ruled that Cruzan's parents could not remove her from life support because she had not clearly expressed her desires previously. Writing for the majority, Chief Justice William Rehnquist stated that it was Nancy's demand to be removed from life support, not her parents' wishes, that the state must respect in such cases.

Planned Parenthood of Southeastern Pennsylvania, et al. v. Casey (1992)

Significance In this ruling the Court upheld its decision in *Roe* v. *Wade* of the right to elective abortion, but allowed the state of Pennsylvania to impose restrictions of notification and consent upon minors.

Background In 1988 and 1989, Pennsylvania revised its laws to require that, to receive an abortion, minors must receive consent from a parent, and married women must notify their husbands. The laws were challenged by several abortion clinics and physicians.

Decision In a 5-to-4 decision, the Court upheld its previous ruling of *Roe* v. *Wade* that women have the right to an abortion in the first trimester of pregnancy, but provided that a state may require that minors have the consent of one parent 24 hours before the procedure. The Court struck down the part of the Pennsylvania laws that required married women to notify their husbands, saying that it could be an "undue burden" upon women.

Vernonia School District v. Acton (1995)

Significance This ruling allowed random drug testing of minors on school property as a safety measure.

Background James Acton, a student athlete in the Vernonia School District, refused to participate in drug testing, stating that the policy invaded his right to privacy and was an illegal search and seizure.

Decision In a 6-to-3 decision, the Court ruled that while on school property, students are subject to greater control of personal rights than are free adults. Furthermore, concern over the safety of minors under governmental supervision outweighs the minimal intrusion into a student's privacy.

Bush v. Gore (2000)

Significance In this ruling, the question before the court was whether ballots that could not be read by voting machines should be recounted by hand. The broader issues were whether the Supreme Court can overrule state court decisions on state laws, and whether an appointed judiciary can affect the result of democratic elections.

Background The 2000 presidential election between Democrat Al Gore and Republican George Bush was very close. Ultimately, the outcome would be determined by votes in the state of Florida. People in Florida voted by punching a hole in a ballot card. The votes were counted by a machine that detected these holes. According to that count, Bush won the state of Florida by a few hundred votes. Florida's Election Commission declared that Bush had won Florida. However, about 60,000 ballots were not counted because the machines could not detect a hole in the ballot. Gore argued in the Florida Supreme Court that these votes should be recounted by hand. The Florida Supreme Court ordered counties to recount all those votes. Bush appealed to the United States Supreme Court, which issued an order to stop the recounts while it made a decision.

The Decision On December 12, 2000, the Supreme Court voted 5 to 4 to end the hand recount of votes ordered by the Florida Supreme Court. The majority said that the Florida Supreme Court had ordered a recount without setting standards for what was a valid vote. Different vote-counters might use different standards. The Court said that this inconsistency meant that votes were treated arbitrarily—based on a person's choice rather than on standards. This arbitrariness, said the Court, violated the due process clause and the equal protection clause of the Constitution. Also, the justices said that Florida law required the vote count to be finalized by December 12. The justices said that rules for recounts could not be made by that date, so they ordered election officials to stop recounting votes.

Gratz v. Bollinger and Grutter v. Bollinger (2003)

Significance These cases considered whether a university violates the Constitution by using race as a factor for admitting students to its undergraduate school and its law school. The ruling affects use of affirmative action programs in higher education. The decisions gave colleges guidelines as to what is permitted and what is not. The decisions were limited to higher education and may not apply to other affirmative action programs such as those for applying for a job or for a government contract.

Background Jennifer Gratz and Barbara Grutter are both white. They challenged the University of Michigan's affirmative action admissions policies. Gratz said that the university violated the Constitution by considering race as a factor in its undergraduate admissions programs. Grutter claimed that the University of Michigan Law School did so.

Decisions In Gratz, the Court ruled 6 to 3 that the undergraduate program—which gave each minority applicant an automatic 20 points toward admission—was unconstitutional. Chief Justice William Rehnquist's opinion held that the policy violated the equal protection clause because it did not consider each applicant individually. "The ... automatic distribution of 20 points has the effect of making 'the factor of race ... decisive' for virtually every minimally qualified underrepresented minority applicant." The result was different when the Court turned to the affirmative action policy of Michigan's Law School, however, which used race as one factor for admission. In Grutter, by a 5-to-4 margin, the Court held that this policy did not violate the equal protection clause. Justice Sandra Day O'Connor wrote for the majority. "Truly individualized consideration demands that race be used in a flexible, nonmechanical way ... Universities can ... consider race or ethnicity ... as a 'plus' factor [when individually considering] each and every applicant." Thus, the law school's policy was constitutional.

United States v. American Library Association (2003)

Significance This case deals with the constitutionality of a federal law called the Children's Internet Protection Act (CIPA). The law was designed to protect children from being exposed to pornographic Web sites while using computers in public libraries. The question before the court was this: Does a public library violate the First Amendment by installing Internet filtering software on its public computers?

Background CIPA applies to public libraries that accept federal money to help pay for Internet access. These libraries must install filtering software to block pornographic images. Some library associations sued to block these filtering requirements. They argued that by linking money and filters, the law required public libraries to violate the First Amendment's guarantees of free speech. The libraries argued that filters block some non-pornographic sites along with pornographic ones. That, they said, violates library patrons' First Amendment rights. CIPA does allow anyone to ask a librarian to unblock a specific Web site. It also allows adults to ask that the filter be turned off altogether. But, the libraries argued, people using the library would find these remedies embarrassing and impractical.

Decision In this case, Chief Justice William Rehnquist authored a plurality opinion. He explained that the law does not require any library to accept federal money. A library can choose to do without federal money. If the library makes that choice, it does not have to install Internet filters. And Rehnquist did not think that filtering software's tendency to overblock nonpornographic sites was a constitutional problem. Adult patrons could simply ask a librarian to unblock a blocked site or could have the filter disabled entirely.

The Dissents Justice John Paul Stevens viewed CIPA "as a blunt nationwide restraint on adult access to an enormous amount of valuable" and often constitutionally protected speech. Justice David Souter noted that he would have joined the plurality if the First Amendment interests raised in this case were those of children rather than those of adults.

Hamdi v. Rumsfeld and Rasul v. Bush (2004)

Significance These cases addressed the balance between the government's powers to fight terrorism and the Constitution's promise of due process. Each case raised a slightly different question:

1. Can the government hold American citizens for an indefinite period as "enemy combatants" and not permit them access to American courts, and

2. Do foreigners captured overseas and jailed at Guantánamo Bay, Cuba, have the right to take their cases to American courts to decide if they are being held legally?

Background In *Hamdi* v. *Rumsfeld*, Yaser Hamdi, an American citizen, was captured in Afghanistan in 2001. The U.S. military said Hamdi was an enemy combatant and claimed that "it has the authority to hold ... enemy combatants captured on the battlefield ... to prevent them from returning to the battle." Hamdi's attorney said that Hamdi deserved the due process rights that other Americans have, including a hearing in court to argue that he was not an enemy combatant.

The prisoners in *Rasul* v. *Bush* also claimed they were wrongly imprisoned. They wanted a court hearing, but Guantánamo Bay Naval Base is on Cuban soil. Cuba leases the base to the United States. In an earlier case, the Court had ruled that "if an alien is outside the country's sovereign territory, then ... the alien is not permitted access to the courts of the United States to enforce the Constitution."

Decision In *Hamdi*, the Court ruled 6 to 3 that Hamdi had a right to a hearing. Justice Sandra Day O'Connor wrote that the Court has "made clear that a state of war is not a blank check for the president when it comes to the rights of the nation's citizens." The government decided not to prosecute Hamdi. In *Rasul*, also decided 6 to 3, Justice John Paul Stevens wrote that the prisoners had been held for more than two years in territory under U.S. control. Thus, even though the prisoners are not on U.S. soil, they can ask U.S. courts if their detention is legal. The *Rasul* cases were still pending when this book was printed.

The Declaration of Independence

In Congress, July 4, 1776
The unanimous Declaration of the thirteen united States of America,

When in the Course of human events, it becomes necessary for one people to dissolve the political bands which have connected them with another, and to assume among the Powers of the earth, the separate and equal station to which the Laws of Nature and of Nature's God entitle them, a decent respect to the opinions of mankind requires that they should declare the causes which **impel** them to the separation.

We hold these truths to be self-evident, that all men are created equal, that they are **endowed** by their Creator with certain unalienable Rights, that among these are Life, Liberty, and the pursuit of Happiness. That to secure these rights, Governments are instituted among Men, deriving their just powers from the consent of the governed, That whenever any Form of Government becomes destructive of these ends, it is the Right of the People to alter or to abolish it, and to institute new Government, laying its foundation on such principles and organizing its powers in such form, as to them shall seem most likely to effect their Safety and Happiness. Prudence, indeed, will dictate that Governments long established should not be changed for light and transient causes; and accordingly all experience hath shown, that mankind are more disposed to suffer, while evils are sufferable, than to right themselves by abolishing the forms to which they are accustomed. But when a long train of abuses and **usurpations**, pursuing invariably the same Object **evinces** a design to reduce them under absolute **Despotism**, it is their right, it is their duty, to throw off such Government, and to provide new Guards for their future security.—Such has been the patient sufferance of these Colonies; and such is now the necessity which constrains them to alter their former Systems of Government. The history of the present King of Great Britain is a history of repeated injuries and usurpations, all having in direct object the establishment of an absolute **Tyranny** over these States. To prove this, let Facts be submitted to a **candid** world.

He has refused his Assent to Laws, the most wholesome and necessary for the public good.

He has forbidden his Governors to pass Laws of immediate and pressing importance, unless suspended in their operation till his Assent should be obtained; and when so suspended, he has utterly neglected to attend to them.

Vocabulary

impel force

endowed provided

usurpations wrongful seizures of power

evinces clearly displays

despotism unlimited power

tyranny oppressive power exerted by a government or ruler

candid fair

He has refused to pass other Laws for the accommodation of large districts of people, unless those people would **relinquish** the right of Representation in the Legislature, a right **inestimable** to them and **formidable** to tyrants only.

He has called together legislative bodies at places unusual, uncomfortable, and distant from the depository of their Public Records, for the sole purpose of fatiguing them into compliance with his measures.

He has dissolved Representative Houses repeatedly, for opposing with manly firmness his invasions on the rights of the people.

He has refused for a long time, after such dissolutions, to cause others to be elected; whereby the Legislative Powers, incapable of **Annihilation**, have returned to the People at large for their exercise; the State remaining in the mean time exposed to all the dangers of invasion from without, and **convulsions** within.

He has endeavored to prevent the population of these States; for that purpose obstructing the Laws of **Naturalization of Foreigners**; refusing to pass others to encourage their migration hither, and raising the conditions of new **Appropriations of Lands**.

He has obstructed the Administration of Justice, by refusing his Assent to Laws for establishing Judiciary Powers.

He has made Judges dependent on his Will alone, for the **tenure** of their offices, and the amount and payment of their salaries.

He has erected **a multitude of** New Offices, and sent hither swarms of Officers to harass our people, and eat out their substance.

He has kept among us, in times of peace, Standing Armies without the Consent of our legislature.

He has affected to render the Military independent of and superior to the Civil Power.

He has combined with others to subject us to a jurisdiction foreign to our constitution, and unacknowledged by our laws; giving his Assent to their Acts of pretended legislation:

For **quartering** large bodies of armed troops among us:

For protecting them, by a mock Trial, from Punishment for any Murders which they should commit on the Inhabitants of these States:

For cutting off our Trade with all parts of the world:

For imposing taxes on us without our Consent:

For depriving us in many cases, of the benefits of Trial by Jury:

Vocabulary

relinquish release, yield

inestimable priceless

formidable causing dread

annihilation destruction

convulsions violent disturbances

naturalization of foreigners the process by which foreign-born persons become citizens

appropriations of lands setting aside land for settlement

tenure term

a multitude of many

quartering lodging, housing

Vocabulary

arbitrary not based on law

render make

abdicated given up

foreign mercenaries soldiers hired to fight for a country not their own

perfidy violation of trust

insurrections rebellions

petitioned for redress asked formally for a correction of wrongs

unwarrantable jurisdiction unjustified authority

magnanimity generous spirit

conjured urgently called upon

consanguinity common ancestry

acquiesce consent to

For transporting us beyond Seas to be tried for pretended offences:

For abolishing the free System of English Laws in a neighboring Province, establishing therein an **Arbitrary** government, and enlarging its Boundaries so as to **render** it at once an example and fit instrument for introducing the same absolute rule into these Colonies:

For taking away our Charters, abolishing our most valuable Laws, and altering fundamentally the Forms of our Governments:

For suspending our own Legislature, and declaring themselves invested with Power to legislate for us in all cases whatsoever.

He has **abdicated** Government here, by declaring us out of his Protection and waging War against us.

He has plundered our seas, ravaged our Coasts, burnt our towns, and destroyed the lives of our people.

He is at this time transporting large armies of **foreign mercenaries** to complete the works of death, desolation and tyranny, already begun with circumstances of Cruelty & **perfidy** scarcely paralleled in the most barbarous ages, and totally unworthy the Head of a civilized nation.

He has constrained our fellow Citizens taken Captive on the high Seas to bear Arms against their Country, to become the executioners of their friends and Brethren, or to fall themselves by their Hands.

He has excited domestic **insurrections** amongst us, and has endeavored to bring on the inhabitants of our frontiers, the merciless Indian Savages, whose known rule of warfare, is an undistinguished destruction of all ages, sexes and conditions.

In every stage of these Oppressions We have **Petitioned for Redress** in the most humble terms: Our repeated Petitions have been answered only by repeated injury. A Prince, whose character is thus marked by every act which may define a Tyrant, is unfit to be the ruler of a free People.

Nor have We been wanting in attention to our British brethren. We have warned them from time to time of attempts by their legislature to extend an **unwarrantable jurisdiction** over us. We have reminded them of the circumstances of our emigration and settlement here. We have appealed to their native justice and **magnanimity**, and we have **conjured** them by the ties of our common kindred to disavow these usurpations, which, would inevitably interrupt our connections and correspondence. They too have been deaf to the voice of justice and of **consanguinity**. We must, therefore, **acquiesce** in the necessity, which denounces our Separation, and hold them, as we hold the rest of mankind, Enemies in War, in Peace Friends.

We, therefore, the Representatives of the united States of America, in General Congress, Assembled, appealing to the Supreme Judge of the world for the **rectitude** of our intentions, do, in the Name, and by Authority of the good People of these Colonies, solemnly publish and declare, That these United Colonies are, and of Right ought to be Free and Independent States; that they are Absolved from all Allegiance to the British Crown, and that all political connection between them and the State of Great Britain, is and ought to be totally dissolved; and that as Free and Independent States, they have full Power to levy War, conclude Peace, contract Alliances, establish Commerce, and to do all other Acts and Things which Independent States may of right do. And for the support of this Declaration, with a firm reliance on the Protection of Divine Providence, we mutually pledge to each other our Lives, our Fortunes and our sacred Honor.

John Hancock	Benjamin Harrison	Lewis Morris
Button Gwinnett	Thomas Nelson, Jr.	Richard Stockton
Lyman Hall	Francis Lightfoot Lee	John Witherspoon
George Walton	Carter Braxton	Francis Hopkinson
William Hooper	Robert Morris	John Hart
Joseph Hewes	Benjamin Rush	Abraham Clark
John Penn	Benjamin Franklin	Josiah Bartlett
Edward Rutledge	John Morton	William Whipple
Thomas Heyward, Jr.	George Clymer	Samuel Adams
Thomas Lynch, Jr.	James Smith	John Adams
Arthur Middleton	George Taylor	Robert Treat Paine
Samuel Chase	James Wilson	Elbridge Gerry
William Paca	George Ross	Stephen Hopkins
Thomas Stone	Caesar Rodney	William Ellery
Charles Carroll of Carrollton	George Read	Roger Sherman
	Thomas McKean	Samuel Huntington
George Wythe	William Floyd	William Williams
Richard Henry Lee	Philip Livingston	Oliver Wolcott
Thomas Jefferson	Francis Lewis	Matthew Thornton

The Constitution of the United States

Preamble

We the People of the United States, in Order to form a more perfect Union, establish Justice, insure domestic Tranquility, provide for the common defense, promote the general Welfare, and secure the Blessings of Liberty to ourselves and our Posterity, do ordain and establish this Constitution for the United States of America.

Article I — The Legislature

Section 1. Congress

All legislative Powers herein granted shall be vested in a Congress of the United States, which shall consist of a Senate and House of Representatives.

Section 2. The House of Representatives

1. Elections The House of Representatives shall be composed of Members chosen every second Year by the People of the several States, and the Electors in each State shall have the Qualifications requisite for Electors of the most numerous Branch of the State Legislature.

2. Qualifications No Person shall be a Representative who shall not have attained to the Age of twenty five Years, and been seven Years a Citizen of the United States, and who shall not, when elected, be an Inhabitant of that State in which he shall be chosen.

3. Number of Representatives Representatives and direct Taxes shall be apportioned among the several States which may be included within this Union, according to their respective Numbers, which shall be determined by adding to the whole Number of free Persons, including **those bound to Service**[1] for a Term of Years, and excluding Indians not taxed, three fifths of **all other Persons**.[2] The actual **Enumeration**[3] shall be made within three Years after the first Meeting of the Congress of the United States, and within every subsequent Term of ten Years, in such Manner as they shall by Law direct. The Number of Representatives shall not exceed one for every

---

Legislative Branch

Article I explains how the legislative branch, called Congress, is organized. The chief purpose of the legislative branch is to make laws. Congress is made up of the Senate and the House of Representatives.

The House of Representatives

The number of members each state has in the House is based on the population of the individual state. In 1929 Congress permanently fixed the size of the House at 435 members.

Vocabulary

[1] **those bound to Service** indentured servants

[2] **all other Persons** slaves

[3] **Enumeration** census or official population count

Note: The parts of the Constitution that have been lined through are no longer in force or no longer apply because of later amendments. The titles of the sections and articles are added for easier reference.

thirty Thousand, but each State shall have at Least one Representative; and until such enumeration shall be made, the State of New Hampshire shall be entitled to choose three, Massachoosetts eight, Rhode-Island and Providence Plantations one, Connecticut five, New-York six, New Jersey four, Pennsylvania eight, Delaware one, Maryland six, Virginia ten, North Carolina five, South Carolina five, and Georgia three.

4. Vacancies When vacancies happen in the Representation from any State, the Executive Authority thereof shall issue Writs of Election to fill such Vacancies.

5. Officers and Impeachment The House of Representatives shall choose their Speaker and other Officers; and shall have the sole Power of impeachment.

Section 3. The Senate

1. Number of Senators The Senate of the United States shall be composed of two Senators from each State, chosen by the Legislature thereof, for six Years; and each Senator shall have one Vote.

2. Classifying Terms Immediately after they shall be assembled in Consequence of the first Election, they shall be divided as equally as may be into three Classes. The Seats of the Senators of the first Class shall be vacated at the Expiration of the second Year, of the second Class at the Expiration of the fourth Year, and of the third Class at the Expiration of the sixth Year, so that one third may be chosen every second Year; and if Vacancies happen by Resignation, or otherwise, during the Recess of the Legislature of any State, the Executive thereof may make temporary Appointments until the next Meeting of the Legislature, which shall then fill such Vacancies.

3. Qualifications No Person shall be a Senator who shall not have attained to the Age of thirty Years, and been nine Years a Citizen of the United States, and who shall not, when elected, be an Inhabitant of that State for which he shall be chosen.

4. Role of Vice-President The Vice President of the United States shall be President of the Senate, but shall have no Vote, unless they be equally divided.

5. Officers The Senate shall choose their other Officers, and also a President **pro tempore**,[4] in the Absence of the Vice President, or when he shall exercise the Office of President of the United States.

6. Impeachment Trials The Senate shall have the sole Power to try all **Impeachments**.[5] When sitting for that Purpose, they shall be on Oath or Affirmation. When the President of the United States is tried, the Chief Justice shall preside: And no Person shall be convicted without the Concurrence of two thirds of the Members present.

7. Punishment for Impeachment Judgment in Cases of Impeachment shall not extend further than to removal from Office, and disqualification to hold

The Vice President

The only duty that the Constitution assigns to the vice president is to preside over meetings of the Senate. Modern presidents have usually given their vice presidents more responsibilities.

Vocabulary

[4] **pro tempore** temporarily

[5] **Impeachments** official accusations of federal wrongdoing

and enjoy any Office of honor, Trust or Profit under the United States: but the Party convicted shall nevertheless be liable and subject to Indictment, Trial, Judgment and Punishment, according to Law.

Section 4. Congressional Elections

1. Regulations The Times, Places and Manner of holding Elections for Senators and Representatives, shall be prescribed in each State by the Legislature thereof; but the Congress may at any time by Law make or alter such Regulations, except as to the Places of choosing Senators.

2. Sessions ~~The Congress shall assemble at least once in every Year, and such Meeting shall be on the first Monday in December, unless they shall by Law appoint a different Day.~~

Section 5. Rules/Procedures

1. Quorum Each House shall be the Judge of the Elections, Returns and Qualifications of its own Members, and a Majority of each shall constitute a **Quorum**[6] to do Business; but a smaller Number may **adjourn**[7] from day to day, and may be authorized to compel the Attendance of absent Members, in such Manner, and under such Penalties as each House may provide.

2. Rules and Conduct Each House may determine the Rules of its Proceedings, punish its Members for disorderly Behaviour, and, with the Concurrence of two thirds, expel a Member.

3. Records Each House shall keep a Journal of its Proceedings, and from time to time publish the same, excepting such Parts as may in their Judgment require Secrecy; and the Yeas and Nays of the Members of either House on any question shall, at the Desire of one fifth of those Present, be entered on the Journal.

4. Adjournment Neither House, during the Session of Congress, shall, without the Consent of the other, adjourn for more than three days, nor to any other Place than that in which the two Houses shall be sitting.

Section 6. Payment

1. Salary The Senators and Representatives shall receive a Compensation for their Services, to be ascertained by Law, and paid out of the Treasury of the United States. They shall in all Cases, except Treason, Felony and Breach of the Peace, be privileged from Arrest during their Attendance at the Session of their respective Houses, and in going to and returning from the same; and for any Speech or Debate in either House, they shall not be questioned in any other Place.

2. Restrictions No Senator or Representative shall, during the Time for which he was elected, be appointed to any civil Office under the Authority of the United States, which shall have been created, or the **Emoluments**[8]

Vocabulary

[6] **Quorum** the minimum number of people needed to conduct business

[7] **adjourn** to stop indefinitely

[8] **Emoluments** salary

whereof shall have been increased during such time; and no Person holding any Office under the United States, shall be a Member of either House during his **Continuance**[9] in Office.

Section 7. How a Bill Becomes a Law

1. Tax Bills All **Bills**[10] for raising Revenue shall originate in the House of Representatives; but the Senate may propose or concur with Amendments as on other Bills.

2. Lawmaking Every Bill which shall have passed the House of Representatives and the Senate, shall, before it become a Law, be presented to the President of the United States: If he approve he shall sign it, but if not he shall return it, with his Objections to that House in which it shall have originated, who shall enter the Objections at large on their Journal, and proceed to reconsider it. If after such Reconsideration two thirds of that House shall agree to pass the Bill, it shall be sent, together with the Objections, to the other House, by which it shall likewise be reconsidered, and if approved by two thirds of that House, it shall become a Law. But in all such Cases the Votes of both Houses shall be determined by yeas and Nays, and the Names of the Persons voting for and against the Bill shall be entered on the Journal of each House respectively. If any Bill shall not be returned by the President within ten Days (Sundays excepted) after it shall have been presented to him, the Same shall be a Law, in like Manner as if he had signed it, unless the Congress by their Adjournment prevent its Return, in which Case it shall not be a Law.

3. Role of the President Every Order, Resolution, or Vote to which the Concurrence of the Senate and House of Representatives may be necessary (except on a question of Adjournment) shall be presented to the President of the United States; and before the Same shall take Effect, shall be approved by him, or being disapproved by him, shall be repassed by two thirds of the Senate and House of Representatives, according to the Rules and Limitations prescribed in the Case of a Bill.

Section 8. Powers Granted to Congress

1. Taxation The Congress shall have Power To lay and collect Taxes, **Duties**,[11] **Imposts**[12] and **Excises**,[13] to pay the Debts and provide for the common Defense and general Welfare of the United States; but all Duties, Imposts and Excises shall be uniform throughout the United States;

2. Credit To borrow Money on the credit of the United States;

3. Commerce To regulate Commerce with foreign Nations, and among the several States, and with the Indian Tribes;

4. Naturalization and Bankruptcy To establish an uniform **Rule of Naturalization**,[14] and uniform Laws on the subject of Bankruptcies throughout the United States;

Vocabulary

[9] **Continuance** term

[10] **Bills** proposed laws

[11] **Duties** tariffs

[12] **Imposts** taxes

[13] **Excises** internal taxes on the manufacture, sale, or consumption of a commodity

[14] **Rule of Naturalization** a law by which a foreign-born person becomes a citizen

THE CONSTITUTION

Vocabulary

[15] **Securities** bonds

[16] **Letters of Marque and Reprisal** documents issued by governments allowing merchant ships to arm themselves and attack ships of an enemy nation

5. Money To coin Money, regulate the Value thereof, and of foreign Coin, and fix the Standard of Weights and Measures;

6. Counterfeiting To provide for the Punishment of counterfeiting the **Securities**[15] and current Coin of the United States;

7. Post Office To establish Post Offices and post Roads;

8. Patents and Copyrights To promote the Progress of Science and useful Arts, by securing for limited Times to Authors and Inventors the exclusive Right to their respective Writings and Discoveries;

9. Courts To constitute Tribunals inferior to the supreme Court;

10. International Law To define and punish Piracies and Felonies committed on the high Seas, and Offences against the Law of Nations;

11. War To declare War, grant **Letters of Marque and Reprisal**,[16] and make Rules concerning Captures on Land and Water;

12. Army To raise and support Armies, but no Appropriation of Money to that Use shall be for a longer Term than two Years;

13. Navy To provide and maintain a Navy;

14. Regulation of the Military To make Rules for the Government and Regulation of the land and naval Forces;

15. Militia To provide for calling forth the Militia to execute the Laws of the Union, suppress Insurrections and repel Invasions;

16. Regulation of the Militia To provide for organizing, arming, and disciplining, the Militia, and for governing such Part of them as may be employed in the Service of the United States, reserving to the States respectively, the Appointment of the Officers, and the Authority of training the Militia according to the discipline prescribed by Congress;

17. District of Columbia To exercise exclusive Legislation in all Cases whatsoever, over such District (not exceeding ten Miles square) as may, by Cession of particular States, and the Acceptance of Congress, become the Seat of the Government of the United States, and to exercise like Authority over all Places purchased by the Consent of the Legislature of the State in which the Same shall be, for the Erection of Forts, Magazines, Arsenals, dock-Yards, and other needful Buildings;—And

The Elastic Clause

The framers of the Constitution wanted a national government that was strong enough to be effective. This section lists the powers given to Congress. The last portion of Section 8 contains the so-called elastic clause.

18. Necessary and Proper Clause To make all Laws which shall be necessary and proper for carrying into Execution the foregoing Powers, and all other Powers vested by this Constitution in the Government of the United States, or in any Department or Officer thereof.

Section 9. Powers Denied Congress

1. Slave Trade ~~The Migration or Importation of such Persons as any of the States now existing shall think proper to admit, shall not be prohibited~~

~~by the Congress prior to the Year one thousand eight hundred and eight, but a Tax or duty may be imposed on such Importation, not exceeding ten dollars for each Person.~~

2. Habeas Corpus The Privilege of the **Writ of Habeas Corpus**[17] shall not be suspended, unless when in Cases of Rebellion or Invasion the public Safety may require it.

3. Illegal Punishment No **Bill of Attainder**[18] or **ex post facto Law**[19] shall be passed.

4. Direct Taxes No **Capitation**,[20] or other direct, Tax shall be laid, unless in Proportion to the Census or enumeration herein before directed to be taken.

5. Export Taxes No Tax or Duty shall be laid on Articles exported from any State.

6. No Favorites No Preference shall be given by any Regulation of Commerce or Revenue to the Ports of one State over those of another; nor shall Vessels bound to, or from, one State, be obliged to enter, clear, or pay Duties in another.

7. Public Money No Money shall be drawn from the Treasury, but in Consequence of Appropriations made by Law; and a regular Statement and Account of the Receipts and Expenditures of all public Money shall be published from time to time.

8. Titles of Nobility No Title of Nobility shall be granted by the United States: And no Person holding any Office of Profit or Trust under them, shall, without the Consent of the Congress, accept of any present, Emolument, Office, or Title, of any kind whatever, from any King, Prince, or foreign State.

Section 10. Powers Denied the States

1. Restrictions No State shall enter into any Treaty, Alliance, or Confederation; grant Letters of Marque and Reprisal; coin Money; emit Bills of Credit; make any Thing but gold and silver Coin a Tender in Payment of Debts; pass any Bill of Attainder, ex post facto Law, or Law impairing the Obligation of Contracts, or grant any Title of Nobility.

2. Import and Export Taxes No State shall, without the Consent of the Congress, lay any Imposts or Duties on Imports or Exports, except what may be absolutely necessary for executing it's inspection Laws: and the net Produce of all Duties and Imposts, laid by any State on Imports or Exports, shall be for the Use of the Treasury of the United States; and all such Laws shall be subject to the Revision and Control of the Congress.

3. Peacetime and War Restraints No State shall, without the Consent of Congress, lay any Duty of Tonnage, keep Troops, or Ships of War in time of Peace, enter into any Agreement or Compact with another State, or with a foreign Power, or engage in War, unless actually invaded, or in such imminent Danger as will not admit of delay.

Vocabulary

[17] **Writ of Habeas Corpus** a court order that requires the government to bring a prisoner to court and explain why he or she is being held

[18] **Bill of Attainder** a law declaring that a person is guilty of a particular crime

[19] **ex post facto Law** a law that is made effective prior to the date that it was passed and therefore punishes people for acts that were not illegal at the time

[20] **Capitation** a direct uniform tax imposed on each head, or person

THE CONSTITUTION

Article II The Executive

Section 1. The Presidency

1. Terms of Office The executive Power shall be vested in a President of the United States of America. He shall hold his Office during the Term of four Years, and, together with the Vice President, chosen for the same Term, be elected, as follows:

2. Electoral College Each State shall appoint, in such Manner as the Legislature thereof may direct, a Number of Electors, equal to the whole Number of Senators and Representatives to which the State may be entitled in the Congress: but no Senator or Representative, or Person holding an Office of Trust or Profit under the United States, shall be appointed an Elector.

3. Former Method of Electing President The Electors shall meet in their respective States, and vote by Ballot for two Persons, of whom one at least shall not be an Inhabitant of the same State with themselves. And they shall make a List of all the Persons voted for, and of the Number of Votes for each; which List they shall sign and certify, and transmit sealed to the Seat of the Government of the United States, directed to the President of the Senate. The President of the Senate shall, in the Presence of the Senate and House of Representatives, open all the Certificates, and the Votes shall then be counted. The Person having the greatest Number of Votes shall be the President, if such Number be a Majority of the whole Number of Electors appointed; and if there be more than one who have such Majority, and have an equal Number of Votes, then the House of Representatives shall immediately choose by Ballot one of them for President; and if no Person have a Majority, then from the five highest on the List the said House shall in like Manner choose the President. But in choosing the President, the Votes shall be taken by States, the Representation from each State having one Vote; A quorum for this purpose shall consist of a Member or Members from two thirds of the States, and a Majority of all the States shall be necessary to a Choice. In every Case, after the Choice of the President, the Person having the greatest Number of Votes of the Electors shall be the Vice President. But if there should remain two or more who have equal Votes, the Senate shall choose from them by Ballot the Vice President.

4. Election Day The Congress may determine the Time of choosing the Electors, and the Day on which they shall give their Votes; which Day shall be the same throughout the United States.

5. Qualifications No Person except a natural born Citizen, or a Citizen of the United States, at the time of the Adoption of this Constitution, shall be eligible to the Office of President; neither shall any Person be eligible to

---

THE CONSTITUTION

Executive Branch

The president is the chief of the executive branch. It is the job of the president to enforce the laws. The framers wanted the president's and vice president's terms of office and manner of selection to be different from those of members of Congress. They decided on four-year terms, but they had a difficult time agreeing on how to select the president and vice president. The framers finally set up an electoral system, which varies greatly from our electoral process today.

Presidential Elections

In 1845 Congress set the Tuesday following the first Monday in November of every fourth year as the general election date for selecting presidential electors.

that Office who shall not have attained to the Age of thirty five Years, and been fourteen Years a Resident within the United States.

6. Succession In Case of the Removal of the President from Office, or of his Death, Resignation, or Inability to discharge the Powers and Duties of the said Office, the Same shall devolve on the Vice President, and the Congress may by Law provide for the Case of Removal, Death, Resignation or Inability, both of the President and Vice President, declaring what Officer shall then act as President, and such Officer shall act accordingly, until the Disability be removed, or a President shall be elected.

7. Salary The President shall, at stated Times, receive for his Services, a Compensation, which shall neither be increased nor diminished during the Period for which he shall have been elected, and he shall not receive within that Period any other Emolument from the United States, or any of them.

8. Oath of Office Before he enter on the Execution of his Office, he shall take the following Oath or Affirmation:—"I do solemnly swear (or affirm) that I will faithfully execute the Office of President of the United States, and will to the best of my Ability, preserve, protect and defend the Constitution of the United States."

Section 2. Powers of Presidency

1. Military Powers The President shall be Commander in Chief of the Army and Navy of the United States, and of the Militia of the several States, when called into the actual Service of the United States; he may require the Opinion, in writing, of the principal Officer in each of the executive Departments, upon any Subject relating to the Duties of their respective Offices, and he shall have Power to grant **Reprieves**[21] and **Pardons**[22] for Offences against the United States, except in Cases of Impeachment.

2. Treaties and Appointments He shall have Power, by and with the Advice and Consent of the Senate, to make Treaties, provided two thirds of the Senators present concur; and he shall nominate, and by and with the Advice and Consent of the Senate, shall appoint Ambassadors, other public Ministers and Consuls, Judges of the supreme Court, and all other Officers of the United States, whose Appointments are not herein otherwise provided for, and which shall be established by Law: but the Congress may by Law vest the Appointment of such inferior Officers, as they think proper, in the President alone, in the Courts of Law, or in the Heads of Departments.

3. Vacancies The President shall have Power to fill up all Vacancies that may happen during the Recess of the Senate, by granting Commissions which shall expire at the End of their next Session.

Presidential Salary

In 1999 Congress voted to set future presidents' salaries at $400,000 per year. The president also receives an annual expense account. The president must pay taxes only on the salary.

Commander in Chief

Today the president is in charge of the army, navy, air force, marines, and coast guard. Only Congress, however, can decide if the United States will declare war.

Appointments

Most of the president's appointments to office must be approved by the Senate.

Vocabulary

[21] **Reprieves** delays of punishment

[22] **Pardons** releases from the legal penalties associated with a crime

The State of the Union

Every year the president presents to Congress a State of the Union message. In this message, the president introduces and explains a legislative plan for the coming year.

Section 3. Presidential Duties

He shall from time to time give to the Congress Information of the State of the Union, and recommend to their Consideration such Measures as he shall judge necessary and expedient; he may, on extraordinary Occasions, convene both Houses, or either of them, and in Case of Disagreement between them, with Respect to the Time of Adjournment, he may adjourn them to such Time as he shall think proper; he shall receive Ambassadors and other public Ministers; he shall take Care that the Laws be faithfully executed, and shall Commission all the Officers of the United States.

Section 4. Impeachment

The President, Vice President and all civil Officers of the United States, shall be removed from Office on Impeachment for, and Conviction of, Treason, Bribery, or other high Crimes and Misdemeanors.

Article III The Judiciary

Section 1. Federal Courts and Judges

The judicial Power of the United States shall be vested in one supreme Court, and in such inferior Courts as the Congress may from time to time ordain and establish. The Judges, both of the supreme and inferior Courts, shall hold their Offices during good Behavior, and shall, at stated Times, receive for their Services a Compensation, which shall not be diminished during their Continuance in Office.

Judicial Branch

The Articles of Confederation did not set up a federal court system. One of the first points that the framers of the Constitution agreed upon was to set up a national judiciary. In the Judiciary Act of 1789, Congress provided for the establishment of lower courts, such as district courts, circuit courts of appeals, and various other federal courts. The judicial system provides a check on the legislative branch: It can declare a law unconstitutional.

Section 2. Authority of the Courts

1. General Authority The judicial Power shall extend to all Cases, in Law and Equity, arising under this Constitution, the Laws of the United States, and Treaties made, or which shall be made, under their Authority;—to all Cases affecting Ambassadors, other public Ministers and Consuls;—to all Cases of admiralty and maritime Jurisdiction;—to Controversies to which the United States shall be a Party;—to Controversies between two or more States —between a State and Citizens of another State; —between Citizens of different States;—between Citizens of the same State claiming Lands under Grants of different States, and between a State, or the Citizens thereof, and foreign States, Citizens or Subjects.

2. Supreme Authority In all Cases affecting Ambassadors, other public Ministers and Consuls, and those in which a State shall be Party, the supreme Court shall have original Jurisdiction. In all the other Cases before mentioned, the supreme Court shall have appellate Jurisdiction, both as to Law and Fact, with such Exceptions, and under such Regulations as the Congress shall make.

3. Trial by Jury The Trial of all Crimes, except in Cases of Impeachment, shall be by Jury; and such Trial shall be held in the State where the said Crimes shall have been committed; but when not committed within any State, the Trial shall be at such Place or Places as the Congress may by Law have directed.

Section 3. Treason

1. Definition Treason against the United States, shall consist only in levying War against them, or in adhering to their Enemies, giving them Aid and Comfort. No Person shall be convicted of Treason unless on the Testimony of two Witnesses to the same overt Act, or on Confession in open Court.

2. Punishment The Congress shall have Power to declare the Punishment of Treason, but no Attainder of Treason shall work **Corruption of Blood**,[23] or Forfeiture except during the Life of the Person attainted.

Article IV Relations among States

Section 1. State Acts and Records

Full Faith and Credit shall be given in each State to the public Acts, Records, and judicial Proceedings of every other State. And the Congress may by general Laws prescribe the Manner in which such Acts, Records and Proceedings shall be proved, and the Effect thereof.

Section 2. Rights of Citizens

1. Citizenship The Citizens of each State shall be entitled to all Privileges and Immunities of Citizens in the several States.

2. Extradition A Person charged in any State with Treason, Felony, or other Crime, who shall flee from Justice, and be found in another State, shall on Demand of the executive Authority of the State from which he fled, be delivered up, to be removed to the State having Jurisdiction of the Crime.

3. Fugitive Slaves ~~No Person held to Service or Labour in one State, under the Laws thereof, escaping into another, shall, in Consequence of any Law or Regulation therein, be discharged from such Service or Labour, but shall be delivered up on Claim of the Party to whom such Service or Labour may be due.~~

Section 3. New States

1. Admission New States may be admitted by the Congress into this Union; but no new State shall be formed or erected within the Jurisdiction of any other State; nor any State be formed by the Junction of two or more States, or Parts of States, without the Consent of the Legislatures of the States concerned as well as of the Congress.

The States

States must honor the laws, records, and court decisions of other states. A person cannot escape a legal obligation by moving from one state to another.

2. Congressional Authority The Congress shall have Power to dispose of and make all needful Rules and Regulations respecting the Territory or other Property belonging to the United States; and nothing in this Constitution shall be so construed as to Prejudice any Claims of the United States, or of any particular State.

Section 4. Guarantees to the States

The United States shall guarantee to every State in this Union a Republican Form of Government, and shall protect each of them against Invasion; and on Application of the Legislature, or of the Executive (when the Legislature cannot be convened), against domestic Violence.

Article V Amending the Constitution

The Congress, whenever two thirds of both Houses shall deem it necessary, shall propose Amendments to this Constitution, or, on the Application of the Legislatures of two thirds of the several States, shall call a Convention for proposing Amendments, which, in either Case, shall be valid to all Intents and Purposes, as Part of this Constitution, when ratified by the Legislatures of three fourths of the several States, or by Conventions in three fourths thereof, as the one or the other Mode of Ratification may be proposed by the Congress; Provided that ~~no Amendment which may be made prior to the Year One thousand eight hundred and eight shall in any Manner affect the first and fourth Clauses in the Ninth Section of the first Article; and that no State, without its Consent, shall be deprived of its equal Suffrage in the Senate.~~

Article VI Supremacy of National Government

All Debts contracted and Engagements entered into, before the Adoption of this Constitution, shall be as valid against the United States under this Constitution, as under the Confederation.

This Constitution, and the Laws of the United States which shall be made in Pursuance thereof; and all Treaties made, or which shall be made, under the Authority of the United States, shall be the supreme Law of the Land; and the Judges in every State shall be bound thereby, any Thing in the Constitution or Laws of any State to the Contrary notwithstanding.

The Senators and Representatives before mentioned, and the Members of the several State Legislatures, and all executive and judicial Officers, both of the United States and of the several States, shall be bound by Oath or Affirmation, to support this Constitution; but no religious Test shall ever be required as a Qualification to any Office or public Trust under the United States.

National Supremacy

One of the biggest problems facing the delegates to the Constitutional Convention was the question of what would happen if a state law and a federal law conflicted. Which law would be followed? Who would decide? The second clause of Article VI answers those questions. When a federal law and a state law disagree, the federal law overrides the state law. The Constitution and other federal laws are the "supreme Law of the Land." This clause is often called the supremacy clause.

Article VII | Ratification

The Ratification of the Conventions of nine States, shall be sufficient for the Establishment of this Constitution between the States so ratifying the Same.

Done in Convention by the Unanimous Consent of the States present the Seventeenth Day of September in the Year of our Lord one thousand seven hundred and Eighty seven and of the Independence of the United States of America the Twelfth In witness whereof We have hereunto subscribed our Names,

George Washington—
President and deputy from Virginia

Delaware

George Read
Gunning Bedford Jr.
John Dickinson
Richard Bassett
Jacob Broom

Maryland

James McHenry
Daniel of
* St. Thomas Jenifer*
Daniel Carroll

Virginia

John Blair
James Madison Jr.

North Carolina

William Blount
Richard Dobbs Spaight
Hugh Williamson

South Carolina

John Rutledge
Charles Cotesworth
* Pinckney*
Charles Pinckney
Pierce Butler

Georgia

William Few
Abraham Baldwin

New Hampshire

John Langdon
Nicholas Gilman

Massachusetts

Nathaniel Gorham
Rufus King

Connecticut

William Samuel Johnson
Roger Sherman

New York

Alexander Hamilton

New Jersey

William Livingston
David Brearley
William Paterson
Jonathan Dayton

Pennsylvania

Benjamin Franklin
Thomas Mifflin
Robert Morris
George Clymer
Thomas FitzSimons
Jared Ingersoll
James Wilson
Gouverneur Morris

Attest:
William Jackson,
Secretary

Ratification

The Articles of Confederation called for all 13 states to approve any revision to the Articles. The Constitution required that 9 out of the 13 states would be needed to ratify the Constitution. The first state to ratify was Delaware, on December 7, 1787. Almost two-and-a-half years later, on May 29, 1790, Rhode Island became the last state to ratify the Constitution.

Bill of Rights

One of the conditions set by several states for ratifying the Constitution was the inclusion of a bill of rights. Many people feared that a stronger central government might take away basic rights of the people that had been guaranteed in state constitutions.

Vocabulary

[24] **quartered** housed

[25] **Warrants** written orders authorizing a person to make an arrest, a seizure, or a search

[26] **infamous** disgraceful

[27] **indictment** the act of charging with a crime

[28] **ascertained** found out

Rights of the Accused

The Fifth, Sixth, and Seventh Amendments describe the procedures that courts must follow when trying people accused of crimes.

Trials

The Sixth Amendment makes several guarantees, including a prompt trial and a trial by a jury chosen from the state and district in which the crime was committed.

Constitutional Amendments

Note: The first 10 amendments to the Constitution were ratified on December 15, 1791, and form what is known as the Bill of Rights.

Amendments 1–10. The Bill of Rights

Amendment I

Congress shall make no law respecting an establishment of religion, or prohibiting the free exercise thereof; or abridging the freedom of speech, or of the press; or the right of the people peaceably to assemble, and to petition the Government for a redress of grievances.

Amendment II

A well regulated Militia, being necessary to the security of a free State, the right of the people to keep and bear Arms, shall not be infringed.

Amendment III

No Soldier shall, in time of peace be **quartered**[24] in any house, without the consent of the Owner, nor in time of war, but in a manner to be prescribed by law.

Amendment IV

The right of the people to be secure in their persons, houses, papers, and effects, against unreasonable searches and seizures, shall not be violated, and no **Warrants**[25] shall issue, but upon probable cause, supported by Oath or affirmation, and particularly describing the place to be searched, and the persons or things to be seized.

Amendment V

No person shall be held to answer for a capital, or otherwise **infamous**[26] crime, unless on a presentment or **indictment**[27] of a Grand Jury, except in cases arising in the land or naval forces, or in the Militia, when in actual service in time of War or public danger; nor shall any person be subject for the same offence to be twice put in jeopardy of life or limb; nor shall be compelled in any criminal case to be a witness against himself, nor be deprived of life, liberty, or property, without due process of law; nor shall private property be taken for public use, without just compensation.

Amendment VI

In all criminal prosecutions, the accused shall enjoy the right to a speedy and public trial, by an impartial jury of the State and district wherein the crime shall have been committed, which district shall have been previously **ascertained**[28] by law, and to be informed of the nature and cause of the accusation; to be confronted with the witnesses against him; to have compulsory process for obtaining witnesses in his favor, and to have the Assistance of Counsel for his defence.

Amendment VII

In suits at common law, where the value in controversy shall exceed twenty dollars, the right of trial by jury shall be preserved, and no fact tried by a jury, shall be otherwise reexamined in any Court of the United States, than according to the rules of the common law.

Amendment VIII

Excessive bail shall not be required, nor excessive fines imposed, nor cruel and unusual punishments inflicted.

Amendment IX

The enumeration in the Constitution, of certain rights, shall not be construed to deny or disparage others retained by the people.

Amendment X

The powers not delegated to the United States by the Constitution, nor prohibited by it to the States, are reserved to the States respectively, or to the people.

Amendments 11–27

Amendment XI

Passed by Congress March 4, 1794. Ratified February 7, 1795.

The Judicial power of the United States shall not be **construed**[29] to extend to any suit in law or equity, commenced or prosecuted against one of the United States by Citizens of another State, or by Citizens or Subjects of any Foreign State.

Amendment XII

Passed by Congress December 9, 1803. Ratified June 15, 1804.

The Electors shall meet in their respective states and vote by ballot for President and Vice-President, one of whom, at least, shall not be an inhabitant of the same state with themselves; they shall name in their ballots the person voted for as President, and in distinct ballots the person voted for as Vice-President, and they shall make distinct lists of all persons voted for as President, and of all persons voted for as Vice-President, and of the number of votes for each, which lists they shall sign and certify, and transmit sealed to the seat of the government of the United States, directed to the President of the Senate;—the President of the Senate shall, in the presence of the Senate and House of Representatives, open all the certificates and the votes shall then be counted;—The person having the greatest number of votes for President, shall be the President, if such number be a majority of the whole number of Electors appointed; and if no person have such majority, then from the persons having the highest numbers not exceeding three on the list of those voted for as President, the House of Representatives shall choose immediately, by ballot, the President. But in choosing the

Vocabulary

[29] **construed** explained or interpreted

President and Vice President

The Twelfth Amendment changed the election procedure for president and vice president.

President, the votes shall be taken by states, the representation from each state having one vote; a quorum for this purpose shall consist of a member or members from two-thirds of the states, and a majority of all the states shall be necessary to a choice. ~~And if the House of Representatives shall not choose a President whenever the right of choice shall devolve upon them, before the fourth day of March next following, then the Vice-President shall act as President, as in case of the death or other constitutional disability of the President.~~—The person having the greatest number of votes as Vice-President, shall be the Vice-President, if such number be a majority of the whole number of Electors appointed, and if no person have a majority, then from the two highest numbers on the list, the Senate shall choose the Vice-President; a quorum for the purpose shall consist of two-thirds of the whole number of Senators, and a majority of the whole number shall be necessary to a choice. But no person constitutionally ineligible to the office of President shall be eligible to that of Vice-President of the United States.

Amendment XIII

Passed by Congress January 31, 1865. Ratified December 6, 1865.

1. Slavery Banned Neither slavery nor **involuntary servitude,**[30] except as a punishment for crime whereof the party shall have been duly convicted, shall exist within the United States, or any place subject to their jurisdiction.

2. Enforcement Congress shall have power to enforce this article by appropriate legislation.

Amendment XIV

Passed by Congress June 13, 1866. Ratified July 9, 1868.

1. Citizenship Defined All persons born or naturalized in the United States, and subject to the jurisdiction thereof, are citizens of the United States and of the State wherein they reside. No State shall make or enforce any law which shall abridge the privileges or immunities of citizens of the United States; nor shall any State deprive any person of life, liberty, or property, without due process of law; nor deny to any person within its jurisdiction the equal protection of the laws.

2. Voting Rights Representatives shall be apportioned among the several States according to their respective numbers, counting the whole number of persons in each State, ~~excluding Indians not taxed~~. But when the right to vote at any election for the choice of electors for President and Vice-President of the United States, Representatives in Congress, the Executive and Judicial officers of a State, or the members of the Legislature thereof, is denied to any of the ~~male~~ inhabitants of such State, ~~being twenty-one years of age~~, and citizens of the United States, or in any way abridged, except for participation in rebellion, or other crime, the basis of representation therein shall be reduced in the proportion which the number of such ~~male~~ citizens shall bear to the whole number of ~~male~~ citizens ~~twenty-one years of age~~ in such State.

Vocabulary

30 involuntary servitude being forced to work against one's will

Abolishing Slavery

Although some slaves had been freed during the Civil War, slavery was not abolished until the Thirteenth Amendment took effect.

Protecting the Rights of Citizens

In 1833 the Supreme Court ruled that the Bill of Rights limited the federal government but not the state governments. This ruling was interpreted to mean that states were able to keep African Americans from becoming state citizens and keep the Bill of Rights from protecting them. The Fourteenth Amendment defines citizenship and prevents states from interfering in the rights of citizens of the United States.

3. Rebels Banned from Government No person shall be a Senator or Representative in Congress, or elector of President and Vice-President, or hold any office, civil or military, under the United States, or under any State, who, having previously taken an oath, as a member of Congress, or as an officer of the United States, or as a member of any State legislature, or as an executive or judicial officer of any State, to support the Constitution of the United States, shall have engaged in insurrection or rebellion against the same, or given aid or comfort to the enemies thereof. But Congress may by a vote of two-thirds of each House, remove such disability.

4. Payment of Debts The validity of the public debt of the United States, authorized by law, including debts incurred for payment of pensions and bounties for services in suppressing insurrection or rebellion, shall not be questioned. But neither the United States nor any State shall assume or pay any debt or obligation incurred in aid of insurrection or rebellion against the United States, or any claim for the loss or emancipation of any slave; but all such debts, obligations and claims shall be held illegal and void.

5. Enforcement The Congress shall have the power to enforce, by appropriate legislation, the provisions of this article.

Amendment XV

Passed by Congress February 26, 1869. Ratified February 3, 1870.

1. Voting Rights The right of citizens of the United States to vote shall not be denied or abridged by the United States or by any State on account of race, color, or previous condition of servitude.

2. Enforcement The Congress shall have the power to enforce this article by appropriate legislation.

Amendment XVI

Passed by Congress July 2, 1909. Ratified February 3, 1913.

The Congress shall have power to lay and collect taxes on incomes, from whatever source derived, without apportionment among the several States, and without regard to any census or enumeration.

Amendment XVII

Passed by Congress May 13, 1912. Ratified April 8, 1913.

1. Senators Elected by Citizens The Senate of the United States shall be composed of two Senators from each State, elected by the people thereof, for six years; and each Senator shall have one vote. The electors in each State shall have the qualifications requisite for electors of the most numerous branch of the State legislatures.

2. Vacancies When vacancies happen in the representation of any State in the Senate, the executive authority of such State shall issue writs of election to fill such vacancies: *Provided*, That the legislature of any State may empower the executive thereof to make temporary appointments until the people fill the vacancies by election as the legislature may direct.

3. Future Elections ~~This amendment shall not be so construed as to affect the election or term of any Senator chosen before it becomes valid as part of the Constitution.~~

Amendment XVIII

Passed by Congress December 18, 1917. Ratified January 16, 1919. Repealed by Amendment XXI.

1. Liquor Banned ~~After one year from the ratification of this article the manufacture, sale, or transportation of intoxicating liquors within, the importation thereof into, or the exportation thereof from the United States and all territory subject to the jurisdiction thereof for beverage purposes is hereby prohibited.~~

2. Enforcement ~~The Congress and the several States shall have concurrent power to enforce this article by appropriate legislation.~~

3. Ratification ~~This article shall be inoperative unless it shall have been ratified as an amendment to the Constitution by the legislatures of the several States, as provided in the Constitution, within seven years from the date of the submission hereof to the States by the Congress.~~

Amendment XIX

Passed by Congress June 4, 1919. Ratified August 18, 1920.

1. Voting Rights The right of citizens of the United States to vote shall not be denied or abridged by the United States or by any State on account of sex.

2. Enforcement Congress shall have power to enforce this article by appropriate legislation.

Amendment XX

Passed by Congress March 2, 1932. Ratified January 23, 1933.

1. Presidential Terms The terms of the President and the Vice President shall end at noon on the 20th day of January, and the terms of Senators and Representatives at noon on the 3d day of January, of the years in which such terms would have ended if this article had not been ratified; and the terms of their successors shall then begin.

2. Meeting of Congress The Congress shall assemble at least once in every year, and such meeting shall begin at noon on the 3d day of January, unless they shall by law appoint a different day.

3. Succession of Vice President If, at the time fixed for the beginning of the term of the President, the President elect shall have died, the Vice President elect shall become President. If a President shall not have been chosen before the time fixed for the beginning of his term, or if the President elect

Prohibition

Although many people believed that the Eighteenth Amendment was good for the health and welfare of the American people, it was repealed 14 years later.

Women's Suffrage

Abigail Adams and others were disappointed that the Declaration of Independence and the Constitution did not specifically include women. It took many years and much campaigning before suffrage for women was finally achieved.

Taking Office

In the original Constitution, a newly elected president and Congress did not take office until March 4, which was four months after the November election. The officials who were leaving office were called lame ducks because they had little influence during those four months. The Twentieth Amendment changed the date that the new president and Congress take office. Members of Congress now take office during the first week of January, and the president takes office on January 20.

THE CONSTITUTION

shall have failed to qualify, then the Vice President elect shall act as President until a President shall have qualified; and the Congress may by law provide for the case wherein neither a President elect nor a Vice President shall have qualified, declaring who shall then act as President, or the manner in which one who is to act shall be selected, and such person shall act accordingly until a President or Vice President shall have qualified.

4. Succession by Vote of Congress The Congress may by law provide for the case of the death of any of the persons from whom the House of Representatives may choose a President whenever the right of choice shall have devolved upon them, and for the case of the death of any of the persons from whom the Senate may choose a Vice President whenever the right of choice shall have devolved upon them.

5. Ratification Sections 1 and 2 shall take effect on the 15th day of October following the ratification of this article.

6. Ratification This article shall be inoperative unless it shall have been ratified as an amendment to the Constitution by the legislatures of three-fourths of the several States within seven years from the date of its submission.

Amendment XXI

Passed by Congress February 20, 1933. Ratified December 5, 1933.

1. 18th Amendment Repealed The eighteenth article of amendment to the Constitution of the United States is hereby repealed.

2. Liquor Allowed by Law The transportation or importation into any State, Territory, or Possession of the United States for delivery or use therein of intoxicating liquors, in violation of the laws thereof, is hereby prohibited.

3. Ratification This article shall be inoperative unless it shall have been ratified as an amendment to the Constitution by conventions in the several States, as provided in the Constitution, within seven years from the date of the submission hereof to the States by the Congress.

Amendment XXII

Passed by Congress March 21, 1947. Ratified February 27, 1951.

1. Term Limits No person shall be elected to the office of the President more than twice, and no person who has held the office of President, or acted as President, for more than two years of a term to which some other person was elected President shall be elected to the office of President more than once. But this Article shall not apply to any person holding the office of President when this Article was proposed by Congress, and shall not prevent any person who may be holding the office of President, or acting as President, during the term within which this Article becomes operative from holding the office of President or acting as President during the remainder of such term.

2. Ratification ~~This article shall be inoperative unless it shall have been ratified as an amendment to the Constitution by the legislatures of three-fourths of the several States within seven years from the date of its submission to the States by the Congress.~~

Amendment XXIII

Passed by Congress June 16, 1960. Ratified March 29, 1961.

1. District of Columbia Represented The District constituting the seat of Government of the United States shall appoint in such manner as Congress may direct:

A number of electors of President and Vice President equal to the whole number of Senators and Representatives in Congress to which the District would be entitled if it were a State, but in no event more than the least populous State; they shall be in addition to those appointed by the States, but they shall be considered, for the purposes of the election of President and Vice President, to be electors appointed by a State; and they shall meet in the District and perform such duties as provided by the twelfth article of amendment.

2. Enforcement The Congress shall have power to enforce this article by appropriate legislation.

Amendment XXIV

Passed by Congress August 27, 1962. Ratified January 23, 1964.

1. Voting Rights The right of citizens of the United States to vote in any primary or other election for President or Vice President, for electors for President or Vice President, or for Senator or Representative in Congress, shall not be denied or abridged by the United States or any State by reason of failure to pay poll tax or other tax.

2. Enforcement The Congress shall have power to enforce this article by appropriate legislation.

Amendment XXV

Passed by Congress July 6, 1965. Ratified February 10, 1967.

1. Sucession of Vice President In case of the removal of the President from office or of his death or resignation, the Vice President shall become President.

2. Vacancy of Vice President Whenever there is a vacancy in the office of the Vice President, the President shall nominate a Vice President who shall take office upon confirmation by a majority vote of both Houses of Congress.

3. Written Declaration Whenever the President transmits to the President pro tempore of the Senate and the Speaker of the House of Representatives his written declaration that he is unable to discharge the powers and duties of his office, and until he transmits to them a written declara-

Voting Rights

Until the ratification of the Twenty-third Amendment, the people of Washington, D.C., could not vote in presidential elections.

Presidential Disability

The illness of President Eisenhower in the 1950s and the assassination of President Kennedy in 1963 were the events behind the Twenty-fifth Amendment. The Constitution did not provide a clear-cut method for a vice president to take over for a disabled president or upon the death of a president. This amendment provides for filling the office of the vice president if a vacancy occurs, and it provides a way for the vice president—or someone else in the line of succession—to take over if the president is unable to perform the duties of that office.

tion to the contrary, such powers and duties shall be discharged by the Vice President as Acting President.

4. Removing the President Whenever the Vice President and a majority of either the principal officers of the executive departments or of such other body as Congress may by law provide, transmit to the President pro tempore of the Senate and the Speaker of the House of Representatives their written declaration that the President is unable to discharge the powers and duties of his office, the Vice President shall immediately assume the powers and duties of the office as Acting President.

Thereafter, when the President transmits to the President pro tempore of the Senate and the Speaker of the House of Representatives his written declaration that no inability exists, he shall resume the powers and duties of his office unless the Vice President and a majority of either the principal officers of the executive department or of such other body as Congress may by law provide, transmit within four days to the President pro tempore of the Senate and the Speaker of the House of Representatives their written declaration that the President is unable to discharge the powers and duties of his office. Thereupon Congress shall decide the issue, assembling within forty-eight hours for that purpose if not in session. If the Congress, within twenty-one days after receipt of the latter written declaration, or, if Congress is not in session, within twenty-one days after Congress is required to assemble, determines by two-thirds vote of both Houses that the President is unable to discharge the powers and duties of his office, the Vice President shall continue to discharge the same as Acting President; otherwise, the President shall resume the powers and duties of his office.

Amendment XXVI

Passed by Congress March 23, 1971. Ratified July 1, 1971.

1. Voting Rights The right of citizens of the United States, who are eighteen years of age or older, to vote shall not be denied or abridged by the United States or by any State on account of age.

2. Enforcement The Congress shall have power to enforce this article by appropriate legislation.

Amendment XXVII

Originally proposed September 25, 1789. Ratified May 7, 1992.

No law, varying the compensation for the services of the Senators and Representatives, shall take effect, until an election of representatives shall have intervened.

Expanded Suffrage

The Voting Rights Act of 1970 tried to set the voting age at 18. However, the Supreme Court ruled that the act set the voting age for national elections only, not for state or local elections. The Twenty-sixth Amendment gave 18-year-old citizens the right to vote in all elections.

Historic Documents

Magna Carta

England's King John angered many people with high taxes. In 1215 a group of English nobles joined the archbishop of Canterbury to force the king to agree to sign Magna Carta. This document stated that the king was subject to the rule of law, just as other citizens of England were. It also presented the ideas of a fair and speedy trial and due process of law. These principles are still a part of the U.S. Bill of Rights.

1. In the first place have granted to God, and by this our present charter confirmed for us and our heirs for ever that the English church shall be free, and shall have its rights undiminished and its liberties unimpaired . . . We have also granted to all free men of our kingdom, for ourselves and our heirs for ever, all the liberties written below, to be had and held by them and their heirs of us and our heirs.

2. If any of our earls or barons or others holding of us in chief by knight service dies, and at his death his heir be of full age and owe relief he shall have his inheritance on payment of the old relief, namely the heir or heirs of an earl 100 for a whole earl's barony, the heir or heirs of a baron 100 for a whole barony, the heir or heirs of a knight 100s, at most, for a whole knight's fee; and he who owes less shall give less according to the ancient usage of fiefs.

3. If, however, the heir of any such be under age and a ward, he shall have his inheritance when he comes of age without paying relief and without making fine.

40. To no one will we sell, to no one will we refuse or delay right or justice.

41. All merchants shall be able to go out of and come into England safely and securely and stay and travel throughout England, as well by land as by water, for buying and selling by the ancient and right customs free from all evil tolls, except in time of war and if they are of the land that is at war with us . . .

42. It shall be lawful in future for anyone, without prejudicing the allegiance due to us, to leave our kingdom and return safely and securely by land and water, save, in the public interest, for a short period in time of war—except for those imprisoned or outlawed in accordance with the law of the kingdom and natives of a land that is at war with us and merchants (who shall be treated as aforesaid).

62. And we have fully remitted and pardoned to everyone all the ill–will, indignation and rancour that have arisen between us and our men, clergy and laity, from the time of the quarrel. Furthermore, we have fully remitted to all, clergy and laity, and as far as pertains to us have completely forgiven, all trespasses occasioned by the same quarrel between Easter in the sixteenth year of our reign and the restoration of peace. And, besides, we have caused to be made for them letters testimonial patent of the lord Stephen archbishop of Canterbury, of the lord Henry archbishop of Dublin and of the aforementioned bishops and of master Pandulf about this security and the aforementioned concessions.

63. An oath, moreover, has been taken, as well on our part as on the part of the barons, that all these things aforesaid shall be observed in good faith and without evil disposition. Witness the above–mentioned and many others. Given by our hand in the meadow which is called Runnymede between Windsor and Staines on the fifteenth day of June, in the seventeenth year of our reign.

From "English Bill of Rights." Britannica Online. Vers. 99.1. 1994–1999. Copyright © 1994–1999 Encyclopaedia Britannica, Inc.

The Mayflower Compact

In November 1620, the Pilgrim leaders aboard the Mayflower *drafted the Mayflower Compact. This was the first document in the English colonies to establish guidelines for self-government. This excerpt from the Mayflower Compact describes the principles of the Pilgrim colony's government.*

The Mayflower Compact

We whose names are underwritten, the loyal subjects of our dread Sovereign Lord King James, by the Grace of God of Great Britain, France and Ireland, King, Defender of the Faith, etc.

Having undertaken, for the Glory of God and advancement of the Christian Faith and Honour of our King and Country, a Voyage to plant the First Colony in the Northern Parts of Virginia, do by these presents solemnly and mutually in the presence of God and one of another, Covenant and Combine ourselves together into a Civil Body Politic, for our better ordering and preservation and furtherance of the ends aforesaid; and by virtue hereof to enact, constitute and frame such just and equal Laws, Ordinances, Acts, Constitutions and Offices, from time to time, as shall be thought most meet and convenient for the general good of the Colony, unto which we promise all due submission and obedience. In witness whereof we have hereunder subscribed our names at Cape Cod, the 11th of November, in the year of the reign of our Sovereign Lord King James, of England, France and Ireland the eighteenth, and of Scotland the fifty-fourth. Anno Domini 1620.

From William Bradford, *Of Plymouth Plantation,* 1620–1647 (Samuel Eliot Morison, ed., 1952), 75–76.

Fundamental Orders of Connecticut

In January 1639, settlers in Connecticut led by Thomas Hooker drew up the Fundamental Orders of Connecticut—America's first written constitution. It is essentially a compact among the settlers and a body of laws.

Forasmuch as it hath pleased the All-mighty God by the wise disposition of his divyne pruvidence so to Order and dispose of things that we the Inhabitants and Residents of Windsor, Harteford and Wethersfield are now cohabiting and dwelling in and uppon the River of Conectecotte and the Lands thereunto adioyneing; As also in our Civell Affaires to be guided and governed according to such Lawes, Rules, Orders and decrees as shall be made, ordered & decreed, as followeth:—

1. It is Ordered . . . that there shall be yerely two generall Assemblies or Courts, the one the second thursday in Aprill, the other the second thursday in September, following; the first shall be called the Courte of Election, wherein shall be yerely Chosen . . . soe many Magestrats and other publike Officers as shall be found requisitte: which choise shall be made by all that are admitted freemen and have taken the Oath of Fidelity, and doe cohabitte within this Jurisdiction, (having beene admitted Inhabitants by the major part of the Towne wherein they live,) or the major parte of such as shall be then present . . .

From F. N. Thorpe, ed., *Federal and State Constitutions,* vol. 1 (1909), 519.

The English Bill of Rights

In 1689, after the Glorious Revolution, Parliament passed the English Bill of Rights, which ensured that Parliament would have supreme power over the monarchy. The bill also protected the rights of English citizens.

Whereas the late King James the Second, by the assistance of divers evil counsellors, judges and ministers employed by him, did endeavour to subvert and extirpate the Protestant religion and the laws and liberties of this kingdom;

By assuming and exercising a power of dispensing with and suspending of laws and the execution of laws without consent of Parliament;

By committing and prosecuting divers worthy prelates for humbly petitioning to be excused from concurring to the said assumed power;

By issuing and causing to be executed a commission under the great seal for erecting a court called the Court of Commissioners for Ecclesiastical Causes;

By levying money for and to the use of the Crown by pretence of prerogative for other time and in other manner than the same was granted by Parliament;

By raising and keeping a standing army within this kingdom in time of peace without consent of Parliament, and quartering soldiers contrary to law; . . .

By violating the freedom of election of members to serve in Parliament;

By prosecutions in the Court of King's Bench for matters and causes cognizable only in Parliament, and by divers other arbitrary and illegal courses;

And whereas of late years partial corrupt and unqualified persons have been returned and served on juries in trials, and particularly divers jurors in trials for high treason which were not freeholders;

And excessive bail hath been required of persons committed in criminal cases to elude the benefit of the laws made for the liberty of the subjects;

And excessive fines have been imposed;

And illegal and cruel punishments inflicted;

And several grants and promises made of fines and forfeitures before any conviction or judgment against the persons upon whom the same were to be levied;

All which are utterly and directly contrary to the known laws and statutes and freedom of this realm; ...

That the pretended power of suspending of laws or the execution of laws by regal authority without consent of Parliament is illegal;

That the pretended power of dispensing with laws or the execution of laws by regal authority, as it hath been assumed and exercised of late, is illegal;

That the commission for erecting the late Court of Commissioners for Ecclesiastical Causes, and all other commissions and courts of like nature, are illegal and pernicious;

That levying money for or to the use of the Crown by pretence of prerogative, without grant of Parliament, for longer time, or in other manner than the same is or shall be granted, is illegal;

That it is the right of the subjects to petition the king, and all commitments and prosecutions for such petitioning are illegal;

That the raising or keeping a standing army within the kingdom in time of peace, unless it be with consent of Parliament, is against law;

That the subjects which are Protestants may have arms for their defence suitable to their conditions and as allowed by law;

That election of members of Parliament ought to be free;

That the freedom of speech and debates or proceedings in Parliament ought not to be impeached or questioned in any court or place out of Parliament;

(continued next page)

That excessive bail ought not to be required, nor excessive fines imposed, nor cruel and unusual punishments inflicted;

That jurors ought to be duly impanelled and returned, and jurors which pass upon men in trials for high treason ought to be freeholders;

That all grants and promises of fines and forfeitures of particular persons before conviction are illegal and void;

And that for redress of all grievances, and for the amending, strengthening and preserving of the laws, Parliaments ought to be held frequently.

From "English Bill of Rights." Britannica Online. Vers. 99.1. 1994–1999. Copyright © 1994–1999 Encyclopaedia Britannica, Inc.

Articles of Confederation

After winning the Revolutionary War in 1777, the newly formed United States of America created a government under the Articles of Confederation. This government allowed the states to have more power than the central government, a situation that would lead to problems later.

Articles of Confederation and perpetual Union between the states of New Hampshire, Massachusetts-bay Rhode Island and Providence Plantations, Connecticut, New York, New Jersey, Pennsylvania, Delaware, Maryland, Virginia, North Carolina, South Carolina and Georgia.

I.
The Stile of this Confederacy shall be
"The United States of America".

II.
Each state retains its sovereignty, freedom, and independence, and every power, jurisdiction, and right, which is not by this Confederation expressly delegated to the United States, in Congress assembled.

III.
The said States hereby severally enter into a firm league of friendship with each other, for their common defense, the security of their liberties, and their mutual and general welfare, binding themselves to assist each other, against all force offered to, or attacks made upon them, or any of them, on account of religion, sovereignty, trade, or any other pretense whatever.

VI.
No State, without the consent of the United States in Congress assembled, shall send any embassy to, or receive any embassy from, or enter into any conference, agreement, alliance or treaty with any King, Prince or State; nor shall any person holding any office of profit or trust under the United States, or any of them, accept any present, emolument, office or title of any kind whatever from any King, Prince or foreign State; nor shall the United States in Congress assembled, or any of them, grant any title of nobility.

VIII.
All charges of war, and all other expenses that shall be incurred for the common defense or general welfare, and allowed by the United States in Congress assembled, shall be defrayed out of a common treasury, which shall be supplied by the several States in proportion to the value of all land within each State, granted or surveyed for any person, as such land and the buildings and improvements thereon shall be estimated according to such mode as the United States in Congress assembled, shall from time to time direct and appoint.

The taxes for paying that proportion shall be laid and levied by the authority and direction of the legislatures of the several States within the time agreed upon by the United States in Congress assembled.

Federalist Paper No. 51

In 1788 the newly written Constitution faced opponents who believed it gave too much power to the federal government. James Madison, Alexander Hamilton, and John Jay wrote, anonymously, a collection of essays that became known as the Federalist Papers. *The following essay, written by James Madison, outlines reasons why the division of power written into the Constitution would keep the government from harming citizens.*

In order to lay a due foundation for that separate and distinct exercise of the different powers of government, which to a certain extent is admitted on all hands to be essential to the preservation of liberty, it is evident that each department should have a will of its own; and consequently should be so constituted that the members of each should have as little agency as possible in the appointment of the members of the others. Were this principle rigorously adhered to, it would require that all the appointments for the supreme executive, legislative, and judiciary magistracies should be drawn from the same fountain of authority, the people, through channels having no communication whatever with one another. Perhaps such a plan of constructing the several departments would be less difficult in practice than it may in contemplation appear. Some difficulties, however, and some additional expense would attend the execution of it. Some deviations, therefore, from the principle must be admitted. In the constitution of the judiciary department in particular, it might be inexpedient to insist rigorously on the principle: first, because peculiar qualifications being essential in the members, the primary consideration ought to be to select that mode of choice which best secures these qualifications; secondly, because the permanent tenure by which the appointments are held in that department, must soon destroy all sense of dependence on the authority conferring them.

Washington's Farewell Address

In 1796 at the end of his second term as president, George Washington wrote his farewell address with the help of Alexander Hamilton and James Madison. In it he spoke of the dangers facing the young nation. He warned against the dangers of political parties and sectionalism, and he advised the nation against permanent alliances with other nations.

In contemplating the causes, which may disturb our Union, it occurs as matter of serious concern, that any ground should have been furnished for characterizing parties by geographical discriminations-Northern and Southern-Atlantic and Western . . .

No alliances, however strict, between the parts can be an adequate substitute; they must inevitably experience the infractions and interruptions which all alliances in all times have experienced . . .

The great rule of conduct for us, in regard to foreign nations, is, in extending our commercial relations, to have with them as little political connexion as possible. So far as we have already formed engagements, let them be fulfilled with perfect good faith. Here let us stop.

From *Annals of Congress,* 4th Congress, pp. 2869–2880. American Memory. Library of Congress. 1999.

Monroe Doctrine

In 1823 President James Monroe proclaimed the Monroe Doctrine. Designed to end European influence in the Western Hemisphere, it became a cornerstone of U.S. foreign policy.

With the existing colonies or dependencies of any European power we have not interfered and shall not interfere. But with the governments who have declared their independence and maintained it, and whose independence we have, on great consideration and on just principles, acknowledged, we could not view any interposition for the purpose of oppressing them, or controlling in any other manner their destiny, by any European power in any other light than as the manifestation of an unfriendly disposition toward the United States. . . .

Our policy in regard to Europe, which was adopted at an early stage of the wars which have so long agitated that quarter of the globe, nevertheless remains the same, which is not to interfere in the internal concerns of any of its powers; to consider the government de facto as the legitimate government for us; to cultivate friendly relations with it, and to preserve those relations by a frank, firm, and manly policy, meeting in all instances the just claims of every power, submitting to injuries from none.

From "The Monroe Doctrine" by James Monroe. Reprinted in *The Annals of America: Volume 5, 1821–1832.* Copyright © 1976 by Encyclopaedia Britannica.

Seneca Falls Declaration of Sentiments

One of the first documents to express the desire for equal rights for women is the Declaration of Sentiments, issued in 1848 at the Seneca Falls Convention in Seneca Falls, New York. Led by Elizabeth Cady Stanton and Lucretia Mott, the delegates adopted a set of resolutions modeled on the Declaration of Independence.

When, in the course of human events, it becomes necessary for one portion of the family of man to assume among the people of the earth a position different from that which they have hitherto occupied, but one to which the laws of nature and of nature's God entitle them, a decent respect to the opinions of mankind requires that they should declare the causes that impel them to such a course.

We hold these truths to be self–evident: that all men and women are created equal; that they are endowed by their Creator with certain inalienable rights; that among these are life, liberty, and the pursuit of happiness; that to secure these rights governments are instituted, deriving their just powers from the consent of the governed. Whenever any form of government becomes destructive of these ends, it is the right of those who suffer from it to refuse allegiance to it, and to insist upon the institution of a new government, laying its foundation on such principles, and organizing its powers in such form, as to them shall seem most likely to effect their safety and happiness.

From "Seneca Falls Declaration on Women's Rights." Reprinted in *The Annals of America: Volume 7, 1841–1849.* Copyright © 1976 by Encyclopaedia Britannica.

The Emancipation Proclamation

When the Union army won the Battle of Antietam, President Abraham Lincoln decided to issue the Emancipation Proclamation, which freed all enslaved people in states under Confederate control. The proclamation, which went into effect on January 1, 1863, was a step toward the Thirteenth Amendment (1865), which ended slavery in all of the United States.

That on the 1st day of January, in the year of our Lord 1863, all persons held as slaves within any state or designated part of a state, the people whereof shall then be in rebellion against the United States, shall be then, thenceforward, and forever free; and the executive government of the United States, including the military and naval authority thereof, will recognize and maintain the freedom of such persons and will do no act or acts to repress such persons, or any of them, in any efforts they may make for their actual freedom. . . .

And I further declare and make known that such persons of suitable condition will be received into the armed service of the United States to garrison forts, positions, stations, and other places, and to man vessels of all sorts in said service.

And upon this act, sincerely believed to be an act of justice, warranted by the Constitution upon military necessity, I invoke the considerate judgment of mankind and the gracious favor of Almighty God.

From "Emancipation Proclamation" by Abraham Lincoln. Reprinted in *The Annals of America: Volume 9, 1858–1865.* Copyright © 1976 by Encyclopaedia Britannica, Inc.

Lincoln's Gettysburg Address

On November 19, 1863, Abraham Lincoln addressed a crowd gathered to dedicate a cemetery at the Gettysburg battlefield. His short speech, which is excerpted below, reminded Americans of the ideals on which the Republic was founded.

FOUR SCORE AND SEVEN YEARS ago our fathers brought forth on this continent a new nation, conceived in liberty and dedicated to the proposition that all men are created equal.

Now we are engaged in a great civil war, testing whether that nation or any nation so conceived and so dedicated can long endure. We are met on a great battlefield of that war. We have come to dedicate a portion of that field as a final resting–place for those who here gave their lives that that nation might live. It is altogether fitting and proper that we should do this.

But in a larger sense, we cannot dedicate—we cannot consecrate—we cannot hallow—this ground. The brave men, living and dead, who struggled here have consecrated it far above our poor power to add or detract. The world will little note nor long remember what we say here, but it can never forget what they did here. It is for us, the living, rather, to be dedicated here to the unfinished work which they who fought here have thus far so nobly advanced.

It is rather for us to be here dedicated to the great task remaining before us—that from these honored dead we take increased devotion to that cause for which they gave the last full measure of devotion; that we here highly resolve that these dead shall not have died in vain; that this nation, under God, shall have a new birth of freedom; and that government of the people, by the people, for the people shall not perish from the earth.

From "The Gettysburg Address" by Abraham Lincoln. Reprinted in *The Annals of America: Volume 9, 1858–1865.* Copyright © 1976 by Encyclopaedia Britannica, Inc.

"I Will Fight No More Forever"

In 1877 Chief Joseph and his group of Nez Percé surrendered to General Oliver Otis Howard. With this surrender, the Nez Percé were removed from their native lands in Idaho to a reservation in Oklahoma.

Tell General Howard I know his heart. What he told me before I have in my heart. I am tired of fighting. Our chiefs are killed. Looking Glass is dead. Toohoolhoolzote is dead. The old men are all killed. It is the young men who say yes or no. He who led the young men is dead. It is cold and we have no blankets. The little children are freezing to death. My people, some of them, have run away to the hills, and have no blankets, no food; no one knows where they are -- perhaps freezing to death. I want time to look for my children and see how many of them I can find. Maybe I shall find them among the dead. Hear me, my chiefs. I am tired; my heart is sick and sad. From where the sun now stands, I will fight no more forever.

Wilson's Fourteen Points

Even before the end of World War I, President Woodrow Wilson announced a 14-point plan to help maintain peace throughout Europe and the world. The goal of his plan was to provide "peace without victory."

Gentlemen of the Congress:

It will be our wish and purpose that the processes of peace, when they are begun, shall be absolutely open and that they shall involve and permit henceforth no secret understandings of any kind. The day of conquest and aggrandizement is gone by; so is also the day of secret covenants entered into in the interest of particular governments and likely at some unlooked-for moment to upset the peace of the world. It is this happy fact, now clear to the view of every public man whose thoughts do not still linger in an age that is dead and gone, which makes it possible for every nation whose purposes are consistent with justice and the peace of the world to avow now or at any other time the objects it has in view.

We entered this war because violations of right had occurred which touched us to the quick and made the life of our own people impossible unless they were corrected and the world secured once for all against their recurrence. What we demand in this war, therefore, is nothing peculiar to ourselves. It is that the world be made fit and safe to live in; and particularly that it be made safe for every peace-loving nation which, like our own, wishes to live its own life, determine its own institutions, be assured of justice and fair dealing by the other peoples of the world as against force and selfish aggression. All the peoples of the world are in effect partners in this interest, and for our own part we see very clearly that unless justice be done to others it will not be done to us. The program of the world's peace, therefore, is our program; and that program, the only possible program, as we see it, is this:

I. Open covenants of peace, openly arrived at, after which there shall be no private international understandings of any kind but diplomacy shall proceed always frankly and in the public view.

II. Absolute freedom of navigation upon the seas, outside territorial waters, alike in peace and in war, except as the seas may be closed in whole or in part by international action for the enforcement of international covenants.

III. The removal, so far as possible, of all economic barriers and the establishment of an equality of trade conditions among all the nations consenting to the peace and associating themselves for its maintenance.

(continued next page)

IV. Adequate guarantees given and taken that national armaments will be reduced to the lowest point consistent with domestic safety.

V. A free, open-minded, and absolutely impartial adjustment of all colonial claims, based upon a strict observance of the principle that in determining all such questions of sovereignty the interests of the populations concerned must have equal weight with the equitable claims of the government whose title is to be determined.

VI. The evacuation of all Russian territory and such a settlement of all questions affecting Russia as will secure the best and freest cooperation of the other nations of the world in obtaining for her an unhampered and unembarrassed opportunity for the independent determination of her own political development and national policy and assure her of a sincere welcome into the society of free nations under institutions of her won choosing; and, more than a welcome, assistance also of every kind that she may need and may herself desire. The treatment accorded Russia by her sister nations in the months to come will be the acid test of their good will, of their comprehension of her needs as distinguished from their own interests, and of their intelligent and unselfish sympathy.

VII. Belgium, the whole world will agree, must be evacuated and restored, without any attempt to limit the sovereignty which she enjoys in common with all other free nations. No other single act will serve as this will serve to restore confidence among the nations in the laws which they have themselves set and determined for the government of their relations with one another. Without this healing act the whole structure and validity of international law is forever impaired.

VIII. All French territory should be freed and the invaded portions restored, and the wrong done to France by Prussia in 1871 in the matter of Alsace-Lorraine, which has unsettled the peace of the world for nearly fifty years, should be righted, in order that peace may once more be made secure in the interest of all.

IX. A readjustment of the frontiers of Italy should be effected along clearly recognizable lines of nationality.

X. The peoples of Austria-Hungary, whose place among the nations we wish to see safeguarded and assured, should be accorded the freest opportunity of autonomous development.

XI. Rumania, Serbia and Montenegro should be evacuated; occupied territories restored; Serbia accorded free and secure access to the sea; and the relations of the several Balkan states to one another determined by friendly counsel along historically established lines of allegiance and nationality; and international guarantees of the political and economic independence and territorial integrity of the several Balkan states should be entered into.

XII. The Turkish portions of the present Ottoman Empire should be assured a secure sovereignty, but the other nationalities which are now under Turkish rule should be assured an undoubted security of life and an absolutely unmolested opportunity of autonomous development, and the Dardanelles should be permanently opened as a free passage to the ships and commerce of all nations under international guarantees.

XIII. An independent Polish state should be erected which should include the territories inhabited by indisputably Polish populations, which should be assured a free and secure access to the sea, and whose political and economic independence and territorial integrity should be guaranteed by international covenant.

XIV. A general association of nations must be formed under specific covenants for the purpose of affording mutual guarantees of political independence and territorial integrity to great and small states alike.

In regard to these essential rectifications of wrong and assertions of right we feel ourselves to be intimate partners of all the governments and peoples associated together against the Imperialists. We cannot be separated in interest or divided in purpose. We stand together until the end.

Brown v. Board of Education

In 1954 a collection of cases came before the Supreme Court under the name Brown v. Board of Education. *These cases challenged segregation in public schools based on the equal protection clause of the Fourteenth Amendment. Chief Justice Earl Warren wrote the majority opinion, which reversed the earlier decision in* Plessy v. Ferguson *that instituted the "separate but equal" doctrine."*

In the instant cases, that question is directly presented. Here, unlike Sweatt v. Painter, there are findings below that the Negro and white schools involved have been equalized, or are being equalized, with respect to buildings, curricula, qualifications and salaries of teachers, and other "tangible" factors. Our decision, therefore, cannot turn on merely a comparison of these tangible factors in the Negro and white schools involved in each of the cases. We must look instead to the effect of segregation itself on public education.

In approaching this problem, we cannot turn the clock back to 1868 when the Amendment was adopted, or even to 1896 when Plessy v. Ferguson was written. We must consider public education in the light of its full development and its present place in American life throughout the Nation. Only in this way can it be determined if segregation in public schools deprives these plaintiffs of the equal protection of the laws.

Today, education is perhaps the most important function of state and local governments. Compulsory school attendance laws and the great expenditures for education both demonstrate our recognition of the importance of education to our democratic society. It is required in the performance of our most basic public responsibilities, even service in the armed forces. It is the very foundation of good citizenship. Today it is a principal instrument in awakening the child to cultural values, in preparing him for later professional training, and in helping him to adjust normally to his environment. In these days, it is doubtful that any child may reasonably be expected to succeed in life if he is denied the opportunity of an education. Such an opportunity, where the state has undertaken to provide it, is a right which must be made available to all on equal terms.

We come then to the question presented: Does segregation of children in public schools solely on the basis of race, even though the physical facilities and other "tangible" factors may be equal, deprive the children of the minority group of equal educational opportunities? We believe that it does.

We conclude that in the field of public education the doctrine of "separate but equal" has no place. Separate educational facilities are inherently unequal. Therefore, we hold that the plaintiffs and others similarly situated for whom the actions have been brought are, by reason of the segregation complained of, deprived of the equal protection of the laws guaranteed by the Fourteenth Amendment.

John F. Kennedy's Inaugural Address

John F. Kennedy became president in 1961, during the middle of the Cold War. In his inaugural address, he spoke to citizens of the United States and the world, asking for peace to be restored for the good of humanity.

[W]e observe today not a victory of party, but a celebration of freedom—symbolizing an end, as well as a beginning—signifying renewal, as well as change. For I have sworn before you and Almighty God the same solemn oath our forebears prescribed nearly a century and three quarters ago.

The world is very different now. For man holds in his mortal hands the power to abolish all forms of human poverty and all forms of human life. And yet the same revolutionary beliefs for which our forebears fought are still at issue around the globe—the belief that the rights of man come not from the generosity of the state, but from the hand of God.

We dare not forget today that we are the heirs of that first revolution. Let the word go forth from this time and place, to friend and foe alike, that the torch has been passed to a new generation of Americans—born in this century, tempered by war, disciplined by a hard and bitter peace, proud of our ancient heritage—and unwilling to witness or permit the slow undoing of those human rights to which this Nation has always been committed, and to which we are committed today at home and around the world.

Let every nation know, whether it wishes us well or ill, that we shall pay any price, bear any burden, meet any hardship, support any friend, oppose any foe, in order to assure the survival and the success of liberty.

This much we pledge—and more.

So let us begin anew—remembering on both sides that civility is not a sign of weakness, and sincerity is always subject to proof. Let us never negotiate out of fear. But let us never fear to negotiate.

Let both sides explore what problems unite us instead of belaboring those problems which divide us.

Let both sides, for the first time, formulate serious and precise proposals for the inspection and control of arms—and bring the absolute power to destroy other nations under the absolute control of all nations.

Let both sides seek to invoke the wonders of science instead of its terrors. Together let us explore the stars, conquer the deserts, eradicate disease, tap the ocean depths, and encourage the arts and commerce.

Let both sides unite to heed in all corners of the earth the command of Isaiah—to "undo the heavy burdens ... and to let the oppressed go free."

And so, my fellow Americans: ask not what your country can do for you—ask what you can do for your country.

My fellow citizens of the world: ask not what America will do for you, but what together we can do for the freedom of man.

I Have a Dream

In 1963 civil rights leaders organized a march on Washington, D.C., that brought attention to the difference between the ideals of the United States and the reality faced by millions of African American citizens. Martin Luther King, Jr. gave the following speech in front of the more than 200,000 demonstrators at the Lincoln Memorial.

I say to you today, my friends, that in spite of the difficulties and frustrations of the moment, I still have a dream. It is a dream deeply rooted in the American dream.

I have a dream that one day this nation will rise up and live out the true meaning of its creed: "We hold these truths to be self-evident; that all men are created equal."

I have a dream that one day on the red hills of Georgia the sons of former slaves and the sons of former slaveowners will be able to sit down together at a table of brotherhood.

I have a dream that one day even the state of Mississippi, a desert state sweltering with the heat of injustice and oppression, will be transformed into an oasis of freedom and justice.

I have a dream that my four children will one day live in a nation where they will not be judged by the color of their skin but by the content of their character.

I have a dream today.

I have a dream that one day the state of Alabama, whose governor's lips are presently dripping with the words of interposition and nullification, will be transformed into a situation where little black boys and black girls will be able to join hands with little white boys and white girls and walk together as sisters and brothers.

I have a dream today.

I have a dream that one day every valley shall be exalted, every hill and mountain shall be made low, the rough places will be made plain, and the crooked places will be made straight, and the glory of the Lord shall be revealed, and all flesh shall see it together.

This is our hope. This is the faith with which I return to the South. With this faith we will be able to hew out of the mountain of despair a stone of hope. With this faith we will be able to transform the jangling discords of our nation into a beautiful symphony of brotherhood.

With this faith we will be able to work together, to pray together, to struggle together, to go to jail together, to stand up for freedom together, knowing that we will be free one day.

This will be the day when all of God's children will be able to sing with a new meaning, "My country, 'tis of thee, sweet land of liberty, of thee I sing. Land where my fathers died, land of the Pilgrim's pride, from every mountainside, let freedom ring."

Let freedom ring from every hill and every molehill of Mississippi. From every mountainside, let freedom ring.

When we let freedom ring, when we let it ring from every village and every hamlet, from every state and every city, we will be able to speed up that day when all of God's children, black men and white men, Jews and Gentiles, Protestants and Catholics, will be able to join hands and sing in the words of the old Negro spiritual, "Free at last! Free at last! Thank God Almighty, we are free at last!"

President Bush's Address to the Nation

On September 11, 2001, terrorists hijacked four passenger planes and used them to attack sites in the United States, including the World Trade Center in New York City. President George W. Bush addressed the country's citizens that evening.

Good evening. Today, our fellow citizens, our way of life, our very freedom came under attack in a series of deliberate and deadly terrorist acts. The victims were in airplanes, or in their offices; secretaries, businessmen and women, military and federal workers; moms and dads, friends and neighbors. Thousands of lives were suddenly ended by evil, despicable acts of terror.

The pictures of airplanes flying into buildings, fires burning, huge structures collapsing, have filled us with disbelief, terrible sadness, and a quiet, unyielding anger. These acts of mass murder were intended to frighten our nation into chaos and retreat. But they have failed; our country is strong.

A great people has been moved to defend a great nation. Terrorist attacks can shake the foundations of our biggest buildings, but they cannot touch the foundation of America. These acts shattered steel, but they cannot dent the steel of American resolve.

America was targeted for attack because we're the brightest beacon for freedom and opportunity in the world. And no one will keep that light from shining.

Today, our nation saw evil, the very worst of human nature. And we responded with the best of America—with the daring of our rescue workers, with the caring for strangers and neighbors who came to give blood and help in any way they could.

Immediately following the first attack, I implemented our government's emergency response plans. Our military is powerful, and it's prepared. Our emergency teams are working in New York City and Washington, D.C. to help with local rescue efforts.

Our first priority is to get help to those who have been injured, and to take every precaution to protect our citizens at home and around the world from further attacks.

The functions of our government continue without interruption. Federal agencies in Washington which had to be evacuated today are reopening for essential personnel tonight, and will be open for business tomorrow. Our financial institutions remain strong, and the American economy will be open for business, as well.

The search is underway for those who are behind these evil acts. I've directed the full resources of our intelligence and law enforcement communities to find those responsible and to bring them to justice. We will make no distinction between the terrorists who committed these acts and those who harbor them.

I appreciate so very much the members of Congress who have joined me in strongly condemning these attacks. And on behalf of the American people, I thank the many world leaders who have called to offer their condolences and assistance.

America and our friends and allies join with all those who want peace and security in the world, and we stand together to win the war against terrorism. Tonight, I ask for your prayers for all those who grieve, for the children whose worlds have been shattered, for all whose sense of safety and security has been threatened. And I pray they will be comforted by a power greater than any of us, spoken through the ages in Psalm 23: "Even though I walk through the valley of the shadow of death, I fear no evil, for You are with me."

This is a day when all Americans from every walk of life unite in our resolve for justice and peace. America has stood down enemies before, and we will do so this time. None of us will ever forget this day. Yet, we go forward to defend freedom and all that is good and just in our world.

Thank you. Good night, and God bless America.

Biographical Dictionary

A

Addams, Jane (1860–1935) American social worker and activist, she was the co–founder of Hull House, an organization that focused on the needs of immigrants. She helped found the American Civil Liberties Union and won the Nobel Peace Prize in 1931. (p. 648)

Aguinaldo (ahg-ee-NAHL-doh), Emilio (1869–1964) Filipino leader and commander of forces in rebellion against Spain, he led an insurrection against the authority of the United States. (p. 699)

Albright, Madeleine (1937–) First woman to serve as secretary of state, she was appointed by Bill Clinton and sworn into office in 1997. (p. 953)

Aldrin, Edwin "Buzz" (1930–) Copiloted the first lunar landing mission, he was the second man to walk on the moon. (p. 898)

Armstrong, Neil (1930–) Commander of the first lunar landing mission, he was also the first person to step on the surface of the moon. (p. 898)

B

Barton, Clara (1821–1912) Founder of the American Red Cross, she obtained and administered supplies and care to the Union soldiers during the American Civil War. (p. 534)

Bell, Alexander Graham (1847–1922) American inventor and educator, his interest in electrical and mechanical devices to aid the hearing–impaired led to the development and patent of the telephone. (p. 617)

Bethune, Mary McLeod (1875–1955) An African American educator and leader who rose to national prominence during the presidency of Franklin Roosevelt, who appointed her director of the National Youth Administration's Division of Negro Affairs. (p. 792)

Bidwell, Annie (1839–1918) American pioneer activist, she worked for social and moral causes and for women's suffrage. (p. 602)

bin Laden, Osama (1957–) A Saudi millionaire and leader of al–Qaeda, the terrorist organization that claimed responsibility for the September 11 attacks on the United States. (p. 956)

Bryan, William Jennings (1860–1925) American lawyer and Populist politician, he favored free silver coinage, an economic policy expected to help farmers. He was a Democratic nominee for president in 1896 and was defeated by William McKinley. (p. 604)

Bush, George H. W. (1924–) The 41st president of the United States, also served as vice president to Ronald Reagan. He led the nation through the Persian Gulf War. (p. 950)

Bush, George W. (1946–) The 43rd president of the United States and son of George H. W. Bush, he was president during the September 11, 2001 terrorist attacks. (p. 954)

C

Carnegie, Andrew (1835–1919) American industrialist and humanitarian, he focused his attention on steelmaking and made a fortune through his vertical integration method. (p. 620)

Carson, Rachel (1907–1964) Author of *Silent Spring* and one of the founders of the modern environmental conservation movement. (p. 933)

Carter, Jimmy (1924–) The 39th president of the United States, his presidency saw a dramatic energy crisis. (p. 934)

Castro, Fidel (1926–) Communist leader of Cuba, came to power through a revolution in 1959. (p. 895)

Chavez, Cesar (1927–1993)
Social activist and founder
of the United Farm Workers,
a leader in the movement
for Hispanic Americans'
civil rights. (p. 882)

Chisholm, Shirley (1924–2005) First African American woman to be elected to Congress, as a Representative from New York. (p. 883)

Churchill, Winston (1874–1965) The prime minister of Britain during much of World War II, he is well–remembered for many speeches made in support of the Allies. (p. 806)

Clinton, Bill (1946–) The 42nd president of the United States, he became the second president impeached by the House of Representatives but found not guilty of the charges. (p. 952)

Coolidge, Calvin (1872–1933) The 30th president of the United States, his presidency helped restore faith in government leaders after the scandals of the Harding administration. (p. 752)

Crazy Horse (1842?–1877) Native American chief of Oglala Sioux, he took part in the Battle of the Little Bighorn, in which General Custer was surrounded and killed. He was killed after surrendering and resisting imprisonment. (p. 595)

Custer, George Armstrong (1839–1876) American army officer in the Civil War, he became a Native American fighter in the West and was killed with his troops in the Battle of the Little Bighorn. (p. 596)

D

Davis, Benjamin O., Jr. (1912–2002) The first African American general in the United States Air Force, he led the Tuskegee Airmen through World War II. (p. 812)

Douglass, Frederick (1817–1895) American abolitionist and writer, he escaped slavery and became a leading African American spokesman and writer. He published his biography, *The Narrative of the Life of Frederick Douglass,* and founded the abolitionist newspaper, the *North Star.* (p. 530)

Du Bois, W. E. B. (1868–1963) African American educator, editor, and writer, he led the Niagara Movement, calling for economic and educational equality for African Americans. He helped found the National Association for the Advancement of Colored People (NAACP). (p. 678)

E

Edison, Thomas Alva (1847–1931) American inventor of over 1,000 patents, he invented the lightbulb and established a power plant that supplied electricity to parts of New York City. (p. 616)

Eisenhower, Dwight D. (1890–1969) The 34th president of the United States, he used his popularity as a war hero of World War II to become president, in which position he led the nation through the Korean War. (p. 816)

F

Farragut, David (1801–1870) American soldier, he was the first commissioned American admiral, and in the Civil War he captured New Orleans and maintained a blockade along the Gulf Coast against Confederate forces. (p. 524)

Ford, Gerald (1913–2006) The 38th president of the United States, he became president upon Richard Nixon's resignation. Ford later pardoned Nixon for his involvement in the Watergate scandal. (p. 930)

Ford, Henry (1863–1947) Founder of Ford Motor Company, he created the moving assembly line and is often credited with helping to create a middle class in American culture. (p. 617)

Francis Ferdinand (Archduke) (1863–1914) Heir apparent to the Austrian emperor, the assassination of him and his wife led to the beginning of World War I. (p. 721)

Friedan, Betty (1921–2006) Author of *The Feminine Mystique,* she pointed out women's dissatisfaction with traditional roles and became a leader of the women's rights movement of the 1960s and 1970s. (p. 883)

Garrison, William Lloyd (1805–1879) American journalist and reformer; he published the famous antislavery newspaper, the *Liberator,* and helped found the American Anti-Slavery Society, promoting immediate emancipation and racial equality. (p. 530)

Garvey, Marcus (1887–1940) African American leader of the black nationalism movement. (p. 763)

Marcus Garvey

Geronimo (1829–1909) Chiricahua Apache leader, he evaded capture for years and led an extraordinary opposition struggle against white settlements in the American Southwest until his eventual surrender. (p. 597)

Gompers, Samuel (1850–1924) American labor leader, he helped found the American Federation of Labor to campaign for workers' rights, such as the right to organize boycotts. (p. 625)

Gorbachev, Mikhail (1931–) Leader of the Soviet Union who introduced perestroika and oversaw the dismantling of the Communist government there. (p. 940)

Gore, Al (1948–) Vice president of the United States and Democratic presidential nominee in 2000. (p. 954)

Grant, Ulysses S. (1822–1885) Eighteenth president of the United States, he received a field promotion to lieutenant general in charge of all Union forces after leading a successful battle. He accepted General Lee's surrender of Confederate forces at Appomattox Courthouse, ending the Civil War. (p. 522)

Guthrie, Woody (1912–1967) Folksinger who expressed the desperation felt by millions of Americans during the Great Depression, especially those rural residents hit by the Dust Bowl. (p. 793)

Harding, Warren G. (1865–1923) The 29th president of the United States, his administration was full of scandals. He died during his presidency while in California. (p. 752)

Haywood, William "Big Bill" (1869–1928) One of the leaders of the International Workers of the World, a Socialist labor union active in the early 1900s. (p. 674)

Hearst, William Randolph (1863–1951) American journalist, he was famed for sensational news stories, known as yellow journalism, that stirred feelings of nationalism and formed public opinion for the Spanish–American War. (p. 645)

Hitler, Adolf (1889–1845) Leader of Nazi Germany during World War II, he rose to power on a platform of intolerance and nationalism. (p. 805)

Ho Chi Minh (1890–1969) Communist leader of North Vietnam during the Vietnam War, his government aided the Vietcong. (p. 898)

Hoover, Herbert (1874–1964) The 31st president of the United States, he was president during the stock market crashes that helped lead to the Great Depression. (p. 757)

Hughes, Langston (1902–1967) African American writer who achieved fame during the Harlem Renaissance for his poetry, which discussed the alienation of African Americans from white American society. (p. 768)

Hussein, Saddam (1937–2006) Socialist president of the Iraqi Republic until captured as a prisoner of war by U.S. forces in 2003. (p. 951)

Inouye, Daniel (1924–) Japanese American who served as Hawaii's first United States senator. He also served in the U.S. Army during World War II. (p. 809)

BIOGRAPHICAL DICTIONARY

Jackson, Thomas "Stonewall" (1824–1863) American Confederate general, he led the Shenandoah Valley campaign and fought with Lee in the Seven Days' Battles and the First and Second Battles of Bull Run. (p. 517)

Johnson, Andrew (1808–1875) American politician and the seventeenth president of the United States upon the assassination of Lincoln, he was impeached for his unpopular ideas about Reconstruction. He held onto the office by a one–vote margin. (p. 557)

Johnson, Lyndon (1908–1973) The 36th president of the United States, became president after the assassination of John Kennedy. Johnson led the nation through the civil rights movement, signing many antidiscrimination bills into law. (p. 879)

Joseph (1840–1904) Native American chief of the Nez Percé group, he became involved in a war with the U.S. Army when his people were removed to a reservation in Idaho. (p. 599)

Kelley, Florence (1859–1932) American reformer, she was active in the settlement house movement and led progressive reforms in labor conditions for women and children. (p. 648)

Kennedy, John F. (1917–1963) The 35th president of the United States, led the country through several cold war crises, but was assassinated in 1963. (p. 876)

Key, Francis Scott (1749–1843) American lawyer who was imprisoned on a British ship during the War of 1812. His poem written about the battle he witnessed has become the national anthem of the United States. (p. R31)

King, Martin Luther, Jr. (1929–1968) Civil rights leader who was committed to a nonviolent approach in bringing about the dramatic change of racial integration. He was assassinated in 1968. (p. 873)

Kissinger, Henry (1923–) Served as secretary of state under President Nixon and helped form the policy of realpolitik. (p. 910)

La Follette, Robert M. (1855–1925) Progressive American politician, he was active in local Wisconsin issues and challenged party bosses. As governor, he began the reform program called the Wisconsin Idea to make state government more professional. (p. 667)

Lee, Robert E. (1807–1870) American soldier, he refused Lincoln's offer to head the Union Army and agreed to lead Confederate forces. He successfully led several major battles until his defeat at Gettysburg, and he surrendered to the Union's commander General Grant at Appomattox Courthouse. (p. 518)

Liliuokalani (li-lee-uh-woh-kuh-LAHN-ee) (1838–1917) Queen of the Hawaiian Islands, she opposed annexation by the United States but lost power in a U.S.–supported revolt by planters that led to a new government. (p. 694)

Lin, Maya Ying (1959–) Chinese American sculptor and architect, designed the Vietnam Veterans' Memorial in Washington, D.C. (p. 912)

Lincoln, Abraham (1809–1865) Sixteenth president of the United States, he promoted equal rights for African Americans in the famed Lincoln–Douglas debates. He issued the Emancipation Proclamation and set in motion the Civil War, but he was determined to preserve the Union. He was assassinated in 1865. (p. 510)

Lodge, Henry Cabot (1850–1924) A U.S. senator from Massachusetts, he was opposed to President Wilson's plan for the League of Nations, fearing it would draw the United States into wars not in the nation's interest. (p. 738)

MacArthur, Douglas (1880–1964) A U.S. general who achieved fame for his actions in the Pacific during World War II and the Korean War. (p. 820)

Malcolm X (1925–1965) African American civil rights leader who advocated using violence if necessary to secure equal rights. Originally a leader of the Nation of Islam, when he broke with the organization, three of its members assassinated him. (p. 880)

Marshall, Thurgood (1908–1993) First African American U.S. Supreme Court Justice, he represented as a lawyer the National Association for the Advancement of Colored People and fought racial segregation. (p. 871)

McCain, John (1936–) American who served as Arizona's United States senator beginning in 1987. He also served in the U.S. Army during the Vietnam War. (p. 902)

McCarthy, Joseph (1908–1957) A U.S. senator from Wisconsin, he led investigations into the spread of communism in American society and within the government itself. He was eventually discredited when he could produce no evidence. (p. 855)

McClellan, George B. (1826–1885) American army general put in charge of Union troops and later removed by Lincoln for failure to press Lee's Confederate troops in Richmond. (p. 517)

Mussolini, Benito (1883–1945) Fascist leader of Italy during World War II. (p. 804)

Nimitz, Chester (1885–1966) Commander of the U.S. fleet in the Pacific during World War II, his strategy helped defeat Japan. (p. 821)

Nixon, Richard M. (1913–1994) The 37th president of the United States, he withdrew troops from Vietnam, ending the hugely unpopular war. He became the first president to resign, after the Watergate scandal affected his credibility. (p. 910)

O'Connor, Sandra Day (1930–) Associate justice of the U.S. Supreme Court, she was the first woman appointed to the Court. (p. 938)

O'Keeffe, Georgia (1887–1986) American artist whose works of flowers and cow skulls became famous. (p. 769)

Olmsted, Frederick Law (1822–1903) American landscape architect who promoted the idea of recreational parks across the nation and helped design Central Park in New York City. (p. 645)

Parks, Rosa (1913–2005) African American seamstress and civil rights activist who began the Montgomery bus boycott by refusing to give up her seat on a segregated city bus. (p. 872)

Paul, Alice (1885–1977) American social reformer, suffragist, and activist, she was the founder of the organization that became the National Woman's Party (NWP) that worked to obtain women's suffrage. (p. 677)

Perkins, Frances (1882–1962) Secretary of Labor under Franklin Roosevelt, she helped draft New Deal legislation and was the first female Cabinet member. (p. 785)

Pershing, John J. (1860–1948) American army commander, he commanded the expeditionary force sent into Mexico to find Pancho Villa. He was the major general and commander in chief of the American Expeditionary Forces in World War I. (p. 709)

Pickett, George (1825–1875) American general in the Confederate army, he was famed for Pickett's Charge, a failed but heroic effort at Cemetery Ridge in the Battle of Gettysburg, often considered a turning point of the Civil War. (p. 539)

Powderly, Terence V. (1849–1924) American labor leader for the Knights of Labor, he removed the secrecy originally surrounding the organization, leading to its becoming the first truly national American labor union. (p. 625)

Powell, Colin (1937–) Appointed the first African American secretary of state by George W. Bush in 2000, he resigned his position over the handling of the Iraq war. (p. 951)

Pulitzer, Joseph (1847–1911) American journalist and newspaper publisher, he established the Pulitzer Prize for public service and advancement of education. (p. 645)

R

Randolph, A. Philip (1889–1979) African American labor leader who proposed a March on Washington during Franklin Roosevelt's presidency. It was called off when Roosevelt barred discrimination in defense industries. (p. 812)

Reagan, Ronald (1911–2004) The 40th president of the United States, his presidency was the result of a rise in conservatism after the dramatic changes of the 1960s and 1970s. (p. 937)

Revels, Hiram (1822–1901) American clergyman, educator, and politician, he became the first African American in the U.S. Senate. (p. 565)

Riis, Jacob (1849–1914) Photographer and journalist who took shocking pictures of the lives of poverty–stricken immigrants, sweatshop workers, and tenement dwellers. These photos were published in *How the Other Half Lives*. (p. 646)

Rockefeller, John D. (1839 –1937) American industrialist and philanthropist, he made a fortune in the oil business and used vertical and horizontal integration to establish a monopoly on the steel business. (p. 620)

Roosevelt, Eleanor (1884–1962) Author, diplomat, humanitarian, and First Lady of Franklin D. Roosevelt, she supported much New Deal legislation aimed at young people and minorities. (p. 787)

Roosevelt, Franklin D. (1882–1945) The 32nd president of the United States, he led the country through the Great Depression and World War II. He served four terms, more than any other president. (p. 782)

Roosevelt, Theodore (1858–1919) Twenty–sixth president of the United States after William McKinley was assassinated, he organized the first volunteer cavalry regiment known as the Rough Riders who fought in Cuba during the Spanish–American War. As President, he acquired the Panama Canal Zone, and announced the Roosevelt Corollary, making the United States the defender of the Western Hemisphere. (p. 680)

Schafly, Phyllis (1924–) A leader of the conservative movement against the Equal Rights Amendment, she spoke out against the forces of feminism that emerged in the 1970s. (p. 883)

Scott, Winfield (1786–1866) American general, he served as commander in the Mexican War and used a two–part strategy against the South in the Civil War; he wanted to destroy the South's economy with a naval blockade and gain control of the Mississippi River. (p. 513)

Seward, William H. (1801–1872) Secretary of state under Abraham Lincoln, he also was responsible for the purchase of Alaska from Russia. (p. 693)

Sherman, William Tecumseh (1820–1891) American Union army officer, his famous March to the Sea captured Atlanta, Georgia, marking an important turning point in the war. (p. 541)

Sitting Bull (c.1831–1890) American Indian leader who became the head chief of the entire Sioux nation, he encouraged other Sioux leaders to resist government demands to buy lands on the Black Hills reservations. (p. 596)

Stalin, Joseph (1879–1953) Communist dictator of the Soviet Union, led that nation through World War II and greatly affected the postwar decisions made about Europe at the Yalta and Potsdam conferences. (p. 805)

Stanford, Leland (1824–1893) American railroad builder and politician, he established the California Central Pacific Railroad and founded Stanford University. (p. 621)

Steinbeck, John (1902–1968) Writer who captured the desperation of Americans struggling through the Great Depression, especially those affected by the Dust Bowl. (p. 793)

Taft, William Howard (1857–1930) Twenty–seventh president of the United States, he angered progressives by moving cautiously toward reforms and by supporting the Payne–Aldrich Tariff, which did not lower tariffs very much. He lost Roosevelt's support and was defeated for a second term. (p. 682)

Taylor, Frederick W. (1856–1915) American efficiency engineer, he introduced the manufacturing system known as scientific management that viewed workers as mechanical parts of the production process, not as human beings. (p. 624)

Truman, Harry S. (1884–1972) The 33rd president of the United States, he became president after the death of Franklin Roosevelt. Truman ended World War II after dropping atomic bombs on Japan. (p. 826)

Tweed, William Marcy (1823–1878) New York city politician known for his control of the corrupt political machine called the Tammany Ring. (p. 663)

Vallejo, Mariano Guadalupe (1808–1890) Californio leader who urged equal rights for Mexicans living in California after the state was captured in the Mexican-American War. (p. 357)

Villa, Francisco "Pancho" (1878–1923) Mexican bandit and revolutionary leader, he led revolts against Carranza and Huerta. He was pursued by the U.S. but evaded General Pershing. (p. 709)

Washington, Booker T. (1856–1915) African American educator and civil rights leader, he was born into slavery and later became head of the Tuskegee Institute for career training for African Americans. He was an advocate for conservative social change. (p. 677)

Wells, Ida B. (1862–1931) African American journalist and anti–lynching activist, she was part owner and editor of the Memphis Free Speech. (p. 677)

Westmoreland, William (1914–2005) Commander of all U.S. forces in Vietnam during the Vietnam War, he began the strategy of search–and–destroy missions. (p. 903)

Willard, Frances (1839–1898) American reformer who helped found the Women's Christian Temperance Union and was also active in the Women's suffrage movement. (p. 676)

Wilson, Woodrow (1856–1924) Twenty–eighth president of the United States, his reform legislation was given the name New Freedom, and it included three constitutional amendments: direct election of senators, prohibition, and women's suffrage. He created the Federal Reserve System, the Federal Trade Commission, and he enacted child labor laws. (p. 682)

Winnemucca, Sarah (1844–1891) Paiute Indian reformer, she was an activist for Indian rights and lectured specifically about the problems of the reservation system. (p. 598)

Wright, Orville (1871–1948) and **Wilbur** (1867–1912) American pioneers of aviation, they went from experiments with kites and gliders to piloting the first successful gas–powered airplane flight and later founded the American Wright Company to manufacture airplanes. (p. 618)

Z

Zedong, Mao (1893–1976) Communist leader of China, he defeated a nationalist army for control of China. (p. 852)

English and Spanish Glossary

MARK	AS IN	RESPELLING	EXAMPLE
a	alphabet	a	*AL-fuh-bet
ā	Asia	ay	AY-zhuh
ä	cart, top	ah	KAHRT, TAHP
e	let, ten	e	LET, TEN
ē	even, leaf	ee	EE-vuhn, LEEF
i	it, tip, British	i	IT, TIP, BRIT-ish
ī	site, buy, Ohio	y	SYT, BY, oh-HY-oh
	iris	eye	EYE-ris
k	card	k	KAHRD
ō	over, rainbow	oh	OH-vuhr, RAYN-boh
ù	book, wood	ooh	BOOHK, WOOHD
ò	all, orchid	aw	AWL, AWR-kid
òi	foil, coin	oy	FOYL, KOYN
aù	out	ow	OWT
ə	cup, butter	uh	KUHP, BUHT-uhr
ü	rule, food	oo	ROOL, FOOD
yü	few	yoo	FYOO
zh	vision	zh	VIZH-uhn

*A syllable printed in small capital letters receives heavier emphasis than the other syllable(s) in a word.

Phonetic Respelling and Pronunciation Guide

Many of the key terms in this textbook have been respelled to help you pronounce them. The letter combinations used in the respelling throughout the narrative are explained in the following phonetic respelling and pronunciation guide. The guide is adapted from *Merriam-Webster's Collegiate Dictionary, 11th Edition; Merriam-Webster's Geographical Dictionary;* and *Merriam-Webster's Biographical Dictionary.*

A

abolitionists people who worked for an end to slavery (p. 529)
abolicionistas personas que trabajaron para poner fin a la esclavitud (pág. 529)

affirmative action an active effort to improve the employment or educational opportunities of members of minority groups and women (p. 933)
acción afirmativa iniciativas para mejorar las oportunidades laborales o educativas de las minorías y de las mujeres (pág. 933)

AIDS Acquired Immunodeficincy Syndrome, a disease that affects the immune system, making patients vulnerable to infections (p. 961)
SIDA síndrome de inmunodeficiencia adquirida; enfermedad que afecta al sistema inmunológico y hace que los pacientes sean vulnerables a infecciones (pág. 961)

Allied Powers a group of nations that allied to fight the Central Powers in World War I, and those countries in opposition to the Axis Powers in World War II (pp. 721, 806)
fuerzas aliadas grupo de naciones que se aliaron para luchar contra las potencias centrales en la Primera Guerra Mundial y los países que se oponían a las fuerzas del Eje en la Segunda Guerra Mundial (págs. 721, 806)

al Qaeda the name of the terrorist organization headed by Osama bin Laden and responsible for the September 11, 2001, attacks (p. 956)
al Qaeda nombre de la organización terrorista encabezada por Osama bin Laden, responsable de los ataques del 11 de septiembre de 2001 (pág. 956)

American Expeditionary Force the U.S. military forces sent to Europe during World War I and led by General John J. Pershing (p. 730)
Fuerza Expedicionaria Estadounidense fuerzas armadas de Estados Unidos bajo el mando del general John J. Pershing que fueron enviadas a Europa en la Primera Guerra Mundial (pág. 730)

American Federation of Labor (AFL) an organization that united skilled workers into national unions for specific industries (p. 625)
Federación Americana del Trabajo organización que unió a obreros especializados en sindicatos nacionales para industrias específicas (pág. 625)

American Indian Movement (AIM) a civil rights group organized to promote the interests of Native Americans (p. 885)
Movimiento de los Indígenas Americanos (AIM) agrupación a favor de los derechos civiles que promueve los intereses de los indígenas norteamericanos (pág. 885)

ENGLISH AND SPANISH GLOSSARY

Anti-Imperialist League a group of citizens opposed to imperialism, and, specifically, to the peace treaty that gave the United States control of Cuba, Guam, Puerto Rico, and the Philippines (p. 700)
Liga Antiimperialista grupo de ciudadanos que se oponían al imperialismo y, más específicamente, al tratado de paz que daba a Estados Unidos el control de Cuba, Guam, Puerto Rico y Filipinas (pág. 700)

apartheid a system of segregation practiced in South Africa (p. 935)
apartheid sistema de segregación practicado en Sudáfrica (pág. 935)

appeasement the policy of giving into the demands of a nation in order to avoid war (p. 806)
contemporización política de ceder ante las exigencias de una nación para evitar la guerra (pág. 806)

Appomattox Courthouse the location where General Robert E. Lee was forced to surrender, thus ending the Civil War (p. 542)
Appomattox Courthouse poblado de Virginia donde el general Robert E. Lee fue obligado a rendirse, dando fin a la Guerra Civil (pág. 542)

armistice a truce or cease-fire agreement between warring nations (p. 734)
armisticio tregua o acuerdo de cese del fuego entre dos naciones en guerra (pág. 734)

arms race a growth in weapons based on the number of weapons an enemy country has (p. 856)
carrera armamentística aumento de armamentos según la cantidad de armas que tiene un país enemigo (pág. 856)

atomic bomb a weapon that receives its explosive power from the splitting of atoms (p. 828)
bomba atómica arma cuyo poder exploivo es generado por la división de átomos (pág. 828)

Axis Powers the coalition of nations in World War II that included Germany, Italy, and Japan (p. 806)
fuerzas del Eje coalición de naciones de la Segunda Guerra Mundial formada por Alemania, Italia y Japón (pág. 806)

B

baby boom a sharp increase in the number of American births during the 1950s and 1960s (p. 858)
boom de la natalidad gran aumento en la cantidad de nacimientos en Estados Unidos durante las décadas de 1950 y 1960 (pág. 858)

Bataan Death March a forced march of American and Filipino soldiers captured by the Japanese along the Bataan Penninsula (p. 820)

marcha de la muerte de Bataán marcha forzada en la península de Bataán de soldados estadounidenses y filipinos capturados por los japoneses (pág. 820)

Battle of Antietam (1862) a Union victory in the Civil War that marked the bloodiest single-day battle in U.S. military history (p. 519)
batalla de Antietam (1862) victoria del ejército de la Unión durante la Guerra Civil en la batalla de un solo día más sangrienta de la historia militar de Estados Unidos (pág. 519)

Battle of El Alamein (1942) a turning point in World War II, in which Allied forces defeated the Afrika Korps of Germany (p. 816)
batalla del El-Alamein (1942) momento decisivo en la Segunda Guerra Mundial, en el que las fuerzas aliadas derrotaron al *Afrika Korps* de Alemania (pág. 816)

Battle of Gettysburg (1863) a Union Civil War victory that turned the tide against the Confederates at Gettysburg, Pennsylvania (p. 537)
batalla de Gettysburg (1863) victoria del ejército de la Unión durante la Guerra Civil que cambió el curso de la guerra en contra de los confederados en Gettysburg, Pensilvania (pág. 537)

Battle of Leyte Gulf (1944) the largest naval battle in history, during which the American fleet destroyed most of the Japanese fleet (p. 822)
batalla del golfo de Leyte (1944) la mayor batalla naval de la historia, durante la cual la flota estadounidense destruyó la mayor parte de la flota japonesa (pág. 822)

Battle of Midway (1942) battle of World War II that ended the Japanese advance in the Pacific (p. 821)
batalla de Midway (1942) batalla de la Segunda Guerra Mundial que puso fin al avance de los japoneses en el Pacífico (pág. 821)

Battle of Shiloh (1862) a Civil War battle in Tennessee in which the Union army gained greater control over the Mississippi River valley (p. 523)
batalla de Shiloh (1862) batalla de la Guerra Civil en Tennessee en la que el ejército de la Unión adquirió mayor control sobre el valle del río Mississippi (pág. 523)

Battle of Stalingrad (1942–1943) a major turning point in World War II; Soviet forces defeated Nazi forces after which the Nazis never recovered (p. 817)
batalla de Stalingrado (1942–1943) momento decisivo de la Segunda Guerra Mundial; las fuerzas soviéticas vencieron a las fuerzas nazis, que nunca más se recuperaron (pág. 817)

Battle of the Bulge (1944–1945) the last German advance of World War II, which was stopped by Allied forces (p. 826)
batalla del Bulge (1944–1945) último avance alemán de la Segunda Guerra Mundial, que fue detenido por las fuerzas aliadas (pág. 826)

Battle of the Coral Sea (1942) the first strategic defeat of the Japanese Imperial Navy by American forces during World War II (p. 821)
batalla del mar del Coral (1942) primera derrota estratégica de la armada imperial japonesa ante las fuerzas estadounidenses en la Segunda Guerra Mundial (pág. 821)

Battle of the Little Big Horn (1876) "Custer's Last Stand"; battle between U.S. soldiers, led by George Armstrong Custer, and Sioux warriors, led by Crazy Horse and Sitting Bull, that resulted in the worst defeat for the U.S. Army in the West (p. 596)
batalla de Little Big Horn (1876) última batalla del general Custer; esta batalla entre las tropas de George Armstrong Custer y los guerreros siux al mando de Caballo Loco y Toro Sentado produjo la mayor derrota del ejército estadounidense en el Oeste (pág. 596)

beats young people, many of whom were writers and artists, who discussed their dissatisfaction with the American society of the 1950s (p. 861)
beatniks jóvenes, en su mayoría escritores y artistas, que debatían acerca de su descontento con la sociedad estadounidense de la década de 1950 (pág. 861)

benevolent society an aid organization formed by immigrant communities (p. 639)
sociedad de beneficencia organización de ayuda formada por comunidades de inmigrantes (pág. 639)

Berlin Wall a barrier of concrete and barbed wire between Communist East Berlin and West Berlin (p. 896)
Muro de Berlín barrera de concreto y alambre de púas que separaba la Berlín oriental comunista de la Berlín occidental (pág. 896)

Bessemer process a process developed in the 1850s that led to faster, cheaper steel production (p. 615)
proceso de Bessemer proceso de producción de acero más económico y rápido, desarrollado en la década de 1850 (pág. 615)

Black Codes laws passed in the southern states during Reconstruction that greatly limited the freedom and rights of African Americans (p. 558)
códigos de negros decretos aprobados en los estados sureños en la época de la Reconstrucción que limitaron en gran medida la libertad y los derechos de los afroamericanos (pág. 558)

Black Power a social movement that called for African American power and independence (p. 880)
Black Power movimiento social que exigía el poder y la independencia de los afroamericanos (pág. 880)

Black Tuesday October 29, 1929, one of the largest U.S. stock market drops (p. 779)
martes negro 29 de octubre de 1929, una de las mayores caídas de la bolsa de valores de Estados Unidos (pág. 779)

Bonus Army a group of World War I veterans that demanded their bonus payments early (p. 781)
Bonus Army grupo de veteranos de la Primera Guerra Mundial que exigía el pago de sus bonos por adelantado (pág. 781)

boomtown a Western community that grew quickly because of the mining boom and often disappeared when the boom ended (p. 588)
pueblo de rápido crecimiento comunidad del Oeste que se desarrolló con gran rapidez debido a la fiebre del oro, pero que desapareció cuando la fiebre terminó (pág. 588)

border states Delaware, Kentucky, Maryland, and Missouri; slave states that lay between the North and the South and did not join the Confederacy during the Civil War (p. 512)
estados fronterizos Delaware, Kentucky, Maryland y Missouri; estados esclavistas ubicados entre el Norte y el Sur y que no se unieron a la Confederación durante la Guerra Civil (pág. 512)

Boxer Rebellion (1900) a siege of a foreign settlement in Beijing by Chinese nationalists who were angry at foreign involvement in China (p. 695)
rebelión de los boxers (1900) asedio a un asentamiento extranjero en Beijing por parte de un grupo de nacionalistas chinos que estaban enojados por la participación extranjera en China (pág. 695)

brinkmanship the Cold War foreign policy designed to "get to the verge without getting into the war" (p. 856)
política arriesgada política exterior durante la Guerra Fría diseñada para "llegar al borde de la guerra sin llegar a la guerra" (pág. 856)

Brown v. Board of Education (1954) Supreme Court decision that ended segregation in public schools (p. 871)
Brown contra la Junta Educativa (1954) decisión de la Corte Suprema que puso fin a la segregación en las escuelas públicas (pág. 871)

buffalo soldiers African American soldiers who served in the cavalry during the wars for the west (p. 596)
soldados búfalo soldados afroamericanos que sirvieron en la caballería durante las guerras del oeste (pág. 596)

business cycle the rhythym in which an economy expands and contracts its production (p. 780)
ciclo económico ritmo al que la producción de una economía se expande y se contrae (pág. 780)

buying on margin the process of purchasing stock with credit, hoping to sell at a high enough price to pay the loan and make a profit (p. 778)
compra a crédito proceso de comprar acciones con préstamos, con la esperanza de venderlas a un precio suficientemente alto para pagar el préstamo y obtener una ganancia (pág. 778)

Camp David Accords (1978) an agreement between the heads of Israel and Egypt that began a process for peace in the Middle East (p. 935)
   Acuerdos de Camp David (1978) acuerdo entre los líderes de Israel y Egipto que dio inicio a un proceso de paz en el Medio Oriente (pág. 935)

capitalism an economic system in which private businesses run most industries (p. 674)
   capitalismo sistema económico en el que las empresas privadas controlan la mayoría de las industrias (pág. 674)

cattle drive a long journey on which cowboys herded cattle to northern markets or better grazing lands (p. 589)
   arreo de ganado viaje largo en el que los vaqueros arreaban ganado para llevarlo a los mercados del Norte o a mejores pastos (pág. 589)

Cattle Kingdom an area of the Great Plains on which many ranchers raised cattle in the late 1800s (p. 589)
   Reino del Ganado área de las Grandes Planicies en la que muchos rancheros criaban ganado a finales de siglo XIX (pág. 589)

Central Powers the coalition of nations in World War I that included the German, Austrio-Hungary, and Ottoman empires (p. 721)
   Potencias Centrales coalición de naciones de la Primera Guerra Mundial formada por los imperios alemán, austrohúngaro y otomano (pág. 721)

Chinese Exclusion Act (1882) a law passed by Congress that banned Chinese from immigrating to the United States for 10 years (p. 641)
   Ley de Exclusión de Chinos (1882) ley aprobada por el Congreso que prohibió la inmigración de chinos a Estados Unidos por 10 años (pág. 641)

Chisholm Trail a trail that ran from San Antonio, Texas, to Abilene, Kansas, established by Jesse Chisholm in the late 1860s for cattle drives (p. 589)
   Camino de Chisholm camino creado por Jesse Chisholm a finales de la década de 1860 que iba desde San Antonio, Texas hasta Abilene, Kansas, para arreos de ganado (pág. 589)

Civil Rights Act of 1866 a law that gave African Americans legal rights equal to those of white Americans (p. 560)
   Ley de Derechos Civiles de 1866 ley que dio a los afroamericanos los mismos derechos legales que tenían los estadounidenses blancos (pág. 560)

Civil Rights Act of 1964 a law that ended discrimination based on race or gender (p. 879)
   Ley de Derechos Civiles de 1964 ley que puso fin a la discriminación en base a la raza o al sexo (pág. 879)

Cold War a period of hostility between Western powers and Communist powers (p. 846)
   Guerra Fría período de hostilidades entre las potencias de Occidente y las potencias comunistas (pág. 846)

collective bargaining a technique used by labor unions in which workers act collectively to change working conditions or wages (p. 626)
   negociación colectiva método empleado por los sindicatos en el que los trabajadores actúan colectivamente para cambiar las condiciones laborales o los salarios (pág. 626)

Communists people who believe in communism, or the political system in which all resources are shared equally (p. 731)
   comunistas personas que creen en el comunismo, es decir, el sistema político en el que los recursos se distribuyen a todos por igual (pág. 731)

Compromise of 1877 an agreement to settle the disputed presidential election of 1876; Democrats agreed to accept Republican Rutherford B. Hayes as president in return for the removal of federal troops from the South (p. 567)
   Compromiso de 1877 acuerdo en el que se resolvieron las disputadas elecciones presidenciales de 1876; los demócratas aceptaron al republicano Rutherford B. Hayes como presidente a cambio del retiro de las tropas federales del Sur (pág. 567)

Comstock Lode Nevada gold and silver mine discovered by Henry Comstock in 1859 (p. 587)
   veta de Comstock mina de oro y plata descubierto en Nevada por Henry Comstock en 1859 (pág. 587)

Congress of Industrial Organizations (CIO) a union that organized workers according to industry, not by skill (p. 788)
   Congreso de las organizaciones industriales (CIO) una unión que ordenó a trabajadores según industria, no por la habilidad (pag. 788)

conservation the planned management of natural resources to prevent their destruction (p. 681)
   conservación administración planificada de los recursos naturales para evitar su destrucción (pág. 681)

containment a foreign policy that attempts to stop the spread of communism without ending it in the countries in which it already exists (p. 847)
   contención política exterior que intenta detener el avance del comunismo sin eliminarlo en los países en los que ya existe (pág. 847)

contraband an escaped slave who joined the Union army during the Civil War (p. 531)
   contrabando esclavo que escapó y se unió al ejército de la Unión durante la Guerra Civil (pág. 531)

ENGLISH AND SPANISH GLOSSARY

Copperheads a group of northern Democrats who opposed abolition and sympathized with the South during the Civil War (p. 532)
copperheads grupo de demócratas del Norte que se oponían a la abolición de la esclavitud y simpatizaban con las creencias sureñas durante la Guerra Civil (pág. 532)

corporation a business that sells portions of ownership called stock shares (p. 619)
corporación compañía que vende algunas partes en forma de acciones (pág. 619)

cotton diplomacy Confederate efforts to use the importance of southern cotton to Britain's textile industry to persuade the British to support the Confederacy in the Civil War (p. 513)
diplomacia del algodón esfuerzos de la Confederación por aprovechar la importancia del algodón del Sur en la industria textil británica para convencer a Gran Bretaña de apoyar a la Confederación en la Guerra Civil (pág. 513)

Cuban missile crisis a threat to national security that occurred when the Soviet Union placed nuclear missiles in Cuba (p. 896)
crisis de los misiles cubanos amenaza a la seguridad nacional que ocurrió cuando la Unión Soviética colocó misiles nucleares en Cuba (pág. 896)

D

Dawes General Allotment Act (1887) legislation passed by Congress that split up Indian reservation lands among individual Indians and promised them citizenship (p. 598)
Ley de Adjudicación General de Dawes (1887) ley aprobada por el Congreso que dividía el terreno de las reservas indígenas entre sus habitantes y les prometía la ciudadanía (pág. 598)

D-Day (1944) an invasion of Nazi-occupied France by Allied forces (p. 819)
día D (1944) invasión de las fuerzas aliadas en Francia, ocupada por los nazis (pág. 819)

deficit the amount by which a government's spending exceeds its revenue (p. 938)
déficit cantidad en la que los gastos del gobierno superan sus ingresos (pág. 938)

deflation a decrease in money supply and overall lower prices (p. 604)
deflación reducción de la disponibilidad del dinero y baja general en los precios (pág. 604)

department store giant retail shop (p. 645)
tiendas por departamentos grandes comercios de venta al público (pág. 645)

détente a period of closer diplomatic relations between the United States and the Communist powers of China and the Soviet Union (p. 928)
distensión período de relaciones diplomáticas más estrechas entre Estados Unidos y las potencias comunistas de China y la Unión Soviética (pág. 928)

Disabled in Action (DIA) a group organized to promote the interests of people with disabilities (p. 885)
Discapacitados en Acción (DIA) grupo organizado para promover los intereses de personas con discapacidades (pág. 885)

domino theory the idea that Communism would spread rapidly throughout Southeast Asia (p. 898)
teoría del dominó idea de que el comunismo se extendería rápidamente por el sureste de Asia (pág. 898)

doves opponents of the Vietnam War (p. 904)
palomas opositores a la guerra de Vietnam (pág. 904)

dry farming a method of farming used by Plains farmers in the 1890s that shifted focus from water-dependent crops to more hardy crops (p. 601)
agricultura sin irrigación método de cultivo que usaban los agricultores de las Planicies en la década de 1890 que provocó un cambio de los cultivos que dependían del agua a otros más resistentes (pág. 601)

Dust Bowl an area of the United States that suffered a severe drought during the 1930s (p. 790)
Dust Bowl área de Estados Unidos que sufrió una grave sequía en la década de 1930 (pág. 790)

E

Eighteenth Amendment (1919) a constitutional amendment that outlawed the production and sale of alcoholic beverages in the United States; repealed in 1933 (p. 676)
Decimoctava Enmienda (1919) enmienda constitucional que prohibió la producción y venta de bebidas alcohólicas en Estados Unidos; revocada en 1933 (pág. 676)

emancipation freeing of the slaves (p. 529)
emancipación liberación de los esclavos (pág. 529)

Emancipation Proclamation (1862) an order issued by President Abraham Lincoln freeing the slaves in areas rebelling against the Union; took effect January 1, 1863 (p. 529)

Proclamación de Emancipación (1862) orden emitida por el presidente Abraham Lincoln para liberar a los esclavos en las áreas que se rebelaban contra la Unión; entró en vigor el primero de enero de 1863 (pág. 529)

Equal Rights Amendment (ERA) a proposed amendment to the Constitution that would provide equal rights to women (p. 883)
Enmienda por la Igualdad de Derechos (ERA) enmienda constitucional propuesta que otorgaría la igualdad de derechos a la mujer (pág. 833)

escalation increased involvment in the Vietnam War (p. 902)
escalada mayor participación en la guerra de Vietnam (pág. 902)

Exodusters African Americans who settled western lands in the late 1800s (p. 601)
Exodusters afroamericanos que se establecieron en el Oeste a fi nales del siglo XIX (pág. 601)

expatriates citizens who leave their country to live elsewhere (p. 768)
expatriados ciudadanos que abandonan su país para vivir en otro lugar (pág. 768)

fascism a political system in which the state or government is seen as more important than the individual (p. 804)
fascismo sistema político en el que se considera que el estado o gobierno es más importante que las personas (pág. 804)

Fair Deal President Truman's legislative plan for the nation that included antilynching laws (p. 850)
Fair Deal plan legislativo para la nación propuesto por el presidente Truman que incluía leyes en contra de los linchamientos (pág. 850)

Fifteenth Amendment (1870) a constitutional amendment that gave African American men the right to vote (p. 563)
Decimoquinta Enmienda (1870) enmienda constitucional que daba a los hombres afroamericanos el derecho al voto (pág. 563)

54th Massachusetts Infantry African American Civil War regiment that attacked Fort Wagner in South Carolina (p. 531)
54to Batallón de Infantería de Massachusetts regimiento afroamericano de la Guerra Civil que atacó el fuerte Wagner en Carolina del Sur (pág. 531)

fireside chats radio programs in which Franklin Roosevelt explained his plan for recovery from the Great Depression (p. 785)
charlas junto a la chimenea programas de radio en los cuales Franklin Roosevelt explicaba su plan para que el país se recuperara de la Gran Depresión (pág. 785)

First Battle of Bull Run (1861) the first major battle of the Civil War, resulting in a Confederate victory; showed that the Civil War would not be won easily (p. 517)
primera batalla de Bull Run (1861) primera batalla importante de la Guerra Civil, en la cual ganó el ejército confederado; demostró que la guerra no se ganaría fácilmente (pág. 517)

flappers young women who challenged traditional ideas of womanhood in the 1920s (p. 759)
chicas a la moda mujeres jóvenes que desafiaron las ideas tradicionales sobre la condición de la mujer en la década de 1920 (pág. 759)

Fort Sumter a federal outpost in Charleston, South Carolina, that was attacked by the Confederates in April 1861, sparking the Civil War (p. 511)
fuerte Sumter puesto de avanzada federal en Charleston, Carolina del Sur, cuyo ataque por parte de los confederados en abril de 1861 dio origen a la Guerra Civil (pág. 511)

Fourteenth Amendment (1866) a constitutional amendment giving full rights of citizenship to all people born or naturalized in the United States, except for American Indians (p. 561)
Decimocuarta Enmienda (1866) enmienda constitucional que otorgaba derechos totales de ciudadanía a todas las personas nacidas en Estados Unidos o naturalizadas estadounidenses, con excepción de los indígenas americanos (pág. 561)

Freedmen's Bureau an agency established by Congress in 1865 to help poor people throughout the South (p. 556)
Oficina de Esclavos Libertos oficina creada por el Congreso en 1865 para ayudar a los pobres del Sur del país (pág. 556)

Freedom Rides a series of integrated bus rides through the South (p. 877)
Viajes de la Libertad serie de viajes en autobús por el Sur en los que se integraban las razas (pág. 877)

frontier an undeveloped area (p. 586)
frontera área que no está siendo utilizada por el ser humano (pág. 586)

fundamentalism a religious belief characterized by a literal interpretation of the Bible (p. 762)
fundamentalismo creencia religiosa caracterizada por una interpretación literal de la Biblia (pág. 762)

genocide the complete destruction of a racial or ethnic minority (p. 827)

    genocidio destrucción total de una minoría racial o étnica (pág. 827)

Gettysburg Address (1863) a speech given by Abraham Lincoln in which he praised the bravery of Union soldiers and renewed his commitment to winning the Civil War (p. 540)

    Discurso de Gettysburg (1863) discurso de Abraham Lincoln en el que alababa la valentía de las tropas de la Unión y renovaba su compromiso de triunfar en la Guerra Civil (pág. 540)

Ghost Dance a religious movement among Native Americans that spread across the Plains in the 1880s (p. 598)

    Danza de los Espíritus movimiento religioso de los indígenas norteamericanos que se extendió por la región de las Planicies en la década de 1880 (pág. 598)

GI Bill of Rights (1944) a law that offered veterans money for school, houses, farms, and businesses (p. 848)

    Declaración de Derechos de los Soldados (1944) ley que ofrecía a los veteranos de guerra dinero para su educación, vivienda, granjas y negocios (pág. 848)

globalization the process in which the United States is becoming more interdependent with other nations (p. 960)

    globalización proceso por el cual Estados Unidos empieza a tener más interdependencia con otras naciones (pág. 960)

global warming an environmental crisis in which the average temperature of the Earth is rising due to pollution (p. 962)

    calentamiento global crisis del medio ambiente por la cual está aumentando la temperatura promedio de la Tierra debido a la contaminación (pág. 962)

Great Depression a severe economic crisis that lasted for the entire decade of the 1930s (p. 780)

    Gran Depresión grave crisis económica que duró toda la década de 1930 (pág. 780)

Great Migration a period of African American movement from the South to cities in the North (p. 763)

    Gran Migración período en que los afroamericanos del Sur se fueron a ciudades del Norte (pág. 763)

Great Society President Lyndon Johnson's legislative plan that included civil rights laws (p. 880)

    Gran Sociedad plan legislativo del presidente Lyndon Johnson que incluía leyes a favor de los derechos civiles (pág. 880)

habeas corpus the constitutional protection against unlawful imprisonment (p. 532)

    hábeas corpus protección constitucional contra el encarcelamiento ilegal (pág. 532)

Harlem Renaissance a period of artistic achievement during the 1920s (p. 768)

    Renacimiento de Harlem período de logros artísticos durante la década de 1920 (pág. 768)

hawks supporters of the Vietnam War (p. 904)

    halcones partidarios de la guerra de Vietnam (pág. 904)

Haymarket Riot a riot that broke out at Haymarket Square in Chicago over the deaths of two strikers (p. 626)

    Revuelta de Haymarket revuelta que se originó en la Plaza Haym arket de Chicago por la muerte de dos huelguistas (pág. 626)

hippies young people who rebelled against the mainstream culture of the 1960s (p. 909)

    hippies jóvenes que se rebelaron contra la cultura convencional en la década de 1960 (pág. 909)

Ho Chi Minh Trail a series of jungle paths that allowed Communist forces to travel from North Vietnam to South Vietnam (p. 902)

    Camino de Ho Chi Minh serie de caminos por la selva que permitía a las fuerzas comunistas ir desde Vietnam del Norte hacia Vietnam del Sur (pág. 902)

Holocaust a program of mass murder in which the Nazis tried to kill all Jews (p. 827)

    Holocausto programa de asesinato en masa ideado por los nazis para exterminar a todos los judíos (pág. 827)

Homestead Act (1862) a law passed by Congress to encourage settlement in the West by giving government-owned land to small farmers (p. 600)

    Ley de Colonización de Tierras (1862) ley aprobada por el Congreso para fomentar la colonización del Oeste mediante la cesión de tierras del gobierno a pequeños agricultores (pág. 600)

Homestead strike (1892) a labor-union strike at Andrew Carnegie's Homestead Steel factory in Pennsylvania that erupted in violence between strikers and private detectives (p. 627)

    huelga de Homestead (1892) huelga sindical en la fábrica de acero Homestead de Andrew Carnegie en Pensilvania, que produjo violencia entre huelguistas y detectives privados (pág. 627)

horizontal integration owning all the businesses in a certain field (p. 621)

    integración horizontal posesión de todas las empresas en un campo específico (pág. 621)

Hull House a settlement house founded by Jane Addams and Ellen Gates Starr in 1889 (p. 648)
Casa Hull casa de asistencia a la comunidad fundada por Jane Addams y Ellen Gates Starr en 1889 (pág. 648)

human rights the basic rights of all people (p. 935)
derechos humanos derechos fundamentales de todas las personas (pág. 935)

hydrogen bomb a thermonuclear weapon that gets its power from splitting a hydrogen atom (p. 856)
bomba de hidrógeno arma termonuclear cuya potencia es generada por la división de un átomo de hidrógeno (pág. 856)

impeachment the process used by a legislative body to bring charges of wrongdoing against a public official (p. 562)
juicio político proceso por el cual un cuerpo legislativo presenta cargos en contra de un funcionario público (pág. 562)

imperialism the practice of extending a nation's power by gaining territories for a colonial empire (p. 692)
imperialismo práctica en la que una nación amplía su poder mediante adquiriendo territorios para un imperio colonial (pág. 692)

Industrial Workers of the World (IWW) a union founded in 1905 by socialists and union leaders that included workers not welcomed in the AFL (p. 674)
Trabajadores Industriales del Mundo (IWW) por sus siglas en inglés) sindicato fundado en 1905 por socialistas y líderes sindicales que incluía a los trabajadores que no admitía la Federación Americana del Trabajo (pág. 674)

Information Revolution an increase in the ability to share information between people and locations brought about by the Internet (p. 961)
Revolución de la información aumento de la capacidad de compartir información entre personas y lugares producido por Internet (pág. 961)

initiative a method of allowing voters to propose a new law if enough signatures are collected on a petition (p. 666)
iniciativa método que permite a los votantes proponer una nueva ley si consiguen suficientes firmas para una petición (pág. 666)

Internet a global system of computers that allows people across the world to communicate (p. 961)
Internet sistema global de computadoras que permite la comunicación entre personas de todo el mundo (pág. 961)

internment the imprisonment of Japanese Americans in special camps during World War II (p. 813)
internamiento encarcelamiento de japoneses-americanos en campos especiales durante la Segunda Guerra Mundial (pág. 813)

Iran-Contra affair a scandal during the Reagan administration in which government officials were accused of selling weapons to Iran and passing the profits to a revolutionary group known as the Contras (p. 939)
escándalo Irán-contras escándalo durante el gobierno de Reagan en el cual funcionarios del gobierno fueron acusados de vender armas a Irán y de entregar las ganancias a un grupo revolucionario conocido como los contras (pág. 939)

Iran hostage crisis a crisis in which Americans were taken hostage by militants in Iran and held for over a year (p. 936)
crisis de los rehenes de Irán crisis en la cual varios estadounidenses fueron tomados como rehenes por militantes iraníes durante más de un año (pág. 936)

ironclad a warship that is heavily armored with iron (p. 520)
acorazado buque de guerra fuertemente protegido con hierro (pág. 520)

island-hopping the strategy used by U.S. forces in the Pacific during World War II that involved taking only strategically important islands (p. 822)
saltos de isla en isla estrategia de las fuerzas de Estados Unidos en el Pacífico durante la Segunda Guerra Mundial que consistía en tomar sólo las islas importantes desde el punto de vista estratégico (pág. 822)

isolationism a national policy of avoiding involvement in other countries' affairs (p. 693)
aislacionismo política nacional de evitar involucrarse en los asuntos de otras naciones (pág. 693)

Jazz Age a name for the decade of the 1920s based on the popularity of jazz music (p. 767)
Era del Jazz nombre que se le dio a la década de 1920 por la popularidad de la música de jazz (pág. 767)

Jim Crow law a law that enforced segregation in the southern states (p. 568)
ley de Jim Crow ley que imponía la segregación en los estados del Sur (pág. 568)

kamikaze Japanese pilots who flew suicide missions during World War II (p. 822)
kamikaze piloto japonés que volaba en misiones suicidas durante la Segunda Guerra Mundial (pág. 822)

Kellogg-Briand Pact an agreement between nations proposing peaceful solutions to conflicts, signed after World War I (p. 754)
Pacto Kellogg-Briand acuerdo firmado entre naciones luego de la Primera Guerra Mundial que proponía soluciones pacíficas a los conflictos (pág. 754)

Knights of Labor secret society that became the first truly national labor union in the United States (p. 625)
Caballeros del Trabajo sociedad secreta que se convirtió en el primer sindicato verdaderamente nacional en Estados Unidos (pág. 625)

Ku Klux Klan a secret society created by white southerners in 1866 that used terror and violence to keep African Americans from obtaining their civil rights (p. 566)
Ku Klux Klan sociedad secreta creada en 1866 por blancos del Sur que usaba el terror y la violencia para impedir que los afroamericanos obtuvieran derechos civiles (pág. 566)

League of Nations a coalition of governments designed to find peaceful solutions to disagreements, proposed by Woodrow Wilson (p. 737)
Liga de las Naciones coalición de gobiernos propuesta por Woodrow Wilson y diseñada para buscar soluciones pacíficas a los desacuerdos (pág. 737)

Lend-Lease Act (1941) a law giving Franklin Roosevelt the power to sell, transfer, exchange, or lease military equipment to any country to help it defend itself against the Axis powers (p. 808)
Ley de Préstamo y Arriendo (1941) ley que dio a Franklin Roosevelt el poder de vender, transferir, intercambiar o arrendar equipo militar a cualquier país para la defensa contra las fuerzas del Eje (pág. 808)

Liberty bonds loans to the government that aided its ability to prepare for World War I (p. 727)
bonos de la Libertad préstamos hechos al gobierno que le permitieron prepararse para la Primera Guerra Mundial (pág. 727)

Lincoln-Douglas debates a series of debates between Republican Abraham Lincoln and Democrat Stephen Douglas during the 1858 U.S. Senate campaign in Illinois (p. 491)
debates Lincoln-Douglas serie de debates entre el republicano Abraham Lincoln y el demócrata Stephen Douglas durante la campaña de 1858 para el Senado estadounidense en Illinois (pág. 491)

Little Rock Nine a group of nine African American students who began the integration of the Little Rock, Arkansas, public school system (p. 871)
los nueve de Little Rock grupo de nueve estudiantes afroamericanos que empezaron la integración del sistema de escuelas públicas de Little Rock, Arkansas (pág. 871)

Long Walk (1864) a 300-mile march made by Navajo captives to a reservation in Bosque Redondo, New Mexico, that led to the deaths of hundreds of Navajo (p. 597)
La Larga Marcha (1864) caminata de 300 millas que hizo un grupo de prisioneros navajos hasta una reserva indígena en Bosque Redondo, Nuevo México, en la que murieron cientos de ellos (pág. 597)

Lost Generation the generation of young people who fought in World War I and eventually became disillusioned with the promise of American society (p. 768)
generación perdida generación de jóvenes que lucharon en la Primera Guerra Mundial y terminaron desilusionados con las promesas de la sociedad estadounidense (pág. 768)

Lusitania a passenger ship bombed by Germany (p. 726)
Lusitania barco de pasajeros bombardeado por Alemania (pág. 726)

Manhattan Project the U.S. effort to build an atomic bomb (p. 828)
Proyecto Manhattan plan de Estados Unidos de fabricar una bomba atómica (pág. 828)

March on Washington a huge demonstration organized by Martin Luther King Jr. to protest racial discrimination (p. 878)
Marcha en Washington manifestación enorme organizada por Martin Luther King, Jr. en protesta por la discriminación racial (p. 878)

Marshall Plan the idea that the U.S. could help rebuild wartorn Europe with loans and other economic aid (p. 847)

Plan Marshall idea de que Estados Unidos podía contribuir con préstamos y otros tipos de ayuda económica a la reconstrucción de la Europa devastada por la guerra (pág. 847)

Massacre at Wounded Knee (1890) the U.S. Army's killing of approximately 150 Sioux at Wounded Knee Creek in South Dakota; ended U.S-Indian wars on the Plains (p. 597)

masacre de Wounded Knee (1890) matanza de aproximadamente 150 indios siux en Wounded Knee Creek, Dakota del Sur; dio por terminadas las guerras entre estadounidenses e indígenas en las Planicies (pág. 597)

mass culture leisure and cultural activities shared by many people (p. 644)

cultura de masas actividades culturales y del tiempo libre que les gustan a muchas personas (pág. 644)

mass transit public transportation (p. 644)

transporte colectivo transporte público (pág. 644)

Mexican Revolution a revolution led by Francisco Madero in 1910 that eventually forced the Mexican dictator Díaz to resign (p. 708)

Revolución mexicana revolución iniciada en 1910 por Francisco Madero, que finalmente obligó al dictador mexicano Díaz a renunciar (pág. 708)

militarism an increase in the importance of the military of a country (p. 721)

militarismo aumento de la importancia del ejército de un país (pág. 721)

mobilize to prepare for war (p. 721)

mobilizarse prepararse para la guerra (pág. 721)

Model T Henry Ford's automobile designed with the average American in mind (p. 755)

modelo T automóvil de Henry Ford diseñado para el estadounidense promedio (pág. 755)

monopoly a complete control over the entire supply of goods or a service in a particular market (p. 622)

monopolio control absoluto de toda la oferta de bienes o de un servicio en un mercado en particular (pág. 622)

Montgomery bus boycott a boycott of the Montgomery, Alabama, public bus system to protest its policy of segregation (p. 873)

boicot a los autobuses de Montgomery boicot al sistema público de autobuses de Montgomery, Alabama, en protesta por su política de segregación (pág. 873)

Morrill Act (1862) a federal law passed by Congress that gave land to western states to encourage them to build colleges (p. 600)

Ley de Morrill (1862) ley federal aprobada por el Congreso que otorgaba tierras a los estados del Oeste para fomentar la construcción de universidades (pág. 600)

moving assembly line an innovation of Henry Ford's that dramatically reduced the cost of production (p. 755)

cadena de montaje móvil innovación de Henry Ford que redujo significativamente el costo de producción (pág. 755)

muckrakers a term coined for journalists who "raked up" and exposed corruption and problems of society (p. 664)

muckrakers término acuñado para nombrar a los periodistas que se dedicaban a investigar y exponer la corrupción y los problemas de la sociedad (pág. 664)

National American Woman Suffrage Association (NAWSA) an organization founded by Elizabeth Cady Stanton and Susan B. Anthony in 1890 to obtain women's right to vote (p. 676)

Asociación Nacional Americana para el Sufragio Femenino (NAWSA) por sus siglas en inglés) organización fundada en 1890 por Elizabeth Cady Stanton y Susan B. Anthony para obtener el derecho al voto de las mujeres (pág. 676)

National Association for the Advancement of Colored People (NAACP) an organization founded in 1909 by W. E. B. Du Bois and other reformers to bring attention to racial inequality (p. 678)

Asociación Nacional para el Progreso de la Gente de Color (NAACP, por sus siglas en inglés) organización fundada en 1909 por W. E. B. Du Bois y otros reformadores para llamar la atención sobre la desigualdad racial (pág. 678)

National Grange a social and educational organization for farmers (p. 603)

National Grange organización social y educativa para los agricultores (pág. 603)

National Organization for Women (NOW) a group that organized to promote the interests of women (p. 883)

Organización Nacional de la Mujer grupo organizado para promover los intereses de la mujer (pág. 883)

National War Labor Board a government agency organized to help settle disputes between workers and employers in war industries (p. 729)

Junta nacional del trabajo en Tiempos de Guerra agencia de gobierno destinada a resolver disputas entre trabajadores y empleadores en las industrias relacionadas con la guerra (pág. 729)

Nazis the National Socialist Party of Germany, headed by Adolf Hitler (p. 805)

nazi Partido Nacional Socialista de Alemania, liderado por Adolf Hitler (pág. 805)

New Deal Franklin Roosevelt's legislative plan to end the Great Depression that included dramatic reforms of government agencies and powers (p. 784)
New Deal plan legislativo de Franklin Roosevelt para poner fin a la Gran Depresión; incluía profundas reformas en las agencias y poderes del gobierno (pág. 784)

new immigrant a term often used for an immigrant who arrived in the United States beginning in the 1880s (p. 636)
nuevo inmigrante término empleado a menudo para referirse a los inmigrantes que llegaron a Estados Unidos a partir de la década de 1880 (pág. 636)

Nineteenth Amendment (1920) a constitutional amendment that gave women the vote (p. 677)
Decimonovena Enmienda (1920) enmienda constitucional que dio a la mujer el derecho al voto (pág. 677)

North American Free Trade Agreement (NAFTA) a treaty that eliminated trade barriers between Canada, the United States, and Mexico (p. 952)
Tratado de Libre Comercio de América del Norte (TLCAN o NAFTA) tratado que eliminó las barreras comerciales entre Canadá, Estados Unidos y México (pág. 952)

North Atlantic Treaty Organization (NATO) an alliance of Western powers (p. 848)
Organización del Tratado del Atlántico Norte (OTAN) alianza de potencias occidentales (pág. 848)

Nuremberg trials the war crimes trials of Nazi leaders (p. 845)
Ensayos de Nuremberg los ensayos de los crímenes de guerra de arranques de cinta nazis (pág. 845)

old immigrant a term often used for an immigrant who arrived in the United States before the 1880s (p. 636)
antiguo inmigrante término empleado con frecuencia para referirse a los inmigrantes que llegaron a Estados Unidos antes de la década de 1880 (pág. 636)

Open Door Policy a policy established by the United States in 1899 to promote equal access for all nations to trade in China (p. 695)
política de puertas abiertas política establecida por Estados Unidos en 1899 para promover el acceso igualitario de todas las naciones al comercio con China (pág. 695)

Operation Desert Storm the military effort to free Kuwait from Saddam Hussein's invasion (p. 951)
Operación Tormenta del Desierto acción militar para liberar a Kuwait de la invasión de Saddam Hussein (pág. 951)

Organization of Petroleum Exporting Countries (OPEC) an alliance of oil rich countries that coordinates oil policies (p. 927)
Organización de Países Exportadores de Petróleo (OPEP) alianza de países ricos en petróleo que coordina las políticas petroleras (pág. 927)

ozone layer a level of the Earth's atmosphere that is being depleted by pollution (p. 962)
capa de ozono nivel de la atmósfera de la Tierra que se está reduciendo debido a la contaminación (pág. 962)

Panama Canal an artificial waterway across the Isthmus of Panama; completed by the United States in 1914 (p. 705)
canal de Panamá canal artificial que atraviesa el istmo de Panamá; Estados Unidos completó su construcción en 1914 (pág. 705)

pardon freedom from punishment (p. 931)
indulto liberación de un castigo (pág. 931)

patent an exclusive right to make or sell an invention (p. 616)
patente derecho exclusivo para fabricar o vender un invento (pág. 616)

Peace Corps a nonmilitary aid program introduced by John Kennedy (p. 894)
Cuerpos de Paz programa de ayuda no militar introducido por John Kennedy (pág. 894)

Pearl Harbor a harbor in Hawaii that serves as the base of the U.S. Pacific fleet and was bombed in 1941 by Japan (p. 808)
Pearl Harbor puerto de Hawai que es la base de la flota del Pacífico de Estados Unidos; fue bombardeado por Japón en 1941 (pág. 808)

Pentagon the headquarters of the U.S. military, located outside of Washington, D.C. (p. 956)
Pentágono sede central del ejército de Estados Unidos, ubicada en las afueras de Washington D.C. (pág. 956)

Pickett's Charge (1863) a failed Confederate attack during the Civil War led by General George Pickett at the Battle of Gettysburg (p. 539)
ataque de Pickett (1863) ataque fallido del ejército confederado, al mando del general George Pickett, en la batalla de Gettysburg durante la Guerra Civil (pág. 539)

Platt Amendment a part of the Cuban constitution drafted under the supervision of the United States that limited Cuba's right to make treaties, gave the U.S. the right to intervene in Cuban affairs, and required Cuba to sell or lease land to the U. (p. 701)
Enmienda Platt parte de la constitución cubana redactado bajo la supervisión de Estados Unidos que limitaba el derecho de Cuba a firmar tratados, le daba a Estados Unidos el derecho de intervenir en los asuntos cubanos y le exigía a Cuba vender o arrendar tierras a Estados Unidos (pág. 701)

Plessy v. Ferguson (1896) U.S. Supreme Court case that established the "separate-but-equal" doctrine for public facilities (p. 569)
Plessy contra Ferguson (1896) caso en el que la Corte Suprema estableció la doctrina de "separados pero iguales" en los lugares públicos (pág. 569)

political machine a powerful organization that influenced city and county politics in the late 1800s (p. 662)
maquinaria política organización poderosa que influía en la política municipal y del condado a finales del siglo XIX (pág. 662)

poll tax a special tax that a person had to pay in order to vote (p. 568)
impuesto electoral impuesto especial que tenía que pagar una persona para poder votar (pág. 568)

Pony Express a system of messengers that carried mail between relay stations on a route 2,000-miles long in 1860 and 1861 (p. 590)
Pony Express sistema de mensajeros que llevaban el correo entre estaciones de relevo a lo largo de una ruta de 2,000 millas en 1860 y 1861 (pág. 590)

popular sovereignty the idea that political authority belongs to the people (p. 476)
soberanía popular idea de que la autoridad política pertenece al pueblo (pág. 476)

Populist Party a political party formed in 1892 that supported free coinage of silver, work reforms, immigration restrictions, and government ownership of railroads and telegraph and telephone systems (p. 604)
Partido Populista partido político formado en 1892 que apoyaba la libre producción de monedas de plata, reformas laborales y restricciones de la inmigración, además de asignar al gobierno la propiedad de los sistemas ferroviario, telegráfico y telefónico (pág. 604)

Progressives a group of reformers who worked to improve social and political problems in the late 1800s (p. 664)
progresistas grupo de reformistas que trabajaron para resolver problemas sociales y políticos a finales del siglo XIX (pág. 664)

Progressive Party a short-lived political party that attempted to institute social reforms (p. 682)
partido Progresista partido político de poca duración que intentó establecer reformas sociales (pág. 682)

Pullman strike (1894) a railroad strike that ended when President Grover Cleveland sent in federal troops (p. 627)
huelga de Pullman (1894) huelga del ferrocarril que terminó cuando el presidente Grover Cleveland envió a tropas federales (pág. 627)

Pure Food and Drug Act (1906) a law that set regulatory standards for industries involved in preparing food (p. 681)
Ley de Alimentos y Medicamentos Puros (1906) ley que estableció normas regulatorias para las industrias de fabricación de productos alimenticios (pág. 681)

R

Radical Republicans members of Congress who felt that southern states needed to make great social changes before they could be readmitted to the Union (p. 559)
republicanos radicales miembros del Congreso convencidos de que los estados del Sur necesitaban hacer grandes cambios sociales antes de volver a ser admitidos en la Unión (pág. 559)

realpolitik a foreign policy in which U.S. interests are put over ethical or principled concerns (p. 928)
realpolitik política exterior según la cual los intereses de Estados Unidos están por encima de los asuntos éticos o de principios (pág. 928)

recall a vote to remove an official from office (p. 666)
destitución votación para sacar a un funcionario de su cargo (pág. 666)

Reconstruction (1865–1877) the period following the Civil War during which the U.S. government worked to reunite the nation and to rebuild the southern states (p. 552)
Reconstrucción (1865–1877) período posterior a la Guerra Civil en el que el gobierno de Estados Unidos trabajó por reunificar de la nación reconstruir los estados del Sur (pág. 552)

Reconstruction Acts (1867–1868) the laws that put the southern states under U.S. military control and required them to draft new constitutions upholding the Fourteenth Amendment (p. 561)
Leyes de Reconstrucción (1867–1868) leyes que declaraban a los estados del Sur territorio sujeto al control militar estadounidense y los obligaban a reformar sus constituciones que defendieran la Decimocuarta Enmienda (pág. 561)

Red Scare a widespread fear of communism and Communists (p. 760)
 Terror rojo miedo ampliamente difundido al comunismo y los comunistas (pág. 760)

referendum a procedure that allows voters to approve or reject a law already proposed or passed by government (p. 666)
 referéndum proceso que permite a los ciudadanos votar para aprobar o rechazar una ley previamente propuesta o aprobada por el gobierno (pág. 666)

reparations financial payments by the loser of a war (p. 737)
 indemnizaciones compensación económica pagada por el bando que es vencido en la guerra (pág. 737)

reservations federal lands set aside for American Indians (p. 595)
 reservas territorios federales reservados para los indígenas norteamericanos (pág. 595)

Roosevelt Corollary (1904) Theodore Roosevelt's addition to the Monroe Doctrine warning nations in the Americas that if they didn't pay their debts, the United States would get involved (p. 707)
 Corolario de Roosevelt (1904) agregado del presidente Theodore Roosevelt a la Doctrina Monroe advirtiendo a las naciones de América que si no pagaban sus deudas, el gobierno de Estados Unidos intervendría (pág. 707)

S

sanctions economic restrictions placed on a country in an attempt to change its policy decisions (p. 935)
 sanciones restricciones económicas aplicadas a un país en un intento de cambiar sus políticas (pág. 935)

Scopes trial a trial in which John Scopes was accused of teaching evolution illegally (p. 762)
 juicio de Scopes juicio en el cual John Scopes fue acusado de enseñar ilegalmente la teoría de la evolución (pág. 762)

search-and-destroy missions the strategy used in the Vietnam War in which enemy targets were located and attacked (p. 903)
 misiones de búsqueda y destrucción estrategia de localización y ataque de objetivos enemigos usada en la guerra de Vietnam (pág. 903)

Second Battle of Bull Run (1862) a Civil War battle in which the Confederate army forced most of the Union army out of Virginia (p. 518)
 segunda batalla de Bull Run (1862) batalla de la Guerra Civil en la que el ejército confederado obligó a gran parte del ejército de la Unión a abandonar Virginia (pág. 518)

Second Industrial Revolution a period of rapid growth in manufacturing and industry in the late 1800s (p. 615)
 segunda revolución industrial período de gran crecimiento en la manufactura y en la industria, a finales del siglo XIX (pág. 615)

segregation the forced separation of people of different races in public places (p. 568)
 segregación separación obligada de personas de diferentes razas en lugares públicos (pág. 568)

Selective Service Act (1917) a law that allowed the president to draft soldiers in times of war (p. 727)
 Ley de Servicio Selectivo (1917) ley que permitía al Presidente reclutar soldados en épocas de guerra (pág. 727)

service economy an economy in which most jobs involve providing services instead of producing goods (p. 960)
 economía de servicios economía en la cual la mayoría de los trabajos consisten en ofrecer un servicio en lugar de producir bienes (pág. 960)

settlement houses neighborhood centers staffed by professionals and volunteers for education, recreation, and social activities in poor areas (p. 648)
 organizaciones de servicio a la comunidad centros comunitarios atendidos por profesionales y voluntarios para ofrecer educación, recreación y actividades sociales en zonas pobres (pág. 648)

Seven Days' Battles (1862) a series of Civil War battles in which Confederate army successes forced the Union army to retreat from Richmond, Virginia, the Confederate capital (p. 518)
 batallas de los Siete Días (1862) serie de batallas de la Guerra Civil en las que las victorias del ejército confederado obligaron a las tropas de la Unión a retirarse de Richmond, Virginia, la capital confederada (pág. 518)

Seventeenth Amendment (1913) a constitutional amendment allowing American voters to directly elect U.S. senators (p. 666)
 Decimoséptima Enmienda (1913) enmienda constitucional que permite a los votantes estadounidenses elegir directamente a los senadores de Estados Unidos (pág. 666)

sharecropping a system used on southern farms after the Civil War in which farmers worked land owned by someone else in return for a small portion of the crops (p. 569)
 cultivo de aparceros sistema usado en las granjas sureñas después de la Guerra Civil en el que los agricultores trabajaban las tierras de otra persona a cambio de una pequeña porción de la cosecha (pág. 569)

ENGLISH AND SPANISH GLOSSARY

Sherman Antitrust Act (1890) a law that made it illegal to create monopolies or trusts that restrained free trade (p. 622)

Ley Antimonopolio de Sherman (1890) ley que prohibía la creación de monopolios o consorcios que restringieran el libre comercio (pág. 622)

Siege of Vicksburg (1863) the Union army's six-week blockade of Vicksburg that led the city to surrender during the Civil War (p. 524)

Sitio de Vicksburg (1863) bloqueo de seis semanas realizado por el ejército de la Unión en Vicksburg para forzar la rendición de esa ciudad durante la Guerra Civil (pág. 524)

sit-down strike a strike in which workers stay at their work stations so that strikebreakers cannot replace them (p. 788)

huelga de brazos caídos huelga en la cual los trabajadores permanecen en el lugar de trabajo para que los rompehuelgas no los puedan reemplazar (pág. 788)

sit-in a form of protest in which African Americans sat at segregated lunch counters and requested service (p. 874)

sentada forma de protesta de los afroamericanos; se sentaban en los comedores que practicaban la segregación racial y pedían servicio (pág. 874)

Sixteenth Amendment (1913) an amendment to the Constitution that allows personal income to be taxed (p. 683)

Decimosexta Enmienda (1913) enmienda constitucional que permite los impuestos sobre los ingresos personales (pág. 683)

social Darwinism a view of society based on Charles Darwin's scientific theory of natural selection (p. 621)

darwinismo social visión de la sociedad basada en la teoría científica de la selección natural de Charles Darwin (pág. 621)

socialism economic system in which the government owns and operates a country's means of production (p. 674)

socialismo sistema económico en el que el gobierno controla y maneja los medios de producción de un país (pág. 674)

sodbusters the name given to Plains farmers who worked hard to break up the region's tough sod (p. 601)

sodbusters nombre dado a los agricultores de las Planicies que se esforzaron mucho para trabajar el duro terreno de la región (pág. 601)

Social Security Act (1935) a law that instituted the pension plan Social Security (p. 787)

Ley del Seguro Social (1935) ley que estableció el plan de pensiones del Seguro Social (pág. 787)

sphere of influence an area where foreign countries control trade or natural resources of another nation or area (p. 695)

esfera de influencia nación o lugar cuyos recursos naturales y comercio son controlados por otro país (pág. 695)

Sputnik the first artificial satellite, launched by the Soviet Union in 1957 (p. 856)

Sputnik primer satélite artificial, lanzado por la Unión Soviética en 1957 (pág. 856)

stagflation a term describing a slowing economy mixed with high unemployment (p. 927)

estagflación término que describe una economía que disminuye su ritmo, acompañado de un desempleo alto (pág. 927)

stalemate a situation in which neither side can win a victory (p. 723)

punto muerto situación en la cual ninguna de las partes puede alcanzar la victoria (pág. 723)

steerage the area on a ship in the lower levels where the steering mechanisms were located and where cramped quarters were provided for people who could only afford cheap passage (p. 637)

tercera clase nivel inferior un barco en el que se encontraban los mecanismos del timón y se ofrecían habitaciones reducidas para las personas que sólo podían comprar un pasaje barato (pág. 637)

Strategic Arms Limitation Talks (SALT) negotiations between the United States and the Soviet Union designed to limit nuclear weapons (p. 928)

Tratados de Limitación de Armas Estratégicas (SALT) negociaciones entre Estados Unidos y la Unión Soviética diseñadas para limitar el número de armas nucleares (pág. 928)

Student Nonviolent Coordinating Committee (SNCC) a group organized to promote civil rights for African Americans through nonviolent protests (p. 874)

Comité Coordinador Estudiantil No Violento (SNCC) grupo organizado para promover los derechos civiles de los afroamericanos con protestas no violentas (pág. 874)

Students for a Democratic Society (SDS) a group organized to protest U.S. involvement in the Vietnam War (p. 908)

Estudiantes por una Sociedad Democrática (SDS) grupo organizado para protestar por la participación de Estados Unidos en la guerra de Vietnam (pág. 908)

suburb a neighborhood outside of a downtown area (p. 644)

suburbio vecindario en las afueras de una ciudad (pág. 644)

Sun Belt the southern area of the United States from Florida to California that experienced an increase in population during the 1970s (p. 858)
Sun Belt área del sur de Estados Unidos, desde Florida hasta California, en la que hubo un aumento de la población durante la década de 1970 (pág. 858)

supply-side economics economic theory that focuses on influencing the supply of labor and goods; it usually involves sharp tax cuts (p. 938)
economía de la oferta teoría económica que pretende influenciar la oferta de mano de obra y de bienes; por lo general, implica grandes reducciones de impuestos (pág. 938)

sweatshops hot, stuffy workshops in which workers prepare materials for low wages (p. 640)
fábricas explotadoras talleres calurosos y con el aire cargado en los cuales los trabajadores preparan materiales por salarios reducidos (pág. 640)

talkie a film that includes sound (p. 766)
película sonora película que incluye sonido (pág. 766)

Teapot Dome scandal a scandal under the Harding adminstration in which government officials were accused of taking bribes to allow oil to be mined from federal lands (p. 753)
escándalo de Teapot Dome escándalo durante el gobierno de Harding en el que se acusó a funcionarios del gobierno de aceptar sobornos para permitir que se usaran tierras federales para extraer petróleo (pág. 753)

Teller Amendment (1898) a congressional resolution stating that the U.S. had no interest in taking control of Cuba (p. 698)
Enmienda Teller (1898) resolución del Congreso en la que Estados Unidos declaró que no tenía intención de tomar el control de Cuba (pág. 698)

Tennessee Valley Authority (TVA) a governmental agency designed to bring jobs and electricity to rural areas of the Tennessee River valley (p. 785)
Autoridad del valle del Tennessee (TVA) agencia del gobierno destinada a proveer empleos y energía eléctrica a las áreas rurales del valle del río Tennessee (pág. 785)

Ten Percent Plan President Abraham Lincoln's plan for Reconstruction; once 10 percent of voters in a former Confederate state took a U.S. loyalty oath, they could form a new state government and be readmitted to the Union (p. 553)

Plan del Diez por Ciento plan de Reconstrucción del presidente Abraham Lincoln; si el 10 por ciento de los votantes de un estado que había sido confederado juraba lealtad a la nación, podían formar un nuevo gobierno y ser readmitidos en la Unión (pág. 553)

terrorism the systematic use of fear or terror to gain goals (p. 953)
terrorismo uso sistemático del miedo o el terror para alcanzar objetivos (pág. 953)

Tet Offensive (1968) a series of attacks by Vietcong forces that proved to many Americans the Vietnam War was not being won (p. 904)
ofensiva del Tet (1968) serie de ataques de las fuerzas del Vietcong que demostró a muchos estadounidenses que no estaban ganando la guerra de Vietnam (pág. 904)

Thirteenth Amendment (1865) a constitutional amendment that outlawed slavery (p. 554)
Decimotercera Enmienda (1865) enmienda constitucional que prohibió la esclavitud (pág. 554)

38th Parallel the boundary between North and South Korea before the Korean War (p. 852)
paralelo 38 límite entre Corea del Sur y Corea del Norte antes de la Guerra de Corea (pág. 852)

Tonkin Gulf Resolution (1964) gave President Johnson the power to send combat troops to Vietnam (p. 902)
Resolución del golfo de Tonkin (1964) otorgó al presidente Johnson la autoridad de enviar tropas de combate a Vietnam (pág. 902)

totalitarianism a form of government in which every aspect of citizen's lives are controlled by the government (p. 804)
totalitarismo forma de gobierno en la cual todos los aspectos de la vida de los ciudadanos están bajo el control del gobierno (pág. 804)

total war a type of war in which an army destroys its opponent's ability to fight by targeting civilian and economic as well as military resources (p. 542)
guerra total tipo de guerra en la que un ejército destruye la capacidad de lucha de su oponente mediante ataques a la población civil y a la economía así como a los recursos militares (pág. 542)

transcontinental railroad a railroad system that crossed the continental United States; construction began in 1863 (p. 590)
tren transcontinental línea ferroviaria que cruzaba Estados Unidos de un extremo a otro; su construcción se inició en 1863 (pág. 590)

Treaty of Fort Laramie (1851) a treaty signed in Wyoming by the United States and northern Plains nations (p. 594)
Tratado del fuerte Laramie (1851) tratado firmado en Wyoming por Estados Unidos y las naciones indígenas de las Planicies del norte (pág. 594)

Treaty of Medicine Lodge (1867) an agreement between the U.S. government and southern Plains Indians in which the Indians agreed to move onto reservations (p. 595)
Tratado de Medicine Lodge (1867) acuerdo entre el gobierno de Estados Unidos y los indígenas de las Planicies del sur en el que los indígenas aceptaron irse a las reservas (pág. 595)

Treaty of Versailles (1919) brought an end to World War I, but was never ratified by the United States (p. 738)
Tratado de Versalles (1919) puso fin a la Primera Guerra Mundial, pero Estados Unidos nunca lo ratificó (pág. 738)

Tredegar Iron Works a large iron factory that operated in Richmond, Virginia, in the early to mid-1800s (p. 419)
Tredegar Iron Works gran fábrica de acero que operaba a mediados del siglo XIX en Richmond, Virginia (pág. 419)

trench warfare a new kind of warfare in World War I that involved troops digging and fighting from deep trenches (p. 722)
guerra de trincheras nuevo tipo de guerra utilizado en la Primera Guerra Mundial en el cual las tropas cavaban trincheras profundas y luchaban desde ellas (pág. 722)

Triangle Shirtwaist Fire a factory fire that killed 146 workers trapped in the building; led to new safety standard laws (p. 673)
incendio de Triangle Shirtwaist incendio de una fábrica en la que murieron 146 trabajadores atrapados en el edificio; este suceso obligó a crear nuevas leyes de seguridad (pág. 673)

Truman Doctrine a policy attempting to contain the spread of communism, beginning with military aid to the monarchies of Turkey and Greece (p. 847)
Doctrina Truman política que intentaba contener el avance del comunismo, ofreciendo inicialmente ayuda militar a las monarquías de Turquía y Grecia (pág. 847)

trust a number of companies legally grouped under a single board of directors (p. 621)
consorcio varias compañías agrupadas legalmente bajo el mando de una sola junta directiva (pág. 621)

Tuskegee Airmen a group of African American pilots who flew missions in World War I; they were the first African American military pilots (p. 812)
Aviadores de Tuskegee grupo de pilotos afroamericanos que volaron en misiones de la Primera Guerra Mundial; fueron los primeros pilotos afroamericanos del ejército (pág. 812)

Twenty-first Amendment (1933) an amendment to the Constitution that ended Prohibition (p. 761)
Vigésimoprimera Enmienda (1933) enmienda constitucional que puso fin a la Ley seca (pág. 761)

Twenty-sixth Amendment (1971) an amendment to the Constitution that lowered the voting age to 18 (p. 911)
Vigésimosexta Enmienda (1971) enmienda constitucional que redujo la edad mínima para votar a 18 años (pág. 911)

U-boats German submarines or "untersee boats" (p. 724)
U-boats submarinos alemanes o "barcos untersee" (pág. 724)

United Farm Workers a group organized to promote the interests of migrant farm workers, it eventually led to the Chicano movement (p. 882)
Trabajadores Agrícolas Unidos grupo organizado para promover los intereses de los trabajadores agrícolas migratorios; con el tiempo, dio origen al movimiento chicano (pág. 882)

United Nations an alliance of nations that attempts to end disputes between countries peacefully (p. 846)
Naciones Unidas alianza de naciones que intenta resolver de manera pacífica las disputas entre los países (pág. 846)

urban renewal a governmental program that attempted to rid innercities of slums and replace them with low- and middle-income housing (p. 859)
programa de renovación urbana programa gubernamental que intentó eliminar las barriadas de los centros urbanos y reemplazarlos con viviendas para personas de recursos bajos y medios (pág. 859)

vertical integration the business practice of owning all of the businesses involved in each step of a manufacturing process (p. 620)
integración vertical práctica empresarial de poseer todas las empresas que participan en cada paso de un proceso de manufactura (pág. 620)

Vietcong the South Vietnam forces that were supported by North Vietnamese Communists (p. 899)
Vietcong fuerzas de Vietnam del Sur apoyadas por los comunistas de Vietnam del Norte (pág. 899)

Vietnamization a policy introduced in an attempt to leave the Vietnam War, in which Vietnamese forces would take over the fighting (p. 910)

vietnamización política introducida en un intento de salir de la guerra de Vietnam, según la cual las fuerzas vietnamitas se harían cargo de la lucha (pág. 910)

Vietnam Veterans Memorial a war memorial in Washington, D.C., dedicated to the veterans of Vietnam (p. 913)

Monumento a los Veteranos de Vietnam monumento conmemorativo de la guerra en Washington D.C. dedicado a los veteranos de Vietnam (pág. 913)

Voting Rights Act of 1965 provided new powers to the federal government to protect African Americans' voting rights (p. 879)

Ley de Derecho al Voto de 1965 dio nueva autoridad al gobierno federal para proteger el derecho al voto de los afroamericanos (pág. 879)

War Powers Act (1973) a law that requires a president to get Congressional approval before sending troops into combat (p. 913)

Ley de Facultades de Guerra (1973) ley que requiere la aprobación del Congreso para que el presidente pueda enviar tropas a la guerra (pág. 913)

War Production Board a government agency set up to oversee production of war materials during World War II (p. 810)

Junta de Producción de Guerra agencia creada por el gobierno para supervisar la producción de materiales de guerra durante la Segunda Guerra Mundial (pág. 810)

Watergate a scandal in which President Nixon resigned over accusations of illegal activity (p. 929)

Watergate escándalo que provocó la renuncia del presidente Nixon por acusaciones de actividades ilegales (pág. 929)

weapons of mass destruction chemical, biological, or nuclear weapons that can kill thousands (p. 957)

armas de destrucción masiva armas químicas, biológicas o nucleares que pueden matar a miles de personas (pág. 957)

Wilderness Campaign (1864) a series of battles between Union and Confederate forces in northern and central Virginia that delayed the Union capture of Richmond (p. 540)

Campaña de Wilderness (1864) serie de batallas entre la Unión y los confederados en el norte y el centro de Virginia que retrasaron la captura de Richmond por parte de la Unión (pág. 540)

World Trade Center a complex of several office buildings that were attacked by terrorists (p. 956)

World Trade Center complejo de varios edificios de oficinas que fue atacado por terroristas (pág. 956)

Yalta Conference a meeting between the leaders of the Allied powers that resulted in a plan for peace after World War II (p. 844)

Conferencia de Yalta reunión de los líderes de las fuerzas aliadas que produjo un plan de paz después de la Segunda Guerra Mundial (pág. 844)

yellow journalism the reporting of exaggerated stories in newspapers to increase sales (p. 697)

prensa amarillista publicación de noticias exageradas en los periódicos para aumentar las ventas (pág. 697)

Z

Zimmermann note a telegram from Germany to Mexico offering Mexico a return of territory in exchange for declaring war on the United States (p. 726)

telegrama Zimmermann telegrama de Alemania a México en el cual se ofrecía a México una devolución de territorios si le declaraba la guerra a Estados Unidos (pág. 726)

zoot-suit riots a series of riots during which Mexican Americans were attacked by whites (p. 813)

disturbios *zoot-suit* serie de disturbios durante los cuales personas de raza blanca atacaron a mexicano-americanos (pág. 813)

ENGLISH AND SPANISH GLOSSARY

Index

INDEX

INDEX

INDEX

Credits and Acknowledgments

For permission to reproduce copyrighted material, grateful acknowledgment is made to the following sources:

Chusma House Publications: From *Soldados: Chicanos in Viet Nam*, edited by Charley Trujillo. Copyright © 1990 by Charley Trujillo.

Doubleday, a division of Random House, Inc., www.randomhouse.com: From *The Diary of a Young Girl: The Definitive Edition* by Anne Frank, edited by Otto H. Frank and Mirjam Pressler, translated by Susan Massotty. Copyright © 1995 by Doubleday, a division of Random House, Inc.

Hill and Wang, a division of Farrar, Straus & Giroux, LLC and electronic format by permission of **Georges Borchardt, Inc., for Les Editions de Minuit:** From *Night* by Elie Wiesel, translated by Stella Rodway. Copyright © 1958 by Les Editions de Minuit; English translation copyright © 1960 by MacGibbon & Kee, renewed © 1988 by The Collins Publishing Group. Originally published as *La Nuit*. All rights reserved.

Alfred A. Knopf, a division of Random House, Inc., www.randomhouse.com; electronic format by Harold Ober Associates Incorporated: "I, Too, Sing America" and "Dream Deferred" ("Harlem") from *The Collected Poems of Langston Hughes.* Copyright © 1994 by the Estate of Langston Hughes.

The Metropolitan Museum of Art, New York, NY: From "Introduction" from *American Paradise: The World of the Hudson River School*, Introduction by John K. Howat. Copyright © 1987 by The Metropolitan Museum of Art, New York, NY.

W. W. Norton & Company, Inc., www.wwnorton.com, electronic format by McCall Corporation: *Thirteen Days: A Memoir of the Cuban Missile Crisis* by Robert F. Kennedy. Copyright © 1968 by McCall Corporation.

Norwegian-American Historical Association: From quote by Gro Svendsen from *Frontier Mother: The Letters of Gro Svendsen*, translated and edited by Pauline Farseth and Theodore C. Blegen. Copyright © 1950 Norwegian-American Association.

Persea Books, Inc.: *Bread Givers* by Anzia Yezierska. Copyright © 1925 by Doubleday & Co., Inc.; copyright renewed 1952 by Anzia Yezierska, transferred to Louise Levitas Henriksen in 1970. Revised edition copyright © 1999 by Persea Books, Inc. Foreward and Introduction copyright © 1999 by Alice Kessler-Harris.

Scribner, an imprint of Simon & Schuster Adult Publishing Group: From *The Great Gatsby* by F. Scott Fitzgerald. Copyright 1925 by Charles Scribner's Sons; renewed copyright 1953 by Frances Scott Fitzgerald Lanahan.

Viking Penguin, a division of Penguin Group (USA) Inc.: From *The Grapes of Wrath* by John Steinbeck. Copyright 1939 and renewed © 1967 by John Steinbeck.

Sources Cited:

Quote by Harold Bryant from *Bloods: An Oral History of the Vietnam War by Black Veterans* by Wallace Terry. Published by Ballantine Books, New York, 1985.

From *Keeping The Faith* by Jimmy Carter. Published by Bantam Books, New York, 1982.

Quote by Maya Lin from "Architect Maya Lin Describes the thoughts Behind the Vietnam Veterans Memorial" by Fernando Quintero from *The Berkeleyan*, 1995.

Quote by Philip Caputo from *CNN Cold War: Interviews*, accessed at http://www.cnn.com/SPECIALS/cold.war/episodes/11/interviews/caputo/

From "The Fall of Saigon" by Ken Moorefield from *To Bear Any Burden: The Vietnam War and Its Aftermath in the Words of Americans and Southeast Asians* by Al Santoli. Published by E.P. Dutton, Inc., 1985.

From quote by Henry Fenner from *You Must Remember This: An Oral History of Manhattan from the 1890s to World War II* by Jeff Kisseloff. Published by Harcourt, Inc., Orlando, 1989.

From *Yesterday: A Memoir of a Russian Jewish Family* by Miriam Shomer Zunser, edited by Emily Wortis Leider. Published by HarperCollins Publishers, New York, 1978.

Quote by a Hungarian immigrant from *This Was America* by Oscar Handlin. Published by Harvard University Press, Cambridge, Mass., 1949.

From "Now I Lay Me Down to Sleep" by Diana Dwan Poole from *Chicken Soup for the Veteran's Soul* by Jack Canfield, Mark Victor Hansen, and Sidney R. Slagter. Published by Health Communications, Inc., Deerfield Beach, FL, 2001.

From *A Life is More than a Moment: The Desegregation of Little Rock's Central High* by Will Counts, Will Campbell, Ernest Dumas and Robert S. McCord. Published by Indiana University Press, Bloomington, 1999.

Quote by Dave Reinemen from "60 Years Later, Okinawa Memories Still Burn" by Tom Berg from *Orange County Register*, 2005.

Quote by Frank Hall from "Hundreds tread site of bloody battle" by Steve Limtiaco. Published in *Pacific Daily News*, accessed at http://www.guampdn.com/apps/pbcs.dll/article?AID=/20050314/NEWS01/503140301/1002.

Quote from *Hard Times: An Oral History of the Great Depression* by Studs Terkel. Published by Pantheon Books, New York, 1970.

Quote by Lawrence Svobida from "Farming the Dust Bowl" from *The American Experience, Surviving the Dust Bowl*, accessed at http://www.pbs.org/wgbh/amex/dustbowl/sfeature/eyewitness.html.

Quote by Louis Ortega from *WWII: The People's Story* edited by Nigel Fountain. Published by Reader's Digest, Pleasantville, NY, 2003.

Quote by Boris Pilnyak from *Our Times*, edited by Loraine Glennon. Published by Turner Publishing, Inc., Atlanta, GA, 1995.

Quote by Michiko Yamaoka, interviewed by Mitsuru Ohba from *Voices of A-Bomb Survivors* web site, accessed at http://www.csi.ad.jp/ABOMB/Hibakusha/h03.html.

courtesy Union Pacific Historical Collection; 625 (b) (Art Reference) © Bettmann/CORBIS, (t) Brown Brothers. **Chapter 20:** Pages 632-633 © Bettmann/CORBIS, 633 (cl) © Joseph Sohm, Chromosohm, Inc./CORBIS, (cr) © CORBIS, (br) © Ted Spiegel/CORBIS; 637 (t) PictureHistory/NewsCom; 638 (cr) Shades of L.A. Archives/Los Angeles Public Library, (cl) National Archives, #90-G-152-2038; 639 (tc) Col. Ernest Swanson Papers, Swenson Swedish Immigration Research Center, Augustana College, Rock Island, IL, (cl) © CORBIS; 640 (bl) Library of Congress, Arnold Genthe Collections, #LC-G403-T01-0363, (br) Library of Congress, Arnold Genthe Collections, #LC-G403-T01-0363; 643 (t) Lake County (IL) Museum /Curt Teich Postcard Archives; 644 (bc) New York State Historical Association, (br) © David Bell/CORBIS; 647 The Granger Collection, New York; 648 Jane Addams Memorial Collection (JAMC neg 227), Special Collections, University Library, University of Illinois at Chicago.

Unit 7. Pages 656-657 Courtesy of the U.S. Naval Academy Museum. **Chapter 21:** 658-659 (t) Elizabeth Cady Stanton Trust; 659 (cl, cr) Janice L. and David J. Frent Collection of Political Americana, (b) The Granger Collection, New York; 663 (t) The Granger Collection, New York; 664 (tl) PRC Archive, (tr) PRC Archive, (cl) PRC Archive, (cr) PRC Archive, (bl) PRC Archive, (br) PRC Archive; 665 (t) © Bettmann/CORBIS; 668 (t) Barnes & Noble, Inc.; 669 (t) Library of Congress/PRC Archive; 671 (b) National Archives/PRC Archive; 673 (t) Courtesy of Steve Latham; 676 (b) © Bettmann/CORBIS; 677 (b) Library of Congress; 681 (tc) Leroy Radanovich/Yosemite Museum, (tl) © W. Perry Conway; 682 (br) White House Collection, copyright White House Historical Association, (bl) White House Collection, copyright White House Historical Association, (bc) White House Collection, copyright White House Historical Association; 687 (t) Library of Congress. **Chapter 22:** Pages 688 (b) © Charles Sleicher; 688-689 (t) © Bettmann/CORBIS; 689 (bl) Press Information Bureau of India, (c) Denver Public Library, Western History Collection; 694 (c) © Douglas Peebles/CORBIS; 695 National Portrait Gallery, Smithsonian Institution/Art Resource, NY; 696 Trustees of the British Museum; 698 (b) © Bettmann/CORBIS, (c) PRC Archive; 700 (tr) Library of Congress; 701 (bl) © Richard Cohen/CORBIS; 703 (br) © CORBIS; 704-705 © Library of Congress; 707 The Granger Collection, New York; 708 (inset) © Bettmann/CORBIS; 710 (b) © Bettmann/CORBIS, (c) © Bettmann/CORBIS; 711 (tr, b) © Bettmann/CORBIS. **Chapter 23:** Pages 716-717 (t) © Bettmann/CORBIS; 717 (cl) © Culver Pictures, Inc., (br) Collection of Colonel Stuart S. Corning/Courtesy of PRC Archive, (bl) Stock Montage, Inc.; 721 The Granger Collection, New York; 724 (t) © CORBIS; 726 ©SuperStock; 728 (t) © Underwood & Underwood/CORBIS, (b) © Patrick BazGetty Images; 729 (t) © K.J. Historical/CORBIS; 731 Sam Dudgeon/HRW; 734 (c) © Hulton/Getty Images, (t) ©Dorling Kindersley Ltd./Courtesy of Spink & Son Ltd., London; 736 (bl) © Michael St. Maur Sheil/CORBIS.

Unit 8. Pages 746-747 Everett Collection. **Chapter 24:** Pages 748 (b) HRW Photo by Lance Schriner; 748-749 (t) The Great White Way, Times Square, 1925 (oil on canvas), Thain, Howard A. (1891-1959)/© New-York Historical Society, New York, USA,;/Bridgeman ARt Library; 749 (bl) Egyptian National Museum, Cairo, Egypt/SuperStock, (cr) Brown Brothers, (bc) © Bettmann/CORBIS, (c) The Granger Collection, New York; 753 The Granger Collection, New York; 754-755 (b) From the Collections of Henry Ford Museum and Greenfield Village; 756 (c) From the Collections of Henry Ford Museum and Greenfield Village; 757 (tr) Janice L. and David J. Frent Collection of Political Americana, (tl) Janice L. and David J. Frent Collection of Political Americana; 759 (t) Library of Congress, (b) TIME Inc./Courtesy of the general libraries, The University of Texas at Austin/HRW photo by Victoria Smith,

(c) © Underwood & Underwood/CORBIS; 760 Library of Congress; 761 © Bettmann/CORBIS; 763 The Phillips Collection, Washington, D.C.; 766 (bl) © Bettmann/CORBIS, (br) The Negro Leagues Baseball Museum; 767 (cl) The Granger Collection, New York, (bl) © Hulton/Getty Images, (cr) The Granger Collection, New York; 768 © Getty Images; 769 © Georgia O'Keeffe Museum, Santa Fe / Art Resource. **Chapter 25:** Pages 774 (b) The Granger Collection, New York; 774-775 (t) © Bettmann/CORBIS; 775 (cl) Janice L. and David J. Frent Collection of Political Americana, (cr) Courtesy Everett Collection, (bl) © Bettmann/CORBIS; 779 (t) © Bettmann/CORBIS; 780 (br) Milton (Pete) Brooks/The Detroit News; 781 (t) Brown Brothers; 786 (t) © Bettmann/CORBIS; 788 (br) Library of Congress, (bl) Library of Congress; 791 (b) NOAA George E. Marsh Album; 792 Library of Congress; 793 (t) Twentieth Century Fox; 795 The Granger Collection, New York. **Chapter 26:** Pages 800 (b) (c) Bridgeman Art Library; 800-801 (t) © CORBIS; 801 (cr) Reuters/HO/Hulton Archive/Getty Images, (bl) AKG-Images, London, (bc) © MPI/Getty Images; 805 © Hugo Jaeger/Timepix/Time Life Pictures/Getty Images; 806 © CORBIS, 808 (cr) © CORBIS; 809 (t) © Brooks Kraft/Corbis; 811 (bc) Picture Research Consultants & Archives, (br) Library of Congress; 812 (bl) © U.S. Air Force/Collection of David Ethell, (t) © CORBIS/Bettman; 813 (tr) © Seattle Post-Intelligencer Collection; Museum of History and Industry/CORBIS; 815 (b) Everett Collection; 816 © Bettmann/CORBIS; 817 (tl) Bettmann/CORBIS, (tcl) Bettmann/CORBIS, (tc) Bettmann/CORBIS, (tcr) Bettmann/CORBIS, (tr) Bettmann/CORBIS, (bkgd) Bettmann/CORBIS; 818 (tl) © CORBIS, (cr) Library of Congress; 818-819 (b) © Keystone/Getty Images; 821 National Archives (NARA); 823 (bl) © Hulton-Deutsch Collection/CORBIS, (tl) © Hulton-Deutsch Collection/CORBIS; 824 ©PHOTOGRAPHER/SuperStock; 826 © CORBIS; 827 © H. Miller/Hulton Archive/Getty Images; 828 © Bettmann/CORBIS; 831, *Night* by Elie Wiesel © Bantam Books, a Division of Random House, Inc.; 833 (r) Joe Rosenthal/AP/Wide World Photos.

Unit 9. Pages 838-839 (bkgd) © New York Times Co./Hulton Archive/Getty Images, 839 (inset) © Lazlo Willinger/SuperStock. **Chapter 27:** Pages 840-841 (tc) © Bettmann/CORBIS; 841 (bl) © Bettman/CORBIS, (cr) AP/Wide World Photos, (bl) © Carl & Ann Purcell/CORBIS, (cl) © Hulton Archive/Getty Images, (cl) © Bettmann/CORBIS; 841 (c) Civil Defense Museum; 845 (bl) © Hulton-Deutsch Collection/CORBIS, (br) UPI/Corbis-Bettmann; 846 (tc) © CORBIS, (tr) AP Photo/United Nations; 847 (c) Editorial cartoon by Tom Little, 1948; courtesy of the Nashville Tennessean.; 848 The White House, Courtesy Harry S. Truman Library; 849 The Granger Collection, New York; 851 (bl) The Granger Collection, New York; 853 (tc) © John Florea/Time & Life Pictures/Getty Images; 854 "FIRE!" from *Herblock: A Cartoonist's Life* (Times Books 1998), Library of Congress; 856 (cl) © Bettmann/CORBIS; 859 (tr) Image courtesy of The Advertising Archives; 860 (tl) © Bettmann/CORBIS, (cl) © Ben Martin//Time Life Pictures/Getty Image, (c) Courtesy Elvis Presley Enterprises, (bl) © Bettmann/CORBIS. **Chapter 28:** Pages 866 (br) Photo by Hank Walker//Time Life Pictures/Getty Images; 866-867 (t) © Flip Schulke/CORBIS; 867 (bc) © Bettmann/CORBIS, (cr) AIMovement, (bl) Sovfoto/Eastfoto; 871 (br) AP/Wide World Photos; 872 (cl) Photos by Will Counts from A LIFE IS MORE THAN A MOMENT; 872-873 (c) Photos by Will Counts from A LIFE IS MORE THAN A MOMENT; 877 (tl) © Bettmann/CORBIS; 878 (all) © Bettmann/CORBIS; 879 (t) LBJ Library Collection; 880 (cl) Gene Herrick/AP/Wide World Photos, (bl) Wisconsin Historical Society; 881 (cl) Bill Hudson/AP/Wide World Photos, (bl) AP/Wide World Photos; 883 © Arthur Schatz/Time Life Pictures/Getty Images; 884 (all) © Bettmann/CORBIS; 885 William Philpott/REUTERS/NewsCom. **Chapter 29:** Pages 890-891 (t) AP/Wide World Photos;

891 (bl) © Hulton Archive/Getty Images, (br) © Dirck Halstead/Getty Images, (c) © Blank Archives/Getty Images; 897 (r) NASA, (bl) © 1996 CORBIS; Original image courtesy of NASA/CORBIS; 900 AP/Wide World Photos; 902 (br) © Sygma/CORBIS, (bl) © LARRY DOWNING/Reuters/Corbis; 903 Courtesy of Charley Trujillo/Chusma House Publications; 905 © CBS Photo Archive/Getty Images; 907 (tr) National Archives (NARA); 909 (tcl) © Leif Skoogfors/CORBIS, (tcr) © Dick Swanson/Time Life Pictures/Getty Images, (tl, tr) © David J. & Janice L. Frent Collection/CORBIS, (bkgd) © The Image Bank/Getty Images; 910 © Paula Bronstein/Getty Images; 911 (tr) © CORBIS, (tc) © Bettmann/CORBIS; 912 (b) © James P. Blair/CORBIS, (cl) © Richard Howard/Time Life Pictures/Getty Images.

Unit 10. Pages 920-921 © Jose Fuste Raga/CORBIS. **Chapter 30:** Pages 922 (cl) © Bill Pierce/Getty Images, (b) © Bettmann/CORBIS; 922-923 (t) Wally McNamee/Woodfin Camp & Associates;923 (cr) Tim Shaffer/AP/Wide World Photos, (br) Lehtikuva Oy/Woodfin Camp & Associates; 927 (t) Jason Laure/Woodfin Camp & Associates; 929 (t) Republished with permission of Globe Newspaper Company, Inc.; 931 AP/Wide World Photos; 933 (t) Bernard Gotfryd/Woodfin Camp & Associates; (c) Janice L. and David J. Frent Collection of Political Americana; 934 (bl) White House Collection, copyright White House Historical Association, (bc) White House Collection, copyright White House Historical Association; 935 Courtesy, Jimmy Carter Library; 936 (t) AP/Wide World Photos, (inset) © Bettmann/CORBIS; 938 Leste Sloan/Woodfin Camp & Associates; 939 (inset) © Bill Gentile/CORBIS; 940 Joh Ficara/Woodfin Camp & Associates; 941 (br) Courtesy Ronald Reagan Library, (br) © Robert Nickelsberg/Getty Images, (bc) NASA, (bl) Chuck Nacke/Woodfin Camp & Associates. **Chapter 31:** Pages 946 (b) Smithsonian Institution, Washington, DC Harold Dorwin 2004-55788; 946-947 (t) © Jeff Greenberg/PhotoEdit; 947 (cl) © Peter Turnley/CORBIS, (bl) David Modell-Katz/Woodfin Camp & Associates, (br) © Derrick Ceyrac/Getty Images; 952 (c) © AFP/Getty Images, (b) © Shelly Katz/Time Life/Getty Images; 953 The White House; 955 (all) © Brooks Kraft/CORBIS; 956 (bl) © Ricky Flores/CORBIS, (bc) © Oleg Nikishin/Getty Images; 957 (bl) © Mirrorpix/Getty Images, (cr) Hasan Sarbakhshian/AP/WideWorld, (bc) Al-Jazeera via APTN/AP/Wide World Photos; 958 Courtesy the White House/Photo by Eric Draper; 960 (bl) © Richard Ross/CORBIS, (br) Custom Medical Stock Photo; 962, © REUTERS/John Gress; 964 (br) © Elise Amendola/AP/Wide World Photos; 965 (bl) © Chabruken/Getty Images, (br) Bizuayehu Tesfaye/AP/Wide World Photos, Rob Schoenbaum/AP/Wide World Photos.

Back Matter: Pages R0-R1; (bkgd) © Royalty-free/CORBIS; Presidents: Pages R23-R27, White House Historical Association (White House Collection); R27 (bc) The White House, photo by Eric Draper; (br) © Ben Baker/Redux Pictures; R30 ©PhotoDisc/Getty Images; R31, The Granger Collection, New York; R33 © Tom Brakefield/Digital Vision/Getty Images; Bio Dic: R82 (l) © Arthur Schatz/Time Life Pictures/Getty Images; R82 (r) © Bettmann/CORBIS; R84 (l) © Bettmann/CORBIS.

Staff Credits. The people who contributed to *United States History, Civil War to the Present* are listed below. They represent editorial, design, intellectual property resources, production, emedia, and permissions. Lissa B. Anderson, Charles Becker, Ed Blake, Gillian Brody, Erin Cornett, Michelle Dike, Mescal Evler, Leanna Ford, Bob Fullilove, Rhonda Haynes, Wilonda Ieans, Cathy Jenevein, Shannon Johnston, Cathy Kuhles, Debbie Lofland, Bob McClellan, Joe Melomo, Richard Metzger, Mercedes Newman, Holly Norman, Nathan O'Neal, Karl Pallmeyer, Shelly Ramos, Gene Rumann, Kay Selke, Ken Shepardson, Michele Shukers, Chris Smith, Jeannie Taylor, Joni Wackwitz, Ken Whiteside, Nadyne Wood